HOLE
In Our
SOUL

HOLE
In Our
SOUL

*The Loss of Beauty and Meaning
in American Popular Music*

MARTHA BAYLES

The University of Chicago Press

Dedicated to
MY MOTHER AND FATHER
who taught me how to dance

The University of Chicago Press, Chicago 60637

Copyright © 1994 by Martha Bayles

All rights reserved. Originally published by The Free Press in 1994

University of Chicago Press Edition 1996

Printed in the United States of America

02 01 00   6   5   4   3   2

ISBN 0-226-03959-5 (pbk.)

Library of Congress Cataloging-in-Publication Data

Bayles, Martha.
    Hole in our soul : the loss of beauty and meaning in American popular music / Martha Bayles.
      p.   cm.
    Originally published: New York : Free Press, © 1994.
    Includes bibliographical references and index.
    1. Popular music—United States—History and criticism.   I. Title.
ML3477.B39   1996
781.64′0973—dc20   95-47139
                                                      CIP
                                                      MN

The author gratefully acknowledges permission to quote lyrics from "Me and the Devil Blues," "Last Fair Deal Gone Down," and "Traveling Riverside Blues," by Robert Johnson. Copyright © 1978, King of Spades Music. All rights reserved.

∞ The paper used in this publication meets the minimum requirements of the American National Standard for Information Sciences—Permanence of Paper for Printed Library Materials, ANSI Z39.48-1984.

Contents

Acknowledgments

My first meeting with my editor and publisher Erwin Glikes was serendipity, but now it feels like destiny. His interest sparked the conception of this book, his skepticism expanded its scope, his encouragement sustained it, and his patience brought it to fruition. For these qualities, and for his friendship, I shall always be grateful.

True mentors are hard to find, but I have been blessed with another, Pearl K. Bell. Frequently I have subjected my work to Pearl's scrutiny, which over the years I have come to prefer to many kinds of praise. In the same vein, I keenly anticipate the scrutiny of two informal teachers, Nathan Glazer and James Q. Wilson, whose understanding of the place of art in society is subtler than that of most social scientists—to say nothing of most cultural critics.

Books often grow out of disagreements, and this one is no exception. I have learned a great deal from Hilton Kramer, though I expect he will find much to dispute in my views of art and popular culture. And I regret that Allan Bloom is not around to read the rest of the argument I once tried to pick with him. His graciousness and generosity are sorely missed.

Authors frequently offer the following demurral, but it is true that *Hole in Our Soul* reflects countless conversations with other people—musicians, writers, industry figures, and aficionados of every stripe—willing to share their experiences and insights with me. My only hope is that those who follow up and read the book don't mind seeing their observations filtered through its strong opinions. Likewise the friends, elders, and colleagues whose promptings helped to shape the final product: Daniel Bell, Walter Berns, Joanne Bickel, Stanley Crouch, Steve Davison, Jeff Gedmin, Ben Gerson, Bob Goldwin, Anne and Max Green, Tom Hines, Robin and

Howard Husock, Randall Kennedy, Kenneth LaFave, Chong-Pin Lin, Grady McGonagill, Andy Meisler, Elvis Mitchell, Steve Miller, Sally Muravchik, Marina and Yuri and Philip Neyman, Pietro Nivola, Wlady Pleszczynski, Mary Kay and Tom Ricks, David Riesman, Carole Robinson, Meta Rosenberg, Bob Royal, Ben Sidran, Bryan Simms, Stuart Spencer, Andy Stark, Terry Teachout, Dan Wattenberg, Seymour Weinstein, David Weiss, and Jonathan Yardley.

To those who read and commented on the manuscript, in whole or in part, my debt is profound: Ken Barnes, Al Basile, Georgia (Jo) Bergman, Peter Dougherty, Gerald Early, Erich Eichman, Gil Friesen, Mark Goldberg, Gertrude Himmelfarb, Steve Lagerfeld, Bruce Nichols, Henry Pleasants, Jay Tolson, John Urda, Jay Walljasper, and Mary and John Walters.

The next list is ungainly but crucial, containing those individuals who offered practical help, moral support, and good humor when these were in short supply: John Berthelot, Mae and Church Churchill, Mike Hartman, c. j. hast, Dot Hines, Anil Kakani, Bob Katzmann, Rita and Yale Kramer, Chris Jarman, Sydnee Lipset, Lydia Lopez, Bobby Newsome, Linda Miller, Lou Ann Sabatier, Jan Ramsey, the staff at Potomac Video's Uptown store (Schelli and Mark), and Dickey Wilson.

From the beginning, this project benefited greatly from the hard work, sly wit, and boundless curiosity of my research assistant, Isaac Green. And toward the end, the author kept her sanity only because of the determination and patience of Stephanie Wilshusen.

At the Free Press, I am grateful to Loretta Denner for clearing up every cloud, Nancy Etheredge for fielding every suggestion, Sue Llewellyn for correcting every mistake, Marion Maneker for answering every phone call, and Paul O'Halloran for keeping every promise. At New River Media, I am obliged to Andy Walworth, Ben Wattenberg, and Jonah Goldberg for tolerating my distractedness.

Going back in time, I remember appreciatively the musical people who opened my ears without imagining that I would ever write a book about music: my brother Howard, my sister Louise, Margaret Angelo, Shelley Erwin, Laval Todd Duncan, Jerry Fightmaster, Cornelia Gaines, Fran Jones, Stephen Lancaster, Steve Luxton, Lewis Opler, and Maurice Page.

To my loyal friends Joanne Bickel, Anne Green, Roland Marandino, and Mary Walters, I have quit trying to add up the debt.

And finally, I thank my husband Peter for making all the love songs come true.

Part One

The Weird Music
of the New World

Chapter 1

Introduction

Hole in Our Soul is not just a history of popular music, although it does, I hope, offer a cogent survey of the major strains from spirituals and ragtime to blues, jazz, country, and gospel; from 1950s rock 'n' roll to 1960s rock; and from 1970s heavy metal, disco, and punk to MTV and rap today. But this book also makes an argument: Taking my title from the old saying, "If you don't like the blues, you've got a hole in your soul," I argue that something has gone seriously wrong, both with the sound of popular music and with the sensibility it expresses. It is still possible to find the tough, affirmative spirit of the blues in contemporary forms. But increasingly, that spirit is rejected in favor of antimusical, antisocial antics that would be laughable if they weren't so offensive.

To the reader who finds nothing offensive in current popular music: Please don't put the book down; you are the person I am most anxious to persuade. To the reader who is repelled by everything out there to the point of giving up: Please bear with me. My intention is not just to rub

3

your nose in the latest swill; any number of critics can do that. Rather it is to explain the situation: to articulate exactly what is wrong, to show where the swill comes from, and to suggest why popular music doesn't have to be this way. Unlike many others who have been knocking popular music lately, I do so from a position of deep and abiding sympathy. In that sense this book is not a tirade, but a labor of love.

This is not to suggest that I sympathize with Madonna's crude headline-grabbing jokes about having been "fucked" by her father; or with "gangsta" rapper Ice Cube's song about "The Nigga Ya Love to Hate" terminating an unwanted pregnancy by kicking the woman and killing the baby; or with hard-core rockers' graphic accounts of rape, mutilation, serial murder, cannibalism, and necrophilia; or with the racial and ethnic hatemongering that has now spread from British punk into American rap and German neo-Nazi rock. Without apology, I am disgusted by these things.

But to dwell on this litany is merely to echo the complaints of others: Beginning with Tipper Gore in the mid-1980s, and continuing with a host of voices from the religious right to the feminist left, many critics have been protesting the obscenity and brutality of contemporary song lyrics and video images. At the same time, few critics have addressed the subject of *sound*—which is, after all, what music is made of. Now, some people believe that this topic was dispatched by the late political philosopher Allan Bloom, whose best-selling critique of higher education, *The Closing of the American Mind*, contains a chapter on the pernicious effects of rock. But as I shall show later, that celebrated chapter displays a near-perfect ignorance of American popular music (whose history hardly begins with rock), and a disappointingly superficial grasp of the European musical classics. Bloom rushed into the critical vacuum, but he didn't fill it.

This neglect of music is regrettable, because just as assaultive as the lyrics and images of contemporary popular music are many of the sounds. From the shrieking clamor of thrash metal to the murky din of grunge, from the cheap, synthesized tinsel of pop ballads to the deadly pounding of computerized rhythm tracks, popular music seems terminally hostile to any sound traditionally associated with music. And herein lies frustration, because for most people the relevant comparison is not between hard rock and Mozart (*pace* Bloom), but between popular music that abuses the ear and popular music that does not. People act on this comparison by tuning in to "oldies" radio—with a defensive shrug, because the media keep insisting that a preference for classic singles is mere nostalgia, but also with a certain quiet conviction that today's sonic abuse will never last as long, or command as much loyalty, as the better "oldies." People act on the same comparison when they embrace new currents—in "rock," "pop," even "rap"—that are actually revivals of richer, more musical sounds.

These statements are based on recent market trends that suggest a wide-spread, possibly growing, rejection of ugly excess in popular music—among both older and younger listeners. Yet few critics note such trends, because few critics see anything positive about the fact that popular music, whatever its artistic claims, is also a commercial product. Indeed, the whole debate over popular music, and popular culture generally, has long been dominated by the tendency of all critics, of all ideological stripes, to blame commerce. Take, for example, the critiques mounted by Gore and Bloom. Hers was liberal and pragmatic, his conservative and philosophical; yet both blamed commerce. Gore styled herself the leader of a grass-roots consumer revolt against greedy corporations whose product was nothing more than a commodity with proven harmful effects, like flammable children's pajamas.[1] Likewise, Bloom denounced record company executives as "robber barons," writing that "the rock industry is perfect capitalism."[2] The same anticommercialism thrives across the political spectrum, from right-wing advocates of censorship to radical rockers accusing one another of selling out. Unfortunately, anticommercialism tells us nothing about what is really wrong with popular music.

How can I let commerce off the hook? First, because I do not use the word *popular* as the opposite of *high, serious,* or *good.* It cannot be stated too often, or too emphatically, that this usage is both illogical and ahistorical. In every period and place, it is possible to cite works that possess both popular-ity and artistic merit. And—to the chagrin of countless phonies, charlatans, and Hollywood producers—artistic inferiority is no guarantee of populari-ty. Historically the categorical put-down "popular" can be traced to the rise of the so-called penny press in eighteenth-century London, when the cheap reading matter produced by the literary hacks of Grub Street caused great alarm among the educated classes, who feared that it would swamp English literature in a flood of sentimental and trivial dreck. It is certainly true that Grub Street produced a flood of dreck. But Grub Street also produced Samuel Johnson, who praised it as the training ground of his critical talent; and later on it produced the English novel.[3] By similar processes many other popular milieus have acquired posthumous halos for having nurtured this or that distinguished art form. Given this history, we might expect the word *popular* to have settled into a more accurate usage.

No such luck. If anything, *popular* has become even more misused since the 1950s, when the phrase "popular culture" became a stand-in for the older, more loaded term "mass culture." The "mass-culture debate" of the 1940s and 1950s, which involved many leading American intellectuals and social scientists, had a definite ideological cast, since most of the participants had grown up steeped in the Marxist social criticism of the 1920s and 1930s—in particular, in the ideas of the Frankfurt School, a group of mostly German-Jewish intellectuals who saw a link between the rise of the electronic mass media, especially radio, and the systematic mind control attempted by the Nazis. Because totalitarian regimes had used the electronic media to attack artistic and intellectual freedoms in Europe, Theodor Adorno, Walter Benjamin, and Herbert Marcuse warned against the same thing happening in the United States, where those media were, if anything, more pervasive. Accordingly a whole generation of American intellectuals learned to draw a sharp, uncrossable line between serious culture and "mass culture." Of course, when these intellectuals jettisoned Marxism, they also got rid of the term "mass culture." But their assumptions about "popular culture" did not change. Even when they championed the triumph of democracy and capitalism over defunct communism, this generation—from the liberal Irving Howe to the neoconservative Irving Kristol—still found it hard to believe that genuine art could emerge from popular culture.

Unfortunately, this intellectual aversion to popular culture received a boost from Marshall McLuhan's contention that the world, and the human mind, are being radically altered by the electronic media. McLuhan was an optimist, but many who share his perspective are not. To communications theorist Neil Postman, for example, contemporary society is becoming a "technopoly," ruled by media that, unlike their print predecessors, are inherently irrational. The discontinuity, the nonlinear nature of these media, Postman argues, interferes with human cognitive and moral development. It was Andy Warhol who said, "If it moves, they'll watch it." To Postman, they'll never be able to do anything else.[4]

The best refutation of this view, gentle reader, is to look at yourself and the people around you. It's clear, from the example of countless educated, literate people who are also fully conversant with the electronic media, that the human mind can, given the opportunity, handle both the new and the old media, just as it can handle more than one language. There is no *inherent* reason why the two cannot coexist, each doing what it does best, in an appropriate balance. The problem, as any parent can tell you, is finding that balance.

Obviously, the growth of the electronic mass media, fueled by the profit motive, has done much harm to art and culture. But it has also done much good. If, for example, we admit that jazz and the cinema are the only truly original American art forms, then we must also admit that neither would have developed as dynamically as it did without the incentives, exposure, and competition provided by the commercialized mass media.

Yet here, too, balance is needed. To say that genuine art can emerge from popular culture is not to say that all popular culture is genuine art. Emphatically, I reject the postmodernist embrace of popular culture as a battering ram against the very idea of artistic standards. For every gray-haired highbrow who denies that art can exist in the schlock-swollen flood of popular culture, there is a wet-behind-the-ears postmodernist who insists that every morsel of schlock belongs in an art gallery or concert hall. One side says that artistic standards cannot be applied to popular culture, the other that they should not. The two sides claim to be in opposition, but if you ask me, they're in cahoots.

In sum, blaming commerce is the easy way out. Forty years ago, commerce was blamed for taking all the sex and violence out of popular culture—for example, movies and TV were criticized for their prudery (showing married couples sleeping in twin beds) and their optimism (attaching happy endings to tragic novels and plays). Today, by contrast, commerce is blamed for putting gratuitous sex, violence, and pessimism into popular culture. My suggestion is this: Instead of explaining a variable (the level of sex, violence and pessimism) by means of a constant (commerce), why not explain it by means of another variable—namely, the deeper cultural changes that have taken place over the same period?

This book offers just such an explanation. But first I must clarify the meaning of another misused word. Even when not preceded by *popular*, the word *culture* contains a built-in ambiguity that, instead of enriching and extending its meaning, fosters confusion. It comes from the Latin root *culti-vare*, meaning to till the soil. But this root supports two different meanings: *culture* in the traditional sense of artistic and intellectual accomplishment; and *culture* in the anthropological sense of the total way of life of a people. I call the first meaning traditional because it is much older than the second, which dates only to the nineteenth century, when Sir Edward Burnett Tylor established it as the core concept of anthropology.

The difference between the two meanings can be described quite clearly. *Culture* in the traditional sense suggests purposeful activity aimed at developing and improving its object, whether that object be an orchid, an individual's grasp of philosophy, or a society's taste in music. Thus its synonyms are evaluative terms, such as *cultivation*, *breeding* and *refinement*. *Culture* in the anthropological sense suggests not the orchid fancier striving for a perfect bloom, but the plant biologist peering with concentration into a tray of experimental seedlings. In the early days of anthropology, one of the biggest obstacles facing European students of non-European societies was their own feeling of superiority. For the sake of collecting accurate data, they struggled to suppress their moral and aesthetic reactions to the customs and rituals they were observing. They didn't always succeed; nowadays it is commonly argued that the scientific approach is itself an arrogation of superiority. Nonetheless, *culture* in the anthropological sense remains the object of study, not evaluation.

Not surprisingly, these two meanings of *culture* are badly muddled in the current debate over multiculturalism. Among the advocates of multiculturalism, we find what amounts to a fast shuffle: typically the substitution of quite ordinary works by this or that "marginalized" group for the towering achievements of "dead white European males," in a process that smuggles the neutrality and relativism of anthropology into the realm of artistic and intellectual endeavor. The Victorian anthropologist suspended taste and judgment in the name of science. The multiculturalist does the same thing in the name of justice. But the latter is a tougher proposition, because instead of declaring taste and judgment irrelevant to the immediate task of gathering data, it rejects them altogether as inherently elitist.

The trouble is, *all* cultural standards—non-Western as well as Western—are elitist. Should they all be rejected? Of course not. Multiculturalists wouldn't dream of asking non-Western peoples to give up their own standards of excellence. That demand is reserved for the West, where it's no longer enough to admit that racial and sexual bias has historically led to mistaken negative judgments. Now the West's positive judgments must be damned as well, and its noblest works reduced to a residue of prejudice. Witness this passage by the journalist Michele Wallace: "It's not a matter of being for or against Western civilization. We are all victims of it. It's time to consider that the classics may, in fact, make more sense to some of us as records of blindness to the plight of the world's majorities, than as sublime masterpieces."[5]

Instinctively, those who would teach such lessons to the young understand that their best weapon is ignorance. The less young people know about Western civilization, the more easily they can be induced to write it off. But the stratagem is a tricky one: Young people are curious, and must be taught something. So the next fast shuffle is to smuggle the evaluative dimension of traditional culture into the realm of anthropology. That is, to treat humble crafts and customs as though they were artistic masterpieces. Of course, such treatment is reserved for those who have been excluded from the Western "canon." Not mistakenly excluded, mind you—just excluded. If the seedling tray has a politically correct label, then perforce, every seedling must be celebrated as an orchid.

Meanwhile, the conservative approach to culture resembles nothing so much as schizophrenia, or perhaps multiple personality disorder. Libertarian conservatives believe (as I do) that the market can have positive effects on culture, in both the traditional and anthropological senses. But they do not believe (as I do) that the market can also have negative effects. Hence the libertarian opposition to censorship is matched by support for the legalization, without regulation, of pornography (including child pornography), drugs, and weapons—a position that adds little to the discussion.

Taking a much stronger stance are the social conservatives, who would willingly regulate culture in both the anthropological and the traditional senses. Like all conservatives lately, social conservatives feel compelled to defend Western civilization at least ten times a day. But the quality of that defense varies greatly, especially with regard to the arts. Historically, it has been a fact of American intellectual life that most people with a working knowledge of the arts have occupied the political left, while most conservatives have displayed a basically know-nothing attitude. This is why the chorus of conservative voices currently touting the superiority of Western art has the genteel, if somewhat nasal, tone of old-fashioned American philistinism. You would never know, from the exhortations of this chorus, that the culture of the West contains more than a set of morally uplifting homilies.

The distinguished exceptions to this rule are, of course, the neoconservatives. But they present problems, too. In their zeal to defend high culture against all perceived enemies, neoconservatives tend to apply an excessively rigorous standard of evaluation. They forget T. S. Eliot's famous admonition that *culture* means different things when applied to the individual, the group, and the society as a whole:

> The difference between the three applications of the term can be best apprehended by asking how far, in relation to the individual, the group, and society as a whole the *conscious aim to achieve culture* has any meaning. A good deal of confusion could be avoided, if we refrained from setting before the group, what can be the aim only of the individual; and before society as a whole, what can be the aim only of a group.[6]

As defenders of democratic capitalism, neoconservatives hardly endorse Eliot's view that the only way to sustain high culture is to restore religious monarchy. Rather they confine themselves to bewailing the public's failure to experience culture on the highest possible level, interpreting all short-comings as evidence of a beetle-browed conspiracy to deface the sacred temple of art—despite the rather curious fact that many of their allies in the "culture war" are people who suspect, without knowing very much about it, that art is bad for "family values."

Join the word *popular* to the word *culture*, and the fog thickens. In the first place, the very popularity of popular culture makes it a part of every-day life in a way that high culture almost never is. Yet this doesn't mean that popular culture can, or should, be reduced to basket weaving. It claims our attention in ways that are always tangentially, and often directly, related to the claims of art. This double aspect of popular culture is well described in a 1954 essay by Robert Warshow, a young participant in the "mass culture debate":

> I have felt my work to be most successful when it has seemed to display the movies as an important element in my own cultural life, an element with its own qualities, and interesting in its own terms, and neither esoteric nor alien. The movies are part of my culture, and it seems to me that their special power has something to do with their being a kind of "pure" culture, a little like fishing or drinking or playing baseball—a cultural fact, that is, which has not yet fallen altogether under the discipline of art. I have not brought Henry James to the movies or the movies to Henry James, but I hope I have shown that the man who goes to the movies is the same as the man who reads Henry James.[7]

It's regrettable that Warshow did not live to see Henry James brought to the movies; his reactions would have been interesting. It's also regrettable that Warshow was only able to contribute a few essays to his stated goal of "resolving the curious tension that surrounds the problem of 'popular culture.'"[8] Almost four decades later, that "curious tension" has risen to a fever pitch, as the "culture war" rages on without a clear definition of *culture* on either side.

My own attempt at resolving the tension requires me to use one or both meanings of *culture*, depending on the context, as well as to make a continual effort to avoid confusion. In that spirit, then, let me sketch the three axes along which the deeper cultural changes of the last several years have affected popular music.

The first axis is the complex racial dynamic of American culture (in both senses). As I shall discuss in chapter 2, this country's distinctive musical idiom was created, and largely dominated, by black Americans. Here it's important to note that, with regard to music, the word *popular* has come to refer to anything in the Afro-American idiom, from the most brilliant jazz to the most idiotic rock, whether or not it is in fact popular.[9] This usage creates the misleading impression that the classics of European music are unpopular (which they are not), and that all Afro-American music is inferior to all European music (which it is not).

Because Afro-American music has been constantly appropriated by the white mainstream, in ways both warmly appreciative and coldly exploitive, the story cannot be told without exploring the tangled conundrum of race and sex that I call the "blood knot." Here our worst problems stem from the tendency, in both its foes and friends, to reduce Afro-American music to a crude caricature of dehumanized sex. Focusing on the simple, pounding beat of hard rock, Bloom implies that all popular music "has the beat of sexual intercourse."[10] Taking exactly the same view, Steven Tyler of the hard rock band Aerosmith boasts: "It's rhythm and blues, it's twos and fours, it's fucking."[11] In general, neither friend nor foe acknowledges that the monotonous beat of hard rock (and, indeed, of much rap) is a travesty of the rich, tireless, complicated rhythms of Afro-American music at its best. All I can say to such people is, if the rhythms of good jazz, funk, blues, or gospel remind you of sexual intercourse, then—well, my hat's off to you.

But I digress. The point is that this caricature of rhythm overlooks the fact that Afro-American music originally functioned in many different spheres, including work, storytelling, celebration, and (most important) religion. To accept such a stereotype is to forget our complex history, and, worse, to insult the people who created the music in the first place.

The second axis of change is the transformation of popular music by high technology—from the clever studio tricks of the 1950s to the multi-track recording and stadium amplification of the 1960s, the synthesizers of the 1970s, and the digital processing and computer sampling of today. For years critics have blamed these devices for everything that is wrong with popular music. Yet here, too, blaming the medium is too easy, because it ignores the message. Superb music has been made using each of these methods, just as superb music has been sold through the commodity system. The fault, dear McLuhan, is not in our machines, but in ourselves.

Which brings us to the third and most important axis of cultural change, the impact on popular music, and popular culture in general, of what I call "perverse modernism." By this phrase, I mean the antisocial, antiart impulses of the European avant-garde, which gave rise historically to such movements as decadence at the end of the nineteenth century; futurism at the start of the twentieth; dada in the 1920s; surrealism and the theater of cruelty in the 1930s; and postwar retreads of these movements, such as happenings and performance art, in the 1950s and 1960s. This part of my thesis is laid out in chapter 3, which separates the perverse strain of modernism from the other two: "introverted" modernism, which tends toward austere formalism and making a religion of art; and "extroverted" modernism, which actively engages both the modern world and the artistic past. In my view, jazz is a modernist art in the latter, more favorable sense. The central argument of *Hole in Our Soul* is that the anarchistic, nihilistic impulses of perverse modernism have been grafted onto popular music, where they have not only undermined the Afro-American tradition, but also encouraged today's cult of obscenity, brutality, and sonic abuse.

This is a difficult argument to make, because it must bridge not one but two generation gaps. The first is the familiar one between the 1960s generation and their parents. According to the standard 1960s myth, this gap opened in the 1950s with rock 'n' roll, only to deepen with the "counterculture" a decade later. Needless to say, this gap still commands more attention than the second, the less visible but more problematic one between the 1960s generation and everyone younger, from thirty-somethings to teens. Here 1960s myth traces a decline from glorious rebellion, high idealism, and excellent music to dull conformity, low cynicism, and terrible music. That is to say, the 1960s generation takes all the credit for what is good about popular music, and none of the blame for what is bad.

I consider it my duty, as a dues-paying member of the 1960s generation, to debunk these myths. First, I dispute the notion that 1950s rock 'n' roll drove a wedge between the generations. In much of the country, especially the South, people of all ages appreciated the continuity between the music and the sensibility of Louis Armstrong, Benny Goodman, and Frank Sinatra on the one hand, and Fats Domino, Chuck Berry, and Elvis Presley on the other. That continuity showed up both in musical elements (such as the ability to swing) and extramusical ones (such as courtesy toward the audience). Not only that, but it persisted in such mid-1960s strains as soul, Motown, and the early Beatles.

The real break came in the late 1960s, when the counterculture went sour, and popular music began attracting people who were less interested in music than in using such a powerful medium for culturally radical purposes. The harbingers of this break were the Rolling Stones, who relished the blues but did not hesitate to make it over in the image of the stale perverse modernism that some of their members had picked up in British art colleges. Thus the Stones enhanced their musical reputation by shocking the public and being arrogantly rude to their audience—behaviors now accepted as part of rock, but thoroughly alien to the blues.

More drastic were the changes wrought by such people as Frank Zappa, the Velvet Underground, and the New York Dolls, American performers steeped in perverse modernism, whose late-1960s stage shows resembled the happenings of Warhol more than they did concerts. Indeed, the Velvet Underground made its name touring with Warhol. Then, in the 1970s, an even more dedicated contingent of cultural radicals climbed aboard the bandwagon. Emerging first in downtown Manhattan and then in art-college London, the strain known as punk effectively turned rock into a species of performance art. Created by a fashion designer named Malcolm McLaren, who had attended six British art colleges but knew nothing about music, the Sex Pistols became famous for attacking music along with everything else. Today the punk legacy persists wherever noise, shock, and ugliness are cultivated for their own sakes, and wherever the fires of adolescent anger and aggression are stoked in ways that are almost totally destructive. It is no accident that Rick Rubin, one of the driving forces behind "gangsta" rap, got his start in a New York punk band called the Pricks.

I have no doubt that the youthful (and not-so-youthful) champions of punk will ignore my efforts to debunk these myths, and simply accuse me of being an aging flower child longing for the music of her youth. My reply is simple: The music I admire the most is not the music of my youth. Nor was it created by my generation, or any single age cohort. It is the best of the living Afro-American tradition, not easily divided into the tidy decades so beloved of pundits and hacks. Its prehistory reaches back four centuries, but its fullest development began at the beginning of the twentieth. Ironically this makes Afro-American music *younger* than perverse modernism, which (despite the claims of today's "postmodernists") has not changed very much in the last hundred years.

Finally I expect to be called a prude and a censor. To the former accusation, my response is simply that there is a world of difference between the human eroticism expressed in Afro-American forms such as the blues, and the dehumanized obscenity that is the perpetual, infantile preoccupation of perverse modernism. In this respect, perhaps more than in any other, the Afro-American tradition has its own distinctive cultural stance—one that, in the long run, will prove truer to civilized values than the European tantrums of the last century.

To the second accusation, my response is that if I believed in censorship, I wouldn't have written this book. If, as some have argued, our only hope is legal censorship, then we're in trouble, because the censorship of popular culture is both a practical and a constitutional impossibility. As the experience of the former Eastern bloc demonstrates, government cannot control the flow of the electronic media. In this country the great bulk of offensive popular music does not fall under the narrow purview of obscenity law as derived from the 1973 Supreme Court decision, *Miller v. California*. There will always be experts willing to defend the "serious literary, artistic, political, or scientific value" of material like the rap group 2 Live Crew's "The Fuck Shop." And there will always be performers like Madonna, who know how to dehumanize sex even before they take off their clothes. And, as fundamentalists and feminists have learned the hard way, the First Amendment stands solidly in the way of any attempt to expand the scope of the law.

Thus I argue that our only hope of reversing the current malignant mood is the market. But I am no libertarian, expecting the market to do magic tricks by itself. It can only respond to a shift in public taste, brought about by the usual combination of things we cannot control and things we can. Optimistically, I count among the latter the old-fashioned tools of persuasion, debate, and education. We need to trace the roots of our present predicament to their true sources in the larger culture. And we need to change our tune about artistic matters. Instead of saying: "I don't know much about art, but I know what I don't like," we need to follow the historian Jacques Barzun, who recommends learning how to say: "It is because I understand this work of art that I dislike it."[12]

Chapter 2

Why Music Is the Wild Card

During the debate over "mass culture" in the 1940s and 1950s, there was a surprising neglect of music. To be sure, most of the cultural intellectuals involved in that debate had literary or visual-arts backgrounds. But there was also an awareness, however dim and unacknowledged, that the relationship between "serious" and "popular" was more complex and problematic in music than in any other field—that American music was, in this particular sense, the wild card in the cultural deck.

Why should this be so? One answer comes from Henry Pleasants, one of the few distinguished music critics of the immediate postwar generation to be equally conversant with the European and Afro-American idioms. In the mid-1950s, after years of writing about the "serious" music composed in Europe and America during this century, Pleasants began to wonder why so much of that music attracted only a minuscule audience, even among people willing to submit to the demands of a highly intellectualized art.

In particular, Pleasants wondered about serialism, the strain of modernist music that rejects the system of tonality that has ordered Western music since the Middle Ages. The moving force behind serialism was Arnold Schoenberg, the Austrian composer who began in the early 1900s to compose "atonal" music—that is, music no longer organized around a particular diatonic (seven-note) scale. Then, persuaded that tonality was a thing of the past, but worried about the formlessness of atonal composition, Schoenberg sought to restore order to music by replacing the diatonic scale with the chromatic (twelve-note) scale. In the end, he combined the new twelve-tone system with tonality, admitting that "a longing to return to the older style was always vigorous in me."[1]

But no such longing was felt by Schoenberg's colleague, Anton Webern, for whom twelve-tone music was a brave new world. Forging ahead, Webern arranged the twelve notes of the chromatic scale into fixed "tone rows" that circumscribed, through rigorously logical permutation, all other aspects of his short compositions. Soon other serialists, such as Pierre Boulez, were applying the same techniques to musical values other than pitch, such as rhythm, timbre, dynamics. By the early 1950s serialism had become a sterile, hypermathematical exercise, well suited to the burgeoning science of electronics but ill suited to the human ear.

Meanwhile, another group of modernists (now identified with John Cage) reacted against this sterility by composing music through random, irrational, processes. But, as it turned out, these "aleatory" compositions were no more listenable. Serialism and aleatory composition are not the sum total of musical modernism, of course. Many of the greatest twentieth-century composers did not reject tonality outright, but rather expanded its resources and possibilities. Nonetheless, the serialists and the aleatory composers often claim to be the sole legitimate heirs of the Western musical tradition.

Pleasants is not the first critic to dispute such claims; anyone with ears can tell you that intellectual rigor is no excuse for musical rigor mortis. But Pleasants is the first to argue convincingly that the twentieth century offers an alternative: "In art and literature the assumed 'modernity' of the contemporary product may well be as bogus as I hold the 'modernity' of contemporary Serious music to be. But neither in the graphic arts, nor in literature, is there a vital so-called subculture to disturb the assumptions of an Establishment."[2]

This "vital so-called subculture" is, of course, the Afro-American idiom. For Pleasants, the essential point is that, unlike the diluted abstract painting now festooning motel walls, or the ersatz surrealist theater now ruling late-night TV, Afro-American music is not a watered-down imitation of European high culture. Yet, as he explains, most "serious" music critics still tend to dismiss all Afro-American music as "popular," meaning artistically inferior:

> This curious obduracy in the face of acknowledged virtues stems, I think, from the persistence of an obsolete terminology. We regard the distinction between Serious and Popular as qualitative when it is, I believe, idiomatic. We are dealing, in my view, not with two grades, the one substantial and the other trivial, but with two separate musical idioms, the one European, the other, Afro-American.[3]

In this book, I define the Afro-American idiom broadly, to include not only such recognizably "black" forms as jazz, blues, and gospel; but also a great portion of twentieth-century music, both high and low. For Pleasants as well as for an increasing number of critics and musicians, "Afro-American" is practically a synonym for "American": This country's ethnically and culturally diverse musics become distinctive only when they acquire the imprint, however light or heavy, of the black idiom.

As we shall see, there are plenty of observers who object to this broad definition—some because they wish to downplay the Americanness of black music, others because they wish to downplay the blackness of American music. I shall consider these objections later. But first let me describe the essential musical characteristics of the Afro-American idiom as it evolved through the first half of the twentieth century. The best way to do this is to focus on the type of Afro-American music that has been most carefully analyzed, and has exerted the most decisive influence on the way people think—or in some cases refuse to think—about the place of music in contemporary culture. That music is, of course, jazz.

What's New—and Old—About Jazz

Significantly, it is harder to distinguish among the various types of music within the Afro-American idiom than to describe the differences between it and European music. To begin with a negative difference, the first thing about jazz that strikes the European-trained ear is the brevity and simplicity of its structures. Almost all jazz performances are a heady mixture of composed, rehearsed, and improvised material built on two simple forms: the thirty-two-bar popular song and the twelve-bar traditional blues. Pleasants himself admits that these rudimentary structures cannot compete with the size and complexity of European musical architecture:

Missing from much of jazz is the *leisurely* buildup of tension that European music achieves—or once achieved—through modulatory structure, thematic development, change of pace and the adding of instruments. Climaxes, in European music, could be prepared over a longer span of time and cover a wider range of dynamics and color.[4]

One exception might be the longer compositions of Duke Ellington, such as *Black, Brown, and Beige* and *The Tattooed Lady*. But, for the most part, these works are suites made up of the often brilliant short pieces for which Ellington is justifiably renowned. Others, notably Thelonious Monk, composed short works with intricate structures. But by the 1950s, John Coltrane, Ornette Coleman, and Cecil Taylor were carrying free-form improvisation to heroic lengths—and proclaiming jazz's proud independence from European-derived notions of musical architecture. Hence the French musicologist André Hodeir's 1954 pronouncement: "Jazz is not constructed music."[5]

Since the elaborate structures of European art music are intimately related to its abundant harmonic resources, it follows that jazz has suffered a disadvantage in this area, too. For many years, jazz relied not only on the structures of popular songs, but also on their relatively unsophisticated harmonies. As Hodeir points out, what passes for harmonic sophistication in the songs of Broadway and Tin Pan Alley is usually watered down from a European source, such as Debussy. But jazz also relies on the blues, whose distinctive pentatonic (five-note) scale creates harmonies that, Hodeir admits, have "a real beauty of their own," one that "avoids banality."[6] Because of the blues, banality is rare in the harmonic explorations of Ellington in the 1920s, Coleman Hawkins and Art Tatum in the 1930s, Charlie Parker in the 1940s, and Miles Davis in the 1950s. Thus Pleasants could write in 1969 that "those who speak disdainfully of the harmonic element in jazz are plainly unaware of what has been going on."[7]

In melody, too, the blues coloration in jazz seduces the ear steeped in European music. From the base metals banged together on Tin Pan Alley in the 1920s, Louis Armstrong alchemized his dazzling melodies of pure gold.[8] And thereafter, the melodic inventiveness of jazz singers and instrumentalists became the chief inspiration behind what is now called the "golden age of American song," deeply influencing such gifted tunesmiths as Irving Berlin, Jerome Kern, Cole Porter, and George Gershwin.[9]

In the context of European modernism, of course, the mere attempt to defend the harmonic or melodic accomplishments of jazz may seem proof of its backwardness. Even the most radical departures from tonality made by innovators such as Taylor and Bill Evans are far less radical than Webern's. As long as serialism is considered the high-water mark of musical modernism, even the most avant-garde jazz will be seen as playing catch-up in a game that "serious" music has long since abandoned.

Of course, jazz's uniqueness does not lie in structure, harmony, or even melody. Let us recall that the structural complexity and harmonic richness of European music were achieved, like all good things, at a cost. Back in the seventeenth century, European music possessed a steady and enlivening beat—as evidenced by the fact that Jean-Baptiste Lully, the official composer and conductor in the court of Louis XIV, died of an infection caused by hitting himself in the foot with his staff-sized baton.[10] In the eighteenth century this explicit beat persisted as a necessary underpinning to the complex melodic counterpoint of Corelli, Vivaldi, and Bach. But with the romanticists of the following century, the emphasis shifted toward a single melodic line, and the rhythmic frame became more plastic. As Pleasants explains:

> The dramatic, reflective and recitative character of nineteenth-century Serious music exacted a price in rhythmic debility. . . . The dynamic faculty of tempo changes, both sudden and gradual, and all the dramatic inflection inherent in various types of acceleration and retardation, while they served an "interpretive" and "expressive" purpose in European music, also contributed to the weakening of the beat as a phenomenon collectively anticipated and collectively experienced.[11]

As for the beat in serialist and aleatory music, it is most accurately described by Groucho Marx's famous line: "Either this man is dead or my watch has stopped."[12]

Enter the Afro-American idiom. All European rhythm, even the liveliest baroque beat, sounds mechanical when compared with Afro-American rhythm. As one European exclaimed on first hearing the tricky syncopation of ragtime: "It has the power and the penetration to inject life into a mummy!"[13] Of course, even ragtime and early jazz sound mechanical when compared with true African rhythm. In the sense that its rhythm has become progressively more complex over the years, jazz has been moving forward into its own African past.[14]

A good description of African rhythm comes from the composer and musicologist Gunther Schuller, who explains: "African music, including its drumming, is wholly contrapuntal and basically conceived in terms of polymetric and polyrhythmic time relationships." Citing the work of the English musicologist A. M. Jones, Schuller continues: "African rhythm is based on additive rather than divisive principles."[15] By "divisive principles" Schuller means the "bar line" that has regulated rhythmic notation—and rhythm—in European music since the Renaissance. When first listening to African music, the Western ear expects the steady "structural" beat to function in the same manner—namely, to mark off regular measures or intervals of time, such as 2/4, which are then subdivided into smaller units, such as 4/4 or 8/4. In other words, we expect African rhythms to be metronomic: little ticks fitting evenly into bigger tocks. But African rhythms do not respect the bar line. They are "additive" in the sense that each vocal or percussive part has a slightly different rhythm, which coincides with, or "crosses," the other rhythms or the structural beat only at strategic moments.

Moreover, the structural beat is frequently implied rather than played, like the dominant in a chord, while the numerous other pulses surrounding the structural beat frequently receive equal, if not greater, accentuation. Schuller uses the phrase "the 'democratization' of rhythmic values" to described this "equality of dynamics among 'weak' and 'strong' elements."[16] The result is a thick rhythmic texture that suggests to the music theorist Leonard B. Meyer "an analogy between the role of the temporal organization in African music and the role of harmony in Western music." Meyer also cites Jones:

> All this rhythm-crossing is the spice of life to the African. It is his real harmony. He is intoxicated by this rhythmic harmony, or rhythmic polyphony, just as we react to chordal harmony. It is this remarkable interplay of mainbeats that causes him irresistibly, when he hears the drums, to start moving his feet, his arms, his whole body. This to him is real music.[17]

The important thing about rhythmic polyphony is that it helps to define that essential quality known as "swing." At some point, every critic tries to unpack Ellington's famous title, "It Don't Mean a Thing If It Ain't Got That Swing." But, like so many other qualities in music, swing eludes verbal definition. Hodeir comes closest when he states that swing depends on five things: "infrastructure" (structural beat), "superstructure" (rhythmic counterpoint), "getting the notes and accents in the right place," "relaxation," and "vital drive." But, as Hodeir then admits: "The first three are technical in nature and can be understood rationally; the last two are psycho-physical, and must be grasped intuitively."[18]

To illustrate the second crucial aspect of swing, "a specific type of accentuation and inflection," Schuller offers a homely but apt comparison: European musicians tend to vocalize their music with syllables containing soft consonants and short vowels, such as *da* and *di*; jazz musicians, by contrast, use syllables with more explosive consonants and fuller vowels, such as *djah* and *bah*.[19] That is, jazz musicians routinely attack their notes with a greater sonority and suggestion of timbre. For the origin of this distinctive attack, historians do not hesitate to go back to Africa. When Africans were first brought to the New World as slaves, their musical practices were tolerated in some regions: New England, the Middle Colonies, New Orleans.[20] But with the development of plantation slavery in the Deep South, African music—especially drumming—was suppressed. The reason was simple: However fanciful the notion of "talking drums" may sound nowadays, Southern slaveowners were well aware that some African drummers had the ability to transmit verbal messages over long distances.

Hence the quality in Afro-American music that the novelist and jazz historian Albert Murray calls a "fusion of incantation and percussion," in which instruments become "extensions of talking drums," and singers "play with their voices as if on brasses, keyboards, strings and woodwinds."[21] For Schuller, this link between incantation and percussion is the source of jazz's expressive individuality:

> Some would refer to this quality as "earthiness," others as "beauty of sound," while still others have seen it as raw and vulgar, since it lacked the "polite" sounds of European art music. But in purely acoustical terms of purity and amplitude, the open-toned, natural quality of African speech and song . . . can be heard . . . in the individuality and personal inflection of the jazz musician's tone. . . . Jazz's strength and communicative power lie in this individuality.[22]

In the European tradition, qualities similar to these were once valued as part of the performer's, as opposed to the composer's, art. But along with rhythm, the art of the performer lost its prominence in European music after the 1930s. Romanticists such as Paganini and Liszt were renowned both as composers and as freely interpretive performers for whom the written score was a point of creative departure. But with modernism, performers became, in the words of Leopold Stokowski, "slaves of little marks on a piece of white paper which we call music."[23] The striking exception, Pleasants reminds us, is jazz:

> In jazz, the relationship between composer and performer, and between musician and audience, has always been based, until recently, on the mutual acceptance of a common language. . . . The jazz musician has had to accept, of course, the discipline of a style, just as Haydn and Mozart did; but within this style he has enjoyed greater freedom than the Serious composer enjoys

today, the latter condemned to the search for a style of his own, or to the acceptance of dogma imposed by other composers.[24]

Jazz and Black Cultural Separatism

I realize that a great many musicians and writers will reject the proposition that Afro-American music is an idiom of Western music, on the grounds that it is, root and branch, totally "black," meaning African. This attitude is usually called "cultural nationalism," but I prefer to call it "cultural separatism," because, instead of affirming Afro-American music by sharing it with the world, it takes a jealously proprietary stance. That is, "black music" is defined as a latter-day talking drum, whose sole function is to communicate among the various black-skinned peoples of the African diaspora. Moreover, black cultural separatism sees that communication in wholly political terms, as part of the ongoing struggle against white racism. Other groups, especially whites, are not invited to eavesdrop—and if they do, they are not expected to understand. In other words, "black music" is coded for black ears only, and there is nothing positive about its having conquered the rest of the globe.

Much as I disagree with this attitude, I appreciate what motivates it: the seemingly endless capacity of whites to carry out self-serving raids on the Afro-American musical storehouse. The sociologist Charles Keil describes the pattern:

> The song and dance [of blacks] . . . were appropriated by white America via the white-controlled music business (record companies, music publishers, radio stations). The examples of this process are legion, and the alienation felt by Negro musicians, resulting largely from this process, is very real. Benny Goodman rose to fame on Fletcher Henderson's arrangements. Elvis Presley derived his style from the Negro rhythm-and-blues performers of the late 1940's . . . And of course the rocking Prince Valiant types from England are notorious plagiarists. These are only a few convenient examples among thousands.[25]

Albert Murray has suggested that, if the intellectual debate over race in America were not skewed toward the social sciences, it would be more evident that cultural resentment lies at the heart of black alienation.[26] He has a point: For every black creator, there's always been a pack of white predators; for every spark of black musical pride, there's always been a billow of resentment against those who profit from the music without returning credit or compensation to its creators. Furthermore, unlike the alienation fueled by poverty, this kind only increases when black people acquire the leisure to study their group's place in society. Rare indeed is the educated black man or woman for whom cultural pride can burn steadily without occasionally flaring into anger.

Nonetheless, the separatist definition of Afro-American music rests on a logical confusion. On the one hand, there is the undeniable fact that the creators of the idiom have been predominantly black. On the other, there is the equally stubborn reality that the musical ingredients of the idiom have been both "black," meaning African, and "white," meaning European.

It would be fascinating to penetrate the mists of time and detail the actual evolution of Afro-American music in the fields, cabins, hush harbors (secret places of worship), camp meetings, wayside inns, and plantation ballrooms of colonial America. Or to tour West Africa, as the folklorist Samuel Charters did in the 1970s, in search of "the roots of the blues." Yet, as Charters discovered, the mists of time are just as thick on the Gambia River as on the Mississippi.[27] Beyond the essential ingredients of rhythmic polyphony, rich sonority, and the intimate role of music in daily life, we cannot with any confidence distinguish between what the first Afro-American musicians inherited from their African forebears and what they picked up from British hymns and marches, Scottish ballads, Irish jigs, French quadrilles, German sonatas, and Italian operas.

Indeed, nothing is more distinctively African about the idiom than its boundless capacity to absorb outside influences. The African musical genius is flexible and inclusive, as Charters notes when he cites Arab influences in the playing of Gambia's *griots*, or tribal bards.[28] And the ravages of European colonialism did not prevent African musicians from absorbing such influences as polkas, marches, sea chanteys, folk ballads, and popular songs—a process that, by 1900, was already giving rise to the "highlife" styles that still dominate West African popular music.[29]

Then there is the fact that jazz not only conquered Europe, Latin America and parts of Asia—it also conquered Africa. The enthusiasm of Africans for jazz hardly suggests an identity with the music they already possessed. More likely, it betokens the human tendency to become fascinated and attracted by that which is both like and unlike oneself. How else to explain the ongoing rivalry between African and American jazz musicians, each madly recycling their resources in a dizzying succession of styles? The more we study this fertile interchange, the less we are able to draw a sharp line between the two continents.

The Afro-American idiom *is* quintessentially African in the sense of sharing the powerfully absorptive capacity of African music. But this is exactly why black American musicians have not traditionally taken a separatist stance toward music that is not "black." In Keil's view, the absorptive capacity of the idiom "derives primarily from a rhythmic substructure that can incorporate with ease the most diverse melodic and harmonic resources."[30] Quite true, but the reasons also go beyond formal aspects, to the basic situation of black people in America. As Ralph Ellison writes:

> Negro musicians have never, as a group, felt alienated from any music sounded within their hearing . . . For as I see it, from the days of their introduction into the colonies, Negroes have taken, with the ruthlessness of those without articulate investments in cultural styles, whatever they could of European music, making of it that which would, when blended with the cultural tendencies inherited from Africa, express their own sense of life— while rejecting the rest.[31]

From this account it is clear that black Americans did reject some of the European music they heard. But that rejection was part of a process of creative synthesis, not a programmatic insistence on preserving the "blackness" of their own tradition. As should be evident to anyone who has studied the cultural history of the twentieth century, the idea of preserving racial purity in cultural matters is not African at all, but rather a European obsession only recently emulated by others.

The Roots of Jazz: Minstrelsy, Ragtime, Storyville

When the spirit of black cultural separatism yearns to fly home to Africa, the place it yearns to escape from the most is the American South. Such yearning is patently explained by that region's tragic history of slavery and racial oppression. But while we should never forget this history, neither should we forget that the South is also the crucible in which black and white Americans jointly forged the nation's most distinctive culture. Not just the music, but also the folkways, oral traditions, and forms of religious worship that we think of as characteristically American have Southern roots.

The black cultural separatist wants to forget the intractably American side of the Afro-American equation. But to forget it is to forget our history. However rich the black strands of Southern culture may be, they are also permanently entangled with the white strands. Indeed, many of the songs, expressions, and customs we think of as "black" have European roots, while many of those we consider "white" go back to Africa. But this does not discredit either. Perhaps the most vital and admirable function of Afro-American culture has been to preserve a sense of dignity and identity among people forced to live in intimate proximity with others who consider themselves superior. To insist that "black" American culture occupy a space radically removed from "white" culture is to deny its unique genius. It is also, as Ellison writes, to commit a kind of violence: "To fashion a theory of American Negro culture ignoring the intricate network of connections which binds Negroes to the larger society . . . is to attempt a delicate brain surgery with a switch-blade."[32]

One subject guaranteed to bring out the switchblades is the ubiquitous form of nineteenth-century entertainment known as minstrelsy. It is not known exactly when whites first got the idea of smearing on burnt cork and imitating blacks for the entertainment of other whites. Nor is it known whether the practice was a British or an American invention. But it is well known that white minstrelsy deliberately appropriated the music and comedy of black slaves. By the 1820s solo white minstrels such as Charles Matthews (an Englishman) and Thomas D. Rice (an American) were corking up to appear on the same stage with popular renditions of Shakespeare.[33] And by the 1840s large troupes such as the Edwin P. Christy Minstrels were offering well advertised public revues in both America and Europe, complete with "Ethiopian melodies" and the comic adventures of such stock characters as the hayseed Jim Crow and the city slicker Zip Coon.

Few would disagree that white minstrelsy, whose popularity peaked before the Civil War, was at best a debasement, and at worst a grotesque parody, of the material it appropriated. To a cultural separatist like Amiri Baraka (LeRoi Jones), the appropriation of black material mattered less than the overall antiblack message: "It wasn't so much the performance that was side-splitting as the very idea of the show itself: 'Watch these Niggers.'"[34] Other writers who set less store by the sheer entertainment value of racism have suggested that white minstrelsy arose partly because black music, dance, and comedy were attractive in their own right. As the music historian Eileen Southern observes:

> The practices of white minstrels in the nineteenth century established unfortunate stereotypes of black men—as shiftless, irresponsible, thieving, happy-go-lucky "plantation darkies." . . . And yet, blackface minstrelsy was a tribute to the black man's music and dance, in that the leading figures of the entertainment world spent the better part of the nineteenth century imitating his style.[35]

Not only that, but knowledgeable whites attested to the superiority of the original. Southern reports that Lewis Paine, a perceptive white chronicler of antebellum plantation life, "dismissed the Fellow's Minstrels (a popular white minstrel group of the 1850s) as not 'bearing comparison' with the plantation slaves, chiefly because of the former's artificiality."[36] If, as Baraka suggests, the only purpose of white minstrelsy was to laugh at black faces, then why would a white observer object to its "artificiality"?

The answer is simple—and complex. On the simple level, it seems evident that antebellum whites were quite appreciative, even picky, about the quality of their black entertainment. As Southern describes, many slaveowners took pride in presenting this entertainment to outsiders: "More often than calling the slaves up to the big house, the slaveowner would take his guests down to the slave quarters to watch a frolic or a shout."[37] Nor was this appreciation confined to the wealthy. Here is the blues historian Robert Palmer's account of the musical tastes of less privileged whites: "In 1838, when the Norwegian concert violinist Ole Bull became the first classical musician to perform in Memphis, the locals received him coolly. 'If he had only . . . played a nigger fiddle,' a budding local critic complained, 'the Norwegian would have captured our . . . amateurs.'"[38]

On the complex side it was unlikely that white appreciation of black culture would lead to social change. To be sure, whites took pleasure in material that would be considered subversive by any self-respecting twentieth-century dictator. Consider the old favorite, "Blue Tail Fly," whose chorus expresses the slaves' lack of grief at their master's death: "Jimmy crack corn, I don't care / Ole Massa's gone away."[39] Or consider the "cakewalk," the dance whose agile contortions are a parody of stately European dances such as the minuet. There were few amusements more beloved by whites than the cakewalk.

Yet at the same time, it seems clear that the mind of the antebellum white possessed one compartment that relished the artistry of blacks, and another that endorsed their subjugation. It would likewise appear that the black mind possessed one compartment that craved the applause of whites, and another that resented their domination. History is full of such paradoxes—only a fool or an ideologue would insist on a neat one-to-one correspondence between what happens in art and what happens in society. By the same token, only a fool or an aesthete would say that there's no meaningful relationship between the two. There is a relationship, a powerful one. But it exists between two realities that move along separate, frequently divergent, paths.

After the Civil War, minstrelsy was drastically transformed by a massive infusion of black talent. All-black troupes arose, as well as troupes that included both black and white acts. Stars like James Bland, Billy Kersands, and Samuel Lucas became international celebrities in an era when most blacks were suffering the collapse of Reconstruction. Such a contrast in fortunes was, obviously, bitter. But, as Southern explains, it would be a mistake to see nothing but racial self-abasement in black minstrelsy:

> It is true that black minstrels blackened their faces with burnt cork (no matter how dark their skins), made up enormous red lips, and used traditional slapstick jokes and gestures, comic patter-songs, and stylized dances. But they also brought to the stage much genuine humor, original dancing, the poignant songs of their people, and superb solo and ensemble performance, both vocal and instrumental. After the war, minstrelsy offered to the creative black man an opportunity to acquire experience in the theatrical arts that could scarcely have been obtained any other way during the period.[40]

And soon black entertainers began shaking off the trappings of minstrelsy. Southern reports that, as early as the 1880s, Bland "dispensed with the blackface makeup . . . and toured the music halls and theatres of England and the Continent as an elegantly dressed singer-banjoist."[41] The 1890s saw the arrival, on Broadway and elsewhere, of all-black musical comedy revues, many of them created by blacks, that had no use for cork.

This change was due largely to the popularity of ragtime. In the first postbellum decades "rag music" was simply black dance music as played in the countless night spots that sprang up along the Mississippi River and elsewhere in the Southeast. Unable to afford bands or orchestras, these saloons, brothels, and gambling places employed the cheapest type of music available: a single "piano thumper" with a left hand able to keep the joint jumping far into the night. Among blacks some of these piano men became legendary, their virtuosity and endurance earning them the title "professor." But rag music reached white ears only through black minstrelsy, where it accompanied the cakewalk.

Then, in the 1890s, rags began to appear in written form as sheet music, both simple songs and more elaborate compositions such as those of the famous "King of Ragtime," Scott Joplin. For whites unable to render the proper syncopation from sheet music (Afro-American rhythms being next to impossible to notate), there was the ubiquitous player piano, with rolls cut by all the best piano men, including Joplin himself.[42] Minstrel comedy persisted into the early days of vaudeville, but by the turn of the century ragtime was a separate entity, the theme music for popular dance crazes sweeping both America and Europe. By 1910 the trend was clear: Tired of being spectators, the white folks were getting in on the act.

Ragtime also influenced band music. Apart from the minstrel troupes whose bands played a broad repertory, it is noteworthy how many other bands—especially dance bands—were black. Southern reports that in some parts of the country, whites avoided going into this line of work because, like barbering, it was seen as the natural province of blacks. In New York, for example, the celebrated bandleader James Reese Europe provided society patrons with "syncopated orchestras" in which the ragtime influence was evident: They introduced banjos, guitars, and saxophones into the usual strings and woodwinds; and, while playing the standard written repertory of the time, they nudged it toward ragtime. In 1914, when the white ballroom team Vernon and Irene Castle popularized the turkey trot, the one-step, and the fox-trot, their favorite band was Europe's.[43]

Then there were the brass bands. In many of America's parks and public spaces today, preserved bandstands still recall the days when, in the absence of electronic amplification, brass bands provided the loud, lusty music needed for outdoor celebrations, public ceremonies and simple Sunday afternoon diversion. Many of these bands were black as well, and sought something livelier than the monotonous "oom-pah-pah" of military music. For example, the U.S. Army's 369th Band, led during World War I by the same James Reese Europe, so impressed the leading military band of France that the French musicians disassembled the Americans' instruments to see if they had been specially adapted for the purpose of ragging John Philip Sousa.[44]

Nowhere were black bands more independent and inventive than in New Orleans. According to legend, jazz was born of a cross between that city's syncopated dance orchestras, which were dominated by the classically trained black Creoles in the genteel "downtown" section, and its brass bands, which were dominated by poor blacks in the parks and gin joints "uptown." In 1894 the city passed Jim Crow laws forcing the upper-crust "downtown" Creoles into the same segregated space as the low-down "uptown" blacks. And in 1899 the city passed another ordinance restricting its time-honored prostitution industry to a single neighborhood, dubbed Storyville after the author of the ordinance, Joseph Story. As the legend goes, it was there, in the brothels and nightclubs of segregated Storyville, that the syncopated dance musicians and their brass-band cousins put their heads together and came up with jazz.

The truth is a bit more complicated, because in New Orleans, both forms of music were already "jazzier" than elsewhere. For example, there was almost no trace of "oom-pah-pah" in brass bands such as Buddy Bolden's, which reportedly played a syncopated, richly sonorous blues as early as 1890.[45] As for the black Creoles, their dances were somewhat less genteel than the turkey trot. From his boyhood the clarinetist Sidney Bechet recalls "cutting contests," in which a group of men would "cut figures" around a jug placed on the floor, to music that was fast and rhythmically infectious. Some scholars have suggested that the black Creoles' love of virtuoso dancing, combined with their classical training, enabled them to play ragtime with greater speed and dexterity than anyone else, thus creating a more propulsive rhythm—in other words, swing.[46] It is certainly true that some of the finest early jazzmen were black Creoles: Bechet, Kid Ory, and the man most often credited with having "invented" jazz, Jelly Roll Morton.

I put quotation marks around the word "invented" because, despite the legend, there was no magic moment when Morton or some other New Orleans musician leaped to his feet and ran down Basin Street yelling, "Eureka!" Machines are invented; forms of music evolve slowly. Nor does a new form immediately replace its predecessors. The cotton gin was a new and better way of carding cotton fiber; jazz wasn't necessarily a new and better way of pleasing audiences. As should be evident by now, the enjoyment of Afro-American music was hardly a novel phenomenon in America—or Europe—at the time of jazz's first appearance.

Still, by the end of World War I, when the paddle steamers had carried it up the Mississippi River from New Orleans to Chicago, and the fledgling recording industry had carried it to New York and Europe, jazz did sweep aside most of its Afro-American predecessors, including ragtime. The farther it traveled from its point of origin, the less it retained of the faster rhythms and stronger blues presence that made it "hot." In a reversal of the white-to-black transformation of minstrelsy, early jazz was soon transmogrified into a dance music called "Dixieland" after its most famous proponents, the all-white Original Dixieland Jazz Band. Dixieland was pretty bland stuff compared with the peppery music of the best New Orleans groups, such as King Oliver's Creole Jazz Band (where Armstrong got his start). Like New Orleans cooking, New Orleans jazz derives its power from deftly balanced ingredients and carefully controlled heat. Consider this description of King Oliver's music by the historian James Lincoln Collier:

> It is, first and foremost, an ensemble music . . . each instrument has a sharply defined role to play. . . . The cornet, in Oliver's hands, set a simple, direct lead, with frequent gaps left for others to fill. The clarinet moved ver-

tically through this horizontal line, roving up and down the harmonies. The trombone underpinned the whole with slurs or very simple harmonic figures in the lower register. The rhythm section set a plain, unembellished, if at times dogged ground beat. . . . It was a disciplined band, and it had to be: with a texture this thick, any irrelevancy would have caused the structure to collapse.[47]

It would be nice to think that the dominant culture appreciated the vitality and discipline of this new type of music. But, just as there are some people in the world who shun spicy cooking on the archaic theory that spices signify corruption in the meat, so there were some people who shunned jazz on the equally archaic theory that lively rhythms and rich sonorities signify corruption in the music. Because jazz made its debut at a time of deep crisis in Western culture, it was perceived in some highly distorted ways. I hope to correct that distortion, both for jazz lovers and for those who are still engaged in the futile task of defending "serious" music against it. But in order to do so, I must depart from what Thomas Mann called "the weird music of the new world" and spend some time with the weird ideas of the old.[48]

Chapter 3

The Three Strains
of Modernism

When F. Scott Fitzgerald called the 1920s the Jazz Age, he didn't mean it entirely as a compliment. To be sure, Fitzgerald's novels glamorized the irreverent hedonism of college youth, upper-class Manhattanites, and idle rich expatriates seeking to free themselves from middle-class morality. But beneath the glittering surfaces he wrote about, Fitzgerald added an insidious current of terror and guilt. His most sympathetic characters, such as Nick Carraway in *The Great Gatsby*, stand uneasily apart from the frenetic gaiety surrounding them, brooding that all this seeming liberation is really a sign of social and spiritual disintegration. In this way, Fitzgerald captured the prevailing mood of a civilization overwhelmed by the waste and horror of World War I. When Fitzgerald attached the word *jazz* to the age, he was merely distilling the general view that the craze for such music was, if not a cause, then certainly a symptom of what Oswald Spengler called (in his book of the same name) "The decline of the West."

In Germany, where war had meant defeat and the collapse of empire, pessimism ran even deeper. In Thomas Mann's 1925 short story, "Disorder and Early Sorrow," an impoverished middle-aged professor of European history takes a worried view of ragtime and jazz while watching his grown children's friends dance at a party in his home:

> They move to the exotic strains of the gramophone, played with the loudest needles to procure the maximum of sound: shimmies, foxtrots, one-steps, double foxes, African shimmies, Java dances, and Creole polkas, the wild musky melodies follow one another, now furious, now languishing, a monotonous Negro programme in unfamiliar rhythm, to a clacking, clashing, and strumming orchestral accompaniment.[1]

Most distressing is the music's ability to "intoxicate and estrange" the professor's beloved five-year-old daughter. After dancing with a handsome youth and becoming roused to a state of passionate excitement inappropriate to her years, the child collapses in a bout of hysterical weeping that strikes mortal agony into her father's heart. Since Mann chooses jazz as the stimulus, first of the young people's indifference to history, and second of the child's trauma, it would seem that he, too, sees a link between "the weird music of the new world" and the decline of the old.[2]

But Mann is too wise to blame all this disorder and early sorrow on jazz. At one point the professor admits that "these mad modern dances, when the right people dance them, are not so bad after all—they have something quite taking."[3] Jazz is merely a detail in Mann's portrait of a cultivated German trying to accept the liberty of the present without abandoning the discipline of the past. When Mann finally wrote his definitive novel about the transformation of Western culture in the twentieth century, the weird music he focused on was not jazz, but that of a composer, modeled loosely on Schoenberg, who dreams of rebuilding Western music from the ground up. Like the professor, the hero of *Doctor Faustus* is a man of profound emotion, but also of reason, who fears and distrusts any form of art, culture, or politics that glorifies the irrational. The novel offers not only a meditation on the difficulty of reconciling reason, will, and passion in any art form, but also a skillfully navigated tour of the currents and crosscurrents of modernism. Such a tour is also needed in the present context, not just because those currents shaped the world's perceptions of Afro-American music seventy years ago, but because they still do.

Today, the so-called postmodernists tout the view that modernism is first, a monolith, and second, a memory. This view is mistaken, on both counts. Modernism has never been a monolith; on the contrary, it contains opposites as extreme as any in cultural history. And there is nothing new about postmodernism; almost all the ideas associated with it have always been part of modernism.[4] These points get lost in the contemporary debate, because the participants rarely stop to define what they actually mean by *modernism*. Some defend (or attack) it as a repository of civilized values; others attack (or defend) it as an assault on those same values. All base their assertions on whatever catalog of modernist works they happen to have in their heads at the time. As Dr. Johnson remarked about two women shouting at each other from adjoining houses on a London street, "They will never agree because they are arguing from different premises."[5]

The word *modernism* is simply too all-encompassing. At its broadest, it includes all the significant artistic currents of the past 150 years, currents that are disorderly within each artistic discipline, unruly as they flow across disciplines, and likely to follow a different trajectory within each art. Critics affix labels, but in the continual flux, only a few stick. Nonetheless, most people who argue about modernism for any length of time end up doing what I am about to do, which is to distinguish between its constructive and destructive tendencies. That both should coexist is hardly surprising, since the modernist period has been, above all, one of intense self-consciousness about the meaning and purpose of art. That is why I begin by explaining, as briefly as possible, where this self-consciousness comes from.

The Birth of Perversity

Art became self-conscious when it began having radical doubts about its relationship with the truth. It was Plato who first subjected the mythical truth sung by the poet to the standard of rational truth set by the philosopher. In the *Republic* he banned poets from his ideal society; in the *Laws* he admitted them on condition that they sing only songs approved by the philosopher-king. As for distinguishing between good singing and bad, Plato did so purely on the basis of philosophical truth. Indeed, his distrust of poetry stemmed from his acknowledgment that, like rhetoric, it can be used to embellish falsehood.

With Aristotle, art was given a realm of its own, with technical rules and standards unique to each discipline. Aristotle also analyzed the effects of art on the audience, for example judging tragedy on the basis of its ability to evoke pity and fear. Yet Aristotle did not depart from Plato's dictum that art is an imitation of nature. Nor did he challenge Plato's assumption that the purpose of art is to serve truth and virtue. Aristotle's aesthetic philosophy is a lot more sophisticated than Plato's, and it gives art a lot more free-dom. But it, too, revolves around the idea that art is subordinate to truth.

This idea held sway until the eighteenth century. There have been myri-ad disagreements—about technique, about how audiences are affected, about what aspects of nature ought to be imitated, and about what consti-tutes truth and virtue. But in all that time, and indeed in all the other civi-lizations of the world, art was never elevated to a position higher than that of other human endeavors such as education, politics, morality, and reli-gion. Only in the West, and only in the last two centuries, has art been placed on the pedestal that it still (somewhat shakily) occupies. Yet the irony of the tale is that it achieved this eminence only by breaking with the truth.

Art did not initiate the break. On the contrary, it was the truth—or, rather, the truth as defined by the rationalists of the Enlightenment—that broke with art, just as it broke with religion. By the early nineteenth centu-ry, rationalism had divided the universe into two zones: that which could be explained by the narrow type of reason called positivism, and that which could not. In the latter zone lay everything human, from the individual psyche to the social order. But that didn't deter the rationalists, who believed it was just a matter of time before everything, including their own souls, would be understood according to the correct methods—those used by Newton to understand optics. As the literary scholar M. H. Abrams observes, this worldview put art on the defensive: "The prevalence of philosophic positivism . . . claimed the method of the natural sciences to be the sole access to truth. . . . To some writers, it seemed that poetry and science are not only antithetic, but incompatible, and that if science is true, then poetry must be false, or at any rate, trivial."[6]

This combination of credulity toward natural science and skepticism toward all other truth claims is central to the condition known as *modernity*. Some people date modernity to the Renaissance, others to the Enlighten-ment, and still others to the Industrial Revolution. However bounded, modernity should not be confused with modernism. On the contrary, modernism is best understood as a reaction *against* modernity. Or, to put it more accurately, modernism is the successor to the original reaction against modernity, which was romanticism.

Now, romanticism was not a monolith either. We will not understand modernism until we understand that romanticism contained two sharply different conceptions of art. The first was that of the German romanticists, who, influenced by Kant, embraced a highly idealized doctrine of art with a capital *A*, summarized here by Abrams: "Poetry has intrinsic value, and as poetry, only intrinsic value. It is to be estimated by the literary critic solely as poetry, as an end in itself, without reference to its possible effects on the thought, feeling, or conduct of its readers."[7]

Today this doctrine of "art for art's sake" is widely believed to be the essence of romanticism: a retreat into foggy aesthetics by sensitive types unable to deal with the real world. But romanticism had a more robust aspect, especially in its early phase. The poet Goethe, for example, used science against itself, proposing organic metaphors for life and art against the mechanistic ones of the positivists. And the English romanticists went further, criticizing the extension of the scientific method into areas where it did not belong, and establishing solid truth claims for art in those same areas. Nor did the early romanticists confuse art with religion. Science may have cast its corrosive doubt upon both, but that didn't make them identical. That happened later, as Abrams notes:

> It was only in the early Victorian period, when all discourse was explicitly or tacitly thrown into the two exhaustive modes of imaginative and rational, . . . that religion fell together with poetry in opposition to science, and that religion, as a consequence, was converted into poetry, and poetry into a kind of religion.

Lost at this point was the older, more robust romanticism, in which "poetry has intrinsic value, but also extrinsic value, as a means to moral and social effects beyond itself."[8]

Having given up its traditional truth claims, art then became polarized. At one extreme was symbolism, a movement in late-nineteenth-century French poetry that sought, by freeing language from logic and meaning, to raise poetry to a radically autonomous, quasi-spiritual realm. At the other extreme was naturalism, an effort to make art into a quasi science by reporting the ills of society with ruthless, clinical detachment. The tension between these two impulses—the former to make art do the work of religion, the latter to make it a tool of scientific progress—was not unproductive. As the critic Edmund Wilson wrote in 1931, "The literary history of our time is to a great extent that of the development of Symbolism and of its fusion or conflict with Naturalism."[9]

Yet because both impulses are fundamentally antagonistic toward life as it is actually lived, their interaction also precipitated a plunge into artistic perversity. The cultural historian Jacques Barzun offers this harsh assessment: "Such, then, are the two streams of lethal influence: idealist and naturalist; or, to pair them in another way, sanctuary art and revolutionary art. . . . Both types of art regard the real world as disastrous, both are intended to make us emigrate, leaving it to its own perdition."[10]

Between them, symbolism and naturalism nurtured the late-nineteenth-century movement known as decadence, in which artists and assorted hangers-on dedicated themselves to Oscar Wilde's proposition: "It is through art, and *through art only*, that we can realize our perfection."[11] (emphasis added) Like the symbolists, the decadents worshiped art in a vacuum, so their ideas about it were ultimately incoherent. But that hardly diminished the appeal of a movement that held everything, including ideas, in contempt. For an incandescent wit like Wilde, it was possible to express that contempt with grace and skill. But the majority of decadents were not that brilliant, and the best they could do was define art in negative terms, as the absence—or better still, the inversion—of other values, especially moral ones. To establish one's creative bona fides, it was no longer necessary to make art; all one had to do was profess to worship beauty, lead a dissolute life, and mock traditional ideas of right and wrong. Meanwhile naturalism, having failed to inspire revolution, offered a vivid account of life in the "lower depths" as a sort of guidebook. Here began the tendency of Western artists to go slumming, not to help the dissolute poor, but to imitate them—the real purpose being, in Baudelaire's deathless phrase, to "shock the bourgeoisie."

Looming in the background, of course, was the philosophy of Friedrich Nietzsche. In his early writings Nietzsche echoed the robust romantic view that the only worthwhile use of reason in art is to confront, wrestle with, and finally incorporate the irrational. But in his later work, especially the tracts written just before he went insane in 1889, he attacked the entire Western tradition for suppressing the passions, inhibiting the will, and blocking the vital sources of human creativity. In his view, the great man, or the great artist, was the one who shattered the mold of tradition, moving "beyond good and evil" and forging a new reality. Needless to say, this idea fueled the decadent identification of art with perversity.

Barzun points out that, a century later, this conception itself has hardened into a mold. Indeed, this "quality of upsetting, inverting, upside-downing" has become "as mechanical and untrue as conventionality, of which it is the mirror image." Not only has it outlived itself, in Barzun's view, it has also eclipsed all previous conceptions of art—including symbolism and naturalism, which, for all their faults, were at least serious. Barzun sees contemporary artists as nothing but shock troops, seeking perversity for its own sake. He argues ferociously that perversity has nothing further to teach us; but he also despairs that it will ever lose its grip.[12]

I applaud Barzun's ferocity, but I reject his despair. Yes, perversity is our Academy. But no, the battle of ideas is not over, because, like all academies, perversity provokes opposition—not just among philistines and moralists, but also among educated people tired of the reigning orthodoxy of shock. Barzun himself hints at the nature of this opposition when he writes about the extraordinarily fertile phase of modernism that preceded World War I. He treasures those years, partly because they coincide with his own childhood (he was raised in an artistic household in prewar Paris), but also because there was something *different* about modernism then. Instead of retreating from the world (symbolism) or denouncing it (naturalism), the art of that period practiced a "new and exact realism," concerned with "the world and the fresh sense of its multiplying parts." Barzun recalls:

> Cubism (using the term inclusively and not just for painting) . . . changed the direction of thought and emotion by subordinating what is individual and subtle to a new desire for structure and solids. Concerned with space and time, Cubism caught and fixed the new perceptions arising from changes in man's command over space and time. And these perceptions it managed not merely to render but to organize.[13]

Some people would disagree, because they see the broken forms of cubism as similar to the confusing images in a symbolist poem: a retreat from shared human sense-experience and meaning, a deliberate refusal to communicate.[14] But there is a difference. Cubism may be baffling to the layman, but it's not a willful abandonment of shared reality. On the contrary, it makes a strenuous effort to bring painting closer to new and modern modes of perception. The great progenitor of cubism was Paul Cézanne, who began as a kind of symbolist, painting fevered, mostly fanciful images, only to end up imposing strict external discipline on his art. Cézanne studied color and light with the impressionists, but then went beyond them, toward a preoccupation with form that was almost mystical in its intensity. Yet as John Rewald observes, Cézanne never ceased to be a realist: "Nowhere in his canvases did Cézanne pursue this abstract concept at the expense of his direct sensations. He always found his forms in nature and never in geometry."[15] Following Cézanne's lead, cubism is also a kind of realism: formally innovative but vitally connected with the world.

Realism is a slippery concept in art history, mostly because Marxist critics have equated it with naturalism.[16] Like naturalism, realism engages, rather than retreats from, the world. But the great realists—Cézanne, Courbet, Millet, Flaubert, Dostoyevsky, George Eliot, Ibsen—were not naturalists. To be sure, their works take a cool, dispassionate stance toward social life and individual psychology, often laying bare the injustices of bourgeois society. Yet, because they retain the capacity for unsparing moral judgment, their art never sinks to the level of crude ideology or thrill-seeking decadence.

Like Barzun, I believe that this realist strain in modernism is the most admirable one. But, unlike him, I do not see it ending with World War I. On the contrary, I see it as a recurring tendency, bound neither by time nor by shifting definitions of particular "isms." By dividing modernism into three parts, I hope to show that the realist strain has survived, along with the perverse strain and the tendency toward art for art's sake. The effort is worth it, because the battle of ideas is still raging in all areas of culture, including popular music.

Before I elaborate on my three strains of modernism, let me say a word about *avant-garde*, the term still used to designate the latest artistic trends. It is ironic that so many so-called postmodernists consider themselves *avant-garde*, since there are few things in the world more *modernist* than the notion of an avant-garde. Yet this use of the term is not surprising. As evidenced by the literary scholar Renato Poggioli's heroic effort to devise a taxonomy of avant-garde movements, *avant-garde* has no consistent meaning with regard to ideas about art.[17] Whenever a different idea gains ground, *avant-garde* acquires a new coloration.

I call my three strains *perverse*, *introverted*, and *extroverted*. *Perverse* I take directly from Barzun, in the hope that it covers the widest possible array of antiart impulses. *Introverted* and *extroverted* I choose not for their psychological connotations (personality types), but for their simple dictionary meanings: "inward turning" and "outward turning." Although my purpose is to establish each strain as an analytic category, not a label for particular artists or periods, I shall nonetheless give concrete examples, to provide ballast against the hot air that inevitably seeps into such discussions.

Introverted Modernism

The first strain is *introverted* modernism, the art-for-art's-sake retreat from the world. This strain pays respectful obeisance to tradition, claiming, with Schoenberg, that "no new technique in the arts is created that has not had its roots in the past."[18] It also keeps, even intensifies, the high seriousness of romanticism. But introverted modernism is also radical, typically announcing itself as the only possible next step. Thus Schoenberg's student Webern did not hesitate to break radically with the past. As the music critic Robert Craft observes: "After his Opus 19 Pieces, Schoenberg was to return to the rhetoric and time-scale of Brahms, whereas Webern inhabited ever after a completely new time-world begotten only with the materials of 12-tone composition."[19] Likewise, the painter Wassily Kandinsky wrote that pure abstraction was "absolutely necessary and can in no way be avoided."[20]

Introverted modernism summarily rejects the shared sense-experience of the world. The shift is most obvious in painting, where, unlike Cézanne and the cubists, the pure abstractionists—or, more accurately, the "nonobjective" painters—sought an ideal realm radically separate from the visible forms of nature. For Kandinsky, this hidden realm was a spiritual one, and nonobjective painting a species of mysticism.[21] For the Russian painter Kasimir Malevich, all that counted was "pure feeling for plastic relationships."[22] For later movements encompassing crafts and architecture, such as de Stijl in Holland and the Bauhaus in Germany, the goal was, in the words of de Stijl founder Theo van Doesburg, "a new plastic beauty . . . in which no image based on phenomena is involved but where numbers, measurements and abstract line have occupied its place."[23]

Significantly these artists conceived of their efforts as approaching the condition of music, exalted by the philosopher Schopenhauer as "the most powerful of all the arts."[24] Music poses a challenge to the introverted modernist, however, because in its "absolute" or wordless form, it is already nonobjective. How, then, shall it be purified?

To the serialists, the answer was clear: Eliminate tonality. Such radicalism was opposed by many other composers and theorists who argued, with Paul Hindemith, that a break with tonality was a break with "the natural laws of sound."[25] Harking back to Pythagoras, such critics still contend that Western tonality is rooted in nature itself, on the grounds that the rudiments of harmony and the diatonic scale can be discerned in the series of "overtones" that accompany any naturally (that is, nonelectronically) produced musical tone. Yet nowadays, most scholars reject this view, noting that Western tonality is but one of many musical systems erected on the same natural foundation.[26]

Nevertheless, I would argue that there is a parallel between representation in visual art and tonality in music, on the grounds that both connect the sense-experience of the artist with that of the larger audience. Whether dictated by "the natural laws of sound" or imposed by the sheer weight of tradition, tonality has refused to die the death prescribed for it by the likes of Webern. And, likewise, serialism has failed to live the life predicted for it—that of a richly communicative artistic language.

We now arrive at another facet of introverted modernism: its cultivated indifference, even hostility, toward the audience. Schoenberg saw himself creating a method that would "secure the superiority of German music for the next two hundred years."[27] But in fact, he created a vacuum: The main impact of serialism has been to alienate the listening public from "serious" music. The serialists have not let this bother them, though. For three-quarters of a century they have followed the example set by Schoenberg in 1918, when he decreed that anyone wishing to attend the concerts of his Society for Private Musical Performances must display a photographic ID before being admitted.[28] In their view the tinier the audience, the finer the music.

At the same time, the introverted modernist is like any other artist in wanting to wield influence. So, while despising the larger public, he demands veneration from a tiny circle of initiates, whom he sees as the vanguard of his artistic revolution. In general, introverted modernism's aesthetic radicalism and its tendency to withdraw from the world cause it to cast its lot with political extremism. At midcentury the Italian futurists and the Russian constructivists shared an ardent faith that art and politics were directly linked, and that upheaval in one area would automatically lead to upheaval in the other. This faith lasted exactly as long as the usefulness of these movements to their totalitarian masters: until the 1920s in communist Russia, the 1930s in fascist Italy. Then they were crushed (a fact that, needless to say, continues to enhance the prestige of artistic radicalism in the minds of intellectuals).

Finally, introverted modernism confounds art with religion, conceiving of the artist's life as an uncompromising quest for what the art historian Barbara Rose calls "the irreducible essence."[29] For Kandinsky, this essence lay in the pure "sensations of colors on the palette," which he believed "became experiences of the soul."[30] For the serialists, it lay in the numerological relationships between tones. About Webern, one of his students insisted, "Ecstasy was his natural state of mind. His compositions should be understood as mystical visions."[31]

Whether mystical in its longing to transcend the world, or gnostic in its claim to possess occult wisdom, this quasi religiosity makes introverted modernism seem very high minded indeed. But the question is: To what purpose? Is there really much spiritual sustenance to be gained from contemplating the formal properties of color and tone? Is there any good reason to believe that art stripped to its bare bones is more "spiritual" that art with flesh and blood attached? Is art God, in the sense that one can seek communion with it by casting aside the things of this world? Such spiritual pretensions well deserve the scrutiny given them by the art critic Hilton Kramer, writing about the nonobjective painter Mark Rothko:

Rothko himself was adamant in that his art went "beyond" color—that its fundamental purpose was religious and spiritual. . . . He had carried painting to a point of extreme reduction, and had made something extraordinary out of what remained, and yet he still yearned for the world of meaning that painting had jettisoned on its way to colonize the extreme position . . . This, I think, helps to explain both the power of the art and its capacity to leave us with a sense of bafflement.[32]

It is interesting to note that Kramer's associate, the music critic Samuel Lipman, feels no such bafflement:

Why, it may be asked, should we aspire to live the life of culture? Why this unremitting labor, this sacrifice of immediate and assured pleasures, this eternal pursuit of unattainable perfection? Because culture, in an age when it is so hard to embrace the divine, when pursued in itself and on its own terms, represents our best secular means of transcendence; because of all worldly activity culture comes closest to revealing, and conserving, the best of which we are capable.[33]

Despite words like "secular" and "worldly," this passage could hardly be more pious in its renunciation of "immediate and assured pleasures" for the sake of "culture." I can offer no better rejoinder than this acerbic comment by Pleasants:

The Establishment's most formidable bastion remains society's acceptance of a concept of art as a kind of mystery—above and beyond the pleasures of the senses, separate and distinct from, and superior to, entertainment, amusement and diversion; of the artist as a source of revelation, a high priest answerable only to his assumed genius. . . . An extension of this curious notion—curious because so much of what we now celebrate as ultimate artistic accomplishment in the masterpieces of earlier times originated as entertainment and diversion—is the notion that art must be serious, sober, solemn and *meaningful*; that *enjoyment*, which may involve a high level of discrimination, is somehow "mindless."[34]

Perverse Modernism

To be fair, Lipman's piety is a reaction against the dominant strain of modernism today, perverse modernism. The first thing to note about this strain is that its attitude toward tradition is neither respectful nor radical—merely contemptuous. The pioneer of this attitude was Arthur Rimbaud, who arrived in Paris in 1871 as a fiery young provincial, seduced one of the symbolists, Paul Verlaine, and outraged the rest by personifying the decadent idea of the poet as social outlaw. Abandoned by his father, raised by his coldly puritanical mother, and educated by a succession of devoted tutors, Rimbaud had both the psychology and the talent to express what Wilson calls "the hysteria of the late nineteenth century in France, . . . an age recently deprived of religious faith, demoralized and embittered by war and already becoming dissatisfied with social utopianism, science and the cult of art as an end in itself."[35]

In a handful of prose poems written when he was between sixteen and nineteen, Rimbaud took symbolism to the very edge of perversity. His art doesn't go over the edge, because it is too brilliant to qualify as antiart. But Rimbaud himself took the leap: In the mid-1870s he burned his manuscripts, denounced books as good only to "cover up the leprosies of old walls," and fled Europe for East Africa, where he spent the rest of his short life in the social limbo between colonizers and colonized.[36] Thus Rimbaud was the first poet in history to be famous not just for his poetry, but for rejecting poetry as "disgusting" and "absurd."[37]

Next came futurism, that gleeful assault on tradition begun in 1909, when the poet Filippo Marinetti proclaimed Italy's intention to shake off "its smelly gangrene of professors, archaeologists, ciceroni and antiquarians."[38] The assault became less gleeful after World War I, when the international movement known as dada expressed the bitter disillusionment of artists at the ambitious political claims of prewar modernism. Beginning with Marcel Duchamp's famous gesture of painting a mustache on the *Mona Lisa*, dada was devoted not to making art, but to debunking it. Barzun calls this impulse "abolitionism"; Poggioli, "nihilism."[39] Whatever the name, it is still with us.

One of the prime movers of dada, André Breton, was also the author of the *Surrealist Manifesto*. Beginning in the mid-1920s, surrealism combined symbolism and Freud in a new conception of art as the direct, spontaneous expression of subconscious desires. Paradoxically, surrealist painters such as Dalí and Magritte became popular: Their subjects were dreams, nightmares, and fantasies; but their techniques were vividly representational. Unlike the nonobjective painters, they made *pictures*.

Not so the surrealist writers: Their technique of "automatic writing" produced mostly gobbledygook. Like futurism and dada, surrealism saw the line between art and life as artificial, crying out to be erased. To his credit, Rimbaud quit calling himself a poet when he quit writing poetry. Not so the perverse modernists of the twentieth century: For them, art is no longer a matter of making objects, but of pointing to objects in the world and proclaiming, "This is art because I say so." Certainly this is what Duchamp did when he placed a urinal in an art galley.

Such pointing and proclaiming has obvious appeal for the untalented. Luigi Russolo, for example, was a mediocre futurist painter until he saw the possibility of becoming a composer without writing music—that is, by celebrating the "noise music" of the city: "the palpitation of valves, the coming and going of pistons, the howl of mechanical saws, the jolting of a tram on its rails, the cracking of whips, the flapping of curtains and flags."[40] Instead of trying to capture the "variety and din" of the industrial age in musical form, Russolo simply signed his name to the racket.[41]

The next challenge was to get one's signature read. Perverse modernists have contempt for the educated audience, but they want desperately to reach the common people, the masses who normally take no interest in art. As the art historians Caroline Tisdall and Angelo Bozzolla write:

> The Futurists turned their backs on the life of the cultivated intellectual. They ridiculed both the servile respect for fossilized learning and the rejection of society implicit in traditional bohemian withdrawal. Instead, like the Dadaists and Russian Constructivists later, they opted for the public arena and demanded instant reaction.[42]

There's nothing perverse about wanting to overcome isolation and reach a larger audience; what's perverse is the blind impatience that demands an "instant reaction." Regrettably, such impatience is the essence of perverse modernism's relationship with the mass media. When the perverse modernist looks at the media, he doesn't see imagery or methods that might stimulate his art, as the cubists did when they incorporated clippings from *Le Figaro* into their brilliantly constructed collages. Instead, the perverse modernist sees only the instrument of his own fame: It's no accident that Marinetti's 1909 *Manifesto and Founding of Futurism* appeared, as a paid ad, on the front page of *Le Figaro*. By using a newspaper not to create art but to publicize himself, Marinetti became the first pure celebrity of the twentieth century—in today's parlance, "famous for being famous."

The inevitable result of such publicity seeking is a leveling of the distinction between high art and low entertainment. When the perverse modernist looks at popular culture, he doesn't see the occasional work that measures up to high aesthetic standards but rather a bludgeon with which to attack tradition, as well as other, more serious artists. It is fascinating to note that Rimbaud was already doing this in the 1870s. In *A Season in Hell*, his most famous prose poem, he strikes a chord instantly recognizable today:

> For a long time I . . . held in derision the celebrities of modern painting and poetry.

I loved maudlin pictures, the painted panels over doors, stage sets, the back-drops of mountebanks, old inn signs, popular prints, antiquated litera-ture, church Latin, erotic books innocent of all spelling, the novels of our grandfathers, fairytales, children's storybooks, old operas, inane refrains and artless rhythms.[43]

Dubbed "camp" in the 1960s, and "postmodernism" today, this relentless leveling has been going on ever since.

So has the commandeering of popular entertainment. In the 1890s the decadents used nightclubs, cafés, and cabarets to get their message across. Ten years later Marinetti dreamed of reaching the masses through a format called "synthetic theater," modeled after the Italian popular theater and the English music hall.[44] In Russia the constructivists turned to the circus.[45] With dada the choice was again cabaret: A group of German dadaists opened the Café Voltaire in Zurich in 1916, as a locus for poetry readings, manifesto declamations, political speeches, skits, dances, and "noise music" performances. Soon dada cabaret was cropping up all over Europe: By the early 1930s the cabarets in Berlin were mounting their attack on the Weimar Republic. And in Paris, the surrealist poet Antonin Artaud hosted the "theater of cruelty": sadistic spectacles staged for the announced pur-pose of shocking the public out of its rational mind.

The only trouble was that the more perverse modernism comman-deered these popular formats, the less popular they became. It wasn't the common people who went to Munich's Café Simplicissimus, the Grand Guignol, Marinetti's "futurist evenings," the Café Voltaire, and Berlin cabaret; it was the political and cultural avant-garde, hoping that this kind of "intimate theater" would, in spite of its unpopularity, foster revo-lution.[46]

And so it did, though not as directly and happily as the avant-garde wished. Like introverted modernism, perverse modernism has a strong affinity for totalitarianism: As mentioned earlier, both futurism and con-structivism went along with the dream of a brand-new, all-powerful state realizing their most cherished schemes for the radical transformation of art, society, and human nature itself. To speed the arrival of that bright future, both movements made maximum use of their pointing-and-pro-claiming skills. For the futurists, the aestheticization of industry was extended to riots, mass demonstrations, and finally war, with special emphasis on the revitalizing power of violence. By the 1930s this tenden-cy was so prevalent in fascism that it drew harsh criticism from Marxist intellectuals, notably Walter Benjamin. But what Benjamin did not admit was that the same process of aestheticization was occurring on the left. As Tisdall and Bozzolla observe:

> The prime example of Russolo's aestheticization of city life took place, not in Futurist or even Fascist Italy, but in the hopeful days of young Soviet Russia. In 1920 the *Concert for Factory Sirens* was performed: work was beautiful, and the sweetest noise for the workers was the orchestrated unison of the sirens that summoned them. This was certainly carried out quite independently of anything Russolo had written, but it illustrates the complexity of both the aesthetics and the politics of those years in which a shared experimental enthusiasm could inspire tendencies which were later to emerge as political polarities.[47]

Again, it wasn't long before these "political polarities" crushed all forms of modernism, including the perverse. In the former Eastern bloc, dadaist gestures have sometimes been made by dissident artists—but, paradoxically, more often during "thaws" than during periods of repression. The paradox is not too puzzling: Under brutal regimes, dissident artists lose their taste for perversity—first, because the state is already perverse enough; and second, because people who risk their lives for art tend not to do it for nihilistic antiart.

To be fair, perverse modernism is not really compatible with totalitarianism. At its core it is anarchistic, hell-bent on disrupting the systematizing power of all organization, social as well as political. After World War II this anarchistic core became dominant, and perverse modernism's reflexive rejection of all authority—and equally its reflexive demand for total freedom—became a fixture in the open societies of the West.

I realize that in some quarters the openness of those societies is still debatable. Perverse modernism has long shared the leftist conviction that Western society is indistinguishable from fascism. In recent years many on the left (and the former left) have come to see this conviction as grossly out of sync with economic, social, and political reality. But few have taken the next step, into cultural reality. Perverse modernism didn't cause two world wars, fascism, and communism. But it did foster a climate in which artists were seen, by themselves and others, as implacably opposed to the values of ordinary people; and in which contempt for morality was seen, by elites and common people alike, as a mark of superiority. In the aftermath of the Nazi holocaust and the Stalinist terror, many artists and critics have been moved to reconsider the quasi-Nietzschean proposition that great personalities can and should generate their own moral values, without regard for the forms those values have taken throughout human history and in all human societies. But, regrettably, many other artists and critics still believe that the sole purpose of their enterprise is, in Lionel Trilling's damning phrase, "a negative transcendence of the human."[48]

The Recourse to Obscenity

That majority includes the many Western artists who now seek "a negative transcendence of the human" while living off taxpayers' money. To judge by the protests routinely voiced by these artists, their peculiar situation has so isolated them from the rest of the world that their ideas never undergo a reality check. On the one hand, they take as their mission the radical disruption of a (presumably) oppressive social and political order. On the other, they complain that the power behind that order—that is, the government—won't pay their bills. The hypocrisy of this position is well skewered by the political scientist Kevin Mulcahy:

> Frankly, there is something disingenuous about the creators of confrontational art or (in Arthur Danto's phrase) "disturbatory" art expressing shock that the taxpayers they meant to offend may themselves be shocked that public monies would be expended to support such works. The most culturally radical person might indeed take a certain pride in having so outraged the bourgeoisie as to be rejected for public funding.[49]

George Orwell frequently observed that there are some ideas so preposterous, only an intellectual can believe them. Today he might add, "Or an NEA grantee."

The true perversity of this situation emerges when we consider the nature of the controversy being stirred up by "disturbatory" art. To listen to its champions, one would think that it was over *ideas*, such as those held by radical anarchists, militant feminists, gay rights activists, and racial separatists. As one such champion wrote recently: "We need more controversial art, not less, to allow the troubling thoughts in our collective unconscious to bubble to the surface nonviolently, to become part of the public debate and, it is hoped, to be resolved."[50]

So deep is the groove worn by modernism that most people automatically assume that art expresses ideas that cannot be expressed in other fields, such as politics, science, philosophy, or religion. In this sense, we still respect the defiant stance taken by art when it was forcibly exiled by positivism. Yet this is the last decade of the twentieth century, and the old defiance is no longer needed. Positivism has faded from most minds, including most scientific minds. Nor do most educated people feel they have much to learn from art; with regard to the important intellectual currents of the day, art is a camp follower. Indeed, it follows at such a distance that it is more accurately described as a straggler.

How, then, shall the straggler persuade itself that it is out in front? By provoking a reaction that resembles, as closely as possible, the original bourgeois reaction to the ideas, sensibilities and formal innovations of modernism. The litany is familiar: The bourgeoisie abused Manet for painting in a nonacademic style; the bourgeoisie censored Flaubert for writing about adultery; the bourgeoisie jeered Stravinsky's *The Rite of Spring*. Nothing gives today's perverse modernist greater pleasure than to identify with these giants—on the grounds that he, too, is shocking the bourgeoisie.

But what is the nature of the shock? Are anarchists, feminists, gay rights activists, and racial separatists banned from contemporary political discourse? Is it forbidden to exhibit paintings that don't employ traditional perspective or depict Christian themes? Do the police enforce laws against the literary representation of extramarital or homosexual sex? Do audiences object to pounding rhythms and pagan rituals in concert halls? Granted, there are some earnest citizens out there who seem never to have heard of modernism—or, if they have, consider it the work of the devil. But such people are increasingly rare. The vast majority accepts, however dubiously, the right of "modern art" to do anything—or just about anything—it wants.

Does this mean that the majority cannot be shocked? No, one thing remains shocking: obscenity. But the first step in understanding obscenity is to shift attention away from an exclusive preoccupation with sex. Current state laws, based on *Miller* v. *California*, define obscenity (or pornography; the terms are interchangeable in this context) as any work appealing mainly to "prurient interest," depicting "sexual conduct" in a "patently offensive way," and lacking any "serious literary, artistic, political, or scientific value."[51] This definition evolved out of a century-long legal battle over the portrayal of sex in serious literature, and its narrow focus represents the decisive victory of art over the notion that any reference to sex, regardless of motive or effect, is inherently obscene.[52] Yet, precisely because *Miller* exempts material possessing "serious artistic value," it is irrelevant to the problem we face today—namely, that perverse modernism makes obscenity and serious artistic value synonymous.

This use of obscenity has a history, as we shall see in a moment. But first let me offer my own definition of obscenity—or rather, my paraphrase of the most useful definition I have found. It comes from the legal scholar Harry Clor, who makes it part of a procensorship argument. My own position is that before we start to *censor*, we should try to *censure*, meaning forcefully and intelligently criticize the use of obscenity by today's "artists." They will cry "censorship," of course. But that is what they always do when other people exercise the right of free speech.

In essence, Clor argues that obscenity does not reside in particular bodily functions or conditions, but in the angle of vision taken toward them. Wisely he begins not with sex but with sensationalist media coverage of fatal accidents, in which dismemberment and death are presented in total detachment from the suffering of the people involved. His other examples include a passage from Joseph Heller's novel *Catch-22*, in which a World War II bomber pilot named Yossarian watches the entrails of Snowden, his fatally wounded crewmate, spill messily onto the floor of their airplane. Quoting Yossarian's appalled cry that "man is garbage," Clor explains why, despite this horror, the passage is not obscene:

> It is true that Yossarian comes to a somewhat obscene conclusion about the nature of man. But he comes to it against his will. . . . The reader, identifying with Yossarian, is . . . not stimulated to give vent to morbid or bestial fantasies and feelings about death. He is encouraged to *think* about death in a human context. . . . Here, then, a fundamental distinction is to be made between a literature which treats of things private or of human debasement and literature which invades privacy and debases man.[53]

Despite its focus on literature, Clor's definition of obscenity is equally relevant to other media:

> Obscenity . . . consists in a degradation of the human dimensions of life to a sub-human or merely physical level. . . . Thus, there can be an obscene view of sex; there can also be obscene views of death, of birth, of illness, and of acts such as that of eating or defecating. Obscenity makes a public exhibition of these phenomena and does so in a way such that their larger human context is lost or depreciated.[54]

As Clor points out, obscenity is a constant in human life. But its use as a surrogate for genuine art—to provoke a reaction similar to that provoked by the original modernists—dates back only about a century, to the decadent substitution of inverted morality for art. Real poets don't need obscenity: Rimbaud's account of the passion he awoke in Verlaine speaks only of "mysterious delicacies," "kindnesses," "kisses and friendly arms," and "a sombre heaven into which I entered and where I longed to be left, poor and deaf and dumb and blind."[55] Even Wilde, that celebrated exponent of gay rights, was outraged when his lover's father publicized the affair.

It's worth repeating that not all obscenity is sexual. In the 1890s, Barzun reminds us, the decadents frequented the Grand Guignol theater, which specialized in "quick skits of cynically atrocious brutality and bloodshed."[56] In the Café Simplicissimus a similar crowd witnessed the extemporaneous performances of Frank Wedekind, a playwright who defied the official censors by excoriating the kaiser, spewing profanity, urinating, masturbating, even going into convulsions onstage. This greatly impressed the future dadaist Hugo Ball: "To me the theatre meant inconceivable freedom. My strongest impression was of the poet as a fearful cynical spectacle: Frank Wedekind . . . was struggling to eliminate both himself and the last remains of a once firmly established civilization."[57] If Wedekind had been an isolated eccentric, his "fearful cynical spectacle" would not be worth remembering. But he was one of the fathers of expressionism. I haven't mentioned expressionism so far, because it stands somewhat apart from the rest of early modernism. But, as the movement most attracted to obscenity, it's worth a brief digression.

The expressionists were a group of German and Austrian painters, composers, and playwrights who combined symbolism and naturalism in a new and different way: Instead of retreating into the rarified realm of art, or exploring the squalid depths of society, the expressionists plunged into the turbid depths of their own psyches. The movement ran parallel with the early days of psychoanalysis, but there was a difference. Freud was ever the scientist, conjuring the irrational in order to strengthen the rational, which he revered as the essence of Western civilization. The expressionists, by contrast, were in open revolt against the "civilized" repressiveness of Austro-German society. So they were both attracted and repelled by the irrational. Beginning with the erotic nudes of Klimt, the movement soon specialized in the haunting, staring, cadaverous figures of Kokoschka and Schiele, which eerily foreshadow the living dead of the Nazi concentration camps.

Not that the expressionists were thinking about public horrors. For them, the horrors of private life, especially sex, were sufficient. As the historian Carl Schorske writes, expressionism was a "subversive and aggressive thrust against an excessively sublimating culture" that tried to "affirm the primary reality of sex as interior personal experience." Yet, because the expressionists were also products of that culture, "the most searing sense of shame . . . is central to the young Expressionist's anguish."[58] Out of shame, artists such as Wedekind felt compelled to torment themselves and others. The literary scholar Robert Corrigan explains:

> German expressionism was schizophrenic in nature. On the one hand, it was idealistic and celebrated in a mystical way the need for love and universal brotherhood in a bewildering and confusing world. On the other, it stri-

dently encouraged the grotesque dramatization of every form of brutality, cruelty, bestiality, and sensuality. . . . Morality is seen as the most lucrative of all rackets, and sexual emancipation is hailed as the only means of curing a diseased society.[59]

Again, this conception of art appeals to lesser lights, both those who lack talent and those who squander it. A good example of the latter is a student of Freud's named Otto Gross, the son of a prominent Prussian criminologist, who rebelled not only against his disciplinarian father, but also against his rationalist mentor. While Freud wanted to tame the beasts of the unconscious, Gross wanted to turn them loose. Like Wedekind, Gross called for revolt against "the patriarchs," meaning all male authority figures from Papa to Bismarck.

Gross's intellect soon degenerated under the influence of cocaine and other drugs. But that didn't stop him from proselytizing the "erotic movement" that, according to the historian Martin Green, formed "the crux of an ideological revolution that seems to have occurred all over Europe between 1890 and 1910."[60] In England this ancestor of today's sexual revolution was touted by the Edwardian "neopagans," Wildean aesthetes such as the poet Rupert Brooke, who visited Munich in 1911 and 1912.[61] It also had a direct impact on Frieda von Richthofen, the young Prussian who had been Gross's disciple before abandoning her husband and children to elope with D. H. Lawrence. It is well known that Richthofen inspired many of Lawrence's heroines. It is less well known that she did so as a self-conscious embodiment of the erotic movement.[62]

To his credit, Lawrence did not share the expressionist attraction to obscenity. On the contrary, his best work makes a sharp distinction between the erotic and the obscene, arguing that sexual repression and obscenity are but two sides of the same coin. Repression, he believed, leads to "sex in the head," an obsession with fantasy that in turn leads to pornography, defined as an "attempt to insult sex, to do dirt on it."[63] Unfortunately, when Lawrence grew older, he made an error typical of latter-day romanticists: He confused sex with religion. As the poet Stephen Spender writes: "Lawrence seems convinced that the forces of the unconscious released by the sexual act might transform the whole world, make men and women become gods instead of being social units."[64]

In the end, the project of erotic liberation fails because it denies shame. In repressive cultures the slightest reference to sex causes undue shame. But do we conclude, therefore, that human beings should never feel shame? Not according to the psychologist Georges Bataille, who reminds us that shame is a natural, universal response to nakedness and eroticism. In most human societies, Bataille notes, these states are regarded as taboo—which does not mean forbidden, but rather sacred and awe inspiring, connected with the mysterious beginnings and endings of life. So the subjective experience of these states is hedged about with barriers and controls:

> Obscenity is our name for the uneasiness which upsets the physical state associated with self-possession. . . . Through the activity of organs in a flow of coalescence and renewal, like the ebb and flow of waves surging into one another, the self is dispossessed, and so completely that *most creatures* in a state of nakedness, for nakedness is symbolic of this dispossession and heralds it, *will hide*; particularly if the erotic act follows, consummating it.[65] (emphasis added)

Note that Bataille says "creatures," not "the bourgeoisie." In his view, the unnatural fruit of Western civilization is not the existence of taboos surrounding sex; such taboos exist in all cultures. Rather it is the deliberate, intellectualized attempt to eliminate them:

> I must first make plain the futility of the common contention that sexual taboos are nothing but prejudice and it is high time we were rid of them. The embarrassment and shame that go hand in hand with a strong feeling of pleasure are supposed to be simply proofs of stupidity. We might just as well say that we ought to make a clean sweep of the whole business and get back to animal habits of eating anything and ignoring filth and excrement. Just as though our whole humanity did not spring from the reaction of horror followed by fascination linked with sensitivity and intelligence.[66]

Today's perverse modernists identify shame with repression because they are committed to obscenity as the only reliable way to get a shocked reaction from the public. They flatter themselves that this reaction is akin to the great scandals of the modernist past. But in fact it comes neither from public resistance to aesthetic innovation, nor from a high degree of prudery in the culture. Instead it reflects the simple fact that most people are not exhibitionists or voyeurs. Most people feel a trace of shame and a strong need for either ritual or privacy when eating, eliminating, making love, suffering, and dying. If that makes them unable to appreciate "art," then the word has lost its meaning.

Extroverted Modernism—and Jazz

The third strain of modernism, which I call *extroverted*, is descended from cubism, realism, and robust romanticism—that is, it represents the survival, even today, of the venerable Western (and non-Western) conception of art as having "intrinsic value, but also extrinsic value, as a means to moral and social effects beyond itself."[67]

To begin with, extroverted modernism is neither aggressively radical nor arrogantly dismissive of tradition. On the contrary, it struggles to reconcile past and present in what Spender calls "a vision of the whole."[68] Consider Picasso, whose cubist experiments were built upon the solid foundation of draughtsmanship he acquired at the Royal Academy in Barcelona. Throughout his tumultuous career, Picasso kept returning to that foundation—seeking, perhaps, the discipline and restraint that make cubism his finest achievement.[69] Likewise, Stravinsky's vital modernism is rooted in the lessons of such mentors as Rimsky-Korsakov and Tchaikovsky.[70] In literature, the best-known statement of this approach is T. S. Eliot's essay, "Tradition and the Individual Talent," which argues that innovation is justified only after a thorough immersion in, and mastery of, the past: "[Tradition] cannot be inherited, and if you want it you must obtain it by great labor."[71]

At the same time, the extroverted modernist relates his art to life as it is actually lived—not just by the privileged few, or by artists, but by everyone. The paintings of Manet, Monet, and Van Gogh depict the daily life of peasants and humble city dwellers; the diction of Eliot and Joyce includes the vernacular speech of the streets and cafés; the music of Bartók, Vaughan Williams, and Falla incorporates folk melodies. All of these modernist efforts contain a tug-of-war between the momentum of formal innovation and the imperative of realism. As Hilton Kramer writes about cubism:

> Much of the high drama that we experience in following the creation of this style and its evolving vision from painting to painting derives from the tension and conflict that we see enacted in the struggle of these artists to retain some residual contact with the representational function of art while feeling more and more compelled to give a fuller and more intense expression to the more formal, abstracting elements of their own discoveries.[72]

This continuing contact with shared sense-experience must not be confused with the perverse-modernist project of erasing the line between art and life. Such confusion was evident in a recent exhibition at the New York Museum of Modern Art called "High & Low" in which masterpieces of cubist collage were placed alongside a re-creation of Duchamp's urinal. Apparently the curators saw no difference between the cubists working the headlines into their art, and the dadaists getting their art into the headlines.

As for the audience, it was Flaubert who declared: "Humanity hates us, we shall not serve it and we shall hate it."[73] Again, antagonism was typical of the original modernists, whose work was routinely abused by the Academy and the Salon, as well as by bourgeois critics mired in such stale repetitions of past glory as sentimental poetry and heroic painting. But, as Kramer persuasively argues, there is no *inherent* reason why nonperverse modernism should remain the enemy of middle-class life.[74] And indeed, it has not. Ever since World War II modernism has occupied the pinnacle of cultural status—and become popular on a scale unimagined by its creators.

Perhaps the most distinguishing characteristic of extroverted modernism is its attitude toward popularity. Extroverted modernism doesn't curry favor with the public, and it can be sharply critical of fashion. But, unlike its introverted counterpart, it doesn't feel compelled to defy popular taste or to overestimate art that is inaccessible to ordinary people. On the contrary, whenever it finds itself pleasing audiences that do not fully comprehend its aesthetic language, it accepts the fact with equanimity. Indeed, extroverted modernism shows itself to be the most traditional strain in openly craving recognition. Manet and the impressionists, for instance, were deeply hurt by the Salon's disfavor, and sought acceptance as ardently as they could without betraying their principles.[75] Lacking introverted modernism's scorn for contemporary experience and the common man, extroverted modernism retains the capacity to please and entertain.[76] Yet, at the same time, it does not stoop to the publicity-seeking antics of perverse modernism. It is didactic in the best sense: Neither withdrawing nor pandering, it seeks to impart a new sensibility to the largest possible audience.

Thus extroverted modernism reminds us that popularity is one of the traditional criteria for judging the value of art. I'm not making it the only criterion, however. On the contrary, the traditional approach to judging art begins by comparing new work with the best of the old. Then it asks whether the new work says something about contemporary reality. And finally it evaluates the work's impact on the audience, with the emphasis on the long term. This latter criterion, the "test of time" as first articulated by Dr. Johnson, is the best kind of popularity test, relying not on the vicissitudes of fashion but on the gradual process by which genuine art moves from its point of origin to its permanent niche in history.

The same is true of popular culture. The difference, of course, is that the masterworks of popular culture begin their career as commodities in the marketplace. But this origin does not, and should not, prevent their finding their rightful place in history. This argument wouldn't sound so outlandish if the two other strains of modernism, introverted and perverse, had not effectively conspired to eliminate the criterion of popularity from our aesthetic judgments.

Finally extroverted modernism does not commit the error of making art into a religion. It remains modest about the presumed transcendence of art in a way that leaves room for genuine spirituality, including orthodox belief. According to the art historian Christopher Green, this modesty stems from a persistent rationalism that refuses to mount the pedestal on which art makes extravagant truth claims that no one really believes.

Comparing cubism with de Stijl, Green writes:

> However much the non-objective painting of de Stijl could be made accept-
> able to the Cubists . . . the definitive metaphysical role given to art (as reli-
> gion and philosophy in the visual mode) simply was not acceptable. . . . At
> its most stubborn the French resistance to abstract and non-objective paint-
> ing stemmed from the shared conviction that art should be founded on the
> concrete, the visible (either nature or the elements of painting or both), and
> the refusal to believe that art could realize abstract universal truths.[77]

Instead of universal truths, extroverted modernism realizes individual truths with sufficient force to render them universal. As the literary critic Fredric Jameson notes: "The great modernists were . . . predicated on the invention of a personal, private style, as unmistakable as your fingerprint, as incomparable as your own body."[78]

In music, we also find individual expression of a very high order—if we know where to look. Pleasants argues that jazz qualifies as a form of musical modernism, but the "serious" music establishment still hesitates. There are three important reasons for this hesitation, one musical and two non-musical, which I shall explore in the rest of part 1. The first reason, the musical one, which I'll explore here, is jazz's failure to have much impact on those modernist composers who, in their exploration of folk sources, took an active interest in the weird music of the New World.

Debussy led the way, copying the syncopation of ragtime in three pieces composed before 1913. After World War I, when New Orleans jazz appeared, similar efforts were made by Stravinsky in Russia, Ravel and Mil-haud in France, Copland and Ives in America. For some jazz enthusiasts, this was a great moment, proof (in the words of one historian) that "the new popular culture was beginning its assault on the musical Parnassus!"[79]

But a more sober assessment is found in Hodeir, who explains why the assault fizzled. First, most of these compositions inserted jazz rhythms, or what were supposed to be jazz rhythms, into settings lacking the steady pulse of a structural beat. "By destroying the basic pulsation," Hodeir writes, "our composers killed the principle of attraction on which the phenomenon of swing depends." Second, these jazz-flavored works were not intended to be performed by jazz musicians. The composers may have wished that symphonic musicians would learn the new idiom, but wishes couldn't supply "that indispensable intermediary, the interpreter." Hodeir explains:

> Anyone who is acquainted with jazz knows that the best-conceived rhythms remain insignificant unless they are performed with swing. Similarly, jazz sonority cannot be expressed by a stereotyped timbre or series of timbres; it must be created anew with each phrase. It takes a long acquaintance with jazz to assimilate its language; what concert soloist, what chamber music specialist has enough time to bring off such an attempt successfully?[80]

If the modernist composers had understood their failure that lucidly, jazz would not have been harmed by it. But they tended to blame jazz's limitations instead of their own. Typical was Milhaud's 1927 declaration: "The influence of jazz has already passed by, like a salutary storm after which the sky is purer . . . renascent classicism is replacing the broken throbbings of syncopation."[81] As Hodeir points out, such declarations were usually based on limited exposure. For example, Milhaud traveled to America during the 1920s, but apparently he never grasped the differences between Broadway revues, diluted dance music, and authentic jazz. Wryly Hodeir recalls: "The French composer was not even curious enough to investigate a certain Louis Armstrong, though people were beginning to talk about him at that time."[82]

Then there was the verdict of Copland, who, after studying composition in Paris, returned to New York to create a music of "conscious Americanism"—meaning, in three works written between 1925 and 1929, the inclusion of superficial jazz effects.[83] Then, in 1930, just as authentic jazz was on the brink of enormously expanding its stylistic and emotional range, Copland wrote it off. Jazz, he declared, "was an easy way to be American in musical terms, but all American music could not possibly be confined to two dominant jazz moods: the blues and the snappy number."[84] Premature though these judgments were, they reflect accurately the relative lack of impact. As Hodeir himself states: "Stravinsky made history when he wrote *Le Sacre du Printemps*; he placed himself in the margin of history when he wrote *Ragtime*."[85]

Nonetheless, it would be wrong to conclude that jazz and modernism had no mutual influence. Indeed, this influence only intensified after the leading composers placed jazz beyond the musical pale. The changes in musical language introduced by jazz were no greater than the changes in pictorial language effected by Cézanne and his heirs; they were actually far less radical than those wrought by Webern. Had the idiomatic difference between jazz and European music been the only obstacle to the former's acceptance, it would have been overcome a long time ago. Imagine that a circle of Parisian composers had created jazz: The music would now occupy a secure niche in modernism, right next to cubism. The fact that it doesn't, that it still occupies a highly ambiguous cultural space, can be explained in nonmusical terms by its origin, which is neither European nor modernist. I now turn to the two aspects of jazz's origin that have proved most troublesome, even to people who admire the music. The first is race; the second, commerce.

Chapter 4

The Obstacle of Race

he deepest roots of the European response to jazz lie in the rivalry between the gods Dionysus and Apollo. According to Greek myth, this rivalry was expressed through their favored musical instruments, each understood to have a drastically different effect on the listener. The first was the *aulos*, or shepherd's pipe, which had come to Greece from Egypt via Crete, and was associated with the rites of Dionysus. The *aulos* produced a combination of two tones, a bass tone, sometimes played as a drone; and a higher, more piercing tone carrying a melody (the usual comparison is with the bagpipe). The second instrument was the *kithara*, or lyre, a harplike instrument sacred to Apollo. As the music historian Christopher Headington suggests, the Greeks had both religious and practical reasons to perceive a conflict between these two instruments:

> Since the gentle tone of the lyre did not mix well with that of the powerful
> *aulos*, they were not often played together. In any case, the cults of Apollo

and Dionysus were different and even opposed. Dionysus represented emotion and the joys of the senses, whereas Apollo was the god of the intellect, of enlightenment, self-control and balanced judgment. According to legend, Apollo protected his style of music, and made King Midas grow asses' ears for daring to prefer the sound of a shepherd's pipe to that of the lyre.[1]

Despite Apollo's efforts, the lyre was not long protected from the pipe. By the 4th century B.C., both the *kithara* and the *aulos* were combined, along with a profusion of other instruments, in a "new style" of Greek music that was more entertainment than ritual. And in later centuries, both instruments were vulgarized for thrills, as the Romans gratified their appetite for coarse entertainment by playing *kitharae* and *auloi* the size of chariots.[2] Rather than speculate about what those monstrosities sounded like, let me stress that the original rivalry between Dionysus and Apollo quickly became a conflict of abstract principles, inhering not in particular musical instruments or styles, but rather in Western civilization's continual effort to sustain the priority of reason over will and passion.

At the beginning was Plato's injunction that the pure elements of music, such as melody and rhythm, be strictly subordinated to words, because only *logos*, or rational discourse, can seek truth.[3] A similar view was taken by the Hebrew prophets, who made a sharp distinction between the sacred and secular uses of music. In Christianity, the result was an abiding distrust of secular music and a constant concern about the power of music to distract worshipers from Scripture. In some Christian denominations, notably Irish Catholicism and Calvinistic Protestantism, this distrust led to a near total ban of music. Most denominations, however, merely tried to draw a line between acceptable, "Apollonian" forms of music that focused attention on the Word, and unacceptable, "Dionysian" ones that distracted or intoxicated the listener.

The trouble was that the line kept shifting. In the early Christian era, the Church allowed only unadorned vocal music, rejecting as corrupt the rich instrumental sound of pagan music.[4] During the late Middle Ages, when vocal music moved toward polyphony, the Church revived Plato's argument that music with more than one melody confuses the mind. But in 1510, when Martin Luther visited Rome as a young monk, the only thing he found to admire about the place was its splendid polyphonic music. Along with instrumental ensembles, Luther introduced polyphony into his own church. Yet, two centuries later, when Bach used the melodic richness of Italian opera to take polyphony to its zenith, he was rebuked by the Lutheran authorities.[5]

By the late eighteenth century, the conflict between Apollo and Diony-sus was given a new twist by romanticism. Ponder this famous speech by the hero of Goethe's novel *The Sorrows of Young Werther*:

> Oh, you rationalists, . . . so calm and so righteous. You abhor the drunken man, and detest the eccentric. You pass by, like the Levite, and thank God, like the Pharisee, that you are not like one of them. I have been drunk more than once, my passions have always bordered on madness; I am not ashamed to confess it; I have learned in my own way that all extraordinary men who have done great and improbable things have ever been decried by the world as drunk or insane.[6]

To Goethe's contemporaries, the illustrious period from Bach to Mozart was "classical," while their own era, ushered in by Beethoven, was "romantic." Among other things, romanticism meant the subordination of words to music—in Schopenhauer's formulation, music accompanying poetry was the "marriage of a prince with a beggar."[7] By this light, romanti-cism was the triumph of Dionysus over Apollo.

Yet we moderns rarely fret about the Dionysian powers of Weber, Schu-mann, Mendelssohn, Berlioz, Liszt, and Wagner. Everyday discourse calls these composers "classical," lumping them with their predecessors almost as if romanticism had never occurred. Even Allan Bloom does this: Defending Plato, he attacks the irrationalism of romantic political philoso-phy, warning that Rousseau and Nietzsche "wanted to cultivate the enthu-siastic states of the soul and to re-experience the Corybantic possession deemed a pathology by Plato." Yet Bloom does not follow this critique with an assessment, pro or con, of those European composers who sought to embody ecstatic possession in music. His target is rock, and he hastens to it, stating that rock "has risen to its current heights in the education of the young on the ashes of *classical* music."[8] (emphasis added)

If pressed, Bloom would have replied that musical romanticism is Dionysian only in the positive sense of wrestling with, and taming, the irrational. Goethe defined art as "demonic," meaning rooted in a life force that is, nonetheless, more good than evil. In this sense, early romanticism was still committed to rationalism. Bloom states it eloquently:

> Civilization, or to say the same thing, education is the taming or domestica-tion of the soul's raw passions—not suppressing or excising them, which would deprive the soul of its energy—but forming and informing them as art. The goal of harmonizing the enthusiastic part of the soul with what develops later, the rational part, is perhaps impossible to attain. But without it, man can never be whole.[9]

With Nietzsche, the "demonic" became the "demoniac," meaning irrational in a destructive sense. Dionysus was not just the god of wine, after all—he was also the god of madness, chaos, and frenzy, whose female worshippers began their revels dancing and drinking in the forested hills outside Thebes, and ended them rampaging through the woods after wild beasts, which they tore to pieces and devoured raw.[10] With expressionism, the line shifted again, and "Dionysian" began to mean a vertiginous dance, a playing with fire, a conjuring of bewitching, distracting, ultimately dangerous passions. Take, for example, the dissonant, atonal pieces written by the young Schoenberg after his wife left him for a painter who then hung himself. According to Schorske, "Schoenberg's desperation . . . lent its force to the radical expansion of musical expression—in this case to encompass a wild oscillation of feeling between tenderness and terror."[11]

The Highbrow Response: Jazz As Dionysian

Such, then, was the state of European musical culture when it first encountered the weird music of the New World. To the objective ear, Schoenberg's "wild oscillation" is a lot more frenzied than the controlled heat of ragtime and jazz. But objective ears were rare, and the main response was to redraw the line, with all European music classified as Apollonian, all Afro-American music as Dionysian. By the 1920s worried responses like that of the professor in Mann's story were second nature to cultivated Europeans. As the historian Neil Leonard summarizes: "The most frightening aspect of jazz was its mysterious power to strike at the heart of rational conduct and moral judgment."[12]

We now arrive at a paradox. In Mann's story, jazz is portrayed as having the power to evoke "disorder and early sorrow" in the soul of a little girl. Yet at the same time, recall Copland's 1930 complaint about the narrow range of emotion in jazz, from "the blues" to "the snappy number."[13] First jazz is damned for being dangerously intoxicating; then it's dismissed for being emotionally shallow and predictable. Mann and Copland were both genuine authorities on music: How could they both be right? Or, to rephrase the question for the jazz lover, How could they both be wrong?

To begin, Copland was right: Most jazz, including the highly developed strains that appeared after 1930, is indeed less emotional than the other forms of music called "Dionysian" at the turn of the century. Romantic music is profoundly emotional, and late-romantic music is even more so—to a fault, some would say. Recall Eduard Hanslick's pungent putdown: "The Prelude to *Tristan und Isolde* reminds me of the old Italian painting of a martyr whose intestines are slowly unwound from his body on a reel."[14] The modernists, including Copland, felt that after Wagner the only hope was to rescue music from excessive emotion.[15] This attitude explains why most modernist music stops short of the emotional heights and depths found in romanticism. But it doesn't explain why modernism, and not jazz, gets admitted to the high-cultural "canon."

Surprisingly, the real reason for jazz's ambiguous status has little to do with Apollo and Dionysus. For the Greeks didn't share the main bias that worked against jazz at its birth: namely, that bodily enthusiasm is bad. It appeared during the late Roman Empire, when a group of extreme ascetic cults (pagan, Jewish, Gnostic, and Christian) arose in response to the grosser and crueler sexual practices of the day.[16] Despite the facile assertions of erotic liberationists from Otto Gross to Camille Paglia, hatred of the flesh is neither the essence of Christianity nor the central legacy of Western civilization. But it is a recurrent theme, and it did color the repressiveness of the era we call Victorian. Among the proper bourgeoisie of Europe and America, jazz was thought to "strike at the heart of rational conduct" not because it stirred the emotions, but because it moved the body.[17] It's no accident that Mann's little girl grows hysterical after dancing; the common assumption was that physical "agitation" had harmful emotional effects, especially in females.

The modernists were divided on the subject of dance: for Stravinsky, whose most influential pieces were the ballets he wrote for Sergei Diaghilev, the truth lay in Ezra Pound's dictum: "Music rots when it gets too far from the dance." But for Schoenberg, "Ballet is not a musical form."[18] Still, the majority of early modernists saw dance (especially "modern dance" as proselytized by Isadora Duncan) as the most humanistic of the arts, harking back to the Greek ideal of spiritual, mental, and physical harmony.

Yet the same credit was not extended to Afro-American dance, even when performed by experts. For example, the kind of dance imported to Paris in the 1920s by the American Josephine Baker was seen as lacking discipline, proportion, and restraint. Indeed, Baker was celebrated as a "primitive," whose movements were shapeless, irrational, and frenzied. Like all primitivism, this judgment overlooks the fact that authentic "primitive" cultures, such as the tribal societies of precolonial Africa, were highly disciplined, ordered, and restrained: Even when they cultivated ecstatic states, they did so in a ritual manner aimed at reinforcing the taboos and rules of their society, not breaking them in the name of instinctual liberation. Precolonial Africans were not perverse modernists.

Neither were black Americans in the 1920s. Despite its long separation from Africa, the weird music of the New World retained a strong ritual dimension—blues and gospel especially offered stylized reenactments of tribulations aimed at driving home the difference between right and wrong. On a more mundane level, no student of classical Greek philosophy, with its emphasis on the link between the habits of practical activity and the virtues of intellect and moral character, should forget that the aboriginal purpose of rhythm in African music was not to stir Dionysian passion, but to accompany work. The better the rhythm, the sooner it revived the weary and reconciled the discordant. In both of these contexts, ritual and work, the motive power of rhythm served a civilizing function.

I realize that by introducing work chants into a discussion of high art, I risk confusing the anthropological and the traditional meanings of *culture*. But I'm not equating work chants with jazz, I'm merely trying to remove the taint from rhythm. Jazz is not intellectualized music, to be sure. Most jazz artists think musically, not verbally, about music; the field has not produced a bumper crop of theoreticians. But the idea that composers must also be theoreticians is the exceptional fruit of German philosophy, not the rule of Western civilization. This idea may have given us introverted modernism, but that scarcely recommends it. Intellect is important in any fine art: It shapes and criticizes the impulses of the imagination, sustains tradition, updates standards, justifies methods. But the intellectualized compulsion to reinvent art from scratch has produced mainly desiccated results.

Jazz is a young art, modest in stature compared with Western music taken as a whole. But it is also an extraordinary art, able to strike a new and wonderful balance between the Dionysian and the Apollonian. What other music tempers such primal rhythmic energy with such precisely controlled counterpoint? What other music carries such intense vocal-instrumental passion on such delicate melodic flights? What other music sustains such terrific tension between the will of the individual and the discipline of the group? The Europeans who first succumbed to these charms no doubt heard, in jazz, the restoration of such classical virtues as wit, playfulness, lucidity, elegance, and emotional restraint. Yet jazz is rarely defended in Apollonian terms, even by those who admire it the most.[19] The next question is: Why not?

The Racist Response: "Jungle Music"

For Neil Leonard, as for most jazz historians (to say nothing of musicians), the short explanation for the misjudgment of jazz is "racism, albeit muted or veiled."[20] Racism isn't the sole motive behind cultural resistance to Afro-American music, but it's certainly an important one. Undeniably it motivated many of the less-cultivated objections, such as this widely quoted 1913 letter to the Paris editor of the *New York Herald*:

> Can it be said that America is falling prey to the collective soul of the negro through the influence of what is popularly known as 'rag time' music? . . . If there is any tendency toward such a national disaster, it should definitely be pointed out and extreme measures taken to inhibit the influence. . . . [This] music is symbolic of the primitive morality and perceptible moral limitations of the negro type.[21]

Unfortunately, no logical barrier separates this racist response from the highbrow one. In 1927 another German, Hermann Hesse, wrote a novel called *Steppenwolf*, in which he describes jazz as "hot and raw as the steam of raw flesh." Then, to drive home the point, he offers this portrait of a jazz musician named Pablo: "His dark and beautiful Creole eyes and his black locks hid no romance, no problems, no thoughts. . . . Presumably, he had not the least idea that there was any music but jazz or that any music had ever existed before it. He was pleasant, certainly, pleasant and polite, and his large, vacant eyes smiled most charmingly." For Hesse, the man who plays jazz is no more rational than the graceful but deadly wild beasts to which he frequently compares Pablo. And Pablo is a light-skinned Creole. Hesse's view of dark-skinned people shows up in an earlier passage comparing the mental and spiritual complexity of his German hero with the simplicity of "the primitive Negro," or (in the same breath) "the idiot."[22]

Ironically, these prejudices against jazz became more crude during the next two decades, just when the music itself was becoming more sophisticated. As Hodeir reminds us, the 1930s and 1940s were a time of concentrated brilliance in jazz, encompassing everything from a revival of the vintage New Orleans style to the big bands with their incomparable soloists:

> Most of the great precursors had become classical figures and were producing their best work; and . . . new leaders were coming up, men in whose work a discerning ear could already tell the direction modern jazz was taking. . . . Never before or since have so many great musicians existed side by side, uniting their efforts to found a marvelously rich and diversified school of jazz.[23]

But brilliance did not protect jazz, any more than it protected any other art. Both the Nazis and the Stalinists carried the prevailing prejudice to the point of lunacy. Consider this official statement by Goebbels:

Now, I shall speak quite openly on the question of whether German Radio should broadcast so-called jazz music. If by jazz we mean music that is based on rhythm and entirely ignores or even shows contempt for melody, music in which rhythm is indicated primarily by the ugly sounds of whining instruments so insulting to the soul, why then we can only reply to the question entirely in the negative.[24]

Of course the Nazis, being Nazis, blamed the Jews as well as the blacks for jazz's defilement of "Aryan" culture. The Czech writer Josef Škvorecký recalls a set of guidelines imposed on all dance bands under the purview of the Third Reich—guidelines that prohibited various musical effects in terms that would be funny if they weren't so vicious. Blues lyrics and tonality, for instance, were denounced as "Jewishly gloomy." Syncopation and swing, those offenses to "the Aryan sense of discipline and moderation," were condemned as "Negroid excesses." Bands were ordered to avoid "the hysterical rhythmic reverses characteristic of the music of the barbarian races and conducive to dark instincts alien to the German people." Equally verboten were "instruments alien to the German spirit" such as "cowbells, flexatone, brushes . . . as well as all mutes which turn the noble sound of wind and brass into a Jewish-Freemasonic yowl." And finally, to show how far Western civilization had come from the ancient Greeks who regarded the plucked strings of the *kithara* as the very essence of Apollonian order, the Nazis also forbade "plucking of the strings" on the grounds that it was "damaging to the instrument and detrimental to Aryan musicality."[25]

Over in the Soviet camp, the official view of jazz was most fully articulated in a 1928 essay by Maxim Gorky, "On the Music of the Gross." There's a highbrow tone to Gorky's potted history of music, summarized by one scholar as "a process of decline that led from Mozart and Beethoven through the waltz to the fox-trot and finally to the convulsions of the Charleston." But Gorky's special eloquence is reserved for describing a "Negro orchestra," in these terms: "The monstrous bass belches out English words; a wild horn wails piercingly, calling to mind the cries of a raving camel; a drum pounds monotonously; a nasty little pipe tears at one's ears; a saxophone emits its quacking nasal sound. Fleshy hips sway, and thousands of heavy feet tread and shuffle." For Gorky, this "music of the degenerate" could only be produced by "an orchestra of sexually driven madmen conducted by a man-stallion brandishing a huge genital member."[26]

Grotesque though this caricature of jazz was, it is even more grotesque to see how handily it survived World War II. Apparently the bad company it kept during the 1930s and 1940s did not diminish its appeal for postwar intellectuals on both sides of the Cold War divide. As suggested earlier, neither the liberals nor the neoconservatives of the war generation have done much to unearth and examine the assumptions underlying their seemingly highbrow aversion to jazz.

Yet the grotesquery gets even worse, because, for all their persistence, the assumptions of a few highbrows would not have proved decisive if they hadn't been taken up, and reinforced, by powerful currents in the culture. That is to say, the enemies of jazz were not the only ones perceiving it to be the crude and lascivious outpouring of a benighted race. With repercussions that still affect us today, the same perception was touted by jazz's friends.

The Primitivist Embrace

Let me begin in 1913, when Stravinsky's *The Rite of Spring* shocked Paris with its imagined celebration of a "primitive" fertility dance. Today, it is common for dancers to interpret Stravinsky's jagged rhythms with movements taken from the Afro-American lexicon, even when costumed as ancient Slavs. But there were no such movements in the original choreography: It is clear, from a recent re-creation by the Joffrey Ballet, that Diaghilev's vision of Dionysian frenzy was expressed through a lot of foot-stomping, frog-hopping, and stork-strutting that now appears more stilted than shocking.[27] There's nothing remotely African about it.

This is not to suggest that Europeans had no impression of Africa in 1913. As the historian Eugene Genovese reports, eighteenth- and nineteenth-century European explorers had been impressed by the central role of sexuality in West African societies, as manifested in "the extent of nakedness; the free use of sexual jokes, allusions and symbols; the apparent ease with which sexual partners could sometimes be exchanged." Concluding from such evidence that "Africans had no standards, no morals, no restraints," many explorers had allowed their imaginations free rein. As Genovese wryly observes, "Before long, Europe and America were hearing lurid tales of giant penises, intercourse with apes, and assorted unspeakable (but much spoken of) transgressions against God and nature."[28]

It's hardly surprising that such images didn't spark the imagination of European artists before the turn of the century. After all, the romantic ideal of natural man was *more* virtuous than his civilized counterpart, not less. The native peoples of North America suited this expectation, at least among French intellectuals residing in France. But the vision of Africa as a jungle vastness teeming with bestial sexual activity was far too bizarre.

Whatever else could be said about Rousseau's "noble savage," he was not generally understood to possess a giant penis.

Recall, however, the decadent and expressionist embrace of dark, destructive, "demoniac" human nature. Exactly parallel to this development runs a change in European attitudes toward Africans, and black people in general. Ahead of his time (as usual), Rimbaud wrote these lines in 1873:

> Yes, my eyes are closed to your light. I am a beast, a nigger. . . . Do I know nature yet? Do I know myself?—*No more words.* I bury the dead in my belly. Shouts, drums, dance, dance, dance! I cannot even see the time when, white men landing, I shall fall into nothingness.[29]

High on the same zeitgeist, Marinetti's multimedia campaign to shock Europe included aggressive publicity about his Egyptian birth, his having been suckled by a Sudanese wet nurse, and his impending inheritance of a fortune accumulated in an Alexandria brothel. Presumably this exotic origin gave Marinetti the strength to survive later adversity, such as three obscenity trials for publishing a novel in which the hero's penis is eleven meters long (just the right length to wrap comfortably around his body while he sleeps).[30] Add inflammatory rhetoric about Italy's duty to conquer Ethiopia, and you have the futurist version of primitivism.

More famous, and legitimizing, was the cubist fascination with African sculpture. By Picasso's own account, his first exposure to such "magical things" as Senufu masks and Basonge statues came as an "epiphany," inspiring his famous 1907 canvas, *Les Demoiselles d'Avignon.*[31] In formal terms *Les Demoiselles* is now seen as the beginning of cubism. This view does justice to the painting's African inspiration, because, as the art historian Paul Wingert explains, "African art is distinctly a sculptor's art . . . clearly derived from and based on the understanding and interpretation of natural forms."[32] Yet *Les Demoiselles* is also seen in psychological terms as a protosurrealist work, a spontaneous expression of Picasso's subconscious desires. This view, Wingert reminds us, is based on a misconception of African art:

> It was . . . the erroneous belief of these young enthusiasts that African sculptures were free, spontaneous creations unhindered by the academic restraints imposed on the artists of Europe. They did not know, when they extolled the freedom of these primitive forms, that this too was an art of traditions.[33]

The same misconception became institutionalized in 1925, when Josephine Baker arrived in Paris. Only nineteen when hired for the Paris premiere of a New York-produced variety show called *La Revue Nègre*, Baker was nonetheless a seasoned performer whose improvisatory skills rested on a solid, if not fully appreciated, foundation. As Phyllis Rose writes in a recent biography:

> [Baker] liked to say later in life that she learned to dance by watching the kangaroos in the St. Louis Zoo . . . but she invoked the zoo and the animals no doubt to please an audience that loved her as a child of nature. . . . By the time she was thirteen, Baker had built up an enormous repertoire of moves. She knew them so well that when she started to dance professionally, it could look like she was making it all up as she went along. But underneath the seeming total spontaneity were known steps and dances—the Mess Around, the Itch, Tack Annie, Trucking—and years of daily practice. When she seemed the most unstrung, there had been the most careful preparation.[34]

As Rose notes, this background meant zip to the Parisians, whose reaction is typified by one eyewitness: "Josephine moved like an animal. An animal doesn't think about how it moves, it just moves."[35]

Rose also notes that the French promoters of *La Revue Nègre* did not like the show at first. To them the precision tap dancing so admired in Harlem was too "disciplined" to be convincingly black; and the figure of the top-billed blues singer, Maud de Forest, was too matronly to be sexy. So a director named Jacques Charles, an "expert in the fantasy life of Parisian males," was hired to make the show blacker—meaning sexier.[36] When Charles asked Baker to appear bare breasted in the final "Danse Sauvage," she threatened to quit. But then, persuaded by flattery, and by the fact that half-naked chorus girls were the custom in Paris, she relented. To judge by this leading review, Charles was an expert:

> In the short *pas de deux* of the savages, which came as the finale of the Revue Nègre, there was a wild splendor and magnificent animality. Certain of Miss Baker's poses, back arched, haunches protruding, arms entwined and uplifted in a phallic symbol, had the compelling potency of the finest examples of Negro sculpture . . . the frenzy of African Eros swept over the audience.[37]

Thus did the Parisians embrace Baker as a purely instinctual being whose thrilling performances flowed, not from her mind and spirit, but from her guts and gonads. There's a resemblance between this response and the long-standing white American fascination with black music and culture, but there's also a difference. For the Parisians, the identification of blackness with eroticism was the latest fad, more the outgrowth of perverse modernism than the result of any real interaction with black people. For white Americans, it was second nature.

The Blood Knot

The Blood Knot is a play by the South African writer Athol Fugard, about two half-brothers, one officially "black" and the other officially "white," whose lives are intertwined in spite of apartheid. Therefore the phrase is an apt metaphor for the tangle of sex and race that has, for more than three centuries, dominated culture in America. Writing about Harlem in the 1920s, the historian Nathan Huggins relates it to minstrelsy:

> The creation of Harlem as a place of exotic culture was as much a service to white need as it was to black. So essential has been the Negro personality to the white American psyche that black theatrical masks had become, by the twentieth century, a standard way for whites to explore dimensions of themselves that seemed impossible through their own *personae*.[38]

It's intriguing to recall how strong the minstrel influence still was in the 1920s. According to one historian, the decor of the Plantation Club, which opened on Broadway in 1923, included "log cabins, Negro mammies, picket fences around the dance floor, a twinkling summer sky, and a watermelon moon."[39] Likewise, the Cotton Club moved only gradually toward its famous "jungle" theme. And few Harlem night spots crossed the line between suggestive and explicit: The naughtiest songs used double entendre; the scantiest costumes bared only legs, arms, and midriffs.[40]

Of course, the gangsters who ran these clubs didn't want to provoke the authorities any more than they were already doing by selling bootleg liquor. But they were also mindful of the sensibilities of their clientele, who were not, for all their champagne and Charleston, Parisians. They were white Americans, and their inheritance, which they shared with the black performers on the stage, was the blood knot. Since we are still rather desperately caught up in this racial and sexual conundrum, it's worth trying to untangle some of its worst misconceptions. But to do that, it's necessary to go back to the beginning—to the original clash of worldviews between Africans and Europeans in the New World.

Genovese suggests that, throughout the Americas, the puritanical outlook of Anglo-Saxon slaveowners made them more restrained than their Spanish and Portuguese counterparts when it came to the sexual exploitation of slave women. But restraint had a cost, especially in cases where such exploitation might have led to deeper feelings. Interracial love was thwarted in the English colonies, Genovese argues, not only by the injustice of slavery, but also by the white culture's powerful association of sex with sin:

Miscegenation poisoned southern race relations much less through those acts of violence which lower-class women—and their men—have always had to suffer in hierarchical social systems, than through the psychological devastation it wrought. . . . What the white men might have viewed, even if perversely, as joyous and lusty, they generally had to view as a self-degradation.[41]

As for the enslaved Africans, most historians agree that the coherence of their original religions was shattered by slavery. But as Albert J. Raboteau notes, it is significant that most North American slaves were not converted to Christianity until the Great Awakening of the 1740s: "In the face of this religious indifference," he writes, "some forms of African religious behavior seem to have continued."[42] Genovese concurs, adding that, even after conversion, most slaves had difficulty assimilating the puritanical view of sex.

This difficulty did not stem from the Africans' savage, concupiscent nature, as was commonly believed by white Americans in the eighteenth century. Instead, it stemmed from the fact that the religions of Africa (like most pre-Christian religions, including those of Europe) placed sex and fertility at the center of the cosmos. However shocking to seventeenth- and eighteenth-century European explorers, the graphic artifacts, dances, and rituals of West Africa symbolized a life force neither wholly material nor wholly spiritual. In the words of a 1970s interfaith study of Christian marriage in Africa:

> In the African worldview sex was not biological only; it was also sacred. It was to be "used" with care; it was mysterious and like all mysterious things it belonged to the gods. The pleasure of sex was, of course, legitimate, but its outcome, whenever possible, was to be children. Childbearing was a religious and social duty. It follows, therefore, that in almost all parts and cultures of Africa, rape, homosexuality, bestiality—all sexual acts which did not fulfill both of these conditions—were condemned and severely punished. They could bring nothing but disaster not only to the people concerned but to the whole community.[43]

According to Genovese, this African worldview persisted among the slaves, who saw sexual misconduct as "primarily a moral offense to the community rather than to God," and who rejected "the denigration of sex as sinful, dirty or anything other than delightfully human and pleasurable."[44] The slaves were not puritans, but neither did they condone sexual excess. Premarital intercourse was tolerated, even encouraged, and there was no stigma attached to its issue. But tolerance did not extend to marital infidelity, by husband or wife; the cure for a bad marriage was dissolution, initiated by either partner. Genovese reports that many slaveowners were well aware of this sexual code among blacks. The more intelligent whites even acknowledged it—some with a trace of self-deprecating humor. Mary B. Chesnut, wife of a prominent nineteenth-century Virginia planter and politician, wrote in her diary that "Negro women are married, and after marriage behave as well as other people."[45]

Not only did the slaves have their own sexual code. They also held definite opinions about the somewhat different code of whites. Above all, they bitterly condemned white male adventurism among their own women. As Genovese writes, this condemnation became violent at times: "Many black women fiercely resisted such aggression, and many black men proved willing to die in defense of their women." In addition, the slaves took a dim view of certain aspects of the white sexual code, notably its insistence on the permanence of marriage and its preoccupation with female purity. About the requirement that brides be virgins, Genovese comments: "That particular pretension, staunchly adhered to by the whites, although much less in their guilt-producing practice than in their hotly maintained theory, the slaves found slightly ridiculous."[46]

The slaves were starkly aware of the gap between word and deed in white sexual morality. The majority of North American slaves lived too intimately with whites to believe that the latter actually abided by the stern morality they professed. Blacks understood all too well that most whites had two moral standards: a rigid one for themselves, from which they frequently fell short; and a lax one for their slaves, with whom they frequently did their falling short.

The blood knot gained another twist after the Civil War, when, as Genovese explains, white attitudes shifted from guilt about sex between white men and black women to terror of sex between black men and white women: "The titillating and violence-provoking theory of the superpotency of that black superpenis, while whispered about for several centuries, did not become an obsession until after emancipation, when it served the purposes of racial segregationists."[47]

Sociologist Calvin C. Hernton describes the ensuing dynamic: the ambivalence warping the white man's perennial exploitation of the black woman; the isolation of the white woman atop a pedestal of sexless virtue; the forbidden-fruit syndrome distorting all contact between the mythically potent black man and the mythically pure white woman; the resentments and hypocrisies afflicting relations between the sexes within each group; and finally the foul mist of irrational violence enveloping the whole.[48]

Especially astute is Hernton's account of how blacks themselves have strengthened the blood knot. He cites the old Southern tale about a group of white men walking through a cornfield, discovering a black couple making love, and joking: "That is another good reason for being a nigger!"[49] Toni Morrison embroiders on this tale in her first novel, *The Bluest Eye*, where instead of merely joking, the white men gather around the (very young) couple and goad the boy to "get on wid it." Naturally, the boy is too terrified to do anything of the kind. But to keep his tormentors at bay, he fakes it. The effect, of course, is to humiliate him before his girl and add another trauma to his life. Yet Hernton's point is that white voyeurism has caused many black people to believe in their own fakery—or, worse. to put on a genuine performance when the white folks jeer: "Make it good, nigger."[50]

The sad truth is that sexual prowess is one of the few traits for which blacks have received tribute from whites—albeit one of spiteful envy. For a people as systematically vilified as black Americans have been, any advantage over the vilifier is bound to exert a certain attraction. Combine that with a clear-eyed view of white sexual hypocrisy, and it seems inevitable that a certain segment of the black population would come to believe that black sexual "immorality" was superior to white "morality." Hence the strain in Afro-American folklore that regards any restraint as a sham, and any license as honest, natural, and authentic. From this strain comes the folk hero Stagolee (the original "bad nigger"), whose sexual swagger is all too frequently imitated by those who lack other sources of pride.

Does this mean that every black performer who pleases a white audience is the same as the boy in the cornfield? Even posing the question is an insult. Yet it needs to be posed, because the blood knot has a way of entangling everyone, white and black, who studies the interaction of black performers and white audiences. Consider this passage from James Lincoln Collier's biography of Louis Armstrong:

> Precisely why white Americans have been drawn to black entertainment is not easy to explain, but two factors are evident. First, the black subculture as it existed in the slave cabins and then in big city ghettos has always seemed exotic to whites. . . . Second, blacks were also seen as more erotic than whites. They were not expected to abide by the sexual proscriptions of white society.[51]

Why should Collier, a white admirer of jazz, find it "not easy to explain" the appeal of black entertainment? No doubt the disclaimer is partly explained by the context, a discussion of the voyeuristic undercurrent of white interest in Afro-American music. Naturally, Collier wishes to distance himself from that undercurrent, with its unflattering image of the white jazz fan as a cold, uptight puritan secretly thrilled by the warm, relaxed sensuality of black performers.

But unfortunately, this undercurrent is real. To be sure, innumerable whites have straightforwardly embraced Afro-American music as an antidote to excessive inhibition—not only in relation to sex, but also to emotion, bodily movement, even religious enthusiasm. Such listeners can appreciate the complex beauties of the music because they can sense the difference between the erotic, which preserves the connections between sex and the rest of life; and the obscene, which severs them. Afro-American music is sometimes erotic, but it is never obscene, because there is always a larger whole—whether spiritual ecstasy, physical exuberance, or emotional catharsis—to which its erotic qualities are joined.

Alas, innumerable other listeners have failed to make this crucial distinction. Some have sought to suppress the whole idiom in the name of suppressing its eroticism; others have isolated and pursued the eroticism for its own sake. To react either way is to sail back to the mythical shores of a Dark Continent that never existed, except in the fevered imaginations of ignorant sailors. Yet it is astonishing how durable these reactions have proven to be.

Chapter 5

The Taint of Commerce

Along with racism and primitivism, jazz also encountered a European cultural sensibility that has long regarded art and profit as radically incompatible. Barzun reminds us that "bourgeois" has been an epithet in the mouths of artists ever since the seventeenth century: "It is not from textbooks of political theory that the artist learns to decry the vices of the bourgeoisie; it is from contact with the stolid playgoer, the greedy middleman, the wayward patron. These are the living obstacles barring the way to fame."[1]

Not surprisingly, such feelings have long been associated with socialism. From the perspective of an English or French romanticist, it was hard to say which was more appalling about the Industrial Revolution—the devastation of the countryside by coal mines and textile mills, or the widening abyss between the wealth of the factory owners and the poverty of the uprooted peasants who were becoming their workers. Socialism promised to heal these traumas, and support art, too.

Of course, socialism divided after 1850, with one side accepting the capitalist system enough to press for changes within it, and the other rejecting any option but violent revolution. Scorn for commerce persisted on both sides, but it was on the latter, which eventually fought the Russian Revolution to erect a permanent barrier between itself and the bourgeois world, that scorn hardened into hatred.

Stalinist Doublethink

We have already seen how the Stalinists, like the Nazis, condemned jazz in both highbrow and racist terms. But because the Soviets had no explicit ideology of race, their theorists had to justify this condemnation in terms of the class struggle—a tricky business at best.

Like modernism, jazz was tolerated by the Communist Party for a brief period after 1917; like modernism, it was attacked as "bourgeois" in the mid-1920s; and like modernism, it was eventually crushed, to make room for the uplifting inanities of socialist realism. But here again jazz was the wild card in the cultural deck. Unlike modernist painting or music, jazz sprang from an extremely oppressed people in an extremely capitalist country. The dilemma for the Party, therefore, was whether to praise jazz as the rallying cry of the black masses, or to denounce it as a tool of capitalist domination. This dilemma was never fully resolved, but in the process the Party contributed an impressive amount of confusion to the world's understanding of what the music is all about.

To point out the horns of the dilemma, the historian S. Frederick Starr quotes an article published in 1913 by a graduate of the Saint Petersburg Conservatory who had emigrated to New York but didn't like the place. True folk music, wrote Ivan Narodny, "mirrors the joys and sorrows, hopes and passions, of the country people. It is moulded under the blue sky, in sunshine and storm." Ragtime, on the other hand, was produced by "an individual whose idea is to make money with its composition. It exults the noise, rush and vulgarity of the street. It suggests repulsive dance halls and restaurants."[2]

This distinction neatly summarizes why so many Europeans admired folk music but scorned jazz. Even among those who admired antebellum spirituals and plantation songs, it was widely assumed that the golden age of Afro-American music had ended with the Civil War, which led not only to the migration of emancipated slaves out of the rural South, but also to the full-blown emergence of industrial capitalism in America. Even sympathetic composers such as Antonín Dvořák (who *did* like New York) focused almost exclusively on the plaintive tonality of "the old Negro melodies." Worse, these Europeans were ignorant of the rhythmic foundations of Afro-American music, so they judged the upsurge of rhythm in jazz to be a function of industrialization and urbanization.

Despite these misconceptions, Europeans were not entirely wrong in seeing jazz as something other than folk music. Unlike true folk music, jazz does not have a centuries-long tradition marked by only small, incremental changes. On the contrary, its history is dynamic, volatile—and, to a surprising degree, urban. Despite sentimental notions about black peasants uprooted from the soil, the deepest taproot of Afro-American music lies in the cosmopolitan port of New Orleans.

Such complex realities did not impede the Stalinists, however. In 1928 the Sixth Comintern called for the American South to rise again—only this time as a black socialist republic, guided into the glorious future by the fraternal hand of Comrade Stalin. It was doubtful, to say the least, that the feeble American Communist Party could foment racial revolution in Dixie, since it had already failed to commandeer Marcus Garvey's back-to-Africa movement in the North. As Starr remarks: "This flabbergasting proposition was the brainchild of Marxist sociologists in Moscow who had been no closer to America than the Lenin Library."[3]

But if the master plan for a "Black Republic of the South" was not destined for longevity, the same cannot be said of its underlying cultural presumptions. Starr continues:

> If the "Colonial Theses" were to be sustained, it was imperative that jazz be defined as proletarian music. Equally important, it had to be presented as a genuine folk music indigenous to the southern Black Belt. But what about its undeniably urban character? Kremlin sociologists could not accept this, so it had to be denied. And what about the intimate connection between jazz, modern communications technology, and commercial distribution? This, too, had to be discounted.[4]

To make matters worse, jazz was popular in the Soviet Union! The Party ideologues not only had to account for the music's origins in America, they also had to rationalize its appeal to the "new Soviet man." As Starr explains, they opted for doublethink:

> The answer revisionist critics proposed was disarmingly simple: there existed not one but two forms of jazz, one proletarian and the other bourgeois. The proletarian was rooted in Negro folk life and bore the scars of past oppression. The bourgeois variant derived not from folk blues but from the

vulgar commercialism of Tin Pan Alley. Bourgeois jazz was popular culture "from above," devised by capitalist exploiters to lull the masses to sleep and stifle their growing class consciousness.[5]

This doublethink became the official Party line in the 1930s, to help highlight the difference between the Party's class-based ideology and the race-based one of Nazism. This difference was glossed over in 1939, when Stalin signed a nonaggression pact with Hitler, only to reappear in 1941, when Hitler invaded the Soviet Union and Stalin suddenly found himself in a wartime alliance with the capitalist homeland of jazz. At that point, the Leader of Humanity not only reopened the churches (to remind the troops that they were defending Mother Russia), he also brought the *dzhazes*, or homegrown jazz bands, back from Siberia.[6] All these hypocritical changes merely reinforced the conviction, on the part of highbrow Marxists not living in the Soviet Union, that the game of jazz was not worth the candle.

The Frankfurt School Mojo

Among Stalinists, the term *bourgeois* was rarely applied to jazz without the adjective *decadent*, meaning cheap, mass-produced diversion used by the capitalists to pacify the workers. Ragtime was "decadent," according to Stalin's Commissar of Public Enlightenment Anatoli Lunacharsky, because it offered an "extreme mechanization of rhythm, . . . pounding your will into a cutlet," and manipulating the worker into living "through his sexual organs, so that during the intervals between work he will be pre-occupied with those sides of his existence." The alternative, as we've seen, was "proletarian" jazz, described as "uncompromisingly lower class but at the same time purged of all links with eroticism and dancing."[7]

If these crude Lunacharskyisms had expired with Stalin, they would scarcely be worth recalling today. But, thanks to the highbrow Marxism of the Frankfurt School, they got refined into a deceptively clear—and astonishingly slippery—substance known as "critical theory." In Samuel Lipman's apt phrase, critical theory represents "the forced marriage of Stalinism and high European culture."[8]

Spooked by Hitler's uncanny ability to use radio, film, and newspapers to spread Nazism into every stratum of society, the refugee intellectuals from Frankfurt gazed with fascinated horror at the American mass media, which they saw as a totalitarianism all the more powerful for being more subtle. As the sociologist Paul Connerton reports, the Frankfurtians drew a parallel between Nazi propaganda and the "marketing psychology" of "organized capitalism." In their view, both systems planted their ideologies in the irrational soil of the individual psyche, which made them impossible to uproot by rational means. Hence the effort by critical theorists to combine the insights of Freud with those of Marx.[9]

Which returns us to jazz. Unlike the Stalinists, the Frankfurtians rejected any notion of jazz as folk music. To them, jazz was as contemptible as the official *völkisch* culture of the Nazis; capitalist America and fascist Germany were identical in this respect. The historian Martin Jay summarizes their view: "Folk music was no longer alive, because the spontaneous *Volk* had been consumed in a process that left popular music, like all popular culture, the creature of manipulation and imposition from above."[10]

Nor could jazz be "proletarian." In the Frankfurtian view art is not the mechanical "superstructure" posited by Marxism, in which a critic may find simple reflections of class bias. Nor is it an autonomous realm, accessible only through quasi-religious contemplation. Instead the Frankfurtians practiced what Adorno called "immanent" criticism; that is, they sought to discover authentic signs of "negation" in art, meaning either an implicit protest against the prevailing social order or an authentic projection of human freedom into the (socialist) future. Sounds simple enough. But the tricky part comes with Adorno's injunction that critics must not be deceived by *phony* negations. Bourgeois capitalism, warned he, is devilishly good at fooling people into thinking they are happy. The Marxist term for such deceptive happiness is "false consciousness." But like most Marxist terms, it got refined by Adorno, into "premature reconciliation."[11]

It was into this bag of capitalist tricks that Adorno stuck jazz—with a vengeance. From the outset, he refused to regard Afro-American music as a new idiom, writing: "Even in the techniques of syncopation, there is nothing that was not present in rudimentary form in Brahms and outdone by Schoenberg and Stravinsky."[12] Thus, jazz did not deserve discussion in aesthetic terms, only "psychosocial critique" as pure "commodity." It was "pseudo-individualistic," because (to his ear) its improvisation offered only the repetition of simple themes. It was "pseudo-democratic," because it substituted "collective" for "individual" fantasies (this from the man who blamed radio for breaking up the collective listening experience of the concert hall!). And finally jazz was "pseudo-erotic," promising only "illusory" sexual emancipation.[13]

This latter condemnation is worth pondering for a moment, because it reveals the contradiction in Adorno's approach. Unlike Lunacharsky, Adorno was not a simple-minded prude. Wearing his Frankfurtian hat, he defined jazz as "desire's surrogate," an "unreal edifice" erected by "the entrepreneurs" to co-opt the true erotic liberation of the masses—which he saw as a good thing, the centerpiece of the updated socialist dream. Yet, unlike some of his fellow Frankfurtians (notably Herbert Marcuse, who became a celebrity in the 1960s for praising that decade's blend of erotic and political protest), Adorno could not readily imagine civilization without its discontents. Wearing his highbrow hat, he condemned the exuberance of jazz as "stylized like the ecstasies savages go into beating the war drums."[14] In other words, jazz was damned if it did and damned if it didn't. As a false erotic liberation, it was helping to oppress the masses. As a true one, it was being carried out by the wrong folks.

There are two reasons why the Frankfurt School has been working its magic charm—or (to use the Afro-American term) its mojo—for so long. First, it enchants its followers with the shrunken heads of both Freud and Marx. Second, it casts a spell in which the highbrow Marxist can have his cultural cake and eat it, too. By insisting that most art, high and low, exists for the sole purpose of reinforcing bourgeois-capitalist consciousness, the "critical theorist" gets to be a revolutionary. But by dictating the handful of exceptions that achieve true "negation," he also gets to be a snob. Moreover, he gets to make these judgments in a way that, thanks to slippery ideas such as "premature reconciliation," need not consider such mundane matters as appearances or common sense.

If the Frankfurt School was the forced marriage of Stalinism and high European culture, then the Popular Front was the traumatic divorce. In 1935 the Seventh Comintern reacted to the rise of fascism by announcing a new phase in the revolutionary struggle that would take a newly positive attitude toward the mass media and popular culture. Such a powerful propaganda machine, it was argued, must be utilized to sway the masses against fascism, even if they did not respond by moving toward communism. The Popular Front strategy—especially in Hollywood and New York—was to make friends and influence people, no matter how tepid their sympathy.

But this strategy did not sit well with the highbrow Marxists, who warned that facile slogans about "people's culture" would lead to artistic leveling. In America their ranks were joined by the "New York intellectuals" associated with *Partisan Review*, who sought to preserve the forced marriage at all costs. To that end, they adopted a version of critical theory, complete with an embrace of introverted modernism and a vehement rejection of popular culture in all its forms.

This approach is crystallized in a famous essay by the art critic Clement Greenberg, entitled "Avant-Garde and Kitsch," which appeared in *Partisan*

Review in 1939. In highbrow dudgeon, Greenberg begins by equating "mass culture" with "kitsch," defined as "popular, commercial art and literature with their chromeotypes, magazine covers, illustrations, ads, slick and pulp fiction, comics, Tin Pan Alley music, tap dancing, Hollywood movies, etc. etc." Kitsch is condemned for three reasons. First, it is commercially produced. Echoing another Frankfurtian, Walter Benjamin, Greenberg writes: "Because it can be turned out mechanically, kitsch is an integral part of our productive system in a way in which true culture could never be, except accidentally." Second, kitsch rips off high culture. Like a parasite, it attaches itself to the "fully matured cultural tradition," from which it draws "devices, tricks, stratagems, rules of thumb, themes, converts them into a system, and discards the rest." And third, kitsch overrides all other types of culture, including folk culture.[15]

These points are well taken, for there *is* such a thing as kitsch—consider Liberace. But Greenberg applies the label to everything popular. He is a true introverted modernist, whose biggest fear is that the masses will like the right art for the wrong reasons. So he defines kitsch as anything that "pre-digests art for the spectator and spares him effort, provides him with a short cut to the pleasure of art that detours what is necessarily difficult in genuine art."[16] The possibility that art might provide both immediate and cerebral pleasures simultaneously, or that an untrained observer might intuit the latter, is ruled out of bounds.

Significantly, Greenberg avoids jazz. As quoted, his list includes "Tin Pan Alley music" and "tap dancing"—but not any of the jazz giants reaching their artistic zenith at the time. At one point, he nods in the direction of jazz, admitting that "kitsch" occasionally produces "something of merit, something that has an authentic folk flavor." But then, perhaps feeling himself tottering on the brink of the Popular Front, he retreats: "These accidental and isolated instances have fooled people who should know better."[17]

In fact, it was Greenberg who should have known better, because jazz is the antithesis of kitsch. Recall that the modernist composers were reacting against the heavy-handed emotionalism of late-romantic music—what Wagner himself called "industrial machinery," a phrase that came back to haunt him in the mouths of his critics, notably Nietzsche. Out of this phrase grew the concept of a "mechanical" music designed to massage and browbeat audiences into a state of passionate exaltation. And out of that concept grew the term *kitsch*, as used by German critics, notably Adorno. The musicologist Carl Dahlhaus offers this apt summary:

> Musical kitsch, whether rousing and high-flown or soothingly sentimental, is a decadent form of romantic music. When the *noble simplicité* of a classical

style descends to the market place, the result is banality—the mere husks of classical forms—but hardly ever kitsch. Kitsch in music has hybrid ambitions which far outreach the capabilities of its actual structures and sounds. . . . Instead of being content with modest achievements within its reach, musical kitsch has pretensions to big emotions, to "significance," and these are rooted in what are still recognizably romantic preconceptions, however depraved.[18]

The point is that jazz, with its classical virtues of wit, simplicity, and emotional restraint, offers relief not just from late romanticism, but also from kitsch. Jazz is rooted in the blues, which is preeminently a music of stoicism, irony, and humor—the very qualities most needful in enduring oppression. And jazz is rooted in gospel, which unleashes powerful emotion for the explicit purpose of containing and redirecting it. As for jazz's exuberance, it is a quality hard won by a people who could ill afford to indulge their passions. Thus it has little in common with the forced exaltation of kitsch.

By 1948 Greenberg was calling himself "an ex- or disabused Marxist." By the 1950s he was one of several *Partisan Review* writers who had come full circle, defending liberal democracy against communism in the heat of the Cold War.[19] But most of these influential intellectuals never became ex- or disabused Frankfurtians. Their belief in the categorical worthlessness of popular culture, and their conviction that the music of Armstrong, Ellington, and Parker bears only a parasitic relationship to "genuine art," remain intact.

Midcult: Curse or Blessing?

The seeming exception is Dwight MacDonald, the literary and film critic who decided in 1960 that the topic of popular culture needed to be reconsidered in the light of such postwar conditions as burgeoning affluence, expanding higher education, and increasing media attention to high culture. His essay, "Masscult & Midcult," is still widely regarded as the definitive putdown of popular culture for neoconservative highbrows who have jettisoned Marxism but not the sharp edge of critical theory. Yet, as I shall try to show, it is far from definitive. Indeed, it's a surprisingly sloppy piece of work.

Here is MacDonald's main thesis:

In these more advanced times, the danger to High Culture is not so much from Masscult as from a peculiar hybrid bred from the latter's unnatural intercourse with the former. A whole middle culture has come into existence and it threatens to absorb both its parents. This intermediate form—let us call it Midcult—has the essential qualities of Masscult—the formula, the built-in reaction, the lack of any standard except popularity—but it decently covers them with a cultural figleaf. In Masscult the trick is plain—to please the crowd by any means. But Midcult has it both ways: it pretends to respect the standards of High Culture while in fact it waters them down and vulgarizes them.[20]

Any resemblance between Midcult and the Popular Front is hardly accidental. The high point of the essay is MacDonald's satirical attack on a true Midcult classic, Ernest Hemingway's *The Old Man and the Sea*. Yet this attack, with its sly mockery of the novella's pseudofolksiness and literary pretension, is full of echoes from the 1930s—in particular, of *Partisan Review*'s many criticisms of the "worker narratives," "folk histories" and "proletarian theatre" churned out by Popular Front sympathizers in federal programs such as the Farm Security Administration and Federal Writers Project.[21]

Of course, a criticism need not be original to be correct. The real problem with "Masscult & Midcult" lies in the many inconsistencies, doubts, and qualifications it throws up while struggling to free itself from the Frankfurtian grip. For example, MacDonald admits in the first few pages that "popular" is not the opposite of "good," declaring that the problem with Masscult is not its popularity, but such unique characteristics as its assembly-line production; its "impersonality"; its failure to provide "emotional catharsis," "aesthetic experience," or even "entertainment"; its "lack of standards"; and its "total subjection to the spectator." These characteristics make Masscult "bad in a new way; it doesn't even have the theoretical possibility of being good."[22]

Sounds dreadful. But then, in the next breath, MacDonald says that "the same writer, indeed the same book or even the same chapter, may contain elements of both Masscult and High Culture." Balzac, he declares, uses "the cheapest, flimsiest kind of melodrama"; and Dickens relies on "the most vulgar kind of theatricality." In other words, these novelists pander to popular taste. But does that mean they display the unique characteristics of Masscult? Is Balzac impersonal and without standards? Does Dickens fail to provide entertainment or emotional catharsis? Are we talking about cheap melodrama and vulgar theatricality (which are hardly new), or about literature that is "bad in a new way"? This part of the essay concludes: "Masscult is a subtler problem than is sometimes recognized."[23] Indeed, it may be too subtle for Dwight MacDonald.

As for MacDonald's doubts and qualifications, they're all over the place. He defends the grubbiness of Grub Street; he applauds the commercial success of modernist painting; he concedes that the hoi polloi sometimes respond to great art; he sees grace and wit in certain Hollywood movies; he suggests that a taste for kitsch might not rule out an appreciation of the avant-garde.[24] Finally he even debunks the idea of "mass culture":

> There is not One Big Audience but rather a number of smaller, more specialized audiences that may still be commercially profitable. (I take it for granted that the less differentiated the audience, the less chance there is of something original and lively creeping in, since the principle of the lowest common denominator applies.) . . . The mass audience is divisible, we have discovered—and the more it is divided, the better.[25]

This is an astonishing statement to find at the end of an essay that begins by depicting America as an atomized mass society in which "large numbers of people are unable to express their human qualities because they are related to each other neither as individuals nor as members of a community."[26] Perhaps MacDonald was temporarily swayed by the better arguments coming out of the "mass culture" debate.

One such argument was set forth by the sociologist David Riesman, whose classic study (with Nathan Glazer and Reuel Denney) of "the changing American character," *The Lonely Crowd*, was one of the most influential texts of the 1950s. Now somewhat dated, the book still poses a vigorous challenge to the begged questions and easy assumptions of the Frankfurtian view. In particular it disputes the much-touted passivity of those on the consuming end of popular culture, arguing instead that popular culture is a highly interactive "taste-exchanging" process through which consumers exert a shaping influence—not only on each other, but also on the producers. Riesman further suggests that this process is capable of climbing, albeit slowly and precariously, up a "taste gradient" extending from the lowest to the highest artistic level.[27]

It is significant that Riesman and his colleagues illustrate their argument with jazz:

> Many critics of the popular arts . . . fail to observe . . . how energetic and understanding are some of the comments of the amateur taste-exchangers who seem at first glance to be part of a very passive, uncreative audience. One of the most interesting examples of this is . . . the large number of young people who, all over the country, greeted jazz affectionately and criticized it fondly. . . . [They] resisted, often violently, and occasionally with success, the effort of the popular-music industry itself to ticket its products:

in the very form of their choices—preference for combos over star soloists, preference for improvisation, distrust of smooth arrangers—they set up their own *standards* in opposition to *standards*.[28]

So much for MacDonald's melancholy decree that nothing exists between Highcult and Masscult except "the tepid ooze of Midcult."[29] It is typical of the whole "mass culture" debate that MacDonald backs up his melancholy view with examples from literature and visual art, while Riesman supports his more sanguine assessment with jazz.

Strikingly, MacDonald admits jazz as exceptional. When deploring the kitschiness of popular music, he cites only the sentimental ballad "I Love You Truly," and the florid virtuosity of Liberace. When he does get around to mentioning jazz, he accounts for its lack of kitschiness by resorting to good old Stalinist doublethink: "The amazing survival of jazz despite the exploitative onslaughts of half a century of commercial entrepreneurs, is in my opinion, due to its folk quality."[30] Unlike Riesman, MacDonald cannot accept the idea that jazz arose from folk sources and passed through the world of commercial entertainment on its way to becoming a modernist art.

Like the Hatfields and McCoys of the Ozark Mountains, the friends and foes of the Popular Front have been feuding for generations. For the last sixty years, critics on both sides have been firing potshots at each other—and whatever stands in the middle, such as popular culture, is now riddled with holes. The heirs of the Popular Front keep trying to use popular culture to send "progressive" messages to the masses. The heirs of the Frankfurt School keep attacking this "politicization," while denying popular culture any claim to artistic legitimacy. And public discourse on the topic keeps getting reduced to the same stupid question: Is popular culture just junk, or is it junk being used as propaganda? It's high time we found an alternative to this tiresome squabbling—namely, proper standards, neither categorically dismissive nor ideologically permissive, by which to judge popular culture. In my view, the best place to start looking is in Afro-American music, where such standards have always existed.

Chapter 6

Cubists and Squares: Jazz as Modernism

Of course, the vast majority of people who appreciate jazz do so without any fancy ideas about it one way or the other. Most people don't relate to music, especially popular music, on an intellectual level. But that is precisely why the misconceptions I've been talking about are so influential. The public, whose opinion is registered in dollars, not ideas, offers little resistance.

Likewise jazz musicians. Along with most artists, jazz musicians accept whatever intellectual acclaim they can get, whether or not it is based on an accurate assessment of their art. In particular, they endorse the Stalinist view of jazz as a folk art corrupted by commerce—largely because it makes room for racial resentment. Too often there *is* a sharp dividing line between the "folk" artist (black) and the "bourgeois" exploiter (white). And too often the memory lingers of the grinning blackface minstrel, bought and sold for the entertainment of whites. What self-respecting jazz musician wouldn't prefer a more heroic image?

85

The Satchmo Smile

It's hard to see anything heroic about Louis Armstrong's famous grin, a masklike expression aptly described by the writer Nat Hentoff as "the broadest and seemingly most durable grin in the history of Western man."[1] Like the minstrel blackface, Satchmo's smile is a grotesque exaggeration of what's underneath—in particular, a smile normally toothy and squinty eyed. Armstrong's squint was especially effective in hiding his intelligence, and as he grew older, he exaggerated it (and his toothiness) to the point where the contrast between the Satchmo mask and his features in repose was really quite startling.

Startling and offensive, because for many jazz lovers the mask was the symbol of Armstrong's having "sold out." As the jazz critic Gary Giddins summarizes: "The standard line about Armstrong . . . goes like this: Louis Armstrong was a superb artist in his early years, *the* exemplar of jazz improvisation, until fame forced him to compromise, at which point he became an entertainer, repeating himself and indulging a taste for low humor."[2] In this view, the Satchmo smile was the "bourgeois" side, the otherwise intelligent expression the "folk" side. Yet Armstrong himself never made the distinction. He rejected burnt cork, but he never rejected show business. On the contrary, he made good use of it, as Giddins explains:

> [Armstrong]'s ability to balance the emotional gravity of the artist with the communal good cheer of the entertainer helped enable him to demolish the Jim Crow/Zip Coon/Ol' Dan Tucker stereotypes. In their place he installed the liberated black man, the pop performer as world-renowned artist who dressed stylishly, lived high, slapped palms with the Pope, and regularly passed through whites-only portals, leaving the doors open behind him. . . . He was as much himself rolling his eyes and mugging as he was playing the trumpet. His fans understood that, but intellectuals found the whole effect too damn complicated.[3]

Most intellectuals balk at the notion of a comic entertainer who is also a musical genius. But that's exactly what Armstrong was. The two faces are conjoined in a way that can only be understood when jazz improvisation is no longer seen as "instinctive" and "spontaneous."

No one disputes Armstrong's greatness as an instrumentalist. Within jazz, the view is summed up by Miles Davis: "You know you can't play anything on a horn that Louis hasn't played—I mean even modern."[4] Symphonic musicians agree: On one famous occasion the brass section of the Boston Symphony went backstage after an Armstrong performance to ask him to repeat a certain passage. He did so, with brilliant variations, and the group was awestruck. One said, "I watched his fingers and I still don't know how he does it . . . playing there all by himself, he sounded as if a whole orchestra were behind him. I never heard a musician like this, and I thought he was just a colored entertainer."[5]

What Armstrong did, in the words of the composer Virgil Thomson, was "combine the highest reaches of instrumental virtuosity with the most tensely disciplined melodic structure and the most spontaneous emotional expression, all of which in one man you must admit is pretty rare."[6] Put another way, it was useless for the Boston visitor to study Armstrong's fingers; because Armstrong's way of playing was akin to Liszt's or Paganini's— a seamless blend of nuanced interpretation, bold variation, and radical invention.

Jazz musicians rarely claim spontaneity for their creations. As Ellington put it, "Anyone who plays anything worth hearing knows what he's going to play."[7] This is why, after praising Armstrong's 1928 solo, *West End Blues*, as "abstract, sophisticated, virtuosic, emotionally expressive, structurally perfect," Gunther Schuller adds that it "did not suddenly spring full-blown from Armstrong's head. Its conception was assembled, bit by bit, over a period of four or five years." Thus Schuller traces the steps by which Armstrong came, by 1926, to consider the jazz solo "in terms not of a pop-tune more or less embellished, but of a chord progression generating a maximum of creative originality."[8] Two years later, Armstrong would be playing a King Oliver standard in a radically new way:

> The block-like polyphonic structures of Oliver's performance, which were broken only by two-bar built-in breaks and revealed no organic development from chorus to chorus, are translated by Armstrong and Hines into an overall new form in which each chorus builds and feeds upon the preceding one. The means are twofold: variation technique combined with gradual dissolution into splinter subdivisions of the original sixteen-bar structures. . . . A necessary corollary to this structural progression was an analogous breakdown of the thematic material.[9]

To read this passage is to recall the cubist project of breaking, dissolving, and splintering forms that had previously been solid. Such a comparison is hardly original—indeed, jazz has been compared with every other invention of the twentieth century, from airplanes (by the futurists) to skyscrapers (by Le Corbusier, who dubbed the Manhattan skyline "hot jazz in stone and steel."[10]) Why not cubism?

Because cubism is "high" and jazz is "low," some critics would say. Yet note that Stuart Davis, universally recognized as the first true American cubist, lists among "the things that have made me want to paint, . . . Earl

Hines' hot piano playing and Negro jazz music in general."[11] Of course, Davis was also inspired by such "low-life" objects as eggbeaters, matchbooks, and light bulbs. But he wasn't a perverse modernist, simply pointing at these things and pronouncing them "art." Nor was he an introverted modernist, reducing objects to their geometric essence. As Hilton Kramer explains, Davis was an extroverted modernist whose involvement in "the life of the times" led neither to "political philistinism" nor to the "metaphysical disposition" of "pure abstraction."[12] Indeed, Davis saw the latter as "inimical to the vitality of art itself."[13]

The question is: How did Davis view jazz? As another "low-life" object in the busy, vulgar American landscape, just waiting to be transmuted into art? Or as an art form in its own right, with something vital to teach America's leading cubist? Both, according to the art critic Barbara Rose. Writing about the influence of jazz on Davis's work, Rose writes that the "tension" and "nervous energy" of his forms "express Davis' concern with *ordering the frenzy he found in the American scene*."[14] (emphasis added) By this assertion, jazz is part of the "frenzy."

But then Rose adds that Davis

> was one of the first artists to appreciate jazz as a distinctly American idiom. The technical means he had disciplined himself to master were now by and large in his grasp. . . . Like Matisse's *Jazz*, Davis' paintings, such as *Hot Still-Scape for Six Colors*, contain an astonishing variety of lively, dancing shapes, sharply contoured and smoothly fitted together in a sequence of syncopated rhythms.[15]

Davis himself would no doubt agree with the latter assertion—as would Ralph Ellison:

> Even though few recognized it, such artists as Ellington and Louis Armstrong were the stewards of our vaunted American optimism and guardians against the creeping irrationality which ever plagues our form of society. They created great entertainment, but for them (ironically) and for us (unconsciously) their music was a rejection of that chaos and license which characterized the so-called jazz age. . . . It is time we paid our respects to a man [Ellington] who has spent his life reducing the violence and chaos of American life to artistic order.[16]

Even apart from Stuart Davis, the similarities between jazz and cubism are striking. Recalling Barzun's praise of cubism as a radically new way of ordering space and time, we can draw a parallel between the brevity of a jazz solo and the shallowness of cubist space: Within each circumscribed arena, the artist carries out a finely modulated work of dissection. The objects being dissected are humble: a bottle, newspaper, or guitar in the case of cubism; a blues, rag, or popular song in the case of jazz. The interest lies in the process of dissection, in which the artist's powers of formal analysis are tested, *along with his aesthetic sense.* I stress the latter because it is not enough simply to take the object apart; the scalpel wielder must also, in Barzun's words, "make beauty and truth out of all possible cases or guesses."[17] The purpose is art, not autopsy.

Equally striking is the way in which both jazz and cubism gain or lose audiences depending on how expressive or cerebral they are. As it happens, the first phase of jazz was the more popular: From Armstrong through the 1940s, the music was strongly colored, richly textured, full of bright lights and deep shadows. The material being dissected remained recognizable, with its emotional power enhanced rather than diminished. Thus the *first* phase of jazz resembles the *second* phase of cubism, the so-called "synthetic" phase initiated by Picasso in 1913, which combined brighter color, denser texture (including that of collage), and greater contrast with more attention to the direct representation of the sensuous appeal of subject matter. Not surprisingly, this phase of cubism still attracts a larger audience than its predecessor, the "analytic" phase that, beginning in 1907, limited itself to a muted palette of browns and grays in order to carry out its highly complex, sometimes unrecognizable dissections.

Which brings us to bebop, the jazz equivalent of analytic cubism. Bebop's great exemplar, the saxophonist Charlie Parker, was criticized for abandoning the fluid, expressive tone of such predecessors as Benny Carter and Johnny Hodges. Parker's tone is not as harsh and dry as some critics claim, but it is lean and spare—for a reason. Like Picasso and Braque, Parker couldn't have done what he did without first limiting his palette. Here is the poet and jazz critic Philip Larkin's account: "Parker found jazz chugging along in 4/4 time in the tonic and the dominant, and splintered it into a thousand rhythmic and harmonic pieces. Showers of sixteenths, accented on half- and quarter-beats, exhibited a new harmonic fecundity and an originality of phrasing that had scarcely been hinted at before." This is not the gushing of a fan. On the contrary, Larkin dislikes bebop for the same reason many art lovers dislike analytic cubism:

> To say I don't like modern jazz because it's modernist art simply raises the question of why I don't like modernist art. . . . I dislike such things not because they are new, but because they are irresponsible exploitations of technique in contradiction of human life as we know it. This is my essential criticism of modernism, whether perpetrated by Parker, Pound or Picasso: it helps us neither to enjoy nor to endure.[18]

Larkin's dismissal of modernism is too simplistic, but there is a grain of truth in his observation that bebop is modernist in a way that earlier jazz is not. For all their genius, the giants of prebebop jazz did not approach music in the self-consciously "artistic" way that Picasso and Braque approached painting. Prebebop jazz presents a paradox: On the one hand it is aesthetically sophisticated; on the other it is culturally innocent (using "culture" in the traditional sense). Armstrong, Basie, Ellington, and their ilk were innocent of modernism in the sense of not taking an adversary stance toward their audiences, or seeing a necessary conflict between art and commerce. They could be bitter about not getting their fair share, but they were not bitter about being popular entertainers. Making a living by pleasing people simply didn't strike them as a problem.

"Mass Culture" as Nurture

Along with anticommercialism, the highbrow aversion to jazz also reflects the Frankfurt School's deep distrust of "mass culture" as purveyed by the electronic media. The only optimist on this topic was Walter Benjamin—and he was a cautious one. His famous 1936 essay, "The Work of Art in the Age of Mechanical Reproduction," argues that the electronic media might, in the right hands, possess revolutionary potential. Compared with the pessimism of Benjamin's colleagues, this qualified optimism has proved appealing to subsequent generations raised on a diet of combined Marxism and popular culture. Thus Benjamin's essay was picked up in the 1960s by the German neo-Marxist Jürgen Habermas, who made it one of the founding texts of the European New Left. And today the bulk of "serious" discourse about popular culture, in both Europe and the United States, still takes its cues from Benjamin's perspective. Too bad these latter-day Frankfurtians almost never ask whether that perspective makes sense when applied to *music*.

I raise the question because, unlike Adorno, Benjamin didn't write about music. He was an art critic, and "The Work of Art in the Age of Mechanical Reproduction" focuses wholly on the objects and processes of the visual media. Its central argument is that the quasi-religious "aura" of the traditional work of art (painting or sculpture) stems from its prehistoric function as a ritual object. In a quick survey of art history, Benjamin traces the gradual emergence of this ritual object from the forbidden inner recesses of sacred temples, to the semipublic settings of houses of worship, to secular exhibition in modern museums.

Then, in a bold formulation, Benjamin declares that the electronic media—in particular, photography and film—have "emancipated" visual art from this ancient ritual function. A photographic negative, he says, possesses no "aura." It is "a work of art designed for reproducibility." What is more, the infinitely reproducible images of photography and film reach people in a new way, one that is less "concentrated," "contemplative," and "optical" than demanded by the traditional art object. And this new type of experience—"distracted," "habitual," "tactile"—has the power, precisely because it affects people indirectly, to "mobilize the masses" for revolution.[19]

Benjamin himself didn't apply this perspective to music, for a couple of reasons. First, this defender of pre-Hitlerian German modernism was predisposed to take film seriously, since his own countrymen had made it an expressionist art form in the 1920s. Second, the Frankfurt School revered Lenin, who considered film the most innovative and influential of the arts.[20] This background was no help in picking up high-cultural and ideological resonances in a strange music created by an alien race in a foreign clime.

Regrettably, when it comes to distinguishing between the revolutionary and reactionary uses of the electronic media, Benjamin's analysis boils down to the same old Party line. He denounces Hollywood's "illusion-promoting spectacles and dubious speculations"; he declares that "the capitalist exploitation of film denies consideration to modern man's legitimate claim to being reproduced"; and he sings the praises of Soviet documentaries that show "not actors but people who portray *themselves*—and primarily in their own work process."[21] In sum, our enlightened critic spurns the golden age of Hollywood for the Stalinist age of steel.

No such concessions are forthcoming from Adorno, who stubbornly refuses to embrace the electronic media. Indeed, his famous 1938 reply to Benjamin, "On the Fetish Character of Music and the Regression of Listening," condemns not only jazz but every other kind of music (including that of his former teacher Schoenberg) the moment it is recorded or broadcast. Strenuously Adorno argues that the process deprives music of its "aura," with a result that is inferior to live performance, and may actually destroy, or "regress," musical taste.[22]

Adorno's pessimism is more understandable when we recall the low quality of recording and broadcast technology in the 1930s and 1940s. In those days one did not have to be a Frankfurtian to have doubts about how well the full symphonic sound of the European classics were faring in the grooves and on the airwaves. The movies were especially brutal: Soundtracks routinely lopped off both the top and the bottom of the musical spectrum, because there was no way to mitigate the harsh effects of treble and bass in the speakers used in theaters.[23] It's too bad that "progressive" thinkers like Adorno had so little faith that such problems could be solved in the future.

Still, Adorno's pessimism suggests a certain integrity. On some level he seems to have recognized that music moves more easily into the electronic media than do the visual arts. And his special horror of jazz suggests an awareness that Afro-American music is at home in the grooves and airwaves in a way the European classics are not. Indeed, it can be argued that the unorthodox trajectory of jazz from folk music to modernism was shaped by "mechanical reproduction." Adorno would not agree that jazz is modernism, but he would certainly agree that many of the musical qualities associated with it are intimately tied to electronic devices, such as the microphone. So it's worth taking a moment to ponder the impact of these devices.

As a singer and historian of European vocal music, Pleasants is aware of the microphone's bad reputation among musical highbrows. Yet he disputes it:

> The most persistent and pervasive prejudice against the popular singer has been his apparent dependence upon the mike, a dependence thought of as a demonstration of vocal infirmity. . . . [But the mike] is a listener, an electronically activated ear, and nothing more than that. As such, however, because it "hears" so well, it is merciless in the exposure of blemishes. . . . But it can also detect and amplify virtues, delicate refinements of melodic line and vocal inflection, minute shadings and subtleties of enunciation and phrase . . . The mike amplifies both good habits and bad, which is why the best of the popular singers sing so well. . . . Working with so candid an ally, they must.[24]

Similar claims can be made for instrumental jazz. Just to cite one example, the subtle and expressive saxophone playing of Lester Young evolved in tandem with the microphone singing of his musical alter ego, Billie Holiday.

In this one respect, jazz would appear to fit Benjamin's definition of an art "designed for reproducibility." But at the same time, jazz exists prior to, and independent of, its own reproduction. When the first jazz bands were assembled for the exclusive purpose of cutting a record, the long history of Afro-American music as live performance did not disappear into the woodwork. As Pleasants explains:

> The impact of the microphone upon vocal technique and upon the articulation of song and text would have been immense in any case. That the coming of radio just happened to coincide with a growing awareness and acceptance of a new Afro-American musical idiom compounded and intensified the repercussions. . . . At the root of the phenomenon is the black

singer's predilection for oral and improvisatory communication, for narrative balladry, exhortatory evangelism and lyrical exaltation.[25]

This last observation returns us to Benjamin's notion that the ritual function of art derives from its origin as a hidden object. However accurate this notion may be with regard to the visual arts (not very, I suspect), it is grossly inaccurate with regard to music, especially Afro-American music. Different arts have different anthropological roots, and it is simply absurd to posit a hidden origin for music and dance. In Europe, Africa, and the rest of the world, these arts trace their ancestry back to public, or at least communal, rituals.

Then there is the question of the "aura." It is a truism to say that the Afro-American musician—whether a gospel shouter, a blues singer, or a jazz soloist—plays a priestly role. This role is sometimes equated with that of the romantic genius, but they are different. The genius is exalted as an individual whose inspired utterances may or may not resonate with the group. The Afro-American musician, by contrast, is elevated chiefly as a conduit for the expression of communal emotion and experience. In both religious and secular settings, he is obliged to interact with his audience through practices such as call and response, collective movement, and the skilled evocation of extreme emotional and mental states.

Because these practices can be traced back to tribal Africa, black cultural separatists often claim that black Americans make no distinction between the sacred and the secular. Such claims hardly describe the generations of black folk who have hotly disputed the type of music that does and does not belong in church. Yet even so, the cultural separatists have a point. The music that blacks have traditionally forbidden in church, notably the blues, is called "Devil's music," a phrase that does not make it secular so much as spiritually malevolent.

The point is that the original ritual "aura" of Afro-American music is difficult to shake. It survives in profane settings, such as the blues joint, nightclub, and dance hall; and it survives electronic reproduction. What Adorno hated most about jazz was what its admirers loved most: its uncanny ability, via radio and records, to penetrate the minds and hearts of listeners far removed in space and time from the original performance. To Adorno this globe-spanning immediacy was fearful; to a less worried mind, like Albert Murray's, it means simply that jazz and blues are "the music that phonographs were all about in the first place."[26]

Less obvious, but far more crucial to the development of jazz, was the impact of the electronic media on musicians themselves. Not only did radio and records capture the finest musicians' achievements in a form that could be studied and emulated, they also broadened the opportunities for study and emulation. Billie Holiday illustrates the point. Growing up in an impoverished section of Baltimore, Holiday spent many childhood hours running errands and doing chores for the proprietress of a local brothel. In an earlier era, a musically talented girl in such straitened circumstances would have few opportunities to hear the best musicians. But Holiday came of age in the 1920s, when the best was accessible. As she writes in her autobiography:

> I'd run all over for Alice and the girls. . . . When it came time to pay me, I used to tell her she could keep the money if she'd let me come up in her front parlor and listen to Louis Armstrong and Bessie Smith on her victrola. . . . I guess I'm not the only one who heard their first good jazz in a whorehouse. But I never tried to make anything of it. . . . In Baltimore, places like Alice Dean's were the only joints fancy enough to have a victrola and real enough to pick up on the best records. I know this for damn sure. If I'd heard Pops and Bessie wailing through the window of some minister's front parlor, I'd have been running free errands for him.[27]

Mention that Armstrong and Smith had a formative influence on Holiday, and her fans will rush to defend the originality of her music. But that's exactly the point. Without early exposure to the best music, Holiday's chances of moving in a truly original direction would have been greatly diminished. I have already emphasized the importance of tradition in extroverted modernism. For someone like Holiday it was not possible to pursue tradition through the Academy, the Studio, the Salon or even the Café. So she pursued it through the Victrola.

Yet it is striking how little this kind of apprenticeship is credited—even by those who served it. In a passage expressing admiration for a group of German jazz musicians she heard in Berlin in 1954, Holiday writes: "The latest American sides they had were from '49 to '50, but those cats can blow. . . . Charlie Parker and people like him, and people like me, we just had it in us. . . . Those cats didn't have it in them. They had to work and study and listen and work some more and get it the hard way."[28]

Such comments are frequently parroted by primitivists who believe that jazz musicians don't think about what they're doing, they just do it. If that were true, then Holiday would not have been obliged to spend several years singing in sleazy nightclubs before making her debut at the Apollo Theatre in 1935. What would be taken as a modest disclaimer coming from a comparably gifted violinist—"I just had it in me"—gets taken as factual statement coming from a jazz musician. Murray objects to such interpretations:

[Blues musicianship] is not a matter of having the blues and giving direct personal release to the raw emotion brought on by suffering. It is a matter of mastering the elements of craft required by the idiom. It is a matter of idiomatic orientation and of the refinement of auditory sensibility in terms of idiomatic nuance. It is a far greater matter of convention, and hence tradition, than of impulse.[29]

It's more than a little ironic that one of the few arts fundamentally shaped by twentieth-century technology should be so widely regarded as the "natural" and "unconscious" outpouring of animal instinct, rather than the product of hard work, discipline, and aesthetic intelligence.

Now the plot thickens, because few jazz apprenticeships would have been served if people hadn't seen profit in it. Back in the 1920s, there were no nonprofit or charitable organizations bringing Armstrong and Smith to the deprived black children of Baltimore. Nor, I hasten to add, were there any cultural commissars dictating which type of folk music was best for these folk. There was, however, a pile of money to be made selling "race records" to the newly discovered black market, as well as to a growing segment of the white market.

The recording industry first established itself in the years before World War I, when the ragtime craze fostered demand for records and phonographs in the home. Between 1914 and 1919 nationwide sales of phonographs grew from $27 million to $159 million. The postwar industry was hoping for the next big expansion in 1920, when a black vaudevillian named Mamie Smith (no relation to Bessie) released a record, "Crazy Blues," that started a blues craze—not for rural Southern blues, but for popular songs with a blues flavor, performed by female singers. Three years later one industry report crowed that "the volume of sales . . . has increased in leaps and bounds for the Columbia Gramophone Company."[30]

Such commercialization was nothing new to black Americans. Before the blues craze, there were the jazz craze, the ragtime craze, the minstrel craze, the brass-band craze—and, during slavery, the cakewalk craze and the fiddle-music craze. Slave musicians were disproportionately represented among runaways, because they knew, from having been hired out to neighboring plantations, that they shared with skilled craftsmen the expectation of making an independent living in the North.[31]

It goes without saying that the image of the slave musician hired out by his owner is a not-so-gentle reminder of America's long and dishonorable tradition of economically disenfranchising black people in general, black

musicians in particular. As painfully as the European modernists suffered
at the hands of the bourgeoisie, their troubles cannot compare with those
of black American musicians exposed to the endlessly bizarre combina-
tions of praise and contempt that white society is capable of dishing out.
Black musicians have also, to a greater degree than European modernists,
seen their work appropriated and diluted for a particularly insulting type of
mainstream acceptance. Indeed, this history would seem to justify a deeply
ingrained anticommercial bias.

Yet the facts are otherwise. The vast majority of black American musicians, past and present, have embraced commerce without compunction.
They have complained of exploitation and a lack of artistic control. But
even the most militant cultural separatists have sought, not to purge the
music of all commercial taint but to pull off a takeover, hostile or otherwise, of those sectors of the music business that profit from black talent.
The bias—and there is one—is profoundly *pro*commercial.

To understand why, it's important to recall that the hireling role played
by the slave musician was not entirely a function of racism. The relationship between black performers and white audiences in the United States
dates back to the early eighteenth century, when, even in Europe, most
musicians were either itinerant minstrels hired by the common people for
special occasions, or (if they were lucky) employees of the church or ser-
vants maintained by noble households for the entertainment of guests.
Either way, musicians occupied the lowest end of the social scale, depen-
dent on the pleasure of others. Thus the Europeans who colonized the
New World regarded their own musicians, white as well as black, in the
same light.

The relationship became explicitly racist in the nineteenth century,
when the European romantic exaltation of the musician was most assured-
ly *not* transferred to the Afro-American context. At that point, it became
the fate of black musicians to be regarded as hirelings simply because they
were black.

Yet the effects of this fate were not wholly deleterious. The political scientist Louis Hartz describes the United States as a "fragment society,"
meaning that it preserves aspects of the historical period during which it
was spun off, so to speak, from Europe. Hartz is concerned chiefly with the
seventeenth-century character of American political institutions.[32] But a
similar view might be taken of Afro-American music, whose evolution
occurred in almost total isolation from contemporary developments in
European art and culture. Hence its cultural innocence.

Again, I mean "innocence" in a very specific way—innocence of the attitudes and beliefs of modernism. Black American musicians have scarcely
been innocent of their own circumstances—which, it so happens, are perfectly summed up in this passage from Barzun: "Historically, the artist has
been a slave, an unregarded wage earner, a courtier, clown and sycophant, a
domestic, finally an unknown citizen trying to arrest the attention of a
huge anonymous mass public and compel it to learn his name."[33] Given
their long experience with the first six alternatives listed here, it's hardly
surprising that black musicians would embrace the seventh. It was Ellington, after all, who came up with this pungent epitaph: "I loved and respected Louis Armstrong. He was born poor, died rich, and never hurt anyone
on the way."[34]

We now arrive at a startling hypothesis. Not only was the most vigorous
form of modernist music created by a people not expected to create anything, it was also nurtured by a process expected to destroy art. This is not
to deny that "mass culture" has been destructive of art. It most certainly
has. But the question is, Compared to what? Commerce and the electronic media have been kinder to art than any other system devised in the
twentieth century. And in the case of jazz, they have been more than kind.
For every occasion on which they stifled or diluted jazz, there has been
another on which they fostered or encouraged it. No matter how promising the raw materials of the Afro-American folk idiom, it would not have
blossomed without this uncelebrated nurture.

Beboppers, Beats, and the Double Audience

As hinted above, the bebop generation did convert to anticommercialism, as
well as to other modernist attitudes not previously found in the Afro-American tradition. For some of bebop's heirs and survivors, this conversion
appears permanent. For others, however, it now appears to have been little
more than an acute, but temporary, growing pain accompanying a drastic
change in jazz's cultural status. Either way, the story has its tragic side.

Bebop was the child of swing, the form of jazz that began when Armstrong joined the Fletcher Henderson orchestra in 1924. Before long the
whole Henderson band was swinging; and by the mid-1930s, its arrangements were being copied by countless other groups, from the sublime to
the ridiculous. As swing became mainstream, it became standardized, and
the more talented musicians began feeling like a small in-group, pitted

against a much larger out-group of managers, bookers, and audiences, whose powers of discrimination were often keener toward skin color than toward music.[35]

Meanwhile, in the Midwest, a number of black bands, such as Walter Page's, Benny Moten's, and Count Basie's, were stripping their arrangements down to the bare bones and allowing their members to fool around with denser percussive and sonorous effects than would have been tolerated in the mainstream. These bands were commercially successful, too—especially among blacks who preferred their bluesier sound to swing's smooth polish. In Kansas City, Missouri, home of round-the-clock nightclubs protected by a city government closely allied with (indeed, indistinguishable from) organized crime, local and visiting musicians routinely met between jobs to hold jam sessions as competitive and educational as they were exhausting.

By 1938, when the rackets were shut down and the action shifted to Chicago and New York, the younger Kansas City musicians had begun to move in a direction that, in Europe, would have been recognized as art for art's sake. Smitten by the work of such outstanding soloists as Lester Young and Charlie Christian, these youngsters strove to establish themselves in a field as crowded as it was brilliant. Instead of being complementary to dance band playing, the "cutting sessions" held by these younger musicians became adversarial, increasing their impatience with the job of entertaining audiences who couldn't always tell the difference between a witty, lucid solo and a flashy, formulaic riff.[36] For a while, young virtuosi such as Parker and John Birks ("Dizzy") Gillespie worked in the better dance bands, where they inspired their peers while also pleasing the paying customers. But as the kudos rose, the ticket sales dropped, and a rift began to open between this new kind of jazz and the popular audience.

At first the challengers reveled in their autonomy. For example, while playing in Cab Calloway's band at the Cotton Club, Gillespie and the bassist Milt Hinton used to spend intermissions on the roof, practicing for cutting sessions at such after-hours joints as Minton's Playhouse.[37] The targets to be "carved" included older figures such as Roy Eldridge (whom Gillespie finally bested after several tries), rivals eager to test their mettle, and snoops out to steal a few nuggets for mainstream swing musicians, usually white. Accordingly, the beboppers had little use for listeners who were not aficionados.

With one notable exception. Bebop's biggest white fans were the beats, a movement of writers based in San Francisco and New York, whose relationship with the older generation of New York intellectuals can best be described as love-hate. As students of these older intellectuals, the beats accepted a highly critical view of American society. But as young hipsters, they also rebelled against their teachers, rejecting both the uplifting banality of the Popular Front and the higher-than-thou modernism of the *Partisan Review*. Instead, Allen Ginsberg and Jack Kerouac revived the spirit of perverse modernism: provoking their elders with dadaist, antiart gestures and shocking the public with unabashed promiscuity and drug taking. And their elders could protest only feebly, since it was they who had been preaching against mindless conformity and joyless puritanism.

Not all of the beats embraced bebop, but to an ardent coterie in Greenwich Village, it was the holy grail. And more than any other bebop musician, Parker, or "Bird," became this coterie's hero. As the jazz impresario Robert Reisner wrote after Parker's death in 1955, "To the hipster, Bird was a living justification of their philosophy. . . . He is to the Second World War what the Dadaist was to the first. He is amoral, anarchistic, gentle, and overcivilized to the point of decadence."[38] To the beat poet Ted Joans, Parker was a fantasy figure: "Bird is not with us tonight but he is in a drawing room at the bottom of the ocean where hipsters like Rimbaud, Appolinaire [*sic*], Whitman, Eluard, and Desnos read poetry and perform erotic oral sex acts with all the dead European whores of the classic era."[39]

The reader will note that Joans does not invite Picasso and Braque to his lower-depths house party. That is because the cubists did not submerge themselves in irrational chaos. Rather they sought an emotionally powerful but rationally ordered exploration of form—which is exactly what Parker sought, although you would never it know it from the tributes of the beats. In recent years the world has been treated to the sordid details of Picasso's personal life, by biographers less interested in art than in aberrance. If these details had been available in the 1950s, Joans would no doubt have admitted Picasso to the beat pantheon, too—for the same reason that Whitman and Rimbaud were admitted: not for being great poets, but for having kinky sex lives. It was on similar nonartistic grounds that the beats eulogized Parker.

Not that there was any slander involved. All observers agree that Parker was a freeloader, a philanderer, a glutton, a liar, an alcoholic, and a drug addict. They also agree that he was generous, chivalrous, candid, and self-denying to a fault. In sum, he was a deeply troubled soul whose creativity was constantly at war with his self-destructiveness. If his mental and physical powers had been any less prodigious, his creativity would never have won any victories at all, and the beats would have taken no more notice of him than of any other human wreckage staggering past on the sidewalk.

At bottom, the beat attitude toward bebop was primitivist. Just ask Norman Mailer, the author of the famous 1957 paean to the hipster life-style, *The White Negro*:

> The Negro . . . could rarely afford the sophisticated inhibitions of civilization, and so he kept for his survival the art of the primitive, . . . relinquishing the pleasures of the mind for the more obligatory pleasures of the body, and in his music he gave voice to the infinite variations of joy, lust, languor, growl, cramp, pinch, scream and despair of his orgasm. For jazz is orgasm, it is the music of orgasm, good orgasm and bad.[40]

In his stronger moments Parker resisted this view of his music. He craved a greater knowledge of European modernism, from Stravinsky to Edgard Varèse, whom he once asked to teach him composition. He refused, except in parody, to play the part of the "primitive Negro." He envied the stability, prosperity, and social respectability enjoyed by classical musicians. He dreamed of settling into a comfortable domestic and professional routine. And he struggled not to go down in flames like some kind of culture-kamikaze.[41]

But unfortunately Parker's strength was not up to the task of denying the only acclaim he ever received from the literary-artistic world outside jazz. So, in his weaker moments, he allowed his hipster friends to identify their alienation with his—even though, as Ellison reminds us, they were not the same:

> The pathos of [Parker's] life lies in the ironic reversal through which his struggles to escape what in Armstrong is basically a *make-believe* role of clown—which the irreverent poetry and triumphant sound of his trumpet makes even the squarest of squares aware of—resulted in Parker's becoming something far more "primitive": a sacrificial figure whose struggles against personal chaos, on stage and off, served as entertainment for a ravenous, sensation-starved, culturally disoriented public which had but the slightest notion of its real significance.[42]

Thirty years later, when the music of Parker and his friends is taught in universities and performed in Lincoln Center, it's hard to imagine the painful marginality they experienced in their youth. American culture had a place for jazz musicians, but not for those whose craving for recognition led them to reject commerce and a pleasing relationship with the audience. When the mainstream media poked fun at bebop as something cooked up by "crazy beatniks," the champions of high modernism did not rush to its rescue. For them the cultural tragedy of the 1950s was the death of Delmore Schwartz, a promising young poet whose struggle against personal chaos was, if anything, less successful than Parker's. With hindsight, it's clear that the small body of writing left by Schwartz cannot compare in significance with the music left by Parker, Gillespie, Mingus, and Monk. But at the time, the creators of bebop were nothing to the *Partisan Review* crowd but a bunch of Negroès in sunglasses playing bongo drums for Allen Ginsberg.

How did the beboppers cope? One survival strategy was to adopt a combination of militant race pride and modernist antagonism, especially toward white audiences. If the white world was going to spurn bebop for being crazy, then bebop would damn well spurn the white world—or at least that part of it within reach. Ellison describes the dynamic by which the beboppers dished it out and the white folks ate it up:

> [The beboppers] demanded, in the name of their racial identity, a purity of status which by definition is impossible for the performing artist.
>
> The result was a grim comedy of racial manners; with the musicians employing a calculated surliness and rudeness . . . and the white audiences were shocked at first but learned quickly to accept such treatment as evidence of "artistic" temperament.[43]

Yet, as hinted earlier, this strategy was never total nor permanent, for the simple reason that not all audiences were white. The beboppers may have ended up playing for white hipsters, but they started out playing for black dancers, black blues fans, and (in some cases) black worshipers. They knew all about the powerful ties binding musicians and audiences in these traditional settings. So they partook of what the poet James Weldon Johnson called "the special problem . . . of the double audience . . . a divided audience . . . made up of two elements with differing and often opposite and antagonistic points of view . . . white America and black America."[44] Much as the beboppers enjoyed laughing at white "squares," they did *not* enjoy being dismissed as too "deep" and "weird" by their fellow blacks.[45] The bond with that audience was not sundered without pain.

Modernist antagonism persisted in free jazz, growing stronger as wide-open experimentation gave way to a cult of musical anarchy. Giddins describes the change:

> Though the great figures of that period—John Coltrane, Cecil Taylor, Ornette Coleman, Albert Ayler, and a few others—could bring off the most demanding improvisational conceits, at least as far as the knowing, sympathetic and determined listener was concerned, they spawned imitators who mistook freedom for license and justified excess with apocalyptic rhetoric.[46]

Pleasants also regrets this phase of jazz, not least for breaking up the continuity between low and high, vernacular and cultivated, that had previously existed in Afro-American music. Recalling that the same continuity existed in European music before the twentieth century, he admits that, in both cases, most of the music reaching the popular audience was dross: "During its natural lifetime . . . the European idiom produced vast quantities of Popular music, most of it more bad than good, and the worst of it fully as bad as the worst that the Afro-American idiom produces today." But Pleasants also makes the essential point that popular forms are not just "vulgar by-products"; without them the higher forms lose vitality.[47]

The better jazz musicians have always grasped this point, precisely because they have always felt tied to the black audience. For every far-out avant-gardist, there is a jazz traditionalist who tries to reconnect with popular forms. As we shall see, the success of these efforts depends heavily on the quality of the popular forms involved. But the failures do not mean that there is something wrong with trying to rebuild the bridges between the blessed isle of jazz and the mainland of popular music. Without such bridges, the idiom as a whole will expire.

Among the original beboppers the most successful bridge builder was Gillespie. Unlike his contemporary Miles Davis, Gillespie never lowered his musical standards to reach a broader audience. I shall return to his musical contribution, which includes the seasoning of bebop with the Afro-Cuban polyrhythms he first encountered when playing in Cab Calloway's orchestra. But for now I want to focus on Gillespie's cultural contribution, which may have done more to help jazz survive than even his music.

As a veteran of bebop Gillespie was not culturally innocent in the manner of his elders. On the contrary, he was hip to modernist attitudes right from the start. But he was also a gifted comedian who had the skill, as well as the desire, to get the attention of a larger audience. Many tales are told about Gillespie's humor, but I especially enjoy this one, related by Neil Leonard:

> In 1963, [Gillespie] arrived unannounced at San Francisco International Airport masquerading as one Prince Ibo in Nigerian robes, tarboosh on his head, and three dark-suited sidemen following at a respectful distance. To the bemusement of officials, the party swept through the lobby, parting crowds on the way to the taxi stand.[48]

After subjecting their cab driver to "pseudo-African double-talk" all the way to the hotel, Gillespie and his companions made a great fuss about not understanding what the fare was. Finally, when the poor man resorted to holding up eight fingers, Gillespie gave him a generous tip and smiled, "Man, why didn't you say so in the first place?"[49]

Jazz snobs who admire Gillespie's music tend to assume that his humor is more acute than Armstrong's. But this assumption underestimates the acuity of traditional Afro-American humor as passed down to Armstrong from such predecessors as Fats Waller. In jazz, humor has long served the purpose of making audiences more receptive to the music. As Gillespie himself explains:

> As a performer, when you're trying to establish audience control, the best thing is to make them laugh. . . . That relaxes you more than anything. . . . When you get people relaxed, they're more receptive. . . . Sometimes, when you're laying on something over their heads, they'll go along with it if they're relaxed. Sometimes I get up on the bandstand and say "I'd like to introduce the men in the band" . . . and then introduce the guys to one another. There's a reason for that.[50]

Leonard notes that the playfulness in jazz serves many other functions: It relaxes the musicians themselves, thereby enhancing their ability to perform; it reduces tensions between group members while maintaining the borders of the jazz world against hostile outsiders; it provides a safety valve for aggression; it fosters musical education and social discipline within the group; and finally it enriches the art form itself. No one has captured this aspect of jazz better than the historian Martin Williams:

> I think that many native American arts and artists have functioned best with a mask, a valid artistic persona, of light-heartedness. And whoever receives that light-heartedness as mere lightness or superficiality will probably not understand our artists, nor appreciate the size and depth of the comments on the human condition which the best of them have made.[51]

Because jazz first appeared during an exceptionally serious period in European musical history, its playfulness was both welcomed (by the public) and deprecated (by intellectuals). To European highbrows raised on the excessive emotionalism of Wagner and the excessive intellectualism of Webern, the comedic streak in jazz seemed proof of a frivolous attitude. Of course, humor is unique among human gifts in that it is rarely appreciated by those to whom it is not given. This sad truth applies especially to art—as acknowledged by the eighteenth-century wit Sydney Smith, when he remarked that others were rising by their gravity while he was sinking by his levity.

Smith also said: "If I were to begin life again, I would devote it to music. It is the only cheap and unpunished rapture upon earth."[52] How perfectly those words apply to jazz!

Part Two

From Rock 'n' Roll to Rock

Chapter 7

The Strange Career of 1950s Rock 'n' Roll

The author of the following passage, Herbert London, is a college professor, so his assertions about 1950s rock 'n' roll sound unusually erudite. But for all its erudition, London's claim is far from unique. On the contrary, the notion that 1950s rock 'n' roll was a "revolution" is conventional wisdom nowadays. London puts it in highbrow language:

> Before the outbreak of revolution in 1789, small groups of trusted friends would meet in Paris cafes to discuss unconventional ideas, engage in hedonistic pleasures, and listen to music that was novel to the ear. . . . In a curiously similar way, the circle of rock adherents—those who embraced the style of rock—shared inner thoughts through the music and formed a strength from the uniformity of those ideas, which formed an emergent ideology. Because of such social circles, the Ancien Régime fell in 1789 and once again a century and a half later.[1]

The journalist Robert Palmer, writing in *Rolling Stone*, is more blunt: "Much has been made of Sixties rock as a vehicle for revolutionary social and cultural change, but it was mid-Fifties rock & roll that blew away, in one mighty, concentrated blast, the accumulated racial and social proprieties of centuries."[2] But both writers make the same claim. If truth were merely a matter of repetition, then the notion that 1950s rock 'n' roll was a social and cultural revolution would be one of the greatest truths of all time. As it happens, it is a myth.

The Overthrow of 1950s Pop

To be sure, 1950s rock 'n' roll did topple one particular ancien régime: that of the six major labels—Capitol, Columbia, Decca, Mercury, MGM, and RCA—that dominated the record industry after World War II. Established in the 1920s, these "majors" had had their ups and downs over the years.[3] But by the early 1950s, they were riding high. They knew their market: an increasingly affluent population eager to buy all the latest consumer goods; and they knew their product: smooth, polished vocal music set to an orchestrated background. This music was called "pop," after the heading on *Billboard*'s "charts," or lists of best-selling records. Thus, I use the term *pop* to describe this smooth, polished sound, not popular music in general.

Pop arose from the ashes of swing, which for various reasons did not survive World War II. In the first place, wartime restrictions such as gasoline rationing and an entertainment tax on nightclubs made it hard for swing bands to keep touring. In response, the American Federation of Musicians (AFM) called a strike between 1941 and 1944. But the strike was ill-conceived, because rather than meet the musicians' demands, the major record companies and radio networks switched to vocalists, for the simple reason that vocalists did not belong to the AFM. The most successful of these vocalists—Frank Sinatra, Perry Como, Doris Day—had started out a soloists with the swing bands, but the demise of swing gave their careers an added boost. By the end of the decade swing was all but extinct, and the industry was reorganized around a new definition of success: the pop song arranged by a producer, played by a small group of in-house musicians, and sung by a vocalist groomed to have the utmost celebrity appeal.

Some 1950s pop lives up to the best legacy of swing. For example, Sinatra's 1953 record "Lean Baby" contains jazz inflections and phrasings reminiscent of good swing. Other pop hits, such as Patti Page's "Doggie in the Window," recall only the banality and standardization of swing at its worst. Sad but true, Page's record sold better than Sinatra's—in fact, for an infamous eight weeks in 1953, "Doggie" was the best-selling song in America.

Perhaps that is why the postwar generation—the baby boomers—rarely distinguish between good and bad pop. When this generation looks back on the 1950s from the perspective of today, the records they deem important are definitely not pop. "Your Cheatin' Heart," for example, by Hank Williams, was recorded for a major label (MGM), but not released to the pop market. Rather it was classified "country & western" (C&W), meaning it was not expected to sell outside a specialized market made up mostly of low-income Southern whites.

In 1953 the term "country & western" was of recent coinage, having been adopted in 1949 as a replacement for the "hillbilly" heading on *Billboard*'s charts. The mentality behind the older term is reflected in *Variety*'s 1926 comment that "hillbillies have the intelligence of morons."[4] Despite such attitudes, the major companies had begun signing "hillbilly" acts in 1929, when the RCA Victor label acquired Jimmie Rodgers and the Carter Family. By the late 1940s Columbia was leading the pack with such diverse acts as Appalachian fiddler Roy Acuff, Western swing bandleader Bob Wills, and "the singing cowboy," Gene Autry. Indeed, it was Autry's decision to suppress the music's "hillbilly" roots in favor of the more glamorous—and marketable—cowboy image that spurred *Billboard* to coin "country & western."

The major labels' interest in "hillbilly" music got a boost in 1940, when the American Society of Composers, Authors and Publishers (ASCAP), concerned about the unlicensed radio broadcast of its members' material, called a boycott of all radio networks and stations. It was one thing to collect royalties on the pressing of records, or to monitor the use of ASCAP-copyrighted material in live broadcasts. It was quite another to keep track of how many ASCAP-licensed records were being played by a new breed of radio hosts called "disc jockeys," or "DJs."[5] ASCAP's boycott was successful in the sense that not one ASCAP song became a hit in 1940. But it failed in the sense that it engendered a powerful rival. In response to the boycott, a consortium of 256 radio stations started its own copyright organization, Broadcast Music Incorporated (BMI).

The founding of BMI changed the face of popular music, because the material licensed by the new organization was different. Most of ASCAP's members were rooted in the world of New York show business—vaudeville, Tin Pan Alley, Broadway—and their musical tastes followed the trajectory leading from swing to pop. BMI's members, by contrast, were rooted in Appalachia, the Southwest, and the Deep South. Not only did they write a different kind of material, they also placed less emphasis on written music than on styles of playing.

For a while, the emphasis on playing didn't matter, because the music industry still operated on the old-fashioned assumption that a written song is an original artwork deserving of copyright, while a record is a mere "occasion of use," like a live performance. When a particular record became a hit, its success was attributed more to the song than to the singer. As long as a major label could obtain the rights to the written song, success seemed assured. Indeed, the practice was to have the song "covered" by a celebrity vocalist in the approved pop style. And most C&W songwriters accepted this practice. For example, Hank Williams was delighted to have his songs covered by Columbia's Tony Bennett.

Of course, the industry's emphasis on written music contains a built-in bias against the Afro-American idiom, in which artistry is partly defined as the ability to give life to mundane material. It would be wrong to say that the industry had no understanding of this fact. Within the jazz field it was well known that the best recordings were every bit as valuable as the best songbooks. But elsewhere the old assumption reigned. When Columbia had Tony Bennett cover a song by Hank Williams, no one expected listeners to prefer hearing the original recording by Williams himself. Bennett's pop cover was considered both musically superior and more appealing to the mainstream. But soon—very soon—this industry calculus would fail.

So far I have been talking about C&W, but the most important source of uncoverable material was "rhythm & blues," the array of musical styles being marketed to another limited sector—in this case, blacks. Like "country & western," "rhythm & blues" was a recent coinage, replacing an older chart heading, "race." It's interesting to note that, unlike "hillbilly," "race" did not start out as an insult: In the 1920s, when *Billboard* first introduced it, "race" was the preferred term of Harlem's leading literary and political lights. By 1949, though, it had lost its luster, and "rhythm and blues" (R&B) was considered an improvement.[7]

Whatever the name, this black-oriented music was of little interest to the major labels. Returning to 1953, we find that three other records now considered important—"Baby Don't Do It" by the Five Royales, "Hound

Dog" by Willie Mae Thornton, and "Money Honey" by the Drifters—
were produced by tiny independent labels with names like Apollo, Pea-
cock, and Atlantic. Some of these "indies" were based in New York, others
in Los Angeles, Chicago, New Orleans—wherever the right concentration
of black talent was found.

By mixing various elements of swing and blues, R&B came up with
three main strains of popular, accessible music. First were the jump bands,
small combos split off from the larger swing bands to play lively dance-hall
music fronted by either a powerhouse blues shouter or a witty vocalist specializing in "jive" lyrics. Second were the club combos, Los Angeles–based
groups playing a smooth style; and third were the Chicago blues bands,
electrifying the rural blues of the Mississippi Delta for a rough, distinctively urban sound.[8]

In addition to these hybrids, R&B also included a vocal style taken
directly from the black church: the close-harmony singing called doo-wop
(a secularization of "do Lord"). These mostly all-male groups, who gathered in stairwells and on street corners everywhere, drew more heavily on
gospel than did such popular predecessors as the Ink Spots.

Along with C&W, R&B made its appearance in the backwaters of a
medium widely believed to be defunct: radio. Like the movies, radio was
left gasping for air by the postwar advent of television; for many local stations the only hope of survival was to hire a colorful, fast-talking DJ to
"spin platters" and deliver energetic spiels for local businesses. Because of
their limited resources and scope, most of these stations restricted their
playlists to either C&W or R&B. This was especially true in the South,
where segregation was still entrenched, and where station owners (all of
them white) saw no reason to mix the two categories. Stations recently
converted to R&B (still a novelty) had little incentive to play "hillbilly"
music; and stations staying with C&W risked incurring white wrath if they
played R&B (routinely referred to as "nigger music").

Yet this strict segregation existed only at the broadcast end. At the
receiving end, radio was rapidly being integrated. In the case of C&W, it is a
well-kept secret that programs such as "The Grand Ole Opry" had been
attracting black listeners since the 1930s. One reason was the lack of other
choices, but another was the undeniable Afro-American flavor of most
C&W. After three centuries of musical cross-fertilization, it should come
as no surprise that blacks all over the country tuned in to the bluesy yodel-
ing of Jimmie Rodgers, the "hillbilly boogie" of the Delmore Brothers, and
the infectious rhythms of Bob Wills.

This is not to say that blacks didn't welcome R&B radio when it came. By the 1930s the first black DJ was broadcasting in Chicago's South Side, and stations in other heavily black areas were starting to sell space to interested advertisers. The journalist Nelson George cites one famous example:

> "King Biscuit Time" [was] broadcast in the early 1940s from the teeming little metropolis of Helena, Mississippi, deep in the heavily black Delta region. At noon, singer-harmonica player Rice (Sonny Boy Williamson) Miller and guitarist Robert Lockwood brought listeners fifteen minutes of blues and greetings from the makers of King Biscuit flour. At one point the broadcast became so popular that a line of Sonny Boy cornmeal was introduced.[9]

Similar practices were found in racially mixed areas, such as West Memphis, Arkansas. It was there, at tiny KWEM, that the blues singer B. B. King got his first radio job, performing a jingle for a patent medicine called Pepticon.[10] Soon KWEM devoted 50 percent of its program time to black-oriented material, inspiring two white entrepreneurs across the river to covert their failing C&W station to wholly black-oriented programming. Their 1948 creation, Memphis's WDIA, was the first Southern radio station of its kind. As the journalist Albert Goldman reports, its influence was great:

> A feeble little 250-watter at seventy-two kilocycles, [WDIA] was just a shout from the bottom of the dial. No radio station in history, however, has ever exerted a greater impact on musical taste. A whole school of subsequently famous performers grew up listening to the station. . . . Not only did they obtain unlimited "exposure" to both the secular and sacred music of black people, they also received a marvelous education in black humor and language.[11]

Because of such exposure young white Southerners were soon flocking to live R&B performances in such numbers that the shows became impossible to segregate.[12] Young whites hired R&B bands for high school dances and frat parties.[13] Then the craze spread to the North, where it was picked up by an enterprising DJ in Cleveland named Alan Freed, who decided to make a splash with an R&B radio show aimed specifically at white youth. To mask the racial origins of the music, Freed borrowed a phrase from the blues that referred either to dancing, or to lovemaking, or (in time-honored fashion) to both: "rock 'n' roll."

Needless to say, Freed made his splash. The success of his "Moondog's

Rock 'n' Roll Party" was evidenced a year later, when he invited his listeners to an R&B concert in a ten-thousand-seat venue (the Cleveland Arena), and more than 25,000 people showed up, a large proportion of them white.[14] It was only 1952, but the aristocracy of pop was already bound for the guillotine.

Music, Lyrics, and Race: The Revolution That Wasn't

The overthrow of the major labels was swift. In 1955 total record sales in the United States were $213,000,000. By 1959 they had leaped to $603,000,000, with most of that growth belonging to the independent labels. In this clearly quantifiable respect, it is easy to see why the British DJ-writer Charlie Gillett calls rock 'n' roll "the dynamite that blew apart the structure of an industry."[15]

But was it a revolution? The question cannot be answered without separating the musical characteristics of early rock 'n' roll from the cultural setting into which it was received, so I begin my discussion with the music. It is simply wrong to suggest that the actual sounds of rock 'n' roll were shocking to mainstream ears. Among the leaders of the jump bands both Lionel Hampton and Louis Jordan were well known to the older generation, Hampton as a veteran of the Benny Goodman Quartet, and Jordan as the head of the popular Tympany Five, whose hits reached the pop chart nineteen times in the 1940s. Likewise, the smooth combo sound echoed the pop success of the Nat ("King") Cole Trio. And a public enamored of the Ink Spots was hardly going to be offended by doo-wop.

The only sound with any real shock potential was the Chicago blues, the R&B style least influenced by swing. Despite the best efforts of Freed and other DJs, this style did not cross over. Indeed, it was not until the 1960s that the Chicago blues had any impact on white taste. If rock 'n' roll was really a musical revolution, then why didn't it emphasize this down-home, gut-bucket sound that was the antithesis of Tony Bennett?

Freed himself once remarked that "rock 'n' roll was merely swing with a modern name."[16] And he was right. By the 1950s America's dance floors had been virtually abandoned—first by the beboppers, with their exploration of rhythms too subtle for human feet; and then by pop, with its preference for mid-tempo ballads. Given this dearth, it is hardly surprising that young whites would seek out whatever dance music was available. R&B

was different from swing in the sense of being played by smaller groups in a bluesier, rhythmically heavier style. But it was similar in the sense of ranging from the sublime to the ridiculous. Bad R&B, like bad swing, reduced the basic elements of a steady beat and repeated melodic riffs to a formula. Good R&B, like good swing, enlivened these elements with rhythmic counterpoint, rich instrumental color, and adventurous solos.

Some of these good qualities made it into the first self-designated rock 'n' roll group, Bill Haley and His Comets. Unlike countless others who borrowed the R&B backbeat, Haley made it swing—with the help of producer Milt Gabler, not only the founder of the renowned Commodore jazz label, but also the producer of Jordan's Tympany Five. Gabler's touch is evident in the fact that Haley's second hit, "Dim Dim the Lights," was the first white record in history to cross *back* to the R&B chart.[17]

But dance rhythms weren't the only reason why young whites gravitated toward R&B. Equally important were the messages and meanings, so different from those of pop. Take showmanship: The war generation had grown up with the flashy zoot suits, pomaded hair, and acrobatic antics of "His Hi-De-Ho Highness," Cab Calloway. But such uninhibited fun had been pretty well purged from 1950s pop. However sweetly he sang, Perry Como in a cardigan was no substitute. As for the lyrics, there were plenty of pop songs about love, but they were mostly treacle. To young ears fed on ditties like "The Little White Cloud That Cried," it was a pleasurable shock to encounter "Sixty Minute Man" and "Work With Me, Annie."

Needless to say, the shock was not pleasurable to all. In response to such material, ASCAP mounted a self-righteous, and self-interested, campaign against BMI. Typical was the comment of songwriter-impresario Billy Rose: "Not only are most BMI songs junk, but in many cases they are obscene junk."[18] This campaign succeeded in keeping BMI songs off a few radio stations, and in scaring the majors into bowdlerizing a few "leer-ics," such as those of Big Joe Turner's "Shake, Rattle and Roll," when it was covered by Haley in 1954. But to take such fitful efforts as proof that rock 'n' roll was a sexual revolution is to freight them with far too much significance. Granted, the lyrics of R&B (and C&W, for that matter) are a bit saltier than those of mainstream pop. But the change was less a revolution than a restoration: The swing era had seen plenty of songs with suggestive lyrics, from Cole Porter's "Let's Do It" to Jordan's "The Chick's Too Young to Fry" to Charlie Barnet's "Scrub Me, Mama, With a Boogie Beat." To focus exclusively on the sugar of the 1950s is to forget the salt of the past.

Nor was rock 'n' roll a racial revolution. To be sure, figures such as Haley, Chuck Berry, Elvis Presley, and Jerry Lee Lewis distinguished themselves by mixing elements of R&B with elements of C&W. Musically, none of these figures was any more or less original than any number of talented people in the crowded R&B and C&W fields. But culturally, they were unique: Unlike their contemporaries, they boldly combined the music labeled "black" with the music labeled "white," an act that for Presley and Lewis especially, violated a strong taboo. At a time when their fellow white Southerners were resisting integration with blacks, they announced it as an accomplished fact.

Yet this change, too, gets freighted with too much meaning. It is true that the 1950s were a high-water mark of white interest in black-dominated music. But such levels had been reached before, without America's racial problems being solved. Like all previous crazes for Afro-American music, the rock 'n' roll craze was marked by the mental compartmentalization described earlier: white pleasure in black performance in one compartment, white prejudice against black people in the other. To the extent that this compartmentalization had depended, since colonial times, on the strict segregation of audiences, it was threatened in the 1950s, when whites and blacks attended shows that were, despite the best efforts of the authorities, not segregated. But the 1950s were also when the electronic media, especially radio, made compartmentalization easier than ever. The mass audience for rock 'n' roll was not formed in a handful of integrated settings, but in thousands of lily-white soda fountains, dance halls, and automobiles, where the undiluted musical culture of blacks was suddenly as accessible as a nickel in the jukebox or a twist of the radio dial. The music may have moved some whites to be more sympathetic to blacks, or to the civil rights cause. But in general, the rock 'n' roll craze was made possible by the technology of private consumption.

To sum up: Nineteen-fifties rock 'n' roll was a "revolution" in the narrow sense of overthrowing the virtual monopoly of the major record labels. But, contrary to myth, it was not a "revolution" in any sweeping musical, sexual, or racial sense. It is simply wishful thinking to claim that this mixed bag of deft, appealing popular music "blew away, in one mighty, concentrated blast, the accumulated racial and social proprieties of centuries."

DJs and JDs: The Theme of Generational Revolt

Most pervasive of all is the myth of rock 'n' roll as a generational revolution: a brand-new music for a brand-new social category: youth. Again, the perception is accurate when applied to the record industry. The overthrow of 1950s pop was largely an assertion of taste, and pocketbook power, by a segment of the population only recently defined as a distinct entity. Championed by market researchers and attacked by intellectuals, the newly emergent "pimple audience" was an undeniable fact of postwar American life. Without it there would have been no rock 'n' roll.

But again, we must ask what kind of revolution we are talking about. Was 1950s rock 'n' roll really the first tremor of the generational upheaval of the 1960s? Or did that upheaval begin elsewhere, in a place far removed from the Afro-American musical tradition?

These questions return us to Bill Haley, accurately described by *Rolling Stone* as "a moon-faced twenty-nine-year-old with a weird spitcurl on his forehead, . . . an unlikely teen idol."[19] In addition to his plumpness, age, and spitcurl, Haley also dressed his Comets in matching plaid jackets with satin lapels, making it painfully clear that he had spent his youth on the C&W circuit. By itself, this image would probably not have earned Haley more than what Giddins calls "a footnote in the recounting of the obstetrics of rock and roll."[20]

But another ingredient got added. In 1955 Haley recorded a song, "Rock Around the Clock," which was going nowhere when its publisher had the bright idea of selling it to MGM for use in *The Blackboard Jungle*, a movie about juvenile delinquents ("JDs") in an inner-city vocational school. Despite being a serious dramatic treatment of a much-discussed social problem, *The Blackboard Jungle* was denounced by organizations and individuals across the political spectrum, from the communist-front Labor Youth League to Clare Boothe Luce, then ambassador to Italy, who objected to its being shown at the Venice Film Festival.[21] All parties accused the film of encouraging criminal behavior among youth, while Haley's record sold three million copies, making him loom forever larger than a footnote.[22]

Since this was the first time a rock 'n' roll song had ever been used on a soundtrack, the question is, What caused all the furor, the movie or the music? To those whose perceptions are shaped by myth, the answer is clear. Here is a typical account from two film historians writing in 1982:

> School teacher Richard Kiley attempts to communicate with his students by playing for them his prized collection of swing records. His students don't want to hear Bix Beiderbecke. *While the soundtrack throbs to the beat of a new sound, rock-and-roll,* the kids make quick work of Kiley's music, leaving him alone to search through the pieces of the broken 78's, shattered memories of a once popular culture.[23] (emphasis added)

Yet these historians are mistaken. Haley's song plays only during the opening and closing credits. In the scene where the JDs smash the teacher's records, the soundtrack doesn't throb to rock 'n' roll, it throbs to Beider-becke's "Jazz Me Blues." And the JDs aren't demanding rock 'n' roll; they're demanding *pop*. The dialogue is explicit: It's Sinatra they want, and Joni James. Another minute, and those evil-eyed hoodlums might have demanded Patti Page.

Now for a few more details. During the bloodiest scene in *The Blackboard Jungle*, when the JDs beat up their teachers in a dark alley, the soundtrack throbs to the Stan Kenton Orchestra, thereby inspiring *Film Daily* to comment: "The use of jazz, bop and swing records as a musical background was a fine idea, forming a properly frenetic background to the steel-age mayhem on the screen."[24] Similar comments were made about the JD movie that preceded *The Blackboard Jungle*: Marlon Brando's 1953 motorcycle film, *The Wild One*. All the throbbing on that soundtrack is provided by the bebop-swing of Shorty Rogers and His Giants.[25] Nor is there a shred of rock 'n' roll in the 1955 release generally considered to be the classic JD movie: *Rebel Without a Cause*. That film features a bebop-swing score by Leonard Rosenman.[26]

I am not implying that Hollywood was afraid of rock 'n' roll. On the contrary, the moment the studios realized the box-office appeal of the new music, they cranked up their sausage machine and began grinding out rock 'n' roll JD movies—most of which, like sausages, do not reward close inspection.[27] The point is not that Hollywood was afraid, but that it hadn't yet made a mental connection between juvenile delinquency and rock 'n' roll—for the simple but forgotten reason that America's worries about juvenile delinquency predated rock 'n' roll by more than a decade.

The historian James Gilbert explains that such worries first arose in the early 1940s, when British social scientists began anticipating the possible destructive effects of World War II on family life and public morality. In the vacuum created by absent fathers and working mothers, these experts feared, the younger generation was being unduly influenced by "mass culture," to the point of fomenting an unprecedented wave of youth crime. In America these concerns were taken up by conservatives, such as FBI Director J. Edgar Hoover, and by leftists, such as the Frankfurt émigrés.[28] Among the latter, the specter of youth crime cast an even more terrifying shadow: incipient fascism. In an influential study published in 1944, the psychiatrist Robert Lindner depicted juvenile delinquency as the "triumphal heavy-booted march of psychopathy," and the wayward American teenager as an "embryonic Storm Trooper."[29]

It might interest the reader to know that the title of Lindner's study was *Rebel Without a Cause*. Optioned by Warner Brothers in 1945, the book sat on the shelf till the early 1950s, when the director Nicholas Ray used it as the basis of his famous film starring James Dean. Ray had his own, less-politicized ideas about juvenile delinquency. But the Frankfurtian perspective remained influential—especially in the many articles, books, and public statements of Frederic Wertham, a German-trained psychiatrist and Frankfurt fellow traveler who singled out "mass culture" as the most important cause of juvenile delinquency.[30] It was partly due to Wertham's influence that the U.S. Senate Subcommittee to Investigate Juvenile Delinquency, organized in 1953 and dominated between 1955 and 1957 by Tennessee Democrat Estes Kefauver, spent two years exploring the link between "mass culture" and delinquency.

Following Wertham, the committee began with comic books, specifically the crime and horror type popular with boys; then it moved on to films and TV. But it never did get around to rock 'n' roll. The members of the committee were concerned about violence and antisocial attitudes in entertainment, not the latest teenage dance craze. Indeed, the majority of public and private institutions debating the problem of juvenile delinquency in the mid-1950s worried a lot more about the impact of comic books and the visual electronic media than about music.[31]

To the extent that music did get drawn into the debate, it was typically assumed that delinquent youth listened to jazz, used slang expressions borrowed from jazz, and (in the case of the leather-jacketed bikers in *The Wild One*) enjoyed scat singing in the manner of Ella Fitzgerald. That seminal film, about a motorcycle gang terrorizing a small California town, is worth a closer look because it embodies, as much as a Hollywood movie can, the Frankfurtian perspective. Produced by Stanley Kramer and directed by a German-trained Hungarian émigré, Laslo Benedek, *The Wild One* features the following dialogue between the bikers and Old Jim, the bartender in the town's humble saloon:

> Old Jim: I mind my own business, listen to the radio—music, that is. The news is no good—excites people. Biker: How about TV? You like TV? Second biker: A new thing, Jim, television. Old Jim: Oh, pictures.... No, no pictures. Everything these days is pictures. Pictures and a lot of noise. Nobody even knows how to talk—they just grunt at each other.

Cut to a close-up (one of many) of the jukebox, playing a jazz record with a scat singer (*not* Ella Fitzgerald) grunting: "Bow-de-lee, bow-de-ooh-bah."

Get it? As in most of Stanley Kramer's movies, it is impossible *not* to get it. These pathetic townsfolk lack the strength to resist the biker/fascist takeover because their brains have been addled by the pseudoeroticism of "mass culture." And the bikers are just as addled, responding like so many laboratory rats to the excitable rhythms of Shorty Rogers and His Giants. What is more, both sides have the same taste—how else explain all those Shorty Rogers records on the town's only jukebox?

Among all the clichés one hears about *The Wild One*, the most accurate is that the main character—Johnny, the softhearted nihilist played by Brando—is the first embodiment, in popular culture, of the beat sensibility. The true model for Johnny is Neal Cassady, the magnetic, bisexual beat who never wrote a page but managed to get written about, to the point of obsession, by all the others, from John Clellon Holmes to Kerouac to Ginsberg to Ken Kesey. It is Cassady's voice we hear when Johnny utters the famous line linking the beat sensibility with that of the biker-JD: "Oh man, we're just gonna go. . . . You don't go to any one special place—that's cornball style. You just *go*."

It's too bad that the beat sensibility hitched a ride on bebop: The arrangement was a free ride for the former, a burdensome drag for the latter. The literary standards of beat poetry were incredibly slack; the musical ones of bebop incredibly stiff. Nonetheless, the two phenomena became linked in the public mind as expressions of spontaneous, uncontrolled impulse. Accordingly, both were injected into Hollywood's first films about juvenile delinquency. Given the conventional wisdom of the day, it seemed only natural that both kinds of irrational expression would appeal to young rebels without a cause.

As it turned out, the beat sensibility was a lot easier to popularize than bebop. Certainly the flyweight nihilism of beat poetry proved more appealing to the average moviegoer than the daunting complexity of a Charlie Parker solo. No doubt this is why these first JD films included so much swing; they needed something more accessible to keep the action going. But swing was old hat in the 1950s—clearly a new theme music was needed for Hollywood's portrayal of troubled teenagers as alienated beats. Hence the propitiousness of adding "Rock Around the Clock" to the *Blackboard Jungle* soundtrack.

Yet the match was a mismatch. Coming as it did out of R&B and western swing, Haley's song is much too cheerful to have worked in the scene where the teacher's records get smashed, much less the beating in the alley. The jazz played during these scenes is inappropriate enough—like many Hollywood movies made in the 1950s, *The Blackboard Jungle* misses the true feeling of jazz by matching it with scenes of foreboding and violence. Still, this particular use of jazz was standard practice at the time; it's not as wildly inappropriate to a scene of back-alley bloodletting as Haley's exuberant, upbeat dance tune would have been. In fact, *The Blackboard Jungle* uses "Rock Around the Clock" rather skillfully. Over the opening credits, the song grabs the audience's attention. Over the closing credits, it follows a scene of reconciliation between another, more tenacious teacher (Glenn Ford) and the natural leader of the JDs (Sidney Poitier). Thus it accomplishes the classic Hollywood purpose of ending with a rush of positive energy.

Despite the mismatch, *The Blackboard Jungle* brought rock 'n' roll within striking distance of replacing bebop as the theme music of the beat JD. At that point, it was simply a matter of time before the right person—*not* Bill Haley—would come along and fuse all three elements in a new way. When he did, the world recognized him at once. His name was Elvis Presley.

The Many Faces of Elvis

The long sideburns and "DA" haircut, the flashy clothes, the curled lip, the uninhibited body language—these visual cues opened a chasm between the stardom of Haley and the supernovadom of Presley. One of the many ironies of the Presley story is the contrast between his image and Haley's. Haley was a fairly sophisticated Northerner—an experienced performer and a radio personality—but his image was hopelessly "hillbilly." Presley, on the other hand, was a totally naive Southerner—a *real* "hillbilly"—but his image was that of the mythical creature sired by social scientists, gestated among beats, and midwifed by Hollywood: the beat JD. One TV producer thought Presley fit this description so perfectly that he dubbed him "a guitar-playing Marlon Brando."[32]

As it happened, Presley's image was his own eccentric creation, based on such Hollywood figures as the suave Italian gangster (he referred to his hairstyle as a "Tony Curtis") and the Latin lover (he admired Rudolph Valentino). But it was no public-relations stunt. On the contrary, Presley's image was, truly, eccentric. In Memphis, where the Presleys moved when Elvis was thirteen, there was nothing to be gained by adopting such a peculiar appearance. The men and boys of Presley's social milieu dressed conservatively and paid frequent visits to the barber. For making himself look like a hoodlum or a foreigner out of the movies, the teenage Presley received only taunts and threats from his high school classmates. It is clear from all accounts that he was regarded not as a rebel or an idol, but a weirdo.[33]

Why did he persist? Why does the weirdo in any high school persist? Usually because he can't help it. One reason why Presley couldn't help it was sociological: To his peers he was already an outcast, the only child of "white trash" parents whose financial difficulties had led to a prison sentence (his father served three years for forgery when Elvis was a toddler) and public assistance (along with the war widows of Memphis, the Presleys lived in a public housing project). The other reason was psychological: To his mother, an uneducated but fanciful woman who had no other children (Elvis's twin brother was born dead) and little use for her unreliable husband, Elvis was quite simply the center of the universe. Thus he was conditioned, even before his fame, to inhabit a dream world in which everything revolved around his charms and his wishes. And he did so quite happily until 1958, when, in a depression over her son's being inducted into the Army, his mother died.

This background would seem an unlikely predictor of overnight megacelebrity. But the world was not studying Presley's background, or his peculiar motives for making himself into a weirdo. Goldman puts it well:

> Instead of characterizing Elvis's triumph in conventional metaphors . . . you are obliged to seek images that suggest speed, violence and, above all, the sheer inadvertence of the man who walks into a room filled with volatile gases, lights a match—and is blown through the ceiling! Clearly, if you want to understand the phenomenon of Elvis Presley or how he "did it," you have to start with the powerfully explosive vapors and not with the puny little match.[34]

Some of those vapors had been stirred up by war. For many Americans, World War II brought unprecedented exposure to people from the other side of the tracks, the other side of the continent, and the other side of the Jim Crow line. The positive effects of this exposure were celebrated in all those Hollywood movies about "bomber crews" from assorted ethnic backgrounds achieving comradeship and heroism together. But there were also negative effects, as evidenced by the (much-debated) degree to which postwar America was subject to a paranoid "fear of the other." In this respect it is striking to note that the high school gang depicted in *The Blackboard Jungle* is itself a "bomber crew" made up of Irish, Italian, Puerto Rican, black, and Jewish JDs.

Because these JDs were also slum kids, *The Blackboard Jungle* makes explicit what was merely implicit in *The Wild One*: that many of the behaviors classified as "delinquent"—especially such noncriminal behaviors as defiance of authority, lack of decorum, preference for pleasure over work, and uninhibited sexuality—were associated with the lower class. Was the war responsible for importing these behaviors into the middle and upper classes? Or was "mass culture" to blame? These questions underlay much of the concern over juvenile delinquency, but they were not articulated until rather late.[35] One reason for the delay may be that, for all its presumed paranoia, the Eisenhower era was also a time of celebration of American democracy. And part of this celebration was a widespread hope that the class and ethnic conflicts of the past would be resolved in the prosperity of the present.[36] We can see this hope reflected in the middle-class setting, psychological (as opposed to sociological) emphasis, and optimistic ending of the film *Rebel Without a Cause.*

For these anxieties Presley was an ideal lightning rod. Precisely because he was not a real JD from a real ethnic slum, he could be attacked, or defended, without reference to Italians, Jews, Puerto Ricans, or some other melting-pot group. Presley's "hoodiness" was an abstract entity existing only in his psyche and in the fevered imaginations of his fans. It is true that he came from lower-class origins, but he was also a Southerner and a WASP, which made him safely immune to the touchy issues of ethnicity and class as they pertained to the problem of juvenile delinquency.

It is now commonplace to mark the further irony that Presley should have been the individual to personify the beat JD. For, unlike James Dean, whose arrogance, egotism, and disdain for convention were impressive even by Hollywood standards, Presley was a coddled mama's boy who never quit saying "sir" and "ma'am" to his elders and social betters—a category that, from his humble perspective, included just about everyone. As Sam Phillips, who produced Presley's first records after years of recording black bluesmen, put it: "[Elvis] tried not to show it, but he felt so *inferior.* He reminded me of a black man in that way; his insecurity was so *markedly* like that of a black person."[37] After dating Presley during his early days in Hollywood, Dean's former girlfriend and *Rebel* costar, Natalie Wood, remarked that the singer was "terribly conventional. . . . He didn't drink. He didn't swear. He didn't even smoke! It was like having the date I never had in high school."[38] In this sense Presley's beat JD image was an inch deep and a mile wide—it suited him ill, but it served him well.

By suggesting that Presley was not the surly and defiant character many people took him to be, I am not endorsing the glorified vision of him as a simon-pure country boy who was destroyed, but never corrupted, by the wicked world of show business. This vision still entrances the cultists who commune with "the King" either at the shrine of his Memphis mansion, Graceland, or in the nation's bowling alleys, hospitals, and convenience stores, where they eagerly await his visitations. To these folk Presley has long ceased to be a popular entertainer: By passing through the earthly trials of wealth, fame, obesity, drug addiction, and death, he has risen to become a semidivine intercessor in touch with such higher divinities as Marilyn Monroe and Liberace. It's too bad that most writers (including this one) cannot resist sarcasm on this topic, because the Elvis cult is not just droll. It is also a fascinating, and disturbing, example of the electronic media's power to lift their favorites into a rarified ether in which they become as immaterial, and immortal, as spirits.

Still, Elvis cultists are not the only ones who resist the beat JD image. The singer's deep attachment to his mother; his undying humility and politeness; his openhearted embrace of the lowliest fan; his patriotic willingness to be drafted into the army; his loyalty to C&W, pop, and white gospel; his intense religiosity—these qualities are constantly stressed in the rosy official Elvis biography as set forth by the star's lifelong manager, "Col." Tom Parker; together with his former wife, Priscilla Beaulieu, and his down-home friends, popularly known as the Memphis Mafia. Yet, like Presley himself, this rosy view would not thrive without the enthusiastic credence of millions of perfectly sane people who remember Presley fondly but do not expect to run into his gold-laméed ghost in a deserted 7-Eleven. I daresay this rosy view, with its insistence on Presley's old-fashioned virtues, provides many people with a much-needed alternative to the myth of 1950s rock 'n' roll as revolution.

Goldman says the explosion Presley touched off was "inadvertent." The mythologizers claim he blew up the whole world. In the glorified and rosy views, there was no explosion. My own opinion, judging from Presley's early performances, is that none of these accounts is accurate. It's immediately evident from these initial glimpses of Presley that he was by no means a "little puny match." He knew exactly what he was doing, although he did it with a certain tentativeness, as though he couldn't quite believe the audience would approve. It is also clear that he was neither devil nor angel. He wasn't trying to offend the audience, but neither was he sprouting wings and a halo. He was deliberately igniting some, but not all, of the volatile gases in the air. The question is, which ones?

Back home in Memphis, nobody ever referred to Presley as "a guitar-playing Marlon Brando." In the South, people knew exactly what to call this weird-looking kid: "the Hillbilly Cat," a name that captures his distinctive blend, not only of C&W and R&B musical styles, but also of white and black styles of personal appearance, dress, and performance. To Southerners, Presley's pompadoured hair smacked less of Tony Curtis than of the "processes" worn by black men, and his eye-catching outfits—black garments set off by pinks, reds, and greens—smacked less of Valentino than of the black "cats" down on Beale Street. Among other Americans, there may have been some hesitation about linking juvenile delinquency with class or ethnicity. But, among white Southerners upset by the civil rights movement, there was no hesitation about linking the corruption of youth with race. As we've seen, the cutting edge of the Southern craze for "nigger music" was right there in Memphis.

Of course, if corruption is defined as white love of Afro-American music, then Memphis has been thoroughly corrupted ever since its founding in 1819, when the white inhabitants were reported to take pleasure in the fiddling and banjo playing of slave musicians. In 1838 it was white Memphis, remember, that gave a chilly reception to the Norwegian violinist who couldn't manage the "nigger fiddle." Throughout its subsequent history Memphis was a prime venue for minstrel shows, dance orchestras, ragtime pianists, riverboat jazz bands, and blues musicians ranging from the 1920s composer W. C. Handy to the 1940s masters of the Delta bottleneck style. The city's position as an inland port, adjacent to the Mississippi River on one side and the heartland on the other, makes it cosmopolitan as well as conservative—the ideal crossroads for all kinds of American music. By the time Presley came along, Memphis was a "blues town" in the sense that black music predominated. But unlike Nashville, the "capital of country music" that until the 1960s frowned not only on black musicians, but also on white musicians with drums, Memphis didn't discriminate. It was willing to listen to anybody, no matter how weird, as long as he had something to offer.

And Presley had something—although the clash of myth with myth makes it tricky to say exactly what. Intellectuals tend to neglect the music altogether, assuming that Presley was a no-talent poseur who just happened to strike a pose containing social dynamite. Popular music writers tend to extol the erotically liberating energies of Presley's rockabilly rhythms, as if such energies were somehow unprecedented in the Afro-American idiom. And the official biographers tend to distill Presley's saintliness from the heartfelt emotion expressed in his gospel tunes and ballads. In a way, these conflicting responses add up to a tribute to Presley's protean talent, which was all the more remarkable for being so unschooled. He did not even serve the apprenticeship typical of his peers. Again, Phillips is candid: "Elvis Presley, probably innately, was the most introverted person that ever came into that studio. He didn't play with bands. He didn't go into this little club and pick and grin. All he did was sit with his guitar on the side of his bed at home. I don't think he even played on the front porch."[39]

As for the influences on that protean talent, they are best summarized by the music chronicler Peter Guralnick:

> Here is the crooner who admired Dean Martin and Eddie Fisher, the devout churchgoer whose single greatest ambition was to sing with the gospel Songfellows, the Beale St. dreamer who listened to R&B "bird" groups and wanted more than anything to be able to sing like Clyde McPhatter, the apprentice bluesman who wanted to feel all that Arthur Crudup had felt. We hear the western clip clop of Scotty Moore's guitar.[40]

On the talent itself, the fairest assessment is from Henry Pleasants, who explains why different people hear different things in Presley. First Pleasants describes Presley's "extraordinary compass . . . about two octaves and a third, from the baritone's low G to the tenor's high B, with an upward extension of falsetto to at least a D flat." Then Pleasants notes that the goal of a classical singer so endowed would be "to achieve a uniform sound as the voice moves up and down the scale," but that Presley did the opposite: He developed his "very wide range of vocal color" into "a multiplicity of voices." It was a logical response to all the influences listed by Guralnick. Pleasants's description is worth quoting at length:

> [Presley] would seem always to have been a naturally assimilative musician, with an acute sense of style. The black rhythm-and-blues style, he has had in hand—and in throat and body—from the very first, along with the heavy breathing, urgent exuberant vocalism and verbal articulation that goes with it, and a natural feeling for appropriate embellishment. Gospel music, and the gospel sound, are second nature to him, too, along with the gospel singer's affectionate mutilation of words. There are songs where he lays into them in a manner worthy of and reminiscent of Mahalia Jackson. . . . Although he commands the country idiom and can color his voice to suit the country cadences, he never sounds to me quite like a country singer. With ballads, he was uncertain at first, and one hears echoes of many other singers. . . . He gained confidence subsequently, as he learned to suit voice to song and to exploit the rich middle area of his range, untapped, as a rule, when he was surging through rhythm-and-blues numbers using more breath than voice. "Now or Never" ("O Sole Mio") . . . is a stunning example of his sense of style. In this famous Neapolitan air he suddenly sounds for all the world like a Neapolitan tenor. And on "That's Where Your Heartaches Begin" he goes into a talking chorus typical of Al Jolson, . . . if closer in its inflections to the fervent oratory of a country preacher.[41]

This passage should be read by (or to) all the rock 'n' roll aficionados who have spent the last thirty years denouncing Presley's eclecticism. Of all the theories offered as to why the singer abandoned rockabilly for schlock, few consider the possibility that he was simply trying to develop his natural gifts. Most (not all) of the schlock in Presley's recorded output is due to tasteless arrangements rather than tasteless singing.

My purpose in defending Presley's vocal ability is not to purge him of other, earthier talents. Only a fool would deny that his initial fame was spurred by the erotic heat of his live performances. Here is an account of a 1955 appearance in Lubbock, Texas, offered by a fellow traveler on the C&W circuit:

> Guitar hanging from his neck, curls dangling over his forehead, eyebrows arching over lidded eyes, [Elvis] grinned seductively at the girls in the front rows. Leaning forward with feet apart and clutching the mike, he warmed up with a slow ballad, then jumped into what the crowd came to see. Hips grinding and shaking, legs jerking and snapping, arms flailing the guitar to a fast beat, he drove the females into hysterics.[42]

This is the quintessential rock 'n' roll moment—and not just for admirers. One year later, when Presley was causing a similar sensation on national television, Jack Gould, the TV critic for the *New York Times*, provided Presley's detractors with this memorable distillation:

> Mr. Presley has no discernible singing ability. . . . His specialty is rhythm songs, which he renders in an undistinguished whine. . . . From watching Mr. Presley it is wholly evident that his skill lies in another direction . . . an accented movement of the body that heretofore has been primarily identified with the repertoire of the blonde bombshells of the burlesque runway.[43]

Gould was not the only pundit to see nothing but blatant sex in Presley's ability to send audiences into states of near-ecstatic enthusiasm. Most educated Americans took a similar view, for reasons that I shall explore later. But first it is necessary to fill in another aspect of Presley's background that, though relatively rare among 1950s rock 'n' rollers, played a highly significant role in both the music itself and the manner in which it was received.

Chapter 8

Rock 'n' Rollers or Holy Rollers?

The most unappreciated fact about the three most galvanizing performers in early rock 'n' roll—Presley, Jerry Lee Lewis, and Little Richard Penniman—is that they all grew up in the Pentecostal church. Presley and Lewis were raised in the predominantly white Assemblies of God, and Penniman in a variety of black Holiness and Church of God sects in his hometown of Macon, Georgia.[1]

Pentecostal churches were a distinct minority in the South during the 1950s, due in part to their style of worship, which aims at achieving a collective trancelike mental state believed to be possession by the Holy Spirit. The name "Pentecostalism" has been in use for ninety years, but the impulse behind this style of worship is ancient. In Jewish tradition, Pentecost is the fiftieth day after Passover and the final day of the spring harvest. In the New Testament, it is also the day when the Holy Spirit appeared to the disciples, in a gust of wind and fire, to grant them the "charismatic gifts" of faith healing and speaking in tongues, powers that were central to early Christianity and all subsequent periods of Christian revivalism.[2]

127

The charismatic impulse made its first appearance in America during the Great Awakenings of the eighteenth century, when the so-called frontier revivalists abandoned the decorum of colonial preaching for a more fervid style intended to engage the "affections" of the congregation.[3] Controversial though the new style was, it came to dominate the West and the South, especially after the Revolution, when these territories were opened up to circuit-riding Baptist and Methodist preachers. Despite doctrinal differences, both of these denominations believed in carrying their message to all people, no matter how lowly, by means of emotional, as opposed to intellectual, appeals. Thus they valued the dramatic skills of oratory— and music. Instead of the staid psalm singing of the colonial era, the Methodists in particular substituted the melodically rich, lyrically compelling hymns of the Englishman Isaac Watts.

The Watts hymns were especially appealing to blacks, and most scholars agree that they influenced the development of the Negro spiritual—which in turn influenced the course of white religious music. In the early 1800s the "camp meeting" movement drew thousands to vast outdoor revivals lasting several days. At these events, blacks (most of them slaves) often outnumbered whites, and the races were physically separated. Nonetheless, the whites got an earful of the blacks' music, often overwhelming in its sheer intensity and duration. Eileen Southern cites this account of a typical 1830s camp meeting:

> By general consent, it was understood that, as to the colored people, that the rules requiring quiet after a certain hour, were, on this last night, to be suspended; and great billows of sound from the tornado of praise and singing rolled over the encampment, and was echoed back from hill and wood for miles away, until the morrow's dawning.[4]

"With the sunrise," Southern elaborates, "the blacks would begin knocking down the plank partitions that separated the white quarters from those of the blacks," and commence a "grand march" around the whole encampment.[5] The eyewitness continues: "Curtains were parted; tents thrown open; and multitudes of faces peered out into the early dawning to witness the weird spectacle. Sometimes the voices of the masters and veterans among the white people would echo back, in happy response, the jubilant shout of the rejoicing slaves."[6]

Shout Unto the Lord

Having started "echo[ing] back" the sounds of black musical worship as early as the 1830s, a certain strain of white Christianity has never ceased to do so. During the late nineteenth century, the revivalist spirit of the camp meetings found its way into the Holiness movement, which arose in protest against the growing complacency of established Methodism. Like the dissenting Baptist sects forming at the same time, Holiness quickly splintered into many smaller sects, each claiming greater godliness than the last. This fragmentation occurred within both white and black Holiness movements, although no sects were integrated. Still, both movements relied on the old revivalist blend of fervid oratory rooted in the British Isles, and ecstatic music rooted in Africa, to create the right atmosphere for receiving the charismatic gifts. These were the sects that gave rise to Pentecostalism. As the historian Sydney Ahlstrom writes: "The Pentecostal awakening is surely an important instance of the direct influence of Afro-American religion on American Christianity."[7]

Pentecostalism got its name in 1901, when a student at a Holiness Bible college in Kansas received the gift of speaking in tongues. The movement quickly spread to Holiness churches, black and white, in Los Angeles, North Carolina, Tennessee, Alabama, Georgia, and Florida. It also attracted many Baptists with its compelling (if essentially Methodist) message that salvation is available to all who seek it. Ahlstrom reports that by 1949 there were eight nationally organized Pentecostal denominations, with a total membership of one million.[8]

Yet, for all its rapid growth, Pentecostalism had few defenders in the 1950s. Unlike the mainstream denominations, or even mainstream evangelicals such as Billy Graham, the Pentecostals paid precious little attention to political and social issues. Their experience of sin and repentance was intensely private, alternating between agonizing soul-searching (when they broke their rigid moral code) and intoxicating rejoicing (when they achieved ecstatic union with the Spirit). Even during the civil rights movement, when so many black churches adopted the "social gospel" of Martin Luther King, Jr., black Pentecostals stayed aloof. Even more aloof were the white Pentecostals—the "holy rollers" who had been seen by the rest of the country as hopelessly backward ever since the Christian fundamentalist attack on the teaching of evolution was publicly discredited during the famous Scopes trial (1925). To the list of benighted traits customarily assigned to this group, the 1950s added the sin of racism.

I will leave it for others to judge whether Pentecostals are more or less racist than other whites. My point is simply that, despite their social attitudes and the segregated nature of their churches, the white Pentecostals of the 1950s were culturally very similar to blacks. As Ahlstrom observes:

The peculiarities of Negro preaching do not stand out. . . . In one case as in the other, the real heart of the sermon—when the Spirit was truly working in the preacher—showed the same ecstatic stress on the joy of being in the Lord, of knowing that the life of sin and death was done and gone, of rejoicing in the still greater bliss to come. Nonverbal aspects of worship may vary, but rhythmic singing and freely responding congregations were not reserved for the blacks alone.[9]

One aspect of this cultural integration was that white Pentecostals wrestled more than other whites with a classic problem of Afro-American Christianity: where to draw the line between sacred and secular enthusiasm, between the ecstasy that was holy and the kind that invited sin.

Historically blacks had drawn the line between particular instruments and practices: They permitted tambourines, for instance, but not drums; they allowed dancing with the feet apart, but not with them crossed. But this line shifted dramatically in the 1920s, when a black vaudevillian named Thomas A. Dorsey got saved at a Baptist convention and decided to incorporate the sounds he knew best into a new genre called "gospel songs." Many people would be surprised to learn that the same man wrote both the salty blues classic, "It's Tight Like That," and the haunting air sung at King's funeral, "Take My Hand Precious Lord." But Dorsey did. Since he incorporated blues into gospel, it has been tricky to say what, apart from song structure and lyric content, distinguishes gospel from blues and other secular strains.[10]

As for Southern whites, most of them drew the line with a vengeance during Reconstruction, when many mainstream white churches (and a few zealously "respectable" black ones) defined all "nigger music" as "Devil music" and reverted to hymn-singing as plain as that of a Puritan perched on a hardwood pew. In the long run, however, this solution proved too drastic for most white Southerners, and they developed their own version of gospel, with sounds borrowed from Tin Pan Alley, C&W, and pop.

The white Pentecostals, by contrast, never compromised. Their style of worship required Afro-American music, and they incorporated everything the blacks did, from Dorsey forward. By the 1950s it was typical of white Pentecostals to believe with all their hearts that R&B was Devil's music, while immersing themselves in identical sounds while attending church, joining community "sings," and listening to gospel radio. For people with a good ear it was well-nigh impossible to appreciate one and not the other. Many preachers knew this, and used the music to win converts. Thus Jerry Lee Lewis's uncle, a moonshiner who made a point of staying away from the Baptist church, joined the Assembly of God in Ferriday, Louisiana, because the preacher let him play the fiddle, accompanied by his wife on rhythm guitar. Soon Lewis's father joined on second guitar, and it was not long before the cousins, little Jerry Lee and the future TV evangelist Jimmy Swaggart, were singing, shouting, "dancing in the Spirit," and pounding the piano for the Lord.[11]

Still, the rigid moral code of Pentecostalism required that a sacred-secular line be drawn—even though the identity of sounds inside and outside the church confounded most efforts to draw it on musical grounds. Again Lewis provides a vivid example. Ashamed of his attraction to a black juke joint called Haney's Big House, the fifteen-year-old Lewis agreed to enroll as a boarding student at Southwestern Bible Institute in Waxahachie, Texas. Like Lewis's home church, the institute belonged to the Assemblies of God. But it drew the line in a different place, as the journalist Nick Tosches reports:

> [Lewis] was called upon to play piano at chapel service, which he gladly did. But when he began playing the Pentecostal hymn "My God Is Real," the preacher shot him a glance of reproach, for he was playing it boogie-woogie style. . . . He beat the boogie so hard that there was nothing left of the hymn, nothing but the sounds of the Holy Ghost that had inspired it, and he cried out the final lyric and raked the keys violently back and forth.
>
> *My god is real, I can feel Him in my soul!*
>
> He was grinning and breathing hard. And then he was expelled from Southwestern Bible Institute.[12]

Lewis's former wife, Myra, reports the singer's confused reaction:

> "I jus' don't understand it," he told his family. "I didn't do anything wrong. I played piano jus' like I always have, the way ever'body has always liked it, only this time they didn't like it. 'Shout unto the Lord, all the earth,' says the Bible. 'Serve the Lord with gladness. Come before his presence with singing.' I served Him gladly. I sang. I shouted. I didn't mean to break any rules, honest."[13]

Needless to say, Lewis's confusion is not shared by those who would mythologize 1950s rock 'n' roll as a "revolution." For such mythologiz-ers—including many hostile critics—the standard interpretation of Lewis's music has little to do with its Pentecostal roots. Both friends and foes pay lip service to the "gospel" contribution to rock 'n' roll, but when it comes to appreciating the larger cultural significance of the music, they join forces in forgetting all about religion. Instead they focus almost exclusively on sex—a focus that distorts both the music and its meaning.

The Uses of Enthusiasm

It would be absurd to argue that 1950s rock 'n' roll is "religious" in the sense of being ethereal, reflective, and contemplative, as opposed to physical, emotional, and erotic. The erotic component in Afro-American music tends to be stronger than in European music, and a puritanical response to this eroticism leads many people to reduce even the most complex and subtle forms of Afro-American music to overt displays of sexuality. The question is, Is this reductionist response any more justified in the case of rock 'n' roll—a music that lacks the complexity and subtlety of jazz? Does rock 'n' roll express anything other than sex? And if not, what distinguishes it from later styles of popular music that resort to blatant obscenity?

These questions apply with special force to the Pentecostal strain of rockabilly, since Pentecostalism is itself Dionysian in the sense of relying on passion and bodily movement rather than reason. Of course, the Pentecostals believe, as did the revivalists of past centuries, that the frenzy stirred up in worship will be subsumed and transcended by the Holy Spirit; that God will channel it into perfect obedience to a strict moral code and total commitment to proselytizing the faith.

The Pentecostals would not deny that there is risk involved. As the Southern historian W. J. Cash observes, this kind of religion can foster a taste for "orgiastic" frenzy that militates against its own moral code. The result, writes Cash, is a psyche torn between hedonism and guilt:

> And of the intellectual baggage [the white Southerner] had brought from Europe and managed to preserve on the frontier, the core and bulk consisted of the Protestant theology of the sixteenth century and the Dissenting moral code of the seventeenth. If he was a hedonist, then, and however paradoxical it may sound, he was also likely to be a Puritan. The sense of sin, if obscured, continued to move darkly in him. . . . Even as he danced, and even though he had sloughed off all formal religion, his thoughts were with the piper and his fee.[14]

A modern version of this conflict shows up in an exchange between Lewis and Sam Phillips, shortly after Lewis had cut his first hit record for Sun. Both were eager for another success, but when Lewis saw "Great Balls of Fire," the new song Phillips had acquired for him, he suddenly decided it was blasphemous. According to a tape made of the session, Phillips tried to mollify him by pointing out that "religious conviction doesn't mean anything resembling extremism," and that even rock 'n' roll can "save souls" if the singer believes in it. To this attempt at sweet reason, Lewis cried: "*No!*

No! No! No! . . . How can the Devil save souls? What are you talkin' about? . . .
Man, I got *the Devil* in me! If I didn't have, I'd be a Christian!"[15]

In this outburst, we glimpse a Jerry Lee Lewis very different from the
rebellious rock 'n' roller celebrated in myth. By saying he has the Devil in
him, Lewis reveals a sense of himself as an unredeemed sinner that is
borne out by various accounts of his being unable, despite sincere efforts,
to respond to the promptings of his church—of looking on in frustration
while others, notably his cousin Swaggart, acquired the charismatic gifts.[16]
The real motivation behind Lewis's defiant "I am what I am" stance may
very well be this undying sense of spiritual failure. Who's to say whether
this inner conflict is more or less deserving of heavenly mercy than the
dull piety of most preachers, to say nothing of the dull hedonism of most
rock stars?

A similar conflict appears in the most galvanizing of the Pentecostal rock
'n' rollers, Little Richard. According to the R&B veteran H. B. Barnum,
who often appeared with Little Richard during the 1950s, nothing could
compare with one of his live performances:

> You knew not, night to night, where he was going to come from. He'd just
> burst onto the stage from anywhere, and you wouldn't be able to hear any-
> thing but the roar of the audience. . . . His charisma was just a whole new
> thing to the business. . . . He'd be on the stage, he'd be off the stage, he'd be
> jumping and yelling, screaming, whipping the audience on. . . . He pulled
> out all the stops. The audiences, they'd rush to touch him. Every night he
> could go to new heights. He could just come out and sing the same song and
> another dimension would happen. I've worked with some top artists, Pres-
> ley, all those, and nobody's ever had that kind of magic.[17]

For countless fans in both America and Europe, the whole point of a Little
Richard concert was the singer's ability to collect the psychic energy of the
audience into a single beam focused on himself. For many, this power indicated a prodigious sexuality, and sure enough, Little Richard was
renowned for an extravagant, mostly gay, promiscuity that, like his stage
charisma, put most competitors in the shade.

Yet Little Richard also excelled at repentance. In 1957 he abruptly abandoned his rock 'n' roll career for the Church of God, only to resume his
rock 'n' roll career in 1962.[18] Then, in the mid-1970s, the piper sent his bill
in the form of a debilitating cocaine habit and the deaths of two family
members, and Little Richard returned to the Church of God, preaching
not only against gay promiscuity, but against all sex—and denouncing rock

'n' roll as "demonic."[19] More recently, he has covered himself again with rock 'n' roll glory—indicating, perhaps, that the conflict of hedonism with guilt is no more stabilizing for him than for Lewis.[20]

Still, instability has not caused these rock 'n' rollers to forget where they learned how to move crowds. They have neither renounced nor denounced the rhythmic fervor of black gospel, and if Mahalia Jackson were alive today, she would probably repeat her 1957 comment about Little Richard:

> I didn't know what to expect in view of Richard's wild reputation as a rock 'n' roll performer, but I was delighted. . . . First of all, his stage demeanor impressed me. I could tell he had been raised right, for he was singing gospel songs the way they should be sung. He had that primitive beat and sound that came so naturally. By primitive I don't mean untamed or wild. I'm referring to the authentic way in which church music should be sung.[21]

Finally, there is Presley, who dealt with his own instability by becoming the spiritual pupil of his hairdresser, Larry Geller, an enthusiast of occult wisdom ranging from theosophy to Hinduism, numerology to Christian Science, Freemasonry to Yoga.[22] Sophisticates who dislike rock 'n' roll may be entertained by the spectacle of Presley's untutored mind trying to digest this gallimaufry.[23] But Presley, like Lewis and Little Richard, was struggling with something real. As Geller remarks, the singer "felt stranded by both his disenchantment with his religious education and the vacuousness of the lifestyle that fame had thrust upon him."[24]

The New Primitivist Embrace

What about sophisticates who like rock 'n' roll? Are they any better at illuminating this particular conflict? A good example is the rock critic Greil Marcus, whose 1975 essay, "Elvis: Presliad," did much to rehabilitate Presley's reputation after his death, and is still routinely quoted by pundits seeking wisdom on the subject. Furthermore, the book in which the essay appears, Marcus's *Mystery Train*, is one of the most highly esteemed books ever written about popular music.

At first glance, Marcus seems to take Presley's background seriously, expressing agreement with "all those who have traced Elvis's music and his hipshake to his religion," and calling Pentecostalism "a source of energy, tension and power." Taking as his models the literary criticism of D. H. Lawrence and Leslie Fiedler, Marcus conceives of American culture as a battleground between puritanical repressiveness and the erotic liberation promised by art. But instead of offering nuanced analyses of this battle in literature, he caricatures America as having been gripped by puritanism ever since the Mayflower scraped her bottom on Plymouth Rock—with no countervailing tendencies, except a "secret revolt against the Puritans" that never broke through the surface until the 1950s. Indeed, Marcus unearths only two musical examples of this "secret revolt" before rock 'n' roll: Robert Johnson, an elusive Mississippi bluesman who boasted of having made a pact with the Devil; and "Harmonica Frank" Floyd, an itinerant C&W singer with a penchant for raunchy lyrics. In Marcus's view, these lonely "ancestors" remained "secret" because the times were not yet ripe. For true liberation, America would have to wait for Presley.[25]

The speediest way to refute this thesis is to point out that it sidesteps practically the entire history of Afro-American music. Marcus says nothing about plantation music, spirituals, minstrelsy, ragtime, jazz, gospel, or swing. About the music immediately preceding rock 'n' roll, he is both evasive and contradictory. In the case of C&W, he avoids the rhythmically energetic strains, mentioning only the "twangs and laments." And about R&B, he avoids all the swing-influenced strains, focusing exclusively on the Chicago-Memphis blues, which he extols for being "loud, fiercely electric, raucous, bleeding with lust and menace and loss." But here Marcus contradicts himself, later dismissing the blues as an expression of black puritanism, full of "fatalism" and "hellfire" and itself needing to be liberated. Finally he credits Presley with overriding the "blues philosophy" of "acceptance" with a brand-new, anarchistic "rage."[26]

In the end Marcus takes an oddly bifurcated view of Afro-American music—a view that is, unfortunately, quite prevalent today. On the one hand, he praises "black music" as a *source* for rock 'n' roll, depicting Presley as the Prometheus who stole its spark, passing it to the white race as it languished in frigid puritanism. On the other, he refuses to regard Afro-American music as a living *competitor* to his beloved rock 'n' roll. His whole argument implies that nothing of any real musical significance occurred between the founding of the Jamestown colony and the release of "That's All Right, Mama." He even claims, at one point, that Presley's singing possesses "an ease and an intensity that *has no parallel in American music.*"[27] (emphasis added) So intent is Marcus on mythologizing the Memphis Prometheus that he ignores the fact that, by the time Presley seized the black musical fire, it had already spent three centuries warming the white folks as well as the black.

With regard to that fire's true nature, Marcus resorts to more caricature, depicting the enthusiasm aroused by 1950s rock 'n' roll as having nothing to do with religion and everything to do with sex. His stance toward the spiritual fervor of Pentecostalism is also bifurcated: He accepts religion as one of the ballyhooed "roots" of rock 'n' roll, but he scorns it as a viable alternative. Contemptuously he dismisses performers who have "returned to the fold after a brief fling with the devil, singing songs of virtue, fidelity, and God, as if to prove that sin only hid a deeper piety—or that there was no way out." For Marcus, the "way out" is clear: "It was [Elvis's] sinfulness that brought him to life." True faith is the "secret revolt"; true hope is "that Saturday night could be the whole show," that we can "trade pain and boredom for kicks and style," that good times won't end as "Saturday fades into Monday."[28] Typically, Marcus restructures the week so that Saturday fades into Monday instead of Sunday, the day when enthusiasm gets put to *non*-hedonistic uses. Ruled out of bounds is the possibility of an enthusiasm that subsumes or transcends the erotic.

Like the primitivist embrace of jazz, this new primitivist embrace of rock 'n' roll slips all too easily into a celebration of obscenity. In the 1982 edition of *Mystery Train*, Marcus cites a song by the American punk band X as "the best song ever written about Elvis . . . the first song about Elvis's place in the American unconscious." Among the lyrics he quotes: "Man in the back says Presley sucked dicks."[29] Also recommended is an "indelibly subversive" book called *Private Elvis*, published in Germany in 1978 and containing "photos of Elvis consorting with whores, actresses, junkies and strippers in a Munich nightclub." Marcus extols these images for depicting the "seamy, erotic smashup of American health with European decay," and offering a "version of the pornographic film Elvis's fans dreamed of for twenty years."[30]

Clearly, Marcus's interpretation of Presley claims to be on the "cutting edge" of contemporary culture. But is it? Ironically, his primitivism is a lot like the initial reaction to rock 'n' roll back in the 1950s. For that decade was the heyday of Freud in American life, a time when countless educated Americans believed that psychoanalysis was the key to every kind of truth. This belief was especially strong in the area of culture. Among thoughtful critics, the Freudian approach could be illuminating. But as Jacques Barzun reminds us, it could also be mechanistic:

> Freud happened to be encumbered with a materialistic notion of science, which gave added color to the crude supposition that at the root of man's being is sex; that all the supposed glamour and significance of love are "romantic," that is to say, spurious; and yet that a man's artistic creations,

political opinions, and individual tastes are the direct, fated outcome of his sexual temperament. There followed the pseudo-psychoanalysis of everyone whose name could be read in the small print of a biographical dictionary.[31]

As it happens, the same crude approach was taken toward people not listed in biographical dictionaries. Indeed, it's easy to see how educated people accustomed to seeing Shakespeare's sonnets reduced to exercises in sublimation might leap to similar conclusions about female adolescents screaming themselves hoarse over Elvis.

Such conclusions were reinforced by the work of Alfred C. Kinsey, who published two provocative (and still controversial) reports on the sexual behavior of his fellow Americans in 1948 and 1953. As the historian William O'Neill explains, it was the second Kinsey report that caused the biggest fuss:

> Kinsey's report on males was controversial but did him little harm. It had long been suspected that men were lustful, and proof of this, however unwelcome, did not shake the moral order. But his report on women made Kinsey notorious. Being mothers women were regarded by many people as practically sexless—the immoral minority excepted—copulating only out of necessity. Kinsey's evidence that women had sexual feelings offended many people, and he would not be forgiven for presenting it.[32]

Again, it's easy to see how a public caught up in an inflammatory debate about female sexuality might be predisposed toward seeing the enthusiasm of female rock 'n' roll fans as nothing but raw libido.

Far be it from me to assert that rock 'n' roll fans—male and female—were *not* feeling their libidinous oats. But here, too, the eroticism of Afro-American music must be seen as part of a larger whole, whether spiritual ecstasy or simply the exuberance of bodily movement. Of all the distortions found in Marcus, the most glaring is his utter indifference to the fact that 1950s rock 'n' roll was, above all, a dance craze.

The extreme ascetic strain in Christianity conceives of everything physical as sexual, and therefore sinful—which is why it distrusts the motive powers of music, especially rhythm. Marcus understands one thing: that this distrust arrived in America with the Puritans. But he doesn't understand two others: first, that puritan distrust has been constantly challenged by the presence, on American soil, of irresistible rhythm; and second, that this challenge has frequently resulted in the overcoming of distrust and the sanctification of rhythm.

In other words, this important and influential critic utterly denies the historic link between American Protestantism and Afro-American music—a link that still causes a great many religious Americans, white and black, to grapple with the problem of drawing a line between the holy and the unholy uses of enthusiasm, between sanctified rhythm and the Devil's drum. The question is: Is this problem of drawing the line more or less profound than Marcus's primitivist reduction of all rhythm, music and fervor to sex? And, of these two conceptions of our music, which is the more puritanical?

The Blood Knot Revisited

At this point the reader may object to my argument that, far from being a "revolution," 1950s rock 'n' roll was seamlessly continuous with its musical and cultural antecedents. Isn't there some essential discontinuity, some markedly unprecedented aspect to the phenomenon that rightly hastens the mythologizers to their task? As Marcus himself writes: "Any musicologist, neatly tracing the development of the music, can tell us that rock 'n' roll did not come out of nowhere. But it sounded as if it did."[33] Doesn't he have a point?

The answer is yes: There *is* something revolutionary about rock 'n' roll. But Marcus cannot say what it is, because he doesn't delve deeply enough into the insidious coils of the blood knot. In the passage quoted earlier, Cash refers to the South's racial-sexual caste system when he says, of the white Southern man, that "the world he knew, the hot sting of the sun in his blood, *the sidelong glances of the all-complaisant Negro woman*—all these impelled him irresistibly toward joy."[34] (emphasis added) Subsequent historians have rejected Cash's assumption that the "Negro woman" was "all-complaisant." But the truth of his gut-level insight remains unaltered—namely, that the erotic pleasures and guilts of Southern white men have always been bound up with the power they exercised over black women. Over the years, the moral hypocrisy inherent in this situation has led to further entanglements, such as the isolation of white womanhood atop a pedestal of sexless virtue; the lynching of black men for unproven sex crimes against white women; and finally, the glorification of black men as avatars of unbridled potency. What Cash reveals, and Marcus ignores, is that all these entanglements stem, ultimately, from the exploitation of black women by white men. This is where we must delve, to find out what sort of revolution rock 'n' roll really was.

The myth of rock 'n' roll as a racial revolution is usually reinforced with images of white rock 'n' rollers boldly crossing the Jim Crow line to learn music directly from blacks—Lewis sneaking into Haney's Big House, for instance, or Presley attending services at the East Trigg Baptist Church. Yet the mythologizers overlook the fact that such interracial contacts had plenty of precedents. Just to cite two: In 1911 Jimmie Rodgers learned the blues from his fellow workers on the Mississippi-and-Ohio Railroad; and in the 1930s, Hank Williams apprenticed himself to an itinerant street singer named "Tee-Tot" (Rufus Payne), who worried that the "little white boss" was spending too much time in the black part of town.[35]

What is more, these direct contacts were probably more important in the old days. Recall that the 1950s saw improvements in the technology of private consumption that made it easier than ever for whites to be on intimate terms with R&B, gospel, and blues without changing their racial behavior one iota. Likewise, the white Pentecostal churches attended by Presley and Lewis were, for all their cultural resemblance to black churches, thoroughly segregated—not to mention thoroughly disengaged from such social realities as the civil rights movement.

Thus the white rock 'n' rollers served a musical apprenticeship that rarely, if ever, required them to set foot on black turf, whether a juke joint, a blues club, or a Baptist church. Neither Presley nor Lewis ever displayed the slightest inclination to march for racial integration. Their program was simplicity itself: They aimed to thrill the crowds, bust the charts, rake in the dough, and beat the pants off the (black) competition. When they succeeded, it was because they were uniquely positioned in both the vanguard of cultural integration and the rear guard of social segregation. That is to say, they were poised to combine the advantage of their black musical skill with the even greater advantage of their white skin. In Presley's case, especially, it was obvious that he held his abilities as an authentic Afro-American musician in very low esteem, compared with such "higher" aspirations as becoming a Hollywood movie star.

There was a moment, when the civil rights movement was getting under way and rock 'n' roll was climbing all three charts simultaneously, when political activism and popular music seemed to be working together to topple the walls of racial division in America. But it was only a moment. In both politics and music, new walls were soon erected that seemed, if anything, higher and more baffling than before. So rock 'n' roll was not a racial revolution in the simpleminded sense of bringing blacks and whites together. Nonetheless, there is a sense in which rock 'n' roll, in its original

Southern context, did foment a social revolution—precisely because it did *not* bring blacks and whites together.

Proper white Southerners condemned R&B as "nigger music" because they associated it not just with black sexuality, but also with the habit of white men to go "slipping around" with black women. In his pivotal study, *Sex and Racism in America*, Calvin Hernton recalls his experience working as a waiter in a Nashville nightclub during the 1950s. The customers were white, the staff black, and their interaction is painfully revealing:

> It was the practice of the patrons, when they became "high," and the night was nearing its end, to call the black women from the kitchen and dance with them. . . . Rebel yells, clapping, and obscene innuendoes would fill the club. . . . The white women wanted to participate, too. . . . And we black boys—I am certain—had reciprocal desires. But it seldom happened . . . the bitter stares of every white man there would be upon you. Finally the dishwasher, a shapely, light-skinned, beautiful Negro of twenty, would be taken onto the floor. . . . The noise and riot would cease. . . . Involuntary sighs and whispers of alien ecstasy would suffuse the quietness of the club—but not from the white women. Envy, jealousy, hatred and repugnant stares would appear on their faces. . . . When the place was empty, the [black] women never failed to express their disgust over what had happened. They knew they were being used as vicarious sex toys, as "Negresses," and not as human females. They "hated" white men; but what could they do? They needed the money.[36]

This spectacle was called "Show Time," and with good reason. With the utmost clarity, this anecdote shows the effects of Southern sexual hypocrisy on each of the participants—white and black, male and female.

Consider for a moment the frustration and humiliation of the white women so vividly captured by Hernton. Southern literature is replete with the suffering—bitter, stoic, neurotic—of white women set up as pure, untouchable paragons by men who then slip around to touch other, "impure" women, often under the same roof. Given the literary sources of Marcus's primitivism, it's remarkable that he overlooks this ubiquitous theme. Perhaps he doesn't find it pertinent to rock 'n' roll because his grasp of sexuality, like that of most primitivists, seems arrested at the stage at which the male has not yet begun to consider the responses of the female. Perhaps this adolescent perspective prevents both Marcus and his fellow primitivists from seeing that the themes of race, sex, music, and enthusiasm converge most strikingly in the white female response to rock 'n' roll.

We needn't ask what kind of music was playing when Hernton's pretty dishwasher and her white partner danced "fast, semifast, then a close-up 'slow drag,' or what is ethnically known as the 'belly rub.' "[37] It was probably

R&B, seen by whites as the theme music of racial-sexual adventurism. Imagine how the white women in that nightclub must have felt about the infectious rhythms and seductive voices of R&B being always directed at some alluring black "mama" or "baby," never at them. No doubt the more timid among them accepted their status as bystanders. But others must have yearned to be the center of all that fascinated male attention, while keenly resenting being excluded from the central erotic rituals of their own society.

Now let me ask: How would these women be likely to react if a white man suddenly appeared who could not only sing as seductively as a black R&B star, but who also made it clear (as no black R&B star could, or would) that his singing was directed not at black women but at *them*? What if, being white himself, this singer made it possible for white women to turn the tables on their men, to reduce those arrogant creatures to passive onlookers while they, the women, abandoned themselves to the sighs, whispers, and screams of "alien ecstasy"? To find the answer, we need only recall that one of the biggest problems on Presley's early Southern tours was security. Along with the frantic adulation of his female fans, he was also endangered by the frantic resentment of the males, who understood all too well that the Hillbilly Cat was not playing by the rules.

By this light, the galvanizing music of the early rock 'n' rollers can be seen as striking a blow, not against sexual morality per se, but against the moral hypocrisies of a color-coded double standard. It can be seen as fostering rebellion, not against society or community in the abstract, but against that particular racial-sexual caste system. It can be seen as helping white men to quit exploiting black women, and white women to get down off their pedestals. It can even be seen as loosening the blood knot enough to give black Southerners a slightly greater margin of privacy and self-respect. To the extent that it accomplished all of these things, rock 'n' roll was revolutionary in the best sense of the word.

Yet this is not the revolution in the myth, because the myth comes not from the Southern context of the music but from the educated preconceptions of the 1950s. Moreover, the myth was not fully articulated until the 1960s, when the music changed both its name and its address. In the 1960s rock 'n' roll became "rock," and ceased to be an expression of the American South, with its agonizing wrestling over the uses of enthusiasm. Figures like Presley, Lewis, and Little Richard, who conceived of life and music as a battleground between God and the Devil, got shunted aside by a new generation with a new battle—or at least, one that was new to the popular mainstream of Afro-American music. It was the battle between Art and Society, especially as carried out by perverse modernism. Needless to say, this new battle is a more appropriate preoccupation for intellectuals and cultural critics than old-time religion ever was. But, as I contemplate its long-term effects on popular music and culture, I can't help wondering: Is it really more interesting, and compelling, than the struggle between good and evil waged by those wild young men roaring out of Ferriday, Macon, and Memphis forty years ago?

Chapter 9

Reaction and Revitalization

o deny that rock 'n' roll was a revolution is not to suggest that it was never attacked. On the contrary, it drew a whole array of hostile responses, including a few that were blatantly racist. On one famous occasion, the executive secretary of the Alabama White Citizens' Council declared before a TV news camera that "the obscenity and vulgarity of the rock 'n' roll music is obviously the means by which the white man and his children can be driven to a level with the niggers."[1] In 1958 a riot broke out in the Boston Arena during a concert organized by Alan Freed; accounts of this donnybrook vary, but most agree that it began with a white girl throwing herself at a black male singer, thereby provoking a violent reaction from both the white boys in the crowd and the white police on duty. [2]

Furthermore, in a replay of the jazz era, these racist attacks meshed all too smoothly with the highbrow bias against rhythm. Public officials and media commentators who wouldn't have been caught dead saying "nigger" didn't hesitate to drag out the old complaint about strong rhythms stirring up uncontrollable passions. For example, the superintendent of police in Bridgeport, Connecticut, defended a 1955 ban on rock 'n' roll dances on the grounds that "teenagers virtually work themselves into a frenzy to the beat of fast swing music."[3] At least the superintendent knew enough to call it "fast swing music." Others just repeated the old refrain: The *New York Times* quoted a respected psychiatrist saying rock 'n' roll was "cannibalistic and tribalistic"; the *New York Daily News* called it "a barrage of primitive, jungle-beat rhythms."[4]

Right on cue, Dwight MacDonald entered the fray, filling several pages of *The New Yorker* with the rather less than original argument that rock 'n' roll was a form of kitsch aimed at exploiting the affluent postwar youth market.[5] This warmed-over mojo proved timely: In 1959 and 1960, the House of Representatives Special Subcommittee on Legislative Oversight held its "payola" hearings, which generated enormous publicity around the charge that DJs such as Freed had artificially initiated and stimulated the rock 'n' roll craze in return for record-company payoffs.

At those hearings, the editor of *Billboard* testified that payola was nothing new, that it was best understood as a continuation of the old (and accepted) practice of "song plugging," by which Tin Pan Alley publishers had once offered incentives to bandleaders to play certain songs.[6] In the same unapologetic spirit, Freed, nearly bankrupt from fighting charges that he had incited the Boston riot, testified that he saw nothing wrong with taking money or favors from the promoters of authentic R&B. As usual he defended the musical superiority of R&B, and argued that payola was the only way the independent labels who produced it could compete against the majors.

But Freed did not prevail. Shortly after refusing to sign an affidavit denying that he had ever accepted payola, he lost his last DJ job in New York (at WABC) and retreated to Los Angeles, where he worked sporadically while sinking into the alcoholic tailspin that caused his death five years later.

Dick Clark, a rich and powerful radio and TV personality, was also summoned to testify before the subcommittee, and it is reported that he forfeited $8 million after being censured by the congressmen. But the fates, or rather the major record labels, were kinder to Clark than to Freed, because they understood that Clark was more willing than Freed to push their bland cover versions of rock 'n' roll over the real thing. Clark's original radio program in Philadelphia had featured covers, and his TV shows, *American Bandstand* and *The Dick Clark Show*, boosted the careers of such major-label "teen idols" as Frankie Avalon, Fabian, and Bobby Rydell.[7] By sticking with this strategy, Clark soon rebuilt his empire.

The Day the Music Died

They're compelling, these tales of gimlet-eyed rednecks and greedy-eyed capitalists plotting against rock 'n' roll, not resting until they have precipitated not only the McCarthyesque payola hearings, but also the lonesome death of Alan Freed, the music's brave champion. And then there's the comic relief of the majors' teen idols, struggling to carry a tune and snap their fingers at the same time. Not surprisingly, these images reinforce a second myth—that of a counterrevolution deliberately set in motion by a "system" terrified at the powerful social and political forces being unleashed by rock 'n' roll.

This second myth acquired its slogan in 1971, when the singer-song-writer Don McLean's hit record "American Pie" used the phrase "the day the music died" to refer to the 1959 plane crash that killed three rock 'n' roll stars (including the promising young Texan Buddy Holly). But to most mythologizers, such as this *Rolling Stone* writer, the music didn't die, it was killed: "It is a measure of Fifties rock's genuine revolutionary potential (as opposed to the revolution-as-corporate-marketing-ploy so characteristic of the Sixties) that while Sixties rock eventually calmed down, was co-opted or snuffed itself out in heedless excess, Fifties rock & roll was *stopped*. Cold."[8]

The core of this scenario is not new: Central to the Afro-American tradition is the fable of the small, risk-taking prospector who lovingly mines a vein of musical gold, only to get shoved aside by a corporate giant intent on plundering the source or, worse, replacing it with fool's gold. How could it be otherwise? Ever since 1917, when RCA Victor began mass-marketing the Original Dixieland Jazz Band, the greater size of the white market has caused the best Afro-American music to be outsold by the dilutions of ill-informed white taste. Now, the scenario changes with rock 'n' roll, because instead of comparing *black* originals with *white* imitations, the counterrevolutionary myth compares *white* originals with *white* imitations. There's nothing wrong with this change, as long as the standard being used to distinguish between authentic and fool's gold is still that of Afro-American musical merit. But for many true believers in this myth, it is not.

Exaggerating the musical distinction between rock 'n' roll and 1950s pop, many mythologizers use the label "pop" as sufficient condemnation in itself, never bothering to distinguish between good and bad pop. This usage leads to glaring contradictions, as when the former *New York Times* rock critic Mike Jahn deplores the late 1950s and early 1960s as a time when "young pop singers masquerading as rock 'n' rollers" stole the limelight. To the usual list of teen idols Jahn adds Bobby Darin, a genuinely talented singer whose "Dream Lover" and "Mack the Knife" topped the charts in 1959.[9] Meanwhile, the mythologizer we started with, Herbert London, credits Darin with having "transformed the soporific harmonies of traditional pop music into . . . rock," thereby taking "a giant step in a cultural revolution."[10] Clearly, one mythologizer's reactionary is another's radical.

The only musical foundation for the counterrevolutionary myth is the fact that most of the rock 'n' roll on the charts after 1958 is not especially rough or erotic. Isn't this proof that the real thing was being suppressed in favor of the fake? Not if we consider that the same proof existed at mid-decade. Take Pat Boone, the much-maligned cover artist who took all the rhythm and blues out of Fats Domino, Ivory Joe Hunter, and (most absurdly) Little Richard. What could be more ersatz than this squeaky-clean fellow in white bucks crooning his way through Little Richard's show-stopping "awop-bop-a-loo-mop / awop-bam-boom"? Boone fits the teen-idol stereotype so perfectly, it's tempting to forget that he *stopped* making rock 'n' roll covers in 1957, two years *before* "the music died."

Or take a black vocal group that seems to fit Jahn's account of late-1950s R&B putting itself through a "bleaching process" by which it "abandoned" its "purity" (meaning, predictably enough, its "roughness" and "straightforward sexual content").[11] It seems inevitable that such a group would produce a harmless ditty called "I'm Not a Juvenile Delinquent," rendered not by grown-up men with deep seductive voices, but by prepubescent boys whose pipings would not have been out of place in the choir loft of Westminster Abbey. It's hard to imagine a smoother, more innocent vocal group than Frankie Lymon and the Teenagers. Yet they came along in 1956, Presley's zenith.

As for the major labels' desire to suppress authentic rock 'n' roll talent, they had a funny way of showing it. After RCA signed Presley in 1955, the others hastened to acquire their own talent rosters. To cite just a few examples: Decca, which had led the way with Bill Haley, signed Buddy Holly, Brenda Lee, and Jackie Wilson; Mercury signed the Penguins, the Platters, J. P. ("Big Bopper") Richardson, and Johnny Preston; RCA signed Sam Cooke; Capitol signed Gene Vincent, the flamboyant "Esquerita," and Johnny Otis; ABC Paramount signed Paul Anka, Lloyd Price, and Ray Charles.

Now, it is true that, along with these acquisitions, the majors felt compelled to manufacture a certain amount of fool's gold. But the reason was simple: They were running out of the real thing. By 1960 the ranks of the original rock 'n' rollers were decimated: In 1956 Carl Perkins's career was derailed by an automobile accident; in 1957 Little Richard returned to the Church of God; in 1958 Presley got drafted; in that year, too, Lewis got blackballed after the British press raised a scandal about his marriage to thirteen-year-old Myra; in 1959 Chuck Berry was arrested and tried on a trumped-up morals charge; later that year Buddy Holly went down in flames, along with the Big Bopper and Richie Valens; and finally, in 1960, Eddie Cochran (who wrote the first song about Holly's death) got killed in a car crash. All these events were unfortunate, some tragic. But only a committed paranoiac could perceive them as tactics in a reactionary plot to suppress rock 'n' roll.

There is also the inconvenient fact that 1960 was the year the record industry began recycling R&B and rock 'n' roll hits. I am not suggesting that this was done out of commitment to musical authenticity. Quite the opposite: It was done for the usual reason—to make money. The "oldies-but-goodies" trend began as a low-budget venture by a tiny California company called Original Sound, which had the bright idea of producing composite albums of hit singles leased on the cheap from expiring independent labels. The trend was encouraged by DJs hoping to retain the loyalty of listeners then entering their twenties.[12] And eventually, the majors got aboard: In 1961, when an unknown group called Little Caesar and the Romans scored a hit with "These Oldies but Goodies Remind Me of You," ABC Paramount released its own nostalgia ditty: "Who Put the Bomp (in the Bomp, Bomp, Bomp)?" On this level the trend was a crude marketing ploy. But it did motivate many companies, including the majors, to rerelease "oldies" that really *were* "goodies." The question is, Would they have done so if they were trying to crush a revolution?

"I Majored in Math": The Paradox of Chuck Berry

If a counterrevolutionary is defined as a calculating businessperson who studies the size and tastes of the white youth market and deliberately formulates a type of music to cash in on that market, then why not indict Chuck Berry? It's unthinkable, of course, to criticize the man about whom John Lennon once said: "If you tried to give rock 'n' roll another name, you might call it Chuck Berry."[13] Along with Lennon, every rock star since the 1960s has cited the eccentric black singer-songwriter from St. Louis as a hero. One of the better rock historians, Charlie Gillett, minces no words: "If importance in popular music were measured in terms of imaginativeness, creativeness, wit, the ability to translate a variety of experiences and feelings into musical form, and long-term influence and reputation, Chuck Berry would be described as the major figure of rock 'n' roll."[14] Even rarer tribute can be found closer to home. In a recent film documentary about Berry, Jerry Lee Lewis quotes his own mother as once having remarked: "You and Elvis are pretty good, but you're no Chuck Berry."[15]

Berry is a figure quite unlike the Pentecostal rock 'n' rollers discussed in the last chapter. But in his own way he is equally fascinating—and misunderstood. His career began in Chicago, where he ventured in 1955 to try his luck with the renowned blues label, Chess, which until then had focused almost exclusively on the Chicago blues—the one type of R&B that was not crossing over to white youth. Chess was owned by two brothers named Leonard and Phil Chess, who had started out as the proprietors of a blues club and were so blues-oriented, they once spurned an offer, made by a hard-pressed Sam Phillips, to buy the entire Sun roster, including Presley, because: "We didn't consider ourselves a hillbilly label at that time."[16]

Ironically, Berry's first hit with Chess, "Maybellene," was the old "hillbilly" standard "Ida Red," given new words and a propulsive R&B rhythm. In his self-penned autobiography, Berry describes how, as a member of the Johnnie Johnson Trio, performing in East St. Louis, he first attracted attention by playing C&W:

> I would . . . impress the audience with my hilarious hilly and basic billy delivery. . . . It could have been because of my country-western songs that the white spectators showed up in greater numbers. . . . Sometimes nearly forty percent of the clients were Caucasian, causing the event to be worthy of publicity across the river in St. Louis.[17]

Soon Berry became known as "the black hillbilly"—a name perfectly symmetrical, and contemporaneous, with Presley's "Hillbilly Cat."[18] After "Maybellene" succeeded, Berry saw his chance and seized it. Just before meeting Presley, Sam Phillips is said to have vowed: "If I could find a white man with the Negro sound and the Negro feel, I could make a billion dollars." Berry's vow was different: "I was trying to shoot for the whole population instead of just . . . shall we say, the neighborhood?"[19] But he, too, sought the alchemy by which "black" and "white" music could be blended into gold.

As we've seen, the alchemy worked more profitably for white rock 'n' rollers. Still, Berry had two advantages over the Phillips-Presley team: He could write songs, and he was conversant with jazz. His remarkable string of 1950s hits, from "Roll Over, Beethoven" (1957), to "Back in the USA"

(1959), still sound fresh, with their crisp, articulate vocals, delivered over the dense cross-rhythms of Johnson's boogie-woogie piano and the jazzy solos of Berry's electric guitar, an instrument that really does (in the words of another song) "ring like a bell." As for Berry's lyrics, they are bold but never barefaced, simple but never simpleminded. They evoke both the craziness and the conformity of youth. For example, both "School Days" and "Sweet Little Sixteen" portray rock 'n' roll as a thrilling but temporary respite from hard work and adult authority, with both of the latter accepted as facts of life. In his 1957 hit, "Rock and Roll Music," Berry echoes Basie's and Goodman's defense of the new style as a danceable alternative to "modern jazz," while also hinting that it is not all that new. As he explained recently: "I definitely catered to the teenagers, but also some to the adults. I didn't leave out the adults, or the swing, the thing that brought me up."[20] In other songs, like "Johnny B. Goode" and "Sweet Little Rock 'n' Roller," Berry brags about the enthusiasm he evokes in his young fans, but also portrays them as innocent.

Since Berry's lyrics are the first fully self-conscious ones in rock 'n' roll, it is remarkable how many people in popular music fail to appreciate his role. To cite one salient example, in a recent film documentary about Buddy Holly produced by former Beatle Paul McCartney, the Rolling Stones' lead guitarist Keith Richards praises Holly, not Berry, for being the first "singer-songwriter" in rock 'n' roll.[21] Given Richards's active participation in the Berry documentary cited earlier, this omission is mind-boggling.

Of course, Holly was a clever songwriter and record producer who died young and full of promise, while Berry's reputation for the past three decades has been that of an embittered oldies act who tours alone and doesn't much care what sort of band he plays with, as long as he gets his money up front. This reputation is partly deserved: Berry's rugged individualism has isolated him as often as it has served him. But a prickly personality does not explain why the rock pundits of the late 1960s should have described him as a primitive, spontaneous, unreflective being—as when Carl Belz called him "a traditional folk artist" who "created art unconsciously" and Jahn called his songs "accidental art."[22]

In part, such comments reflect the longevity of the racist and primitivist responses discussed earlier—reinforced, no doubt, by Berry's open violation of racial-sexual taboos. Despite his long and stable marriage, Berry has had numerous affairs with white women, some of them underage. His adventures were never as flamboyant as Little Richard's, nor were they carried out on the massive scale associated with later groups such as the Rolling Stones.[23] But Berry's penchant for bragging about his "Brown

Eyed Handsome Man" appeal for white females outraged a lot of people. Even Richards, that veteran backstage Don Juan, sneers when recalling Berry in the company of "a little piece of white tail."[24] No doubt this side of Berry provoked the lynch-mob atmosphere surrounding his arrest, trial, retrial, and two-year imprisonment for a dubious violation of the rarely enforced Mann Act (a law that prohibited transporting minors across state lines for immoral purposes).

Still, the most important reason why rock pundits disparage Berry is because he presents a paradox not easily reconciled with the myth of rock 'n' roll as a thwarted revolution. On the one hand, his music is as galvanizing as Pentecostal rock 'n' roll—in fact, it wears better because of its jazzier texture. But on the other, Berry's whole approach to rock 'n' roll smacks of the tendency rock critics most deplore about the late 1950s: the premeditated manufacture of pleasing, accessible music that flirts with rebellion but ends up reinforcing the status quo. Berry, who was almost thirty when he recorded "Maybellene," was too old to sing "I'm Not a Juvenile Delinquent." But to a large extent that was his message. London gets the story right (for once) when he writes: "He surely wasn't a critic of capitalist values and neither was his music . . . Berry may have been all passion and sizzling discontent, as some rock critics have suggested, but his lyrics are as irrepressibly conformist as the proverbial 'organization man.'"[25]

Berry would agree. Indeed, he is proud of having earned a diploma in business management while in prison.[26] In the documentary *Hail, Hail, Rock 'n' Roll* there is a sequence in which Little Richard and Bo Diddley (Berry's contemporary at Chess) confess their youthful naïveté in the face of sharp business practices. Berry listens coolly, then hints, not too subtly, that he was too smart to get ripped off. "I majored in math," he says. The spotlight is immediately stolen by Little Richard's hilarious retort: "Well, *I* majored in *mouth!*" But the point remains clear: Berry would rather be respected as a shrewd businessman than adulated as a wild rock 'n' roller.[27]

Finally Berry disproves the myth because he sees himself as solidly within the Afro-American tradition. When confronted by interviewers eager to sing the praises of his "revolutionary" achievement, he is self-deprecating. When asked about his songwriting, he dismisses it as a mere moneymaking venture.[28] And when asked about his musical sound, he explains that it was the best he could do, given his lack of real talent for jazz, blues, or even pop.[29] Like most 1950s rock 'n' rollers he has nothing but admiration for the finer pop singers, stating with all sincerity: "If I had only one artist to listen to through eternity, it would be Nat Cole."[30]

Admittedly it was Berry who bragged that rock 'n' roll would "Deliver us from the days of old." But when pressed, the man whose name is synonymous with 1950s rock 'n' roll rejects the notion that his music represents a radical break with the past. On the contrary, he offers this clear-eyed assessment:

> They say that's a Chuck Berry song because it's . . . [*hums his trademark guitar riff*]. Well, the first time I heard that was in one of Carl Hogan's riffs in Louis Jordan's band. We have T-Bone Walker; I love T-Bone Walker slurs, and he's bluesy. So put in a little Carl Hogan, a little T-Bone Walker, and a little Charlie Christian—the guitarist in Tommy Dorsey's band [*sic*]—together, and look what a span of people that you will please! And that's what I did, in "Johnny B. Goode," "Roll Over, Beethoven." And making it simple is another important factor, I think, that resulted in a lot of artists understanding and being able to play my music. If you can call it my music. Ain't nothing new under the sun.[31]

Back to the Well: Motown vs. The Wall of Sound

Charles Keil has asserted that "each successive appropriation and commercialization of a Negro style by white America" forces a return, by blacks, to the well of their tradition to draw forth fresh material that will remain off limits to whites, at least for a while. Writing in 1966, Keil further asserts that this "appropriation-revitalization process" has been a constant source of renewal for American popular music and, indeed, for American culture as a whole.[32] Yet with today's hindsight, the question becomes: Did that revitalizing process survive rock 'n' roll?

If the key conflict following rock 'n' roll was between white originals and white imitators, then where did that leave blacks? As Keil notes, black performers were historically accustomed to inhabiting an economically disadvantaged, but creatively privileged, sphere. Was that sphere no longer theirs at the beginning of the 1960s? Was the well of tradition now equally the property of whites?

The initial answer to these questions was no, because, along with the black performers still holding their own in established R&B styles (notably doo-wop), a new form of black-dominated music appeared that promised to appeal to whites while also being beyond their reach. Its name was Motown.

Motown founder Berry Gordy Jr. was the third Berry Gordy to make his independent way in the world. His grandfather, Berry Gordy, was the offspring of a Georgia cotton farmer and a slave woman who, thanks to the education provided by his white father, bought himself out of the share-cropping system in the 1890s. The son of this freeholder, Berry Gordy II [*sic*], grew up to take his father's place as the manager of a prosperous family farm—no mean feat in Oconee County, Georgia, where black economic independence was, to say the least, discouraged. The fortunes of the Gordy family increased over the years, but so did the discouragement they faced. By 1922 they decided, after a lucrative timber deal provoked threats of lynching, to sell the farm and move to Detroit, where Berry II bought the family a house and started three businesses.[33] With this background their son, Berry Gordy Jr. [*sic*], did not need to major in math.

Apart from his family the two other formative influences on Berry Gordy Jr. were the Ford Motor Company, famous for paying blacks an equal wage and pioneering the assembly-line method of production; and the diverse music scene in Detroit. Gordy worked on the Ford line as a young man, while also pursuing a keen interest in music, specifically bebop. He started his own jazz label, but soon realized that the only money in music lay in R&B. He began as a songwriter, selling a couple of songs to R&B star Jackie Wilson. But soon he was persuaded by his associate, the young singer Smokey Robinson, that the only way to prevent exploitation was through expansion. By 1960 Gordy had incorporated his own publishing company, record label and subsidiaries, talent management outfit, record manufacturing plant, and distribution firm.

Beginning in 1961 with Robinson's "Shop Around" and continuing through 1971, Motown releases made the top ten listings in the pop chart no less than 110 times. Given this remarkable success, one would think that Motown would have an impressive collection of gold records. But it doesn't. Nelson George explains why:

> Motown would be very strict about who had access to its books. Artists would only be allowed to review them two times a year and no industry regulatory group, such as the Recording Industry Association of America, the organization that awards gold and platinum albums, would be allowed to audit the company's books (a policy that didn't change until the late seventies, which is why none of Motown's hits of the sixties was ever certified gold).[34]

George describes Gordy's management style as paternalistic, even autocratic, toward the Motown "family" (which included many of his relatives) and distrustful, even paranoid, toward outsiders. To some degree, this portrait fits George's general depiction of self-made black businessmen as "suspicious both of white authority and of black deceit or incompetence."

Because such suspicion can drive these businessmen to the point of "doing a poor job of utilizing and motivating personnel," George hints that it may be one reason, apart from white racism, why there have been so few successful black record companies.[35] Yet, as George himself makes clear, this profile of the distrustful black businessman fits a lone wolf like Chuck Berry better than it does Gordy, because Gordy did, in fact, know how to use talent and delegate responsibility. No doubt this is why he is still respected, even by cultural separatists, as the black David who slew the white Goliath of the record industry.

Yet, like Chuck Berry, Gordy presents a paradox: The whole purpose of his tightly managed "production line" was to refine black musical talent into a standardized product that would sell in white markets from Eastport, Maine, to Chula Vista, California. Indeed, Gordy was the very image of a counterrevolutionary: Just as the major labels were taking Italian kids off the streets of Philadelphia and molding them into Fabians and Frankie Avalons, so Gordy was taking black kids off the streets of Detroit and molding them into Miracles, Temptations, and Supremes. Only Gordy went even further, hiring professional choreographers and finishing-school instructors to drill his teen idols in precision dance moves and upper-middle-class body language. In the oft-repeated motto of Maxine Powell, Motown's director of Artist Development, these carefully groomed acts "were being trained to perform in only two places: Buckingham Palace and the White House."[36]

As for the records, they were meticulously engineered in the studio. Motown was not the leader in studio technique at the time; that title must go to Phil Spector, the boy wizard who spent the early 1960s perfecting the art of overproducing rock 'n' roll. I say "overproducing" because, as far as musical values are concerned, Spector's early hits depart from the Afro-American tradition in one crucial respect: They do not emphasize the distinctive expressive qualities of individual voices and instruments. With the exception of the lead singers in his "girl groups" (the Crystals and Ronettes), Spector treated voices as mere units of manipulable sound. And that went double for instruments, as described by the musician-writer Andy Mackay: "Spector used a large number of musicians, all playing much the same part. The musicians were deliberately tired out by long sessions and repetitive parts, in order to produce an impersonal element in the wall of sound, the phrase most often used to describe the echo-laden, quasi-orchestral texture of Spector's records."[37]

Motown borrowed some of Spector's techniques, such as limiters and equalizers to squeeze more volume into the narrow frequency range of the transistor radio. As might be expected from a company based in Detroit, Motown was acutely aware that (in George's words) "fifty million radios were rolling around the country in car dashboards." Reporting that no Motown record was ever pressed until chief engineer Mike McClain had quality-checked it on his own "minuscule, tinny-sounding radio designed to approximate the sound of a car radio," George states that the "high-end bias of Motown recordings can be partially traced to the company's reliance on this piece of equipment."[38] No doubt this "high-end bias" explains why, apart from looks and hustle, Diana Ross became lead singer of the Supremes. As another Motown star, Marvin Gaye, recalls, "Diana's voice was the perfect instrument to cut through those sound waves."[39] Certainly her pennywhistle soprano has no other discernible claim to superiority over the richer, gospel-inflected voices of Mary Wilson and (especially) Florence Ballard.

These decidedly counterrevolutionary practices are likely reasons why our dyed-in-the-denim 1960s rock critic Jahn dismisses Motown as "a black-owned version of popular schmaltz."[40] Yet the goal of Motown's electronic tinkering was less to build a featureless "wall of sound" than to project distinctive voices and instruments through a limited medium. We need only recite a few names—Mary Wells, Smokey Robinson, the Four Tops, Marvin Gaye, Gladys Knight, the Temptations, Stevie Wonder—to recall the success of this approach. From the heights of Robinson's gauzy countertenor (which succeeds in combining "high-end bias" with musicality) to the depths of Temptation Melvin Franklin's resonant bass, the voices of Motown are recognizable even when the names and faces are not.

Motown also used superior instrumentalists. Here is George's account of how William ("Mickey") Stevenson, Motown's director of Artists and Repertory (A&R), acquired his session players:

> Stevenson helped Berry inaugurate a jazz label called Jazz Workshop, and, using it as an inducement, Stevenson got several players under dual contract as recording artists *and* staff musicians. For Motown, it ensured a reliable, skilled group of players who were always on call. For the musicians, many of whom were bebop fanciers from the fertile East Coast jazz scene, Jazz Workshop held the promise that they would be able to record the music they really loved. So they tolerated playing Motown's "Mickey Mouse music" for session fees . . . [and] for the often-illusory opportunity to record jazz.[41]

Disingenuous though this strategy may have been, it is hardly in the same category as Spector's habit of rehearsing his session men into a malleable stupor.

Finally Motown stressed songwriting. Like the New York music publishers whose offices filled the Brill Building on Broadway in the early 1960s, Gordy organized a contemporary version of Tin Pan Alley. Robinson was the first, and in some ways the most gifted and prolific. But there were plenty of others: Stevenson, Gaye, the team of Holland-Dozier-Holland, Barrett Strong, Norman Whitfield, and so forth. Gordy knew how to pit all these talented people against one another in a fierce but creative competition.

Jahn calls Motown music "popular schmaltz" because it was produced by techniques similar to those used by the majors when producing ersatz rock 'n' roll. Yet, despite its unblushing reputation as a "hit factory," Motown at its best managed to produce music of considerable wit, fervor, and vitality. Even more than Chuck Berry, the example of Motown suggests that commercialism is a neutral, rather than a negative, factor. The most vigorous periods in popular music occur whenever someone like Milt Gabler, Sam Phillips, or Berry Gordy comes along to show that business acumen can indeed be combined with taste. The anticommercial bias of high culture insists that this combination is impossible. But I would reply that it is simply, like all good things, rare.

Back to the Well: Southern Soul

Let us return for a moment to 1959, the year the music supposedly died. As George observes, a more accurate view of that year reveals a compelling sign of life: "Many rock & roll historians, with their characteristic bias toward youth rebellion, claim that the last two years of the fifties were a musically fallow period. But that claim only works if you're willing to ignore Ray Charles's brilliant work."[42]

The smooth harmonies and heightened emotions of doo-wop recall various strains of gospel quartet singing. But quartet is only one side of gospel. The other side is the tradition of solo evangelism, a combination of preaching and singing against the spontaneous but stylized responses of the choir and congregation.[43] Quartet and solo evangelism have never been mutually exclusive: Often the lead singer of a quartet doubles as an evangelist. As we've seen, there is also an abiding priestly dimension to the role of the performer in blues and jazz. Whether or not he plays this role for white audiences, the black musician in these secular fields rarely succeeds with his own people if he neglects its proper rituals and communal atmosphere. Yet this does not mean that the sacred and secular roles are identical. There have always been significant differences—at least until the end of the 1950s, when black singers like Sam Cooke, James Brown, and Ray Charles came along with the popular style known as soul.

More than the others, Cooke came directly from gospel. The son of a Chicago minister, he was raised in choirs and reached the zenith of gospel success in 1950, when, at age fifteen, he was chosen to replace Rebert H. Harris as the lead singer of the Soul Stirrers. With his father's approval, but to the dismay of many in the gospel field, Cooke began recording secular music in 1957. Almost immediately he had a hit, "You Send Me," and in 1960 he signed with a major label, RCA, which did not know what to do with him. Because he was young and handsome, RCA tried to squeeze Cooke first into the teen-idol mold, and then into the pop crooner mold. For a couple of years the singer floundered, searching for a popular style that would utilize his rich, velvety voice with its seemingly effortless melisma. If he hadn't been shot under dubious circumstances in 1964, Cooke might well have found his way back to the sanctified style that was his true medium. To compare his gospel recordings with his better secular recordings is to be struck by the resemblance, and in some cases, the identity between the two.[44]

Next is the "Godfather of Soul," James Brown. According to the gospel music historian Anthony Heilbut, Brown was greatly influenced by Ira Tucker of the legendary gospel quartet, the Dixie Hummingbirds, whose range extended from mellow quartet harmonizing to solo evangelizing in the style known as "hard singing": shouting, keening, moaning, screaming, and exhortation. Tucker was also known for jumping off the stage, racing up and down the aisles, dropping to his knees, and writhing in ecstasy. Except for Little Richard, Brown was the first secular performer to adopt such "Devil-destroying" routines.[45]

In the early 1960s, however, Brown's popularity with whites was limited compared with that of his contemporary, Ray Charles. Although Charles started out in the late 1940s trying to croon like Nat ("King") Cole, he lacked Cole's natural vocal gift. So, after signing with Atlantic in 1954, he moved toward a rougher style, described by Pleasants as "an extraordinary assortment of slurs, glides, turns, shrieks, wails, breaks, shouts, screams and hollers, all wonderfully controlled, disciplined by inspired musicianship, and harnessed to ingenious subtleties of harmony, dynamics and rhythm."[46] In addition, Charles introduced into popular music a new kind of song structure, described here by the British critic Iain Chambers: "From gospel, soul music took the use of a repetitive harmonic pattern which often employed only a pair of chords ('harmonic ostinato'). The song was perpetually threatened by a resolution which never arrived, the chords rolling to a summit and then falling away again. It often produced a seemingly 'timeless' structure."[47]

Many blacks objected to this new style, seeing it as a sinful secularization of sacred music. As the blues singer Big Bill Broonzy put it, Charles shouldn't have been "mixin' the blues with the spirituals," but "singin' in a church."[48] Yet, as discussed earlier, the line between sacred and secular has always been tricky to draw on strictly musical grounds. Charles himself insists that the gospel-blues distinction is artificial: "This was not a thing where I was tryin' to take the church music and make the blues out of it or vice versa. . . . I was raised in the church . . . singin' in the church and hearin' this good singin' in the church and also hearin' the blues, I guess this was the only way I *could* sing."[49]

Still, it's important to recall that, even more than blues, gospel was the exclusive property of blacks in the early 1960s. The main reason why blacks objected to Charles's style was probably uneasiness about the speed at which something sacred was being packaged and sold to whites. By 1959, when Charles's rhythmic shouter "What'd I Say?" became a pop hit, the trend was clear. Not only was sanctified music moving out of church, it was also moving out of the neighborhood.

The term *soul* had been circulating in elite jazz circles for the previous decade, where, like the literary term *négritude*, it summed up a mystique of blackness that is hard to define intellectually, but serves the psychological, political and philosophical function of turning a negative stigma into a positive standard.[50] In jazz *soul* referred to the black reaction against the cool style pioneered by Miles Davis in the early 1950s but subsequently dominated by whites such as Dave Brubeck. Cool jazz softens bebop's hard-edged intensity through an emphasis on pure tone, lyrical melody, rich chromaticism, and the use of classical structures such as the rondo and the fugue.[51] Since these changes move jazz closer to European music, it was inevitable that at least some black jazz musicians would want to move it back toward African rhythms and down-home strains of blues and gospel. Charles was well aware of these developments (for example, he and Charles Mingus both recorded for Atlantic), so it is no accident that he was the one to inject gospel into the popular mainstream.[52]

Nevertheless, there are important differences between the elite soul jazz of the 1950s and the popular soul music of the 1960s. Like bebop, soul jazz tended to be anticommercial; and like free jazz, it inclined toward black cultural separatism. Soul music, by contrast, kept a hungry eye on the market, including the white market. Not only that, but it violated the cultural-separatist standard of racial purity by being the product of intimate collaborations between black and white entrepreneurs, producers and musicians. And finally, because most of these collaborations took place in the South, soul music was also different from the distinctly Northern phenomenon of soul jazz. Indeed, it is best understood as a regional as well as a racial revitalization.

Just to illustrate the point, here are a few words from Jim Stewart, the former C&W fiddler who founded the greatest soul label of all, Stax Records in Memphis:

> I had scarcely seen a black till I was grown. I didn't know when I started, I didn't know there was such a thing as an Atlantic Records. I didn't know there was a Chess Records or Imperial. I had no desire to start Stax Records, I had no dream of anything like that. I just wanted music. Just anything to be involved with music—one way or the other.[53]

With the help of Rufus Thomas, a DJ on Memphis's pioneer black radio station, Stewart and his business partner (and sister) Estelle Axton soon began producing hit records featuring the talents of black R&B musicians and young Memphis whites equally steeped in the music. For example, the black keyboardist Booker T. Jones and the white guitarist Steve Cropper created the sound later immortalized as "Memphis Soul Stew."[54] To this zesty concoction was soon added the essential vocal ingredient. As Gillett recalls:

> Otis Redding's "Pain in My Heart" (1963) showed producer Steve Cropper closer to working out a suitable arrangement and instrumental sound to back up gospel-styled singing. Repetitive piano chords still linked the song to earlier types of ballads, but Cropper's guitar was now assuming the role of gospel group, answering, echoing, and developing vocal phrases in much the same way Ray Charles's band had substituted for a gospel group in "I Got a Woman" ten years earlier.[55]

Similar ingredients came together in the tiny Fame studio located in Muscle Shoals, Alabama (the birthplace of Sam Phillips). And it was not long before both tiny Southern labels were joining forces with the strongest surviving R&B label, Atlantic. Having survived the rock 'n' roll years by signing performers such as Big Joe Turner, Bobby Darin, the Drifters, and Ray Charles, Atlantic was well positioned to channel Southern soul into the mainstream.

Actually "channel" is not the right word, because although its interracial collaborations broke up rather bitterly at the end of the decade, the story of

Southern soul is not, as some would have it, simply a tale of rapacious white businessmen exploiting noble black artists. That plot was played out. But so were many others. Few chroniclers have more sympathy for the economically powerless black musician than Guralnick; yet he credits Atlantic with playing a creative role, writing that the label's trademark was "a kind of downhome sound with a sophisticated twist."[56]

Finally, the most important fact about Southern soul is that during the late 1950s and early 1960s, it was the only form of American popular music not tailored exclusively to youth. Soul emerged from collaborations that were not only interracial and interregional, but also intergenerational. Of course, there were older people involved in making teen-idol and girl-group rock 'n' roll. But it was only in soul that the elders did not lower their standards in an effort to reach the youth market. For this reason, soul qualifies as a true revitalization. Rhythmically, it asserts Afro-American complexity against the increasingly simplified backbeat of rock 'n' roll. Vocally, it asserts the power and expressiveness of gospel and blues against the feeble pipings of most teen idols and girl groups. And lyrically, it asserts a broader range of emotion and experience than could be found in the narrow compass of the industry's market research. Thus Southern soul not only refutes the counterrevolutionary myth, it also reinforces the argument that in popular culture, the bad does not always drive out the good. When the circumstances are propitious, the public can and will reject fool's gold in favor of the twenty-four-carat real thing.

Chapter 10

Another Country
Heard From

Although I have challenged the term *revolution* as applied to 1950s rock 'n' roll, I cannot quarrel with the term *British Invasion* as applied to the swift transformation of the American popular music market in the mid-1960s. From the point of view of native talent, it was definitely an invasion—and an ill-timed one at that. Between Motown and Southern soul, records by black performers maintained a constant presence on the pop charts throughout the early 1960s: Between 1955 and 1963 the number reaching the top ten increased by more than 50 percent; in 1963, thirty-seven of the 101 top ten hits were by black acts.[1] As for British imports, a handful had made the American charts during the previous five years, but not one in 1963. British rock 'n' roll was regarded as yet another form of fool's gold, and the idea of a British act capturing the American market would have struck most people as laughable.

Then came the deluge. In 1964 the number of black top-ten singles dropped to twenty-one, their lowest level since 1956. And the number of British records reaching the top ten climbed to thirty-one, almost a third of the total.[2] Motown and Southern soul put up some resistance, but as I shall try to explain in the next two chapters, the British Invasion was better armed culturally, if not always musically.

The Purists Across the Pond

In the 1950s most middle- and upper-class British fans of Afro-American music preferred older styles. As Gillett writes:

> There had been a tradition in Britain since the twenties, maintained by a substantial minority of people, of being interested in declining forms of Negro popular music. As a succession of stylistic trends in the United States rendered various styles virtually obsolete, a group of enthusiasts in Europe devoted themselves to perpetuating the music by collecting records, by importing, if possible, the original performers to Europe to make a tour or even take up residence, and by playing the music themselves.[3]

Along with this preference for older styles went a fastidious purism that rejected all subsequent styles, and deplored the forces (especially the commercial ones) that had fostered the change. Not surprisingly, the next step was factionalism, as described by the sociologist Iain Chambers:

> Traditional jazz, the music of a pre–First World War New Orleans, played in strict ensemble, employing march times and containing no instrumental solos, had its high priest in Ken Colyer. . . . Trad jazz grew out of a deep aversion to "swing" and its "decadent commercialism." . . . The debates and acrimonious disputes that raged in British jazz in the 1950s completely excluded any modernist tendencies. The struggle was between "trad" and "revival" jazz. The latter being the jazz of the 1920s following its migration north to Chicago. It was most widely associated with Louis Armstrong's Hot Five. In both cases, a stern morality scorned the subsequent commercialisation of a one-time "folk" music and insisted upon the "authenticity" of the respectively championed musics.[4]

Ultimately these purist distinctions derived from the Stalinist double-think of the 1930s—as did the purism of those British folk music fans who worshiped Appalachian ballads and country blues to the exclusion of all other popular forms. Many British folkies were hard-shell leftists who not only preferred the old folk styles, but also wanted the lyrics to focus on hard times and class exploitation rather than on such frivolous topics as gambling, drinking, the traveling life, or the battle of the sexes. Thus British folkies adored Josh White, a former gospel and cabaret singer whose association with Woody Guthrie and Pete Seeger in the early 1940s had enriched his repertory with protest numbers such as "Bad Housing Blues," "Jim Crow Train," "Uncle Sam Says," and "Defense Factory Blues."[5] The fact that these were not traditional blues did not deter folk purists concerned less with the depth of a singer's roots in the Afro-American tradition than with his willingness to sing about social injustice.

Even British folkies who were not rigid leftists preferred their blues strictly acoustic and country, without any of the trappings of show business or the modern urban environment. This was a pretty tall order, given the central role played by the blues in every type of Afro-American music from vaudeville to jazz, gospel to R&B. The blues historian Paul Oliver explains:

> Were the blues a simple folk music local to one area, native to a small social group and tied to a firm tradition of standardized form and instrumentation, as is the case with many forms of folk music in various parts of the world, the identification and appreciation of its peculiar properties would present no undue difficulty. But the blues was sung and played in districts that are literally thousands of miles apart. . . . It was a music that was common to persons living under the most primitive rural circumstances and in the high pressure of modern city life.[6]

Ironically, the purism of the folkies was skillfully mined by such enterprising bluesmen as Big Bill Broonzy, one of the most popular "race" recording artists of the 1930s. Recording on the independent Bluebird label in Chicago, Broonzy had moved easily between the acoustic blues of his native Mississippi and more swing-oriented music, actually making his best records with a small jazz combo. Broonzy did not, however, make the 1940s transition to electrified blues, leaving that field to his protégé, Muddy Waters. Still, he did not retire. In the time-honored Afro-American tradition, he spent the 1940s hustling himself a new gig. In his astute history of the Mississippi blues, Robert Palmer describes how

> a left-wing and generally naive young audience accepted [Broonzy], along with Leadbelly, Sonny Terry, and Brownie McGhee as true folk artists. Broonzy's dozens of Bluebird records with bass, drums and jazz band backing were conveniently forgotten, and he played the role of the folk bluesman fresh from the cotton fields to the hilt.[7]

The only drawback to this strategy was the loss of vital contact with audiences intimate with the blues. Imagine the dismay felt by even the most gifted bluesman in a situation like this one described by Keil:

> An affair I witnessed in London featured an array of elderly bluesmen, a few of them quite decrepit. . . . The same show presented to a Negro audience in

Chicago (assuming they could be enticed into watching such a parade of invalids in the first place) would be received with hoots of derision, catcalls, and laughter. The thousands of Englishmen assembled for the event listened to each song in awed silence; the more ludicrous the performance, the more thunderous the applause at its conclusion.[8]

When asked about the authenticity of his material, Broonzy's standard reply was: "I guess all songs is folk songs. I never heard no horse sing 'em."[9] Helped, no doubt, by his wry humor, Broonzy remained a fixture on the British folk circuit until 1958, at which point his health failed, and he suggested to his sponsors that they replace him with Muddy Waters.

Muddy Waters readily agreed, since (as we've seen) his brand of blues had never crossed over to the white American audience. Yet regrettably, he knew nothing of British purism. Palmer describes how, assuming that his new fans were primed for the loud, gritty, electrified sound of Chicago blues, Muddy Waters "cranked up his amplifier, hit a crashing bottleneck run, and began hollering his blues."[10] The reaction was outrage: Such "decadent commercialism" was not to be tolerated. Fortunately, Muddy Waters proved as flexible as Broonzy had before him. "Now I know that people in England like soft guitar and the old blues," he commented. "Next time I come I'll learn some old songs first."[11]

I hasten to add that not everyone in Britain was worried about "decadent commercialism." There were plenty of ordinary people who would gladly have enjoyed it, if only they'd had the chance. But there was a big difference between Britain and America in the 1950s: While America had a fertile, decentralized popular culture, Britain had a strong, centralized cultural authority and no popular culture to speak of. Gillett explains:

> The reaction to rock 'n' roll in Britain had been slightly different from the reaction in the States, where it had evolved gradually out of relationships between audiences and performers, which had expressed themselves through secondary channels of communication, the specialist radio stations and maverick disc jockeys. In Britain, there was no comparable network of secondary media. There was an establishment, and virtually nothing else.[12]

The elitism of the British cultural establishment still confers certain advantages. As any admirer of the British dramatic arts will attest, it makes possible something that occurs only sporadically in America: the circulation of top theatrical talent through both the film and television industries. But such a system is poor at growing talent from the grass roots. Unlike Afro-American music, British folk music had never taken dynamic commercial form. As the historian Ian Whitcomb writes, "There was no Welsh hillbilly, no cornish ragtime, no Highland jazz."[13] During the late 1940s and early 1950s, when young Americans were twirling their radio dials to catch the vivid sounds of C&W, R&B, blues, and gospel, the government-owned BBC offered British radio listeners only two choices: a classical channel and the "Light Programme," which featured 1950s pop at its most insipid. The sole alternative was Radio Luxembourg, a continental station whose commercial English-language programming was dominated by the four major British record companies.[14]

Just as there were no small local radio stations in Britain, there were also no small independent record labels. Two of the majors, Decca and EMI, began importing American rock 'n' roll after the success in Britain of the film *The Blackboard Jungle*. By the late 1950s there was a small rock 'n' roll presence, imported and homegrown, on the Light Programme and in a few record stores. And American groups such as Bill Haley's were touring Britain quite successfully. But during the key period of the late 1940s and early 1950s, when R&B was attracting a mass following in America, it was virtually unknown in Britain. That's why rock 'n' roll sounded so radically new when it arrived.

New and dangerous. Long-standing British fears about juvenile delinquency were revived when rioting and vandalism broke out in theaters showing *The Blackboard Jungle*. According to Gillett, this and subsequent American films with rock 'n' roll soundtracks "provoked audiences in some working class areas to rip out the movie seats in order to give themselves room to jive."[15]

Yet, as the word "jive" suggests, these fears were exaggerated. The salient fact is that in Britain, as in America, rock 'n' roll was primarily a dance craze. But, precisely for that reason, it precipitated a crisis between restless British youth and a cultural establishment that, in true highbrow fashion, permitted only "strict tempo" dance music to be played in public halls.[16] Lacking a setting in which to jitterbug and jive, the rowdier segments of British society created their own. To take this as proof that rock 'n' roll causes delinquency is to endorse the puritanical notion that dance and physical exuberance are by definition wicked. A more balanced assessment would be that, in a replay of the European crazes for ragtime and jazz, working-class British youth welcomed rock 'n' roll unself-consciously as an aid in overcoming physical inhibitions (not just sexual ones) ingrained in their culture. And they didn't worry too much about the taint of commerce, because from their war-weary point of view, the commercial trappings of rock 'n' roll were simply part of its affluent, all-American allure.

The British Meaning of "Pop"

Here again, the experience of the majority had zero impact on what the elite decided to think about popular culture. The British elite, both in the cultural establishment and among folk purists, knew exactly what to think about rock 'n' roll. Perhaps because they felt so overwhelmed by American popular culture in general, they failed to make any distinction between the small, independent companies that had fostered R&B, and the large, monopolistic firms that had tried unsuccessfully to resist it. From the elite perspective, rock 'n' roll was no better than the 1950s pop purveyed in the dance halls and on the Light Programme. Both were tainted, so both were "pop."

It is crucial to note at this juncture that the British meaning of "pop" comes not from the American (or British) record industry, but from the visual arts. Specifically it comes from the peculiar environment of the British art colleges, unique institutions that had been occupying a sort of cultural no-man's-land since the Victorian period, when they were founded by the government for the express purpose of improving the international competitiveness of British industrial design. This mission seems clear enough, but as the sociologist Simon Frith explains, it was complicated by the fact that artistically talented people in the nineteenth century were distrustful of commerce and industry: "The Schools of Design were intended for artisans, not artists, but even they were well-versed in the creative stance. Romanticism, in all its political and stylistic shades, gripped the nineteenth-century artist's imagination: art education became the natural setting for the bohemian battle with convention."[17]

The battle continued, under different guises, right through the end of World War II, at which point the art colleges became the first British institutions to react to the influx of American popular culture. As the art historian Carol Anne Mahsun reports, this reaction gave rise to the term "pop":

> The British critic Lawrence Alloway has laid claim to having coined the term "pop." Originally it referred to popular culture or the mass media and became commonly used in reference to works of a group of artists interested in redeeming popular culture. . . . The term was employed in conjunction with an expansionist aesthetic that strove to integrate art and the manmade environment of the fifties. . . . The group drew criticism at the time because an admiration of American films, ads, science fiction, and commercial photography was equated with being pro-American.[18]

Significantly, Mahsun's list of American imports does not include music. In the beginning, British pop art focused almost exclusively on the visual media. Yet the art college crowd overlapped with the folkie crowd, so it was inevitable that the sensibilities of the pop art movement would spill over into the folk music movement, where they posed a direct challenge to purism: If pop art's "expansionist aesthetic" applied to American commercial art and advertising, then why not to the styles of American music defined as "decadent commercialism"[19]

Over the years, this visual-arts orientation has made it extremely difficult for Britons to take show business in their stride, the way Big Bill Broonzy did. Whether rushing to embrace "pop" or vehemently rejecting it, Britons have tended to go to self-conscious extremes. Winston Churchill summed up this mentality very well when he remarked about his countrymen: "Some see private enterprise as a predatory target to be shot, others as a cow to be milked, but few see it as a sturdy horse pulling the wagon."[20]

From Skiffle to Ed Sullivan: The Rise of the Beatles

Without the vital network of secondary media that existed in the United States, it was hard for the United Kingdom to grow its own rock 'n' roll talent in the 1950s. After the success of *The Blackboard Jungle*, the big record companies began developing rock 'n' roll acts. But most were like Tommy Steele, imitations of American imitations, with little to offer musically. Still, there were a few, notably Cliff Richard, who managed to capture some of the excitement of the original. Ironically, but not surprisingly, these better "pop" performers honed their skills among the purist folkies.

The link was Lonnie Donegan, a member of two highly regarded trad jazz bands who enjoyed remaining on stage between sets to instruct the audience about the roots of trad jazz. Singing the usual Appalachian ballads and country blues to the accompaniment of an old, battered guitar, Donegan would invite the audience to play along on handmade instruments, such as jugs, washboards, kazoos, jerry-built banjos, and basses made of boxes, broomsticks, and string. The idea was to re-create the so-called "spasm band" street music of turn-of-the-century New Orleans, a form that survived long enough to be recorded in the 1920s under the name of "jug" or "skiffle" music.

Skiffle, as it came to be called in Britain, started out as a purist phenomenon, abjuring all taint of commercialism in "factory-made instruments."[21] But the craze soon spread to the nonpurist majority, who not only used whatever instruments they could get their hands on, they also played whatever material struck their fancy. Before Ken Colyer could say "decadent commercialism," the whole country (including Cliff Richard) was happily thumping away at skiffle versions of R&B, rock 'n' roll, even pop standards. Like the Afro-American idiom whose eager stepchild it was, skiffle respected few barriers—not even the quintessentially British ones of social class. As Chambers writes:

> Although deeply despised by the purists in both the jazz and folk worlds, and largely excluded from the Hit Parade by the increasingly professional organization of pop music, the popular format of skiffle . . . offered a major democratisation of music-making. With little money and limited musical skill it became possible to become directly involved in a popular music. By 1957, there were numerous amateur skiffle competitions being regularly held everywhere in Britain and literally thousands of groups.[22]

Out of those thousands it was inevitable that some would develop a more sophisticated style. It was not by chance that this occurred in the industrial North, since that was the part of England most saturated with Afro-American music. In particular, Liverpool had a large Irish population interested in Appalachian ballads, and a smaller black population fond of the blues. Liverpool was also a port city teeming with merchant and military seamen, including many Americans with a taste for the latest C&W, R&B, and rock 'n' roll. When these visitors weren't trading records with the locals, they were seeking ways to spend their dollars on live music—an opportunity not lost on the city's skiffle players.[23] As working-class pubgoers rather than middle-class clubgoers, those amateurs had no purist compunctions about transferring their talents to more up-to-date instruments. The new style, dubbed "Merseybeat," is here described by the London music impresario, Alexis Korner:

> There was a certain brashness about the Liverpool music which stamped it almost immediately—they played it the way they speak English, you know! . . . The Mersey Sound was basically a guitar sound: lead guitar, rhythm guitar, bass guitar and drums was the Liverpool setup. What really caught on was not so much the Mersey Sound but guitars, purely and simply guitars, electric guitars.[24]

Playing countless rough gigs in the cellar clubs of Liverpool, as well as across the North Sea in Hamburg, Germany (another watering hole for U.S. sailors), the Merseybeat groups demonstrated a hungry dedication to both music and business that would have won them respect on America's chitlin circuit.

The difference, of course, was that Merseybeat groups had even slimmer prospects of breaking into the big time than the denizens of the chitlin circuit. But, as it happens, Liverpool was blessed with the British equivalent of Sam Phillips: a middle-class striver named Brian Epstein, who had begun in the late 1950s to sell records out of his family's furniture store. In 1961 Epstein picked up the local enthusiasm for a particular Merseybeat group called the Beatles, who had evolved from a skiffle group known as the Quarrymen. He went to hear them and decided that they had a little something extra that was otherwise lacking in Merseybeat music. He then proceeded, in the amazingly short span of three years, to sell that little something, first to his fellow Britons, and then, on a scale beyond even his wildest dreams, to the rest of the world.

No one can study Epstein's activities between 1961 and 1964 without reeling in amazement at his audacity and persistence. He began by hiring a Hamburg photographer to clean up the image of the greasy-haired, T-shirted, leather-jacketed quartet. With tidy collarless suits and girlish hair-cuts, John Lennon, Paul McCartney, George Harrison, and Pete Best soon resembled a cross between choirboys and the zoot-suited working-class youth who had begun calling themselves "Teddy boys" in the mid-1950s. Epstein's next moves were to replace Best with a new drummer named Ringo Starr (Richard Starkey); to cajole a contract out of the powerful British label EMI; to book the group with maximum publicity into venues throughout the UK; and to woo and bully the media into paying attention, encouraging the use of such tabloid expressions as "Moptops," "Fab Four" and "Beatlemania."

Epstein was especially adept at parlaying the Beatles' humble origins into a selling point, both for working-class youth and for middle- and upper-class youth intrigued by a certain postwar cultural mystique of working-class life initiated by the playwrights known as Angry Young Men and then popularized through JD films and attempted British clones such as Billy Fury and Marty Wild. Only Epstein was smart enough to make his Young Men not Angry but Cute. It is sometimes suggested that Epstein's own sup-pressed homoeroticism gave him an instinct for bringing out the Beatles' cuteness. This may be the case, but it is also true that the group offered a refreshing update on the working-class mystique. In Gillett's words:

> Their social message was rarely expressed, but hung about their heads as an aura of impatience with convention and evident satisfaction with wealth and fame. ... . Where the [Angry Young Men] had shown working-class youth as caged within a harsh physical world, resentful towards those they believed had made it that way, but resigned to their place in such a world, the Beatles presented working-class youth as loose and free, glad to be out, unafraid to snub pretension, easily able to settle in comfortably where a rest could be found.[25]

These qualities were on triumphant display when the Beatles toured Europe in 1963, then returned home to give a Royal Command Performance at which Lennon famously asked Queen Elizabeth and her next of kin not to applaud, "just rattle your jewelry."[26]

Some observers have attributed this "cheekiness" to the irreverent comedy of the British music hall (similar to vaudeville).[27] Others have stressed the influence of postwar American popular culture. Either way, the question soon became: Would the Beatles play in Peoria? Epstein decided that they would. Having too much respect for the anarchy of American radio to break the group there, he zeroed in on America's most centralized medium: television. Ed Sullivan had witnessed Beatlemania in Britain, and commented to the press that it reminded him of the Presley craze. So Epstein made Sullivan an offer he couldn't refuse: three appearances on Sullivan's weekly variety show at half the going rate. Sullivan accepted, and the first Beatles appearance on American television attracted a record-breaking viewership of 73 million.[28]

But Epstein didn't stop to savor that victory; he was too busy end-running EMI's American subsidiary, Capitol Records, which had declined to issue the Beatles' first few singles. Taking full advantage of the anarchy of the American music business, Epstein released the singles on the black-owned independent label, Vee Jay—which nearly went bankrupt trying to pay for enough pressings to meet the demand. Vee Jay's grip on the Beatles lasted only until Capitol sniffed pay dirt; then the Beatles switched labels, and Epstein began priming Capitol with bright ideas about how to spend an unprecedented promotional budget of $50,000.[29] After a wildly successful American tour in 1964, Epstein kept the pressure on: rushing the film *A Hard Day's Night* into quick release, keeping new singles and albums coming, and in general oiling his contacts with American opinion makers.

It would be a mistake, though, to attribute the Beatles' rise entirely to Epstein's business acumen. For, like Sam Phillips before him, Epstein had made a real discovery. Musically the Beatles *did* have an edge over the other Merseybeat groups. In keeping with the skiffle craze, and indeed with most British efforts to assimilate the Afro-American idiom, the majority of Merseybeat players emphasized instrumental over vocal proficiency. Transferring the techniques of skiffle to the electric guitar, they specialized in playing rock 'n' roll hits in the loud "rave-up" manner required by the rough young crowds in Liverpool and Hamburg.

The Beatles aspired to playing in the rave-up manner, too, but their real musical strength lay elsewhere. In the EMI studio, with an inspired producer named George Martin, they began to focus on a flair for vocal harmony that had been introduced into the group by Lennon. Significantly, Lennon was the only Beatle to have attended art college, and he hadn't liked it. Between 1957 and 1960, he had been an insecure—and resentful—working-class student at the predominantly middle-class Liverpool College of Art. But, for the Beatles' purposes, Lennon had not wasted his time. To express his resentment he had spent those years sneering at the trad jazz scene and ferreting out every form of politically incorrect music he could find—from Presley, Berry, and Little Richard to C&W and R&B sources unheard by British ears.[30] In particular, Lennon urged his fellow Beatles to study American vocal groups, from the Everly Brothers to Motown, from Buddy Holly and the Crickets to doo-wop, from the Delmore Brothers to Alex Bradford's Greater Abyssinian Baptist Choir.[31]

To list these influences is not to disparage the Beatles' initial accomplishment. On the contrary, they lived up to their many predecessors in the Afro-American idiom by stressing creative recombination over radical innovation. From Berry and Holly they took electric-guitar riffs and the importance of writing their own material; from the vocal groups and gospel, they took the knack of mixing harmony with rhythm and the use of a mid-tempo range to maximize the effect of their singing; from Motown and Phil Spector, they took an emphasis on studio technique; from skiffle, they took a preference for self-played instrumentation over lavish studio arrangements. Given Martin's guidance and the group's natural talents, not to mention Lennon's and McCartney's gift for collaborative songwriting, these elements combined in a nifty new style.

I use the word "nifty" in a deliberate attempt to avoid the hyperbole that inflates most writing, past and present, about the Beatles. Basically the group replicated the experience of the first white rock 'n' rollers: their splendid early style qualified as a truly original contribution to the Afro-American idiom, one of the few arising from a nonblack source. But it wasn't as original as their fellow Britons thought, due to two factors: first, the lack of British exposure to R&B; and second, the passionate desire for a distinctively British style of music capable of reversing the rock 'n' roll trade deficit. As Gillett recalls, this combination of ignorance and patriotism made the Beatles the Great British Hope:

> The gospel-harmony groups had very little success in Britain, and the result for the British audience was a sound with a familiar rhythm and a novel vocal style. The way the Beatles echoed one another's phrases, dragged out words across several beats, shouted "yeah", and went into falsetto cries, was received in Britain as their own invention; it seemed that Britain had finally discovered an original, indigenous rock and roll style.[32]

Then there was the cultural establishment, wearing the usual blinkers toward Afro-American music. According to Lennon, "the first intellectual reviewer of the Beatles" was a *London Times* critic named William Mann, who "wrote about aeolian cadences and all sorts of musical terms" that impressed "the middle classes and the intellectuals." Like the masses of Beatlemaniacs, Mann displayed little awareness of the Beatles' musical sources, basically crediting the group with having invented the combination of quartet singing and propulsive rhythm. But unlike the Beatlemaniacs, who imagined this combination to be uniquely British, Mann imagined it to be uniquely European. That is, he praised the Beatles for restoring the European emphasis on harmony and melody to what he otherwise regarded as a barbarous cacophony of rhythm. Among those members of the elite who had been gazing with horror on the spectacle of British youth lost to Dionysian revels, Mann offered the hope that the spirit of Apollo, breathing through the "aeolian cadences" of this new group, would restore civilization.

Of course, no self-respecting rock 'n' roller would accept such a compliment, which is why Lennon called Mann "a bullshitter."[33]

A Touch of Camp: The Apotheosis of the Beatles

At this point, we depart from the musical question and move on to the cultural one. Here again, the Beatles' experience replicates that of the white rock 'n' rollers, in the sense that their musical originality was not the only, nor indeed the most important, cause of their fame. On both sides of the Atlantic, extramusical factors were equally crucial. As we've seen, one of these was the dazzling hype cloud whipped up by Epstein. But even the mightiest thunderhead of hype cannot create a phenomenon like the Beatles if the timing is less than perfect. For the Beatles, however, the moment was just right: Like the vapors ignited by Presley a decade before, the cultural atmosphere of the mid-1960s was in a highly volatile state, needing only the right spark to set it off.

As already mentioned, the Beatles' brash-but-cute image had powerful reverberations in Britain that went beyond the specific appeal of their musical style. Not only did they project a fresh update on the working-class mystique, they also exerted an undeniable homoerotic attraction for an establishment known to be top-heavy with gay men. In the United States these charms mattered less than the simple fact that the group was British. As with the Presley craze, the sheer scale of American Beatlemania moved a few highbrow pundits to drag out the old litany of warnings against "jungle rhythms" and "mass culture." But the most remarkable thing about the Beatles' conquest of America was how quickly it silenced these complaints. Faster than anyone could say "John-Paul-George-Ringo," the Fab Four were enjoying the one type of crossover success never achieved by America's native rock 'n' rollers. In the words of Jahn, "The Beatles, by being noticeably intelligent, proved that rock could have intellectual appeal."[34]

Jahn's phrase, "noticeably intelligent," captures the essence of the moment. The Beatles' predecessors, from Presley to Berry, had plenty of native intelligence. But the intelligence of poor white Southerners and blacks was hardly "noticeable" to America's educated elite. Along with plain old racism, that elite also suffered from chronic Dixiephobia—as illustrated by a 1956 *New York World Telegram* article beginning with the headline PRESLEY DRIVES 'EM WI-ULD WITH HIS SINGIN', WIGGLIN'.[35] At the same time, educated Americans suffer from a chronic Anglophilia that causes them to hear Shakespeare himself in the accents of anyone hailing from the British Isles.[36]

But most of all the Beatles' intelligence became "noticeable" when they distanced themselves from their exploding commercial success. Unfortunately for the black Americans who had cast their lot with Motown, the mid-1960s were a bad time to be straightforward and sincere about show-business glitz and upward mobility. This was certainly true in Britain, where a 1965 Motown tour failed to attract audiences and got dismissed by one Glasgow critic as "reminiscent of production numbers in pre-war Hollywood films." Ironically, all those charm-school lessons aimed at preparing ghetto youngsters to play Buckingham Palace led to one London critic's writing that Motown was too polished, lacking "the rough-edged common touch which is the vital link between the Beatles . . . and the audience."[37]

In America as well, the mid-1960s were a time of new attitudes toward commerce and culture. Hilton Kramer notes that 1964 was a pivotal year in this respect, seeing not only the debut of American pop art (as personified by Andy Warhol), but also the publication (in *Partisan Review*) of Susan Sontag's famous essay, "Notes on Camp." As Kramer explains, both pop art and camp involved a self-conscious rejection of high culture, combined with an equally self-conscious embrace of popular culture—the kitschier the better.[38] Sontag leaps about quite nimbly trying to delineate the shared camp attributes of the French Academy, Flash Gordon comics, Busby Berkeley musicals, and Japanese horror films. But it is Kramer who cuts to the heart of the matter, writing that camp offers "'forbidden' pleasure in objects that are corny, exaggerated, 'stupid,' or otherwise acknowledged to have failed by the respectable standards of the day," while also excluding "the 'straight' public." Thus camp skips the challenge of genuine art while keeping the avant-garde "distinction between 'us' and 'them'."[39] What Kramer knows, and Sontag's essay pretends not to know, is that 1960s camp was nothing new. Another name for it is perverse modernism.

I'm not saying that the Beatles took a camp attitude toward Afro-American music—that would come later. But they did add a touch of camp to their act, just enough to give them an edge on the black American competition. At a time when Motown performers were giving only happy-talk interviews to the press, the Beatles were putting on an equally calculated, but more up-to-date, show. Skilled in the art of deflecting British criticism of their craven "pop" commercialism, they (correctly) regarded the American media as a piece of cake. As Lennon later recalled: "When we arrived here we knew how to handle the press. The British press are the toughest in the world; we could handle anything."[40]

Boy, was he right! When asked by American reporters to sing, the Beatles grinned, "We need money first." When asked to explain their popularity, they retorted, "We have a press agent." When asked about possible female leads in an upcoming film, they quipped, "We're trying for the Queen. She sells."[41] Equally seductive was their stance toward high culture. Chuck Berry may have written "Roll Over, Beethoven," but few American journalists ever bothered to ask him what he actually thought of classical music. Berry's autobiography says that the song was inspired by his boyhood impatience at having to wait to use the family piano until his sisters finished practicing their Beethoven.[42] But this detail was never part of Berry's image. For one thing, the white stereotype of blacks simply does not include little girls playing sonatas. For another, Berry was a phenomenon of the 1950s, when all rock 'n' rollers were seen as coming from the backward South. How many reporters ever asked Presley or Lewis what they thought of Beethoven?

The Beatles, however, were different. Never mind that they were working-class blokes from Liverpool, no more likely than working-class blacks from St. Louis to have sisters practicing Beethoven. The Beatles looked like British schoolboys, so their American interlocutors assumed that they would have something to say about high culture. Needless to say, few Americans ever remarked on the complete evasiveness of Ringo's droll reply: "I think Beethoven's lovely . . . especially his poems."

Ill informed though it was, elite enthusiasm for the Beatles soon came to dominate public opinion in America. Combined with the genuine appeal of their music, the Beatles' touch of camp inspired hyperbole even in such highbrow critics as Richard Poirier, writing in a 1967 issue of *Partisan Review* that the group's genius was so great that it could not possibly be contained by any existing musical style, instrumentation, or recording technology.[43] Other, equally bedazzled scribblers credited the Beatles with having restored American optimism after the assassination of President John F. Kennedy.[44] In sum, as Gillett writes, "A large proportion of the Western world was determined to imbue the Beatles with all the qualities that could possibly be ascribed to any and all kinds of popular music."[45]

Of course, there were people in America who knew all about the Beatles' musical sources. But even here, the Beatles made conquests by consistently deflecting the hyperbole of less-than-knowledgeable pundits. Gillett reminds us that the foursome "kept telling anyone who would listen [that] there was nothing particularly new or startling in any of their records."[46] By paying frequent tribute to their Afro-American sources, the Beatles did a very smart thing: In 1964, just as the civil rights movement was making banner headlines, they distanced themselves from the old pattern of white appropriation without credit or compensation. Ironically, their music conformed to the pre-rock 'n' roll pattern of emphasizing harmony and melody over sonority and rhythm. (In this respect the *London Times* "bullshitter" had a point.) But at the same time the Beatles never let their audience forget that their most important sources were black. In this way they profited from both old and new patterns of white appropriation: They didn't dispute the highbrow perception that their music was more "civilized" than R&B, but they also came off as racially enlightened.

When we recall the various ups and downs that jazz experienced on the way to high-cultural status, the sudden apotheosis of the Beatles seems a case of history repeating itself as farce. However appealing their early style, it rarely approaches the musical artistry of jazz. To the question of why the group was taken so seriously, the answer lies not in their aesthetics, but in their attitudes.

Although America's white rock 'n' rollers lacked the musical sophistication found in jazz, they had a pretty clear idea of where they stood in the cultural hierarchy. Carl Perkins put it best when he said: "Rockabilly's simple music but it's not that easy to play."[47] By this light, the Beatles' true significance is not that they invented rock 'n' roll, or brought it to a level of distinction never before achieved by Afro-American music, or any of the other ridiculous claims made in their name. Instead, the Beatles' significance is that, in their charmingly flippant way, they began the process by which popular music would achieve an elevated cultural status for reasons that have little or nothing to do with Afro-American musical quality.

Chapter 11

Blues, Blacks, and Brits

he Beatles' astonishing success led record companies on both sides of the Atlantic to open their doors to any and all semblances of Merseybeat. Companies signed dozens of mop-topped look-alikes, such as Peter and Gordon, Gerry and the Pacemakers, Chad and Jeremy, who departed ever further from the Afro-American roots of skiffle. The resulting combination of music-hall melodies (without a touch of blues), archly affected lyrics, and rhythms reduced to a vapid tick-tock certainly fits my definition of fool's gold.

These Merseybeat clones sold a lot of records, but at the same time, their inanity made room for a reassertion of the musical advantages of Motown and Southern soul. The Supremes, the Four Tops, Marvin Gaye, and the Temptations all maintained a strong presence on the pop charts during the mid-1960s. And Southern soul entered its most fertile period just as the British Invasion occurred. Unfortunately, as we shall see, this resistance was short-lived.

The Triumph—and Temptation—of Soul

The best soul records of the mid-1960s are by the male singers whom Atlantic's renowned talent scout Jerry Wexler discovered in various parts of the country and brought South to record at either Stax or Fame. Most of these already had careers in gospel and R&B, but their releases on the Atlantic label made their names nationally known: Solomon Burke, Wilson Pickett, Otis Redding, Sam and Dave, Percy Sledge, Joe Tex. Depending upon which of their records became hits, each of these singers got identified with a certain type of sound. For example, Burke was known for his mellifluous love ballads, Pickett for the piercing shrieks of his "hard singing." As Pickett explains: "I got to be known as a screamer. And once you get known for something special, well, now, *that* would be your hood ornament."[1] Yet it is important to recall that these "hood ornaments" weren't the whole car. Pickett could also sing in a mellow voice, and Burke could rasp and shout with the best of them. Coming as they did from the solo evangelist tradition, soul singers defined vocal artistry as the ability to move across the whole spectrum, while also perfecting the "sandpaper and silk" of the middle.

Some of this vocal artistry got lost in the transition to soul, for the obvious reason that a solo evangelist delivering a sermon has long stretches of time, sometimes an hour or more, in which to demonstrate his virtuosity; while a soul singer cutting a single record has only three minutes. As it happens, the best soul records are those in which the singers accept this time limit and don't strain after extremes that, in church, would be meaningful only after a lengthy buildup. Nor did the best soul singers *need* to strain; their middle range was already more expressive than anything coming out of Britain.

Yet, like gospel, soul is not a music of limits. Its rich middle range was not enough to satisfy most fans—including most black fans. I specify the latter because, however much the producers of soul hoped to reach the white audience, they had no intention of skipping over the black one. Indeed, people like Wexler pitched soul deliberately at black record buyers, who (in Gillett's dry formulation) "were not interested in the songs composed by British singers using the techniques of rhythm and blues."[2] To know what those record buyers *were* interested in, we need only recall that the mid-1960s were tumultuous times for black Americans: Their angers, sorrows, and triumphs had less to do with heaven and hell than with social and political conflict. But emotions were no less intense for being worldly. The lyrics of soul were not political (at least not then), so the burden of conveying the passions of the times was placed on the music—creating a built-in incentive for soul singers to go to the extremes that Wexler dubbed "over-souling."[3]

As for white audiences, they, too, wanted passion. Here is Gillett's account of how Redding responded to his first crossover hit, a cover of the Rolling Stones' "Satisfaction":

> He later told an interviewer that he had not wanted to make the record, which was a crude, harsh parody of his earlier performances. But the record . . . was played on the pop stations, and Redding's reputation began to soar. But none of the records he made after 1965 were comparable to those he had already made. . . . "I Can't Turn You Loose" had a good fast bass line, but an unjustified hysterical vocal; "Try a Little Tenderness" (1966) began with a searing interpretation that was irresistible, yet it too built up to a frenzy that bore no relation to the words or mood of the song.[4]

To Redding's credit, he retreated from over-souling the moment his success seemed assured. In 1967, after a triumphant appearance before a white rock audience at the Monterey Pop Festival, he joined forces with Steve Cropper in writing and recording his most memorable song, an eloquent ballad entitled "(Sitting on the) Dock of the Bay." The record shot to number one on the pop chart in early 1968—right after Redding was killed in a plane crash.

As one of the best soul singers, Redding was a difficult artist to cover. Indeed, only the foolishly intrepid have presumed to cover "Dock of the Bay." But on one famous occasion, Redding did admit defeat by another singer. When he heard Aretha Franklin's 1967 version of his 1965 hit, "Respect," he said to Wexler: "I just lost my song. That girl took it away from me."[5] This comment pleased Wexler, since it had been his idea to make the Franklin version—as part of Atlantic's effort to find the right musical format for a young woman considered at the time to be the most promising, but also the most disappointing, singer of her generation.

Both the promise and the disappointment stemmed from the same source: Franklin's exceptional upbringing as a child prodigy of both sacred and secular Afro-American music. The daughter of C. L. Franklin, a prominent Baptist minister whose preaching was renowned throughout the country, Franklin's girlhood was divided between touring as a soloist in her father's choir, and associating with the luminaries, not only of gospel, but also of blues, jazz, R&B, and pop—all of whom were welcomed into the Franklins' Detroit home by her music-loving father. The first fruit of this background was that Aretha spent the early 1960s in the same limbo as her friend and mentor, Sam Cooke. Signed to Columbia by the veteran producer John Hammond, she made two albums exploring Ray Charles's jazz-gospel blend. These were interesting albums, but when they failed to sell, Franklin agreed to shift in the direction of 1950s pop, with results that were disastrous, both commercially and musically. The relationship ended in 1966, and then it was Wexler to the rescue, signing Franklin to Atlantic and taking her down to Muscle Shoals for a recording session that would, in his phrase, "put her back in church."[6]

That session is famous, for two reasons. The first was musical: As was typical at the Fame studio, all the assembled musicians were white, and only one of them (the singer Dan Penn) had ever heard of Aretha Franklin. So expectations were low and the atmosphere casual. But as Penn later recalled, the mood of the session changed the moment Franklin arrived:

> When she come in there and sit down at the piano and hit that first chord, everybody was just like little bees buzzing around the queen. You could tell by the way she hit the piano the gig was up. It was, "Let's get down to serious business." . . . It was beautiful, better than any session I've ever seen, and I seen a bunch of 'em.[7]

The second reason for the session's fame was racial: It turned from "beautiful" to ugly when one of the white musicians (a stand-in trumpet player) tried to get fresh with Franklin in front of her husband and manager, Ted White. One thing led to another, and soon tempers were flaring on all sides—one of many imbroglios that would contribute to the eventual breakup of soul's interracial collaboration.

Yet, portentous though it was, the incident did not break up Wexler and Franklin. A few weeks later the sessions resumed in New York City, with as many of the Stax and Fame musicians as Wexler could summon. He set the stage, but that was all he did. By his own account it was Franklin who ran the show:

> She'd take the song—she found most of them—or she'd write it. And she would work out a layout, working at home with her little electric piano and the girls. So you had three major ingredients: First of all, you had the arrangement implicit in the piano bars, you had her lead vocal, and you had the vocal background leads. She brings all this into the session . . . All we did was start to shade in drums, bass, guitar. We might make small changes, but it would always be by agreement with her. . . . Those records were so damned good because she took care of business at home.[8]

In terms of sheer musicianship, Wexler places Franklin in a class by herself, or rather in a class that contains only one other person: Ray Charles.[9] Both Franklin and Charles subsume the roles of singer, musician, songwriter, arranger, and producer. And both defy musical categorization, having ventured successfully into a number of fields.

But there is a difference. As mentioned earlier, Charles developed his eccentric singing style partly to compensate for a limited natural endowment. Franklin, on the other hand, has a superb vocal gift that sometimes gets wasted on the pyrotechnics of gospel and soul. Praising Franklin's "warm and velvety" mezzo-soprano, Pleasants regrets "the compulsion to achieve, or seem to represent, a state of ecstasy" that "tempts her to sing continually outside her normal range."[10] But Pleasants also confesses himself awed by the virtuosity with which Franklin yields to that temptation, adding ruefully that "Aretha knows her idiom. . . . She didn't achieve her present eminence singing for the European-schooled, opera-bred, sixtyish likes of me."[11]

Unfortunately for popular music in the 1960s, the temptation noted by Pleasants was not limited to gifted musicians. On the contrary, it was felt by a whole generation of young whites endeavoring to escape the perceived confines of middle-class life. Writing in 1974, Pleasants gives a sympathetic account of these efforts:

> Centuries of Western European civilization . . . with its emphasis upon decorous comportment and behavior, upon the assumed virtues of restraint and moderation, and upon the assumed felicity of favoring others by keeping one's own troubles and ecstacies to oneself, have conspicuously diminished the white man's powers of exuberant self-expression. This debility has been strongly felt and deeply resented by younger whites, hence the attraction, for them, of the unembarrassed fervor of the black American's music, especially that part of it most vividly reflected in the soul-baring characteristics and devices of gospel.[12]

What this account misses is the fact that those same young whites were largely oblivious to the religious roots of soul. Despite the enthusiasms of the 1950s, it was not until the live soul performances of the mid-1960s that the non-Southern, non-Pentecostal white majority got exposed to anything like the intensely emotional communalism of Afro-American worship. And even then, they did not associate the experience with religion. Some blacks damned soul as a shameful secularization; others blessed it as a timely put-down of rock 'n' roll. Either way, they knew where soul was coming from: Behind each cry of "Baby!" they heard the echo of "Jesus!" Whites, on the other hand, knew only that soul was coming from blacks, and that it gave people a thrill. As on so many previous occasions, it was all too easy for whites to reduce that thrill to sex. It would be heartening to think that blacks responded by reminding whites that soul had a spiritual dimension transcending the erotic. But generally they did not, because the more popular soul became with whites, the more constricting became the coils of the blood knot.

As we've seen, the historic disparity between African and Puritan world-views gave rise to three harmful distortions: the exploitation of black women by white men; the fear of mythically potent black men violating mythically pure white women; and the rejection of all sexual morality in the name of black sexual braggadocio. If, as some historians have claimed, the first distortion ruled during slavery and the second after Emancipation, then I would claim that the third came to rule during the 1960s. Even Ray Charles, one of the heroes of popular music, has declared that, for him, sex is nothing but a healthful pastime that should not be limited or curtailed by moral considerations: "Sex needs to be open and fun, free and happy. . . . No restrictions, no hang-ups, no formalities, no forbidden fruit—just everyone getting and giving as much as he and she can."[13]

Of course, Charles made this declaration in the early 1970s, at the height of the so-called "sexual revolution." It's possible that his views (like many other people's) have been tempered by the sour fruits of that revolution. Yet even if his views haven't changed, there is still a difference between Charles's philosophy and that of the movement that grew up around his music. Based on his many encounters with women all over the world, Charles vouchsafes the wisdom that racial differences are of no erotic significance: "It's all a matter of individual chemistry—you and her—and none of the clichés are worth a damn."[14]

By "clichés" Charles means the myths and distortions of the blood knot. Needless to say, his judgment that they are "not worth a damn" was not prevalent in the 1960s. On the contrary, they were worth a great deal, in both politics and culture, to those who were willing to trade on them. With regard to soul music, the myth of black hyperpotency was a definite selling point for what the writer Gerri Hirshey aptly calls "a great roster of macho marquee titles: the Wicked, the Midnight Mover, the Man and a Half, the Godfather, the Sex Machine, the Ice Man, the Big O, Love Man."[15] No doubt many young blacks felt gratified by the sight of young whites going into raptures at the bidding of "soul men." It must have been tempting to forget all about church.

Far be it from me to condemn white enthusiasm for Afro-American music. As stated earlier, that enthusiasm is a good thing when it is either unself-conscious or respectful of the artistry involved. But when it spills over into primitivism, enthusiasm can become pernicious. So far, the only primitivism discussed in this book has been that of nonmusicians (such as highbrow critics). This is because, before the 1960s, the musicians who apprenticed themselves to Afro-American music were of two kinds: those who tried to live up to the idiom's standards of musical excellence; and those who diluted it to appeal to genteel taste. Not until the 1960s did a new generation of white musicians begin distorting the music to appeal to primitivist taste.

The New Purism: The Rise of Early Rock

If a mad marketing genius had surveyed the American popular music scene in the mid-1960s and decided to invent a new chart-busting style, he might have come up with the second stage of the British Invasion. I call it "second" for the sake of analysis only; it really began at the same time as the first. For the fact is that the Beatles were not the only British group to sweep the American charts in 1964. Along with their smooth harmonies came a rougher import—records such as "Do Wah Diddy Diddy" by Manfred Mann, "The House of the Rising Sun" by the Animals, and "You Really Got Me" by the Kinks sounded, to white ears at least, like the Chicago blues with a smidgen of soul. Yet the faces on the album covers were just as shaggy and British as the Beatles'. In other words, these groups combined the selling points of blackness and Britishness.

There is a sense in which this second stage *was* the concoction of a mad marketing genius. But not entirely. Along with primitivism (about which more later), its real source was British anticommercialism.

It all started when Muddy Waters plugged in his guitar and split the British folk music movement in two. I have already described the folkie purist reaction, which was horror at such "decadent commercialism." There was also a pro-Muddy reaction: Groups such as Alex Korner's Blues Incorporated, the Yardbirds, and the Animals plugged in their own guitars and began playing not only Chicago blues but also rock 'n' roll covers of Chuck Berry, Little Richard, and another Chess performer turned rock 'n' roll, Bo Diddley.

Yet purism dies hard. Even though these groups played rock 'n' roll along with their blues, they still resisted the label "pop," reserving that for the much-maligned Beatles. The journalist Philip Norman parrots this new purism nicely:

> On January 12, the Saturday-night pop show "Thank Your Lucky Stars" provided its snowed-in bumper audience with the spectacle of that absurd new pop group the Beatles, looking even more outlandish in their mop-top haircuts and crew-necked suits, lip-synching their new record . . . [and] jiggling about absurdly, grinning at the camera and each other.[16]

The new purists did not object to the Beatles' playing of electrified genres; indeed, they played them themselves. What they did object to was (you guessed it) the "commercialization" of those genres—meaning the Beatles' smooth harmonies, skilled playing, and crowd-pleasing manner. Under this new dispensation it was these qualities, not electric instrumentation per se, that made music "pop." And it was roughness and crudeness per se that made something "blues." I prefer to call the music created by these new British purists "early rock," because it quickly set itself apart, not only from the Beatles, but also from Muddy Waters.

Early rock really began when Alexis Korner's circle attracted a motley crew of young would-be musicians who were bored with skiffle and seeking something new and exciting. Many (not all) hailed from such London suburbs as Richmond and Surrey, where if one's prospects in life were not uniformly rosy, neither were they working-class grey, as in the council-housing environment of Liverpool. Most of these children of the lower-middle class had been expected to complete business and technical degrees in order to climb the next painful rung of the ladder from respectability to gentility. But most (not all) had rebelled against those expectations, not by dropping out of school entirely (which would have meant getting a job), but by enrolling in art college.

According to Frith, postwar educational reforms opened many art colleges to working- and lower-middle-class youth who "had neither academic nor occupational qualifications but whose 'awkwardness' seemed to have some sort of creative potential."[17] These students not only lacked the habit of sustained effort, they also lacked the motivation, for a couple of reasons. First, their humbler origins meant that the doors of the elite cultural establishment were closed pretty tightly, even if they studied hard and got their degrees. Second, the time-honored battle between fine art and commerce had been turned on its head by pop art. For the first time in art college history, the taste of the masses—their penchant for popular culture—was considered avant-garde. As Frith writes, John Lennon was typical of many such students who "played up their supposed working classness . . . using rock 'n' roll as a sign of their contemptuous vulgarity."[18]

It was in this defiant spirit that crowds of restless art students and assorted hangers-on flocked to Korner's Marquee Club, listening to Korner and his fellow blues fanatics Chris Barber, Cyril Davies, and John Mayall—not to mention the occasional visiting dignitary from Chicago. Their goal was "contemptuous vulgarity," and it was not long before they found a way to achieve it.

Just as the Beatles emerged from the pack of Merseybeat groups, so one group emerged as the undisputed leader of early rock. The Rolling Stones got their first break in 1962, when Blues Incorporated were invited to perform live on a regular Thursday-night BBC radio program, and Korner asked a couple of the band's apprentices if they would substitute at the Marquee Club. Among those who eagerly accepted were two art students named Keith Richards and Brian Jones, and a boyhood friend of Richards who occupied a higher rung on the career ladder, having done well enough in grammar school to enroll as a business student at the London School of Economics. His name was Mick Jagger.

Soon the Rolling Stones were making the rounds of the suburban London clubs, doing their best to drive the crowds crazy with their covers of blues, soul, and R&B hits. In this they resembled all the other early rock bands. But just as the Beatles owed their preeminence to a combination of creative advantage and aggressive promotion, so did the Stones benefit from both a slight edge in talent and the help of a world-class hustler. In some ways Andrew Loog Oldham resembled Brian Epstein: He was a young would-be impresario whose inexperience was exceeded only by his chutzpah. But in other ways Oldham did not resemble Epstein. Most significant, he had no real interest or taste in Afro-American music. Whereas Epstein had gotten his start selling records in music-obsessed Liverpool, Oldham entered the music business from the tangential fields of fashion and public relations. From the beginning, he showed a flair for crude publicity stunts: Norman reports that one concert promoter fired Oldham for "inviting journalists to view cinema seats which, during a particularly well appreciated package show, had been slashed with razors and drenched with female urine."[19]

Taking a lesson from his American idol, Phil Spector, Oldham retained the right to record the Rolling Stones anywhere he chose.[20] Sensing that the Stones would not thrive in the cautious atmosphere of British Decca (where they had been quickly signed by an executive still chafing at having passed up the Beatles), Oldham took the group, which now included bassist Bill Wyman and drummer Charlie Watts, on a pilgrimage to that bastion of blues authenticity, the Chess studio in Chicago. There they cut a few blues covers, notably a version of Howlin' Wolf's famous "Little Red Rooster."

Compared with the originals, the Stones' covers are amateurish; no blues fan would ever place their "Rooster" above Howlin' Wolf's. But soon Oldham was urging the Stones to quit making covers and start beating the Beatles at their own game—songwriting. Richards and Jagger accepted the challenge, and the breakthrough occurred after Oldham had taken the group to Los Angeles in 1965. There, in the RCA studios, they used a "fuzz box," or electronic sound-blurring device, to roughen the sound of their first original number one hit, "(I Can't Get No) Satisfaction." Soon to follow were several others: "Get Off My Cloud," "Nineteenth Nervous Breakdown," "Paint It Black" and "Mother's Little Helper." And suddenly the new purist music was enjoying "pop" success.

The Stones also beat the Beatles at paying tribute to their black American sources. They weren't always graceful about it, as when Jagger wrote, in a 1964 letter to *Melody Maker*, "These legendary characters wouldn't mean a light commercially today if groups were not going round Britain doing their numbers."[21] But even after becoming megastars, the Stones often performed with blues acts—boasting, not without justification, that by featuring these acts on their American tours, they were carrying burning coals back to Newcastle. And it's true: Countless young white Americans would never have been exposed to the Chicago blues if they hadn't seen its leading exponents opening for the Stones. As Muddy Waters himself admitted, "They stole my music, but they gave me my name."[22]

But there were problems with all this tribute. First was the fact that its sincerity was rarely tested. In Britain the cloak of blues purism that the Stones wrapped around themselves was also the costume with the best commercial prospects—not because the general British public loved the blues, but because a small but influential audience was still seeking an alternative to the "pop" commercialism of the Beatles. Jagger had this audience in mind when he insisted, in the aforementioned letter, that the Stones were *serious* students of Afro-American music, not "just a beat group who came up overnight, knowing nothing about it."[23] It was abundantly clear which "beat group" he meant.

In the United States the problem was different: How to deal with the originals? Here the Stones' custom of using their black heroes as opening acts had the unfortunate effect of relegating those heroes to the secondary, by-now-familiar role of "rock forerunners." However loud the applause for Muddy Waters, he was still expected to fade into the wings when the Stones got ready to make their grand entrance. Most white fans came to believe, after seeing this same scenario played out a hundred times, that the Stones were more musically sophisticated than their black opening acts—even though that wasn't true.

What's So Pure About the Blues?

Having criticized British blues purism, am I now making an equally arbitrary distinction between Muddy Waters and the Rolling Stones? The answer is no, because my distinction is not made on the basis of anticommercialism.

Unlike jazz, which has been the object of scholarly research since the 1920s, the blues has been systematically studied only since the 1950s. Nonetheless, most scholars trace its origins to two sources: to Afro-American religion and ritual, including spirituals, ring shouts, field hollers, work chants, sermons, and toasts; and to early forms of American popular culture, including plantation music, minstrel "coon songs," and popular ballads performed by itinerant street singers for hatfuls of pennies.[24]

That is, the origins of the blues are both noncommercial and commercial. The form as we know it—one performer, usually male, singing and playing a guitar—dates back to the years immediately after the Civil War, when emancipation sent former slave musicians out on the road to earn a living. This image of the solo, itinerant bluesman appeals to aficionados steeped in the romantic ideal of the lonely artist pitted against a hostile society. But the blues rarely fits this ideal, for two reasons. First, the blues has always been played by groups as well as by individuals; and second, it has never ceased to sell itself. For more than a century, the blues performer's motto has not been "art for art's sake" but "make way for the paying customers." The latter have included everyone from travelers waiting at a railroad depot to sharecroppers crowded onto segregated benches for a country "medicine show," from families gathered for a barbecue on a Mississippi cotton plantation to lowlifes raising hell in a Memphis juke joint, from city dwellers strolling in a public park to transplanted Southern factory workers in a hole-in-the-wall Chicago club.

In recent years the blues performer most frequently forced into the art-for-art's-sake mold has been the renowned Mississippi Delta bluesman, Robert Johnson. Because Johnson was a lone wolf who wrote many of his own lyrics, some of them strikingly original, reissues of his 1930s record-ings have been greeted with glowing tributes depicting him as a true romanticist.[25] The deflating truth, however, is that Johnson spent most of his career working as a human jukebox. Guralnick cites one of Johnson's contemporaries recalling that the bluesman "was as likely to perform 'Tumbling Tumbleweeds' or the latest Bing Crosby hit as one of his own compositions. 'You didn't play what *you* liked, you played what the people liked. That's what you had to do.'"[26] Johnson died in 1938. If he had lived, he might have been one of the first Delta bluesmen to perform on radio. The price of appearing on tiny KFFA was singing jingles for the King Bis-cuit Flour Company, and allowing your face to adorn a cornmeal label. But Johnson would have paid it, as did his stepson and protégé, Robert ("Jr.") Lockwood.[27]

Unlike folk purists, musicians have always defined the blues as a musical structure, as a way of playing and singing, and (perhaps most important) as a ritualized way of coping with the harshness of life.

Crystallized in the early twentieth century, the traditional blues struc-ture is a three-line, twelve-bar stanza, with lyrics following a variety of rhyme schemes, usually *aab*. Typically in the key of E or A, the blues stanza starts with four bars on the tonic, with the fourth shifting to the dominant 7th; then it proceeds to two bars on the subdominant, two more on the tonic, two on the dominant 7th, and two final bars back on the tonic. Not all blues have this structure—far from it. The oldest known blues are almost free-form, and many "classic" blues, such as those recorded by Bessie Smith and others in the 1920s, have the familiar structure of the thirty-two-bar popular song.

But blues artistry consists of more than strumming a simple sequence of chords and singing the somewhat constrained melodies that arise from them. First and foremost the blues is polyrhythmic, possessing the elusive but essential quality of swing. Second the blues is characterized by distinc-tive vocal and instrumental techniques, such as "moaning" and "string bending," which produce a rich variety of timbres and microtonal shad-ings. Like polyrhythm, these techniques are indisputably the heritage of Africa. As a slave musician remarked to a white visitor in the 1830s, "Notes is good enough for you people, but us likes a mixtery."[28] That "mixtery" is especially pronounced in blues vocalism, which, like the vocalism in solo evangelism and soul, ranges over a wide spectrum, from tones pure enough to pass muster in a European concert hall to "impure" textures evocative of every imaginable emotional state.

Emotion brings us to the spirit of the blues, a subject frequently misunderstood, even by its admirers. The music gets its name from the Elizabethan phrase "the blue devils," meaning a fit of bad temper or melancholy. But bad temper and melancholy are merely the starting point of the blues, not its destination. Of course, some people regard the blues as depressing, as would befit the "Devil's music." This view prevails in the gospel field, where many agree with Mahalia Jackson's judgment: "Blues are the songs of despair, gospel songs are songs of hope."[29] It is more sympathetically expressed by the blues historian Paul Oliver: "The blues is primarily the song of those who turned their backs on religion."[30] But both evaluations miss the point. If the blues teaches us anything, it is that despair is not the only alternative to faith. For all the emotionalism found in blues performance, the music's basic philosophy is stoic.

To put the matter another way, "having the blues" is not the same thing as "playing the blues." The former refers to a negative state of mind, such as loneliness or grief, anger or fear, disappointment or jealousy; the latter, to the art of leavening, tempering, or (possibly) transforming such a state. Because it does not expect to achieve heavenly bliss, the blues aims lower than gospel, at what can be achieved in this world—usually enough irony or humor to give a modicum of freedom within even the grimmest circumstances. As Albert Murray explains:

> The church is not concerned with the affirmation of life as such. . . . The church is committed to the eternal salvation of the soul after death. . . . But the Saturday Night Function [the blues performance] is a ritual of purification and affirmation nonetheless. Not all ceremonial occasions are solemn. Nor are defiance and contestation less fundamental to human well-being than are worship and propitiation. Indeed they seem to be precisely what such indispensably human attributes as courage, dignity, honor, nobility and heroism are all about. . . . The most immediate problem of the blues-bedeviled person concerns his ability to cope with even the commonplace. What is at stake is a sense of well-being that is at least strong enough to enable him to meet the basic requirements of the workaday world.[31]

Robert Johnson's blues never suggest any hope that coping with trouble in this world will lead to rewards in the next. One of his best known lyrics goes, "You may bury my body down by the highway side / So my old evil spirit can catch a Greyhound bus and ride."[32] But Johnson makes it just as clear that if despair is allowed to rule in small things, it will rule in large: "If you cry about a nickel / You'll die 'bout a dime."[33] Like gospel, the blues involves both performer and audience in a communal, ritualized reenactment of extreme emotional states. But, also like gospel, the purpose of the blues ritual is to *return* from those states—to *survive* trouble, not succumb to it. The difference is that, unlike the preacher, the bluesman tempers every extreme. His stoic stance toward life eschews pain. But his focus on bitter realities also distrusts joy.

Historically, the topics addressed by the blues make for a very long list. Here are just a few, taken from Oliver's landmark study of traditional blues lyrics: employment and the lack thereof; the need to migrate, usually by railroad, and the personal costs thereof; color prejudice, among blacks as well as whites; standards of beauty and dress; flirtation, romance, courtship, and marriage; fidelity and infidelity; sex in all its permutations, including sexual boasting and insult; folk beliefs, magic, and "hoodoo"; gambling; carnivals, juke joints, and vaudeville; liquor, prohibition, and drugs; conditions in various regions and cities; prostitution and vice; weapons and fighting; gangsters and crime; the Ku Klux Klan; prison and convict labor; the abuses of the criminal justice system; prison escape and family breakup; capital punishment; the Mississippi River; floods, tornadoes, dust storms, and hurricanes; housing, insurance policies, and fires; military service, wars, and veterans; diet, working conditions, injury, and disease; death, funerals, and cemeteries; heaven and hell; bereavement and hero-worship.[34]

Because the blues has long been embraced as an authentic "folk art" by the political left, its stoicism tends to get overlooked. Old Leftists from Anatoli Lunacharsky to Amiri Baraka have interpreted the blues as a form of coded political protest, thereby foisting on the music a programmatic optimism about human affairs that is simply not present. And New Leftists from Greil Marcus to the black nationalist Ron Karenga have dismissed the blues as passive acceptance of injustice, thereby missing the hard gleam of resistance at its core.

When the rural Southern blues moved to the urban North in the 1940s, both its sound and its lyric content changed. In Chicago, practitioners of Johnson's Mississippi Delta style such as Muddy Waters and Howlin' Wolf began using electric amplifiers to make themselves heard over the conversational din of clubs and saloons. At the same time one theme came to dominate the lyrics: relations between the sexes. There were commercial reasons for this change; as Charles Keil explains, "Radio stations and other commercial interests have been most energetic in reshaping blues styles." But there were other reasons, too; Keil adds, "male roles in the [Northern] Negro community are confused, anxiety-laden, and in need of redefinition."[35] In other words, sex became the focus of the urban blues not just because sex sold, but also because sex was (and is) freighted with meanings about the stability, and instability, of life in the urban North.

Many people miss these meanings because they are taken aback by the idiom's sexual frankness. What Oliver says about country blues is equally true of the urban styles: "As with all other subjects the blues, when dealing with matters of love and sex, is forthright and uncompromising. It was this open declaration of subjects that the conventions of polite society decreed should be kept hidden from view which caused so much offense."[36] Since prurience is the flip side of puritanism, Oliver's observation can be easily updated for the age of the sexual revolution. Today many primitivist blues fans assume that the essence of the form—its real *truth*—is raw sex. For both kinds of listeners, there is nothing but a crude leer in the famous Johnson lyric: "You can squeeze my lemon 'til the juice run down my leg."

Yet such listeners miss the point. Like all blues lyrics, "squeeze my lemon" must be interpreted in context. The line appears in Johnson's "Traveling Riverside Blues," a song of wry complaint. The singer has a woman in every Mississippi port, but the one in Friar's Point has "got a mortgage on my body, now, a lien on my soul." "Squeeze my lemon" expresses lust, all right, but in a deliberately banal way suggestive of what casual sex has become for this heartsick traveling man. The next (and last) line is crucial: "But I'm goin' back to Friar's Point, if I be rockin' to my head."[37]

From the perspective of black audiences, Chicago blues was only one strain in the 1950s and 1960s. Indeed, it was a rather specialized, even mannered strain, appealing chiefly to the uprooted Mississippians of that city.[38] Equally if not more popular were several other strains whose roots lay outside Mississippi, and whose topical focus was not quite so narrow. These include the spare Texas blues of Sam ("Lightnin'") Hopkins, the sprightly guitar figures of Jimmy Reed, and the lyrically swinging Texas and Memphis sounds of T-Bone Walker, B. B. King, Little Johnnie Taylor. Yet, like the Chicago blues, these other strains also seek to mitigate the pain of sexual relations though resignation, irony, and self-parody. Their sexual focus is not prurient because, as in most other forms of Afro-American music, it represents a ritualized effort to cope.

The Rolling Stones Paint It Black

Needless to say, stoicism was in short supply in 1960s London. Among the folkie blues purists, it was well understood that true blues artistry can be acquired only through hours of practice and years of immersion in the idiom. Indeed, they argued endlessly whether Britons, or white people in general, could *ever* acquire that artistry. Some concluded that authentic blues feeling was right up there with "natural rhythm" as a trait that could only be inherited with dark skin. Others labored to disprove this view through slavish, note-for-note imitations of the masters. Either way the folk scene offered a combination of rigid standards and social inaccessibility that, ironically, resembled the closed doors of the elite cultural establishment. So here, too, early rock took a short cut.

The first step was to single out the Chicago strain of blues—especially as fashioned by the Chess songwriter and producer Willie Dixon. To repeat: Most forms of Afro-American music take pride in negotiating the spectrum from sweet to salty, smooth to rough, pure to gritty, soft to loud, slow to fast. Dixon's contribution, in the competitive heyday of R&B, was to emphasize the latter qualities. And in lyric content he emphasized male braggadocio more than most other blues strains. One result of this emphasis was a negative reaction among Chess musicians; according to Guralnick, Muddy Waters himself grew tired of Dixon's approach and, in the early 1960s, returned to a broader, mellower style closer to that of the Delta.[39]

Yet while Muddy Waters was broadening the Chicago blues, his British admirers were narrowing it to the point of caricature. The British journalist Charles S. Murray makes an important distinction between the folkie purists, who "regarded any departures from the gospel according to their favourite bluesmen as near-blasphemy," and early rock, which swiftly succumbed to the "fetishization of lead guitar playing as an athletic event (who could be faster, louder, and more audacious?)."[40] The first step toward guitar "fetishization" was getting rid of all the other instruments. The typical Chicago blues band contained two (sometimes three) guitars, drums, acoustic bass, harmonica, and piano. Muddy Waters's sound in particular would have been inconceivable without the harmonica of Little Walter Jacobs and the piano of Otis Spann. Most early rock groups, by contrast, chose to strip away this instrumentation, ending up with a sound that was, like Merseybeat, totally guitar centered.

The Rolling Stones followed this pattern at first. They started out with a piano player, a Blues Incorporated veteran named Ian Stewart. But when it came time for their British television premiere, Oldham dropped Stewart—because, as Philip Norman explains, "his short hair, beefy arms, and pugnaciously sensible face looked 'too normal.'"[41] Now, as it happens, Otis Spann also had short hair, beefy arms, and a pugnaciously sensible face. But it would never have occurred to Muddy Waters to drop the best blues pianist in Chicago on the basis of his looks.

Still, to their credit, the Stones did not carry guitar-centeredness much further. Neither mulishly purist nor aggressively "progressive," they opted for a "two-guitar" sound in which neither Richards nor Jones stood out as a soloist. Some critics cite noble democratic reasons for this arrangement, which continued when Jones was replaced by Mick Taylor, and later by Ron Wood. Others disparage it by saying that none of these guitarists had the ability to stand out.[42] My own view is that the Stones were trying, in this one area at least, to stay loyal to the blues.

The Stones also retained Stewart as an unofficial member of the band. And they never abandoned the practice initiated by Jones before his drug-induced death in 1969, of playing with other musicians, including some very good ones. Thus they sustained a musical sound that was undeniably bluesier than those offshoots of guitar "fetishization," hard rock and heavy metal.

But as Jones himself used to say, sound is only one aspect of music. To be exact, Jones said that sound was the *only* aspect of Afro-American music that held any interest for him. In an early press interview, he gave this answer to the question "How did you come to play R&B?":

> It's really a matter for a sociologist, a psychiatrist, or something. . . . If you ask some people why they go for R&B you get pretentious answers. They say that in R&B they find "an honesty of expression, a sincerity of feeling," and so on, for me it's merely the sound. . . . I mean, I like all sorts of sounds. . . . It doesn't express damn-all to me, really. . . . But I like the sound.[43]

Rather than say something "pretentious" myself, let me quote Muddy Waters on the subject of his young white acolytes:

> I think they're great people, but they're not blues players. Really, what separates them from people like Wolf and myself, we're doing the stuff like we did way years ago down in Mississippi. These kids are just getting up, getting stuff and going with it, you know, so we're expressing our lives, the hard times and the different things we been through. It's not real. They don't feel it. I don't think you can feel the blues until you've been through some hard times.[44]

Note well that Muddy Waters does *not* define blues feeling as a function of skin color, geography, social class, or relationship to the means of production. For him, blues feeling is the product of long hard experience, with life as well as with music. However loyal the Stones were to blues instrumentation, they were disloyal to the eventual goal of achieving blues feeling.

The difference shows up most starkly in the human voice. Most pundits dutifully report that Jagger learned to sing from Muddy Waters and Howlin' Wolf. Yet the only black singer Jagger ever came close to imitating was the lightweight soul singer Don Covay, and even so, the only thing Jagger added was a quality not found before in the Afro-American vocal tradition: snideness.[45] And he has subtracted a lot. All too accurate is Murray's generalization: "British blues bands ran the emotional gamut from A (I'm feeling sorry for myself) through B (I'm well 'ard, me) to C (I'm not tough really but I'm going to pretend that I am) to D (I'm pissed off)."[46] Or, as Muddy Waters himself summed it up: "These white kids can . . . run a ring around you playin' guitar, but they cannot vocal [*sic*] like a black man."[47]

Ultimately, the Rolling Stones transmogrified the blues along the two axes that most distinguish the Afro-American idiom from perverse modernism: the relationship between the artist and the audience, and the treatment of the erotic.

With regard to the former, recall that the Stones' main concern was to define themselves as blues purists, meaning not "pop." From that standpoint, the Beatles' commercial success was purchased at the inexcusably high price of becoming entertainers. Their charming cheekiness was no better than the droll working-class humor traditionally aimed at the upper classes from the music-hall stage; and their campy attitudes toward high culture and commerce, however appealing they might be to American elites, were too tame for the art college crowd. Hence Oldham's decision to define the Stones as the opposite of the Beatles. Here he found his true vocation, registering every fear aroused by rock 'n' roll in the bosom of the cultural establishment and making it part of the Stones' media image. As Norman writes: "Coverage of the Stones from 1964 onward testifies to Andrew Loog Oldham's artful success in making their name synonymous with surliness, squalor, rebellion and menace."[48]

Nor were these threats aimed just at the establishment. The real genius of the Stones lay in their cultivated contempt for their audience. Instead of grinning at the camera, they scowled. Instead of signing autographs, they spat. Instead of ending their televised performance at the London Palladium with the show-business ritual of going out on the revolving stage to greet the fans, they turned their backs and stalked off. The success of such gestures is reflected in Iain Chambers's awed assessment:

> The outrageous behavior of the Rolling Stones . . . was a novel and disturbing form of deviancy. Working-class delinquency or gang fights was one thing, but this disdainful refusal not of the fruits of the consumer society but of the traditional means—hard work, servile gratitude, sacrifice and dedication—for obtaining them, was something else. Physical surliness and rude

grudges were to be occasionally expected, widespread ideological disaffection was far more serious.[49]

The irony, of course, is that the Stones wrapped themselves in the cloak of blues authenticity while rejecting the crowd-pleasing manner that is an essential part of every bluesman's stock in trade. Granted, that manner takes a different form when removed from its original all-black setting. But it always reflects a basically positive disposition toward whatever audience happens to be out there. Even the notoriously moody Howlin' Wolf never failed to behave courteously when performing for his newly acquired white fans. Like all bluesmen, he lived by the old adage: "The people can make you, and the same people can break you." Just to underscore the contrast, here is another of the Stones' heroes, Chuck Berry, describing his first meeting with Muddy Waters:

> We paid our fifty-cents admission and scrimmaged forward to the bandstand, where in true living color I saw Muddy Waters.
>
> He was playing "Mo Jo Working" at that moment and was closing the last set of the night. Once he'd finished, Ralph boldly called out from among the many people trying to get Muddy's autograph and created the opportunity for me to speak with my idol. . . . It was truly the beginning as I continued to watch his most humble compliance in attempting to appease his enthused admirers. The way he communicated with those fans was recorded in my memory, and I've tried to respond in a similar way to fans of my own.[50]

What Chambers calls "servile gratitude" and Berry calls "humble compliance," I would call, simply, graciousness. But whatever the name, it was not a quality emulated by the Stones. As their first "official biography" noted in 1964:

> Many top pop groups achieve their fame and stardom and then go out, quite deliberately, to encourage adults and parents to like them. This doesn't appeal to the forthright Stones. They will not make any conscious effort to be liked by anybody at all—not even their present fans if it also meant changing their own way of life. The Stones have been Rebels With A Cause . . . the cause of rhythm'n'blues music.[51]

To fathom the cynicism behind this last claim, we need only ask: Were the Stones really motivated by what Chambers calls a "fierce loyalty to the blues"?[52] Or were they cynically exploiting the negative symbolism of race?

I said earlier that the 1960s were the first time that primitivism became the province of musicians, as opposed to critics and observers. At the core of what the Stones did to the blues is the by now familiar pattern of a racist response to Afro-American music devolving into a primitivist embrace, with both reactions isolating and exaggerating the element of eroticism.

To be sure, the Stones picked up on cues that were already there. When Presley realized that his bodily movements were galvanizing the audience, he accentuated them. So did Lewis. And Little Richard used his gift for enthusiasm as a spur to promiscuity, aided by drug abuse. More recently the soul singers of the 1960s made no effort to dispel the youthful white perception that their music was an expression of hypersexuality cut loose from any moral context.

Yet in each of these cases, the process of debasement was counteracted by the presence—in the musician's own mind, if nowhere else—of Afro-American religion. Even at their most hedonistic, none of these people ever forgot that what they were fooling around with was a means of spiritual transcendence.

The Rolling Stones, by contrast, had zero interest in religion. For them the only kind of Afro-American music that mattered was the blues, which turned its back on religion and talked about sex with startling frankness. And the only kind of blues that mattered was the Chicago strain, which carried sexual braggadocio to extremes. That extreme was what the Stones wanted, and nothing but. If 1950s rock 'n' roll loosened the coils of the blood knot by fostering a healthier eroticism between white Southern men and women, the Stones retightened those coils. Instead of mitigating the historic white obsession with black sexuality, the Stones did their best to intensify it. Like the soul singers, the Stones understood that the myth of black hyperpotency was a hot item in the 1960s. But, unlike the soul singers, the Stones didn't have to deal with the complications and disadvantages of actually being black. For them it was easy to market the myth: Just play at being "black," as defined by their own—and their audience's—primitivist fantasies.

The gambit began with Jagger's stage persona. Recalling the singer's debut with Blues Incorporated, Korner suggests that, whatever Jagger was studying in those early days, it was not blues artistry: "The thing I noticed about him wasn't his singing. It was the way he threw his hair around. He only had a short haircut, like everyone else's. But, for a kid in a cardigan, that was moving quite *excessively*."[53] According to Norman, Oldham saw a similar quality in Jagger. When Oldham made the aforementioned decision to drop Ian Stewart for looking "too normal," an associate suggested that he drop Jagger, too, "in favor of a vocalist who could *really* sing."[54] But Oldham resisted, vowing to keep Jagger because some things are more important than singing. As he explains: "It was always the sex in rock 'n' roll that attracted me . . . the sex that most people didn't realize was there. Like the Everly Brothers. Two guys with the same kind of face, the same kind of hair. They were meant to be singing together to some girl, but really they were singing to each other."[55] Clearly it was not Jagger's command of the blues idiom that put £ signs in Oldham's eyes; it was his visual appeal as a loose-limbed, pouty-faced, smoky-eyed androgyne.

As we've seen, the homoerotic approach to cultural eminence was hardly new in Britain. What was new, though, was the addition of racial overtones to the mix. And what was harmful was the impact that addition had on all subsequent perceptions of the blues—as seen in Norman's 1984 account of Jagger's early potential as a blues singer:

> The Jagger of this first album is simply a singer with the band, stepping back to allow others their turn. But in every syllable he sings, there are signs of the Jagger to come. There are signs, most powerfully, in "I'm a King Bee," a slow blues, torrid with sexual warning—"I'm a king bee, baby, buzzin' round your hive"—intoned by Jagger in a somnolent drawl, *his tongue and lips playing an audible, almost visible part.*[56] (emphasis added)

Without shame, this passage revives the hoary assumption that "black" music is a function of "black" bodily characteristics, especially those associated with sex. On the same assumption, the Stones made Jagger's full, bee-stung lips the centerpiece of their stage act, and in 1971 made those same lips, complete with lolling tongue, the official logo of their new record label.[57] The associations could hardly be more obvious: Jagger has a "black" mouth, which means that he can sing the blues. Add the parallel assumption that the blues is nothing but sex, and you have the conclusion that Jagger's singing is pure prurience.

But don't take my word for it. Take Oldham's, describing the first time he laid eyes on the Stones: "It was just a blues roots thing. . . . Even so, I knew what I was looking at. It was sex."[58] Or take the word of Mike Jahn, declaring in 1973 that Jagger was a better "imitation black blues" singer than Eric Burdon, because he had "more aggression, more obvious sexuality. . . . He was skinny, with big flappy lips, and danced around the stage with an intensity unmatched by anyone save the American soul singer James Brown."[59]

With regard to the dubious equation of Jagger's vamping with Brown's Devil-destroying showmanship, recall that it was Brown himself who said: "I never gave a dirty show in my life."[60] Like any master of gospel, soul or the blues, Brown takes pride in being able to guide his audience through the emotional as well as the musical spectrum: from humble to boastful, saintly to sinful, passive to aggressive, tender to cruel. Here, too, the willed isolation of the latter elements as "black" is simply a distortion perpetrated by people obsessed with the shock effect that a blues or soul performance has on their own constrained sensibilities. In the case of early rock, this distortion is perpetuated every time a critic equates "blackness" with "aggression," "obvious sexuality" and (don't forget) "big flappy lips."

Poor Jahn. He is hardly the only 1960s rock critic to have been hypnotized by the ersatz "blackness" of the Rolling Stones. One British reviewer exclaimed, "Never before has there been a sound to rival this—Except, perhaps, in the jungles of darkest Africa!"[61] Another Stones biographer, Stanley Booth, uses his background as a white native of Little Richard's hometown of Macon, Georgia, to authenticate the Stones' racial mystique. Booth calls Keith Richards "the world's only bluegum white man, as poisonous as a rattlesnake."[62] And, lest we forget the history of the blood knot, Booth regales us with this description of the R&B star Tina Turner, opening for the Stones at the Los Angeles Forum in 1969:

> Here came Tina down the hall, wearing a gold-and-silver fringed dress, very short . . . filling the air with a scent so sweet, so musky, as to equal the evil black funk of her husband Ike. . . . She and the Ikettes started to dance in their near-Egyptian way, . . . arms folded over breasts, bucking, making little grabbing movements with their thighs as their skirts rose higher, higher, almost high enough to reveal the heavenly mink-lined wet black cunt. The lights went out, a strobe started to flicker, Tina and the Ikettes writhed and thrusted, caught in their mad nigger poses, crotch flashing, smoke bomb—
> Next, the Rolling Stones [,] . . . inciting the crowd to orgasm."[63]

To give young Jagger his due, he was extremely skillful at balancing the somewhat contradictory personae of seductive schoolboy and hypersexed stud. Too often, though, he did so by mixing effeminate vamping with cruel sexual boasting. In this respect his real models were not Muddy Waters and James Brown, but Ike and Tina Turner, R&B veterans who succumbed with special eagerness to the new primitivist embrace. After years of recording and touring in the United States, Ike and Tina finally made it big in the mid-1960s, when they followed in the footsteps of Little Richard and conquered England with a combination of infectious rhythm and flamboyant eroticism. Only, as Norman reports, their eroticism was more explicit:

> Ike and Tina Turner [were] black soul music's most blatantly sexual performers, a laconic guitarist standing by, apparently indifferent, while his half-

naked Zulu princess wife teased a hand microphone into an erect phallus, fondling it with bejeweled fingers, flicking it with her tongue as she murmured and gurgled an act of fellatio, communicable to thousands. Of all the influences on Mick Jagger's stagecraft, none was so great as Tina Turner.[64]

Ike Turner's compulsive pattern of infidelity, wife-beating, and cocaine abuse would soon wreck his career and push Tina to the brink of suicide. Without excusing this behavior, it is worth noting that it was very much a product of the blood knot. Ike's father was a Baptist minister in Clarksdale, Mississippi, whose own infidelity got him into fatal trouble when he took up with a black woman already claimed by one of the local whites. Ike was still a toddler when a gang of whites came to his home, dragged his father into the yard, and beat him so badly that he was bedridden until his death three years later.[65]

When Tina first met Ike, his band, the Rhythm Kings, was performing for mostly female fans, white as well as black.[66] It was under his tutelage, therefore, that she learned how to titillate an audience. But she also learned about music. For whatever else may be said of Ike Turner, he produced solid, brassy R&B in the classic 1950s mold. The British art college crowd appreciated this music, of course. But there was always that undercurrent of primitivism, that obsession with what Eric Clapton would call "the spade sex thing."[67] By the time Jagger began studying the Turners' "stagecraft," that undercurrent had become uppermost, and the lessons were more about "the spade sex thing" than about R&B. From Tina, he learned titillation, from Ike, menace and cruelty. It did not matter that these things were causing agony in private; in public they were causing ecstasy. In the eyes of both the Rolling Stones and their fans, Ike and Tina Turner were the ideal black couple.

As for the blood knot, it came full circle in 1970, when the Stones released "Brown Sugar," a song that inspires this tribute from Norman:

> "Brown Sugar" was an instant Jagger-Richards classic, fusing Keith's indolently repetitive opening riff with Jagger's hip-shaking Dixie drawl in a paean of racist sexism that could have been about Marsha Hunt [Jagger's black girlfriend], or brown Mexican heroin, or cunnilingus on a female plantation slave with Jagger as Simon Legree . . . "Brown Sugar" was the stickiest treat to be found on *Sticky Fingers*.[68]

Not surprisingly, Norman skips over the lyric about the "scarred old slaver" taking pleasure in midnight whippings of slave women. Some treats are a trifle too sticky.

In the end, the eroticism of early rock could not be less bluesy. Despite the boastful tone of such Chicago hits as Muddy Waters's "I Just Want to Make Love to You" or Howlin' Wolf's "Little Red Rooster," both renditions preserve, by means of finely tuned vocal and instrumental techniques, that "mixtery" of sound and emotion that suggests a playful disinterestedness toward the boastful impulses in man. In the Stones' hyped-up covers of these same songs, there is nothing but boastfulness, in a vocal so harshly weak that it forces our attention back to the guitar, which is being played louder and faster than the original, but certainly no better.

Add the guitar-centeredness of the rest of early rock, and you have a significant shift: away from an emotionally expressive vocalism and toward an athletically aggressive instrumentalism. With hindsight, we can see some rather striking sexual connotations in this shift. The controlled vocalism of genuine blues suggest power, intensity, and energy being harnessed—as opposed to repressed. The runaway instrumentalism of early rock suggests a lot of blocked, undifferentiated energy being released, in an uncontrollable rush. Blues performers know how to stop and take a breath, even in the midst of apparent ecstasy. They never lose their ability to address the audience, either by singing, playing, or talking. It is here that we find the sexual connotation. The capacity to communicate, even in the midst of passion, is what separates human lovemaking from dehumanized sex. Thus, even at their saltiest, blues performers always maintain a sense of reciprocity with their audiences. The guitar virtuosos, by contrast, lose themselves in a masturbatory fantasy. This contrast in performance style parallels the distinction between eroticism and obscenity—a distinction that would soon be lost on the youthful avatars of rock.

Part Three

Inspiration and Polarization

Chapter 12

Words and Music: The Rise of the Counterculture

By refuting the myth that 1950s rock 'n' roll was a social and cultural "revolution" anticipating the upheavals of the 1960s, I am not suggesting that there is no connection whatever between American culture in the 1950s and the so-called counterculture of the following decade. On the contrary, the connection is abundantly clear to anyone familiar with the intellectual undercurrents that surfaced during the Eisenhower years. My point is simply that these undercurrents came from one source, rock 'n' roll from another. It was not until the tumultuous 1960s that the two became conjoined.

The New Radicalism

The late 1950s were a time when many American intellectuals, especially those on the left, were profoundly weary of politics. The first generation of New York intellectuals had lived through the communist enthusiasms of the 1930s and the deadly splits over Stalin; the second had grown up amid the postwar debates about democracy and the bitter feuds over McCarthyism. For many of these people the Old Left was bankrupt: The real question was how best to deal with the triumph of the "bourgeois" West.

Yet, at the same time, many found it hard to abandon that old radical impulse—especially when the alternative was to accept American society as it existed under Eisenhower. So they rummaged around for a new radicalism, one that would focus less on "political economy" as understood by Marxists and more on "social psychology" as understood by Freudians. One of the most influential writers of the day was Herbert Marcuse, the eccentric Frankfurtian who articulated a vision of human liberation *within*, as opposed to *from*, consumer society. Another was Wilhelm Reich, the former psychoanalyst who posited a free-floating erotic energy, known as "orgone energy," that was both the cause of all human problems (from neurosis to nuclear weapons) and the potential solution (if discharged through more and better orgasms). In a similar vein, a professor of humanities named Norman O. Brown developed an erotic-liberationist theory of history and called for revolution, not against class oppression but against sexual repression. Finally there was the novelist Norman Mailer, who incorporated all these themes into his literary-journalistic persona; and the beat poet-proselytizer Allen Ginsberg.

The only one of these new radicals to set forth a political, or quasi-political, program was Paul Goodman, a social analyst who advocated the dismantling of the "organized system" of advanced technological society in the name of human freedom and wholeness, especially the sexual kind. An anarchist, Goodman was more adept at criticizing small institutions (which he sought to reform) than large ones (which he sought to destroy).[1] Yet, at the same time, he took a dim view of the beats, criticizing their "defensive ignorance of the academic culture" and their "cynicism and neglect of ethical and political goals." In his view the beats were no better at resisting the "system" than were the juvenile delinquents, and no less conformist than the "organization men" of big business and government.[2] Like the older generation of New York intellectuals, Goodman respected reason, high culture, the work ethic, and the idea of social progress.

Yet it was the irrational, debunking, anarchistic side of Goodman that most appealed to the young. According to the literary critic Morris Dickstein, the elite college students who flocked to hear Goodman in the early 1960s did not see him as all that different from Ginsberg. Like the poet Goodman was scruffy, poor, and accessible; he preached and practiced free love; he wrote and spoke in a way that rejected "the false neutrality of the social scientist" and "the hyper-cultivated Brahmin tone of the literary intellectuals."[3] Dickstein notes that there were important intellectual differences, not only between Ginsberg and Goodman, but among Marcuse, Reich, Brown, and Mailer. But from the perspective of the students, the important thing about these writers was what they had in common:

> Because these men were intellectuals, because we were budding intellectuals, they had made a startling conjunction for us—which they also embodied—between the world of ideas and a new mode of experience, a new consciousness. . . . [They] spoke with special urgency to our newness to the world of ideas—we who knew their vocabulary but had never seen it used with such animating directness—and to our late adolescence, for we knew that at bottom their gospel was a sexual one, that sex was their wedge for reorienting all human relations.[4]

Like Otto Gross at the turn of the century, these students wanted to overthrow not only sexual repression, but also the Freudian notion that sexual repression was necessary. Dickstein explains:

> The Freud who emerged . . . was not the Freud of the fifties whose dark view of human nature and the necessity of restraint provided the underpinning for a new social quietism. . . . Nor was it the liberal revisionism which, in departing from Freud's instinctual theories, tended to de-emphasize sex and to find happiness in the successful "adjustment" to society's demands.
>
> The new Freudian radicalism stressed the repressive character of society, but without the later Freud's tragic and stoical belief that these repressions could never be transcended . . . The key change since Freud's death is the tremendous expansion of technology which . . . points toward . . . the diminution of human labor, creating the possibility of a society built more on leisure and pleasure.[5]

To Norman Podhoretz, a contemporary of Dickstein's who is now a leading neoconservative, the secret of the new radicalism's appeal was that it "could survive perfectly well, and indeed even thrive, without the help of Marx or the Communist Party or the Soviet Union."[6] Yet Podhoretz overstates the case. The new radicals were nothing if not conversant with the Frankfurt School's ongoing efforts to combine Marx and Freud. However well they got along without the Communist Party and the Soviet Union, they were not about to jettison Marx. Writes Dickstein: "The end of the fifties saw the first publication in English of Marx's early writings, which emphasized 'alienation' rather than the laws of political economy, and which gave much impetus to the development of a new humanism that would steal Marx away from his orthodox keepers."[7]

It's not easy to synthesize Marx and Freud, but it is tempting. Writing in 1987, Allan Bloom offers this pungent assessment:

> Freud talked about interesting things not found anywhere in Marx. The whole psychology of the unconscious was completely alien to Marx, as was its inner motor, eros. None of this could be incorporated directly into Marx. But if Freud's interpretation of the cause of neuroses and his treatment of the maladjusted could itself [*sic*] be interpreted as bourgeois errors that serve enslavement to the capitalist control of the means of production, then Marx would move in on the Freudian scene. What Freud said were permanent contradictions between human nature and society could be set in motion dialectically, and in a socialist society there would be no need for the repression that causes neuroses. So Freud was neatly enrolled in the Marxist legions, adding to the charm of economics that of eros, and thereby providing a solution of what men are going to do after the revolution—a problem left unsolved by Marx.[8]

For Bloom, the real influence behind the new radicalism was Nietzsche, although the intellectuals of the 1950s did not acknowledge it, swayed as they still were by a simplistic condemnation of Nietzsche as the philosopher of Nazism.[9] This view of Nietzsche was challenged in the 1950s, most prominently by Walter Kaufmann, who showed that the philosopher had in fact abhorred racism, anti-intellectualism, and arrogant nationalism.[10] Kaufmann's careful scholarship set the stage for a new reading of Nietzsche, but unfortunately, there were many people for whom this new view turned out to be just as simplistic as the old. By the time the 1960s counterculture was in full swing, Nietzsche was widely seen as the philosopher of Dionysian abandonment, of unlimited sexual activity construed as the true source of artistic creativity, and of art as unfettered self-expression. Those who knew better were outnumbered, even in academic and intellectual circles, because the 1960s were also a time when careful scholarship went out of fashion.

"Modernism in the Streets"

The difference between the new radicalism of the late 1950s and the counterculture of the 1960s was, needless to say, one of scale. What began as the preoccupation of a tiny elite became the property of the public at large, with a speed that astonished all but the most prescient observers. The most prescient of these was Lionel Trilling, the literary dean of the New York intellectuals, who graduated from Columbia in 1925 and returned to teach

English there in the 1950s. Trilling never ceased to admire the achievements of the great modernist writers, or to analyze their affinities with Marx, Freud, and Nietzsche. Yet by the late 1950s Trilling was already asking some hard questions about the future of modernism. Having coined the phrase "adversary culture" to describe the generally hostile stance of modernism toward the rest of society, he began to express misgivings about the role played by educators like himself in transforming the anti-establishment literature of their youth into the established university curriculum.

In the first instance, Trilling worried about modernism losing its edge as it became "domesticated" into an "orthodoxy of dissent" shared by millions of educated—and semieducated—Americans.[11] But he also worried about that edge falling into philistine hands. The older New York intellectuals were troubled by the nihilistic agenda of the beats. But it was Trilling who suggested, in a 1961 essay called "On the Teaching of Modern Literature," that his own career might have contributed to "the socialization of the anti-social, or the acculturation of the anti-cultural, or the legitimation of the subversive."[12] He had good reason, since one of his most influential former students was Ginsberg. Trilling's conclusion puts the problem eloquently:

> I venture to say that the idea of losing oneself up to the point of self-destruction, of surrendering oneself to experience without regard to self-interest or conventional morality, of escaping wholly from the societal bonds, is an "element" somewhere in the mind of every modern person. . . . But the teacher who undertakes to present modern literature to his students may not allow that idea to remain in the *somewhere* of his mind; he must take it from the place where it exists habitual and unrealized and put it in the conscious forefront of his thought. . . . I press the logic of the situation not in order to question the legitimacy of the commitment, . . . but to confront those of us who do teach modern literature with the striking actuality of our enterprise.[13]

Reading this essay, one gets the eerie feeling that Trilling saw the late 1960s coming and perceived in advance that it would be a time when (as he wrote in 1969) "everything that was speculatively implied in literature" would be "actualized in politics, in social action."[14]

Trilling took a gloomy view of what he called "modernism in the streets," assuming that modernism could not be popularized without being debased.[15] It is striking to see Dickstein, a former student of Trilling's, view the same phenomenon through his generation's rose-colored granny glasses:

> For the impatient students . . . whose "counterculture" actually inherited
> many of the ideas of the "adversary culture," . . . culture was to be seen
> above all in its practical and political possibilities. If literature had its
> utopian and subversive import, if literature was full of incitement to rebel-
> lion and self-creation, if it taught us to judge man's life by the standard of
> quality rather than quantity, by the standard of imagination and full
> humanity rather than material success, then such visions could not be left
> to literature alone; they could be fulfilled in actuality. It was paradise now
> or never.[16]

Whether filtered through a gloomy or a rosy lens, this perspective on the
counterculture is important. Certainly it is more cogent than the 1960s
generation's vain belief that its ideas were brand new. This belief is now an
insufferable media cliché, in part because it was reinforced, back in the
1960s, by respected liberals.

One of these was Arthur M. Schlesinger, Jr., the eminent historian who,
writing in 1969, criticized the *political* radicalism of the New Left for being
driven by "anarchistic impulse" and "historical illiteracy" while at the same
time praising the *cultural* radicalism of the counterculture as a wholly fresh
response to "the velocity of history." Accepting the extravagant claim that
family, education, and religion had "lost their hold," Schlesinger endorsed
young people's efforts "to evolve their own values" and "to live according
to their own standards of authenticity."[17] Needless to say, his failure to see
any link between such efforts and the presence of Nietzsche, Blake, Freud,
Diderot, and Pirandello on undergraduate reading lists opens *him* to the
charge of historical illiteracy.[18]

Yet for all his neglect of the intellectual sources of the counterculture,
Schlesinger did make one important point. He observed that the students
of the 1960s "find in music and visual images the vehicles that bring home
reality."[19] Apart from quoting a couple of undergraduate effusions about
the Beatles and Bob Dylan, he had little to say about the nature of the
musical vehicle. But at least he noticed it.

Likewise Dickstein. Unlike his intellectual elders, Dickstein understood
from the beginning that the heart of the counterculture was not literature,
visual art, or even film, but music. Indeed, he argues that 1960s rock "kept
developing the complexity and subtlety of its resources," until it became
the medium through which

> the elite religion of modernism . . . was assimilated and—horrors!—popu-
> larized. A mass audience was created that was as tolerant of obscurity—as
> mystically addicted to it—as the audience of the early part of the century was
> indignant at it. Surrealism lost its shock-value—though not its hostility to

the audience—and became another language of verbal discourse, the royal road to the unconscious and the irrational.[20]

Nowadays, both the critics and defenders of the counterculture stress the importance of music. Allan Bloom and Camille Paglia, for example, disagree about many things—but not about the Rolling Stones being the ultimate expression of Dionysian energy. Of course, neither pays any attention to Muddy Waters. But that's exactly the point. Once again, the intellectuals debating the significance of cultural change do not stop to interrogate their own assumptions about popular music. Older intellectuals decrying rock music's influence depict it as the whole-cloth creation of the Beatles; Dickstein implies that American popular music lacked "complexity and subtlety" before the 1960s; and speculators such as Bloom and Paglia see rock as a kind of seizure contracted by reading the wrong (or right) books.

As for Trilling himself, he had the good grace to admit feeling overwhelmed. In a public forum in the early 1970s, he was pressed by Hilton Kramer and Podhoretz to explain why he was not more forceful in attacking the counterculture. His reply was a simple one: "Fatigue." Then he added: "Subjects and problems got presented in a way that made one's spirits fail. It wasn't that one was afraid to go into it, or afraid of being in opposition—I suppose I am speaking personally—but rather that in looking at the matter one's reaction was likely to be a despairing shrug."[21]

Was this a "failure of nerve," as Kramer later called it? Or was it an honest confession of bewilderment by a man who had always taken pride in being a seismographer of culture?[22] Did Trilling suspect that "modernism in the streets" was not a complete explanation for what happened in the 1960s—that there might be a hidden dimension to the counterculture that, despite his best efforts, he had not been able to fathom? There is room for this interpretation in Mark Krupnick's overview of Trilling's career:

> The early essays are informed by an acute sense of immediate social and political issues; the late essays rely on large general notions of "the self." It has been the fate of cultural criticism to become more refined, less material, *as the social context of culture becomes less accessible to rational comprehension.* Criticism falls back on "the self" *when the culture itself becomes more heterogeneous and resistant to interpretation.*[23] (emphasis added)

Far be it from me to claim that Trilling would have been less fatigued and despairing if he had understood the musical vehicle ridden so hard by 1960s youth. But I am convinced that the period he found so bewildering becomes a lot less "resistant to interpretation" when such an understanding is achieved. A friend of Trilling's recalls an incident in 1973, when, after sitting through a movie with a powerful rock soundtrack, Trilling rose from his seat and cried: "How can the novel compete with *that*?" I never knew Lionel Trilling, but I would like to think that what follows is a partial answer to his question.

Bob Dylan's Coffeehouse Blend

Despite their popularity in the early 1960s, Motown and Ray Charles did not capture the allegiance of young whites who had grown up on rock 'n' roll but were now looking for something more "serious." For this group the only vehicle worth jumping aboard was the folk music bandwagon gathering steam on both sides of the Atlantic. In the United States as in Britain, this movement favored old material, Appalachian ballads, and country blues, played on "authentic" (meaning acoustic) instruments. Exceptions were made for new songs with "progressive" (meaning protest) lyrics, but any other signs of contemporary taste, such as electrified instruments or up-to-date love lyrics, were not tolerated.

The hero of the folk movement was Woody Guthrie, the famous Depression songwriter whose best lyrics grew out of harsh personal experience: as a penniless "Okie" being turned back at the California border ("Dough-Re-Mi"); as a half-starved farmworker being cheated by wasteful growers ("Pastures of Plenty"); as a union organizer being bullied by company thugs ("Union Maid"). Musically, Guthrie borrowed many of his tunes from "hillbilly" and gospel sources, which he did not see as a problem because he neither claimed nor respected copyright. Guthrie was never a member of the Communist Party, although he traveled in the same circles for many years.[24] But his music is an almost perfect embodiment of the Popular Front—no doubt because he really was one of "the folk," coming from humble origins in rural Oklahoma.

Being one of the folk was more problematic for another leading light, Pete Seeger, whose background was politically leftist but also privileged. As his half-sister Peggy once remarked about their upbringing among New York City's WASP elite, it was necessary for the Seegers to learn "who 'the folk' really are."[25] Still, it helped that Pete, a loyal member of the Party till 1951, got blacklisted during the McCarthy years. Such credentials sustained his good reputation among leftist folkies quick to condemn any performer suspected of "selling out."

Actually, Seeger's first priority has always been *singing* out. Despite his somewhat rigid politics, he is musically less a purist than a popularizer.

During the 1950s and 1960s, he cofounded the folk movement's premier magazines, *Sing Out!* and *Broadside*. He also fostered countless careers (including that of Guthrie, whom he met in 1940), and did his best to keep up with the times—even if that meant occasionally venturing into the forbidden territory of "decadent commercialism." In sum, Seeger played a key role in bridging the gap between the elite folk movement of the 1950s and the mass counterculture that followed.

That gap began closing in 1958, when a group called the Kingston Trio placed a folk song, "Tom Dooley," at the top of the pop chart. Their success was spurred by their image as all-American boys from California (*not* Greenwich Village), wearing crew cuts and collegiate outfits (*not* overalls and workshirts) and singing old Tennessee ballads (*not* protest songs). There was also more room on the chart, since the original rock 'n' rollers were fast decamping from the scene. Not sorry to see them go, the national media and the major record labels were strongly attracted to the idea of a folk music craze, providing it was purged of the Old Leftist taint.[26] By 1962 the Kingston Trio, the Limelighters, Peter, Paul & Mary (described by one critic as "the Kingston Trio with sex appeal"), Judy Collins, and Joan Baez had all emerged from the coffeehouses into the big time, including profiles in *Newsweek* and contracts with companies such as Capitol and Warner.[27]

Leftist politics were not the only thing purged from this first wave of "popular folk music."[28] Also purged were many Afro-American sounds. Not all of these performers fit the narrow clean-cut stereotype: the Limelighters were obviously Jewish; Peter and Paul sported "beatnik" beards; Mary, Judy, and Joan all had the long straight tresses that would soon be flowing on every American campus and suburb. But appearances could be forgiven when the voices and guitars were crystal clear, the melodies hummable, the harmonies sweet, and the lyrics intelligible. Because they sounded so pretty, these popular folk singers gained elite approval the way the Beatles later did: by promising to woo young listeners away from rougher, bluesier, more rhythmic sounds.

The promise was only temporary, though, because one young folkie was about to reinject the music with all these sounds and more. In 1961 a nineteen-year-old named Robert Zimmerman, the son of an appliance store manager in Hibbing, Minnesota, came East on a pilgrimage to the bedside of Guthrie (then incapacitated with the Huntington's chorea that was to kill him six years later). Intent on becoming Guthrie's heir, Zimmerman began hanging around every coffeehouse in Greenwich Village, playing for pennies and promoting a mythic identity as "Bob Dylan," a precocious drifter who had spent his youth traveling the highways and byways and learning folk music directly from the folk.

The truth is that Dylan, like most of his generation, learned most of his folk music from records, in particular those of Ramblin' Jack Elliott, a native of Brooklyn who was the first to drop his Jewish name (Elliott Adnopoz) and become Guthrie's heir.[29] Like Elliott's, Dylan's manner of singing, self-accompanied on guitar and harmonica, was too rough to cross over to the mainstream. But to folkies bewitched by the blues, roughness epitomized authenticity. Compared with a country blues master such as John Lee Hooker, Dylan was the rankest amateur. But the distinction was lost on pundits such as Robert Shelton of the *New York Times*, who wrote in 1961: "Mr. Dylan's voice is anything but pretty. He is consciously trying to recapture the rude beauty of a Southern field hand musing in melody on his porch. All the 'husk and bark' are left on his notes and a searing intensity pervades his songs." And Elliott offered his own seal of approval: "There was not another son of a bitch in the country that could sing until Bob Dylan came along. Everybody else was singing like a damned faggot."[30]

Even more authenticating were Dylan's politics. Most of the major labels avoided politicized folk music, but there was one notable exception. The eminent John Hammond offers this straightforward explanation of his—and Dylan's—reasons for teaming up in 1962:

> Well, it was partly that my politics are left, you see, and Bobby was in his protest days. . . . He was not respectful of the Establishment. . . . And the only reason Bobby was willing to come to CBS was that I had signed Pete Seeger when he was still blacklisted. Columbia Records proved its independence from CBS by signing Seeger. So Bobby figured he couldn't go wrong if he went to CBS, and he didn't go wrong.[31]

Accordingly, Columbia gave some leeway to Dylan's protest side. The company did veto two of the songs on Dylan's first album of original material, *The Freewheelin' Bob Dylan* (1963).[32] And Dylan got censored by the higher-ups at CBS-TV, who refused to let him play his "Talkin' John Birch Society Blues" on the Ed Sullivan show. Nonetheless, *Freewheelin'* retained four songs that became instant protest classics: "Masters of War," "Ballad of a Thin Man," "A Hard Rain's A-Gonna Fall," and "Blowin' in the Wind"— which even scaled the pop chart when covered by Peter, Paul & Mary. And Dylan's second protest album, *The Times They Are A-Changin'* (1963), carried him to triumph at that year's Newport Folk Festival, where he was celebrated as the unchallenged bearer of the Guthrie-Seeger mantle.

But then a strange thing happened: the mantle bearer became a turn-coat. In 1964 Dylan released *Another Side of Bob Dylan*, which contained no protest songs at all, not even vaguely poetic ones like "Blowin' in the Wind." Instead the lyrics focused on the singer's troubled feelings about personal relationships and life in general. The only song that could be called topical was "My Back Pages," the confession of a former know-it-all who now realizes that neither he nor anyone else has all the answers. Not surprisingly, this new effort moved the diehard folkies at *Sing Out!* to accuse Dylan of "selling out." Yet Dylan was not doing that, he was merely updating himself. By introducing songs with psychosexual themes and rather cryptic lyrics, he was both breaking with the objective certainties of the Old Left and announcing his involvement with the subjective myster-ies of the new radicalism.

Dismaying though this change of lyrical emphasis may have been, it was nothing compared with the musical change that followed. By 1965 Dylan's fans were accustomed to seeing his songs climb the pop chart when cov-ered by Peter, Paul & Mary. But then a new kind of cover appeared: A West Coast group called the Byrds, who had started out as a folk group but were now moving toward rock, covered an unreleased Dylan song called "Mr. Tambourine Man." As Charlie Gillett describes, the move toward rock got a boost in the studio:

> The [Byrds] were already playing "Mr. Tambourine Man" in their live set, but [Columbia] producer Terry Melcher had doubts that it could hold the steady time-pulse needed for a danceable radio single. The necessary profes-sional feel was supplied by three of Los Angeles's top sessionmen, whose experience included most of Phil Spector's sessions: Larry Knechtal played the elegant and captivating bass-line, while Hal Blaine kept time on drums; Leon Russell's first instrument was piano, but here he played guitar, blend-ing in with the distorted clang of [Byrd leader] McGuinn's twelve-string guitar. . . . The rest of the group stood around shaking tambourines and singing along with the chorus.[33]

When "Mr. Tambourine Man" reached the top of the pop chart, the reaction was predictable. After all, it was only a few years earlier that Muddy Waters's electrified Chicago blues split the British folk movement. American folkies had experienced the same split, and Dylan's original admirers were those who rejected electric blues and, needless to say, deplored the very existence of rock 'n' roll. Thus they were appalled when Dylan—Guthrie's heir—allowed one of his songs to be turned into a "danceable radio single."

The Authenticity of Electricity

Then Dylan himself went over the edge, deciding in 1965 to perform with electric instruments. In March of that year he released *Bringing It All Back Home*, a remarkable album featuring acoustic guitar on one side, electric guitar and drums on the other. Unlike his earlier LPs, this one sold more than a million copies. Flushed with confidence, Dylan arrived at the Newport Folk Festival that July accompanied by the Paul Butterfield Blues Band, a white American group honorably apprenticed to the Chicago blues. It was a bold move, and it caused great distress: the crowd hissed and booed; Seeger was "brokenhearted and angry"; Dylan was again attacked in *Sing Out!*[34]

But the move also won converts—including Seeger, who recorded his own electric blues album the following year.[35] However distressing Dylan's triumph may have been to the purists, it is readily comprehensible to anyone not allergic to commercialism. There are two senses in which Dylan really *did* bring it all back home. For other Americans, he reclaimed the blues from captivity in Great Britain (in the background of the photo on the cover of *Bringing It All Back Home*, the discerning eye can pick out the record sleeve of Columbia's 1961 reissue of Robert Johnson). And for young people on both sides of the Atlantic, Dylan reclaimed the distinctive sound of the Afro-American idiom from both the incipient distortions of early rock and the prettiness of popular folk.

These achievements are impressive when we consider that Dylan is at best a mediocre musician. The roughness of his voice may remind naive listeners of the blues, but as we've seen, there's a lot more to the blues than roughness. The same must be said of his guitar and harmonica—he will never be in demand as a session musician. But natural endowment and technical skill comprise only one side of musical talent. There is another side, manifested in the two areas where the young Dylan did excel: songwriting and tastemaking.

It is ironic that Dylan should have started out in the purist folk movement, because his best songs stand in the finest tradition of C&W, from Jimmie Rodgers and Hank Williams to Johnny Cash and Willie Nelson. There is also a trace of Broadway in the way he combines pungent blues honesty with acerbic Jewish wit. The results are complex emotions rendered in spare, elegant ballads: "It Ain't Me Babe," "Don't Think Twice, It's All Right," "Girl from the North Country," "Boots of Spanish Leather," "Tomorrow Is a Long Time." Of course, this mixture of C&W and Broadway is nothing new: Except for the oldest hymns and ballads, country music has long been permeated with the influence of commercial popular song. As for the blues, Dylan had a better understanding than the Rolling Stones of the lyric versatility of the masters: "You can say it in a different way, you can say it with more words, but you can't say anything better than what they said. And they covered everything."[36]

Given Dylan's flair for writing ballads of gemlike clarity, it is regrettable that he was mentored by Ginsberg during his Greenwich Village period. For Dylan's more rambling, free-associative lyrics display the typical vices of beat poetry: deliberate obscurity, self-indulgence, pretentiousness, and (most damning) indifference to the aural texture—the *music*—of words. Since Dickstein is primarily a literary critic, it is interesting to note his cool assessment of Dylan's poetry amid his otherwise warm enthusiasm for 1960s rock: "[Dylan] produced nothing which could be anthologized in any first-class collection of verse. Verbally, whatever Dylan did well during that period [1964–66] had already been done better by a whole line of *poètes maudits* from Blake, Rimbaud, and Lautréamont to his friend Allen Ginsberg."[37]

Yet here again Dylan snatched victory from the jaws of defeat. His early attempts at "poetic" lyrics, such as "Ballad in Plain D," are not only verbally overstuffed, they are musically threadbare—the listener soon tires of his monotonous guitar and harmonica playing. After 1965, however, the monotony was relieved: *Bringing It All Back Home, Highway 61 Revisited* (1965), and *Blonde on Blonde* (1966) all benefit from excellent musical support.[38] As Gillett explains, Dylan's decision to "go electric" depended upon other people's willingness to go "sifting through the available musicians in search of people who could adapt to Dylan's primitive musical technique without either smothering him or exposing his limitations." Gillett cites the example of *Blonde on Blonde*, which backs Dylan with some of Nashville's "best young session men including pianist 'Pig' Robbins, bass player Wayne Moss, drummer Norman Putnam and guitarist Jerry Kennedy, supplemented by Robbie Robertson and Al Kooper from earlier associations, and Joe South from Atlanta."[39] I repeat Gillett's list of names because, with the exception of the last three, they are not likely to be recognized by the millions who regard *Blonde on Blonde* as Dylan's masterpiece—the work, as one critic put it, of an "astonishingly gifted young man."[40] Of course, Pig Robbins and the others may well regard their work with Dylan as their main claim to fame: Their playing enlivened his material, but it *was* his material, and there was nothing else like it at the time. Nonetheless, an intelligent critic like Dickstein should know better than to treat the musicians' contribution as mere fluff:

Take a favorite song of mine, "I Want You" (on *Blonde on Blonde*), which combines a terribly simple, hard-driving refrain, consisting mainly of the words in the title, with the most surreal and inaccessible stanzas, some whose lyrics can't even be made out, much less understood. With its overpowering rhythm it's a great song for dancing, as well as a riveting expression of intense sexual need. But the tune, the rhythm, and the refrain would be hollow without the suggestive, bizarre poetic fragments of story and metaphor that create the mood, build up feeling, and intimate deeper meanings. It's as if Dylan needed esoteric mysteries to support the pop refrain.[41]

In spite of having judged Dylan a mediocre poet, Dickstein claims that this album would be "hollow" without the "feeling" and "deeper meanings" provided by the words. It may be that Dickstein is one of those people who admire words more than music, also finding the sound of an Italian opera or a German *lied* "hollow" without the libretto or poetic text. But I doubt it. More likely he is dismissing the music of Nashville sessionmen because they are . . . well, Nashville sessionmen. And he is giving undue credit to Dylan's "poetic fragments" because they are . . . well, "poetic fragments." The music itself? Fit only for dancing or the "expression of intense sexual need."

This exegesis would not be necessary if Dickstein's bias were unique. But it isn't. The majority of those who champion the 1960s counterculture end up belittling Afro-American music as the humble accompaniment of the "poetic" expression of "serious" figures like Dylan. Indeed, the appeal of Dylan's musical sound gets forgotten in the ongoing cottage industry of pseudo-literary analysis of his "texts." To his credit, Dylan never fell for such foolishness. Here is his reaction, in a 1969 interview with *Rolling Stone*:

Q: There's a cat named Allen Weberman who writes in the "East Village Other." He calls himself the world's leading Dylanologist. You know him?

A: No . . . Oh, yes, I did. Is this the guy that tears up all my songs? Well, he oughta take a rest. He's way off. . . . let me tell you, this boy's *off*. . . . I bet he's a hard-working fellow, though. I bet he really does a good job if he could find something to do, but it's too bad it's just my songs, 'cause I don't really know if there's enough material in my songs to sustain someone who is really out to do a big job. . . . I mean, a fellow like that would be much better off writing about Tolstoy, or Dostoevsky.[42]

For all his sarcasm, which is legendary, Dylan never took the fatal step of being sarcastic about music. He never lost his boyhood taste for C&W, R&B, and 1950s rock 'n' roll—all those "commercialized" categories of

Afro-American music that propelled him out of the narrow folk music orbit. Nor did he ever lose touch with the blues. In 1963, when the Rolling Stones were busy reducing it to a primitivist caricature, Dylan was telling Nat Hentoff:

> The way I think about the blues comes from what I learned from Big Joe Williams. The blues is more than something to sit home and arrange. What made the real blues singers so great is that they were able to state all the problems they had; but at the same time, they were standing outside of them and could look at them. And in that way, they had them beat. What's depressing today is that many young singers are trying to get *inside* the blues, forgetting that those older singers used them to get *outside* their troubles.[43]

Recently Dylan's rare public appearances have been depressing: his corroded voice has lost whatever narrow range it once possessed, and his face and body seem older than his years, wracked by nameless, perhaps unnameable, demons. And his behavior toward all forms of tribute can only be described as perverse. But the man still attracts the support of excellent musicians, people willing to step out of their own spotlight and play backup, working overtime to make the faded legend sound good.

As for the substance of that legend, it has left two legacies, one unfortunate and the other fortunate. The unfortunate legacy is the tendency, on the part of the post-1960s popular music culture, to neglect music in favor of words. For all its talk of "peace and love," the counterculture was really rooted in the assumptions of the new radicalism: that the "system" was rotten; that happiness within it was illusory; that compromise would yield a living death; and that the only hope lay in negation and revolt, the more radical the better. Those who shared these assumptions were bound to take a highly selective view of Afro-American music. Like Mailer declaring that "jazz is orgasm," they took what they wanted from black music (and, I might add, from black people) and left the rest. If the music didn't suit, they were only too happy to debase it. The fact that some blacks assisted in the process didn't make it any less of a debasement.

The fortunate legacy is the effort, on the part of many subsequent musicians, to follow Dylan's example in tempering the negative sensibility of the new radicalism with the affirmative sound and spirit of Afro-American music. I shall return to this legacy later. But for now, suffice it to say that the young Dylan was more interesting than a lot of 1960s rock stars because he was genuinely torn between the musical tradition he loved and the counterculture that loved him.

Chapter 13

Art and Religion, 1960s Style

When Dickstein wrote that rock "kept developing the complexity and subtlety of its resources" in the 1960s, he meant that on both sides of the Atlantic, technological change was fostering a new, self-consciously "artistic" phase of the music.

By the 1950s, "serious" music had been transformed by electronics: computers, synthesizers, tape recorders. Postwar serialists like Karlheinz Stockhausen and Milton Babbitt used the new technology to achieve higher levels of mathematical order. Aleatory composers like John Cage used it to explore randomness and chance. Both were fascinated by electronic methods of creating sound. And the commercial record industry carried out its own, market-oriented research. It was inevitable that rock would be affected.

The first sign of change came in 1965, when Brian Wilson of the Beach Boys withdrew from live performance into his state-of-the-art studio, where he spent six months crouched over the latest four-track tape machines and Moog synthesizers, finally emerging with "Good Vibrations," a remarkable single that swept the charts in 1966 and is still regarded as one of the most technically accomplished singles ever produced.[1]

Yet it is significant that, like Phil Spector, Wilson was a shy middle-class kid with no special talent or liking for live performance. Until the rock era, it was not really possible to succeed as a musician in the Afro-American idiom without learning how to handle oneself in front of an audience. This does not mean that all prerock musicians were natural performers. On the contrary, many were shy types who got their satisfaction from the music, not the applause. But all the same, they had to go out there and play for the people. The option of withdrawal did not exist—at least, not until music making got transformed into a laboratory science.

To the extent that rock 'n' roll was invented in Sam Phillips's Sun Studio, it started out as electronic music. But because rock 'n' roll was also continuous with the Afro-American tradition, its musical values existed quite apart from electronics. As we saw in the case of Motown, the best use of the new technology was the "traditional" one of projecting voices and instruments through limited media such as the transistor radio. But Wilson and Spector didn't take this route, preferring to make music independent of the gifts, and failings, of actual musicians. The advantage for the producer is obvious, but so is the danger. By removing Afro-American music from the discipline of singing and playing for others, the studio of the 1960s removed it from the taproot of its strength.

The best example is the Beatles. Two albums, *Rubber Soul* (1965) and *Revolver* (1966), were feats of songwriting by the individual members of the group, and of studio wizardry by George Martin, who basically created multitrack recordings on four-track tape (eight- and sixteen-track were not yet available). Then, in 1967, Martin and the Beatles outdid themselves with their most celebrated album, *Sergeant Pepper's Lonely Hearts Club Band*. Mackay explains how the process worked by then:

> The technique was, in simple terms, to record on all four tracks and transfer them to one or two tracks of another four-track machine. This left spare tracks available which could be used and transferred. . . . The four composite tracks could then be mixed to stereo. All this was very time-consuming, especially since the *Sergeant Pepper* album used a lot of special tape effects as well as orchestral and other instruments.[2]

Even more multilayered than its predecessors, *Sergeant Pepper* still has remarkable clarity and shape. The sounds that are closest to the listener, such as the vocals, are crisp and palpable. Those that are furthest removed, such as the hurdy-gurdy in "For the Benefit of Mr. Kite," are delicately cobwebbed with static. The result is a montage of diverse sounds that sustains the illusion of coherence and depth. By combining the technical (if not the musical) emphasis of Motown with that of Spector and Wilson, *Sergeant Pepper* is both a wall of sound and a bas-relief.

Yet the album is also a withdrawal. Philip Norman suggests that its many references to carnival and music hall can be seen as compensation for the fact that the Beatles were finished as a live band.[3] They were finished for a technical reason: Having become (in Lennon's provocative phrase) "more popular than Jesus," they could play only in the largest venues; typical was their 1966 Shea Stadium concert, where 55,000 fans strained to hear the music over a PA system that would be deemed barely adequate for a large nightclub today.[4] And the Beatles were finished for a personal reason: Having taken the world by storm, they now felt stormed by the world; Lennon and McCartney in particular itched to escape their role as prize attractions in an international entertainment conglomerate.

The Beatles' problems were unique, of course. But the sheer scale of their success inspired grandiose, if not megalomaniac, fantasies on the part of others. According to *Time*, the Beatles' previous music had "blended monotonously into the parched badlands of rock." But now, with *Sergeant Pepper*, they had transformed rock into "an art form."[5]

Art Rock, Art Damage

The usual term for the music that followed *Sergeant Pepper* is "art rock," though some wags in the record industry use the phrase "art damage" to describe its presumed unmarketability.[6] In fact, art rock has often proved surprisingly marketable. Still, "art damage" remains an apt description of its musical impact.

Along with technological change, art rock was also fostered by social change. When the working-class Beatles received MBE (Member of the British Empire) honors at Buckingham Palace, it suddenly seemed as though Britain's "rock royalty" would be able to leap tall class barriers at a single bound. But, like race friction in America, class friction in Britain does not disappear so much as change shape. We've seen how the lower-middle-class Rolling Stones scorned the "pop" taste of the working-class Beatles. In a similar way, countless upper-middle- and upper-class Britons greeted both groups' success with the suspicion that someone with the "proper background" could do rock "better." As the music became the province of older, more educated, and affluent youth, many with training in classical music, "better" was (predictably) defined as more European.[7]

Not all the art rockers had classical training. But a few did: Gary Brooker of Procol Harum studied piano, as did Keith Emerson of Emerson, Lake, and Palmer, and several members of Yes. Rick Wright and Roger Waters of Pink Floyd were admirers of Stockhausen. And Ian Anderson of Jethro Tull was a virtuoso flutist. Gillett explains that art rock emerged from a new kind of cellar club in London that showcased the talents of

> middle class musicians who had only recently noticed pop music's existence . . . [and who were] less concerned with the repetitive chords of American dance music than with finding musical structures for free-form poetry and melodic improvisations. . . . At the Middle Earth and UFO in London's West End, the audience took acid or smoked dope in the gloom. . . . The erratic rhythms of the musicians threw the audience into spasm-dance movements, while the guitarists carried themselves off into space.[8]

As this account suggests, art rockers did not serve long apprenticeships in live performance. Even before London narcotics squads began raiding the clubs, the genre responded to the siren call of the studio. After *Sergeant Pepper* the rock album was viewed in a new light: Rather than a collection of singles, it would now become a unified whole, like a symphony. Obviously it was time for people with the "proper background" to get busy creating lasting works of art.

Ironically, the most lasting creations turned out to be a handful of hit singles: "Your Move" by Yes, "Nights in White Satin" by the Moody Blues, and "A Whiter Shade of Pale" by Procol Harum (based on a melody by Bach).[9] In most art rock it is clear that the goal is the musical Big Time, meaning romanticism. Because art rock strives for exalted, oceanic emotion, the critic John Rockwell accuses it of "sentimentality" and "late-romantic bathos."[10] In that sense, art rock is kitsch. But it is also perverse modernism, because it glories in shapelessness, in what Murray calls "a wholehearted assault on the very notion of structure, which—in musical terms—served as a useful metaphor for the unacceptable face of authority."[11] Like free jazz, art rock proves once again that total freedom is enabling for a handful of geniuses, but disabling for everyone else.

In this respect, it's useful to compare art rock with classic American popular song. Songsmiths such as Kern, Gershwin, and Porter derived complex melodies and coloristic harmonies from romanticism, but they also submitted them to the thirty-two-bar form and the polyrhythmic requirements of swing. Art rock borrows the same elements, but it doesn't submit them to any discipline. Instead it simply embellishes them until the available space—a multitrack tape the length of an LP side—is filled. Thus art rock mimics the superficial effects of romanticism while ignoring the demands of musical architecture. It is hardly surprising that the genre's most celebrated successes consist of decoration added to existing compositions, such as Emerson, Lake, and Palmer's *Pictures at an Exhibition* (music by Mussorgsky).

Eventually the pressures of popularity returned art rock to live performance, but in a manner as remote from the older tradition as the chariot-size instruments of the Romans were from the Greek *aulos* and *kithara*. The biggest swing band, the loudest Chicago blues, the brassiest R&B revue, the mightiest gospel choir—none approaches the sheer scale, volume, and technical sophistication of an early-1970s rock concert. Driven by the challenge of venues like Shea Stadium, the sound engineers of the late 1960s developed hugely powerful amplification systems capable of filling gigantic sports arenas—or, in the case of Woodstock, acres of farmland. Needless to say, there was (and is) a mismatch between such systems and the virtues of Afro-American music. It's hard to tell which loss is more troublesome: that of audience interaction, or that of sound quality—not that the two are unrelated.

Art rock didn't suffer these losses, because it didn't have these virtues to begin with. As Andy Mackay explains:

> By the early 1970s, the pattern of the monster, touring rock band had been established. . . . The major groups set out with fleets of articulated lorries carrying the equipment to build night by night a multi-media show of formidable proportions. Groups vied with each other to stay ahead in the league of technological overkill: . . . Emerson, Lake & Palmer [traveled] with a revolving drum kit and a complete symphony orchestra individually amplified with contact mikes. . . . Pink Floyd developed lights, special effects, the use of tapes and multi-directional speaker set-ups to a new level of sophistication.[12]

Art rock was not the only genre to turn itself into a multimedia extravaganza. But it was foremost in adding pretension to grandiosity. As might be expected, the art rockers were not content with mere music—even when supplemented by truckloads of hardware, computerloads of software, and the trappings of grand opera. Roger Waters of Pink Floyd explained in 1969 that "the performance becomes more theatrical. And it needs special material—it can include melodrama, literary things, musical things or lights."[13]

Wagner would have put it more eloquently, I daresay. But the goal was undeniably Wagnerian—or rather pseudo-Wagnerian, since it didn't involve the labor of coherent musical composition.

Art rock did not, for the most part, realize its aspirations. Some groups played with symphony orchestras, but the results won few converts. Ironically, the group that came closest to winning high-cultural status was the Who, art-college contemporaries of the Rolling Stones who started out playing crude imitations of soul music for the working-class "mods" of London's East End. The Who made their biggest mark in 1968, with the release of a two-record set called *Tommy: A Rock Opera*. Despite the name, *Tommy* does not mix rock with European music. On the contrary, it is dominated by the Who's mature style: ponderous, rhythmically monotonous hard rock, relieved only by a scrap of memorable melody (the haunting "feel me, touch me" refrain) and Elton John playing boogie-woogie piano.

All the same it was *Tommy* and not Pink Floyd that appeared on the stage of New York's Metropolitan Opera in 1970. Why did *Tommy* succeed while other, more musically pretentious concoctions failed? There are two reasons, both having to do with the cultural climate of the late 1960s. First, *Tommy* was considered more authentic, precisely because it consists of hard rock, rather than doctored-up Mussorgsky.[14] Second, *Tommy* avoids the typical pseudoromantic themes of art rock (fairy-tale bliss and apocalyptic angst) in favor of the more up-to-date subject of popular culture itself.

The plot is clumsily contrived: A boy is struck blind, deaf, and dumb (when his father is murdered by his mother's lover); finds salvation in his sense of touch (developed by playing pinball); gains celebrity as a pinball champion; sets out to save the world; is thwarted by greed and violence; and retreats into his private realm. All of this is delivered without drama or character development, only heavy-handed visual symbolism accompanied by leaden music. Still, the critics raved, one calling *Tommy* "a major milestone in the evolution of rock from a relatively mindless form of entertainment to an art form that deals with the complexities of modern life."[15] Translated, such praise means that *Tommy* is a work of pop art, accurately reflecting that movement's self-conscious ambivalence toward commercialized culture.[16] Not surprisingly its most compelling scene is the one in which a mob gathers in a cathedral to pay obeisance to Marilyn Monroe.

Tommy does not use the cathedral setting to make a religious statement, merely to comment on the idol-worshiping ways of the masses. This detail raises an important difference between British and American rock in the late 1960s. In Britain rock musicians aspired to *art*, to breaking down the doors of the elite cultural establishment. In the United States, by contrast, where the divisions of class and culture were less rigid, rock musicians aspired to *spirituality*.

I realize that spirituality is not part of the 1960s counterculture as described so far. But as the movement evolved, even its intellectual founders noticed that it had a religious dimension. Goodman, for example, wrote in 1970 that the real insurgency of the time was a spiritual one.[17] Dickstein argues that the poetry of the 1960s expressed a new "spiritual seriousness."[18] And Schlesinger departed from his criticism of the New Left's disorganized, ahistorical politics long enough to praise the counter-culture's plunge into disorganized, ahistorical religion.[19] As the reader may guess, my own view is that the much-vaunted spirituality of the counter-culture was really pseudospirituality, with the most important ingredients missing. Certainly this is the picture that emerges from the evolving rituals of 1960s rock.

West Rips Off East: Minimalism and San Francisco Rock

While art rock looked to Europe for inspiration, spiritualized rock looked to Asia, in particular to the raga music of the Indian sitar master Ravi Shankar. By the mid-1960s Shankar's teaching and playing had impressed a great many jazz musicians, as well as such non-jazz composers as Philip Glass. In the case of jazz, the influence consisted of a few borrowed elements: scales, melodic and rhythmic patterns, and drones added to the basic vocabulary of jazz.[20] In the case of Glass, a graduate of Juilliard who broke with European music after contracting to transcribe a Shankar raga for a film score, the result was a style of composition that makes a virtue of repetition.[21] As Glass explains, the idea is to "take very small units and add them together.... Then you join cycles of different beats, wheels within wheels, everything going at the same time and always changing."[22]

Since tape recorders are better at repeating themselves than live musicians, similar ideas occurred to composer-engineers such as Terry Riley, Steve Reich (both American), and Mike Oldfield (British), whose experiments proved surprisingly lucrative when rock fans rushed out to buy Riley's *A Rainbow in Curved Air* and Oldfield's *Tubular Bells*.[23]

The name for this trend is *minimalism*, a word that elicits mixed responses because the impact of this trend on our musical culture has been uneven. On the lowest level, minimalism can be blamed for "new age" music, best described as upscale Muzak. On the middle level, minimalism has contributed some of the most riveting and evocative film music ever heard, such as the passages from *Tubular Bells* used in the stylish horror film *The Exorcist*, and Glass's stunning scores for *Koyaanisqatsi* and *Hamburger Hill*. On the highest level, however, the jury is still out. Minimalist composers see themselves writing concert music that, according to Steve Reich, should "facilitate closely detailed listening."[24] The same presumption animates (if that is the word) Glass's collaborations with the stage designer Robert Wilson, in which the former's painstakingly crafted, glacially evolving sound patterns accompany the latter's slow-motion tableaux vivants. Unfortunately the vivant quality often eludes audiences struggling to keep their eyes open.

I realize that the last comment brands me as the type of philistine who would snore through *Einstein on the Beach*. All I can say is that, even wide awake, I remain skeptical about the quasi-spiritual claims of introverted modernism. Like the blank canvases of radical nonobjective painters, the monotonous compositions of minimalist composers are routinely praised for inducing the aesthetic equivalent of a religious trance.[25] But, as I asked earlier, to what purpose? The unavoidable fact is that, without a meaningful connection with the symbols and disciplines of a shared religious tradition, such as Hindus possess when they listen to ragas, most of us (including most music lovers) find it hard to stick with trancelike music for its own sake. We may become mesmerized for a while, but when nothing much happens, we become unmesmerized.

Unless, of course, we are stoned. In the streets, parks, and clubs of San Francisco during the mid-1960s, "psychedelic" or "acid" rock groups such as the Grateful Dead and the Jefferson Airplane aspired to spirituality in the form of high guruship in the "expansion" of their generation's "consciousness." Quick to seize on the sitar, especially after George Harrison strummed one in "Norwegian Wood," these San Francisco groups made that instrument's shivery arpeggios into musical code for the drug experience. It is worth noting that when Shankar saw the sitar being used in this way, he "gracefully withdrew from that scene."[26]

Afro-American sounds were put to similar use. The Grateful Dead was started in 1965 by Jerry Garcia, an accomplished guitarist and bluegrass banjoist, and the group quickly became famous for their live performances at the many "peace and love" celebrations of the mid-1960s. Having started out as a folkie jug band and then graduated to being the "'acid test' house band" of novelist (and former beatnik) Ken Kesey and his LSD-taking

Merry Pranksters, the Dead were masters at managing the moods of a stoned crowd.[27] First they would rouse their listeners with some foot-stomping bluegrass; then they would befuddle the happy dancers with an irregular jazz rhythm; then they would get the aggressive types screaming through a hard-rock solo; then they would cool the mob down with a mellow folk ballad; and then finally they would inspire mass cloud gazing with an hourlong pseudoraga. So skilled are the Dead at crowd pleasing, they are still the top-grossing live act in the United States, spending six months of the year playing lengthy concerts for loyal "Dead-heads," some of whom are young enough, despite their tie-dyed garb, to be the children of the original hippies.[28]

More recordable than the studio-shy Dead was the Jefferson Airplane. Signed early to RCA, the group attracted critical attention as the first rock band to perform at the Newport Jazz (not Folk) Festival, where their solid musicianship was praised by a number of jazz critics who otherwise detested rock.[29]

Yet, despite the staying power of the Dead and the sophistication of the Airplane, the "San Francisco sound" never established itself as a distinctive musical force like that of Memphis, Motown, or Liverpool. It captured the media spotlight with the hippie movement, but as Gillett reports, all that spotlight really did was dazzle a lot of businessmen who should have known better: "When the dust had settled after the record industry had swept through San Francisco . . . there was surprisingly little musical content to justify all the fuss. . . . Beneath all the hair and behind the clouds of smoke, the musicians were mostly playing the same old rhythm and blues grooves."[30]

It was lost on the revelers at Woodstock that Country Joe and the Fish's antiwar anthem "I-Feel-Like-I'm-Fixin'-to-Die" was musically identical to "Muskrat Ramble," the New Orleans jazz standard by Edward ("Kid") Ory. In the studio, however, where people did recognize "Muskrat Ramble," the challenge was to come up with something musically new to put on record. At that point it became clear that most San Francisco groups were "general business" bands—the kind that people hire for weddings and bar mitzvahs. The only difference was that the hippies were hiring them for drug trips.[31]

Soul Goes Psychedelic

So far it may appear that Western religion didn't loom very large in the counterculture. Didn't the hippies arise in San Francisco, the home of the beats? Wasn't their spirituality derived from the beats' fascination with Zen Buddhism, mixed with equal parts dime-store mysticism and ecological pantheism? And didn't the "peace and love" generation reject everything associated with Western civilization, especially American Protestantism? The answer to these questions is yes. But, at the same time, the counterculture drew heavily on one of America's oldest religious traditions: ecstatic communalism. Didn't the Monterey Pop Festival take flight in response to Otis Redding's secular solo evangelism? Wasn't the group solidarity experienced by 1960s youth largely induced by the enthusiasm-building techniques of good old Southern gospel? And doesn't that communal feeling persist as one of that generation's fondest memories? The answer to these questions, too, is yes.

Not all black gospel singers became soul singers in the early 1960s. Some stayed in gospel, and others gained a broader audience by traveling the folk circuit. And, unlike the soul singers, they did so without abandoning their religious repertory. This was possible for two reasons. First, most folkies found black religion more acceptable than white (a bias reinforced, I might add, by the sight of black Southern Christians mounting morally righteous protests against their white segregationist counterparts). Second, the sexual focus of soul struck most folkies as vulgar and commercial; their mood of hopeful idealism was better suited by the uplifting energy of pure gospel. As their fame grew, groups such as the Staple Singers and the Chambers Brothers began covering soul and even rock hits. But they also combined spirituality with social significance in an important genre known as the "message song."

These groups did not invent the message song. Back in the 1940s gospel quartets sang tributes to President Roosevelt, and reminded their listeners that there was "No Segregation in Heaven." And in the 1950s gospel stars such as Dorothy Love and June Cheeks sang explicitly pro-civil-rights material.[32] Still, the standard for message songs was set in 1964, when Sam Cooke wrote and recorded "A Change Is Gonna Come," released as a single after his death in 1965. A poignant ballad masterfully performed, the record captures the delicate balance between spiritual affirmation and hope for social change that marked the early civil rights movement. Yet Cooke, who was not well known to the folkies, was also influenced by folk taste. Peter Guralnick reports that Cooke reacted to Dylan's "Blowin' in the Wind" by saying: "I got to write something. Here's a white boy writing something like this."[33]

"A Change Is Gonna Come" was (and is) a hard act to follow. But that's exactly why it challenged other soul performers, such as Curtis Mayfield, to move away from sexual themes—not toward the explicitly Christian themes of heaven, hell, and salvation but toward the vague yet hardly un-Christian ones of brotherhood, self-respect, and justice. Gillett reports that Mayfield's "adaptations of gospel imagery . . . [were] delivered with such subtlety and grace that the notoriously conservative white radio program-mers let them on the air."[34]

It was not long before the message song became part of the hippie ritual. In 1967 a Texas-born gospel prodigy named Sylvester ("Sly") Stone assem-bled a talented crew of women and men, whites and blacks, relatives and friends, who dressed up like gypsies and called themselves Sly and the Family Stone. Signed by Epic Records (a CBS subsidiary), Stone insisted that the group not be marketed as soul—and, sure enough, Sly and the Family Stone did not play soul. Musically they disrupted soul's traditional call-and-response pattern of melody-defining lead singer and harmony-providing backup by having everyone participate in what Charles Murray describes as a "pass-the-parcel succession of lead voices," combined with "outbreaks of bom-bom-bom scatting." They also added jazz-inflected trumpet and saxophone, electronic effects on lead guitar and organ, and the remarkable percussive electric bass of Stone's cousin, Larry Graham.[35]

Thematically Sly and the Family Stone revved up the message song with witty lyrics, as in the song "Don't Call Me Nigger, Whitey (Don't Call Me Whitey, Nigger)."[36] Such wit may help to explain why the group held together through the early 1970s, even after the breakup of Southern soul. In the end the only obstacle to its continued success was Stone's troubled personality, which caused him to flee the limelight as often as he sought and captured it.[37]

Stone's success made a deep impression on other black artists trying to reach the countercultural audience—notably the Motown songwriter and producer Norman Whitfield, who between 1968 and 1972 worked with the Temptations on a series of musically intense, volatile message songs that deftly appealed to the alienated feelings of both black and white youth by portraying ghetto life in sympathetic but unsentimental terms. "Papa Was a Rolling Stone" was the only such song to reach the top of the pop charts, but the others did well enough to disprove the cliché that meaning-ful lyrics cannot sell.[38]

The next step was a declaration of independence by Motown's best-known male performer. By 1971 a decade of chart successes had given

Marvin Gaye the leverage to produce his own album, *What's Going On.* Despite Motown's initial objections (Gaye says they "didn't like it, didn't understand it, and didn't trust it"), this remarkable album was in the company mold in one sense: It made maximum use of studio technology to project Gaye's voice—or rather, voices. As David Ritz points out, Gaye's "multitracked voices were startling . . . a one-man Moonglows, . . . singing duets and trios with himself, juxtaposing his silky falsetto and sandpapery midrange."[39] Also standard for Motown was Gaye's mixture of strings and R&B instrumentation.

Yet Gaye also broke the Motown mold: Instead of focusing on singles, he produced his own version of the art rock album, conceived as a whole greater than the sum of its parts. And he succeeded—in part because he kept Gordy's unkept promise to the jazz musicians who played for Motown. *What's Going On* is not a jazz record, but it does give some talented musicians room to stretch out.[40] Gaye even took the step, unheard of at Motown, of putting their names on the album cover. Perhaps this is why the LP won kudos not only from rock critics, but also from some jazz critics, such as Stanley Crouch of the *Village Voice*, who otherwise took little notice of Motown's products.[41]

To top things off, Gaye's eccentric creation yielded three top ten singles and sold more copies than any previous Motown album.[42] This success came as a surprise to the company, because Gaye's lyrics venture into forbidden territory: poverty, pollution, the Vietnam War, and the "generation gap." At the same time, *What's Going On* preserves the message song spirit, ending with a prayer for understanding and forgiveness that is truly heartfelt, in part because it stemmed from the singer's troubled relationship with his father.

A typical error of rock critics is to assume that, after the Beatles, all musicians in the Afro-American idiom took their cues from rock. From this perspective *What's Going On* is merely soul music's answer to *Sergeant Pepper.* But, as anyone in the field of jazz knows, soul musicians in the 1960s got their inspiration from other sources, notably a new kind of spirituality in jazz. Some of this spirituality was Christian, as when Ellington began in the mid-1960s to compose full-length concerts of sacred music. Some was a mixture of East and West, as when Eric Dolphy and John Coltrane pursued idiosyncratic spiritual quests. Coltrane in particular was an insatiable reader who ignored ethnic boundaries: Along with the Bible of his Protestant minister grandfathers, he assayed Zen, Hindu, and Muslim texts, as well as Plato, Aristotle, and the Cabala.[43] It's too bad this open-minded eclecticism has been forgotten by those who idolize "Trane" as a patriarch of black cultural separatism. And it's too bad that another aspect of Coltrane's example got forgotten, as well. An important fruit of his quest was his recovery from both heroin and alcohol addiction. As Hentoff writes, "During his huge musical ascent, which was about to start, Coltrane was clean and stayed clean. That's power."[44]

A different kind of power was in evidence at Woodstock, when Sly and the Family Stone took the 1960s generation to church. The gospel historian Anthony Heilbut describes the group's landmark performance: "The embodiment of the Woodstock Experience, getting the freaks together, was Sly Stone, a graduate of store-front churches who sang 'I Want to Take You Higher.' Change his slang and his clothes, and Sly's a stoned gospel singer, teasing, worrying, provoking a congregation to shout themselves happy."[45] The difference was that Stone took people "higher" on drugs, not in the Spirit. Unlike Greil Marcus, who somewhat begrudgingly admits that Stone's later troubles were due to his involvement with "bad dope," Stone himself knew perfectly well that his problem was *good* dope.[46]

Gaye knew it, too. Raised by zealously religious parents in the House of God (a sect even Pentecostals find marginal), Gaye's life was a constant tug-of-war between his upbringing and his celebrity life. Trained to seek ecstasy in music, he added drugs and promiscuity to the mix, only to suffer debilitating guilt. It would be nice to say that Gaye went from strength to strength after the success of *What's Going On*, but he did not. The album derives much of its emotional power from his hope of winning his father's approval, and when that hope failed, Gaye's problems grew worse until 1984, when he was shot to death by his alcoholic father. Ritz puts the whole sad tale in a nutshell:

> The final battle, long suppressed, had been building for four decades. The smoldering acrimony had reached a boiling point. Both sick victims of different chemical addictions, both highly spiritual men who had fallen from their own set of lofty moral standards, father and son saw their own demise in one another's eyes. Their primal love for each other had turned to primal hate.[47]

Still, for all their instability and for all the puritanical rigidity of their moralism, Stone and Gaye were better off than some of their contemporaries. At least their spirituality possessed a moral dimension that could be applied to their own behavior. At least they knew that the exaltation of their music was in *tension* with the hedonism of their lives, not *tandem*. Even at their lowest, they understood that chemical intoxication bears the same relation to rejoicing in the Spirit that jumping off a cliff bears to flying. The two experiences feel the same at first, but they end up differently.

Who was worse off? Those who told themselves that addiction could be joined with spirituality, that jumping off a cliff was the same as flying. This fatal lesson was imparted to 1960s youth by Timothy Leary, the Harvard professor and LSD guru who once told a young audience: "You're the first generation in human history to know how to control your own nervous system, change your own reality. Blow your own mind."[48] And it was reinforced by many well-meaning liberals who should have known better. So detached was elite opinion from "organized religion," it actually saw drugs as a viable alternative.[49]

Of course, some people experiment with drugs and suffer no ill effects, perhaps actually achieving a greater appreciation of spirituality. But such experiences lack the most important dimension of religion. One of the main reasons why young people quit the hippie life was its lack of moral guidance and authority.[50] Like the beats who admired Zen but had no use for its mental and physical discipline, the eclectic pseudospirituality of the hippies was not tied to the behavioral or moral requirements of *any* faith. Their worldview was highly moralistic, but in a politicized way that directed attention away from the behavior of individuals.[51] Old-time religion may be faulted for ignoring social issues, but at least it places the soul of the believer at the center of the drama. The moralism of the 1960s was the other way round—so smitten with its apocalyptic vision of the "system" that it tolerated suicidal excess in the name of opposition. Even within their own framework of "love and peace," the flower children had no operative definition of what loving and peaceful actions actually were. Still less did they know how to place constraints on hostility and aggression, in a setting where these were often aggravated by drug abuse. Thus, their rudderless quests often ran painfully aground.

"Electric Sky Church": The Loneliness of Jimi Hendrix

No account of the 1960s would be complete without the pivotal figure of Jimi Hendrix. Unlike the British guitar heroes with whom he is usually lumped, Hendrix had a spiritualized view of music that was rooted, like his extraordinary guitar playing, in his Afro-American background. Yet, unlike his contemporaries in soul, he didn't learn about music in church. Instead Hendrix spent his Seattle boyhood absorbing the tastes of his father, a semiprofessional tap dancer who had performed with respected jazz and swing bands. Born in 1942, when his father was away at war, the infant Hendrix was farmed out to relatives because his mother was ill with tuberculosis. His father retrieved him at war's end, but then his parents divorced, and when Hendrix was ten his mother died. By adolescence Hendrix was emotionally withdrawn, and so attached to his guitar that he talked and slept with it. As he told *Life* in 1969: "I got the guitar together 'cause that was all I had. I used to be really lonely."[52]

Hendrix joined the army paratroopers in 1961 but failed basic training because of psychological problems and a back injury. Deciding to become a professional musician, he spent the next couple of years playing backup for an array of soul, R&B, and rock 'n' roll acts, notably Little Richard, James Brown, and the Isley Brothers. He learned a lot, but his career foundered on two obstacles. First, he was a mediocre sideman, talented but inclined to ignore his fellow musicians, either drifting off to the point of solipsism or showing off to the point of exhibitionism. The other obstacle, fatal in soul and R&B, was Hendrix's inability to sing. Working in New York, he was close to dropping out when he began hanging around Greenwich Village. It was there that he discovered the four things that would transform him from a failed sideman to a countercultural demigod: the ear-splitting sound of British hard rock, the beat-poetic lyrics of Dylan, free jazz, and drugs.

Hendrix's first apotheosis was British. John Hammond, Jr., a blues folkie and the son of the venerable Columbia producer, hired Hendrix to play electric-blues backup for him at the trendy Café Au Go Go. Encouraged by Hammond, and emboldened by playing with white musicians for a mostly white audience, Hendrix began closing each night's performance with a wild solo in which, according to Charles Murray, he "played the guitar behind his neck or back, between his legs or with his teeth," making it "squeal, roar and chuckle at its master's most casual gesture." Before long his performances attracted the visiting British rock royalty, including Chas Chandler, a bassist with the Animals who was thinking of becoming a manager. Chandler knew the British rock scene inside out, and he persuaded himself—and Hendrix—that the latter could take it by storm. So, in the fall of 1966, Hendrix flew off to London (in Murray's words), "the city in which the ugly duckling of the chitlin circuit would become a gorgeous, psychedelic swan."[53]

A nice metaphor but inaccurate, because the image of Hendrix peddled by Chandler was far from swanlike. The British press heaped racial stereotypes on Hendrix, calling him everything from "Mau Mau" to "Wild Man from Borneo"; Chandler encouraged the process by releasing only the most depraved-looking publicity photos; and Hendrix obliged with onstage erotic antics meant to overwhelm the competition, as well as offstage conquests meant to boost his image as an imported black stud.[54]

Then, backed by two British musicians in a "power trio" called the Experience, Hendrix returned to the United States to deliver a powerful performance at the 1967 Monterey Pop Festival which climaxed when he set his guitar on fire.

As for Hendrix's catering to primitivism, that reached its nadir in 1968, when the Plaster Casters, a group of female fans from Chicago, made a plaster model of his erect penis. Hendrix was not the only star to be immortalized in this way; several others submitted (more or less successfully) to the same treatment. But, although the model itself crumbled, the artisans touted Hendrix as the most impressive specimen they had ever encountered.

Yet, as time went on, Hendrix grew weary of such fame. About the naked women pictured on the cover of his 1969 album, *Electric Ladyland*, he told a British reporter: "I wouldn't have put this picture on the sleeve myself."[55] And about his onstage antics, Clapton's oft-quoted comment is worth quoting again:

> It was the perfect combination, just what the market wanted, a psychedelic pop star, who looked freaky . . . and then, English people have a very big thing about a spade. They really love that magic thing, the sexual thing. Everybody and his brother in England still sort of think that spades have big dicks. And Jimi came over and exploited that to the limit. . . . He'd do a lot of things, like fool around with his tongue or play his guitar behind his back and run it up and down his crotch. And he'd look out at the audience, and if they were digging it, he wouldn't like the audience. He'd keep doing it, putting them on, playing less music.[56]

When Hendrix *did* play music, his medium was not just the electric guitar, but also the enormous amplification systems developed for stadium rock. Such systems cause the electromagnetic pickups on instruments (especially guitars) to receive two different kinds of signals: those manually produced by the musician, and those produced when the instrument recycles its own sound after the sound issues from the loudspeakers—in other words, "feedback," a sustained tone that is both distorted and shrieking with high harmonic overtones.[57] Feedback and other colorful electronic effects, such as reverb, were used by art rockers (including Keith Emerson, who used them on the organ) and by other guitar heroes. Yet, as the American blues musician Mike Bloomfield explains, Hendrix's approach to these sounds was uniquely rooted in the blues:

> He was into pure melodic playing and lyricism as much as he was into sounds. In fact, he had melded them into a perfect blend. . . . [He] uses an

immense vocabulary of controlled sounds, not just hoping to get those sounds, but actually controlling them as soon as he produces them. I have never heard such controlled frenzy, especially in electric music.[58]

Charles Murray illustrates the point in his description of Hendrix playing the "The Star-Spangled Banner" at Woodstock:

> He begins to play the tune—one which every American has heard several thousand times.
>
> Or rather, he *tries* to play it, but somehow it gets ambushed along the way. That clear, pure tone—somewhere between a trumpet and a high, pealing bell—is continually invaded by ghostly rogue overtones; the stately unreeling of the melody derailed by the sounds of riot and war, sirens and screams, chaos and alarm. . . . Time and again, the rich, clean statement of the melody would resurface, a proudly waving flag standing above the *melee*, and time and again . . . the feedback and distortion ate into the melody like acid, corroding everything it did not consume.[59]

At that moment Hendrix was a true extroverted modernist, whose intense engagement with both past and present allowed him to experiment with a boldness and flair rarely achieved by the electronic serialists. Barzun, no admirer of the blues, admits that the serialists' creations tend to be lifeless exercises with a "laboratory smell."[60] No one would ever say that about Hendrix.

Yet the moment was brief. Murray says that Hendrix's "gauntlet is still lying where he left it."[61] I would add that the main person who failed to pick it up was Hendrix himself. A brilliant self-taught musician, he craved, but also avoided, opportunities to learn and expand.[62] After Woodstock he retreated to upstate New York to surround himself with nonrock musicians, including Billy Cox, an R&B bassist whom he had befriended in the army. In Cox it seemed that Hendrix was seeking a path away from rock, which he described in 1970 as "too heavy, almost to the state of unbearable."[63] One Hendrix biographer, David Henderson, suggests that Cox also provided emotional and moral support:

> The bass lines were not difficult, but the feeling and philosophy behind them were. It was a subtle thing. String-bending nuances only brothers who had played in the South knew. . . . Jimi knew that Billy Cox was a down-to-earth, Southern homeboy with simple tastes and few excesses. . . . Jimi hoped that Billy's mind would not be blown by the sudden wealth and weird scenes. Jimi hoped that he succeeded in communicating to Billy that he was not as much into the weird scenes as it seemed, or as many thought.[64]

At the same time Hendrix sought out jazz musicians, most notably Gil Evans, the arranger and bandleader who had worked with Miles Davis in his prime. Evans thought highly of Hendrix, and four years after the guitarist's death, he produced *The Gil Evans Orchestra Plays the Music of Jimi Hendrix*—an album that would be a lot more interesting if it didn't have a gaping hole where Hendrix's guitar should have been.[65]

Finally Hendrix sought out free jazz, with negative results. In a replay of Charlie Parker's story, Hendrix's craving for adulation led him to suffer fools who praised not the discipline but the apparent chaos of his music, and who—worse—glorified the all-too-real chaos of his life. So when his music finally did fall into chaos, many of his drug-besotted fans failed to notice. They quite literally let him get away with musical murder.

Hendrix's ambitions may have faltered when his old friend Cox dropped his first tab of acid in Holland, only to be rushed to the hospital for a massive dose of the tranquilizer Thorazine, which put him into a semicoma for several weeks.[66] Cox recovered, but the incident was a warning, one of several that began hitting home in the late 1960s. Needless to say, it came too late for Hendrix. There is nothing but bitter poignancy in his vague hopes of founding a new "Electric Sky Church": "We're trying to save the kids . . . to help them realize a little more what their goals should be. We want them to realize that our music is just as spiritual as going to church. The soul must rule, not money or drugs. You should rule yourself and give God a chance."[67]

Hendrix died in London at the age of twenty-eight; the coroner reported that he choked on his own vomit after overdosing on sleeping pills. It is probably significant that no one played "Electric Sky Church" music at his funeral. Instead, during the private service at the Dunlap Baptist Church in Seattle, a friend of the family sang spirituals with a gospel accompaniment. At the cemetery a choir sang "When the Saints Go Marching In." And at the reception afterward, the assembled mourners, including several British and American musicians, held a "freewheeling jam session" whose purpose, New Orleans–style, was "to keep spirits high and the atmosphere light."[68] Perhaps on that occasion Hendrix found relief from unbearable heaviness.

Revolving Doors: Why Jim Morrison Keeps Coming Back

Hendrix would seem to be the quintessential icon of the 1960s counterculture: He spanned the whole trajectory, from the down-home roots of Afro-American music to the spaced-out fringes of hippiedom; he combined patriotism, radicalism, the blues, and the electronic avant-garde in a single galvanizing performance; he attracted every lightning bolt of racial and sexual energy in the air at the time; and he was fiercely talented. Yet Hendrix's name was scarcely mentioned during the recent round of nostalgia that began with the twentieth anniversary of Woodstock and ended with the release of a Hollywood movie celebrating the good old days of "sex, drugs, and rock 'n' roll." When the director of that movie, Oliver Stone, looked around for the counterculture's ultimate avatar, he didn't pick Hendrix. Instead he picked Jim Morrison of the Doors—the 1960s rock star with the least interest in, or connection with, Afro-American music.

Despite my criticism of the Rolling Stones, I cannot imagine making a film about them without at least some reference to black American musicians, whether Chuck Berry, Muddy Waters, or Tina Turner. But with Morrison I can. And indeed, Stone's *The Doors* is just such a film. Afro-American music was important to the Door's three instrumentalists: guitarist Robby Krieger, drummer John Densmore, and organist Ray Manzarek. Yet *The Doors* shows us nothing about their backgrounds—an omission that is especially glaring in the case of Manzarek, who boasts of having learned the blues in South Side clubs while studying classical piano at the Chicago Conservatory. Manzarek was the one who talked Morrison into starting a rock band. But, as the film accurately depicts, Morrison was always more interested in words than in music. He gave the band its name, taken from William Blake's line "the doors of perception" (also the title of Aldous Huxley's famous essay about the revelatory effects of mescaline), and he wrote most of the Doors' lyrics, even though his efforts usually needed drastic revision.

As for Morrison's vocalism, it was quite impressive at first. On early records such as "When the Music's Over," his expressive baritone ranges, blues fashion, from rich, buttery tones to rasping whispers and piercing cries. Yet Morrison's goal was not musical but dramatic—or, more accurately, histrionic. His later performances are ordeals of frantic declamation during which he turns his back, literally and figuratively, on the music. And that was foolish, because the Door's best performances gain their emotional power from the mesmerizing swirl of Manzarek's organ, the precise punctuation of Krieger's guitar, and the staccato punch of Densmore's drums.[69]

Ironically, Morrison's penchant for declamation was a boon to the group. Because he wanted every syllable to be heard, the Doors did something practically unheard of in the late 1960s: They played *quietly*. If their distinctive talents had been allowed to mesh and mature, the group might effectively have updated the beats' attempted synthesis of verbal and musical expression. The beats failed because they declaimed their poetry to bebop, a music that was far too complex and sophisticated to serve as a cushion for speech. The Doors came closer to succeeding because the musical spell woven by the band did for Morrison's lyrics what minimalist music does for film: provide the right emotional ambience without being too distracting.

Yet this potential was never realized, because Morrison felt mostly contempt for the musical idiom into which he had so propitiously stumbled. According to Jac Holzman, who signed the group to Elektra Records, Morrison "wanted to be remembered as a poet" and complained that "this rock 'n' roll thing had gotten far beyond his ability to control the public's perception of him."[70] Sympathetic rock critics have concurred, in predictable fashion elevating Morrison's poetry over the group's music. This is a mistake, because at best Morrison's poetry is a case of arrested development. Before he became a rock star, he showed some promise as an imagist—notably in "Horse Latitudes," an oft-quoted fragment about mustangs being jettisoned from a Spanish galleon in the Sargasso Sea. But the handsome, well-edited volumes currently bearing Morrison's name contain nothing but fragments and scraps, half-formed images, and free-associative meanderings. Morrison never made the sustained effort needed to write even passable free verse, and his emotional range—from petulant narcissism to dead-serious angst—is far narrower than that of the least of his poetic idols. He certainly never approaches the concise elegance and wry tenderness of Dylan's best ballads. Nor does he achieve the beats' studied attitude of "cool."[71] From such idols he absorbed only a sloppy disregard of syntax.[72]

The sole distinguishing characteristic of Morrison's writings is psychological waywardness—derived, it appears, from his unhappy childhood as the son of an aloof naval officer whose career forced many family moves and fatherly absences. According to his biographers, Morrison's chief boyhood pleasure was defying, confounding, and tormenting other people.[73] And he never outgrew these impulses, because, from an early age, he began drinking heavily instead of wrestling with his emotional problems. As often happens with youthful alcoholics, booze became the formaldehyde in which his adolescent hang-ups were preserved.

Much has been made of Morrison's reading, which was certainly more wide-ranging than that of other 1960s rock idols. But, as clearly implied by his biographers, Morrison focused less on the literary accomplishments of his favorite authors than on their personal failures. Mostly he sought high-minded excuses for his own self-destructive behavior:

> The romantic notion of poetry was taking hold: the "Rimbaud legend," the predestined tragedy, were impressed on his consciousness; . . . the alcoholism of Baudelaire, Dylan Thomas, Brendan Behan; the madness and addiction of so many more in whom the pain married with the visions. . . . *To be a poet entailed more than writing poems.*[74] (emphasis added)

The only trouble was, for Morrison, being a poet entailed *less* than writing poems.

Unlike the beats, who were anti-intellectual in a way that only educated people can be (remember that Ginsberg was a student of Trilling's), Morrison was pseudointellectual. Rock critics are impressed by his knowledge of Nietzsche, for example.[75] But that knowledge did not extend to the passage in which Nietzsche contrasts the true Dionysian spirit with the phony one. Walter Kaufmann finds that passage utterly central to Nietzsche's thought. I find it utterly damning of the 1960s counterculture:

> "Giving style" to one's character—a great and rare art! It is exercised by those who see all the strengths and weakness of their own natures and then comprehend them in an artistic plan until everything appears as art and reason, and even weakness delights the eye . . . Conversely, it is the weak characters without power over themselves who *hate* the constraint of style. . . . Such spirits . . . are always out to interpret themselves and their environment as *free* nature—wild, arbitrary, fantastic, disorderly . . . only in this way do they please themselves. For one thing is needful: that a human being *attain* his satisfaction with himself . . . only then is a human being at all tolerable to behold. Whoever is dissatisfied with himself is always ready to revenge himself therefor; we others will be his victims.[76]

Words to ponder while recalling the spectacle of Morrison lurching drunkenly about the stage of a Los Angeles nightclub, screaming that he wants to "kill" his father and "fuck" his mother.[77]

As Morrison's mind and body degenerated under the influence of alcohol and drugs, he resorted to greater exhibitionism—including the famous 1969 concert in Miami during which he is reputed to have exposed himself. Since the occasion led to a lawsuit that stymied his career, it matters legally whether or not Morrison actually unzipped his fly after several minutes of fondling himself and shouting abuse and obscenities at the crowd. But it hardly matters culturally. At that point anyone could see that Morrison's dissatisfaction with himself and the world *was* his art. He had no other.

I am not forgetting that some of the greatest figures in the Afro-American tradition have been self-destructive.[78] Bessie Smith, Billie Holiday, Lester Young—these and many other lives were ravaged by alcohol, drugs, promiscuity, and violence. But from bitter experience the traditional black audience knew better than to confuse these depredations with the art of music. It was only when Bird met the beats that self-destructive behavior got held up as an exemplary spiritual quest. To quote Ellison again, Parker was "a sacrificial figure whose struggles against personal chaos, on stage and off, served as entertainment for a ravenous, sensation-starved, culturally disoriented public."[79] Subtract the musical artistry, and you have a fair assessment of what rock became in the person of Jim Morrison.

Still, one thing can be said for these lost souls of the 1960s: They didn't just gaze into the abyss—they leaped. Their wild behavior stemmed from wild states of mind, as evidenced by the fact that they sometimes shocked even themselves. Witness Hendrix's revulsion at his "show-time" act, and his refusal to perform it on cue. As he said, "I can only freak when I really feel like doing so."[80] Likewise Morrison: Most of the crazy things he did were the product of inchoate, spontaneous impulse, not conscious calculation. And he, too, resented being trapped in what the rock writer Lester Bangs calls the "implicit absurdity of the rock 'n' roll bête-noire badass pose."[81]

However absurd, the self-immolation of these rock idols was real. For true absurdity—and perversity—we must now turn from the dead to the living, from the shades of Hendrix and Morrison to the flesh and blood of someone like Oliver Stone, who trades in the stale fantasy of art as self-destruction without placing his own life, or ego, in any danger. Consider the climax of *The Doors*, the dizzying scene in which Morrison drives a San Francisco audience into Dionysian frenzy and then suddenly decides to join the fray. Stage diving into the crowd, he leads a half-naked bunny hop while chanting, "Break on through to the other side!" into his hand-held microphone.

It's a spectacular moment, but I can't help noticing that it's technically impossible. All Hendrix had to do was brush his guitar against his microphone stand, and his entire sound system would fill with deafening shrieks. Here Morrison knocks over a whole stack of loudspeakers . . . and the sound remains perfect. He also boogies, microphone in hand, to the back of the surging audience . . . in the days before the cordless microphone was invented.

It's only a movie, of course—an illusion. But it's a pernicious illusion. Mere mortals such as Hendrix and Morrison had to wait until the end of the show to wreck their equipment. In Stone's fantasy, there's no need to wait, because there's no such thing as destruction. The "artist" can smash his speakers again and again, and the volume will keep on pumping. He can smash his life again and again, and his celebrity will keep on growing. And the spectator is reduced to a thrill-seeking voyeur, relishing the show but refusing, with extreme bad faith, to face any of the real-life consequences.

Chapter 14

Hard Rock Becomes
a Hard Place

A gainst those who see the 1960s counterculture in wholly
literary-philosophical terms, I stress the animating role of
Afro-American music. Yet, against those who see a seamless compatibility between the new radicalism and the musical tradition
that produced jazz, blues, country, and gospel, I also stress their incompat-
ibility. In some cases a balance was struck: 1960s youth appropriated the
music for their own purposes, but without sacrificing its integrity. For
example, "Muskrat Ramble" sounds just as sprightly when accompanying
Country Joe MacDonald's black-comic antiwar lyrics as when played by a
New Orleans jazz ensemble. But people like MacDonald had a knack for
the music that soon dropped out of the equation.

Bludgeoning the Blues

Most popular music pundits believe that blues vocalism was alive and well
at the end of the 1960s, its torch having been passed to Janis Joplin,

described on the cover of one biography as "the greatest white, female, blues singer in history."[1] Joplin was routinely rated a genuine blues "shouter" in the mold of Big Joe Turner or Big Maybelle. She was also touted as a soul singer: The *Village Voice* wrote in 1968 that her "belting, grooving style combines Bessie Smith's soul with the finesse of Aretha Franklin covered all over with a James Brown drive."[2] Such praise sounds a mite startling when we consider that Joplin, a middle-class dropout from the Gulf Coast of Texas, was barely holding her own on the coffeehouse circuit when she shot to fame as "the Queen of California rock."[3] Was her singing really that good?

As discussed in the last chapter, music was not exactly the focus of the San Francisco hippie scene, where Joplin first made her reputation. Nor was it Joplin's. She paid constant tribute to Bessie Smith, even helping to erect a stone on Smith's long-unmarked grave in Philadelphia's Mount Lawn Cemetery.[4] But vocally Joplin could not have named a less appropriate model. Smith, whose vocal range barely exceeded one octave, was a stunning practitioner of blues "mixtery," shading every note and beat with rich nuance.[5] Joplin started out with a strong three-octave voice, but rather than develop its potential she began her career doing imitations of Smith—only without nuance in a painfully high register.[6]

Yet even this effort sounds better than Joplin in her heyday, when she cauterized her vocal equipment with a singing style that consisted almost entirely of screaming. She screamed to make herself heard over her first electrified band, a third-rate Grateful Dead clone called Big Brother and the Holding Company. But she also screamed on principle, in the name of the blues—even though the noise failed to impress those who actually knew something about the blues. Reviewing a double bill in London featuring B. B. King and Joplin, Pleasants compared the former's "consummate musicianship" with the latter's reliance on "a sound that little boys of four or five produce when trying to determine just what degree of aural torture will finally drive Mommy or Daddy into giving them a smack in the teeth."[7] After giving her top billing at a 1968 revue put on by Stax in Memphis, the creators of Southern soul walked out after her third number.[8]

Why, then, was Joplin lionized? In part, because the commercial success of early rock led to a revisionist view of the blues. Consider the judgment of David Dalton, a *Rolling Stone* writer and Joplin biographer who dismisses the "deadpan formality" of the blues, which might have been "lyrically consoling" for oppressed blacks, but was clearly "an anachronism" when imposed on the protean Joplin. Echoing Greil Marcus, Dalton describes Joplin as so caught up in "a myth of freedom and a disdain for boundaries" that she needed to "experience not just the blues but the original impulse that created it: the violence, eroticism, craziness and sputtering of rage before the blues had been codified and ironized."[9] In other words: Forget the craft of Bessie Smith's singing; what matters is the turbulence of Bessie Smith's emotions. Joplin herself agreed:

> Young white kids have taken the groove and the soul from black people and added intensity. Black music is understated. I like to fill it full of feeling—to grab somebody by the collar and say "Can't you understand me?" . . . I was brought up in a white middle class family—I could have anything, but you need something in your gut, man.[10]

Unfortunately, all Joplin had in her gut at the time of her death in 1970 was hard liquor, hard drugs, and hard feelings toward the world for not loving her enough. It would be nice to think that her legacy has been a revival of interest in female blues vocalism. But all she really left behind was the widespread impression that singing the blues is the same as throwing a tantrum in public.

As for *playing* the blues, rock "improved" on that, too. For all his brilliance as a soloist, Hendrix's chief rival, Eric Clapton, is one of those people whose love for the blues outstrips his capacity. He's a better singer than Hendrix, which isn't saying much. But Clapton has limited skill as a rhythm guitarist. According to one Hendrix biographer, this incapacity was a point of dispute between the two stars:

> Clapton could never seem to understand what Hendrix was getting at when he stressed rhythm accompaniment. Hendrix felt that Clapton was too intellectual about it, . . . insisting the guitar was now an instrument of the virtuoso, just like in classical music. Jimi tried to get across the message that the funk, the feel, and the boogie of the blues came from a subtle rhythmic combination of which the guitar played an essential role but never got the credit, . . . where the guitar put the electric fire crackling over the bass and drums, creating the dynamic that made folks want to dance and shout and get it all out.[11]

There's very little subtle crackling in Cream, the power trio started in 1966 by Clapton, Jack Bruce (bass), and Ginger Baker (drums). Cream was known mostly for virtuosity and volume—"a wall of noise," writes one critic, "that was physically palpable, and . . . almost literally bowled audiences over."[12]

Yet it's possible that Clapton *did* understand. Despite their huge success, selling more than fifteen million albums in the United States, Cream disbanded in 1969.[13] To his disappointed fans, Clapton explained that the group had developed that particular line of music as far as it could go.[14] And for all his diverse musical activity since then, he has never returned to the hard rock sound that culminated in Cream. I say "culminated" because, although this sound became dominant in the 1970s, it did so without progressing musically. Instead, a great many people, musicians as well as businessmen, took careful note of Cream's commercial success, and proceeded to turn hard rock into a new brand of fool's gold.

I argued earlier that fool's gold rock 'n' roll was not a counterrevolution but simply a market filler, quickly supplanted by something better: Motown, Southern soul, the Beatles. But back in the early 1960s the competition was still a musical one: Audiences were still buying whatever sounded best on the jukebox, at the sock hop, over the radio. A decade later the situation had changed. Rock had become an overblown ritual, laden with meanings that had nothing to do with music.[15] And the distortions begun with hard rock had gotten carried to extremes that still remain impervious to musical competition.

The process began with groups such as Steppenwolf and Grand Funk Railroad (in the United States) and Led Zeppelin and Black Sabbath (in Britain), which basically simplified, and amplified, Cream's "wall of noise." A few others, such as Vanilla Fudge and Iron Butterfly (in the United States) and Deep Purple (in Britain), added some arty organ noodling. But as the 1970s became the 1980s, a seemingly endless parade of groups— Aerosmith, Judas Priest, Def Leppard, Iron Maiden, Twisted Sister, Poison, Mötley Crüe, Guns N' Roses—prospered with a no-frills style described by the critic Jon Pareles as "stylized and formulaic, a succession of reverberating guitar chords, macho boasts, speed-demon solos and fusillades of drums."[16]

Some bands were more virtuoso than others, but even the more accomplished were confirmed primitivists. As Steven Tyler of Aerosmith boasts: "It's twos and fours, it's fucking. You know, you can really fuck to a good Aerosmith song."[17] To the first MTV generation, this stuff is "rock 'n' roll," as evidenced by Twisted Sister's album title, *You Can't Stop Rock and Roll*. Needless to say, it sounds nothing like the music of the 1950s. But sound is no longer the point. To these fans, "rock 'n' roll" isn't music; it's *attitude*.

And where did this attitude originate? Not, it turns out, in Afro-American music. Instead it emerged from the decadent pseudoliterary sensibilities of certain performers. The proper term, *heavy metal*, was first used in a song by Steppenwolf, a hard-rock band founded by an East German émigré, John Kay, who named the group after Hermann Hesse's novel (the one that describes jazz as "hot and raw as the steam of raw flesh"). Kay borrowed the phrase "heavy metal" from one of William S. Burroughs's fictional celebrations of pedophilia, sadomasochism, heroin addiction, and ritual murder—associations that would soon become endemic.

It would be nice to be able to pin heavy metal on the Germans—or the British, who first bludgeoned the blues. But it was the American market that bought Cream: According to Gillett, the smart money in late-1960s Britain defined rock with "America appeal" as "stadium-oriented music [that] reduced the blues formula to ever more basic elements, delivering macho lyrics with crude posturing and ear-splitting volume."[18] Surprisingly, the U.S. record company quickest to pick up on heavy metal was Atlantic. Not only did it seize the American rights to Cream, it subsequently signed Led Zeppelin, Vanilla Fudge, and Iron Butterfly. By one account, Jerry Wexler stayed loyal to the "unspoiled energy" and "honesty" of Afro-American music, while Atlantic president Ahmet Ertegun was attracted to "paradox and anomaly and incongruity and excess of style."[19] Ertegun won out, and Atlantic led the way in selling heavy metal to the world. The music now has loyal fans in places as diverse as Poland, Japan, Russia, and Brazil.

The Eyes Have It

All observers, friend and foe, agree that heavy metal is not just music. From a more-or-less neutral point of view, Pareles writes: "For many heavy metal bands, the music tells only part of the story. Heavy metal concerts are theatrical events, community rituals."[20] From a prometal standpoint, Led Zeppelin biographer Stephen Davis describes metal as "creating its own private universe for its fans. The music was only one part of it. Something else was going on."[21] And from the ranks of those offended by the genre, Tipper Gore adds: "In concert, the most strident bands not only play their music at the highest decibel levels, but perform what they describe as 'vaudeville acts' that glamorize explicit sex, alcohol and drug use, and bloody violence. Some depict the most extreme antisocial behavior imaginable."[22] To put it another way: Heavy metal bands don't just scream, they also provide reasons to scream.

As we've seen, the visual emphasis in rock came largely from Britain. Commenting about audiences there, Hendrix objected:

> The main thing that used to bug me was that people wanted too many visual things from me. I never wanted it to be so much of a visual thing. . . . I just wanted the music to get across, so that people could just sit back and close

their eyes, and know exactly what was going on, without caring a damn about what we were doing while we were onstage.[23]

The opposite tack was taken by the Who, described here with refreshing honesty by their lead guitarist, Pete Townshend:

> When the Who first started we were playing blues, and I dug the blues and I knew what I was supposed to be playing, but I couldn't play it. . . . I could hear the notes in my head, but I couldn't get them out on the guitar . . . It used to frustrate me incredibly. I used to try and make up visually for what I couldn't play as a musician. . . . I'd hold my arm up in the air and bring it down so that it really looked lethal, even if it didn't sound too lethal. . . . I got to jump about, and the guitar became unimportant. I banged it and I let it feed back and scraped it and rubbed it up against the microphone, did anything. . . . It didn't deserve any credit or any respect. . . . And one day it broke.[24]

When Hendrix abused his guitar, it was because he wanted to make a new sound, not distract people from the sound he was making. Townshend himself admits: "Jimi took some of our stuff, but he was doing a whole different thing with it. He took what I was doing and turned it into music."[25]

The Who's approach prevailed, largely because the British love for Afro-American music has long expressed itself in visual terms. Since the 1920s ordinary fans have displayed their musical loyalty through such visual cues as hairstyles, fashions, dance steps, body language, and demeanor. Given the priorities of pop art in the 1960s, it was inevitable that such display would attract the attention of artists, filmmakers, fashion designers, TV producers, and advertising honchos—people more at home in the visual media (their baby) than in Afro-American music (someone else's baby).

The talents of these people had a huge impact. By 1965 the UK was taking the lead, not only in rock-oriented TV programming but also in making the short promotional films that would eventually give rise to rock video.[26] By the early 1970s British rock had reached the point of defining whole styles, such as "glam" and "glitter," in terms of looks rather than sounds. Indeed, the superstar of this phase, David Bowie, was renowned less for his eclectic musical borrowing than for his snakelike image shedding. By metamorphosing from bisexual drag queen to spaced-out extraterrestrial to cocaine-sniffing "thin white duke" to blue-eyed soul brother to electronic avant-gardist, Bowie became the archetypical figure of the decade, exerting an irresistible fascination for British writers like Simon Frith, whose highly intelligent books about "pop" say next to nothing about music.

Rising to prominence in the late 1960s, when huge stadium audiences needed something to look at besides puny figures (however well costumed) strutting and fretting upon the far-off stage, Bowie put on a remarkable show, with surprisingly high musical standards (whatever the style being borrowed) and in total control of his simple, but always striking, stagecraft. Often criticized for being "cold," he actually had remarkable audience rapport, achieved partly through sheer theatricality, and partly through his endearing habit of breaking unexpectedly into boyishly sunny smiles.[27]

Unfortunately, these positive qualities got lost in the heavy-metal wasteland. That genre, too, fills gigantic stadiums with visual and theatrical effects, but the effect is rarely simple or striking. The overall tone was set by Black Sabbath, a Birmingham-based group that spent the mid-1960s calling itself Earth and playing jazz-flavored rock in small British and Continental venues. Discontented with its limited success, and inspired by the supergroup Led Zeppelin, Earth decided in 1968 to change its name to Black Sabbath, adopt the heavy-metal sound, and titillate the media with rumors of Satan worship and occult magic. Critics derided the band's "anguished screeching about war pigs, rat salads, iron men and similar gloomy topics set to an endlessly repeated two-chord riff."[28] But capacity crowds flocked to see them, and it was only when one of the musicians got restless and tried to add keyboards and horns that Black Sabbath ran into trouble. Lead singer Ozzy Osbourne departed, taking the stage act with him, and continued to have solo success into the early 1980s—when, during one famous concert, he bit the head off a bat.[29]

I cannot resolve the ongoing dispute over whether or not the unfortunate bat was alive at the time. But I can point out that Black Sabbath was far from unique in getting trapped in a particular visual-theatrical gimmick. Other groups, like the Blue Oyster Cult (specializing in smoke bombs and lasers) and Kiss (known for their startling black-and-white face makeup), found themselves in the un-Bowie-like position of being unable to jettison the gimmicks that were the only things distinguishing them from hundreds of sound-alike competitors. Most heavy metal bands with an iota of talent wind up chafing against the rigidity of their fans' expectations—a rigidity best explained by Pareles's reference to heavy metal as "a community ritual."

Hellhounds for White Folks

How different is heavy metal ritual from its immediate predecessor, the massive outdoor rock festival of the late 1960s? Every rock fan knows about Altamont, the December 1969 concert held at the Altamont Speedway, a grubby stock-car racetrack forty miles outside San Francisco, which was marred by escalating violence that climaxed when members of the Hell's Angels motorcycle gang murdered a black youth named Meredith Hunter (who may or may not have been wielding a gun). Altamont is commonly viewed as the end of the hippie era, the turning point when the counterculture moved beyond "peace and love" into a darker, more pessimistic phase. This view is accurate enough, in the sense that Altamont took the bloom off rock festivals for investors and media pundits. But the change didn't happen in a day.

The headliners at Altamont were the Rolling Stones, who—regretful about having priced themselves out of Woodstock and stung by criticism that they were charging too much for tickets on their current American tour—decided to boost their countercultural credentials (and their standing vis-à-vis the San Francisco rock scene) by sponsoring a free concert, dubbed "Woodstock West," in the heart of hippiedom. For a while it looked as if the event would indeed revive the ecstatic communalism of the dying decade. Joining the Stones on the bill were four talented California bands: Santana, the Jefferson Airplane, the Flying Burrito Brothers, and Crosby, Stills, Nash & Young. Opening the program was Carlos Santana's jazz-based group, whose Afro-Cuban rhythms never failed to bring audiences to their feet. And sure enough, the crowd responded with what one witness called "almost pure ecstasy."[30]

But the moment was short-lived. No one, including the Stones, had bothered to ask whether it was a good idea to invite the Hell's Angels to serve as an informal security force. As it turned out, the Angels were not into ecstasy—at least not the kind evoked by Santana. While the hippies danced, the gang members used them for target practice, lobbing full beer cans into the crowd. And while subsequent acts played, the Angels escalated their violence, assaulting people at random with a variety of weapons. It was dark by the time the Stones made their calculatedly belated entrance, bathed in a blood-red spotlight. They were in top form, Jagger the wickedest of schoolboy imps, singing "Sympathy for the Devil," "Under My Thumb," and "Brown Sugar" while the Angels hacked and stomped eighteen-year-old Hunter to death.[31]

Even before the murder, the Hell's Angels committed more mayhem at Altamont than the Chicago police committed during the 1968 Democratic Convention. Yet there was never an equivalent amount of outrage. On the contrary, Altamont is recalled with a curious mixture of wistfulness (at the demise of flower power) and awe (at the Stone's presumed Dionysian powers). And whatever footage exists of the Chicago riot, it has never been edited into a feature film with an exciting rock soundtrack—like *Gimme Shelter*, the Altamont concert film famous for including the actual murder and after-the-fact rationalizations by the Stones.

Nor did anyone at Altamont (with the notable exception of Marty Balin of the Jefferson Airplane) try seriously to stop the carnage. People were scared, of course. But they were also paralyzed by their own myths. After all, the Hell's Angels were not hated symbols of authority, they were semi-glorified symbols of pop-Nietzschean freedom. As Norman explains:

> [The Angels] had acquired a certain chic, thanks to writers like Hunter S. Thompson and Emmett Grogan, who perceived in their impenetrable brutishness and grubbiness a candor otherwise absent from modern American life. So it was politic, but also "groovy" to set these real-life urban bandits in visual counterpoint to the mythic outlaws and vagabonds of rock.[32]

No heavy metal groups played at Altamont, but clearly, it was one of those occasions on which the "real-life" and the "mythic" converge. And in that convergence heavy metal found much of its inspiration.

In their ongoing effort to be naughtier than the Beatles, the Rolling Stones began making satanic allusions in 1967. Titles such as *Their Satanic Majesties Request* and "Sympathy for the Devil" attracted the attention of the film-maker Kenneth Anger, who proposed casting Jagger and Richards as Lucifer and Beelzebub in his film *Lucifer Rising*, while trying to get them interested in his hero, Aleister Crowley, modern Britain's most notorious Devil-wor-shiper, who spent his life provoking the public with self-advertised satanic practices such as sex orgies, drug marathons, and Black Masses.[33]

The Stones spurned Anger's entreaties, suspecting, no doubt, that they could get along without that type of publicity. But their flirtation set a precedent for others. Jimmy Page, the lead guitarist of Led Zeppelin, was a Crowley fan even before he accepted the *Lucifer Rising* job. The film project collapsed, but that hardly mattered. Encouraged by Anger, Page became a tireless advocate of Crowley's occult powers, enhancing his own mystique by purchasing a former Crowley estate on Scotland's Loch Ness. By this route satanism became heavy metal's semiofficial religion, observed by groups from Black Sabbath to Judas Priest, Kingdom Come to Slayer.[34]

Heavy metal also contains another pseudospiritual strain, one that didn't come from the Stones. Instead, some of the more literary art rock groups inspired Led Zeppelin to take an interest in pre-Christian mythology, especially Celtic and Norse. At first that interest fostered a moody, quiet phase in the band's otherwise deafening music. But the main impact was not musical. Led Zeppelin soon reverted to its former sound, with the mythology setting what Davis calls "the tone of overwrought Dark Ages fantasy . . . that would be the standard psychic backdrop for all the heavy metal bands to come."[35]

It's hard, listening to the heavy-metal-influenced music of Europe's neo-Nazi youth movement, to ignore the chillingly fascist flavor of this blood-and-soil backdrop. Equally troubling is metal's long-standing posture as an aggressively "white" music, in hostile opposition to whatever "black" music happens to be competing with it. To be sure, heavy metal started out paying homage to the blues. But that was exactly the problem. Nothing breeds resentment like homage. Rolling Stones biographer Stanley Booth remarked to Mick Jagger in the late 1960s: "Well, that's the dream, we all want to be black, what we think black is." And Jagger replied, with characteristic coolness, "*I* don't. I'm not black and I'm proud of it."[36]

This reply speaks volumes about the transition from early rock to heavy metal. Jagger himself was never smitten with "blackness" so much as skilled at manipulating others who were.[37] But those others were legion, and by the end of the 1960s, it is likely that they were tired of the whole musical, folkloric, and (especially) sexual mystique of "what we think black is." What a relief, then, to be able to recast primitivism as an affair of wild white savages lurching through the primeval mists of Europe!

As for the blues, the very extremes to which heavy metal carries its occult themes suggests a radical break. For the fact is that Afro-American culture takes a very different attitude toward the Devil and the supernatural than the one taken by the West. During centuries of persecution by the medieval Church, the various pagan religions of Europe, from Greek and Roman cults to Teutonic and Celtic nature worship, were cast as heretical, evil, and totally malevolent. As one scholar writes: "It is absolutely necessary to realize that nobody whatever doubted the actual existence of these old pagan gods. They existed as truly as the great God; but whereas the pagans had taken them for gods, the Christians knew them to be devils."[38]

In Afro-American culture, by contrast, these centuries of persecution did not occur. So the comparable beliefs—the "old pagan gods" that came to the New World with the Africans—ended up in a different, more syncretic relationship with the dominant religion. The legendary voodoo of New Orleans is the most salient North American manifestation of non-Christian African folk religion existing alongside, and frequently intertwined with, Christianity.[39] There are European as well as African sources for voodoo, and very little of it can be traced directly back to Africa. But voodoo does reflect its African origin in one sense: It sees supernatural beings as neither inherently good nor inherently evil, but capable of going either way, depending on the skill and intentions of the conjurer. As Paul Oliver explains: "In Louisiana and Alabama there were undetermined numbers of men and women versed in the lore and beliefs of voodoo who practiced their arts for both good and evil."[40]

Reflecting its folk origins, the blues depicts Satan as a conjurer or trickster, wicked but also vain, mercurial and susceptible to human wiles.[41] Lawrence Levine reports that, during slavery, "songs of the Devil pictured a harsh but almost semicomic figure (often, one suspects, a surrogate for the white man), over whom [the blacks] triumphed with reassuring regularity." The folktale hero known as High John the Conquerer is always encountering, and outwitting, the Devil.[42] Emerging from these sources is a strain of wry humor toward Satan and his works that pervades the blues—including Robert Johnson's.

The point is that people like Johnson came by their supernaturalism naturally. Blues such as "Hell Hound on My Trail" and "Me and the Devil Blues" emerged from a living tradition; they were not dug out of a sourcebook for the self-conscious purpose of shocking the public, as when Mötley Crüe adopted the Satanic symbol the pentagram in the hope that, as one band member allowed, "it would be able to get a rise out of normal citizens."[43]

Boys Will Be Boys—Or, Meet Me in the Moshing Pit

The most strikingly false note of heavy metal paganism is its male-centeredness. Even the most superficial dabbler knows that the ancient pagan cults of Europe were centered around nature and fertility, and therefore worshiped female deities as well as male. But the Great Goddesses don't make it into the heavy metal pantheon, for reasons that have less to do with the genre's historical sense than with its psychological priorities.

Charles Murray indicates these priorities in this comparison between "You Need Love," a classic Chicago blues by Muddy Waters, and "Whole Lotta Love," the heavy metal version by Led Zeppelin:

> The former is a seduction, . . . warm and solicitous: [Muddy Waters] suggests that the woman to whom he is singing is both sexually inexperienced and starved of affection, and volunteers to remedy both conditions. . . . Led Zeppelin, by contrast, come on like thermonuclear gang rape. . . . The woman is strictly an abstract, faceless presence; she is an essential part of the intercourse kit, but not as an individual. 'Love,' in this context, is a euphemism for something measurable with a ruler.[44]

And that was back in 1970. By the 1980s heavy metal had quit bothering with euphemisms—or with intercourse, for that matter. Good old promiscuity went the way of the dodo bird, as "speed metal" and "death metal" groups beefed up their act with bloody sadism. The mid-1980s were the heyday of rock videos depicting female victims chained, caged, beaten, and bound with barbed wire, all to whet the appetites of twelve- and thirteen-year-olds for onstage performances such as the famous one in which the group W.A.S.P. sang its hit song, "Fuck Like a Beast," while pretending to batter a woman's skull and rape her with a chain saw. Offstage, performers regaled fan magazines with stories of strange sex acts with groupies, involving wine and beer bottles.[45] Metal stars bragged about having intercourse during performances, recording sessions, and video tapings.[46]

This aspect of the genre attracted plenty of criticism, including some from feminists eager to denounce it as an unvarnished affirmation of patriarchal attitudes. As a result many people now believe that antifemale violence is the whole point of the heavy metal ritual.

But is it? Because feminism now appears on the rock establishment's list of approved political causes, this kind of criticism has made a dent. In 1985, for instance, when Gore accused Twisted Sister of selling T-shirts depicting a woman in chains, lead singer Dee Snider was outraged: "We *never* had a shirt like that. I've always tried to eliminate the sexism of heavy metal."[47] Since most heavy metal stars are masters of hypocrisy, it's hard to take Snider's comment seriously. Yet there is a grain of truth to his insistence that sexism is not the whole picture. If we set aside the feminist obsession with female victimization, we may be able to see heavy metal for what it really is: a ritual venting of hostility against all of society, not just women, for blocking the natural aggressive instincts of young males.

Of course, to say anything about this subject we also have to set aside the feminist conviction that male aggression, whether natural or learned, is irrevocably bad. For the sake of argument, let us assume that it is natural, even good, for young males to be aggressive, energetic, and competitive with each other. And let us admit that, apart from a few sanctioned outlets such as athletics and the military, our society represses these natural tendencies. Young males spend the bulk of their time in environments in which the only way to win approval is to sit still, obey instructions, study hard, and get a good job. It's a tribute to the flexibility of human nature that most of them adjust. But many do not. Many get into trouble, and many succumb to the blandishments of music that is, in Davis's words, "loud, Anglo-Saxon, violent, 4/4, *martial*."[48]

Now, male aggression is also present in older forms of Afro-American music—especially those that encourage forceful virtuosity in male performance and dance. But in those older forms, aggression is mixed with its opposite: loudness with softness, fast tempos with slow tempos, wild abandon with tender emotion. The idiom's great strength is its ability to play these contrasts off against each other, evoking extremes but also tempering them. Unfortunately this strength was lost when "rock" became the antithesis of "pop." Right from the beginning, "pop" was condemned not only for being commercial, but also for appealing to female listeners. And "rock" succumbed to an adolescent obsession with "hardness," meaning not "hard singing" in the gospel sense, but the need to prove one's masculinity by avoiding sounds that might be construed as "soft." It's no accident that the chief substitutes for heterosexual dancing at heavy metal concerts are all-male workouts, such as "headbanging" (snapping the head up and down to the beat), "slam-dancing" (violently jostling one another), and "moshing" (pushing and shoving in the "pit" below the stage).[49]

We now arrive at an odd pass. If heavy metal represents exaggerated masculinity—"cock rock" carried to the point of "penile dementia"—then why do so many stars wear lipstick?[50] Not only lipstick but heavy eye makeup and rouge; elaborately teased, frizzled, and coiffed hair; skin-tight garments suggestively sliced, ripped, and stuffed; and flashy jewelry, feather boas, women's lingerie, and enough accessories to stock a medium-size department store?

Cross-dressing has always been part of British popular entertainment, from the "heroes" of Christmas pantomime played by women in fishnet stockings to the Rolling Stones' penchant for sporting feather boas and makeup in their early videos.[51] With the rise of glam rock in the early 1970s, this tradition of "gender-bender" performance gained a new self-consciousness among the theorists of "pop," and writers such as Iain Chambers began using Frankfurtian language to extol the "image of artful disturbance" created by Bowie, which succeeded in "loosening the sexed male subject from previous, more predictable, moorings."[52]

Hard rock's initial reaction to glam was to declare itself its mortal enemy. As one writer for *Melody Maker* chided, "If you wanna hear a rock and roll band, wipe off that bloody silly makeup and go see Zeppelin."[53] But cross-dressing soon proved irresistible to heavy metal, devoted as it is to getting "a rise out of normal citizens." In the United States there was also the example of late-1960s underground groups such as Alice Cooper and the New York Dolls, who used transvestism to get a rise out of everyone, including the most jaded rock fans. Because these "shock rock" groups were self-consciously avant-garde in a way that heavy metal is not, I shall return to them later. But for now let me note that their cross-dressing was more radical than that of glam rock, precisely because the practice is less at home in the United States. Unlike Jagger and Bowie, whose feminine prancing never interfered with their mass popularity, shock rock was a fringe phenomenon for several years.

Heavy metal stars remain ambivalent about cross-dressing. The glam or "fashion" bands, which sport heavy makeup, elaborate hairstyles, and exhibitionist costumes, defend their appearance on the grounds of hypermasculinity—either bragging that it is a sign of true "balls" or insisting that it helps to soften up groupies.[54] As for the "macho" bands, they simply declare that full-blown transvestism is "wimpy." Yet they, too, flirt with gender-bending. Sebastian Bach, the golden-tressed lead singer of Skid Row, does his best to explain: "Yeah, they call me 'pretty boy.' But I can't help the way I look. But I don't act like a pretty boy. I sure as hell don't act like a girl. . . . A lot of these heavy-metal people wear five layers of makeup. You might say those guys look like girls. They don't look so macho. I wear a little bit of eye liner and that's all." Less convoluted, and more revealing, is Bach's account of why he joined a heavy metal band: "I'm like a racing car that's always in overdrive. I have energy to burn. . . . I didn't need school. I knew what I wanted to do—rock 'n' roll. . . . My parents didn't understand where I was coming from. My father said finish school or get out of the house. So I got out."[55]

A young man thrown out by his father is bound to feel angry, but he is also going to feel hurt. Anger is expressed by macho defiance, of course. But how many contemporary fathers are going to be upset by hard-drinking, skirt-chasing behavior on the part of their sons? To really punish Dad, a boy has to violate a real taboo, and there aren't many left. So, before he goes out after the booze and the girls, he dresses up like a girl. Not only does this tactic call extra attention to his rebellious actions, it also eases the pain of rejection, as he relishes his power to cause sexual and emotional consternation in older males.

This scenario does not apply to every headbanger, of course. But it does suggest that the motives behind the ritual are more complicated than the feminist view admits, and that it is not entirely hypocritical for these performers to denounce sexism while pursuing their usual excess. With or without lipstick, they are acting out aggression, not just against females, but against everyone—parents, teachers, police, authority figures of all stripes—who keep young men idling in "overdrive" when they have "energy to burn."

How Heavy Is It?

As for leaping into the abyss, some heavy metal stars, such as Led Zeppelin's John Borham, have followed Jim Morrison's example.[56] But most stop several yards short of the brink. They scream a lot about death and despair; they engage in a certain amount of substance abuse, promiscuity, and mischief. But they also get clean, get married, and get their lives together more frequently than their public image suggests.

Sometimes there's an element of coercion in the conversion. When the lead singer of Mötley Crüe quit drinking in 1985, it was after being convicted of alcohol-related vehicular manslaughter.[57] And when the heavy metal impresario Doc McGhee started the antidrug Make a Difference Foundation in 1988, it was after being convicted of large-scale marijuana smuggling.[58] But sometimes the impulse comes from the performers themselves, as when Blackie Lawless of W.A.S.P. contemplates the lessons of his brief apprenticeship with the New York Dolls: "They were scary, the only band I knew that could sit in an airplane terminal and miss five planes in a row. They showed me what not to do."[59]

I am not knocking such restraint. On the contrary, I have nothing but sympathy for the sentiments expressed by Lawless. But as his stage name suggests, it's not easy for heavy metal stars to adopt a life-style of playing their gigs and then going home for a good night's sleep. Most of them would prefer not to advertise their newfound taste for health food and mineral water. As Nikki Sixx of Mötley Crüe remarked after taking part in McGhee's antidrug concert in Moscow, "I was very worried that people were going to say we had turned into Pat Boone because we weren't drinking and raising hell."[60] Like the antisexism sentiments quoted above, the clean-living pronouncements of heavy metal smack of hypocrisy. But at the same time they also reflect a growing sense of unreality pervading the genre's celebration of destructive excess.

Even more unreal is heavy metal's celebration of violence. After all, how many performers have been prosecuted for sadistic torture, rape, or murder? Ever since the 1950s the question has repeatedly been raised as to whether the violence in popular culture has any impact on actual behavior. Today, when the violence in Hollywood movies is depicted with a vividness unimaginable in the 1950s, the usual defense is that the whole thing is just a cartoon. As Lawless said about his famous simulated chainsaw rape, "It's just a goof."[61]

The most obvious flaw in this defense appears whenever a puffed-up concert promoter or industry honcho insists that popular music has the power to change the world—a claim that underlies every rock-missionary effort of recent history, from George Harrison's 1971 concert for Bangladesh to the colossal Live Aid concert of 1985 to Pink Floyd's on-location paean to the dismantling of the Berlin Wall in 1989. Such claims have been exaggerated ever since the folk movement sought to radicalize the masses with song. But that doesn't make them groundless. Only a fool would argue that music—especially music combined with gut-wrenching spectacle—has no impact on audiences. Yet this is exactly what the defenders of heavy metal do when they suggest that a steady diet of gleeful sadism does no harm.

Of course, whatever harm heavy metal does cannot be scientifically proved in the way some critics wish. In response to the constant charges of censorship aimed at her by the music industry, Tipper Gore did her best to frame her campaign in the practical language of consumer advocacy, defining heavy metal and other offensive rock as unsafe commodities whose measurable toxic effects could be eliminated if only record manufacturers would apply better quality control. Gore reinforced this consumer advocacy approach with empirical data purporting to measure the direct behavioral effects of media portrayals of sex and violence—in particular, clinical psychological studies suggesting that violence, with or without sex, increases male aggression toward women.[62]

Now, if Gore had been acting as a social scientist, she would have had to admit that this type of evidence cannot be conclusive in any serious policy debate.[63] But she wasn't acting as a social scientist, she was acting as a lobbyist—one whose résumé included helping another consumer group, Action for Children's Television, persuade the FCC to regulate the violence in cartoons and other children's TV programming back in 1972. On both occasions Gore understood very well that the rhetoric of "hard data" is helpful in winning valuable allies, such as the American Academy of Pediatrics and the National Mental Health Association—to say nothing of the national PTA.

Yet Gore undermined her consumer advocacy stance every time she took a principled stand against censorship. If heavy metal had really been just an unsafe commodity, she would have had no qualms about yanking it off the shelves—by government action, if necessary. But by taking an anti-censorship stance, she implicitly acknowledged that the commodity in question was also a form of artistic expression, however debased. Because Gore lacked the wherewithal to tackle the cultural question, her star began to fade around the time Bloom published *The Closing of the American Mind*. At least he wrestled with the problem in the right arena.

In recent years others have taken the same consumer advocacy approach, only to run into the same obstacle—namely, the defense of "artistic freedom" mounted by industry spokesmen all too willing to call their critics philistines as well as prudes. This strategy was employed by Danny Goldberg of the American Civil Liberties Union and its offshoot, the Musical Majority, when he equated Gore's proposal of a voluntary labeling system with the banning of *Ulysses*, and warned of a new "McCarthyism" bound to have a "chilling effect" on "artists."[64]

In addition, there are always a few graduates of the Jim Morrison School of Pseudo-Intellectualism willing to place heavy metal in the same league as high modernism. Only a trace of modesty qualifies this boast from David Lee Roth, former lead singer of Van Halen:

> The real good stuff, the 100 percent pure, straight-to-the-medulla-oblonga-ta art, is always slammed, at least for the first 12 years that it exists.
>
> When they rioted and tore the chairs out of the floor during the "Rites of Spring" [*sic*] for Stravinsky, when Dali did the Andalusian and whatever and they literally tore the screen off the wall, when Michelangelo unveiled the Statue of David, when Henry Miller was banned for 27 years, and on and on.
>
> Am I in that class? Probably not. Can I ascend to it? You bet.[65]

Even if we accept Roth's fantastic notion that the Parisians of 1913 expressed their outrage at *The Rite of Spring* by ripping up the seats in the Théâtre des Champs-Élysées, it's important to remember that Stravinsky didn't want a riot. Indeed, he took comfort in the fact that when the audience booed, his fellow composer Florent Schmitt shouted, "*Taisez-vous, garces du seizième!* [Shut up, you society bitches!]"[66] Heavy metal, by contrast, regards itself as an abject failure if all hell *doesn't* break loose.

Since heavy metal lacks aesthetic sophistication in the realms of music, language, visual art, and theater, its sole claim to artistic seriousness lies in its perversity. "Some art is perverse; heavy metal is perverse; therefore, heavy metal is art." This dysfunctional syllogism may be as old as the century, but it's still going strong, in part because, as Trilling once noted in his diary, the assault it mounts is no longer against the armored complacency of the nineteenth-century bourgeois, or even against "mature, already shaped persons who were able to resist or contain it." Instead the assault is mounted against a more vulnerable target: angry, troubled adolescents.[67]

We now arrive at the most persuasive defense of heavy metal, the one that shifts the ground from Art to Therapy. To the more intelligent purveyors of the genre, the fact that heavy metal is a distillation of youthful male aggression provides not only an explanation of its appeal for a particular demographic group, but also a justification for its excess. As the record producer Tom Werman put it to the *Los Angeles Times*, young people

> need to be angry, they need to have music they can clench their fists by, to pump themselves up by. They're not always happy. They're confused and alienated. I'm confused and alienated a lot of the time too.
>
>   They need an outlet like hard rock. I need it, too. I haven't outgrown my need for it—nor will I ever outgrow my need for it.[68]

Werman implies that heavy metal works by allowing its adherents to vent negative feelings that would otherwise cripple and distort their personalities. In other words, heavy metal can be defended (as pornography sometimes is) as an escape valve, an "outlet" that keeps already antisocial types from engaging in even more antisocial behavior.

This argument sinks beneath the weight of examples such as Jeffrey Dahmer of Milwaukee, the serene young psychopath whose constant indulgence in heavy metal did nothing to prevent his indulgence in murder, necrophilia, and cannibalism. I'm not saying that heavy metal *caused* Dahmer's hideous crimes any more than it causes the teen suicides with which it is sometimes linked. But neither did it prevent them. At the very least, it's worth pondering that such a person found heavy metal a suitable accompaniment to his deeds.

Of course, Dahmer was a loner, and the type of therapy heavy metal is supposed to provide is preeminently group therapy. One of the leading practitioners of group therapy, the psychiatrist Elisabeth Kübler-Ross, describes how the process ideally works: "In one-third of my workshops, we have a potential mass murderer. When he vents his rage, he makes a horrible sound you never forget. But afterward he'll never hurt a fly. So when I hear the sound, to me it's like Mozart."[69] In this vein the champions of heavy metal seize on the idea of ritual and set forth the argument that heavy metal is therapeutic because it functions as the modern equivalent of a puberty rite. It's "a vital and reliable rite of passage," writes Mikal Gilmore of *Rolling Stone*.[70] It's "a community ritual," writes Pareles, that teaches troubled youth that they are not alone, that others feel the same disturbing, sometimes terrifying emotions.[71]

Given my own view of heavy metal as driven by frustrated male aggression, I have a certain sympathy for this defense—but only up to a point.

Both group therapy and puberty rites are intended to help people cope with real life. The same cannot be said of heavy metal. On the contrary, the young people most deeply involved with the genre, such as the dropouts, runaways, and "throwaways" who congregate in places like Hollywood Boulevard in Los Angeles, seem incapable of coping with anything. As a number of observers have noted, these youngsters display a grotesque combination of vaunting ambition and drooping despair, based on the conviction that the only alternative to rock stardom is death in the gutter.[72] Nor do the stars provide much guidance. They're just as nihilistic as their followers, only instead of getting punished for self-destructive behavior, they get rewarded.

I would also point out that we do not live in a tribal society. Like heavy metal, puberty rites are intensely communal affairs in which trauma, humiliation, and terror—sometimes to the point of ritual death—are used to make a deep impression on young minds. But there the resemblance ends. Werman says that heavy metal helps young people "feel angry." But he also implies that they are already angry, that society has made them angry. Does heavy metal offer a release for anger that is already there? Or does it whip up even more anger? And does whipping up more anger offer greater release? And what happens afterward? Does the headbanger go home after the concert with his troubled emotions under control, ready to face the sometimes tedious demands of daily life? I don't think so. I don't believe that this kind of "rock 'n' roll" functions the way Chuck Berry's did back in the 1950s: as a brief, high-spirited respite from the necessary routines of home and school. Heavy metal doesn't offer a respite, it offers an *alternative*.

Puberty rites inflict painful ordeals in order to inculcate young people with the values of the tribe: to drive home the very clear, specific rules by which manhood, womanhood, and proper behavior are defined. Heavy metal, by contrast, offers a gigantic spectacle, geared to the maximum involvement of thousands of onlookers and arousing many of the troubling passions and treacherous currents of contemporary life, with the sole aim of *immunizing* the young against shared values—that is, of *preventing* their socialization.

At this point the defenders of heavy metal usually quit praising its therapeutic power and say instead that most headbangers eventually grow out of their obsession. This is their final argument, and it may very well be true. But it doesn't explain how those same young people are supposed to make up for the months and years they wasted in the grip of something so ugly and useless. Heavy metal offers ritual death, but at the end of the ordeal, there is no rebirth.

Chapter 15

Soul Loses Its Soul

It would be reassuring to think that the core of the Afro-American tradition kept right on swinging along through all the changes just described. But unfortunately, it did not. The styles created by black musicians in the 1970s and 1980s have transformed the idiom almost as dramatically as hard rock and heavy metal have done. Most observers, black and white, see these transformations as a legitimate reaction against the distortions of "white" taste and a return to authentically "black" music. But are they? The question now becomes whether the black-dominated genres that emerged after soul reaffirm the excellence of the tradition, or whether they succumb to the antimusical tendencies of new technology and old racial stereotypes.

The Great Soul Crack-up

Soul survived into the 1970s; many fine performers and songs date from that decade. Soul also expanded its audience after the 1960s, especially in places such as northern England, where it still has ardent fans.[1] Yet most sources agree that its "golden age" ended in 1968.[2] As with rock 'n' roll, there was a specific day the music died: In 1967 Otis Redding and several Stax musicians were killed in a plane crash, demoralizing both rivals and friends.

There was also a fool's-gold scenario: In the fall of that year, Atlantic was sold to the giant Warner Brothers/Seven Arts conglomerate. And, despite assurances that nothing would change, the negotiations revealed that Atlantic had already gutted its small Southern partners. At Stax, for example, Stewart and Axton found, in the small print of their contract, a provision giving Atlantic ownership of their entire catalog of master tapes, as well as the recording rights to such popular acts as Sam and Dave. Their response was to pull out of the Warner's deal and sell Stax to Paramount, and thence (after much infighting and recrimination) to Columbia.[3]

Such moves were typical, which is why some pundits see the breakup of soul as another counterrevolution. But again, being picked up by the majors was not always a disaster. Some of the best soul music of the 1970s was produced in the North, at a black-owned label recently annexed by Epic. Clive Davis, the head of CBS at the time, had no real feeling for soul music—by his own admission, he had "no claim to having 'ears.'"[4] Yet he did have a feeling for business, and in 1971 he decided, on the basis of a study conducted for CBS by the Harvard Business School, that the company had been missing out on the soul phenomenon.[5] It was not long afterward that Columbia entered into a funding and distribution agreement with Philadelphia International Records (PIR), a soul label started in 1967 by black entrepreneurs Kenny Gamble and Leon Huff. The deal proved happy for both parties: Gamble and Huff got a hefty production budget, access to the CBS distribution network, and (after some hard bargaining) control of all PIR promotion; Davis got a crack at the soul market, with four gold singles from PIR the first year.[6]

Musically, PIR took a page from Motown's book, packaging its gospel-derived sound in shiny wrappings for mass consumption. Some critics deride PIR as no better than Motown. In my view, it is no worse—and that is a compliment. For Gamble and Huff took just the right page from Motown, building the "Philly Sound," as it came to be called, around fine studio musicians and powerful vocalists, such as Eddie Levert of the O'Jays and Teddy Pendergrass of Harold Melvin and the Blue Notes. This small label's experience certainly suggests that moving into the big time does not automatically bleach the soul out of soul.

Peter Guralnick's excellent history of Southern soul places great emphasis on another reason why Southern soul broke up in 1968: It was in April of that year that Martin Luther King, Jr., was assassinated—in Memphis. As Guralnick reports, the event was traumatic for everyone at Stax. For example, the black songwriter Isaac Hayes told him: "I couldn't write for about a year—I was filled with so much bitterness and anguish." The white bassist Duck Dunn described his dismay at trying to speak with Hayes outside the Stax building, only to have the Memphis police pull up and threaten Hayes with a shotgun.[7] The whites who had previously felt at home at the modest studio and office on East McLemore Street found their comings and goings cut off by hostile black crowds. And even when the crowds dispersed, the hostility remained.

Nowhere were these heightened racial tensions more evident than four months later, at the Miami convention of the National Association of Television and Radio Announcers (NATRA), an organization of black DJs that had devoted itself to schmoozing and partying until 1965, when a caucus of concerned members persuaded it to adopt a politically activist agenda.[8] Never a terribly cohesive outfit, NATRA saw activism turn to chaos in August 1968, when (as Guralnick reports) "a group calling itself the Fair Play Committee . . . surfaced on the second day of the convention with the avowed intent of wresting money and power from the white colonialists who still controlled the black music."[9] Among the "white colonialists" attacked were the New Orleans record entrepreneur Marshall Sehorn, who was pistol-whipped; Jerry Wexler, who was hung in effigy and subjected to death threats; and Phil Walden, Otis Redding's longtime friend, manager, and business partner, whose account of the event illustrates the reaction of many whites:

> One guy really hurt me, a black guy we had helped get two or three jobs as a DJ—he was finally in a major market—he just hit me with this constant barrage of crap, this racist-slanted stuff, some insinuation that I was probably responsible for Otis's death—it made me *sick*. . . . You know, if I was a young black, I'd probably have been the most militant sonofabitch in the black race. But I just got tired of being called whitey and honky, because I knew in my heart what I had done and I knew in my heart I was right. . . . You know, back then I wouldn't even listen to a white record. I hated that crap. The first time I heard the Rolling Stones, I said, "You've got to be kidding. Who'd want to be listening to this when you could be listening to a great soul singer?" But after that I just decided I'd get into white rock 'n' roll, and that's what I did.[10]

The activist leadership of NATRA disavowed any connection with the Fair Play Committee.[11] But that didn't keep members from applauding the attacks. A deep well of resentment was being tapped, and many blacks felt that all whites were fair game.

The end of the 1960s was therefore also the end of the "white Negro" in the record business. I have already mentioned that Wexler and Ertegun closed out the decade by signing a number of hard rock and heavy metal groups; they also signed some British art rock bands. And Phil Walden was not the only white Southerner to abandon the R&B and soul fields. The widespread defection of the Southerners in particular had a positive impact on the so-called "country" strain of rock, as we shall see later. But it also spelled the breakup of a real, if fragile, interracial community. For Guralnick the loss of that community is the real reason for soul's decline. As he writes, the music lived, and died, with "the Southern dream of freedom."

Nelson George agrees that soul music was hurt by a loss of community. But from his perspective, that community was black: the network of black independent labels, promoters, distributors, and DJs that had emerged with R&B and continued to function during the soul era. George acknowledges the role of figures such as Wexler, but sees them as marginal. In his view the quality of Afro-American music is inextricably linked with the solidarity of the black community and the health of black entrepreneurship. That's why he wrote a book about Motown, and that's why he praises the Philly Sound chiefly because it was produced by smart black businessmen who knew how to play hardball with big-leaguers like Clive Davis.[12] In this respect, George shares the procommercial bias of the older Afro-American tradition. But he, too, is a child of the 1960s, and, although he doesn't spout separatist rhetoric the way the Fair Play Committee did, there is an undeniable separatist thrust to his plea that blacks in the music business ought "to free themselves from the comforts of crossover, to recapture their racial identity, and to fight for the right to exist on their own terms."[13] Like the original advocates of Black Power, George is not opposed to commerce in principle. He just wants to change its color.

But as the Black Power movement learned the hard way, this change cannot be accomplished by fiat. People who combine good musical taste with business acumen have always been rare, and, like it or not, the realities of racism have made them rarer among blacks than among whites. Certainly James Brown considered these to be the odds in the late 1960s, when he infuriated Black Power leaders by telling his fellow musicians, "If you don't have the white man in your business, you're going to blow it."[14]

Brown's prediction was borne out at Stax and other labels, even Motown, on those occasions when people interpreted Black Power to mean that white business partners could be dispensed with—only to discover, down the line, that nobody was keeping track of the money.

Yet not even in our wildest dreams should the record industry be depicted as the innocent target of black extremism. If the Fair Play Committee was out of line in 1968, so were the mysterious characters who beat up the executive secretary of NATRA on the eve of the convention. As George suggests, not all the provocation came from the black side.[15] In the end it seems clear that the gangster element in the record business was trying to undermine NATRA at the same time that NATRA was playing footsie with similar elements in the Black Power movement. Perhaps the two sides deserved each other. But soul music didn't deserve to get caught in the middle.

The same pattern was evident in the mid-1970s, when another payola scandal erupted. This time the investigation focused on the record companies—especially CBS and its soul music partners, PIR and Stax. As mentioned above, Stax failed where PIR succeeded, in part because its newly installed black management interpreted Black Power to mean "take the money and run," meaning run the business into the ground. Still, both labels were in trouble when it came to payola. Charged with using CBS funds to grease the palms of DJs, they had no real defense. In the time-honored tradition of R&B (and, I might add, of all other forms of popular music), they had been doing exactly that. One highlight of the investigation was when James Brown, asked to testify about his own promoter's activities, replied that the only reason he could think of to give money to a DJ was to get him to play James Brown records.[16]

Such scandals are bound to recur, because turf battles are bound to continue in a business as unstable as it is lucrative. For some critics, the mere existence of sharp practices and wily deceptions is an adequate explanation for everything that is wrong with popular music. And indeed, it's tempting to say that popular music is sick and sadistic because the business is run by hoodlums. The only trouble is, the business has always been run by hoodlums: in the 1920s, when jazz first flowered, it was on the vice-ridden Mississippi riverboats; in the 1930s, when swing matured, it was in the graft-funded nightclubs of Kansas City; in the 1940s, when bebop bloomed, it was in the Mafia-run nightclubs of Fifty-second Street. And so on.

It is also significant that shady dealings sometimes speed public acceptance of new and better music. And critics judge them accordingly. For instance, the champions of rock 'n' roll forgive Alan Freed for taking payola from small-time hustlers pushing R&B, but they condemn Dick Clark for having a similarly cozy relationship with major labels pushing white-bread covers. The foes of rock 'n' roll, on the other hand, see Freed as abetting consumer fraud and debasing popular taste, and credit Clark with trying to put music back into responsible hands. Today Freed's taste is considered superior to Clark's. But it could have been the other way around, with the inferior music making the conquest. The music doesn't justify the methods, any more than the methods justify the music. Each must be judged by the appropriate standard: ethics in business, aesthetics in music. It would be tidy to trace a direct line between the purity of the money invested in popular culture and the quality of the result. But the example of Hollywood should be enough to remind us that no such line exists.

From the perspective of this book, sharp practices must be viewed in the same light as legitimate ones—as harbingers of increased competition in a changing market. The system is cutthroat and corrupt, and its excesses should be prosecuted. But within certain limits corruption is simply part of the way things get done. To eradicate it altogether would be to undermine the competitive free-for-all that allows the rare individual with both taste and integrity to succeed with those qualities more or less intact.

As I have repeatedly stressed, the market is both friend and foe to art, in the sense that its power to amplify, magnify and accelerate changes in taste is, obviously, good or bad, depending on the nature of those changes. But the market cannot initiate such changes, any more than it can resist them. That is why it is not enough to blame the record industry for what happened to soul. The racial tensions of the late 1960s did have an impact on the way people did business. But, more important, they had an impact on the way people made music.

Loveless Love Men

The first reaction of soul performers to the increased militancy following King's assassination was to alter the content of message songs. Instead of love and brotherhood, the theme became anger and distrust in songs by Sly and the Family Stone, the O'Jays, Stevie Wonder, and certain Motown groups working with Norman Whitfield. One memorable example is "Smiling Faces Sometimes," performed by a short-lived trio called Undisputed Truth, in which Whitfield used echo and overdubbing to add demonic cackling and rattlesnake chirring to a powerful rhythm track and a lyric warning the listener to trust no one, especially no one who smiles, shakes your hand, and pats you on the back.

Other soul performers bucked this trend, sensing that it cut against the spirit of a music that was, after all, based in gospel. But although the musical skill and survivalist spirit of Mayfield, Donny Hathaway, Bill Withers, the Commodores, Al Green, the Staple Singers and Earth, Wind and Fire kept their records at the top of the charts, the same qualities kept these performers out of the media limelight. The traditional gospel emphasis on feeling good and doing right was just not in sync with the official post-1960s mood: despair at the dashing of utopian hopes, and headlong hedonism as the preferred response.

First to adapt to the new mood was Isaac Hayes, the Stax songwriter who was so affected by King's assassination that he dropped out for a year. When he returned it was to a new Stax, under black management and committed to producing no fewer than twenty-seven albums for Paramount during the first month of their agreement.[17] There were truckloads of cash coming in and acres of vinyl to be grooved, so aspiring house musicians, including Hayes, were given all the studio time they wanted to record whatever they wanted. Hayes set to work and produced *Hot Buttered Soul*, an album that was not taken seriously by anyone; it was barely mentioned at the splashy promotional party thrown by Paramount in May 1970 to announce the new Stax lineup. But then it went triple platinum, outselling every other album in Stax history and catapulting Hayes into unexpected stardom. As he told Guralnick, "I could have wrote my own ticket."[18]

To a large extent he did. His next few albums resembled *Hot Buttered Soul* and sold almost as well, giving rise to a new genre of soul: the lengthy, drawn-out monologue, half-spoken and half-sung against a dense, throbbing, quasi-orchestral background. The real triumph of *Hot Buttered Soul* is its eighteen-minute version of "By the Time I Get to Phoenix," a Jimmy Webb song that had recently been taken to the pop chart by the pop-country singer Glen Campbell. Hayes appreciated the song, about a man's painful exit from an unhappy marriage, and, like most good Afro-American musicians, he refused to be deterred by chart categories. As he told writer Gerri Hirshey:

> I was doing a gig in a black club. . . . I knew they were going to think I was crazy doing a song by a white pop singer, so I figured I'd explain. And I started talking. Explaining why, as a black man, there were things I could draw on in the song, weaving in some personal stuff. . . . And pretty soon they quieted down, and they were listening to me. So I sang the song, and at the end people went crazy. Some were crying. It was wild and very gratifying. I tried it again in a white club, and the response was the same.[19]

Hayes gave "Phoenix" a lush, multitracked production in the studio, but it's worth noting that the performance was first honed, blues fashion, in a live setting. Equally important is the fact that "Phoenix" is a good song to begin with, blessed with a strong melody and a lyric that is a gem of compressed storytelling.

Unfortunately, these qualities did not remain the stuff of the new soul. Hayes's expansion of soul's musical resources did yield a few triumphs, notably his soundtrack for the movie *Shaft*, and similar efforts by Mayfield and Quincy Jones. And, to the extent that Gaye's *What's Going On* was inspired by Hayes, the new genre can be said to have produced one masterpiece.[20] But most soul performers did not bring Gaye's rare talent to the new multitracked, album-length format. Like their predecessors in free jazz and art rock, they convinced themselves that shapelessness was freedom, and ended up becoming self-indulgent and pretentious. Only this time the self-indulgence and pretension were not about Art, they were about Sex. The piercing emotional intensity of soul was left behind as soul men became "love men."

If Hayes turned soul to butter, Barry White turned it to oleo. Performing with a trio of female singers and a sludgy forty-piece orchestra known as Love Unlimited, White's early 1970s records ooze their way through endless numbers like "Love's Theme," "Can't Get Enough of Your Love, Babe," "Love Serenade, Part I," and (you guessed it) "Love Serenade, Part II." Rock critics dislike White, and for once they are right. The music is closer to Muzak than soul, and, as the critic Lester Bangs observes, the sensibility is a cross between soft soap and soft porn: "[White's] technique: slide ever-so-gently, like a palm going down a shoulder to a tit in a movie house, from simple declarations of undying devotion into the realm of prurient interest . . . truly titillational stuff: 'Take it off. . . . Baby, take it *all* off. . . . I don't wanna see no panties. . . . Take off that *brassiere*, my dear.'"[21] In music as in life, things rarely stop at this stage. The real test of a love man like White was whether he could produce the boudoir equivalent of a live sportscast, in which the announcer for the championship game also happens to be the top scorer.

Even more unfortunate was the fascination this dreck held for Gaye. As suggested earlier, Gaye was deeply conflicted about sexual matters, craving love and attention but shrinking from adoring female fans.[22] Needless to say, this conflict did not get resolved when *What's Going On* boosted his celebrity without bringing about the desired reconciliation with his father. The demands became greater, and so did the guilt, at a time in Gaye's life when his real sexuality was troubled by a bitter divorce with his first wife,

Anna (Motown president Berry Gordy's daughter), and feelings of inadequacy toward a new girlfriend who clearly threatened him with her liberated attitudes and musical ambition.

We've seen how performers with religious backgrounds like Gaye's tend to be highly unstable, either retreating back into the church to seek forgiveness, or plunging into celebrity hedonism with the conviction that they're already damned. This instability got worse in the 1960s, when large numbers of whites either ignorant of or indifferent to the religious background of soul perceived its enthusiasm to be wholly erotic, and many black performers did their best to reinforce that perception. Still, it wasn't until Gaye went off the deep end over White that the process became irreversible. In a desperate attempt to shake his sexual guilt, Gaye transformed himself into a circuit-riding preacher in the new 1970s religion of liberated sex, stating his credo in the liner notes of his 1973 album, *Let's Get It On*: "I can't see what's wrong with sex between consenting anybodies. I think we make far too much of it."[23] For a loyal fan like David Ritz, Gaye's music redeems the banality of this message. But as Ritz himself admits, the banality shows up in the music:

> [Gaye] loved fully orchestrated, wildly romantic music. . . . By now he had mastered multitrack vocalizing, the art of playing with his voices, a skill perfectly suited for an album so rooted in masturbatory imagery. The use of moaning women in the background sounded childish, but sexual noise was an integral part of the little-boy fantasy which lay at the heart of what seems to me a work of rare beauty.[24]

Gaye is a special case, of course. But the same forces that propelled this troubled artist into the ooze made "love men" out of many other talented musicians, such as Larry Graham (the bassist for Sly and the Family Stone) and Teddy Pendergrass of PIR. From a business point of view, the genre promised to win a niche on the pop chart by offering an old-fashioned type of masculine sex appeal that was clearly missing from hard rock and heavy metal. The assumption was that any woman in her right mind would prefer the love man's smooth-talking, satin-sheets-on-the-waterbed approach to the ear-blistering screeching of white boys with roadkill hair.

But what a choice. Given the fact that this "loving" genre appeared at a time when love (as in "love and peace" and "love your enemy") was going out of fashion, the question arises: Was love really the point? From a woman's point of view, there is something unconvincing about the sound of a man so enamored of his own powers of seduction that his partner is reduced to a faint chorus of orgasmic chirps. There were a few "love ladies," notably Millie Jackson, but their tendency to confess and complain kept them with one foot in the blues. Unadulterated love man music is not about pain, it's about fantasy, as Gaye himself discovered when the confessing-and-complaining album he made about his divorce was a flop.[25]

The exemplary love man is not sadistic like the headbanger, but he is no less self-absorbed. All alone in his dream world, he may express trembling passion and profound adoration for his sackmate, but that doesn't make her any more real than the pliant victims of the heavy-metal stage. In both cases the agenda is not really sex between man and woman. For the headbanger it's aggression against society, and for the love man it's a not-so-veiled put-down of the white boys.

From the gospel perspective soul never had any spark of its own, anyway; it just borrowed the power of the Spirit to sing about earthly pleasures, and was bound to sputter out eventually. For Al Green, one of the most successful soul singers of the 1970s, who returned to the gospel fold in 1980, the only way to retain the spark was to reconnect with the source: Today Green calls his Memphis church his "battery," and insists that the "electricity" in his music has "nothing to do with sex; that's something to do with the other realm." Green willingly admits that his secular career has made him a more disciplined performer. But in his view discipline isn't enough:

> I took what I learned from the rock 'n' roll: the ingenuity, the class, the charisma, the movement, the hesitation. . . . Yes, you take all of this that you learn in pop, rhythm & blues, and you use it to your best advantage. But it doesn't give you the fire. You can't create the charisma for fire. Either you have the fire or you don't have the fire, the spiritual fire.[26]

In typical gospel fashion Green overstates the case, implying that all secular Afro-American music lacks inspiration, which is clearly not true. But gospel *is* special, in the sense of tolerating more extreme emotions than other forms of Afro-American music. In gospel, suffering is the path to God, and God will respond to the most agonized cry by turning it into the most jubilant shout. So there's no reason to hold back. Needless to say, the resulting taste for extremes takes on a very different cast when transferred to the realm of sexual pain and pleasure.

Then there's love, the much-maligned subject of popular music since Day One. Love complicates the picture because it has both a sexual and a spiritual side. But that is exactly why gospel-influenced vocalists, male and female, have such a powerful effect: when they sing in that sanctified manner, they express both sides of love, freeing popular music from the sterile, hearts-and-flowers, Tin Pan Alley sentimentality that denies sex; while also evoking something greater than vainglory about the singer's own prowess. In the 1970s this doubleness got lost, and characters like White began extracting the eroticism from soul with all the efficiency and beauty of a strip-mining operation. It may be that Green became a gospel purist for the same reason that Gaye became a love man: it was either drown in the ooze or go back to church. At least, that is the choice Green recalls in a recent interview:

> My spiritual beliefs were as much a part of the records I made in the '70s as they are a part of what I'm doing now, so I have no idea why the public's perception of me has changed. My audience today isn't as big as it was during the '70s, but the concentration is heavier. It's like the difference between regular and premium gas—you get better mileage with gospel.
>
> "Baby come shake your thing, let's shake our thing together"—that's great fun, but with gospel you're talking about something with substance that means something to people who already shook their thing and left that behind.[27]

Deliverance to Decadence: James Brown to P-Funk

Most black musicians in the late 1960s were separatist in the sense of feeling threatened by the accelerated pace of white appropriation. They felt exhilarated at seeing so much of their music "getting over," but they also understood all too well that history was repeating itself: that the white-dominated majors were taking most of the profits, and that the industry had every incentive to replace black musicians with white ones as soon as possible. The love man genre promised some relief—as we've seen, it was hard for whites to steal. But it was also hard for many blacks to stomach. Another style was needed to affirm black pride without insulting black intelligence. So attention became focused on the one figure who, despite his best efforts, had never been fully accepted by whites; who had not been invited to perform at Monterey or Woodstock; and who had spent the week before the King assassination not at the Fillmore West but in West Africa: James Brown.

There are a couple of reasons why Brown never crossed over as massively as his Motown and soul contemporaries. One was his politics. Not only was he more outspoken than most of his peers, he was also more baffling, since his combination of support for the system and pride in blackness was definitely out of joint with the late 1960s. He released a record called

"America Is My Home" right after the King assassination. He called himself an "American patriot" at the height of the Vietnam War. He endorsed Hubert Humphrey for president in 1968, Richard Nixon in 1972.[28]

Still, the main reason for Brown's limited acceptance among whites was his music. Sometimes the stumbling block was the lyrics, as when his famous record, "Say It Loud, I'm Black and I'm Proud," alienated white fans who, by his own testimony, "didn't understand it. They thought I was saying kill the honky."[29] But most of the time it was Brown's distinctive sound that was simply too rich for the white folks' blood—a fact that endeared him to militants even when they detested his politics. One black historian wrote in 1968 that Brown "symbolizes the vast differences between black and white cultural and aesthetic values."[30] And that same year LeRoi Jones (not yet Amiri Baraka) wrote that Brown's music was alien to whites because it represented the pure essence of blackness:

> If you play James Brown . . . in a bank, the total environment is changed. Not only the sardonic comment of the lyrics, but the total emotional placement of the rhythm, instrumentation and sound. An energy is released in the bank, a summoning of images that takes the bank, and everybody in it, on a trip. That is, they visit another place. A place where Black People live . . . a place, in the spiritual precincts of its emotional telling, where Black People move in almost absolute openness and strength.[31]

Predictably, Jones's rhapsody ignores the fact that Brown eagerly courted white fans by appearing in TV shows like *Shindig* and Hollywood movies like *Ski Party* (starring Frankie Avalon and Dwayne Hickman).[32] Nor does Jones anticipate Brown's stated pride in knowing that his "funky" music is now as "American as apple pie."[33]

Yet the militants did have a point. Ever since its inception, "funk" has been better appreciated by blacks than by whites. In Britain the word means a bad mood; but in the United States it means a strong odor, especially tobacco or bodily smells; and among black Americans, it has long been used, along with "dirty," "nasty," "low-down," and "gut-bucket," to refer to the rough, bluesy, and above all, polyrhythmic end of the musical spectrum. In the early 1950s, when postbebop jazz musicians began returning to their musical roots, "funk" was adopted as their badge of authenticity against the third stream and the avant-garde. For example, Milt Jackson of the Modern Jazz Quartet called his 1954 album *Opus de Funk*. Horace Silver also used the term, as have his acolytes Lee Morgan and Herbie Hancock.[34]

By the early 1960s the concept of funk was well established in both jazz and soul. But Brown claimed it as his specialty in songs like "Ain't It Funky Now" (1969), "Funky Drummer" (1970), and "Make It Funky" (1971). It's a sound in which melody and harmony are reduced to a thin membrane covering the gnarly, muscular, whiplash rhythms that are the music's real strength. According to Brown, that strength first emerged during the 1965 recording of "Papa's Got a Brand-New Bag":

> We stopped to listen to the playback to see what we needed to do on the next take. While we were listening, I looked around the studio. Everybody—the band, the studio people, *me*—was dancing. Nobody was standing still. . . . I was still called a soul singer . . . but musically I had already gone off in a different direction. I had discovered that my strength was not in the horns, it was in the rhythm. I was hearing everything, even the guitars, like they were drums. I had found out how to make it happen . . . when I saw the speakers jumping, vibrating in a certain way, I knew that was it: deliverance.[35]

No doubt Brown flags that moment because "Papa's Got a Brand-New Bag" was his first pop chart hit. But the sound had been evolving for over a decade, during which he and his highly disciplined band had become as tight and seamless as the best 1930s swing bands. As Stanley Crouch writes, Brown is "the Fletcher Henderson and Count Basie of rhythm and blues."[36]

Yet Brown's performance style also retained that gospel spark. Guralnick describes the singer's "trademark" as the moment near the end of each performance when "a weary James Brown, assailed with the cares, worries, and woes of the world, collapsed under the weight of his burdens, then somehow found the strength to go on." Usually this moment would arrive when, after a thirty- or forty-minute version of a soul classic such as "Please Please Please," Brown would sink to the floor in (unfeigned) exhaustion and wait for his aides to come out and enfold him in a satin cape (a trick borrowed not from church but from the boxing ring).[37] Slowly he would rise and, supported by his minions, limp painfully toward the exit. Then, when he was almost offstage, the band would revive the rhythm groove with deliberate, delicious hesitation. At first Brown would ignore the summons, hanging his head and staggering slightly, clearly a man from whom every drop of physical and spiritual energy had been drained. But the band would persist, and by now the audience would be screaming and begging for more. At the last possible moment Brown would relent. He would stop, stand frozen amid the fulminating rhythm, and wait to be struck. Then, with a gesture as old as spirit possession itself, he would cast off the cape and deliver a reprise that was less an encore than a resurrection.

Brown's performances rarely failed to move crowds to ecstasy, but as the 1960s segued into the 1970s, funk, too, began to acquire a different sensibility. Brown still dominated, and his worldview did not change. But he came to share the spotlight—and several band members—with a rival named George Clinton. Clinton, who started out with a New Jersey vocal group called the Parliaments, claims Brown as his first hero. But after moving to Detroit, where he "dropped a whole lotta acid" as part of the local hippie scene, Clinton acquired two more heroes: Jimi Hendrix and Sly Stone. Convinced that white youth were ready for "a total rejection of the smooth and slick Motown-type sound," Clinton mixed Brown's funk with Stone's and Hendrix's psychedelic trappings.[38] His overlapping bands, Parliament and Funkadelic, didn't get much radio exposure, on account of being unclassifiable in either the "soul" or the "rock" format. But that didn't stop Clinton from building a "P-Funk Empire," trading musicians with Brown and in general setting the pace for state-of-the-art dance music.[39]

Clinton's other hero was Sun Ra, one of the true eccentrics of jazz. A veteran of the swing era, Sun Ra became, in the 1950s, a pioneer in both the use of electric instruments and structureless improvisation. He was also a pioneer in pseudospirituality, claiming to be a native of Saturn and, in the race-conscious 1960s, adding the ritual trappings of Egyptian sun worship to his stage productions.

It may sound strange to lump Brown, Stone, Hendrix, and Sun Ra into the same category, but in one important respect they all resemble one another more than they do Clinton. Consider this statement of purpose from Brown's autobiography: "When I'm on a stage, I'm trying to do one thing: bring people joy. Just like church does. People don't go to church to find trouble, they go there to lose it. Same thing with a James Brown show."[40] Stone, Hendrix, and Sun Ra propelled themselves into orbits untraveled by Brown, to be sure. But they, too, saw their purpose as celebration and survival. Even at their spaciest, they stuck to Brown's basic dictum: "I always try to do something positive with my music."[41]

With Clinton this dictum became a joke. The process began when the talented bassist William ("Bootsy") Collins (who had played with Brown but chafed under his discipline) began enlivening P-Funk shows with mocking impressions of Hendrix mumbling his way through a stoned sermon on "cosmic love vibrations."[42] Granted, Hendrix took 1960s pseudospirituality to an extreme that cried out for parody. But the mockery did not stop there. Clinton's special genius, and the thing that still sets him apart from his heroes, is his thoroughgoing cynicism. Like Hendrix and Sun Ra, he made frequent allusions to space travel. But, like David Bowie, he saw these as pure camp, pop art borrowings from cheap science fiction, unencumbered by genuine spirituality. Instead of God, Jesus, the Pentecostal Holy Spirit, or even "cosmic love vibrations," Clinton sang about the lustful adventures of the "Maggot Overlord" aboard his "Mothership." The overall tone of his act can be deduced from a few early album titles: *Free Your Mind and Your Ass Will Follow* (1970), *America Eats Its Young* (1972), and *Cosmic Slop* (1973).

Clinton's empire has lasted for two decades, in part because nothing stays in fashion longer than the ability to turn everything into a joke. Yet, at the same time, P-Funk's fairly stringent musical standards began to look impossibly high during the latter half of the 1970s, when a huge segment of the audience began marching to a different, and greatly inferior, drummer.

Disco: Invasion of the Sex Robots

People did try to dance to heavy metal in the 1970s, but as we've seen, the result was mostly headbanging, slam-dancing, and moshing. Such was the impact of the misguided distinction between "rock" and "pop": Danceability got caricatured as a "pop" quality—cheap, commercialized, crowd-pleasing, easy to produce (just play a repetitive beat), and inherently mindless. In the early 1970s this caricature got disproved every time a soul or funk musician produced a song both lyrically intelligent and rhythmically exciting. But such material became rarer as the decade wore on, for two reasons. First, the black inheritors of soul and funk proved as willing as anyone to sell their musical birthright for a mess of primitivist pottage. And second, advances in studio technology put rhythmic excitement, or at least a simulacrum thereof, into the hands of every hack who could afford the equipment. Soon these tendencies converged in a new kind of music that really does fit the "pop" mold.

"Disco" was a place before it was a music. The word comes from the French *discothèque*, meaning record library. It was used in Paris during the Nazi occupation to describe a hideaway where jazz fans could gather to drink wine and share prized-but-forbidden record collections. Of course, the idea of playing recorded music in a social setting was nothing new in the United States—the first jukebox appeared in a San Francisco saloon as early as 1900.[43] By the 1930s the modern type of machines were ensconced in drugstores, bars, and restaurants all over the country; by the late 1940s the "mobile DJ" had become a familiar figure at social functions, such as teenage "record hops."

Nonetheless, the idea of a nightclub in which records were played did not become prevalent in America until the 1960s, when countercultural nightclubs began springing up, mostly in New York but also on the West Coast, modeled on the highly successful Electric Circus in the East Village. It was in these places that the craft of mixing San Francisco–style light shows with a broad selection of recorded music was first perfected. But when the counterculture went sour, so did these establishments, becoming the province of inner-city youth and gay men pursuing hard drugs and an aggressively hedonistic life-style. The trend did not become mainstream again until the late 1970s. But then it did so with a vengeance. In 1977, when the hit movie *Saturday Night Fever* was released, there were twenty thousand disco clubs and more than two hundred disco radio stations in the United States; the following year disco records made up 20 percent of *Billboard*'s top one hundred hits.[44] At that point the mainstream disco was a glitzy bar with a roomy dance floor and a pulsing, computerized light show, smoothly coordinated with loud, nonstop dance music played by a DJ in an illuminated "spinner's booth," who strove for expertise at jiving the audience while blending the last few beats of each record with the first few beats of the next.

Such establishments proliferated in hotels, resorts, and shopping malls everywhere. But they were only worth visiting in the early days, when the DJs played genuine soul and funk. As the craze grew, so did the demand for new material. Soon lesser soul, funk, and even rock talents were climbing on the bandwagon, producing a sound best described by James Brown, whom it hurt in both pride and pocketbook:

> Disco is a simplification of a lot of what I was doing, of what they *thought* I was doing. Disco is a very small part of funk. It's the end of the song, the repetitious part, like a vamp. The difference is that in funk, you dig into a groove, you don't stay on the surface. Disco stayed on the surface. See, I taught 'em everything *they* know but not everything *I* know.[45]

The most musically influential disco group was Chic, a black quintet signed to Atlantic in 1976, who stripped the rhythm down to a tense, mechanical rasp and leached all the emotion out of the vocals, which consisted of cryptic one-liners ("le freak, c'est chic") chanted with deadpan irony. The rock critic Ken Tucker sums up the effect: "If, as its detractors said, disco was wallpaper for the ears, Chic manufactured the most refined and minutely detailed wallpaper of all."[46] Yet even this wallpaper possessed quirky life, compared with what came next. For, as disco boomed, the new technology made it possible to mass-produce wallpaper that positively glistened with fool's gold.

Actually, one of the first uses of a so-called "drum machine," or a pulse electronically emitted by a synthesizer instead of manually produced by a drummer or bassist, was in Sly and the Family Stone's hit single, "Family Affair." And no one has ever accused that song of sounding lifeless, just as no one has ever accused Motown's Stevie Wonder of denaturing the music when he brandished his mastery of the Moog and ARP synthesizers in a remarkable series of albums that made him one of the most popular and respected musicians of the 1970s. I lead off with these examples to show that I am not a Luddite who condemns all music that is not, in the words of one *New York Times* critic, "stone-ground and preservative-free—made of wood, metal, animal hide and human effort."[47]

But neither do I share the attitude expressed by Nile Rodgers, the guitarist-producer who, after graduating from Chic, became an influential purveyor of synthesized sound:

> It's all just paint, right? You just have to grab all the colors you can get. If somebody introduces these new metallic colors that have bits of metal flake in them and gold leaf and stuff—all of a sudden you're starting to get a texture to your work that you didn't have before when you just worked with these primary, oil-based paints with no other textures in them.[48]

It would appear, from the knowledge of painting displayed here, that Rodgers would also consider black velvet an improvement over canvas. Fortunately he's not a painter. But he is a musician, which makes it all the more troubling that he should seem to dismiss the traditional materials of that art:

> Technology just allows composers especially to be more creative than they have been. I mean, I can't play the French horn but I have some great French horn sounds in my Synclavier. It allows me to interpret the French horn the way I hear it. In the old days . . . sometimes it was damn frustrating to write out the arrangements and listen to them played poorly all day. . . .
>
> Of course, the other side of the coin is that sometimes you get an interpretation from a musician that *you* would never have thought of. . . . Somebody in the back makes a mistake and you go, "Wait a minute, what was that again?" . . . You look at the paper and the copyist copied it wrong, but it sounds hip and you use it. Of course, you lose that spontaneity.[49]

Despite using words like "interpretation" and "spontaneity," Rodgers comes uncomfortably close to implying that the only musical quality lost when live musicians are replaced by synthesizers is human error. Obviously, this is not the assumption guiding the communalism of Afro-American music-making.

Human error is hardly the point, anyway. As randomness, it can easily be programmed into a computer—indeed, such programs are called "humanizers." No, the real problem with the new technology of the disco era was that it facilitated the manufacture of musical tinsel for people with tin ears. To listeners unacquainted with the range and texture of traditional instruments, the ringing tones generated by frequency modulators are pretty. To dancers unfamiliar with the seething momentum of a hot rhythm section, the microtimed beat patterns stuttered out by a drum machine are danceable. Rodgers is right to say that machines are better than bad musicians. But what about good musicians?

At the height of the disco boom, the most uncreative forces in the industry spewed out disco literally by the premeasured unit, introducing the infamous labeling system known as beats-per-minute (bpm), so that even the most inept DJ could segue from one record to the next. In Nelson George's view the low point was reached when the Europeans got into the act:

> At least the Philly disco records sounded like they were made by humans. Soon, Eurodisco invaded America, initially from Munich, and later from Italy and France. It was music with a metronomelike beat—perfect for folks with no sense of rhythm—almost inflectionless vocals, and metallic sexuality that matched the high-tech, high-sex, and low passion atmosphere of the glamorous discos that appeared in every major American city.[50]

The only trouble with George's color-coded judgment is that it doesn't explain why so many *black* listeners gravitated toward Kraftwerk, a quartet of West Germans from Düsseldorf who, as self-conscious popularizers of Stockhausen's electronic avant-garde, heavily influenced the Eurodisco sound.[51] In New York Kraftwerk enthralled young black audiences with "live" performances consisting of a stage full of electronic equipment and department-store mannequins rigged to look as though they were being operated by the computers, rather than vice-versa. As the journalist David Toop writes, "The George Clinton funk empire and its theatre of excesses had taken sex, sci-fi and comic-book abandonment about as far as it could go: four Aryan robots pressing buttons was a joke at the other extreme."[52]

Soon not all the robots were Aryan. As the musical warmth ebbed out of disco, it was replaced by an extramusical substitute. Next to the white Australian group the Bee Gees, the biggest disco star was Donna Summer, a black American singer who was hired by Europe's top disco producer, Giorgio Moroder, to do the vocal for "Love to Love You Baby," a huge hit that introduced a new type of performer: the "disco queen" who doesn't sing so much as specialize in the orgasmic sound effects developed by the love man genre. Summers, who *could* sing, led the way for many others who could not: panting, sighing, yelping, moaning amateurs like Gloria Gaynor, Loleatta Hollaway, and Grace Jones. Even the R&B veteran Esther Phillips got into the act, ruining a perfectly good imitation of Dinah Washington's mellow 1960 hit, "What a Difference a Day Makes," with a whomping disco beat and a ludicrous overlay of (you guessed it) panting, sighing, yelping, and moaning. Here was a new kind of robot, one that automated sex as well as music in numbers such as "Get It Up for Love," "Open Up for Love," "Hot for You" and "More, More, More."

In 1979 the disco boom went bust, taking several companies with it and dragging the whole industry into the red. Two reasons were overexpansion and sheer hype.[53] But another was an antidisco backlash, fueled partly by antiblack feeling, as in the heavy metal "disco sucks" campaign; and partly by antigay feeling.[54] For the heyday of disco was also the heyday of recklessness in the gay male life-style. Gay men did not invent the gleeful promiscuity of the 1970s, and in recent years many have rejected it in favor of a moderation more suited to the plague years of AIDS. Still, it cannot be denied that the late 1970s were when gay sexual behavior was at its most "liberated."[55] Nor can it be denied that many gay men saw disco as the theme music of their collective orgy, with the attitude that straights weren't really at the party. Groups such as the Village People appealed to the mainstream, but their coded messages were really for the clubs, where (as one chronicler reports) musical taste inclined toward "the driving rhythmic beat of the conventional disco sound."[56] It's ironic that, for all their mutual antipathy, heavy metal and disco came to resemble each other in this respect: pounding, monotonous rhythm that carries sexual feeling to dehumanized extremes.

Yet the backlash was not just antiblack and antigay.[57] In a 1980 handbook for would-be disco proprietors, the *Billboard* reporter Radcliffe A. Joe describes mainstream discos as pleasure palaces where the public can "abandon themselves to the tidal wave of raw animal emotions that engulfs them." Then Joe offers this warning, in a chapter helpfully entitled "Club Safety":

Another hazard . . . is the growing problem of damage to noses caused by excessive use of cocaine. "Coke" is among the commonly used drugs on the disco scene. Plastic surgeons in hospitals in major disco cities testify to an increasing demand for bridge restoration work to be done on noses damaged by abuse of the drug.[58]

It's hard to say which rings hollower nowadays, Joe's blithe prescription for mass hedonism or his implicit assumption that noses are the only things harmed by cocaine.

Whatever Happened to Black Music?

The disco bubble burst, but the music survived. The name was replaced by more euphemistic chart headings, such as "urban contemporary," "dance music," and "R&B" (even though the latter has practically nothing in common with the R&B of the 1940s and 1950s). Apart from rap, which I shall explore later, the styles falling under these three headings are what older people have in mind when, after reminiscing about their favorite soul, funk, and original R&B favorites, they switch on the radio and lament: "Whatever happened to black music?"

Part of the answer is technology, though I want to make clear what I mean by this statement. As we've seen, Afro-American music has long been at home in the electronic media. Computer-driven modifiers and synthesizers are now extremely complex and powerful, for which we are grateful whenever they rescue another jazz or blues classic from a dusty grave of distortion and static. But that does not mean that these and other high-tech devices have engendered a new, improved musical aesthetic.

Consider the case of Luther Vandross, a contemporary R&B singer who specializes in pitting his voice against state-of-the-art instrumental textures and rhythm tracks devised by a leader in the field, Marcus Miller. According to Peter Watrous of the *New York Times*, this team produces an "ecstatically lush" sound, "stacked with huge choirs, layers of percussion, odd and lingering melodies, and a surfeit of his [Vandross's] agile and sinuous tenor."[59]

Watrous is right about Vandross's voice: a rich, glossy sound overlaid with a delicate purr (the aural equivalent of satin swathed in gauze), it is supple enough to fit into every one of Miller's precision-tooled nooks and crannies. The contrast flatters Vandross, but that's exactly the problem. The emotional sterility of the backdrop leaves the voice isolated in a quest for feeling that quickly dead-ends in empty virtuosity. The result may saturate the ear, but it doesn't satisfy the soul.

Even more serious is the rhythm problem. Listening to Vandross interact with the snap-crackle-pop of Miller's computerized rhythm tracks is like watching a pro tennis player take the court against a ball-serving machine. No matter how skillfully the pro returns the serve, the interaction never develops into a rally.

Or, as Ellington put it, "It Don't Mean a Thing If It Ain't Got That Swing." Recall Hodeir's definition of swing as the complex interaction between a basic structural beat and a rhythmic counterpoint, or "superstructure," in which success requires "getting the notes and accents in the right place." Described thus, it sounds tailor-made for the computer—Hodeir himself admits that the "technical" side of swing "can be understood rationally." But then Hodeir explains that the more elusive qualities of swing, "relaxation" and "vital drive," are "psycho-physical, and must be grasped intuitively."[60] In other words, swing is a matter of feeling as well as mathematical precision. And feeling is a hard thing to program.

Again, I'm not denying the existence of people who can use programmed rhythms without sacrificing swing. But typically they do so by fitting synthesized beats into a live rhythm groove, rather than the other way around. But if they do that, they might as well record with real musicians. And I don't mean studio hacks; I mean good musicians. There's nothing wrong with Luther Vandross's singing that collaboration with equally gifted instrumentalists wouldn't cure.

It's important to add, however, that such collaboration would have to include a different class of songwriters. For, next to excessive reliance on synthesizers, the biggest weakness of contemporary R&B is songwriting. Vandross writes much of his own material, although not very well; and the majority of his peers simply wait passively for the producer to provide their material, both sides sharing the disco-era faith that witless lyrics and melody "hooks" are adequate, as long as the package is polished to a blinding—or rather, deafening—gloss.

It's interesting to note the parallel between this kind of music and 1950s pop. Now, as then, the producer is the most important figure, responsible for every step in an intensely studio-bound process, and dangerously prone to self-indulgence. What has changed is the pattern of that self-indulgence. In the 1950s the worst producers were like little boys in a candy store, dripping syrupy strings and gooey choral voices over material that was already loaded with sugar. Today they are like little girls in a boutique, playing dress-up with every conceivable kind of synthesizer frippery.

In disco's most direct descendant, "dance music," the vocalist's role is reduced even further, to a level slightly below that of the disco queen, while producer superteams, such as Jimmy Jam and Terry Lewis or L. A. Reid and Babyface, write the songs, program the computers, tell the singers (and occasional musicians) what to do, supervise the multitrack recordings, and then mix and remix the result until it acquires their distinctive stamp. Too often the result is a stultifyingly predictable blend of mechanical rhythms, glittery metallic sounds, and voices delivering one part melody to nine parts panting, gasping, and moaning. The overall effect is that of Minnie Mouse abandoning herself to the tender ministrations of a Kraftwerk robot.

The best that can be said about these postdisco genres is that in recent years they have expressed doubts about narcissistic hedonism. By the mid-1980s widespread concerns about AIDS, teenage pregnancy, and sex crime among inner-city youth prompted many in the record industry to become a trifle defensive about the messages propagated by their music.[61] To the extent that producers and musicians shared these concerns, the lyrics of contemporary R&B and "dance music" became as likely to warn against youthful promiscuity as to encourage it. Another indication of the new mood was the fact that inspirational songs by high-tech gospel groups like the Winans have had considerable success on the R&B chart. Needless to say, such efforts win kudos from critics weary of listening to orgasmic mice.

Yet musically, the disco mentality still dominates both the sacred and the secular charts, to the point where most of the new messages sound just as banal as the old. Later I shall explore the possibility that this return to an older and wiser lyric sensibility is inspiring a parallel return to older and richer music. I'm not suggesting—or prescribing—that black musicians turn back the clock in a simple revival of past genres. They have traditionally left this "moldy fig" strategy to whites, and there is every reason to expect them to go on doing so. I am suggesting, however, that black musicians who try to engage the popular audience in a constructive, as opposed to a destructive, manner are likely to run into trouble. Not only will they find themselves artistically short-handed, after twenty years of vapid, clichéd songwriting and emotionless, slick sounds. They will also encounter resistance from mainstream white listeners who have spent the same number of years rejecting the Afro-American aesthetic in favor of one that is, in many ways, its opposite.

Part Four

The Triumph of Perversity

Chapter 16

Their Art Belongs to Dada

We now arrive at the breaking point, where popular music veered most sharply away from any semblance of connection with the Afro-American tradition. To give a proper account of how this happened, it is necessary to return to the 1950s, when—cultural light-years away from the popular music of the time—there was a resurgence of perverse modernism in the arts.

During World War II, Europe saw a cessation of such prewar entertainments as dada cabaret and Artaud's "theater of cruelty"; no doubt the war itself provided a surfeit of blood, abuse, and irrationality. After the war, however, the emergence of abstract expressionism as the dominant style of visual art prompted a new round of dadaism from the younger generation in Europe. Abstract expressionism (also called the New York style because it was created by European artists in exile and their American students), fused the psychological concerns of surrealism with the formal discipline of cubism. For some people, as it turned out, the result was both too serious and too American.

287

Bloody Fluxus

The art historian RoseLee Goldberg describes the attitude of the 1950s movement known as Fluxus:

> It came to be considered socially irresponsible for artists to paint in secluded studios, when so many real political issues were at stake. This politically aware mood encouraged Dada-like manifestations and gestures as a means to attack establishment art values. By the early sixties, some artists had taken to the streets and staged aggressive . . . events in Amsterdam, Cologne, Düsseldorf and Paris. Others, more introspectively, created works intended to capture the "spirit" of the artist as an energetic and catalytic force in society.[1]

Goldberg does well to put "spirit" in quotes: By all accounts, European Fluxus was a lackluster affair. The high point came in 1961, when an Italian artist named Piero Manzoni sold ninety cans of his own feces (each weighing thirty grams and marked "Made in Italy") to art patrons willing to pay at the same rate as the current price of gold.[2]

It's hard to imagine anyone improving on that gesture, but plenty of people tried—in both Europe and America, as Fluxus spread to New York and captured the attention of a certain disenchanted segment of that city's art world. By the early 1960s New York art patrons were enthralled by "happenings," quasi-theatrical events staged for the purpose of breaking down the barrier between art and life. The redoubtable Susan Sontag attended several of these, and praised them as a new theater of cruelty:

> Only in our dreams do we nightly strike below the shallow level of what Artaud calls, contemptuously, "psychological and social man." But dreaming does not mean for Artaud simply poetry, fantasy; it means violence, insanity, nightmare. . . . Artaud shows the connection between three typical features of the Happening: first, its supra-personal or impersonal treatment of persons; second, its emphasis on spectacle and sound, and disregard for the word; and third, its professed aim to assault the audience.[3]

In other words, the art lovers who bought Manzoni's dada doodoo got off easy. Those who showed up at New York happenings were not treated kindly at all. Sometimes the weapon was boredom, as at Allan Kaprow's *18 Happenings in Six Parts*, which required the audience to spend an entire evening sitting on folding chairs and listening to performers, half-hidden behind plastic partitions, march up and down, repeat meaningless phrases, ring bells, set off explosions, and (for a climax) emerge from behind the partitions and stand pointing at the floor. Sometimes the trick was physical harassment: Patrons were doused with water, pelted with pennies, choked with sneezing powder, singed with acetylene torches, ordered to walk the plank, locked in cattle cars, and otherwise treated as "impersonally" as possible.[4]

The parallel with futurism is irresistible. It was Marinetti, after all, who insisted that the success of "futurist evenings" be measured by abuse, not applause. Even more important for our present purposes is the revival of noise music at happenings. Russolo's manifesto, *The Art of Noises*, was translated into English by the Fluxus performer Robert Filliou.[5] And John Cage, the composer most closely associated with Fluxus, spent the 1950s reviving (exhuming?) the futurist gimmick of pointing to noise and proclaiming it music.

Cage's experiments were all the more alluring for being wrapped in the mantle of Zen Buddhism, an approach that greatly impressed the beats, since they, too, justified their artistic methods—or lack thereof—with quotations from the Zen masters. Unfortunately, neither Cage nor the beats distinguished between a certain Zen approach to spiritual enlightenment (*Rinzai*) and the Zen practice of the arts. In the former the master uses surprise, nonrational dialogue, even physical blows to jolt the student out of conventional patterns of thinking. In the latter the artist spends years practicing his craft before he can create a poem or painting with the perfect spontaneity of nature. Zen masters do not equate surprise, irrational dialogue, and physical blows with art; and the Zen poets and painters do not expect to achieve perfection quickly, in the manner of *satori* (sudden enlightenment).[6]

Mostly, what Fluxus took from Zen were new ways to humiliate disciples. And new ways were needed, too, because, unlike the crowds who hurled insults and rotten tomatoes at Marinetti when he told them to "spit on the Altar of Art," the audiences at happenings did not fight back.[7] Indeed, Sontag reports neither outrage nor offense at happenings—only laughter. To her this response suggests a cosmic (dare we say Zen?) sense of humor.[8] To me it suggests unthinking reverence before what was still, undeniably, the Altar of Art. The worried psychologists who studied the "authoritarian personality" in postwar America should have taken a gander at these happening-goers, trooping back and forth across Manhattan, or out to the suburbs on weekends, to obey whatever senseless, boring, insulting orders their artistic masters were pleased to give them.

Those same masters made lofty pronouncements about the impact of their art on "the public."[9] But in fact the public wasn't present. Sontag reports that the audience for happenings was "loyal, appreciative, . . . experienced"—and minuscule: "One sees mostly the same faces again and again."[10] If happenings were really going to have an impact on more than a coterie of followers, then somebody was going to have to figure out a way to make them more entertaining. It wasn't very long before somebody did.

Happenings Happen to Rock

Say the word *happening* today, and most people will not think of Kaprow, Claes Oldenburg, or any of the other visual artists who first staged this kind of event in New York. Instead, they will think of Andy Warhol, who hired a rock band called the Velvet Underground to perform in his 1966 happening, the *Exploding Plastic Inevitable*. The Velvet Underground were more than primed for the job when they met Warhol in 1966: The lead singer and songwriter, Lou Reed, was a poet who, in spite of having studied with Delmore Schwartz, styled his own writing after the beats. Reed had found, after a stint trying to write songs for the music publishers housed in the Brill Building, that his dark, cynical sensibility was not selling.[11] But it meshed perfectly with that of a viola player named John Cale, the first rock musician in history to come directly from the musical avant-garde. Born in Wales and conservatory trained, Cale had spent a number of years working with the minimalist composer LaMonte Young when he met Reed.

Reed's and Cale's combined talents made for limited success on the metropolitan rock circuit, but the band impressed the beat poet Gerard Malanga, who recommended them to Warhol. Warhol's contribution was to add a German model, actress, and "chanteuse" known as Nico, whose quavery voice contributed less than her striking looks and decadent aura. When one reviewer likened a performance by the Velvet Underground to Berlin cabaret, the band's reputation was made.[12] Popular music had met and married perverse modernism, and for many observers, it was a great leap forward for rock. Consider, for example, the comment made by Kraftwerk in 1975, when asked what kind of American music they admired. The Velvet Underground, they replied, because its "German dada influence" raised it above "American popcorn chewing gum."[13]

Musically, Cale and Reed were attracted to the basics of rock 'n' roll: the steady beat, the simple chord changes, the occasionally sweet melodies. As John Rockwell notes, "this fascination with the basics was merely a rock extension of the whole lower-Manhattan art world's devotion to minimalism and rigorous structuralism." At the same time, no one would confuse the Velvet Underground's sound with rock 'n' roll. Instead of embellishing the simple structure with rhythmic counterpoint and blues "mixtery," Cale added a ragalike drone, sped up the beat to an unaccented 4/4, and broke up the monotony with occasional dollops of feedback.[14] As Charlie Gillett observes, this "deliberately primitive musical accompaniment seemed to have filtered all the black influences out of rock 'n' roll, leaving an amateurish, clumsy, but undeniably atmospheric background."[15] Indeed, the sound was atmospheric enough to make happenings more palatable to the public.

The Velvet Underground also attracted people tired of the bombast of late-1960s rock. Like the Doors, they played quietly hypnotic backup for the declamations of an aspiring beat poet (Reed) whose words could actually be understood. The whole effect was a relief to the ear: Like Warhol's colorful silkscreens of Marilyn Monroe, Velvet Underground songs such as "Sunday Morning," "Femme Fatale," and "There She Goes Again" are deliberately appealing, even pretty. Yet they escape being "pop" by having lyrics guaranteed to keep the band off the radio. As the critic Karen Schoemer writes, the Velvet Underground embodied "a dark, devastating glamour that absolutely reflects a time and place—New York City in the mid to late 60's—that are gone forever. In a dry, dispassionate voice, Mr. Reed recounted details of his mundane life, which just happened to be full of drag queens, pimps and hypodermic needles."[16]

The deadpan tone of Reed's songs, especially the grimmer ones, such as "Heroin" and "Venus in Furs," represents the complete abandonment of the spiritual high ground staked out, however ineptly, by the 1960s counterculture. That is why most effective scene in Oliver Stone's film *The Doors* is a downtown Manhattan party at which Morrison is introduced to Warhol. The contrast between Morrison, the supposed Dionysian demigod, and Warhol, the smiling nihilist, is perfectly captured when Warhol hands Morrison a toy phone, saying: "I can talk to God on this phone, but I don't have anything to say."

Like the telescope, perverse-modernist rock was invented in three places simultaneously. The second place was Los Angeles, where the late Frank Zappa released his first album, *Freak Out!*, in 1966. Unlike Reed, Zappa was a multitalented musician who spent his formative years immersed in all kinds of music, from R&B to bebop to free jazz to the electronic experiments of Varèse and the bizarre explorations of his friend and associate, Don Van Vliet ("Captain Beefheart"). In another personality, these ingredients might have blended into a brilliant musical career. But in Zappa they yielded only patches of brilliance, because his musical taste was ever in thrall to his compulsive need to satirize everything in sight.

Much of his satire was well aimed, as when he famously defined rock journalism as "people who can't write interviewing people who can't talk for people who can't read." Zappa's best moment came in 1967, when he put out an album called *We're Only in It for the Money*, which made merciless fun of two sacred cows: the hippies (romanticized in the media) and the Beatles (riding the triumph of *Sergeant Pepper*). Zappa also gets some credit, believe it or not, for the survival of democracy in Czechoslovakia. In 1969, after the Soviet invasion that crushed the Czech dissident movement, the most effective voice of protest was a rock band, the Plastic People of the Universe, who took their name, and some of their style, from Zappa. Indeed, Zappa was long one of Czech president Václav Havel's heroes: In 1990 he offered Zappa a job as special ambassador to the West on trade, culture, and tourism.[17] But, like all compulsions, Zappa knew no limits. And the result, paradoxically, was a lack of critical judgment. He would attack anything, it seems, except his own shortcomings.

Zappa began, in the mid-1960s, to impress certain pundits as a wildly original character. How original, the reader may judge by reading *Life* magazine's description of a concert by Zappa's band, the Mothers of Invention:

> On stage there is the possibility that anything can happen. Dolls are mutilated. A gas mask is displayed. A bag of vegetables is unpacked and examined. There are spaced intervals of "honks" and suddenly the Mothers perform "Dead Air." They stop, sit down, and ignore the audience. Zappa might get a shoeshine from Motorhead, the percussionist. They keep this going for as long as it takes for the audience to become unsettled, uncomfortable, and angry. Then Zappa calmly approaches the mike and says: "It brings out the hostilities in you, doesn't it?"[18]

Like the Velvet Underground, Zappa was not strictly speaking a noise musician. For some people his virtuosity was proof of superiority, and Zappa was justified in telling audiences: "You wouldn't know good music if it bit you on the ass."[19] Of all genres, whether European or Afro-American, Zappa was an expert parodist, devoted (in Iain Chambers's words) to "mirroring contemporary culture—from Sinatra to Varèse—as a giant scrap heap of disposable consumer trash."[20] The question is: by what authority did Zappa place others on the scrap heap? Could he play a finer blues than Howlin' Wolf, whose sound he and Beefheart mimic at the start of a 1969 song called "Willie the Pimp" (on the LP *Hot Rats*)? And, nine minutes later, when Zappa finishes a prolonged workout on the wah-wah pedal, does he prove himself a better guitarist than Hendrix? Zappa's blues may appeal to people who have never heard the original, or who prefer to take their music without feeling. But "Willie the Pimp" is neither an improvement nor a parody of anything in need of parodying.

Zappa also pioneered the use of obscenity. If "Willie the Pimp" is shocking, it's not because of any musical or political commentary; it's because the lyrics sound for all the world like, "Hot ass, hot tits," even though the record sleeve coyly prints them as "Hot rats, hot zitz,"[21] Zappa was using song titles like "Why Does It Hurt When I Pee" and "Shove It Right In" back when today's metal fans were still headbanging in their playpens. And he could even claim credit for having invented disco queen vocalizing: Back in 1969 he was already perfecting his own sexual sound effects—not an orgasmic mouse so much as . . . well, a hot rat. In "Tengo Na Minchia Tanta," the band plays a Latin dance number while Zappa works his way through four minutes of artful sighing, grunting, panting, and groaning.[22] By the time he reaches his climax, the listener is more than ready to leave the men's room and go back to the dance.

Zappa's big comeback in the 1980s was as a foe of Tipper Gore's consumer crusade against obscene rock lyrics. It wasn't much of a contest, given Gore's obtuseness on the subject of culture and Zappa's adroitness at leaping back and forth between the high ground of "artistic freedom" and the low ground of "it's only entertainment." What one rock critic has called Zappa's "puerile sexism" was also very much in evidence.[23] After ridiculing Gore and her associates at the Senate hearing, Zappa wrote an article for *Cash Box* dismissing their campaign as an "ill-conceived housewife hobby project."[24] Not content to skewer Gore's weaknesses, he indulged his own weakness for "broadside japes," as another critic calls them.[25] Typical was his response to Susan Baker, wife of then Treasury Secretary James Baker: He regaled the Senate committee with a poor imitation of her Southern accent. This particular jape boomeranged in 1990, when Secretary of State Baker visited Czechoslovakia and shared the anecdote with President Havel, who decided to look for a more diplomatic ambassador.[26]

I realize that Zappa's sniping at Gore only enhanced his reputation in the eyes of many rock fans. But what about his arrogance toward his peers? Take, for example, his view of working musicians. During the disco era he relentlessly (and expertly) parodied robotistic synthesized music in songs such as "Dancin' Fool." Yet he had even less use for the human beings who were replaced by synthesizers. In a recent interview he declared that most session players are "sight-reading cretins" who deserve to be put out of work. Yet he also denounced highly skilled session players as money-grubbing "A-teams" who hog all the best jobs.[27] From this and countless other tirades against the self-interested motives of others, it is clear that nothing aroused Zappa's ire more than the thought that somebody besides himself might be making money in the music business.

John Lennon's wit was always sharper than Zappa's, because it was more selective in its targets. But as Lennon's career moved beyond the Beatles stage, he became the third person to join happenings with popular music.

As the only Beatle to have attended art college and acquired a serious taste for things avant-garde, Lennon reacted to the group's astonishing commercial success with a bitter sarcasm that created considerable tension between him and the others. McCartney in particular did not share Lennon's anti-commercial bias, or the garbled leftist politics that went with it. Indeed, one need search no further than this for the reason why the 1960s rock establishment has never lionized McCartney the way it has Lennon, despite the fact that McCartney is, if anything, more musically talented.

At any rate, Lennon's frustrated perverse modernism got a new lease on life in 1966, the same year Zappa released *Freak Out!* and Warhol hired the Velvet Underground. For that was when, at a London art gallery, Lennon met his future wife Yoko Ono. In their case there was nothing metaphorical about rock marrying perverse modernism, because Ono—the daughter of a prominent Japanese banker—had dropped out of Sarah Lawrence in the 1950s to join the Fluxus movement in New York. At first she was a patron, sponsoring happenings and noise music concerts in her downtown loft. Then she became an "artist" in her own right—at least according to the standards of Fluxus.

Her ideas were hardly original: In 1957 a French Fluxus artist named Yves Klein lit a firecracker in front of a blue canvas, calling it *One Minute Fire Painting*; in 1961 Ono asked visitors in a Madison Avenue art gallery to light a match in front of a white canvas and study the smoke.[28] During the late 1950s and early 1960s, Fluxus artists gave absurdist instructions to their audiences; in 1966 Ono staged a "Do It Yourself Fluxfest," telling patrons to "breathe," "watch the sky," and "carry a stone until you forget about it." Also during the late 1950s, Cage staged performances of aleatory and noise music; during the 1960s Ono staged a "conceptual" concert of random noises made by people moving about on a darkened stage, and something called "Sky Piece," in which a group of musicians was bound together with bandages and dragged from the stage before any of them could play a note.[29]

Thus Ono was right in step with the herd of independent minds when she had the great good luck to meet Lennon. It was good luck because, like all perverse modernists, Ono's most malleable medium was celebrity— and Lennon had plenty. As he told a reporter in 1969, "Publicity is my trade."[30] This is not to suggest that their relationship was anything but loving and sincere. But it was also a boon to Ono's career.

Perhaps due to her upbringing, Ono did not naturally gravitate toward obscenity, although she did cause a minor scandal at a 1967 London film festival with a film called *No. 4, Bottoms*, composed entirely of ten-second exposures (in both senses) of 365 celebrity derrières. With Lennon such mildly naughty gestures stirred up a much bigger fuss. For example, the cover of *Two Virgins*, a photo of the couple standing together in the nude, marked a low point for Lennon, due to mounting tensions with his fellow Beatles, a recent conviction for marijuana possession, and the FBI's decision to open a file on the pair that made it hard for them to do business in the United States.[31] But it was a high point for Ono, making her the center of attention beyond the wildest dreams of the ordinary untalented avant-gardist.

Was Ono untalented? What about her much-vaunted musical collaborations with Lennon, which he himself defended against a legion of fans who felt betrayed by them? Lennon's confusion on this score is worth exploring, because it reflects a larger confusion that would soon engulf popular music. Unlike McCartney, whose ambition did not then extend beyond the "pop" goal of reworking the vocabulary of the Afro-American idiom, Lennon was a man with high hopes, serious hopes, *artistic* hopes. Unfortunately, he pinned them all on Ono.

The turning point came at the Toronto Rock and Roll Festival in 1969. Appearing live for the first time since 1966, and solo for the first time since 1957, Lennon was sharing the lineup with his idols Chuck Berry, Bo Diddley, Jerry Lee Lewis, and Gene Vincent. Accordingly, he was extremely nervous: "I just threw up for hours before I went on."[32] Yet once he took the stage and heard the wild applause of twenty thousand fans, he became his old self, launching into roaring covers of three 1950s hits: "Blue Suede Shoes," "Money," and "Dizzy Miss Lizzy." Yet, just as the old excitement was returning, who should take the stage but Art—a mysterious figure in a white shroud who turned out, after a few baffling moments, to be the source of the thin, off-key whinnying that kept creeping in at all the wrong moments. A computer programmed to miss every note and muff every beat could not have done a better job.

And that was only the beginning. The next step was a real-life enact-ment of every musician's nightmare: the star's tone-deaf girlfriend getting up to sing with the band. When Ono cast off her shroud and joined Lennon in a new creation called "Cold Turkey," the whinnying gave way to gobbling, choking, gibbering, squawking, screaming, yowling, yipping, keening—and finally, over the droning background of a number called "John, John, Let's Hope for Peace," the cry of a baby rabbit being tortured to death. The audience swallowed it, because at that point the audience was swallowing anything Lennon dished out. Even so, he seemed a bit worried: He announced Ono's solo performance by saying, "Now Yoko is going to do her thing—all over you." And at the end of the set, he joined Clapton and the other musicians for a hand-rolled smoke, perhaps to stave off another attack of nausea.[33]

Two years later Lennon told *Rolling Stone*: "I like rock & roll, man. I don't like much else. . . . There is nothing conceptually better than rock & roll. No group, be it Beatles, Dylan or Stones, have ever improved on 'Whole Lot of Shakin'" [*sic*] for my money."[34] He added that he and Ono had taught each other a lot; perhaps one of the things he taught her was that there *is* a distinc-tion between music and noise. Over the next ten years Lennon's life mel-lowed; he did not quit writing songs, and Ono did not quit doing her thing all over people. But their union seemed happy enough till Lennon was mur-dered by a deranged fan in 1980. Regrettably, the same cannot be said of the marriage between popular music and perverse modernism.

Shock Rock and "Stoopid Noizes"

In "A Reasonable Guide to Horrible Noise," published in the *Village Voice* in 1981, Lester Bangs calls the Toronto performance "Interesting . . . for John's churning blues-unto-feedback guitar riff and how far ahead of her time Yoko was vocally."[35] What Bangs finds interesting I find portentous. For Lennon's acceptance of Ono's noise gave the stamp of legitimacy to a movement that would end up devouring the very thing he loved.

At first the movement was called "shock rock," with groups cropping up everywhere at the end of the 1960s. In Phoenix, Arizona, a band called Alice Cooper (after the transvestite stage persona of their leader, Vincent Damon Furnier) began combining hard rock with stage antics reminiscent of Zappa. Naturally Zappa was impressed. Indeed, he signed Alice Cooper to his Straight Records label after the group caused a mass walkout at the trendy Los Angeles nightclub, Cheetah. Not only did Alice Cooper display the requisite contempt for the audience, they were also scornful of Afro-

American music, especially the blues. "We're not going to play Delta blues," Furnier told the *Berkeley Barb* in 1970. "I couldn't care less how many times his baby left him. We were upper middle class suburban brats that had anything we wanted. We never had a blues. The whole end is that we are what we are now—a living social criticism."[36]

Compared with the tribute paid by metalheads who have long since forgotten what the blues sounds like, this cynicism is almost refreshing. But there's nothing refreshing about shock rock. Moving beyond the Velvet Underground, who scrubbed the blues but added a trace of melody and minimalist hypnosis; and even beyond Alice Cooper, who did produce a few catchy singles; the bulk of the new genre offered little but hard rock clichés, played at deafening volume with the utmost rhythmic monotony, relieved only by uncontrolled bursts of feedback. Had they been straight rock bands, MC5, the New York Dolls, and Iggy Pop and the Stooges would probably not have made it. But they knew better than to hang their hopes on music. Instead they stressed "social criticism." For MC5 (short for "Motor City 5," though the group came from Ann Arbor, not Detroit), the trademark was New Left politics: The only band to perform for the antiwar demonstrators at the 1968 Democratic Convention in Chicago, MC5 was managed by John Sinclair, the head of an abortive organization called the White Panthers, and their chief contribution to the revolution was to reach number 82 on the 1969 pop chart with a song called "Kick Out the Jams," which contained the word *motherfucker* until it was removed by the record label (Elektra).[37]

The New York Dolls were a different kettle of fish, dabbling less in political than in cultural radicalism. By carrying Alice Cooper's transvestism to flamboyant extremes, they established themselves as the darlings of the downtown Manhattan arts scene after the Velvet Underground broke up. Musically they were less appealing than the Velvet Underground, but their audience came to appreciate their aesthetic of ugliness, and several rock critics soon tumbled for the idea. Here is a typical compliment, paid by Ken Tucker to the group's first album, *New York Dolls*:

> The album's sound may be kindly termed muddy, with [David] Johansen's ragged roar rising up from the depths of the murk. In its sloppy, crude way, it was a thrilling record; in fact, it was thrilling in part because it was so sloppy and crude—in the face of an increasingly sophisticated record industry, the Dolls blew a big, wet Bronx cheer.[38]

A richer mixture of bodily fluids was forthcoming from Iggy Pop and the Stooges, also from Ann Arbor. Their leader, James Osterberg, boasts of having served a blues apprenticeship, playing drums for various black bands on Chicago's South Side. About the people he met there he has this to say: "Good musicians, but . . . children, complete children . . . it's just like playing with a bunch of 10-year-olds who've got knives and guns and things."[39] True to the spirit of primitivism, Osterberg was more interested in the chaos of black musicians' lives than in their musical craft; instead of learning to play like his mentors, he assembled a band of nonmusicians for the express purpose of accompanying his own plunge into chaos. Mike Jahn describes a typical performance:

> The Stooges' music, for all practical purposes, is one big noise that throbs. . . . The important thing about their music is that it fills the room and provides a context for Iggy Pop, who is watched by the audience with intense fascination. . . . He writhes. He moans. He seems totally self-involved. He rubs his body, he contorts, bending over backward until his head nearly touches the floor. He rolls his tongue around. He makes grotesque shapes with his lips. He acts very ugly and precociously sexual. . . . Earlier in the show, he took a drumstick and raked it across his chest until he started to bleed. After another concert he was heard to lament that he hadn't bled enough.[40]

That was in 1970. In 1991 Iggy Pop got this rave from the *Boston Globe*:

> Last night Pop gave sweat and blood, the latter coming from a self-inflicted head gash ("not a serious injury," he said later), spilling a red stream onto his bare chest. It was 45 minutes of pure, compacted ferocity, . . . and one, it seemed, fueled by the frustration of looking into the front sections and seeing seated fans. . . . Mike stands were kicked over; bad words flew through the air; the energy level hit 11 on a 10 scale.[41]

It's no wonder this routine lasted twenty years; it was almost a century old when Iggy Pop adopted it. Not that Iggy Pop was a student of expressionism, the Grand Guignol, or the theater of cruelty. For him inspiration came from a parallel strain of happening, called "performance art," that began in Europe and migrated to the United Sates at about the same time as Fluxus. Yet, as RoseLee Goldberg's account suggests, older perverse-modernist movements lie at the root of performance art:

> [The performances] of the Austrian artist Herman Nitsch, beginning in 1962, involving ritual and blood, were described as "an aesthetic way of praying." . . . His *Orgies, Mysteries, Theatre* projects were repeated at regular intervals throughout the seventies. A typical action would last several hours:

it would begin with the sound of loud music—"the ecstasy created by the loudest possible created noise"—followed by Nitsch giving orders for the ceremony to begin. A slaughtered lamb would be brought on stage by assistants, fastened head down as if crucified. Then the animal would be disembowelled; entrails and buckets of blood were poured over a nude woman or man. . . . Such activities sprang from Nitsch's belief that humankind's aggressive instincts had been repressed and muted through the media. . . . These ritualized acts were a means of releasing that repressed energy as well as an act of purification and redemption through suffering.[42]

Other practitioners of this strain sought to recreate a bloodier version of the "fearful cynical spectacle" of Frank Wedekind going into convulsions at Munich's Café Simplicissimus. The logic was clear: If art lovers were impressed by animal blood, they'd be thrilled by the performer's own. Hence the Parisian performance artist Gina Pane slashed and burned her body "in order to reach an anaesthetized society"; and the Austrian Rudolf Schwartzkogler tried so hard to create human "wreckage" that he ended up killing himself in 1969.[43] By the time Iggy Pop came along, violent obscenity was de rigueur in certain avant-garde circles. And it conferred the same advantage as sexual obscenity: the power to "shock the bourgeoisie."

To their credit, most 1960s rock critics were disgusted by shock rock. But they were in a weak position to defend Afro-American music, because, more often than not, they had been the ones identifying the genuinely affirmative spirit of the music with the woolly headed utopianism of Woodstock. When the attack came, these Woodstockians were helpless: Any defense of good music seemed, perforce, a defense of mindless "peace and love." Likewise, the charge that rock had "sold out" was unanswerable. Rock had indeed become big business: Its Dionysian revels had been transformed into Roman circuses, with millionaire stars blasting countercultural bathos at stadiums full of shaggy fans as long in the tooth as they were spaced in the head.

The whole scene was ripe for an apostate like Lester Bangs, who got the drop on his generation when he accused them of pretending to be "loose, liberated, righteous and ravenous," while actually succumbing to "the whole damn pompous edifice of this supremely ridiculous rock 'n' roll industry." Yet when it came to finding a way out, the apostate was no more help than the Woodstockians. Like Lennon, Bangs was quick to defend Afro-American music against Commerce. But when the damage was done by Art, he crumpled. With Greil Marcus (the editor of his posthumous selected writings), Bangs shared the blinkered assumption that nothing of any musical or cultural significance occurred before the 1960s generation discovered rock 'n' roll. Strikingly ignorant of both the Afro-American musical past and the history of the European avant-garde, Bangs's sole prescription for what ailed mainstream rock fans was a stronger dose of what they were already taking:

> They sit there, wide-eyed vegetative Wowers or sullen in a carapace of Cool, afraid or unable to react, to get out there in that arena which is nothing more than life, most often too cowed to even hurl a disappointing hoot stageward. And that is why most rock bands are so soporifically lazy these days, and also why the Stooges, or any other band that challenges its audience, are the answer. Power doesn't go to the people, it comes *from* them, and when the people have gotten this passive nothing short of electroshock and personal exorcism will jolt them and rock them into some kind of fiercely healthy interaction.[44]

By this route, Bangs became the chief exponent of what Dave Marsh calls "stoopid noizes."[45] In 1976, when Lou Reed made a solo album called *Metal Machine Music*, consisting entirely of electronic feedback, Bangs called it "the greatest album ever made."[46] No doubt Bangs, a loyal fan of the Velvet Underground, recalled the use of noise on such early songs as "Heroin," which concludes with a harsh squeal like that of a braking New York subway train. But Bangs overlooks the key distinction. In "Heroin," the Velvet Underground incorporates noise into music—the strategy, as we've seen, of both extroverted modernism and the blues.

It is often claimed that Reed made *Metal Machine Music* to get out of his RCA contract.[47] Regrettably, that did not stop anyone—Reed or his fans—from defending it in perverse-modernist terms. Zonked on amphetamines, he boasted to Bangs that the LP's blistering harmonics contained all the world's great music: "Just sit down and you can hear Beethoven right in the opening part of it. . . . It's down here in, like, you know, the fifteenth harmonic. But it's not the only one there, there's about seventeen more going at the same time."[48]

If only Reed had been able to stare speed-trippingly into a vat of discarded oil pigments, he might have seen all the world's great paintings. To Bang's credit he didn't buy this particular nonsense. For him *Metal Machine Music* was great simply because it got a rise out of people, even record company executives, at a time when nothing else could. Like obscenity, which Bangs also admired, "horrible noise" was a sure thing, a guaranteed shock, a fleeting impression that somebody somewhere was doing something creative.

CBGB and the Cult of Incompetence

If you're wondering what came next, the answer is simple: more of the same. Nonetheless, it is notable that the next generation of shock rockers came more from the ranks of would-be poets and painters than from those of musicians. Now the locus shifts back to New York, most notably to a hole-in-the-wall nightclub called CBGB, which opened on the Bowery in 1973. The club's full name, CBGB-OMFUG, was short for "Country, Bluegrass, Blues and Other Music for Uplifting Gourmandizers," because the owner, Hilly Kristal, was a veteran folkie who hoped to make the club into a venue where the downtown arts crowd could hear such groups as they passed through town.[49]

It didn't turn out that way. There were a few competent musicians among the headliners at CBGB, but most of the styles they played can be classified only as "Other." For example, a group called Television got hired after their manager, an associate of Warhol's named Terry Ork, told Kristal that the band played country, bluegrass, and blues. But the lead guitarist, Tom Verlaine (Tom Miller of Wilmington, Delaware) specialized in free-jazz-derived soloing; the closest Television ever got to the blues was when CBGB's official poet, Patti Smith, said, "Tom plays the guitar like a thousand bluebirds screaming."[50]

Still, Television had more musical substance than most of the bands at CBGB. Television's vocalist, Richard Hell (Richard Meyers, also of Wilmington), split from the group in 1974 because he was less interested in music than in becoming "a sexy drunken poet like Dylan Thomas."[51] No Dylan Thomas, Hell did achieve fame in 1977, when his new band, the Voidoids, made a record called *Blank Generation* that gained a cult following, especially in Britain. In a pattern already familiar from the Doors and the Velvet Underground, Hell's nihilistic commentary and the simple but atmospheric music of the Voidoids proved mutually reinforcing. Likewise Patti Smith: Her first album, *Horses* (1975), benefits from a pulsating background produced by John Cale of the Velvet Underground.

Without such reinforcement, or with the wrong reinforcement (Smith later switched to hard rock), these CBGB poets sound drearily inane.[52] At least Reed has written some compelling song lyrics (which is to say, not poetry). Smith has written neither. *Dream of Life*, a comeback album released in 1988, was praised for showing the "reflective" side of her "poetic imagination."[53] But the only poetic thing about it is a quote from Rilke on the sleeve. Inside, there is only ersatz beat drivel.[54]

In sum, music was important without being important at CBGB. To most of the SoHo audience, what mattered was the performance art, not the music. Musicians could provide either "the loudest possible created noise" for hysterical frenzy, or an eerie throbbing backdrop for verbal meanderings. But they rarely sounded bluesy, soulful, or rhythmically complex. The one band that did sound that way, Mink DeVille, met with initial opprobrium.[55]

Was this sensibility racist? Yes, says Bangs in a 1979 essay called "The White Noise Supremacists," which describes how the racial polarization of popular music, combined with the growing pathology of life in New York, led to vehement antiblack feelings among the CBGB regulars. Bangs reports the use of racial slurs such as "boon" ("Baboon") among people who spent the rest of their time bewailing social injustice. And he describes a taste for swastikas and other Nazi regalia among CBGB performers inspired by the sporting of such symbols by Iggy Pop and the New York Dolls. Bangs confesses that he found these things bracing at first, a refreshing antidote to hippie "love and peace." But in 1976, when he gave a party for the CBGB crowd, their comments raised a few doubts:

> When I did what we always used to do at parties in Detroit—put on soul records so everybody could dance—I began to hear this: "What're you playing all that nigger disco shit for, Lester?"
>
> "That's not nigger disco shit," I snarled, "that's *Otis Redding*, you assholes!" But they didn't want to hear about it.[56]

The corresponding European view was expressed by the Velvet Underground's Nico when she told a reporter in 1979 that she thought of blacks as "a whole different race. . . . I don't like the features. They're so much like animals . . . it's cannibals, no?"[57] With such attitudes afloat, it's no wonder Bangs writes: "Most of the SoHo bands are as white as John Cage."[58]

But this is not to say that the downtown crowd clamored to hear Cage perform. Ironically, Cage was too highbrow for people inspired by Warhol to use popular culture as a battering ram against genuine art. So, while the CBGB audience rejected Afro-American music, they also wanted to call what they were doing "rock 'n' roll." What they needed was something tacky and déclassé to love, which did not in any way resemble "nigger disco shit." It was a clever band from Forest Hills, New York, that came up with the formula. Calling themselves the Ramones (after an early pseudonym of Paul McCartney) and adopting "Ramone" as their surnames, the quartet came up with a distinctive, if exceedingly limited, sound. According to Joey Ramone (Jeffrey Hyman), the group admired shock rock. But they also admired rock 'n' roll: "We missed hearing songs that were short and exciting . . . and good! We wanted to bring back the energy to rock & roll."[59]

Too bad the Ramones couldn't play well enough to capture that energy. As Joey explains: "We just couldn't figure them out, so we decided to write our own, and we had to make them basic enough so we could play them."[60] Here is an apt description from *Rolling Stone*'s Ken Tucker:

> From the start, the Ramones distinguished themselves from the general run of loud, fast upstarts by becoming much louder and much faster. . . . Johnny and Dee Dee Ramone [John Cummings and Douglas Colvin] whipped up deafening storms of sound with only two or three guitar chords; Tommy Ramone [Tom Erdelyi] slammed the beat with metronomic precision. Joey Ramone—impossibly tall, limp haired, and ungainly—leaned into this hurricane and bleated songs with titles like "Beat on the Brat," "Gimme Gimme Shock Treatment," and "Now I Wanna Sniff Some Glue." Most of the Ramones' songs didn't last more than two minutes; their average performance clocked in at less than thirty minutes, *but it was arguably the most exhilarating half hour in rock and roll.*[61] (emphasis added)

Recall that Tucker also finds the "crude and sloppy" sound of the New York Dolls "thrilling." But I don't mean to single him out. Many popular music pundits have praised the "energy" of the Ramones' "thrash" sound, despite the fact that the sole musical source of that energy is speed and volume.

Thus the Ramones' main contribution to rock was an amazingly simpleminded approach to rhythm. As Bangs discovered, the fans of this music do not just reject the mechanized rhythm of disco, they reject all Afro-American rhythm. Indeed, they prefer the jackhammer beat of thrash on the grounds that it is, perforce, a greater stimulant. Typically, they measure the beats-per-minute of disco (126–132 bpm), compare it with the rate found in thrash (250–300 bpm), and argue that the latter is superior because (as they claim) it produces more adrenaline in the listener.[62]

It was an insult to jazz when Adorno described its rhythms as having "convulsive aspects reminiscent of St. Vitus' dance or the reflexes of mutilated animals."[63] But it's no insult to thrash. Indeed, the same remark would probably be taken as a compliment. Thrash fans often brag that what the genre really does is take old rock 'n' roll and speed it up—play it live at 78 rpm, instead of 45. Yet what they are speeding up is not the sound of the real thing, with blues and swing excitement built in; it's the rhythmically monotonous, bland sound of the white-bread cover—Pat Boone instead of Fats Domino. Only a fool with a tin ear, or a conformist terrified of not being on the "cutting edge," would credit the Ramones with recapturing the old energy.[64] It is a pity that the CBGB crowd's disgust with the bombast of hard rock and the mechanization of disco led them, not toward better music, but toward a cult of incompetence. But don't take my word for it, take Hilly Kristal's:

> I thought it was very crude music. It was not that it was strange, but it was hard to take. It was very loud and abrasive. . . . They were not musicians. They were kids who used music—even if they couldn't play their instruments—to express themselves. The fundamental thing was a form of expression. . . . It was creative. They were making their own melodies, and it was very inspirational to have it here, though it was very hard to take, to listen to.[65]

Chapter 17

Punk: The Great Avant-Garde Swindle

The Ramones toured Britain twice in the mid-1970s, and many CBGB loyalists insist that those visits, and other contacts with the New York scene, were the real inspiration for the media explosion known as *punk*, which tore through Britain in the late 1970s with a force that can still be felt today. (It was also called *new wave*, but the meaning of that term was later to change rather drastically.) Yet the New York influence took hold only because a critical mass of Britons were already primed for such an outburst. As usual, the story begins in that cultural hall of mirrors, the British art college.

Futurism Ain't What It Used to Be: British Punk

The initiator—some would say perpetrator—of British punk was Malcolm McLaren, an entrepreneur and fashion designer who spent the 1960s in art college: eight years in six schools, to be exact, with two expulsions.[1] In McLaren's own words: "I learned all my politics and understanding of the world through the history of art. . . . Art schools were the islands of the dispossessed. I discovered an incredible critique that has stayed with me up to today."[2] Since the words "understanding" and "critique" suggest the constructive use of reason, they do not really describe what McLaren learned in art college. A better phrase is "perverse modernism," because British punk is best understood as the most spectacular realization to date of the old futurist dream of the sudden, subversive media blitz. It also, as we shall see, shows the destructive futility of that dream.

McLaren's career as a "serious" artist was brief: His first gallery exhibition, mounted in 1965, was a variation on the Allan Kaprow happening described earlier—a maze of partitions intended to trap visitors and defeat their expectation of seeing works of art. After that McLaren tried his hand at filmmaking, but it was in 1968, during the student uprising in Paris, that he found his true calling. He focused on Paris because, a born cynic in the mold of Frank Zappa, he had no use for the higher aspirations of 1960s rock, British or American. Nor did he have any special love for Afro-American music, although he brags of having spent all of his arts grant money on rock 'n' roll records.[3] What really caught McLaren's eye was "situationism," one of the pet ideologies of the French student left, a combination of structuralism (then in its heyday) and neo-Marxism—in particular, a revival of Walter Benjamin's hopes for a revolutionary use of mass media.

As we've seen, such hopes are as old as the media themselves. For Marinetti the strategy was to force the modernization of Italy by placing a manifesto on the front page of a leading Paris newspaper. For Benjamin it was to inspire the masses through the "progressive" use of cinema. For the situationists it was to infiltrate the established media and turn their power against them. Unlike the architects of the Popular Front, whose goal was to transform the media into a conduit for Stalinist propaganda, the situationists' goal was anarchistic: to become ensconced in the media, then to use structuralist methods to disrupt, debunk, and demystify the shared consciousness of society—both its moral values and its basic sense of reality. In other words, they took the Frankfurtian concept of "negation" and ran with it, not toward a utopian future but down the steep slope of nihilism.

I say "nihilism" despite of the efforts of punk theorists to identify the movement with anarchism.[4] Historically there's an important difference: The goal of anarchism is to topple the large, centralized, bureaucratic institutions of society, and leave the small, organic ones standing. Recall that this message, as preached by Paul Goodman, was part of the new radicalism. Goodman was dismayed at how quickly the 1960s counterculture forgot the constructive side of the message. Punk went even further: Apart from an occasional nod in the direction of punk "community" (something that, by all accounts, never existed), the movement showed precious little concern for what was supposed to be left standing in its wake.[5] Destruction was the thrill, the messier the better; therefore the proper word is "nihilism."[6]

The first thing McLaren did with situationism was start a clothing boutique—because he was also inspired by Mary Quant, purveyor of mod fashion to the swinging Londoners of the 1960s. In 1972, when McLaren and his partner, designer Vivienne Westwood, first opened Let It Rock, their shop in the seedy World's End section of King's Road, the idea was not to deconstruct society's consciousness but to cash in on the latest revival of the "Teddy boy" craze of the 1950s. But as Westwood recalls, "Malcolm began to get bored with the idea of Teddy boys . . . he thought they were some kind of expression of revolt, and he just got rather tired in the end of them all talking about which record had come out on the same label."[7] Thus the next step was a reprise of what had actually happened in the 1950s: a shift away from music toward the JD mystique. Reviving the "rocker" style of the early 1960s, McLaren and Westwood renamed their shop "Too Fast To Live, Too Young To Die" (the motto of the James Dean cult), and filled it with black-leather biker gear.

Then our situationist couturiers found an even hotter idea: Nazi chic.[8] Brought back from their sojourn in New York, this gambit made quite an impression on the art college crowd. One convert recalls: "It was always very much an anti-mums and anti-dads thing. We hated older people—not across the board but particularly in suburbia—always harping on about Hitler. . . . It was a way of saying, 'Well, I think Hitler was very good, actually' . . . a way of watching someone like that go completely red-faced."[9]

Sensing that he was on a roll, McLaren returned to New York in 1974 to design costumes for the New York Dolls. In theory his idea should have worked: By dressing the band in the colors and insignia of Maoist and Soviet communism, he was literally waving a red flag in the face of the American public. But in practice it sputtered. The Dolls were half dead from drugs (one had already died), and the trend was shifting to CBGB.[10] McLaren followed the trend and became smitten with the stage persona of Television's Richard Hell: short spiky hair, beatnik sunglasses, and a ripped T-shirt bearing a scrawled message ("Kill me"). At that moment, British punk was conceived: In the words of one New York Doll, McLaren "copied the New York groups; he loved Richard Hell."[11]

On his return to London, McLaren renewed his contacts with a group of working-class kids trying to put together a rock band. Only one could play, but that wasn't a problem. The important thing, as the journalist Jon Savage explains, was the interest the kids sparked in McLaren:

> Pop is one of the very few areas of English society where members of different classes can mix on anything resembling equal terms. Its history is full of interactions between middle class, often Jewish, often homosexual entrepreneurs and working-class, male performers. If sex is not involved, another kind of fantasy is: the performer, Trilby-like, can often act out what the manager himself is unable to do, because of either age or inhibition.[12]

Since Savage is one of those British writers who focus almost exclusively on the visual side of "pop," he ignores the changes that had taken place since Epstein took a similar interest in the Beatles. As we've seen, Epstein the entrepreneur did transform the scruffy, leather-jacketed Quarrymen into the fresh-faced, Eton-collared Beatles. But that was only after Epstein the record man had judged their music to be the finest in Liverpool. Those priorities got reversed when Andrew Loog Oldham looked at the Rolling Stones, saw "pure sex," and promptly kicked out the fine keyboardist Ian Stewart for looking "too normal." With McLaren the question of music never even arose. Describing the first time McLaren heard the New York Dolls play, Savage writes: "It was awful, he thought, but so awful that it crashed through to the other side, into magnificence. Upon this inverted aesthetic his interest in pop was fully rekindled."[13]

Hence McLaren's bold decision to turn his lads into a walking, spitting, screaming, pill-popping advertisement for his boutique. First he dubbed them the Sex Pistols, then he sacked the one tolerable musician in the group (Warwick Nightingale), on the grounds that he was too serious about writing songs and playing guitar. Then McLaren presented the others (guitarist Steve Jones, drummer Paul Cook, and bassist Glen Matlock) with their new lead singer: an especially wild street kid named John Lydon, whose voice was a snarl, but whose bitterly antisocial personality mesmerized McLaren. Almost before Lydon was brought into the group, he was renamed "Johnny Rotten." Here is Savage's account of his "audition":

> Lydon was hesitant and nervous but . . . allowed himself to be steered back to the shop. There he was placed in front of the jukebox, with a shower attachment in his hand as a microphone, and told to sing along to Alice Cooper's "Eighteen." . . . He froze, but then . . . he began to jump up and down in a spastic fashion, gabbling improvised lyrics: "I'm eighteen, sex in

the grass, I'm eighteen. . . ." Jones growled further threats of violence and, under considerable stress, Lydon launched into a sequence of hunchbacked poses—screaming, mewling and puking. . . . The group wasn't sure, but McLaren was. "I had an eye," he says, "and my eye saw Rotten's ability to create image around himself."[14]

What McLaren's eye really saw, of course, was Richard Hell. The hair, the sunglasses, and the T-shirt ("I Hate") were all in place when the Sex Pistols staged their first few appearances—happenings, really—in various art colleges where McLaren had connections.

It's worth noting that, for all their reputation as street rebels, the Sex Pistols rarely ventured beyond the "playpens" of the art colleges.[15] They were terrified to perform in the rough environment of the council housing estates, knowing all too well that in such places crude obnoxiousness was not an art form but a team sport. After the group began making (and breaking) record contracts, the releases of their records were frequently held up by spontaneous walkouts on the part of pressing plant workers offended by their content.[16] And the tabloids, those garbled organs of mingled working-class conservatism and decadence, blasted the group.

As a class phenomenon, therefore, punk was neither a working-class revolt nor an outbreak of under-class anarchy. Rather it was, as Simon Frith reminds us, "the ultimate art school music movement." As we've seen, the art colleges were repositories of class resentment, but it was predominantly the lower-middle-class kind: a volatile mixture of poor education, frustrated ambition, and stale avant-gardism. Punk is best described as a middle-class panic touched off by a middle-class trickster well acquainted with middle-class fears of social chaos during high unemployment. Frith adds that those fears got amplified when the media chose to depict punk "as a street and not a college movement, an eruption from the gutters of inner-city recession (rather than bored suburbia)." As the media swelled with sensationalist reportage about punk, and the various groups, especially the Sex Pistols, got censored and banned, the "dole queue" young did adopt the look and some of the attitudes of punk—including, unfortunately, its fascination with Nazi imagery. But as Frith concludes, "Punk as a youth subculture has a different history from punk as pop style."[17]

"Empty and Sad, Almost": Punk Obscenity

The real kerosene of the punk explosion, however, was neither art nor politics, but our old standby, obscenity. Along with the swastika, McLaren had been charmed by the New York Doll's use of sadomasochism as a fashion statement. By seizing upon that theme (resonant, needless to say, with certain elite British sensibilities), McLaren found the core truth of contemporary perverse modernism: if art and ideas don't shock 'em, obscenity will. He renamed his shop "Sex"; stocked it with rubber bondage gear, whips, vises, and "tit clamps"; festooned the walls with images from hard-core pornography; and transferred the same images to designer T-shirts. Savage writes:

> There was a naked black footballer with pendulous cock, Alex Trocchi's fervid lesbian fantasies, or the troubling image of a twelve-year-old boy, suggestively exhaling a cigarette, which came from *Boys Express*, a small paedophile magazine sold openly with a contact address in Essex. . . . One blatant design acted as an implicit graphic manifesto for the Sex Pistols. . . . Two cowboys pose outside a dancehall, on Saturday night. Both wear cowboy hats, long boots and no trousers . . . two large, flaccid penises are a whisker away from contact.[18]

Even McLaren's friends were offended by the T-shirt depicting the hood worn by a brutal rapist then terrorizing Cambridge. True to form, his response was to silkscreen even more rapist T-shirts, only this time adding the Beatles' song title, "A Hard Day's Night." Then, when Sex got raided by the vice squad, and the Sex Pistols got banned from playing the famous Marquee Club, McLaren moved swiftly to book the group into a grimy strip joint, advertising the show with a handbill featuring a photo of Johnny Rotten ripping the blouse off the buxom shop assistant.[19] Not even the Sex Pistols' attack on the queen (in their first album, *Anarchy in the UK*) won them as much publicity as their next coup, a brief spew of profanity aimed at the drunken host of a television talk show.

Of course, the word *obscenity* never crossed our intrepid retailers' lips. To hear Westwood reminisce, you'd think she and McLaren had been D. H. Lawrence, reviled for the love scenes in *Lady Chatterley's Lover*: "If there is one thing that frightens the Establishment, it's sex. Religion you can knock, but sex gives them the horrors."[20] But what Westwood means by "sex" would give D. H. Lawrence the horrors. For punk was not only intent on getting explicit material into circulation, it was devoted to making that material as repulsive as possible. Search the lyrics, the images, the critical commentary, the films, and the books of punk, and you will find few, if any, depictions of sex as a positive occurrence between two people fond of each other.

The first explanation for this is psychological. Punk followed the pattern roundly condemned by Lawrence, of sexual repression leading to an infantile obsession with sex—in other words, of prudery and pornography as two sides of the same coin. Thus, along with celebrations of obscenity, Savage's book about punk contains several references to the "puritanism" of the punks, including this comment by a young woman: "I became asexual, I think many people were, it was an incredibly asexual movement."[21]

The second explanation for punk's rejection of positive sexuality is ideological. Since situationism is basically another shake of the Frankfurt School mojo, the punks worried a lot about whether they were subverting the commercial mass media or selling out to them. More ink has been spilled on this question than it deserves, since it is the wrong question. But one thing is certain: the punks rejected any alluring or emotionally positive evocation of sex as "pop." Even the Damned, who screamed like the Sex Pistols, but about the breakdown of relationships instead of society, were damned as "pop." Their hit, "Love Song," got lambasted when Lydon (embarked on a solo career after splitting with McLaren) sneered his way through a single called "This Is Not A Love Song."

Closely related to the punks' attitude toward sex was their attitude toward Afro-American music. Their distinctive blend of know-nothing contempt and racist primitivism is revealed in Savage's description of 1950s rock 'n' roll as "brutality and sheer sexual explosiveness," "big, bad noise" and "the brutal beat."[22] Even more revealing was a 1988 exhibition at the downtown New York Museum of Contemporary Art: "Impresario: Malcolm McLaren and the British New Wave." In one room of that show (mounted with McLaren's assistance), a cluster of video monitors played tapes of black music-making: a West African tribal dance, a Jamaican reggae festival, and an American high school cheerleading contest. At first the display seemed inoffensive, and therefore out of place. But a second look uncovered its purpose: In each tape the camera sought out the most lascivious angle, using the zoom lens for closeups of the bare breasts of the African women, the shaking thighs and buttocks of the Jamaican dancers, and the bare knees of the American teenagers. And each tape kept cutting to McLaren's leering face. Above the display ran the caption: "I'm Taking Their Culture and Exposing It in the Right Way."

Yet the ultimate obscenity of punk was not sexual. At a 1976 show at a nightclub called the Nashville, the Sex Pistols attracted a sizable audience and, more important, reporters and photographers from the influential

New Musical Express. Because the band was just beginning to attract attention, it was a key moment. No wonder McLaren and Westwood became
worried when, as Savage reports, "Neither the group's performance or the
audience were particularly inspired."[23] But then inspiration struck Westwood. As one witness later recalled, Westwood suddenly began, "for no
reason," to slap the young woman next to her. Immediately the woman's
boyfriend began to slap Westwood. Next McLaren and Lydon leaped in,
and before you could say "publicity," a general row ensued. Clearly Westwood did have a reason: As the same witness added, "It was extremely electrifying. Up until that point it was just another date."[24] And in the next
issue of the *NME*, the Sex Pistols got a feature story, complete with action
photos.[25]

Accordingly, the shop on King's Road underwent another transformation in early 1977. Renamed "Seditionaries," it acquired the look of a
prison fortress on the outside, a war zone on the inside. The walls were
papered with enlarged photographs of fire-bombed Dresden, the ceiling
sported a jagged hole filled with spotlights, and the racks held new (and
pricier) attempts at terrorist chic. In the eyes of one fashion-oriented
chronicler: "*Seditionaries* presented a vision of an apocalyptic utopia that
sought to locate punk on the precipice of cultural collapse."[26]

The reality is more cogently described by Bob Geldof, an Irish musician
who arrived on the scene in 1978:

> We were playing at the Music Machine in London. It was at the time when
> the aggression of the punk era was being manifested not in posturing or in
> spitting, which had been one of the original marks of the movement I could
> not tolerate, but in actual physical violence. The people on the balcony had
> begun dropping beer glasses. . . . Girls were crying and people were leaving
> with serious gashes . . . We could hear that running battles had developed on
> the dance floor. The atmosphere was foul. . . . A character from one of the
> earlier bands walked on stage and punched me in the face. . . . We went
> straight into "Lookin' After Number One" and sang with special emphasis,
> with the blood pouring down my face, the refrain, "I don't want to be like
> you." They used the picture on the cover of the *NME* the next week with a
> holier than thou article on "Now the Violence Has to Stop," which was iron-
> ic considering that they had played a large part in inciting the phenomenon.[27]

Earlier I contrasted the self-immolators of the late 1960s with those
hypocritical individuals who, having quit or avoided such behavior themselves, still tout it as the essence of true art. This hypocrisy took even more
cynical form in the relationship between McLaren and the two members

of the Sex Pistols whose antisocial personalities most fascinated him: Lydon (Johnny Rotten) and John Ritchie, the pathetic nonmusician who replaced Matlock, and became "Sid Vicious" under McLaren's tutelage.

Of what did that tutelage consist? Describing the heavy use of amphetamines among the punks, Savage comments: "The Sex Pistols and their followers were playing with a gun loaded by McLaren and Westwood. Drugs also fragmented already frail teenage identities."[28] Or, as Geldof recalls:

> The Sex Pistols seemed to me to be one of the few genuinely nihilistic bands around. The atmosphere in their camp seemed to be permanently poisonous. I once saw them at a university gig. They were fighting before the concert. Steve hit Sid Vicious; he was fed up being in a band with someone who hadn't a clue how to play bass. Malcolm wanted him there simply as a catalyst, so when Steve hit Sid, Sid was doing his job properly. The concert was awful. It was empty and sad, almost. As they were leaving, Sid and Nancy walked over to the bus door and Malcolm slammed it in Sid's face and told him he could fuckin' walk back for all he cared.[29]

Geldof adds, "I liked Johnny Rotten. He was an extraordinary character with a fierce intelligence."[30] Perhaps it was Lydon's intelligence that led him to break with McLaren. The alternative was to end up like Ritchie: a weak, scared rat in a maze, drugged, prodded, and jolted to ever greater behavioral extremes. It would seem, by all accounts, that Ritchie's only protest was to take up with Nancy Spungeon, an American prostitute who got him hooked on heroin, thus slowing him down and wreaking havoc with McLaren's plans.

The whole scenario is a nightmare version of the old Motown gambit of picking young people off the street and making them over in the image of show business. Only Berry Gordy sent musically talented teenagers to charm school to clean up their act, while McLaren thrust mentally unstable young people into crazy, disorienting situations to dirty up theirs. Then the dirt was marketed: After Spungeon's death, Westwood brought out a T-shirt, now a collector's item, pretending to quote Sid Vicious: "She's dead, I'm alive, I'm yours."[31] It was only when the experiment failed and the rats began whimpering for help that our masterminds moved on to other projects.

The year 1979 marked the end of middle-class panic at the specter of "anarchy in the UK." McLaren boasted, in the title of a film he was making about the Sex Pistols, that he had pulled off *The Great Rock 'n' Roll Swindle*. But in fact the group had self-destructed. Lydon and McLaren were feuding, and Ritchie died of a heroin overdose after being charged with the stabbing murder of Spungeon. At the same time the record industry was taking a dive—due not to the depredations of punk but to the bursting of the disco bubble. It was clear, as those who had led the punk assault on the profit system went into costly litigation over the profits, that punk had become the creature of the system instead of the other way around. Needless to say, this outcome has been a continuing source of dismay to the movement's situationist champions.

Another source of dismay has been the fact that punk attitudes quickly became diluted by "pop," meaning ear-pleasing forms of Afro-American music. For many of the British and American groups comprising the post-punk new wave—Blondie, the Talking Heads, Elvis Costello and many others—the strategy was simple: play whatever form of "pop" you like, but also distance yourself from it, through the Warhol-approved posture of camp. Other postpunk groups, such as the Clash, the Specials and the Police, focused on strains of Afro-American music (such as Jamaican reggae) not sufficiently commercial to be "pop." I shall return to these strategies later. For now, suffice it to say that their caption reads: "We're Taking Their Culture Because We Want to Sell Records."

The Punk Legacy: A Dull Cutting Edge

It would be wrong to suggest that punk has no distinct musical legacy. Many of its heirs returned to the "pop" fold, but many did not. For the latter true punk music still comprises the "white as John Cage" strains developed at CBGB, and the thing to be avoided at all costs is the affirmative spirit of Afro-American music. They still associate that spirit with the hated 1960s counterculture, and they still evince a vehement anticommercialism tinged with racism. That leaves a musical legacy composed of three strains: noise (usually electronic but sometimes vocal), the speeded-up thrash of the Ramones, and the atmospheric minimalism developed by the Velvet Underground. Since the first two usually occur together, I shall discuss them first.

Noise and thrash are mixed in the American offshoot of punk known as "hardcore," concocted in 1978 by a San Francisco band called the Dead Kennedys. According to their leader, "Jello Biafra" (Eric Boucher), the Dead Kennedys were inspired by both the Sex Pistols, who toured the United States in 1977, and the Ramones, who taught Biafra that "all you gotta do is pick up a guitar and turn up the knobs . . . you're gonna blow people out the door."[32] The extramusical sensibility of the group is reflected in its name, as well as in titles like "Too Drunk to Fuck" and "Kill the Poor." In brief, the Dead Kennedys combined the attack-dog humor of Zappa with a crude sound requiring none of Zappa's proficiency. Not surprisingly, the band was endlessly cloned throughout the 1980s.

In a genre so devoted to "turning up the knobs," it was perhaps inevitable that the next step would be the fusion of hardcore and heavy metal. Musically this fusion, known as "thrash metal" or "speed metal," is heavy metal played at 78 rpm, with sweltering sheets of electronic noise substituted for blues-bludgeoning guitar solos. Anxious to maintain the "do-it-yourself" ethos of punk, thrash metal performers eschew "guitar heroics" in favor of sheer speed and volume. And their predominantly male fans don't dance, they headbang, slam-dance, and mosh with an extra degree of aggressiveness. Indeed, thrash metal concerts are marked by a persistent tension between the orderly, ritualized aggression associated with heavy metal, and the punk taste for real blood. The usual outcome is a higher level of mayhem, tolerated until someone—the band or the concert promoter—starts feeling threatened in the pocketbook.

Needless to say, both hardcore and thrash metal raise the same question asked earlier: What is the point of whipping up all this anger? The question gets addressed with a modicum of self-consciousness in these genres, thanks to their art college inheritance. Rather than fall back on the mindless "party till you puke" hedonism of heavy metal groups such as Mötley Crüe, hardcore and thrash metal bands claim a higher significance for what they do. That significance is derived from punk—specifically, from the latter days of British punk, when the movement split into two parts: the "lefties," who believed in channeling anger into political protest; and the "arties," who (actually truer to the spirit of punk) went on believing in rage and nihilism for their own sake.[33]

In the United States the "lefty" route is taken by thrash metal bands such as Metallica, with the result that they suddenly become legitimate in the eyes of their elders—especially those 1960s elders who still believe in the rock "revolution." It's ironic how some of those elders, after years of hating heavy metal, learn to love it the moment a metal group becomes "intelligent," meaning politically correct.[34] Among hardcore bands, the same advance in "intelligence" is achieved whenever a group switches from just plain screaming to screaming about current events.

As for the "arty" route, it is taken by the variant of thrash metal known as "death metal," a form that impresses those 1960s elders whose ideals have curdled into cynicism. Ponder this passage by Robert Palmer:

The darkness in the music holds up a mirror to the darkness in society—the empty pieties and alienating double speak of politicians and self-appointed spiritual guardians. The best death-metal bands may be anathema in some quarters. But there can be no question of their artistic intent. As the author William S. Burroughs once remarked when asked about his own proclivities for horrific imagery, "Look around. Just look around."[35]

Reluctant though I am to defend the 1960s counterculture, I feel obliged to point out that Burroughs was not one of its original gurus. Unlike the new radicals, he never held up a vision of social progress. He was (and is) a thoroughly decadent figure, a believer in sadomasochism and drug addiction as the only relief from the oppressiveness of the "system" or (depending on the context) from the absurdity of existence. Well known to the beats, Burroughs didn't make the countercultural scene until the early 1970s, when utopianism was devouring its children—and then, the part he played was that of the specter at the feast.[36] His main contribution to popular music was to call heavy metal "magical and evocative" at a time when most rock critics loathed it.[37] Now, it would seem, those same critics have come around to Burroughs's way of thinking. And the perverse-modernist itch to erase the line between art and life has taken a new twist: Because horror and evil exist in life, art has the right—indeed, the obligation—to concentrate exclusively on them.

To be fair, even the supplicant race of rock critics is occasionally taken aback by the death metal sensibility. In a 1990 interview with the Los Angeles band Slayer, *Rolling Stone*'s Mikal Gilmore followed Palmer's logic in praising the band's decision to "to write more about the human and social horrors of the modern world."[38] But, as Gilmore pursued the topic with the band's lyricist, Tom Araya, he found himself in a moral free-fall. Here is Araya's part of the interview, an explanation of why he wrote a song about the serial killer Ed Gein:

> I sit there and I ask myself, "Now, how would it feel if I really wanted to kill somebody?" And I know: I'd feel an exhilaration. I'd feel awesome. . . . The fact that he could seriously skin these people and preserve their body parts . . . that's just fucking amazing, to do things like that with no heart at all. And then I came across another book about this guy named Albert Fish, who murdered these little boys and then ate their penises. He said he tried eating their testicles, but he found them too chewy.[39]

I don't know whether there is an end point to this process, but a culmination of sorts has been reached in the genre known as "grindcore," which, like Araya, takes violent obscenity to extremes that would be comical if they weren't so morally repugnant. Released on the aptly named Earache label, British and American groups such as Napalm Death, Morbid Angel, Massacre, Nocturnus, Carcass, and Godflesh vie for the dubious honor of being the loudest, ugliest, and sickest kids on the chopping block. Here again, it's a challenge for even the most jaded rock critic to remain appreciative. Even *Spin*, the magazine that lists Burroughs as a contributing editor, subtitles an article on grindcore: "Heavy Metal Goes Too Far."[40]

Of course, once a group commits itself to the mindless aesthetic of shock, there's no such thing as going too far. The imperatives of "art" demand it. As Godflesh's leader declares:

> I think the only way we fit into this whole Earache thing is the fact that we provoke extreme reactions. But too many of the other bands on the label are extreme in a bad way, it's just sensationalism. . . . I think we've got a lengthier vision of where music can go, whereas a lot of these bands are already working within a set of confines.[41]

I leave it to the reader to imagine what might constitute a "vision of where music can go" among "artists" bored with serial murder and cannibal feasting on the private parts of little children. My only hope is that, whatever it is, it sneaks up on them first.

The Punk Legacy: The Return of Art Rock

More influential than either noise or thrash has been the atmospheric minimalism developed by the Velvet Underground. Indeed, it has been the mainstay of the punk musical legacy, in the sense that most "alternative" groups play some variation on the formula set down by Cale and Reed: a thudding 4/4 beat, shards of melody set against dissonant chords, and repetition taken to the point of near-hypnosis. Noise and thrash are present, but in alternative bands throughout the 1980s, they were used mostly for effect: the speed and volume of thrash for "energy," occasional bursts of electronic or vocal noise for proof of avant-garde boldness. The alternative formula still appeals to young people with limited musical ability who, in another era, might have aspired to become poets or painters, but who understand all too well that today's cultural limelight shines most brightly on the popular musician. These beginners need only cobble together the basic elements of the formula to stake out a position in popular music, because music is no longer the point.

More recently, alternative rock has given way to grunge, the Seattle-based genre that entered the big time in 1991, when a band called Nirvana released an album called *Nevermind*. Expected to sell about 200,000 copies, *Nevermind* knocked Michael Jackson off the top of the album chart and subsequently sold over 10 million copies. Since then, Nirvana has been wrestling with success in a way that reveals the punk legacy at its most stultifyingly antimusical.

The immediate forerunners of grunge were Sonic Youth, an alternative band that added a heavier dose of thrash and noise to the mix, while retaining the melodic prettiness of the Velvet Underground. Like Sonic Youth, Nirvana crossed the forbidden line into "pop" by writing songs containing scraps of melody, pretty guitar chords, and harmony singing. Suspecting (correctly, no doubt) that these elements contributed to their commercial success, Nirvana quickly retreated back into thrash, noise, and an emotional gamut running from A (for angst) to B (for blitzkrieg).

Like the Velvet Underground and the Doors, grunge bands showcase the histrionic abilities of their lead singers. To the extent that this emphasis reflects a hunger for serious poetic expression, I sympathize. But I also fear that grunge will starve on the fare provided. If the genre were really a breeding ground for young poets, then the lead singer of Nirvana, Kurt Cobain, would not so readily admit that his lyrics are "just a bunch of gibberish."[42] Like all post punk songwriters, Cobain is not just hostile to music, he is also hostile to the music of words. Some grunge singers, notably Eddie Vedder of Pearl Jam, have strong, expressive voices reminiscent of Jim Morrison. But the lyric sensibility of the genre is even narrower than Morrison's.

Narrower and nastier, because grunge is also heir to punk nihilism and the heavy metal compulsion to shock. Nirvana's latest album, *In Utero*, has a cover graced with bodily organs and fetuses, and lyrics evoking rape and a new twist on cannibalism: the eating of a cancer tumor.

In performance, grunge bands take their cues from the bald-headed, doe-eyed sweetheart of alternative rock, Sinead O'Connor. Possessing a thin but tolerable voice, O'Connor performs her songs by lurching back and forth between whispery crooning and eruptions of shrieking, wailing, gobbling, and gibbering. In the same vein, many of Nirvana's songs begin quietly, with Cobain intoning over a strummed guitar and old-fashioned backbeat. Then all of a sudden they "turn up the knobs," blasting the ear with screaming, thrash, and feedback. In O'Connor, this shtick is touted as a pure product of her brooding Irish soul. In Nirvana, it is praised as a distillation of Seattle despair. In fact, it is a cliché of expressionist theater, passed down through performance art (via Yoko Ono) to punk. As a theatrical device it well deserves the judgment rendered by the playwright and Brecht scholar, Eric Bentley:

> The German actor's habit of screaming his head off whenever he is faced with some problematic lines . . . [is] a priceless way of evading the issue. The favorite mannerism of the screaming type of actor is the sforzando: he is talking in a slow and hushed voice, as slow and hushed as only a German actor's voice can be, when before you know it he has hit a single word or line with all the violence he can muster. The hope, apparently, is that the audience will gasp and say, "*This* is acting!"[43]

Apparently the grunge rockers hope their audiences will gasp and say, "*This* is singing!"

I am not denying the possibility of musical creativity within atmospheric minimalism: If the Velvet Underground had stayed together for a decade, refining and varying each element in their formula, they might have developed a rich, enveloping sound like that of U2. The Irish band that gave O'Connor her first break (by letting her sing backup on an early album), U2 was started in Dublin during the punk era, only to become one of the most popular bands by 1985, when *Rolling Stone* knighted them "Our Choice: Band of the '80s."

U2 is blessed with a limited but resourceful lead guitarist, Dave ("The Edge") Evans, and a vocalist, Paul ("Bono") Hewson, who doesn't sing so much as carry poetic declamation to heights undreamed of by Jim Morrison, Lou Reed, and Patti Smith. But the group's recorded sound depends heavily on the magic of the modern studio. Like O'Connor, who uses computer techniques to thicken her reedy voice, U2 also uses high-tech devices to enhance its sound. I make this observation not to disparage the results but to report how radically these postpunk performers have departed from the movement's original "do-it-yourself" ethic.

The departure was even greater in U2's 1992 world tour, which showcased the band in precisely the kind of full-blown, multimedia stadium extravaganza that so offended the punks in the 1970s. Though their fans will not like to hear it, what U2 has really become is an art rock band. And it's a loss, because all those light shows and giant video screens flashing images and "buzzwords" obscure the group's most distinctive quality, apart from its sound: Bono's way with *real* words. For example, U2's first number one single, "With or Without You," features a refrain—"And you give yourself away"—that deftly rebukes the singer's lover for deceiving him, while also informing her that she is *not* deceiving him. Like all great lyrics, this refrain wrests a morsel of genuine poetry from ordinary speech.

Not only that, but "With or Without You" is a genuine song. Like another U2 hit, "I Still Haven't Found What I'm Looking For," it possesses a conventional song structure and a shapely melody. But regrettably these two songs are like the handful of hit singles that emerged from art rock: Their shapeliness only proves the general rule of shapelessness. And, also like art rock, U2 attracts champions who defend shapelessness in highbrow terms that scorn the traditional uses of popular music. In the words of Eamon Dunphy, the band's worshipful biographer, these two singles are merely "songs that would be sung at parties." A more objective observer might describe them as songs that could be *sung*, period. But to Dunphy singability is a necessary but regrettable concession to popular taste, not to be placed in the same class with "Bullet the Blue Sky," a tuneless drone whose sole claim to artistic "seriousness" is its denunciation of U.S. policy in Nicaragua.[44]

Needless to say, U2's "lefty" stance endears it to rock elders such as those at *Rolling Stone*. But equally important to younger fans has been the group's unapologetic spirituality. During the band's formative years, three of its members belonged to a Dublin Pentecostal community called Shalom, in which they prayed, called on the Holy Spirit, spoke in tongues, and adopted a rigorous morality. As Dunphy recalls: "We knew about the tyranny of personal freedom, the dreadful empty oppression of sexual promiscuity. We knew about the depression that ambushed you on the other side of a drug induced high."[45]

For Irish fans, this spirituality had special force because of the Irish Catholic Church's long-standing bias against any form of musical liturgy. Rooted in the historical repression of Irish Catholicism by England, that same bias has, unfortunately, been inherited by the Irish-dominated Church in the United States.[46] In both countries it's easy to see how young people with no real exposure to musical worship would fall for U2's special brand of rock ritual—especially since that ritual could not be more different from either the Dionysian "love-ins" of the 1960s or the Roman circuses of the 1970s. U2 do not preach their strict personal morality, but their struggles with it are well known, and the atmosphere of their early concerts conveyed a high-minded sobriety that couldn't help but appeal to young people fed up with self-indulgence.

For these reasons U2's admirers credit the group with having restored the hopes, and avoided the vices, of the 1960s counterculture. Yet here again the comparison with art rock is revealing. U2's music seeks the same exalted, oceanic emotion sought by art rock, but it also has the same weakness: romantic grandiosity unsupported by romantic musical architecture. Like the worst of art rock, the worst of U2's music is hollow and pretentious, a form of kitsch reaching for, but failing to grasp, the "big emotions." Despite the wry title and the best efforts of high-tech producers Brian Eno and Daniel Lanois, U2's 1992 album, *Achtung Baby*, chooses art rock grandiosity over the modest but realizable ambitions of the popular song. The verses and choruses are printed out for the eye to see, but not shaped for the ear to hear. Listen to the first thirty seconds of any track, and you will have heard the rest. Laden with vocal histrionics and sonic trim, the album is little more than state-of-the-art aural wallpaper.

Even more telling is the comparison with an older musician greatly admired by U2. In Bono's words: "I'm in awe of a musician like Van Morrison. I had to stop listening to Van Morrison records for about six months before we made *The Unforgettable Fire* because I didn't want his very original soul voice to overpower my own."[47] This awe is shared by O'Connor, who defines "universal spirituality" as "the feeling that someone like Van Morrison leaves you with after seeing his concerts or listening to his records."[48]

One would think that such tribute would lead to emulation, but it cannot, because none of these postpunk performers have anything like Van Morrison's background, talent, or craft. As Bono admits: "I have no musical background. My record collection started in 1976 with Patti Smith's *Horses*. U2 grew up saying 'Fuck off' to the blues."[49] And most grunge rockers simply equate "black music" with rap.

Van Morrison, by contrast, grew up steeped in Afro-American music, because his parents, Jehovah's Witnesses living in Belfast, Northern Ireland, sang gospel and collected American records. A professional musician from the age of fifteen, Van Morrison toured Europe with American blues and rock 'n' roll acts, then briefly joined the ranks of early rock with a group called Them. But by the late 1960s he was unwilling to move in the direction of hard rock, so he withdrew from the scene in order to forge a swirling blend of soul music and jazz that (except for the vocal element) invites comparison with Marvin Gaye.

The point is that Van Morrison does successfully what postpunk art rock only pretends to do. Having mastered the Afro-American idiom, he added melodic and harmonic elements (as well as a lyric sensibility) from his own Irish background, which infuse his music with certifiably romantic emotions such as melancholy, nostalgia, even mystical yearning. It helps, of course, that, unlike the "gibberish" of alternative rock and grunge, Van Morrison's lyrics avoid cliché and respect the music of words. But most important is Van Morrison's fluency in his adopted idiom, which keeps his feet on the ground, his humor intact, and his exaltation free of kitsch. At his best he sounds like exactly what he is: a sorrowful amateur poet who's been dunked in the life-giving waters.

In their 1988 album, *Rattle & Hum*, U2 made a conspicuous effort to connect with major figures in the Afro-American idiom: Billie Holiday, B. B. King Bo Diddley, Elvis Presley, Sam and Dave, the Beatles, Bob Dylan, Jimi Hendrix. Yet the result was a travesty, for reasons best summarized by Pareles: "The problem isn't one of race or geography, but of talent and inclination. Other white performers from across the Atlantic . . . have managed to personalize blues and soul. *U2, however, tries to adopt the perceived sincerity of soul while ignoring its musical standards.*"⁵⁰ (emphasis added)

This summary crystallizes the unfortunate legacy of punk. Taken together, the three strains I've been describing represent a backlash against Afro-American music. Noise and thrash mark the triumph of perverse modernism over musical values of any kind, and atmospheric minimalism replaces the stoic spirit of the blues with the overblown kitsch of art rock. It may be that this backlash was bound to occur, and that these are the only sounds capable of expressing the sensibilities of young people today. The defenders of this music say that the kind of affirmation found in older music is no longer possible. The choice, they insist, is between screaming protest, screaming nihilism, or morbid romanticism. The world is a grim place, and popular music must reflect that fact.

But is the world a grimmer place than it used to be? Maybe so, if you're a white middle-class youth looking back at the utopianism of white middle-class youth in the 1960s. But as I have repeatedly stressed, Afro-American music is not the creation of white middle-class youth. And, despite its long association with commerce and its adoption by the woolly-headed counterculture, the affirmation it embodies is real. The punk legacy justifies its ugliness and nihilism by talking about tough times: war, recession, pollution, and prejudice. All I can say is, times were also tough for the people who created blues, jazz, country, and gospel. London in a recession produced the Sex Pistols; Kansas City in a depression produced Count Basie. Unemployment statistics do not explain the difference.

Chapter 18

High on High Tech

o Theodor Adorno, all music becomes "mechanical" the
moment it comes into contact with electronic recording
and broadcasting. Whether fascist propaganda or capitalist
commodity, the result, he insisted, could not possibly be art. After criticizing this view with regard to older Afro-American music, I must be careful
not to succumb to it now. Undeniably, high-tech devices such as synthesizers and video have shifted the emphasis away from the expressive uses
of sound and toward the self-conscious, self-referential uses of mixed
media, with sound itself getting reduced to a mere accessory. But here, too,
the machines are only as good as the people programming them. The computer hacker's slogan still applies: Garbage In, Garbage Out.

The New Wave Goes to Camp

In the good old days of futurist theater and dada cabaret, popularity was
measured in the hundreds: If a café filled with cheering (or heckling)

spectators, then the artist could claim a public impact. In the days of British punk, by contrast, a record had to make it onto the pop chart or it failed the test of the subversive media blitz. Along with the greater scope of the mass media came more accurate ways of determining whether a given performance was actually reaching the masses. Thus the Sex Pistols' greatest triumph came in the summer of 1977, when their sardonically titled single, "God Save the Queen," reached the top of the UK pop chart during Queen Elizabeth II's silver jubilee. That triumph was heightened by the fact that, having been banned by the BBC and censored by the press, the record climbed the published chart as an empty space. Punk's champions understood that without that hot minute, they might just as well have been back in art college. They also realized that a hot minute was all they were going to get. The problem wasn't censorship—indeed, the banning of "God Save the Queen" boosted sales. No, the problem was captured by McLaren when he said: "Christ, if people bought the records for the music, this thing would have died the death long since."[1]

Hence the "new wave," the motley musical movement that followed punk, and that champions of punk routinely condemn for having retreated from anarchic noisemaking back into traditional music-making. If the story were that simple, I would praise the new wave on the same grounds. But anarchic noisemaking did not disappear, and traditional music-making remained on the defensive, because most new wave performers shared punk's warped attitude toward Afro-American music. Like Bono, they "grew up saying 'Fuck off' to the blues." Yet, at the same time, many new wave performers could not bring themselves to dismiss all forms of listenable music as "pop." So they resorted to camp: playing, or hiring others to play, their favorite "pop" style, while sending the message (more or less) that the whole thing was a joke (more or less). Needless to say, that "more or less" contains the essence of the tale.

Camp had a history, of course. If the Beatles caught a touch of it from pop art, then the glam rockers of the early 1970s came down with a terminal case. Two of the biggest stars of the decade, Elton John and David Bowie, distanced themselves from the music through visual-theatrical means. John was flamboyant and hilarious about it, Bowie cool and detached. This stylistic difference helps explain why the new wave adored Bowie and despised John, seeing the former's commercial success as a feat of Warholian manipulation, the latter's as crude pandering.[2] It probably mattered that John's popularity was a mass phenomenon, while Bowie's was something of a cult. But even more, it mattered that John did not always sustain the attitude of camp. On the contrary, he ventured into the forbidden territory of love songs. There are no Bowie ballads like John's "Your Song" or "Daniel," which combine shapely melodies and heart-tugging lyrics in the style of 1950s pop. Predictably the new wave judged this side of John to be pure schlock—just as it condemned his American contemporary, Billy Joel, who shares John's background in classical piano and mastery of Afro-American genres but plays his music straight, without the implicit insult of camp.

That insult was explicit in the case of Roxy Music, the extremely influential new wave band started in 1971 by three British musicians and two art college students. One of the latter was Brian Eno, the studio whiz who "treated" the group's sound electronically to make it both familiar and strange, like Warhol's slightly altered mass media images. In strictly musical terms the quality of the result can be assessed from this comment by Chris Blackwell of Island Records: "When I first *heard* the Roxy Music tape I must say I wasn't that crazy about it. When I *saw* the album sleeve I became very crazy about it. I could *see* the concept of what it was."[3] (emphasis added)

When Eno left in 1973, Bryan Ferry, the other art student, carried on in the same vein. Indeed, as Dave Marsh reports, Ferry had studied with the British pop artist Richard Hamilton, whose "vision of pop art, a distanced comment on the mass society in which the artist lived but did not willingly participate, is very much the spirit of Roxy Music."[4] From this perspective, the fact that the musicians in the band were pretty good could be seen as a drawback. As long as Eno was there to "treat" their sound, distance and irony were assured. But after his departure it was up to Ferry to enforce the joke. Marsh offers this wry account:

> Ferry learned to manipulate the rudiments of pop without sullying his work with the taint of emotion or sentiment. Except that he had this damn band to work with which . . . kept inserting passion into the mix. Ferry fought this manfully and on his late eighties solo albums finally found the complete desiccation he'd long sought.[5]

The pop art inspiration was equally direct in the case of the CBGB band known as Blondie, which made its debut at CBGB in 1974. Inspired by Warhol's Factory, the group's singer, Deborah Harry, presented herself as a mass media cliché: the bleached-blond sex bomb. And the group's first album, *Blondie*, wore the same point literally on its sleeve: a collage of B-movie and cartoon images, including the comic strip of the same name. As for Blondie's music, it followed the same pop art logic by sticking to fool's gold genres: first teen idol rock 'n' roll, then disco. Even when the musicians played well, Harry's singing was always as flat and affectless as Bryan Ferry's.[6]

Also debuting at CBGB was Devo (for "de-evolution"), a musically amateurish band from Kent State University that made its name dressing and jerking about like a clutch of crazed automatons. Like Kraftwerk, Devo was merely repeating one of the most reliable clichés in the history of avant-garde theater: mechanical men strutting about making pronouncements on the mechanization of society. Renowned for its campy sci-fi videos, the group survived into the 1980s. But they never really succeeded in transferring their sight gag to sound. Their music is robotistic: repetitive synthesizer riffs and vocals reduced to a reedy sneer. But it's not in the same league as Kraftwerk's, unfolding with all the spontaneity and warmth of an electronic cash register reading a bar code.

Thus, the link between camp and robotistic sound was firmly forged by the end of the 1970s. Yet it's important to note that this sensibility existed quite apart from the high-tech methods: one of the first British bands to imitate the sound of Kraftwerk was Joy Division, a Manchester group that played not synthesizers but the usual punk lineup of guitar, bass and drums. Taking its name from the Nazi term for concentration-camp brothels, Joy Division specialized in robotistic sounds and morbid themes even before its singer, Ian Curtis, committed suicide in 1980. They did produce one starkly affecting song, "Love Will Tear Us Apart." But after Curtis died they renamed themselves New Order (another Nazi term), took up the electronic cudgels, and began producing a lightweight version of Kraftwerk that was quickly dubbed "synth-pop."

The problem for subsequent synth-pop bands such as Human League, Depeche Mode, Orchestral Manoeuvres in the Dark, the Gang of Four, and Nitzer Ebb, was how to distinguish between their robotistic music (which is "art," after all) from equally robotistic schlock (such as "dance music") being sold and distributed through identical industry channels. The solution was partly musical: Stick with the minor mode, add dissonance and distortion, and (above all) make sure the beat either chatters like a machine gun or pounds like a migraine headache; and partly lyrical: angst, angst, and more angst. But mostly the gimmick was visual: The main function of synth-pop, throughout the 1980s, was to accompany "cutting-edge" video.

MTV: Surrealism in Every Home

Music video has been around only since the late 1970s, but already the artistic verdict seems to be negative. The highbrow view, as expressed by Allan Bloom, is that "Nothing noble, sublime, profound, delicate, tasteful or even decent can find a place in such tableaux."[7] As usual Bloom overstates the case. But he's right about the overall banality, vulgarity and offensiveness of the medium. Indeed, the insider verdict is not all that different. Georgia (Jo) Bergman, the Warner Records executive who pioneered music video in the United States, states unequivocally that it has not lived up to its potential: "It began as advertising, but many people hoped it would go beyond that. It didn't."[8]

Both Bloom and Bergman blame commerce, but while his judgment is part of a sweeping condemnation of popular culture, hers is a more nuanced view. As a former aide to both the Beatles and the Rolling Stones, Bergman understands very well that commercial incentives fostered the rise of video. In the late 1960s short promotional films of the British supergroups helped to satisfy a global market that included Britain, the United States, Western Europe, Australia, and Japan. In the early 1980s the new all-video cable channel, MTV, demonstrated a power to sell records that surpassed that of radio.[9] So Bergman has reason to say that the industry's goal in sponsoring music video is not to underwrite the fine art of blending motion pictures with music.

Yet Bergman also has reason to suggest that video was more creative in the early days, when demand exceeded supply and the good people in the advertising department had not yet tightened the screws. Unfortunately that creativity rarely sprang from musicians. Instead it sprang from those restless toilers in the vineyards of film, fashion, television, and advertising who had been trying, since the 1960s, to enliven those media with avant-garde ideas. Understandably, many of these *cinéastes manqués* welcomed the brand-new, white-hot medium of video as a godsend. Seizing this opportunity *was* more important than making money—or, for that matter, making music.

Presumably the film medium offers total freedom to combine visual images and sound. But ironically that freedom wasn't there in the early days of sound, when the technical difficulties of recording placed severe constraints on what had been a freewheeling silent medium. These difficulties were soon overcome, however, and the visual freedom of film reasserted itself, with a vengeance.[10] Indeed, sound became second banana—as Aaron Copland commented about his own experience writing scores: "Music is like a small flame put under the screen to help warm it."[11]

Music video claimed to reverse these priorities. Instead of adding music to visual images, the videomaker was supposed to add visual images to music.[12] But the task was never as straightforward as that, in part because the visual associations triggered by music are different with each listener. As the critic Brigid Brophy has quipped: "Almost the only thing music can represent unambiguously is the cuckoo."[13] Of course, when lyrics are present, the obvious solution is to illustrate them. Opera has always done this; so have the musical theater and the publishers of sheet music. But precisely because it is obvious, this solution did not appeal to the pioneers of video. To their way of thinking, anything was better than, say, the Andrews Sisters singing "Don't Sit Under the Apple Tree" while sitting under an apple tree.[14]

As it happened, there *was* something better, right there in the art college curriculum. The exception to the paralysis of early film by sound were the French surrealists, who incorporated sound technology into films aiming not at logical sequence but at bizarre juxtapositions that would stir the subconscious. By the 1930s, when surrealism became the creature of the political left, these same French filmmakers embraced the familiar avant-garde goal of transforming society through a sudden eruption of irrational, liberating energy.

Surprisingly, this surrealist influence showed up very early, in the heavy metal videos that first dominated MTV. In "You Can't Stop Rock and Roll" by Twisted Sister, a Nazi-like "Taste Squad" pursues the band, only to stop when its music is pumped into their headphones. Soon the headphones are smoking, the pursuers are headbanging, and Twisted Sister is escaping. In "Cum on Feel the Noize" by Quiet Riot, a young metalhead's bedroom is literally blown apart by the music—an image that harks back to such French films as René Clair's *Á Nous la Liberté*, in which a "liberating wind" blows away all repressive authority. Likewise, Clair's and Jean Vigo's famous sequences blending school, factory, and prison (seen as identical under capitalism) influenced heavy metal video via such British films as *If . . .* and the art rock classic, *Pink Floyd: The Wall*.

It was not long before MTV viewers were taking their surrealism straight. The "concept video" had been pioneered in America in the 1970s, by Devo and a group of San Francisco performance artists calling themselves the Residents. But it was the British who really reduced the word "music" to a mere adjective before the all-important noun, "video." By the mid-1980s, hundreds of art college portfolios were opening, spilling their contents onto the airwaves in videos that neither followed any logical visual sequence nor had any discernible relation to the song they were accompanying. It was during this "rush of gratuitous imagery" (Brian Eno's phrase)[15] that the saying became common: "Great video, shame about the song."

Not surprisingly, the musical genre of choice for concept videos was synth-pop; already denatured and roboticized, it was, to say the least, user friendly. As one performer told the journalist Michael Shore, "We were composing soundtracks for films that we weren't able to make just yet."[16] Synth-pop spawned the "haircut" band Duran Duran, whose records sold only in markets penetrated by MTV.[17] Many others followed, and the ranks of videomakers swelled with the likes of McLaren, dressing one band as pirates, another as Apaches, and (as ever) keeping his distance from anyone afflicted with musical talent. In 1985 McLaren cheerfully predicted that the day was approaching "when somebody turns off the sound and just watches images, maybe focuses on the socks the singer is wearing, and then runs out and finds he can't get those. Does he want to buy the record? It doesn't even occur to him."[18]

Even though McLaren's prediction hasn't come true, the video era does raise the question of whether visual stimuli don't automatically take priority over auditory ones. Not all the music promoted by video has been bad. But strait is the gate and narrow the way through which good music may pass without injury into MTV.

Sometimes music is injured by tribute. The most celebrated videos of the 1980s combine strong musical statements with costly, clever minifilms clearly intended to do the music justice. The videos are so stimulating, however, that they distract from the music. In Dire Straits' droll cartoon "Money for Nothing," it's clear that the same effect could have been achieved with much duller music (as indeed it has been, by hundreds of synth-pop bands). The distraction is even more bothersome when the images are rivetingly surreal, as in Peter Gabriel's clay-animated "Sledgehammer." And when the music is stunning all by itself, as in Paul Simon's "Boy in the Bubble," the temptation is simply to close one's eyes and listen.

Even so, tribute is better than trivialization of the sort inflicted on veteran black musicians deemed "pop" by videomakers. Tina Turner, for example, regained the summit of popularity in 1984 with her single, "What's Love Got to Do With It?" Now, this punchy, astringent song needs no assistance whatsoever from the visual arts. But assistance was provided all the same, by videomakers who swatched its knife-edged sound in softcore, soft-brained visual erotica.[19] The black videomaker Alvin Hartley offers this criticism of what his peers did to Gladys Knight: "[She] is someone a lot of black folks grew up on, she's *heavy*. . . . she's too great to be overshadowed by break dancers spinning around while she's singing a serious love song." Instead Hartley prefers the old-fashioned approach of illustrating the lyrics—admitting that it may be "too literal for some people," but insisting that it's the only approach Knight's fans "can relate to."[20] Significantly the same literal approach is taken in country music, which shares with soul a heritage of putting the music first.

It's no accident that the most successful use of video has been in "dance music." In the early days of MTV, when most of the fare was either heavy metal or surreal synth-pop, one outstanding exception was "Mickey," an exuberant production number about high school cheerleaders made by Toni Basil, a TV choreographer whose "all-singing, all-dancing . . . aesthetic," writes Michael Shore, was "a welcome relief from the oppressively chic, ambiguous image-mongering of most rock videos."[21] Other "dance music" videos were slow to follow, because most of the people making such music in the early 1980s were not white, and MTV was trying to appeal to an audience for whom antidisco feeling was inseparable from antiblack feeling. The company's founder, Robert Pittman, explains: "Our research showed quite simply that the audience for rock music was larger, and that the mostly white rock audience was more excited about its music than the mostly black audience was about its music, rhythm & blues or disco or whatever you want to call it."[22] Translated, this meant: "No black faces." I state the case this strongly because, as the journalist J. Randy Taraborrelli points out, the criteria being used were not musical, but epidermal:

> It was acceptable [on MTV] to have Phil Collins sing The Supremes' "You Can't Hurry Love," and [white soul singers] Hall and Oates sing other black-sounding material. But the real thing was unacceptable. When videos of black artists were submitted, they were quickly rejected by MTV as not being "rock and roll." . . . Bob Pittman may not have been a racist, but he and MTV certainly catered to white suburban racism.[23]

Videogenic: Michael Jackson, Prince, and Madonna

Then came the deluge, led by the young graduate of Motown who is still the most commercially successful video star: Michael Jackson. Sixteen years old when the rest of his family act, the Jackson Five, left Motown for Epic in 1975, Jackson was already a seasoned, zealously ambitious performer who, with the help of Quincy Jones, launched a solo career that astonished the world when his second album, *Thriller* (1982), became the best-selling recording in history, with sales now approaching forty million.

Musically, *Thriller* sustains the Motown precedent of making new technology live up to old standards. But, unlike his Motown predecessors, Jackson had to deal with the camera as much as the tape recorder. At first, there was no problem—on the contrary, Jackson was drawn to video as a moth to a flame. An extraordinary dancer since 1971, when the Jackson Five appeared on the Ed Sullivan show and the host remarked, "The little guy in the front is incredible," Jackson was even more incredible in 1983, when his breakthrough solo performance on Motown's twenty-fifth anniversary TV special dazzled millions of viewers—including two of his idols, Fred Astaire and Gene Kelly.[24]

Nothing succeeds like success, but in Jackson's case the brave new world of video also had a warping effect. After CBS bullied MTV into airing his "Thriller" video, Jackson vowed to succeed in every possible medium, not just music and dance. But unfortunately his remarkable talent was not enough to surmount the fact that, as a bona fide product of Berry Gordy's Hit Factory, his universe simply did not include the culturally sophisticated attitudes of the British new wave—either its anticommercial commercialism, or its campy stance toward Afro-American music. Indeed, Jackson's lack of avant-garde credentials has attracted many unkind cuts: Greil Marcus has defined "the Jacksonist pop explosion" as "a version of the official social reality, generated from Washington as ideology, and from Madison Avenue as language";[25] the British press has dubbed the star "Wacko Jacko"; and the editors of the *New Republic* have sneered about his plan to write an autobiography: "Write, hell. Can Michael Jackson read?"[26]

Jackson's real problem, I suspect, is that he can read well enough to be hurt by such comments, but not well enough—in the culturally sophisticated sense—to understand where they are coming from. Yearning to be taken as seriously as some of the British video stars, he cannot see why he is dismissed as a lightweight. The resulting frustration may help to explain some of his eccentricities, such as his adventures in plastic surgery. Much ink has been spilled on the topic of this strange black youth's obsession with narrowing his features and (possibly) bleaching his skin.[27] But to me the most important message conveyed by Jackson's pale, carved, haunted face is that the visual dimension of popular music has become so important that it's no longer enough to be a prodigiously gifted musician and dancer.

The prevailing sensibility of the video culture is that of surrealism: the project of blowing the lid off civilization through abrupt releases of irrational, libidinous energy. It's a poor fit with Jackson, the latest in a long line of Afro-American performers to be caught between a strict religious upbringing (Jehovah's Witnesses) and the pressures of show business. For Jackson the conflict is all the more intense for having begun in childhood, when promiscuity and cutthroat manipulation invaded his own family. His greatest triumphs were mildly controversial: The "Thriller" video, a mini-horror-movie about living corpses, upset his coreligionists; the lyrics of "Billie Jean," about a young man denying paternity, worried some critics. But compared with most of what was appearing on video at the time, this material was downright wholesome.

Unfortunately the same cannot be said of such recent efforts as "Bad" and "Dangerous," which strain grotesquely to live up to their titles. After witnessing these videos, in which Jackson ceaselessly grabs his crotch, smashes car windows, and zips up his fly (in that rather unconvincing order), most people shake their heads and say he's out of touch. To be sure, he's always been somewhat out of touch: Witness his ludicrous attempts to regain credibility after being accused of child molesting. It's a sad situation. Still, the saddest thing about Jackson today is how his struggle to keep up with the video culture has put him out of touch with his own musical inheritance.

More comfortable in the video culture is Prince Rogers Nelson, the Minneapolis wunderkind often compared with Jackson because of his light skin, delicate build, and androgynous persona. But anyone subscribing to the notion that these two stars are interchangeable need only watch them in action. As Pareles writes: "They sing, they dance, they're utterly different."[28]

Prince has been running his own show since 1976, when, at age seventeen, he became the youngest person ever to wrest creative autonomy from a major record label (Warner's). He has also been mixing every musical genre from soul to heavy metal to funk to synth-pop, with more flair than any competitor, including Jackson. Yet, with the exception of his dazzling 1984 album, *Purple Rain*, Prince has never gained anything like Jackson's mass popularity, because, as Jackson himself puts it, "I could never be like [Prince] on stage. I'd never want to be. Sometimes he can be really gross."[29] Even the relatively inoffensive *Purple Rain* contains "Darling Nikki," the song whose reference to masturbation shocked Tipper Gore into starting her campaign.[30] Prince's exhibitionism seems to have psychological roots: The only child of divorced parents, he spent his adolescence bouncing from relative to relative, until he was finally taken in by the mother of his best friend, who gave him refuge in her basement, where, by his own account, he began composing "sexual fantasies. . . . Because I didn't have anyone around me . . . there were no people. No anything. When I started writing, I cut myself off from relationships with women."[31] Later on Prince's first recording engineer would take credit for having suggested "naughty implied sexuality" as a publicity gambit.[32] But clearly the impulse runs deeper.

At his most appealing, Prince tries to reach out, sharing the spotlight with his fellow performers—especially the women, who clearly welcome the chance to do more than gyrate and coo. And recently he has recorded and performed with superior vocalists such as the gospel veteran Mavis Staples, whose gorgeous, raspy voice is a welcome change from Prince's own tendency to bleat like a priapic baby goat. But it's clearly a struggle. Even when Prince succeeds in singing like the young Smokey Robinson, his visual persona still prances on cloven hooves.

Nonetheless, Prince's goatishness is preferable to the icy decadence purveyed by Madonna. Michael Jackson may disapprove of Prince's antics, but he is bound to respect the latter's music. About Madonna, the high priestess of hype whose supernova has lately come to eclipse his own, Jackson is both disapproving and contemptuous: "She just isn't that good. Let's face it. She can't sing. She's just an okay dancer. What does she do best? She knows how to market herself."[33] For all his crotch grabbing, Jackson is disgusted by such marketing gambits as the tabloid spat between Madonna and his untalented sister LaToya over whose breasts are bigger (with or without implants). Reportedly he asked his staff never to talk about the incident.[34]

If the members of Jackson's staff do not talk about Madonna, they are unique. For Madonna Louise Ciccone from Bay City, Michigan, is one of the most talked-about celebrities in the world. Despite her cultivated image as a blue-collar Italian American, Madonna was raised in a middle-class suburb on piano and ballet lessons—the latter winning her a scholarship to the University of Michigan in the mid-1970s. Quitting college soon afterward, she moved to New York, where through talent, hard work, good looks, and a few strategically placed affairs, she made herself into a late-arriving disco queen, presiding over "urban contemporary" radio and the predominantly gay club scene. By 1984 she had two hit singles, and by 1985 she was selling millions of singles, LPs, and movie tickets for what is still her best role, that of a SoHo hoyden in *Desperately Seeking Susan*.

Despite a few lapses (notably her subsequent films), Madonna has more or less stayed on top. Musically she claims to have grown up listening to Motown, but if so, it was Motown after Diana Ross quit being the hood ornament and became the whole car. Like Ross, Madonna thrives on the disco sound: peppy but predictable synthesizer-driven rhythms, enhanced (somewhat) by live musicians, and rendered instantly recognizable by her voice, an instrument not unlike Ross's in its piercing, high-end recordability.

But it is in the extramusical realm that Madonna really made her name. Her first image, taken from Cyndi Lauper, a singer and art student who was her video rival for a while, was that of a sexy ragamuffin given to showing her underwear while chirping blithe protofeminist messages. But then Madonna switched to a heavy-duty pop art image, that of the blonde bombshell celebrated in Warhol's *Marilyn* series and CBGB's Blondie. Like David Bowie she is renowned as a changeling. But unlike Bowie she knows better than to change her sound. At first, her loyalty to disco drew venom from rock critics.[35] But the strategy has paid off, because after all, this is the video age, and what matters is not one's musical statement but one's relation to the visual arts. That is why pundits, professors and preachers go cross-eyed trying to interpret Madonna's mutations, taking her far more seriously than they would ever take any number of more musically inventive performers (Prince, for example).

Accordingly, Madonna is exhibitionistic to a degree unimagined even by Prince. For a while her exhibitionism had a "serious" side, as in such over-wrought videos as "Like A Prayer" and "Oh Father," which purport to express such topics as the grief and spiritual doubt caused by her mother's early death. But the big problem with these videos is the widening gap between their emotionally freighted themes and a sound that is still, with very few exceptions, fizzy upbeat "dance music."

Perhaps that is why, in a reversal of Jackson's situation, Madonna is most at home in decadence. Her most convincing work, in terms of form expressing content, celebrates the gay male life-style at its most hedonistic. For example, her video "Vogue" sets a spare, Chic-influenced sound against a deadpan display of black-tie preening as practiced in gay clubs. More recently, "Justify My Love" and some of the songs on the album *Erotica* use a whispery vocal and a chicken-scratch beat to underline a deliberately vacuous celebration of sadomasochism. These were also feats of marketing: "Justify My Love" received a major sales and rental boost after being banned by MTV, and the X-rated book *Sex* was sold coyly shrink-wrapped in Mylar plastic. On such occasions Madonna is impressive: The black-leather bimbo cracks her whip, and the media lion jumps through her hoop.

But lately there is something desperate about Madonna's whip cracking, something reminiscent of the fading hooker fighting to keep her street corner. But don't misread the metaphor—this working girl does not have a heart of gold. On the contrary, one learns from Madonna's most emotionally exhibitionistic work, the self-filmed documentary, *Truth or Dare*, that she is a selfish, manipulative person whose concern for others and faith in God are expressed only when they suit her immediate purposes. One moment she is declaring how protective she feels toward her "babies," the young, mostly gay male dancers who perform with her in "Keep It Together," an anthem to emotional commitment. The next it becomes clear why that song is performed in S&M gear: Madonna's good-byes to her "babies," when their term of employment is over, are professionally final. One moment Madonna is singing "Happy Birthday" to her father before thousands of fans, and literally prostrating herself at his feet. The next she is cracking sardonic jokes about his being a hopeless alcoholic and informing a visitor that he "fucked" her when she was a little girl grieving for her mother. It's hard to tell, from the shrieks of laughter that follow this last remark, whether the accusations are true. But it's easy to tell that Madonna has a cruel streak a mile wide, and that her "art" is largely a matter of acting out unresolved psychosexual conflicts.

Worst of all is Madonna's incurable shallowness. She may claim to be taking her fans on "an emotional journey, portraying good and bad, light and dark, joy and sorrow, redemption and salvation." But I can't help noting that she truncates the last pair of opposites. A truly daring artist would include *perdition* with redemption, *damnation* with salvation. But not Madonna. She is still, I fear, the neurotically defensive daughter who, when her father dismisses her raunchy stage antics as "art," snaps angrily: "It's got nothing to do with art!"[36]

Samplers and Virtuosos: "A Race of Freaks"

Madonna is wrong, of course. The excesses of the video era have everything to do with art, in the sense of perverse-modernist impulses shaping the uses to which high-tech devices are put. This is not say that technological changes have no impact: Clearly synthesizers and video have offered incentives to devalue musicianship. But as we move to the next step in the high-tech process, the deciding factor continues to be not the medium, but the message.

The big news is that synthesizers are now old hat, compared with the latest high-tech method, computer "sampling." Growing out of post–World War II research and development in tape recording, and given a tremendous boost by the recent simplification of the process via digital sound processing, sampling presents a radically different proposition, one that may render moot much of what I have been saying about high-tech music-making. In the first place, sampling doesn't suffer from the musical limitations of synthesizing. On the contrary, it is a device for accessing the entire universe of recorded sounds, musical as well as nonmusical. All the sampler user need do is lift the desired sound out of its original context and place it into a new one assembled by him. The process is similar to that of moving a paragraph from one document to another with a computer word processor. And, similarly, a sampler also allows the user to alter any passage, including the borrowed one.

Today the best known use of sampling in popular music is in rap, to which I shall turn in the next chapter. But first we should examine a relatively obscure genre, "industrial rock,"which combines high-tech methods, especially sampling, with the nihilistic sensibility of punk. Industrial rock can be traced back to CBGB, where a band called Suicide added tape-recorded noise to the usual bashing of guitars, drums, heads, and psyches.[37] Tape recorders were not popular at CBGB, due to the "do-it-yourself" ethos. But soon many young people (Europeans in particular) realized that they had long been part of the musical avant-garde—not just in Stockhausen, but also in the noise music of Cage and the French sound engineer Pierre Schaeffer, who presented the first taped "concert of sounds" in 1948. As electronic music-making evolved, the term *musique concrète* came to refer to any montage of recorded, often altered sounds, as opposed to purely synthesized ones (obviously, the two techniques can be combined). At its best, *musique concrète* can be a form of extroverted modernism, an aural version of cubist collage in which sound fragments are put together in a formally complex yet humanly expressive manner.

Industrial rock claims to be in this league, but all it really does is recycle perverse-modernist clichés. Its leading light in Britain, Neil Megson ("Genesis P-Orridge") served his apprenticeship in the Fluxus movement before starting a performance-art group known as COUM, whose brief moment in the media limelight was achieved by mounting a sexually obscene art exhibit.[38] Megson's account of the early days of his industrial band, Throbbing Gristle, has a familiar ring:

> Throbbing Gristle's studio was in a factory next to London Fields . . . where a lot of the plague victims were buried . . . But we always saw the Death Factory as a metaphor for industrial society as well. When we'd finished producing the tapes, I went outside at Martello Street as a train passed on the railway line. . . . [I heard] a sawmill cutting up wood, and a dog barking, and

I just said, "We haven't invented anything. We've just put down what's here all the time."[39]

Industrial rockers rarely mention the futurist origin of their ideas, because they don't want to be associated with fascism or (worse) optimism. Dada, on the other hand, is frequently cited—other groups have called themselves Cabaret Voltaire and Père Ubu. Pure noise collection, with an emphasis on harsh factory sounds, has remained the prime focus of German groups like Einstürzende Neubaten ("collapsing new buildings) and British groups like Test Dept., SPK, and Throbbing Gristle. But other groups have used disco-era methods to produce a more marketable hybrid: factory noise set to that ever-reliable computerized beat. Audiences were not appreciative at first; one member of Cabaret Voltaire was badly injured in a protest melee.[40] But as punk has made the idea of ugly music more acceptable, other groups have followed suit, using either drum machines or repeated tape loops to create the monotonous thud that now gives industrial rock its reputation as "dance music"—although headbanging, moshing, and stage diving are the only possible responses to outfits like Nine-Inch Nails, Skinny Puppy, and Meat Beat Manifesto.

Other industrial rockers have ended up surfing on the new wave, sampling music as well as noise. *Spin* magazine reports, with unwitting irony:

> CDs found in the "industrial" section of the local record store now incorporate elements as disparate as pop song formats . . . , rap and hip hop . . . , jazz . . . , reggae and dub . . . , and new age. . . . Unbelievably, even disco now ranks as an influence . . . The tools of the trade are the same; what these groups choose to do with them has definitely become a matter of user discretion.[41]

As this passage suggests, the most obvious problem with sampling is legal: For every eager borrower using the new technology as a license to steal, there is an injured party bringing a lawsuit. Yet, surprisingly, most such suits have been ineffective: The amount of material borrowed tends to be sufficiently small, and the borrower's claims of originality tend to be sufficiently convincing (especially when the sound has been altered), that the law becomes fuzzy.[42] There is also the problem of sheer scope, as favorite passages move through the industry like computer viruses. As one musician comments: "How do you negotiate something that has unlimited use? The computer will use it as a file, and we don't know whether it's going to be part of a movie soundtrack, a jingle or somebody's harmony class at a university."[43] Important though this legal issue is, the practice of sampling has become so widespread that some sort of resolution seems likely—perhaps an industry-wide measure such as a flat rate of royalties for all artists, in compensation for all potential sampling use.[44]

Less likely to be resolved, in my view, are the aesthetic and cultural issues raised by sampling. On its face, the very ease of sampling seems to have foreboding implications. Like all musical traditions, the Afro-American one has, until recently, assumed that becoming a musician required learning how to sing or play an instrument. Of course, the Afro-American tradition has been unusual in one unhappy sense: Its master practitioners have too often seen their work appropriated without proper credit. But at least the appropriators of the past were obliged to serve some kind of apprenticeship. With sampling, it becomes possible to nick other people's music without an iota of respect, discipline, or care. The question is: Will sampling lead to a further devaulation of musicianship?

Again, the answer lies not in our machines, but in ourselves. We already live in a culture in which musicianship is devalued. Since the 1970s popular music has suffered a severe polarization of attitudes toward the proper nature of musical eloquence. At one extreme we have the "do-it-yourself" ethos of punk, which equates true art with impassioned incompetence. At the other we have the cult of bloodless virtuosity that free jazz bequeathed to hard rock, leading to the abandonment of feeling in favor of empty athleticism.

This cult of virtuosity is evident in high-level hard rock groups such as Living Colour, the black New York band that seeks to prove its racial bona fides by aggressively including Coltrane and Hendrix in the hard rock pantheon. Living Colour is renowned for its fast-and-furious pastiche of styles, including slices of free jazz. But because the musical values displayed by the group are mostly speed, dexterity, and volume, the result is a species of camp. These young virtuosi have no intention of mocking their heritage. But they have a funny way of showing respect.

Even funnier is the respect shown by the up-and-coming West Coast genre called "funk-punk." The pioneers in this field were a black Los Angeles band called Fishbone, whose rip-roaring, frequently hilarious accelerations of pastiche are particularly well suited to video. All funk-punk groups, including the predominantly white bands Red Hot Chili Peppers, Faith No More, and Jane's Addiction, pay tribute to Hendrix and Coltrane. But they are closer to George Clinton in their hyperactive stage antics and caustic humor.

Musically, funk-punk subscribes to the belief that whipping through a shopping list of musical styles is better than sticking to just one. Self-conscious about having grown up in the 1980s, the decade of channel-zapping, the genre lays claim to a unique "postmodernist" sensibility that knows more, and grasps more, than any previous generation.[45] Unfortunately, they have not grasped the distinction between pastiche, typically parodic in intent, and the creation of a genuinely new style.

The real impetus behind today's bloodless virtuosity is not zapping, anyway, but Zappa—whose recorded output, already the product more of science than of art, has now been digitally remastered down to the last morsel in the up-to-date home studio of the master. Like funk-punk, the Zappa reissues currently crowding the nation's record bins are more robotistic, in their not-quite-human way, than anything bleeped out by a synthesizer.

It was the romantic composer Robert Schumann who said: "Would to heaven that a race of freaks could arise in the race of artists, with one finger too many on each hand; then the dance of virtuosity would be at an end."[46] In other words, only the prospect of superhuman virtuosity can teach some musicians that music involves more than technical skill. Today the race of freaks has arrived, in the form of high-tech methods. So far, though, it has not had the desired humanizing effect. The woods are full of virtuosi who will not become human until they venture into the open meadows of emotion. But they're scared to do so, because their culture defines all emotion (except anger) as "pop." And the antidote, blues feeling, is ignored because it is no longer considered "black."

As for what *is* considered "black," that subject has become so problematic that it deserves a chapter of its own.

Chapter 19

Rap: Trying to Make It Real (Compared to What?)

o be precise, the term *rap* refers to rhyming words chanted, or "rapped," by a lead performer to a heavily rhythmic musical accompaniment known as hip-hop. *Hip-hop* is also the preferred term for the urban youth culture that began in the late 1970s, with its rapidly changing styles of dance, slang, fashion, graffiti, and videogenic attitude. I try to respect this distinction in the following discussion, but at certain points I succumb to the widespread tendency to call the whole thing *rap*.

Whatever the name, rap is notable for having revived the idea of "blackness" as something whites must buy from blacks because they cannot steal it. When Nelson George mourns "the death of rhythm and blues," he is really mourning a time—from the 1940s through the 1960s—when an astonishing amount of good Afro-American music was carried, in unfiltered form, by the electronic media. In his view, this period of musical vitality was the result, ironically, of racial segregation in the production, distribution, and consumption of popular music. Hence his campaign for a

341

return to black control of black talent. Perhaps this strategy would foster better, less exploitive treatment of musicians—or, given human nature, perhaps it wouldn't. One thing is certain, however: By itself George's strategy would not necessarily improve musical quality.

Why not? For two reasons. First, contemporary "black" styles are easier than ever to steal: Instead of spending years singing in church or performing on the chitlin circuit, the white appropriator need only master the studio. Second and more important, the tastes of the white audience have changed. The old strategy of sweetening and diluting Afro-American music still works with some white listeners. But not with the children of punk. What they crave are aggressive, noise-dominated sound; obscene, violent lyrics; and emotions ranging from sadistic lust to nihilistic rage. The salient fact about hip-hop is that, over the years, it has learned how to satisfy this craving. And in the process it has redefined "blackness" for a whole generation. But, to quote the title of Eugene McDaniels's pungent message song, "Trying to Make it Real" raises the question, "Compared to What?"

Low-Tech, High-Skill: The Genesis of Hip-Hop

In the mid-1970s, when hip-hop first emerged in the inner-city nightclubs of New York, the answer to McDaniels's question was clear: hip-hop was real compared with the brainless robotism of disco. Like all disco DJs, those who presided over dances, block parties, and social clubs in the Bronx worked with two turntables, in order to change records without interruption. But instead of simply playing one record after another, a young Jamaican immigrant known as "Kool DJ Herc" cooked up a novel approach. The most popular part of any dance record is the "percussion break," when the singing stops, the rhythm section takes over, and the flashiest dancers disport themselves on the floor. In the journalist David Toop's apt phrase, Herc

> ate the cherry off the top of the cake and threw the rest away. A conga or bongo solo, a timbales break or simply the drummer hammering out the beat—these could be isolated by using two copies of the record on twin turntables and playing the one section over and over, flipping the needle back to the start on one while the other played through.[1]

The next step was taken by "Grandmaster Flash" (Joseph Saddler), the son of Barbadian immigrants who studied electronics in school, and got inspired by the sight of another DJ using a switch to bring the sound of both turntables into his headphones. By his own recollection, Flash flashed:

> I had to go to the raw parts shop downtown to find me a single pole double throw switch, some crazy glue to glue this part to my mixer, an external amplifier and a headphone. What I did when I had all this soldered together, I jumped for joy—I've got it, I've got it, I've got it! . . . My main objective was to take small parts of records and, at first, keep it on time, no tricks. . . . After that, I mastered punch phrasing—taking certain parts of a record where there's a vocal or drum slap or a horn. I would throw it out and then bring it back, keeping the other turntable playing. . . . The crowd, they didn't understand it at first but after a while it became a thing.[2]

Atop his "wheels of steel," Grandmaster Flash was not a musician in the sense of being able to sing or play. But he was a skilled percussionist, working with turntables and records the way another performer might work with a drum kit. His materials were cheap and available, but unlike the punks, he didn't consider the crudeness of his tools an excuse to abandon craft. By the time he ended one of his galvanizing sessions with a medley of soul ballads—because, as he says, "After you sweat and you're tired you appreciate it"—he had given his listeners a far more exciting experience than could be had at the top-dollar discos downtown.[3]

The Caribbean connection is important, because by setting up as mobile DJs running their own shows, these pioneers were drawing upon a practice long established in the islands. Since the 1940s the Caribbean DJ has been much more of a celebrity-performer than in the United States. Since most islanders were too poor to buy records or record players, and most radio stations were controlled by the upper classes with a highbrow fastidiousness worthy of the BBC, DJs traveled the countryside with their record collections (local and imported) and their souped-up "sound systems," competing for the trade of outdoor celebrations and dance halls. The more successful were also the owners of the only recording studios available to island musicians. So they enjoyed something close to a monopoly.

Along with a high level of professional self-esteem, the immigrant Bronx DJs also imported technical ideas. From Jamaica came the practice of remixing "break" versions of American soul and R&B hits, twelve-inch records on which the favored instrumental part would be prolonged and accented with additional rhythm instruments. Also from Jamaica came "dubbing," the practice of removing the vocal part, so that the DJ could substitute his own vocal presence, which was usually not singing but talking, in the stylized manner known as "toasting."

Actually, this term, with its connotation of a brief tribute over a glass of champagne, fails to do the form justice. For Jamaican toasting is a species of improvised oral poetry whose roots run deep, back through Trinidadian calypso to the West African *griots* who (like the bards of ancient Ireland) could recite detailed clan histories, offer elaborate praise songs, and insult prominent people with such skill that the better ones made a handsome living just keeping their mouths shut. Under slavery this latter function blossomed into the acerbic social commentary for which calypso has been famous since the eighteenth century.[4] And praise turned to boasting, carried to competitive extremes.

Both of these tendencies survived into hip-hop, along with a taste for masquerade. Like Mardi Gras in New Orleans and Carnival in Brazil, Caribbean calypso contests are replete with costumes, pageantry, false names, and mock-royal titles. Hence the prevalence of outlandish costumes and nicknames in hip-hop, as well as its early obsession with graffiti—which some have defended as a significant form of public art, although beleaguered commuters might not agree.[5] In any case, hip-hop qualifies as the first Afro-American genre to compete with the British in the visual realm. Not surprisingly, it has had a decisive impact on video.

But I am getting ahead of myself. Hip-hop didn't make it to video until 1986. First it had to make it to records, which was not easy. For a while, the only way to preserve what Grandmaster Flash and his ilk were doing was to make noisy tapes of their live shows. But then the disco bubble burst, and a few hardy prospectors began panning for the next nugget. It appeared in the form of the first hip-hop record, "Rapper's Delight," released in 1979 on the tiny R&B label Sugar Hill. It was hardly authentic: two voices reciting radio patter from the 1950s, while a studio band played the instrumental part of Chic's "Good Times." But this lack of authenticity did not keep "Rapper's Delight" from reaching number 36 on the pop chart.

As one might expect, this success rankled the hip-hop pioneers. Grandmaster Flash had been reluctant to record, seeing studio production as more sophisticated than what he was doing.[6] But "Rapper's Delight" changed his mind. His remarkable 1981 single, "The Adventures of Grandmaster Flash on the Wheels of Steel," laboriously captures the sound of Flash actually "cutting and scratching" among several different records. But soon the studio took over, and the most influential records, from Afrika Bambaata's "Planet Rock" to Flash's "The Message," were artful blends of live music and dramatic rapping with synthesized and tape-recorded sounds—even *musique concrète*, as in the shattering glass and greedy coke sniffing heard on Flash's powerful antidrug single, "White Lines."

The point is that hip-hop was low-tech by necessity, not choice. The pioneers' objection to disco was not that it was made by high-tech methods, but that it was vapid and repetitive. So as soon as they arrived in the studio, they embraced sampling as the easiest way to incorporate great rhythm "breaks" into their records. Instead of recording a rapper actually talking over a James Brown dub, it was now possible to fit Brown's rhythm groove, along with the rapper's voice and any number of other sounds, into a brand-new mix. So prevalent became this practice that Brown is justified in saying: "[Hip-hop] is the next thing, but it's all from me."[7]

Predictably hip-hop borrowing provoked a flurry of lawsuits: If Chic was upset by Sugar Hill's live re-creation of "Good Times," imagine how they felt about having it sampled. Brown has also taken legal action. Yet here, too, the legal problems raised by sampling may prove more solvable than the aesthetic and cultural ones. Consider the change that occurred when hip-hop entered the studio. In his live show, Grandmaster Flash had to keep up with the best rhythm sections, such as Brown's, if he was going to use their records. With sampling, this element of musicianship gets lost. The computer permits any sound to be inserted, with the utmost precision, at any point, to create a thickly textured aural montage. And if it doesn't fit exactly, it can always be altered.[8] The process requires skill, needless to say. But not always musical skill. And the result is not always judged by musical standards.

The standards that do exist in hip-hop depend on the judge's prior orientation. Critics steeped in older Afro-American forms deplore the lack of swing in the computerized rhythms that now dominate, while connoisseurs of such rhythms insist (with reason) that they are better in hip-hop than in synth-pop and "dance music." And rock critics admire the way hip-hop incorporates the sounds of heavy metal—which it has been doing since the beginning, when Flash's "punch phrasing" included blasts of feedback, power chords, and drum breaks. In 1986, when a hip-hop trio from Queens called Run-DMC took the genre to the upper reaches of the pop chart for the first time, it was largely through increasing the dose of heavy metal. Run-DMC's hit single, "Walk This Way," was made with Aerosmith—and the video featuring both groups (white faces as well as black) was hip-hop's first appearance on MTV.

Finally there are the countless influential critics who listen more to the rap than to the hip-hop. Justifying this approach is the fact that, like atmospheric minimalism, hip-hop subjugates music to words. Yet even here the studio spelled change. Like Flash's turntable skills, the skills of the pioneer rappers were improvisatory, a blend of timing and verbal inventiveness that can still be found whenever one of them performs. As one critic wrote about a rare live appearance by LL Cool J (James Todd Smith): "His clear tenor and astounding machine-gun articulation cut through the torpor of the room like an electric knife."[9] Since written poetry is, as a rule, more sophisticated than improvised, one might expect improvement now that most raps are written down and recited. But no such luck. Rap "poetry" is a cut above punk, but most of it merely confirms the fact that an inability to improvise does not confer an ability to write.

But verbal incompetence is the least of hip-hop's problems nowadays. Some of the differences between hip-hop and the rest of Afro-American music stem from its roots in the oral (as opposed to the musical) tradition, and in the Caribbean (as opposed to North America). But as hip-hop evolved, it also departed from these roots in ways as drastic as they are disturbing. One cause of this departure, as I shall show, is the increasing perversity of popular music in general. But another well worth considering is the social pathology that has gradually engulfed the black poor since the end of the civil rights era.

Overdose: Popular Culture in the Ghetto

Revived after the civil disturbances in Los Angeles in 1992, the debate about the troubling changes that have occurred in America's inner cities since the 1960s sputters on. Most people agree that skyrocketing rates of crime, drug addiction, unemployment, and teen pregnancy mean that things have gotten worse.[10] But few agree about causes. Because so many inner-city residents are black, some people argue that the cause is white racism, pure and simple.[11] Others stress structural economic change, saying that racism is less important than the departure of low-skilled jobs from urban areas.[12] Still others point to the unintended effects of civil rights victories: the fact that fair housing laws and affirmative action have aided the flight of middle- and working-class blacks from the segregated enclaves where they once set a positive example for those less fortunate.[13] And politicians dispute which policy orientation is more harmful, wrongheaded liberal activism or calculated conservative neglect.

The only ray of hope, albeit a slim one, is the amount of agreement being voiced on three matters that would have been hotly disputed back in the late 1960s: first, that funding cuts and institutional withdrawal from the inner cities have been politically feasible in part because ghetto culture has become repellent and frightening; second, that it is bad for the poor to be isolated from the rest of society; and third, that all levels of American culture are suffering from a breakdown of civic and personal responsibility.

Reinforcing this consensus is the observation of sociologist Elijah Anderson that since the early 1970s, poor black communities have lost their "old heads"—meaning the men whose "acknowledged role was to teach, support, encourage, and in effect socialize young men to meet their responsibilities with regard to the work ethic, family life, the law, and decency"; and the "wise and mature" women who provided "an important source of instruction and social sanction."[14] In their place, Anderson says, are new "role models":

> The man derides family values. . . . In fact he considers it a measure of suc-
> cess if he can get away without being held legally accountable for his out-of-
> wedlock children. . . . Self-aggrandizement consumes his whole being and is
> expressed in his penchant for a glamorous life-style, fine clothes, and fancy
> cars. . . . The high life holds out thrills for young girls, many of whom also
> seek independence from households with their mothers and sisters and
> brothers. Involved in sexually active peer groups, many settle for babies and
> participate in status games for which a "prize"—a cute baby—is the price of
> admission.[15]

Such patterns of behavior are hardly new in poor black communities, as countless sociological studies and blues lyrics attest. But they have not, for the most part, been dominant. The question is: What has brought them to the fore?

Sociological studies rarely mention popular culture, so it's striking to see Anderson blame TV commercials for fostering materialism, soap operas for teaching false ideas about male-female relationships, and rap for encouraging youthful male aggression in public spaces.[16] One does not have to be a sociologist to reach the commonsense conclusion that, in this one respect, the inner city is anything but isolated: Popular culture rushes in where even police and firemen fear to tread. Few inner-city residents can afford CD players or cable, but most have TV, tape players, and radio. So their children, growing up without direct contact with the outside world, spend their formative years on intimate terms with the thousands of characters, entertainers, and celebrities populating the airwaves. In the absence of traditional supports such as family, school, community, and church, it seems likely that these youngsters will overdose on the worst aspects of popular culture, their own sense of reality making it hard to give credence to anything better.[17]

But even worse is the loss of cultural continuity once provided by the "old heads." That is, the young are losing contact with their own musical and oral tradition as handed down through channels other than the electronic media. This seems to be true even in the rural South, where the grip of tradition is loosened by the popular culture pouring in from the outside. Because this culture expresses values radically different from those taught by the "old heads," the most vulnerable young blacks are now almost as cut off from their heritage as the most prejudiced young whites.

Pink Ears and Sexual Delirium

By 1987, when Run-DMC had made it onto MTV and sold three million records, it looked as though hip-hop was poised to conquer the larger white audience. But then the crossover dream turned into the appropriation nightmare, as Run-DMC's own label came up with the bright idea of white hip-hop. The lead rapper for Run-DMC, Joseph Simmons, and his brother Russell, who co-owned the tiny label Def Jam, were middle-class college students wise in the ways of the market. So they readily agreed to the proposal, put forth by Russell and his white partner Rick Rubin, of a white, punk-oriented group called the Beastie Boys. At least, it seemed like a good idea at the time.

The Beastie Boys were four refugees from suburban Long Island who, like Rubin, started out in New York's hardcore scene. Typical of that scene was "Cookie Puss," the group's first single, described by David Toop as "a nasty pornographic scratch record . . . [that] brought together oral sex, telephone violence, food and sexually transmitted diseases as well as an implied racism."[18] Signed to Def Jam, the Beastie Boys mutated into hip-hop's official gross-out act, spewing beer on audiences and taking promotional cues from Duran Duran, whose X-rated nightclub videos included topless models clambering on a giant inflated phallus.[19] Outside the New York venue of their 1987 tour, the Beastie Boys erected a similar structure, sprayed it with whipped cream, and invited young female fans to lick it clean.

There was no visible animosity between the Beastie Boys and Run-DMC when they appeared together on that same tour. But it must have been galling for Run-DMC to see their carefully crafted third album outsold by the Beastie Boys' debut, a sloppy mixture of hip-hop and hardcore called *Licensed to Ill*. Likewise, a new album by LL Cool J sold only two million copies compared with *Licensed to Ill*'s four. Suddenly old fears began to surface. How was hip-hop going to achieve the traditional double-edged goal of reaching white listeners while resisting white appropriation? In the good old days "blackness" was a cluster of musical skills, honed in settings that were off limits to whites. In 1987 "blackness" would have to be something else. But what? The answer was painfully obvious.

Sexual boasting had always been part of rap, but in 1988, it became more explicit. A rapper from the mean streets of Philadelphia named Schooly D released a single called "Mr. Big Stuff," in which he inflated his own member beyond the wildest dreams of the Beastie Boys' promotional staff. And in June of that year an Alabama record retailer was convicted of selling pornography in the form of *Move Somethin'*, an album by a then obscure rap group called 2 Live Crew. In 1990, when 2 Live Crew's next LP, *As Nasty as They Wanna Be*, was ruled obscene by a federal judge in Florida, the group complained of having been singled out on racial grounds. Given the arbitrariness of most obscenity prosecutions, that complaint appeared justified. But at the same time, 2 Live Crew benefited from the publicity: Even before the ruling was overturned by a jury, they sold 1.7 million copies of an album that would otherwise have had only limited appeal.

Predictably, the defenders of obscene rap portray it as solidly within the Afro-American tradition. Toop, for example, offers Screamin' Jay Hawkins—an R&B performer known for leaping out of a coffin and shrieking swamp-voodoo lyrics in a voice that would make Little Richard blanch—as evidence that R&B was equally shocking: "Screamin' Jay Hawkins was at the apex of the kind of music that struck terror into the hearts of white American parents in the 1950s—the idea of their children pressing their pink ears to the loudspeaker of a radio that was blasting out this blatantly sexual and demonic delirium was too much to bear."[20]

Typical of this defense is the use of the bland word *sex* to cover everything from flirtation to flagellation. Ponder this passage from the constitutional law scholar Kathleen M. Sullivan:

> You cannot take the sex out of rock-and-roll or rhythm-and-blues. True, the quality of the mixture spans a wide range. 2 Live Crew's lyrics are crude, vulgar, and blunt. They can't hold a candle to the infinitely more clever double-entendre and subtle innuendo of earlier and greater sexually suggestive songs. . . . But which is more "obscene," sexual lyrics that are coded or blunt? No court should ever start down the road toward an answer.[21]

The obvious reply to such equivocation is that the courts have been traveling down precisely that road for many years. Indeed, the burden of proof lies with those who would repeal the law against offensive crudity, not with those who would enforce it.[22]

Still, the point is not that 2 Live Crew's material is legally obscene (a question that would only be worth debating if the laws were fairly enforced), but that it represents a new stage in the debasement of Afro-American music. Like the love men, the obscene rappers are less interested in seducing women than in silencing the white boys, and less concerned with promoting black pride than with peddling primitivist stereotypes. But unlike the love men, they have no use for consensual (or sensual) acts. The stereotype they peddle is ugly, sadistic, and criminally violent—"blackness" filtered through heavy metal and punk. Among male rappers it is now standard practice to boast about one's mighty sexual organ ripping asunder the bodies of "bitches" and "ho's." Ice-T screams about his "Evil Dick"; N.W.A. (Niggaz With Attitude) rap about a "preacher's daughter" who offers to "take a broomstick up the butt," allows herself to be raped by "a gang of niggers," and (for good measure) "licks out their asshole."

Thus obscene rap also attacks the vestiges of communal emotion in Afro-American music. R&B, gospel, and blues have different ways of dissecting the heartsore turmoil of passion, of bringing what is hidden to light. But all share the same goal, which is to aid the survival of the aberrant individual by drawing on the strength of the group. "All our troubles are the same," is their message. The contrast could not be starker with obscene rap, whose goal is to punish the group for the aberrance of the individual. Like heavy metal and punk, its message is: "You made me what I am, and I'm going to make you pay."

Some rappers argue that they are creating a new communalism, "the black network we never had."[23] Such claims reveal a disturbing ignorance of the real impact that obscenity has on human community.[24] The original hip-hop DJs presided over broad-based social functions, such as block parties, in the mid-1970s. But as the ghetto environment became more forbidding, hip-hop moved into nightclubs attracting only young people, including many teenagers, whose immersion in that wild scene worried their parents. The result was an antirap bias among older ghetto dwellers that is rarely acknowledged or respected in the "new black network." For example, a favorite target of rap insult has been black-oriented radio, which has frequently resisted playing hip-hop.[25] Yet the reason for that resistance, ignored by rappers, is that black radio is less divided by age than white radio, so playing rap risks alienating older listeners.

The Jamaican-born sociologist Orlando Patterson makes a similar point:

> I [have] been reflecting on the differences between the lyrics of dance-hall reggae—which is quite lewd . . . and rap music. . . . These two proletarian

musical forms from the diaspora now mutually influence each other (to the dismay of the folks back home). . . . Before rap, dance-hall lyrics were harm-lessly erotic, something I could listen and dance to with my daughters. Rap lyrics, as you know, are incredibly brutal. . . . There is a horrible sickness here, and . . . it has nothing to do with any acceptable form of humor.[26]

The most persuasive defense of obscene rap comes from people well versed in Afro-American culture, who defend it as part of the oral, as opposed to the musical, tradition. Testifying at the 2 Live Crew trial, the literary scholar Henry Louis Gates, Jr., traced a clear connection between obscene rap and a streak of raunchy humor running through calypso, toasting, and such North American customs as "signifying," "sounding," and "playing the dozens."[27] The same streak pervades popular culture, from nineteenth-century minstrelsy to vaudeville, "party records," and stand-up comedy. The performers themselves stress the link: Like the Rolling Stones trotting out Muddy Waters, 2 Live Crew pay tribute to such older comedians as Rudy Ray Moore and "Wild Man" Steve Gallon, whose graphic sexual comedy was popular in the 1970s.

To those who would defend obscene rap, this link with the past justifies any excess. But such reasoning overlooks the fact that, like all cultures, Afro-American culture has different standards for different settings. For example, the great black comedians have always accepted such restraints as the rule against profanity in the broadcast media. From Moms Mabley to Richard Pryor, they could be as funny, or funnier, when required to "clean up their act" as when performing in more permissive situations. Not so the obscene rappers; they are lost without their Anglo-Saxon monosyllables. When 2 Live Crew tried to capitalize on their notoriety by offering a "clean" performance in a regular venue in Georgia, the show fizzled, because rather than milk every drop of humor from the situation, as Pryor would have done, all they could do was tell their drunken fans to yell "fuck" in all the right places.[28]

The great performers have also known how to adapt their material to private gatherings, to the nightclub stage, to records, and to the public air-waves. Of course, they were bound by legal and regulatory requirements. But very often those requirements suited their sense of propriety. As James Brown says, "I feel solidarity with the breakers and the rappers and the whole hip hop thing—as long as it's clean."[29] Even Marvin ("Sexual Heal-ing") Gaye drew a line between private and public, amusing friends with a satirical ditty called "Dem Niggers Are Savage in the Sack," but never ship-ping it platinum to the nation's retail outlets.[30] As for Moore and Gallon, they insist that their party records were never intended for all ears. In a recent interview, Moore admitted that his own mother has never heard his X-rated records, and he doesn't want her to, because "I wasn't brought up like that."[31] Indeed, Moore and Gallon offer their own criticism:

> [Moore:] We're not in the same bag, and if you think they are, you don't know nothin' about show business. The things that Steve and I did on records, we called them ghetto expressions and a form of art. We don't say [expletive] this, [expletive] that, [expletive] this.
>
> [Gallon:] Or say it just to say it.
>
> [Moore:] We use it as a punch point where it has the greatest impact. . . .
>
> [Gallon:] I wouldn't dare take my mother *near* 2 Live Crew. And they got the women up there naked. That's not entertainment to me. That's porno. . . . We have a gentleman's approach to our comedy. And we're basically there to make you laugh, not to insult you or to insult your integrity.[32]

The relation of standards to settings becomes even more important when the obscenity is abusive. As Toop reports, some toasts and stories are "violent, scatological, obscene, misogynist."[33] To this extent the abusiveness comes from Afro-American culture, in the anthropological sense. But does that make it culture in the traditional sense? Stanley Crouch reminds us that just "because it's a tradition, that doesn't mean it's something to aspire to."[34] Most obscene rap possesses neither wit nor musicianship—only obscenity. By the standards of the Afro-American past, that is not enough to qualify it as art. But by the standards of perverse modernism, it is. As we've seen, obscenity is the preferred weapon of those willing to do anything to get a rise out of the public. The faces are black, but the strategy is European: Seek out a submerged, antisocial custom that is considered marginal even by its participants, drag it kicking and screaming to the surface, and celebrate it as "art."

Guns 'n' Poses: The "Gangsta" Mystique

In my own city of Washington, D.C., the plague of black youth violence is now so overwhelming that the Children's National Medical Center reports "a 1,740 percent rise in the number of children and teen-agers treated for knife and gunshot wounds since 1986."[35] Again the policy debate sheds more heat than light, but the most astute observers now include popular culture in their analyses. Mark Naison, a professor of Afro-American studies who coaches in a Brooklyn youth program, offers this capsule history of the plague's origins:

> By the mid-1970s, the Black Power movement . . . survived on the street largely through a distorted symbolic shorthand: images of crime as rebellion and working-class (or middle-class) Blacks as "suckers." The left intelligentsia, caught up in disappointments and fantasies of its own, did little to challenge this destructive ideological brew. . . . And the lifestyle and language of hustlers was designated a frontier of Black resistance by filmmakers and folklorists alike. . . . As the community consciousness of the Black Power era faded, restraints against violent assaults on other Blacks, which previous generations of hustlers had respected, fell completely by the wayside. A true "outlaw culture" was now in place.[36]

Because hip-hop appeared at roughly the same time as the outlaw culture, the two were linked in the popular mind in a way that was, at first, unfair. Although Run-DMC dressed like gang members, their lyrics offered unambiguous counsel against drugs and crime. And in 1986, when one of their concerts erupted into a pitched battle between rival Los Angeles gangs, they tried to persuade the media that they did not sanction violence.

But it was too late: Rival rappers were already sending the opposite message. The following year saw the release of *Criminal Minded*, an album by the New York group Boogie Down Productions, which featured, among other things, a rap about the thrill of using a nine-millimeter pistol to kill someone at close range. When one member of the group was shot to death, the lead rapper, KRS-One, switched to an antiviolence message. But again it was too late. Encouraged by the success of *Criminal Minded*, voted one of the year's top ten albums by Britain's *New Musical Express*, hundreds of other rappers seized on the "gangsta" mystique as a way to "sucker" the competition.

Then the action shifted to Los Angeles, the site of the original bloodletting. What had been a badge of shame in 1986 became a medallion of pride three years later, when a rapper called Ice-T (Tracy Marrow) released *Rhyme Pays*, an album of foul-mouthed raps about drug deals, sadistic sex, and drive-by shootings in South Central. If Ice-T's statements are to be believed, he has been a member of both the Bloods and the Crips, a drug pusher, a street hustler, a pimp, a jewel thief, a college graduate, and a veteran of the U.S. Army. Some critics take such self-mythologizing with a grain of salt. Others, like Greg Tate of the *Village Voice*, simply gush:

> [Hip-hop] is the song and dance of an incipient warrior culture. Hiphop represents the black male treating his pariahhood as if social vilification were a superheroic emblem. . . . Ice-T is the first gold rapper to emerge from a bona fide black criminal enterprise, the gangs of Los Angeles. . . . Ice-T's background gives him an advantage over all the wannabee gangsters in East Coast hiphop. When he slips into the killcrazy heads of the Bloods and the Crips, . . . you know he's talking reality.[37]

Without using the word, the defenders of "gangsta" rap see it as a form of naturalism—a cold, clinical look at life in the "lower depths." As one member of N.W.A. put it, "We're like reporters. We give them the truth."[38] Here, too, there is a clear Afro-American precedent. Indeed, the roots of "gangsta" rap's stark realism show up in Lawrence Levine's distinction between the "social bandit" of white folklore (Robin Hood, Jesse James) and the "bad man" of black folklore (Stagolee): "Black legend did not portray good bad men or noble outlaws. The brutality of Negro bad men was allowed to speak for itself without extenuation . . .They preyed upon the weak as well as the strong, women as well as men. They killed not merely in self-defense but from sadistic need and sheer joy."[39]

Yet, as Levine goes on to explain, such legends offered "no hope of social redemption. Black singers, storytellers and audiences . . . were not beguiled into looking to these asocial, self-centered, and futile figures for any permanent remedies."[40] Instead black folklore sought redemption in a very different figure, the "moral hard man" personified by the steel-driving giant, John Henry:

> John Henry is a much more fully developed hero figure than the bad man. In many ways he is a secular version of the Biblical heroes who were traditionally so important in black thought. He is bestowed with extraordinary powers, forced to undergo a superhuman test, is momentarily plagued by doubt, and then faces his ordeal and ultimate martyrdom stoically and with complete faith. Above all, he is a culture hero. The bad man's contests tend to be individual; they are *his*. While the folk may derive vicarious rewards from his direct, violent approach, they remain separated from his life, in which they are often his victims, and detached from his death which they greet with no particular dismay. John Henry's epic contest is never purely individual. . . . His victory is shared and his demise is mourned. . . . It is this representative quality that gives his struggle epic proportions and makes John Henry the most important figure in Afro-American lore.[41]

Levine traces the descent of John Henry through the real-life black heroes of the twentieth century, starting with Jack Johnson and Joe Louis, and continuing through the civil rights era, including such figures as Martin Luther King, Jr., Malcolm X, and Muhammad Ali. The moral hard man's basic stance is to beat the white man at his own game, meaning to prove himself superior according to physical, mental, and moral standards that both races respect—or at least profess to respect.[42] Thus, the devoutest hope placed in any black leader has always been that he would take the countless Stagolees of America's streets and prisons and turn them into an army of John Henrys.

Whether or not they recall such legends, most aspiring young rappers would probably rather play John Henry than Stagolee. But they don't have much of a chance, squeezed as they are between the outlaw culture of the streets and the hardcore taste of the music business. Consider the Geto Boys, a Houston group whose breakthrough is described by the journalist David Mills:

> Houston's Ghetto Boys did harmless dance raps until James Smith, local recording entrepreneur, caught a whiff of the money gangsta rappers were raking in. Next thing you know, the Ghetto Boys were doing for Houston's crime-plagued 5th Ward what N.W.A. did for Compton. The Boys' violent tales made them an underground sensation.
>
> Compounding the cynicism, Rick Rubin last year picked up the group for his Def American label, hoping to exploit the tremendous publicity surrounding 2 Live Crew. The re-named Geto Boys combined N.W.A.'s overblown gangsterism with 2 Live Crew's sexist raunch, plus a new element—slasher movie gross-out imagery. Bushwick Bill is probably the first rapper ever to allude to necrophilia.[43]

Rubin has learned his lesson well. When the manufacturer refused to press the Geto Boys' first album, he made good use of the publicity, signing with another distributor and bragging, "If the record had been made by a white group like the Beastie Boys, it would never have caused a sensation."[44] Sensation is, of course, his food and drink: Def American also carries the shock comic Andrew Dice Clay and the thrash metal group Slayer. But the Geto Boys, being black, pack an extra punch.

Strikingly, the core audience for "gangsta" rap is increasingly white.[45] Indeed, Ice-T's most recent efforts, *Body Count* (the 1992 album containing the notorious single, "Cop Killer") and *Home Invasion* (the 1993 album that terminated his relationship with Time Warner), feature thrash metal, not hip-hop. Predictably, most of the people revolted by Ice-T's lyrics do not stop to consider that he is now playing a style of music that is not popular among inner-city blacks.[46]

Unlike that of police organizations, politicians, and pundits, my revulsion at "gangsta" rap does not stem from fears that its fans will start gunning down cops. Such fears are not to be dismissed, but to focus exclusively on them is to play into the hands of cynical manipulators like Rubin and Ice-T, who know all too well that whites fear rap simply because they fear blacks—especially young black men. No, my revulsion stems from the spectacle of young black men who are not brutal criminals posing as such, in order to sell thrills to whites. Or. more disturbingly, from the fact that rappers are now getting involved in criminal activity—with the perverse result that being arrested, indicted, and convicted boosts both their image and their record sales. Sometimes police are the victims, as in the alleged 1993 shooting of two Atlanta officers by rapper Tupac Shakur. But most of the time, the victims are peers: the female host of a TV show, beaten by former N.W.A. member Dr. Dre; a cousin, shot by the popular rapper Slick Rick; the victim of a drive-by shooting, allegedly murdered by Snoop Doggy Dogg's bodyguard while the rapper himself was driving.

The whole "gangsta" rap strategy is summed up in the Capitol Records press release that promised "mean-tempered diatribes on violent 'gangsta' lifestyles [that] challenge middle-class norms by rubbing their noses in the reality of the contemporary urban jungle—a place most suburbanites don't dare tread." Or in the *Rolling Stone* headline: "Dr. Dre and his protégé, Snoop Doggy Dogg, take hardcore rap from South Central L. A. to your house."[47] Anyone, black or white, who worries that the outlaw culture is encouraging American society to disinvest in black youth, can only feel dismay at this particular marketing gambit.

I realize that by protesting this way, I'm inviting some hip kitty to say, "Chill out, lady, it's just a joke." And sure enough, Rubin says of the Geto Boys: "The images in their lyrics, whether it's sleeping with seven women or cutting someone up with a chainsaw, are exaggerations. It's not any more real than a horror movie. The guys are just having fun."[48] Also just for fun is "Momma's Gotta Die Tonight," Ice-T's song about a son setting his mother on fire, hitting her with a baseball bat, and carving her into pieces. From this viewpoint the only people who take this stuff seriously are fuddy-duddy critics and psychopaths already planning to dismember their moms.

But the logic is no better than heavy metal's. Switching expertly to the other side of his mouth, Rubin also touts "gangsta" rap as the authentic voice of ghetto rage. And Ice-T's reason for dicing Momma is she's a "racist bitch" who taught him not to trust white people. Obviously, a pinch of politics makes it easier to cover one's keister in a crisis: Having denounced the federal government between gang rapes and chain saw massacres, the Geto Boys can then respond righteously to being dropped by Geffen Records: "They can't hold us back. . . . The truth can't be stopped."[49]

By now I expect it's superfluous to say that "the truth" has precious little to do with this process of reducing Afro-American music to a minstrel version of grindcore. Writing about black jazz musicians in the 1940s, Gerald Early says they wanted "no part of being the collective unconscious garbage heap of neuroses for whites."[50] I doubt that future historians will be as generous toward "gangsta" rap.

Blackface Punk

Accuse British punk of nihilism, and its fans will leap to its defense as a "progressive" force, recalling that Malcolm McLaren denounced the neo-fascist National Front, that the Clash started a movement called Rock Against Racism, and that most punks rejected the xenophobic "skinheads" who helped to inspire neo-Nazism.[51] What punk fans will not admit, however, is that neo-Nazism was partly nurtured in the poisonous atmosphere of punk, that there is a difference between fascism and parliamentary government (even under Conservatives), and (hardest of all) that the dream of socialist revolution is dead.

In other words, you can defend the politics of punk only if your own views are naive, crazy, or outdated. I wish hip-hop were different, because the people for whom it claims to speak could use some constructive political engagement. But just as punk's "lefty" heirs embrace the defunct extremism of the British left, so do hip-hop's "progressive" voices embrace the defunct extremism of the Black Power movement.

By "extremism" I don't mean the intermittent efforts of "gangsta" rappers to send "positive messages" to ghetto youth. It was heartening, in the past, to see efforts such as the Stop the Violence Movement, which donated the proceeds of a single called "Self-Destruction" to the National Urban League; or the decision of several Los Angeles rappers to tape a video, "We're All in the Same Gang," at the violence-torn Nickerson Gardens housing project in Watts.[52] But as one rapper commented at Nickerson Gardens: "It's not going to stop anything. . . . The older ones are too set in their ways. No one can tell them what to do."[54] To judge by the growing trend toward criminal activity, the real gansters on the street are having more influence on the rappers than vice-versa. Indeed, the latter seem compelled to prove that they're not "busters" (posturing do-nothings).

Instead, what I mean by "extremism" is the style of black politics that fosters rage and despair among blacks, contempt and cynicism among whites. Crouch offers this pungent summary:

> Whereas once merely speaking out against injustice was itself an incendiary act that could bring violence or death to the speaker, over the last 20 years, or at least since Malcolm X, the gleeful or pompous haranguing of power has become a vocation. The image of the professional adversary has damaged the freedom black politicians have to make deals, to compromise, to really shape, influence, or wield power. Probably the worst effect of unrelenting rabble-rousing and the constant attempt to manipulate white Americans through the imposition of guilt was the destruction of the developing national identification with the problems of black Americans that had result-ed from the efforts of civil rights leaders like Martin Luther King. In the wake of his death, telling white people off frequently became more impor-tant than changing power relationships.[55]

As Crouch makes clear, this style of politics was self-defeating, even tragic, the first time around. It's tempting to quip that its recurrence in hip-hop is a case of history repeating itself as farce. Certainly it has its farcical side. But, given the intractable problems of the black poor, it's more accurate to say that the tragedy is ongoing.

Because it was detached from any real effort to organize or mobilize black communities, the original extremist rhetoric of Black Power flowed easily into popular music through such figures as the Last Poets and Gil Scott-Heron—the latter a talented musician best known for his line, "The revolution will not be televised." As it happens, Scott-Heron got it back-wards: There is no revolution, but it *is* being televised. Public Enemy wouldn't have it any other way.

To anyone old enough to remember the hellfire sermons of James Bald-win, the antiwhite tirades of pre-Mecca Malcolm X, and the quasi-Marxist fulminations of the Black Panthers, the nonstop verbiage of Public Enemy's lead rapper, Chuck D (Carlton Ridenhour), was full of echoes when it ruled the rap scene in the early 1990s. To young listeners unfamil-iar with these sources, Chuck D delivered quite a wallop—not least because he rapped against some of the densest, most intimidating sound montages ever created. And each sonic punch packed a visual counter-punch, as the group's videos spliced real footage of historic racial con-frontations (mostly in the United States and South Africa) with highly fanciful—and distorted—reenactments of current headlines. By such means Public Enemy sought to make hip-hop into what one observer called "a highly charged theater of race."⁵⁶

It hadn't started out that way. In the late 1980s, when Chuck D and his fellow rapper Flavor Flav (William Drayton) were college students in suburban Long Island, hip-hop was just a lark. Explaining why he signed them to Def Jam, Rubin recalls: "There wasn't any politics in the music at the time. [Chuck D] was just doing some real good, real funny raps, about driving around in his [Olds] 98 . . . I think the politics became very much of an angle. They were looking for something to make them different from the other rap groups."⁵⁷ Here again, the punk legacy was decisive. Indeed, Robert Hilburn reports that Chuck D's friend Bill Stephney "pushed for the group's tough, even radical stance because he was a fan of alternative rock and had long yearned for a hip-hop equivalent of the Sex Pistols or the Clash."⁵⁸

For "tough, radical" rhetoric capable of lobbing a media bomb, the group turned to Professor Griff (Richard Griffin), a follower of the Nation of Islam under Louis Farrakhan, who obligingly told the *Washington Times* in 1989 that "Jews are responsible for the majority of wickedness that goes on across the globe." In the explosion that followed, Chuck D announced the departure of Griff and wrote a letter to CBS (Def Jam's distributor) insisting that Public Enemy did not mean "to offend anybody, but to offend the system that works against [blacks] 24 hours a day, 365 days a year."⁵⁹ Of course, what Public Enemy were really doing was making the system work for them: their second album, *It Takes a Nation of Millions to Hold Us Back* (1989), sold 1.1 million copies and swept the *Village Voice* critics' poll;⁶⁰ and their third, *Fear of a Black Planet* (1990), went platinum the first week.

Such explosions were hard to sustain, though, as evidenced by the monotony of the group's live shows. They opened impressively, with the paramilitary-looking "S1W" twirling their Uzis like so many Third World drum majorettes. But soon there was nothing but flashing lights, deafening (taped) sound, and Chuck D's resonant ranting, relieved only by the clowning of Flavor Flav, who was supposed to play "the Joker" to Chuck D's "Lyrical Terrorist" but whose spastic parody of ghetto speech and mannerisms rarely elicited more than an embarrassed smile from onlookers.⁶¹

Still, Public Enemy would not have been the same without Flavor Flav, because his clownish incoherence was the truest emblem of its politics. At their zenith the group was accused of many rhetorical excesses, including recycled anti-Semitism. But serious criticism was blunted by the sheer difficulty of picking an argument with people who have nothing invested in clarity, everything in obfuscation. For example, Public Enemy endorsed both the black-supremacist ideology of Farrakhan and the memory of Malcolm X, seemingly oblivious to the latter's bitter break with the Nation of Islam.

Likewise, Chuck D claimed to have had his political consciousness raised at a boyhood summer camp with counselors who were former members of the Black Panther Party. But he couldn't have earned many merit badges, for he showed no sign of having read the party's founding text, Eldridge Cleaver's prison memoir, *Soul on Ice*. In particular he seemed to have missed the passage in which Cleaver recalls his own reaction to Malcolm X's break with the Muslims: "At a secret meeting of the Muslims in Folsom, I announced that . . . I was throwing my support behind Brother Malcolm. I urged everyone there to think the matter over and make a choice, because *it was no longer possible to ride two horses at the same time*."[62] (emphasis added)

Too bad the brothers at Folsom didn't have Public Enemy to show them how to ride two horses, a donkey, an elephant, and a load of bull besides. To contemporary political discourse, Public Enemy's chief contribution has been a new species of video, in which young hero-worshipers effectively deconstruct the hard-won convictions of their heroes. Along with dislocated images of protest and snippets of once-coherent speeches, Public Enemy videos jumble political ideologies as though they were all equally meaningful.

Or meaningless—as in the group's 1992 video, "By the Time I Get to Arizona." Described by Chuck D as a "revenge fantasy" against that state's officials for opposing a holiday in honor of Martin Luther King, Jr., the video shows Public Enemy poisoning a state senator, blowing up the governor with a car bomb, and ambushing several state legislators with semiautomatic weapons. As it happens, the King holiday proposition had broad white support and lost by a narrow margin. But that didn't stop Public Enemy from spewing venom at the entire state—which, needless to say, would have appalled King. The head of the Arizona NAACP called the video "a disservice"[63]; and Warren Stewart, the Baptist minister who led the proholiday movement, denounced it as "an insult to the memory of Dr. King and a *terrible* lesson for our young people." Hoping that the voters would discount the video as "a public relations stunt," Stewart nonetheless warned against such cynicism: "Public Enemy is getting millions of dollars of free publicity at the expense of the legacy of Dr. King and our efforts to build a coalition and win a holiday in 1992."[64] Even Malcolm X's admirers objected. As one historian chided, "Malcolm X always made it clear when it came to violence that he was talking about self-defense."[65]

Chuck D and his imitators remain indifferent to such criticism because ultimately they're indifferent to politics. Their act is sheer bluster, and so are their defenses. First, they claim special knowledge of what King and Malcolm X would be thinking if they were alive today. (In case you're wondering, it's the opposite of what they were thinking at the height of their powers.) Second, they claim special access to the collective mind of the black race—a mind that, according to Chuck D, has no need of clarity. As he explains, making oneself "perfectly clear" is for whites only: "I might say things that the media understands or the white man understands, but then I might not be communicating with the black audience."[66]

Of course, Chuck D is not consistent even on this point, asserting in the next breath that his raps are better than the message songs of Marvin Gaye, Stevie Wonder, and Curtis Mayfield, because "All that was just singing. It's not as direct. With rap, there is no way to miss the point."[67] Perhaps he was thinking of his protégée, a young female rapper named Sister Souljah (Lisa Williamson), who made her point very directly in the spring of 1992, when she justified the Los Angeles riots by telling the *Washington Post*, "If black people kill black people every day, why not have a week and kill white people?"[68] As everyone knows, that comment was blasted by Democratic presidential candidate Bill Clinton in a strategic attack on Jesse Jackson, whose Rainbow Coalition had invited Sister Souljah to appear on a panel. Many other voices, black and white, soon joined the fray, but no one expressed the problem better than Stanley D. Henderson, a D.C. resident who wrote a letter to the *Washington Post* right after the Souljah interview appeared:

> As a young black man, I've experienced the frustrations and setbacks that impede black people's struggle to succeed in a society originally designed to exclude them. . . . [Yet the] greatest and saddest threat facing black people in America today is self-destruction. To suggest that we take a break from murdering our own in order to commit acts of savagery against whites is not a solution I am willing to propose to black youth, who are in need of much more constructive options than "revenge" against those they perceive (correctly or incorrectly) as the cause of their problems. Does [Sister Souljah] suggest that after a week of killing people for no reason other than their ancestry we return to the job of self-annihilation? . . . If rappers like Sister Souljah fancy themselves leaders of black youth, they need to stop sending destructive, unproductive and contradictory messages to those they profess to serve.[69]

Some people define "hip-hop" very broadly, as any kind of sound montage assembled through computer sampling techniques. Among other things, this definition lends an air of authenticity to high-tech avant-gardists with no real connection to the "street." More typical, though, is the narrower definition of hip-hop as a particular type of sound montage: Afro-American speech fitted to Afro-American rhythms, and addressing the problems of growing up black. Clearly, there are those who would narrow the term still further, to eliminate any positive approach to those problems. But, precisely because hip-hop is part of the Afro-American tradition, many black observers have resisted this further narrowing. From journalists to religious leaders to the managers of radio stations, black opinion-makers have begun to express their disgust at obscene and violent rap. And the same disgust has been felt within the ranks of young black performers. That is why I am glad to report that there is a place for hip-hop in the next chapter, which discusses the survival of Afro-American music despite the depredations of the last twenty-five years.

Chapter 20

You Don't Miss Your Water (Till Your Well Runs Dry)

he title of this chapter comes from an old Southern proverb, also the title of the 1962 Memphis soul classic by William Bell. In its laconic way, the proverb marks the point at which we have now arrived. After the bad news of the last several chapters, the reader may wonder whether the musical well has run dry, or become so polluted that it no longer has the power of self-replenishment. That is why I now turn to the good news: the diverse, sometimes paradoxical, ways in which the fount keeps springing anew. I cannot say whether it is bottomless. But I can suggest that it is a lot deeper, and purer, than the source presuming to replace it.

Resisting Perversity

To survey the contemporary landscape of black-dominated popular music, from hip-hop to contemporary R&B, is to discover a surprising resurgence of older sounds, from Motown soul to the "Philly sound," R&B to gospel—even jazz. Ironically this return to the music of the past is being facilitated by the technology of the future: sampling.

As we've seen, the hip-hoppers of the mid-1980s seized on sampling as a way to get the best possible rhythm tracks onto their records. Like imitation, sampling is the sincerest form of flattery. Still, hip-hop has flattered rhythm too much, the other elements of music not enough. A typical Ice Cube or Public Enemy record offered the auditory equivalent of a Dagwood sandwich: a monster rhythm track stuffed with every variety of sampled sound effects, with only a few skilled rappers able to bite it off. "Pop" rappers such as Fresh Prince offered a sweeter, sprightlier version of the same dish. Yet in both cases the lack of melody or harmony limited emotional expression beyond anger and aggression on the one hand, playfulness and fun on the other. Hip-hop competition being what it is, a new formula was bound to appear.

By the mid-1980s, the sounds of contemporary R&B were being added to hip-hop in a style called "new jack swing," exemplified by the rapper-dancer Bobby Brown. Unfortunately, the typical new jack swing star was part love man, part Prince, playing the male stripper and inviting screaming female fans onstage for simulated sex. One exception was the immensely popular Hammer (Stanley Kirk Burrell), the Oakland Navy man who danced better than anyone and kept his act clean in the manner of James Brown, not Bobby. Hammer's most popular album, *Please Hammer Don't Hurt 'Em*, sold nine million copies and relied totally on sampling—indeed, it would have been the target of many a lawsuit, had Hammer not secured all the rights. Hammer then switched to a live band and began performing message songs, old and new, with gospel choirs. But then his star faded—in part because he was lambasted as "pop" by his fellow rappers, and in part because his success carried within it the seed of its own destruction. By fostering a return to expressive musicianship, Hammer, a poor singer, priced himself out of the market.

A similar pattern has emerged within hip-hop itself, as East Coast groups such as Queen Latifah, P. M. Dawn, and Arrested Development have expanded hip-hop's expressive range by sampling a greater variety of music. Arrested Development's 1992 album, *Three Years, Five Months and Two Days in the Life Of . . .*, not only samples the psychedelic soul of Earth, Wind and Fire and Sly and the Family Stone, it also ventures into singing—both the melodic chanting of the lead rapper, Todd ("Speech") Thomas, and the downhome gospel of Dionne Farris. In efforts such as the group's hit single, "Tennessee," sampling looks less like a high-tech gimmick than a path leading back to the ancestral well.

Sampling is a poor substitute for real musicianship, to be sure. But it's better than synthesizers and drum machines at connecting young nonmusicians with the past. As the editor of *Keyboard* comments, "[Sampling is] putting amazing music into the hands of a lot of people."[1] Yet, like Hammer's, these performers' own musical limitations may open them to challenge by the real thing. As "gangsta" rap migrates to the white suburbs, black audiences are gravitating toward a new generation of singers who neither rap nor trap themselves in the studio.

The best so far have been Boyz II Men, a talented quartet who honed their rich sound on traditional gospel and classical choral music at Philadelphia's High School of the Creative and Performing Arts. When their first album, *Cooleyhighharmony*, was released by Motown in 1992, critics praised it as a return to that label's original high standards—and with reason. The weaker songs still smack of contemporary R&B, vocal curlicues bouncing around inside a Nintendo game. But the stunning hit single, "Motownphilly," lives up to its title by doing what Motown and Philadelphia International Records did in their prime: placing the studio at the service of the voice, instead of the other way around.

Thus, both hip-hop and contemporary R&B seem to be rediscovering their musical heritage. By cracking open the rhythm-dominated shell of hip-hop and pouring in a torrent of soulful melody and harmony, sampling allows young hip-hoppers to express more feeling than previously allowed in the genre. And by singing either a cappella or with musically vital accompaniment (both sampled and live), the new vocalists are digging more deeply into musical memory than last week's charts. To the extent that this new power and depth arise from principled resistance to perversity, nothing could be more welcome.

Equally welcome, and better known, is the self-renewal occurring in jazz. Since the early 1980s a group of young jazz musicians known as "neoclassicists" have been rediscovering both the greater jazz tradition and the greater jazz audience. The name topping the charts is, of course, Wynton Marsalis, the New Orleans trumpeter who dazzles listeners with his facility in both the European classics and jazz, especially bebop. In addition to providing a role model for other young talents, Marsalis (together with such mentors as Stanley Crouch and Albert Murray) carries on a persuasive public relations campaign in favor of jazz as "America's classical music." Even more persuasive is the music itself: the remarkable mixture of improvisation and composition pouring forth from Terence Blanchard, Roy Hargrove, Donald Harrison, Marcus Roberts, and the World Saxophone Quartet, to name a few. At times it seems that the neoclassicists have succeeded in redefining jazz in their image.

At other times, however, it doesn't. Like all jazz, neoclassicism is in a commercial slump right now. More important, it has been criticized as a giant step backward, a retreat from the innovations of free jazz. Especially galling to free jazz advocates is the fact that most major jazz festivals now focus on the music of older figures whose mature styles developed before free jazz, or on neoclassicists rooted in such styles. A good example would be New York's JVC Jazz Festival, which, after a period of experimentation, now relies on tributes to artists such as Clifford Brown, Art Blakey, Betty Carter, Doc Cheatham, pre-1960s Miles Davis, Jon Faddis, Stan Getz, Dizzy Gillespie, Dexter Gordon, Lionel Hampton, John Lewis, Wynton Marsalis, Thelonious Monk, Gerry Mulligan, Billy Strayhorn, Clark Terry, and Sarah Vaughan. Stellar though this lineup is, it does not always suit those who fancy themselves on the "cutting edge." For them the real action is in the downtown "performance space" called the Knitting Factory, where musicians such as Tim Berne, Ned Rothenberg, and Thomas Chapin pursue free jazz's motley legacy.

Yet the fascinating thing about these contemporary jazz avant-gardists is that, unlike their counterparts in avant-garde rock, they do not routinely abuse audiences, resort to obscenity, or wallow in predigested nihilism. However inaccessible their sounds may be, they do not attack musicianship as such. Unlike the cultural free-fall occurring in other "performance spaces" such as the Kitchen, the Knitting Factory festival tends, on the whole, to display an active and respectful engagement with the jazz tradition, to seek a positive relationship with the audience, and (most strikingly) to take a craftsmanlike approach toward the making of music. In this way, it, too, resists perversity.

As for neoclassicism, it is neither a revival nor a revolution, but a return to the deep, dynamic traditionalism of jazz at its finest. Its heroes are those figures who have, over the past forty years, exerted a steady counterpressure against antimusical perversity. After Parker's death in 1955, Monk, Charles Mingus, and Sonny Rollins decided that the best way to move jazz forward was to reach back—into stride piano and gospel (Monk), blues (Mingus), and swing (Rollins). Others reached out to the broader audience. For example, the adoption of modal scales in the cool jazz of Miles Davis and Gil Evans was seen as radical at the time, but it was really an attempt to simplify: like the blues scale, archaic modal scales provide a basis for improvisation that the everyday listener can sense, even if he wouldn't know a Doric mode if it were wired into his doorbell. The result is closer to the jazz of the great big band soloists: uncluttered, expressive, unpredictable, subtly embellishing something that feels solid underneath.

Then there was hard bop, reacting to the "Europeanization" of cool jazz by infusing bebop with African, Latin, and Caribbean rhythms, as well as with harmonies and vocal inflections from blues and gospel. Initiated by Art Blakey and Horace Silver on the Blue Note label, this soul, or funk, style soon proved as capable as cool jazz of attracting a broad spectrum of listeners. Indeed, as we have seen, it was this phase of jazz that directly inspired Ray Charles and James Brown.

Broadly speaking, then, neoclassicism is nothing new. In its effort to incorporate blues, gospel and older jazz forms into a highly sophisticated bebop-based music, it seeks to reconnect jazz with both the past and the people.

The Futility of Fusion

Now the question arises: Will these various trends converge? Will the gap between popular music and jazz become narrower, perhaps even close, as it did during the heyday of swing? And would this be a good thing?

Taking the long view, Henry Pleasants argues that, yes, the gap should be narrowed, because popular music and art music have always needed each other. We've seen how jazz's ambiguous cultural status—as both entertainment and art—has been the source of its vitality. Pleasants reminds us that it was the loss of a similar vital connection that hastened the decline of European art music into self-indulgence and sterility. But Pleasants also has a specifically musical reason for seeking a rapprochement between jazz and popular music:

> Pop has thus far been predominantly a vocal style, . . . which is all to the good—and jazz, having divorced itself from the Popular singer at the close of the swing era, has been too exclusively instrumental. Pop needs the jazz musician's instrumental skills and experience if it is to grow, and jazz needs the vocal and melodic innocence of pop. . . . The jazz musician will find his way back to the mainstream or perish in the more or less benign lunacy of the avant-garde; and the pop musician can use him in achieving musical maturity.[2]

What I find most striking about this passage is its optimism. Writing in 1969, Pleasants clearly felt, despite his grim prognosis for avant-garde jazz, that the prospects were bright for a restored connection between jazz and popular music.

If only he could have seen what was coming. Again, only hindsight reveals the degree to which Afro-American music would be trampled by the three horsemen of the cultural apocalypse: primitivism, motivating black performers to accept and act out racist stereotypes; perverse modernism, turning musicians against music itself; and high tech, turning music-making into a bloodless exercise. Taken together, these three have blocked jazz's path back to the mainstream.

To its credit, jazz tried getting there anyway. Leading the pack was Miles Davis, the only bebop figure to become a popular music icon. To an exacting critic like Crouch, Davis's efforts to reach the popular audiences of the 1970s and 1980s were nothing but pandering. There was an all-too-perfect fit between Davis's aloof, sardonic personality and the incipient punk culture that began, at the end of the 1960s, to hate everything associated with "peace and love."[3] Other critics argue that the "rock fusion" of such albums as *Bitches Brew* (1969) offers a dense harmonic and rhythmic texture unlike anything seen before in jazz, while mercifully avoiding the rhythmic monotony of rock.[4]

Crouch would reply that all Davis really did was thicken funk with electronic noise, while forcing his horn into the upper register, where it's clear he's no Dizzy Gillespie.[5] Nonetheless, Davis's rock fusion is infinitely preferable to that developed by two of his sidemen, drummer Tony Williams and guitarist John McLaughlin. In the latter's early-1970s group, Mahavishnu Orchestra, rhythm was reduced to hard rock tedium, textural density to guitar heroics. To describe the result, Charles S. Murray resorts to heavy irony: "In general, fusion combined rock's elasticity with jazz's concision; jazz's populist impulse urge with rock's elitist ambitions; bebop's catchiness and danceability with rock's appropriateness as a showcase for marathon solo improvisations. God, it was awful. And many people are still blaming Miles Davis."[6]

More palatable was the "funk fusion" launched by four other Davis sidemen: saxophonist Wayne Shorter, and keyboardists Joe Zawinul, Chick Corea, and Herbie Hancock. Most successful has been Hancock, a jazz musician in his own right, whose electronic funk for the Blue Note label earned these kudos from the label's founder, Alfred Lion: "Maybe it's not the most advanced jazz, but it's good funky music."[7] "Good funky music" is still played by both jazz musicians and funk veterans; new recordings, along with the Blue Note originals, are frequently heard on the better jazz radio stations.[8]

Yet not all funk fusion lives up to Lion's standard. Starting in 1966, when Blue Note was sold to the Liberty label, the genre became insipid in the hands of newcomers such as Ronnie Laws and Earl Klugh. Gone was the melodic and harmonic sophistication inherited from bebop, and gone was the rhythmic complexity injected by Blakey and Silver. In their place was a growing dependency on musical clichés and high-tech tinsel.[9] In the late 1980s, *Billboard* finally started listing "fusion" separately from "jazz." But the best term is "fuzak"—it captures the genre's true functions: as a sedative for yuppies waiting in line at their favorite brunch spot, and as fodder for "Jazzy" or "Wave" radio formats, clearly designed to help weary commuters make it through the rush-hour traffic without committing murder. Fuzak is no more likely to spark interest in jazz than Muzak does in Bach.

Davis went into seclusion in 1975, becoming addicted to drugs and promiscuity in the manner of many another icon at the time. Then in 1980 he reemerged and declared his readiness for the next round of fusion—this time with contemporary R&B. The price he paid can be measured by listening to *Tutu* (1986), a lifeless album that merely inserts Davis's trademark sound into a Nintendo game, studio-crafted by Marcus Miller. When Miller's own supple bass playing enters, it almost fills the gulf between Davis and the surrounding sterility—almost, but not quite. Davis's trumpet has always been introspective, even lonely; here, it is an exile's voice, muttering in his native tongue while growing old in an alien land.

Finally, there is hip-hop fusion, attempted by Davis in the last year of his life. After his death in 1991, Warner released the spotty results of his collaboration with the rapper Eazy Mo Bee. That album, called *Doo-Bop*, does little more than squirt Davis's horn, like mustard, into a state-of-the-art Dagwood rhythm sandwich. Likewise, Quincy Jones's 1990 album, *Back on the Block*, purports to introduce Parker and Coltrane to the hip-hop crowd through rapped tributes and sampled snippets. Apart from the obvious commercial motive (for which, incidentally, both Davis and Jones received more rebuke than return), such ventures are clearly motivated by the desire to reach out to the young. As Jones told *Parade*, "Black people, we have no sense of our musical history. And that's a shame, man. I just hope, before I get out of this world, that I can do something about it."[10] Yet this approach is exactly the wrong one: instead of enriching hip-hop with real music, the way hip-hop youngsters have been doing, these jazz elders are stripping the emotion from music in order to cram it into the hip-hop mold. It's merely the latest of several bad examples set by Davis: attempts to "fuse" jazz with popular forms that have already diluted, or distorted, Afro-American music to the point of insult.[11]

That is why the neoclassicists look before they leap. The movement had its first crisis in 1984, when Wynton Marsalis fired his brother Branford from their original quintet because Branford had accepted an invitation to tour with the British rock musician Sting (Gordon Sumner). Since then, Branford's fluid saxophone has been mingled with popular sounds from Caribbean R&B to bluegrass, Brooklyn hip-hop to revived western swing. In 1992 he joined the ultimate lowbrow medium of television, leading a funk fusion band on Jay Leno's *Tonight Show*. And while Wynton's back-to-New-Orleans album, *The Majesty of the Blues*, showcases the octogenarian banjoist Danny Barker, Branford collaborates with a very different banjoist, the young, experimental Bela Fleck. Today the Marsalis brothers are reconciled, at least to the extent that Branford seems to have persuaded Wynton that he's not dragging the good name of jazz through the mud.

Wynton may seem overly fastidious, but neither he nor Branford would deny that there's plenty of mud out there. It's one thing for jazz musicians to mix it up with the fertile loam at their musical roots; it's quite another to besmirch it with dreck. So we must modify the question asked earlier: *Under what circumstances* would it be good to close the gap between jazz and popular music? Again Pleasants can help with the answer. Recall the specific musical reason he gave—that popular music needs "the jazz musician's instrumental skills and experience," and that jazz needs "the vocal and melodic innocence of pop." Today it seems that jazz comes well equipped: Who can dispute the instrumental prowess of the neoclassicists? But what about popular music? What does it bring to the table? Here is where the Marsalis brothers' disagreement lies, but here is also where any hope of renewal must be found.

The key, as always, is the audience. I don't mean jazz aficionados, with their sharp ears and reverent attitude; nor do I mean postpunk diehards, with their contempt for music and craving for the next jolt of outrage. I mean the casually discriminating audience, the kind of people who partied and danced to the Duke Ellington Orchestra back in November 1940, when one of that band's wintry one-nighters was captured on record at the Crystal Ballroom in Fargo, North Dakota. Ellington once remarked that his band played best at dances: "If I hear a sigh of pleasure from the dance floor, it becomes part of our music."[12]

Where do such audiences come from? Not out of thin air: They must know the idiom well enough to enjoy fluency and to delight in eloquence, and they must be able to communicate that joy and delight back to the performers. Obviously such responsiveness is unlikely from an audience that speaks only the language of primitivism, high tech, and perverse modernism. But is this an accurate description of today's audience?

Surprisingly, the answer is no. Even younger listeners who grew up on heavy metal, punk, and rap seem, on the whole, to be musically bilingual. I make this brazen assertion on the basis of radio market research that has long revealed an "overwhelming" preference, among young and old alike, for "oldies."[13] In part this pattern reflects the loyalty of heavy metal fans for every hard-rock track ever recorded. And in part it reflects the undying appeal of schlock ballads, too many of which get played on "oldies" radio. But "oldies" radio also plays a more or less wide-ranging collection of classic singles. Because the classics tend to move at mid-tempo without assaulting the ear, they get lumped with the schlock as "light," "easy," or "soft"—misnomers that, I need not repeat, stem from rock's adolescent obsession with being "heavy" and "hard." Setting those misnomers aside, what the "oldies" craze really represents is the survival of a widespread taste for music powerfully connected to the Afro-American source.

To those aggressively marketing the "cutting edge," this taste is mere nostalgia. But that's illogical in the case of younger listeners, insulting in the case of older ones. What the taste for "oldies" really means is that the contest isn't over. The three horsemen are popular, to be sure. But the majority still seeks the same things that people have always, in all times and places, sought in music: not the formal complexity of high art, but not mud either. Instead, people seek the elemental, the primal things: the motive power of dance, and the emotional power of song. Where can these be found nowadays?

The Trip Home from Camp

Afro-American music reasserts itself every time a culturally sophisticated performer decides, for whatever reason, to drop the ironic distance and play the music straight. This pattern appears in some unlikely places: in Frank Zappa's 1968 album, *Cruising With Ruben and the Jets*, described by one critic as "a send-up of fifties rock 'n' roll, though with an affection that even Zappa could not deny"[14]; in Lou Reed's late-1970s albums *Coney Island Baby* and *Rock and Roll Heart*, two R&B albums acknowledged to be "surprisingly warm"[15]; in David Bowie's 1984 tour, *Serious Moonlight*, featuring a fine band and the changeling dressed in a white suit no campier than Cab Calloway's; and even in David Johansen's transmutation from a

New York Doll into "Buster Poindexter," a campy persona used as a cover for playing music, such as Trinidadian *soca*, that Johansen happens to like.

Even at CBGB, music reasserted itself in groups such as Mink DeVille, who were nearly thrown out by an Andy Warhol lickspittle for the crime of playing R&B, but who stayed to become one of the most popular groups in the club, featured in no less than three tracks on the LP put together by Hilly Kristal, *Live at CBGB's*. As Willy DeVille summed up his renegade attitude: "I think rock 'n' roll moves your tail and makes your heart go boom! boom! boom! . . . If it doesn't move you emotionally, I have no use for it."[16]

Equally renegade was Boy George (George Alan O'Dowd), one of the "new romantic" fashion performers who dominated British video after punk. Hired by Malcolm McLaren because he looked pretty in lipstick, Boy George turned out to be interested in music—which killed the deal with McLaren, because (as usual) the latter was allergic to the stuff. Unfazed, Boy George started his own band, the Culture Club, renowned not just for its leader's skill at cross-dressing, but also for its heartfelt revival of the Motown-Philly sound.

Likewise, a mixed British and American band, the Eurythmics, became famous for a gender-bending fashion statement: the elegant men's clothes worn, and discarded, by lead singer Annie Lennox. Yet the Eurythmics were also a soul powerhouse. Lennox is no Aretha Franklin, but her partner, Dave Stewart, made her sound very good, backing her up with gospel singers and top-notch musicians, including himself. Unlike Blondie or Roxy Music, the Eurythmics never deadened the music with deadpan performance; rather they hypnotized audiences with their suave but celebratory stage presence.

The Eurythmics were part of the "new wave" mentioned earlier as the diverse field of postpunk musicians who, in Bill Flanagan's words, "decided they were not going to limit themselves or pretend that playing music every night does not make you a better musician."[17] Many new wave performers came from "pub rock," an umbrella term for the countless groups that spent the punk years playing music for audiences more interested in having a good time than in fomenting anarchy. The punks detested the pub rockers—first because they could play, and second because they made money. As Bob Geldof recalls, the pub rockers returned the compliment:

> By going on *Top of the Pops* we were . . . in danger of being smeared with that most awful of accusations, commercialism. . . . The Sex Pistols were pre-

tending they didn't want to go on the show; the reality was that they were desperate to appear, but couldn't get on simply because of who they were. Finally, after "holding out" for a year, the Pistols "decided" they'd go on *Top of the Pops* as a radical gesture. In fact, they made a video acceptable to the BBC who allowed it to be played. This was hailed as a "revolutionary triumph" by the press: our appearance, a year before, was apparently a "sell-out.". . . They could all go and fuck themselves as far as I was concerned. I wanted to sell records, I wanted as many people to hear and see us as possible.[18]

For such talented and successful new wave groups as the Pretenders and Dire Straits, Geldof's bluntness says it all. But for two of the most eminent new wave graduates, "that most awful of accusations" has remained burdensome. Elvis Costello, a gifted musician who has written and recorded hundreds of songs in a dozen different genres, has only intermittently escaped what he once described as "this *anti* attitude," which he inherited from his father, a frustrated jazz musician who spent his adult life playing strict tempo dance music for the nobility, including the royal family.[19] And David Byrne, another genuinely talented graduate of CBGB, only frees himself from irony when abandoning himself to the African and Caribbean rhythms for which he has a genuinely creative passion.[20]

Other new wave musicians made the trip home from camp by concentrating on styles of Afro-American music not considered "pop" (meaning commercially successful). Chief among these was Jamaican "ska," an early form of reggae perennially popular in British working-class dance halls, where it is played at "all-niters" alongside Motown and soul. Ska was the original Jamaican response to R&B in the 1950s, deriving its name from a distinctive way of playing the R&B backbeat—not coming down hard, as rock musicians do, but "chopping," or bouncing off the beat, with a calypsolike syncopation. In its original form ska retained the melodic interest, vocal emphasis, and jazz-based instrumentation of R&B.

Reggae, which supplanted ska in the 1960s, shows the influence of rock by making the chopped backbeat heavier and slower, and by dispensing with R&B melodicism. Reggae is also a vehicle for protest. It began as party music, toasting and boasting set to the "reggay," or "regular," beat. Then, in the mid-1960s reggae entered a phase that anticipated American "gangsta" rap by celebrating the "rude boy" street culture—first of Kingston and then of London and other British cities where Jamaican immigrants faced diminishing opportunities and rising hostility from whites. For a brief time in the late 1960s, the rude boy phase of reggae was popular with British "skinheads," an interracial flirtation that was cut short by the stardom of

Bob Marley, who infused reggae with the separatist spirit of the Jamaican religious cult, Rastafarianism.

All this took place before punk, but the memory of black rude boys and white skinheads making common cause against the authorities did not fade: As punk split into "lefties" and "arties" in the late 1970s, the former seized on ska and reggae as a medium of protest. A Coventry band called the Specials was the first to blend ska and punk, but the group really taking up the political cudgels was the Clash, a band composed of two working-class members, who had grown up in racially mixed Brixton; and Joe Strummer (John Mellors), the son of a British diplomat whose political radicalism (including support for the terrorist Baader-Meinhof gang) had been molded in elite public schools. The Clash emerged as leaders in the Rock Against Racism movement, stalwartly defending nonwhite immigrants against neofascist attacks.[21] But at the same time they made good use of the producers and publicists at CBS. By 1979 they were on the cover of *Rolling Stone*, and their album *London Calling* was being extolled as "the *Blonde on Blonde* of its generation."[22] But then the politics took over—in accordance with the direction that reggae itself was taking. A few reggae musicians, notably Marley and Augustus Pablo, have combined reggae rhythms with beautiful melodies. But more typical is the prolonged repetition of the reggae backbeat as an accompaniment for politicoreligious harangues. In this latter mode, the Clash's three-disc release, *Sandinista!*, proved inspirational to political rappers such as Public Enemy. Too bad it sounds like a reeducation session for apparatchiks stoned on ganja.

More musically creative in their use of reggae was the Police, a British trio often compared with David Byrne's Talking Heads. Started by art rock veteran Stewart Copeland, the Police also included Sting, later associated with Branford Marsalis. An amateur jazz bassist, Sting has said that he "found the rock music of the time abhorrent. It was all Led Zeppelin and Deep Purple. I hated it."[23] But neither were the Police inspired by the supposedly liberating energies of punk. The Specials had tried to mix ska and punk by speeding up the former and interspersing it with noise, but the Police took a different tack, blending reggae with sophisticated jazz rhythms and harmonies. Despite the pretentiousness of Sting's lyrics, the music remains fresh. Of course, the group was labeled "pop" the moment its records went platinum—a fate avoided by the Clash, who staked their commercial success on constantly reminding the world how anticommercial they were.

Folkies, Outlaws, and Root Doctors

In the United States, where the camp impulse was never as strong as in Britain, the survival of Afro-American music followed a different path, one closer to the folk movements of the 1960s and 1930s. This path took a number of sharp, even paradoxical turns, as diverse musicians searched for "authentic" alternatives to such mainstream trends as heavy metal and disco. Indeed, it may seem odd to put Bruce Springsteen, Paul Simon, Willie Nelson, and Mac "Dr. John" Rebennack under the same heading. But despite their musical differences, these and many other veterans of the last twenty-five years share a deep traditionalism that has helped their music endure—and, possibly, prevail.

Among these seekers of authenticity, the least impressive musically is Springsteen, the embodiment of the all-American attitude that hard rock is the ultimate folk music. As heavy metal took over in the 1970s, many Americans reacted by getting all misty eyed for its immediate predecessor. Some truly missed the sound, but others missed the celebratory communalism of the mass concerts, and longed for the feeling (however illusory) of generational solidarity in protest. Enter Springsteen, signed to Columbia by John Hammond in 1972 after several years of building a loyal following among white youth old enough to recall the upheavals of the 1960s but too young to have participated in them. Springsteen also came from a blue-collar social stratum more likely to have fought the Vietnam War than to have protested it, but that only enhanced his populist image in the sour wake of the counterculture.

Dave Marsh, the author of not one but two Springsteen biographies, describes the singer's music as "soul," on the grounds that the singer's renowned E Street Band included organ, keyboards, backup singers and the honking saxophone of Clarence Clemons. Yet Marsh also cites "Springsteen's nervous aversion to syncopation, which he conscientiously avoided."[24] Or, in the words of the old Irving Berlin tune, "He Ain't Got Rhythm." Hard rock was what the audience wanted, and hard rock was what they got. For years Springsteen's trademark sound was that of many instruments blending into a single monotonous pounding that Marsh aptly calls "that dinosaur beat."[25] To be sure, Springsteen's best songs have a melodic force capable of defying gravity, in effect lifting the dinosaur off the ground and making it fly—albeit heavily, like an overfed pterodactyl. And whenever Springsteen departs from hard rock, his true if limited muse leads him in the direction of melancholy ballads, some of them quite affecting. But such departures have a cost, because for Springsteen's core audience, the only authentic sound on earth is that dinosaur taking flight.

More impressive musically is the search for authenticity that takes popular musicians to the far corners of the globe. In jazz, there is nothing new about cross-fertilizing with Africa, the Caribbean, and Latin America. But "world beat," as it is called, represents a new trend in popular music. A similar term, "world music," refers to the stepped-up circulation, in Western Europe and the United States, of traditional ethnic forms such as ritual drumming from Burundi, women's choral singing from Bulgaria, and faith-healing chants from Morocco. "World beat," by contrast, refers to the incorporation of traditional sounds into established popular genres, with electronic instrumentation added. Thus it is the larger and more significant category.

Some world beat music is pretty bad. Paris in particular is famous for taking the rich popular music of West Africa and the Caribbean and reducing it to "dance" fodder. As Pareles writes: "Put a foursquare disco beat under the music, and Americans might dance to it; exchange a long, intricate melody for a short, repeated hook and more Westerners will think it's catchy. But follow that recipe too closely, and you end up with Stacey Q singles."[26]

At first glance this process fits the folkie scenario of pure native cultures being despoiled by commercialization. But the fact is, most of the music in question has already been commercialized—by the natives. To cite just one example, a highly dynamic interaction of folk and popular strains (including American imports) has, since 1900, produced such diverse West African styles as highlife (Ghana), *juju* (Sierra Leone), *soukous* (Zaire), *mbalax* (Senegal), Afro-beat (Nigeria), and *mbaganga* (Zulu South Africa). It would take a longer book than this one (horrors) to trace the intricate history of what the writer John Collins calls "syncretic African music."[27] But the point is simply that Africa's popular music is just as eclectic and commercialized as America's. Indeed, the cross-fertilization has been so extensive, the term "Afro-American" ("Americo-African"?) could now be applied to the whole.

World beat entered the mainstream in the early 1980s, when David Byrne, Brian Eno, and the British art rocker Peter Gabriel began adding African, Caribbean, Latin American, and Middle Eastern sounds to their records. But it took off when Paul Simon, a former folkie who (with his partner Art Garfunkel) had been hugely popular in the 1960s, brought three decades of musical exploration to fruition in *Graceland*, a stunning collaboration with South African musicians that sold seven million copies and won several Grammys.

For some critics it's not enough that Simon spent his entire career (in Gillett's words) "commendably avoiding any trace of parody and often stimulating investigation by his audience of his sources."[28] Because he is white, Simon is routinely accused of "stealing" other people's music—even when the accusation is groundless, as it certainly is in the case of *Graceland*. Not only did Simon discuss his plans with antiapartheid leaders and the de facto musicians' and producers' unions in South Africa, he also paid his South African collaborators triple union scale and direct royalties for all songwriting credits.[29]

Now, before Simon sprouts wings and a halo, I should add that he's not a great singer: The sound of his sweet but thin fluting atop the amazing music he assembles can be tiresome, causing the listener to long for less of Simon and more of such collaborators as Milton Nascimento, the Brazilian singer who worked with Simon on the 1990 album, *Rhythm of the Saints*. A gifted musician in a country replete with gifted musicians, Nascimento chimes in only briefly on "Spirit Voices," a song he cowrote. But it's plenty long enough for his nightingale voice to put Simon's in the shade.

Some purist critics accuse Simon of inauthenticity because he blends diverse sounds from diverse cultures and continents.[30] But here the comparison with Nascimento is apt, because he has been doing exactly the same thing for years. Indeed, as a Brazilian, Nascimento grew up in a country where music remains a seamless whole, with no barriers between popular song, folk music, and jazz—and no *musical* notion of racial, ethnic, or national purity. From his own reply to purist criticism, it's clear that Simon grew up in a similar country:

> For me this was not an intellectual concept. . . . It was instinctual, visceral. It's only later, when I looked back on it, that I began to take an overview.
>
> The sound of percussion is the sound of "Iko Iko" and Louisiana music, which I really liked when I was a kid, not aware of where this music comes from. And yes, the reason this music is syncopated and sounds like that is because Louisiana connects into the Caribbean, which connects into West Africa. But I didn't know any of those things. This is just what I love.[31]

Simon grew up in 1950s America—the country where viewers tuning in to see Elvis Presley perform "Hound Dog" on the Ed Sullivan Show also caught Mitzi Gaynor singing highlights from *South Pacific*;[32] the country where mainstream outlets like Sullivan did not feel compelled, as MTV now does, to split into separate channels in order to protect the adherents of mutually hostile subgenres from inadvertent exposure to enemy taste; the country where rock 'n' roll was born out of unruly intercourse between "black" and "white" genres of popular music.

By the end of the 1960s, though, this same country was divided by moats, firewalls, and barbed-wire fences imposing apartheid on supposedly incompatible styles of music. One of the biggest barriers—a virtual Berlin Wall—was erected between blues-based rock and country music. The times demanded a strict separation between music considered "revolutionary" and music considered "reactionary," and the 1960s heirs of Commissar Lunacharsky were more than willing to enforce it. In the process, they nearly blotted out the memory of hundreds of country musicians—from Jimmie Rodgers to Bob Wills, Bill Monroe to Hank Williams, Buck Owens to Merle Haggard—who had learned at least part of their trade from the blues.

Fortunately, there were some wall jumpers around, beginning with Johnny Cash, Bob Dylan, and Kris Kristofferson, and continuing with the Band, Gram Parsons, Chris Hillman, and Linda Ronstadt. Not all these people were Southerners, but they all shared Parson's Florida-bred disgust at hearing Northern rock fans disparage country as "shit-kicking music."[33] Some of the best albums of the late 1960s and early 1970s blended country and rock; and soon a new genre, country rock, was offering stiff competition to heavy metal and disco.

Epitomizing the new sound was Crosby Stills Nash & Young (CSN&Y), the first group to blend subtle vocal harmonies with an accompaniment of combined acoustic and electric guitars. To some extent this sound resembles the white gospel harmony of older C&W groups such as the Louvin Brothers, who influenced both early rock 'n' roll (Buddy Holly, the Everly Brothers) and Merseybeat (the Searchers, the Hollies). But, as the critic Robert K. Oermann notes, the rough edges are missing: "Generally speaking, country-rock is characterized by smoother vocals than hard country, and . . . the characteristic close-harmony group singing on choruses is as reminiscent of the Beach Boys as of Nashville."[34] Even smoother were subsequent groups such as the Eagles, the Doobie Brothers, and America—who made many fine records, but who also pushed country rock close to a creamy blandness reminiscent of such earlier white-bread forms as Paul Whiteman's "swing" and Pat Boone's "rock 'n' roll."

Not surprisingly, the country rockers who best avoided this fate were the ones most steeped in the blues. Indeed, the pick of the genre is Creedence Clearwater Revival, a San Francisco group so fluent in the blended language of country, bluegrass, R&B, and blues that they were often assumed to hail from Louisiana or Mississippi. It's hard to say which was more refreshing, the group's knack for knocking off hit singles when album rock was at its most pretentious, or their buoyant return to the spirit of the 1950s when the 1960s were at their heaviest.

Meanwhile, the best country musicians were struggling to avoid a different kind of creamy blandness, that of the "Nashville Sound," here described by Oermann:

> The advent of rock 'n' roll in the mid-1950s sent country music reeling. It dropped drastically in popularity as more and more radio stations switched over to playing the new teenage music. In response, several Nashville producers began to produce country records for the adult buyers of easy-listening pop music. . . . The procedure was to smooth over the roughness of the country style of a singer with violin sections, soft background voices, sophisticated arrangements, and studio technology.[35]

Some outstanding performers, such as Patsy Cline, sang with "heart" despite this treatment.[36] But others succumbed, and by the 1960s the Nashville Sound was the cliché summarized by Peter Guralnick as "the whining steel, the swelling choruses, the same familiar sidemen playing the same familiar licks that are stamped on every record."[37] A quick way to spot the difference: If the music is animated by hardworking fiddles, it's either old-time country or bluegrass; if it swoons on a cushion of violins, it's the Nashville Sound.

Fortunately, there were alternatives. Bluegrass, the distinctive upbeat style created by Bill Monroe in the 1940s, offered a refuge for fans of lively music who wanted no part of either rock 'n' roll or rock. But, by the same token, bluegrass was too much of a refuge—indeed, a purist bastion—to attract many wall jumpers. More influential was honky-tonk, the Texas strain of country that was heavily influenced by R&B. During the 1950s, the most respected names in country—Ernest Tubb, Lefty Frizzell, Hank Williams, and George Jones—retained those R&B influences, even when besieged by violins. And by 1959 honky-tonk was poised to make a comeback, as the commercial success of Buck Owens's bluesy, swinging sound enabled him to build a recording empire in Bakersfield, California, and to foster the 1960s careers of other honky-tonk stalwarts, notably Merle Haggard.[38]

Thus there was strong precedent for the so-called "outlaws" of the 1970s, including such Nashville fixtures as Hank Williams, Jr., and Waylon Jennings. Inspired by the songwriter Willie Nelson, who pointedly left Nashville for his native Austin, Texas, in 1971, Williams and Jennings decided to kick over the traces and forge a new style capable of bringing rock and country fans together. Unfortunately, however, they did to honky-tonk what Springsteen did to soul: They took its rich instrumentation and sacrificed it to the dinosaur beat. The result, sometimes called "redneck rock," may seem authentic compared with the Nashville Sound. But it's not honky-tonk. The abiding weaknesses of country music are two: love of sentimental cliché, rooted in its turn-of-the-century link with Tin Pan Alley, and fear of polyrhythm, rooted in white racism. Honky-tonk's blues influence provides a welcome tonic for both ills. But "redneck rock" cures only one: sentimentality. Rhythmically, it's no more complex than the Nashville Sound—only louder.

Happily, the most influential outlaw was Nelson himself, an iron-willed character who, having resisted the Nashville Sound, was not about to succumb to hard rock. In 1976 he let RCA talk him into participating in an album called *Wanted: The Outlaws*, which was the first country LP to sell a million copies. But then Nelson struck out for the territory, recording *Stardust*, an album of jazz standards with the Stax soul veteran, Booker T. Jones, which went multiplatinum. Just as happily, this success inspired hundreds of other talented people to start using country as a base from which to explore everything from vintage New Orleans jazz to doo wop, boogie-woogie to blues, spirituals to swing. If the term "outlaw" means musical freedom, then the "country" category today includes more outlaws than law abiders.

Yet Roseanne Cash, Mary-Chapin Carpenter, Nanci Griffith, Emmylou Harris, Wynona Judd, k.d. lang, Lyle Lovett, Kathy Mattea, Ricky Scaggs, and Randy Travis don't call themselves "outlaws." On the contrary, they tend to attach a negative meaning to the word, because, for their generation, it connotes the spectacle of talented individuals such as Williams and (especially) Jennings abandoning themselves to the worst excesses of the counterculture.

There have always been excesses in country music, to be sure—Hank Williams, Sr., drank himself to death at the age of twenty-nine. Yet, as we've seen, the Afro-American tradition does not consider excess a substitute for art. Like the blues singer, the honky-tonk singer may or may not live the life he sings about. What matters to his listeners, who know better than to romanticize that life, is how well he sings. Recall that country music's most direct retorts to the counterculture—the hit singles "Okie From Muskogee" (1969) and "The Fightin' Side of Me" (1970)—came not from the Nashville establishment, but from Merle Haggard, ex-convict and self-described "White Man Singin' the Blues." In honky-tonk, confession is motivated by a God-given sense of sin, not an Art-given taste for self-immolation.

Of course, this sense of sin is exactly what rock critics find so reactionary—or, as Robert Christgau once said, "fascistic"—about country.[39] No longer the music of white Southerners alone, country nonetheless displays the old fundamentalist tendency to stand apart from the rest of American society, maintaining its own institutions and organizations, and effectively filtering out everything that doesn't fit its worldview. Hence the term "new traditionalist" for these younger performers. Along with reaffirming older sounds, some of them also reaffirm older values, such as family love and duty, the work ethic, the wages of sin, patriotism, even old-time religion.

Perhaps because I know the difference between social conservatism and fascism, I am not bothered by this extramusical reaffirmation. Nor am I bothered by country music's unapologetic embrace of commerce.[40] But I am troubled by its seeming racial exclusivity. To behold the lily-white complexion of this otherwise lively and diverse scene is to feel concern, either that black Americans no longer share the values being reaffirmed, or that racism is alive and well in Nashville.

To the first concern my response is that, if social-scientific survey data are to be believed, black Americans are more socially conservative than is commonly supposed.[41] Certainly there is a conservative side to the hip-hop and contemporary R&B self-renewal described above. There may even come a point at which these young musicians rediscover what their grandparents still remember: that, in the words of William Bell, "There's not much difference between country and western and r&b. Not when you really analyze it and break it down lyrically to what it is really saying."[42]

To the second concern my response must be tentative. I cannot assert that any part of the music industry, including the Nashville establishment, operates without white racism. But there is more than one kind of racism in popular music. Which is more degrading to black performers, country's apparent exclusiveness, or "gangsta" rap's increasingly sick primitivism? Moreover, it is not evident that the country audience rejects black performers out of hand. Beginning in 1965 the black country star Charley Pride sold more records than anyone on the RCA label, except Elvis Presley. It is also true that, despite the fondness for country music expressed by such legendary black artists as Charlie Parker and Ray Charles, the genre's pale complexion is partly an artifact of black attitudes.[43] In 1992 the aspiring black country singer Cleve Francis made an astute observation: "Maybe Nashville did discriminate against black singers, but in the black community, nobody encouraged you to sing country music—it's a two-way street."[44]

Of course, both Pride and Francis are musically conservative to the point of tedium. In this respect country audiences resemble rock audiences: They are more tolerant of musical freedom in white performers than in black. But here again the charge of racism is too easy, because the best country musicians use their eminence to reaffirm their Afro-American roots. And these reaffirmations, whether Nelson doing a TV special with Ray Charles or Randy Travis singing a duet with B.B. King, contain none of the leering primitivism found in the standard postpunk rock "tribute." This is because, despite the racial polarization that makes country lily white, places like Nashville, Austin, and Bakersfield provided a safe haven for many of the core values of the Afro-American musical tradition at a time when those values were under assault.

As any music lover knows, there is another city that qualifies as a haven, New Orleans. New Orleans is not socially conservative, to be sure. But it is musically conservative in the best sense, meaning that it conserves interconnectedness—not just across genres, but also between generations. Thus, the spirit of New Orleans presides over the musicians I call root doctors, whether or not they actually come from there. Growing up in the 1950s and 1960s, these people fell in love with Afro-American music and remained stubbornly loyal to it without being purist. Now in their forties or older, they are as seasoned, in their way, as the blues, R&B, gospel, and country figures they first admired. Their careers have been swamped, sometimes capsized, by the upheavals of their times. But the familiarity, in the 1990s, of names such as Van Morrison, the Neville Brothers, Dr. John, Bonnie Raitt, and Ry Cooder suggests that maybe they were doing something right all along.

The salient fact about the root doctors is that, unlike such rock icons as Jagger, they are not perceived as "old." They're not getting any younger, I'll admit. But their music is not perceived as "old" in the sense of being forced, stale, repetitious, or anachronistic. Instead, it occupies a special niche only slightly below that of Ray Charles, B. B. King, and Willie Nelson. Most listeners, young and old, understand that the root doctors have paid their dues.

The subject of interconnectedness returns us to the question raised earlier, about whether or not the gap between jazz and popular music ought to be closed. Like all popular musicians since Day One, the figures discussed in this chapter know how to satisfy the human craving for dance and song. Yet does that mean they have anything to teach today's superbly equipped jazz musicians? When Pleasants made his comment back in 1969, jazz was immersed in "the benign lunacy of the avant-garde," and its link with popular music was tenuous indeed. Today the finest jazz musicians, avant-garde as well as neoclassicist, have tremendous respect for the great entertainer-artists of the past: Armstrong, Ellington, Basie. Indeed, Wynton Marsalis frequently seeks to conjure their spirits, urging worshipful audiences to loosen up and act more like the folks in Fargo, North Dakota. "Don't just sit there," he exhorts, "tap your toes, clap your hands, get happy." In the same vein Marsalis and his peers—notably Blanchard and Harrison—acknowledge the importance of song, working long and hard to restore to their playing the "singing" or "vocal" qualities that distinguished the great swing-era soloists.

Yet the neoclassicists still share certain attitudes inherited from bebop. Marsalis does his exhorting from the stage at Lincoln Center, not the bandstand in the Rainbow Room. For these heirs of Birdland and Minton's, it is hard not to see a dance floor as a paddock for musical philistines. Likewise, the neoclassicists will occasionally accompany a virtuoso vocalist like Betty Carter. But in general, they don't take kindly to sharing the spotlight with a singer. One suspects that this is because they still retain the bebop conviction that instrumental music takes priority, and that the best singers are those who use their voices "like a horn."[45]

It takes an old-timer like Pleasants to remind us that this priority is backward:

> The art of the jazz musician, in my view, is an instrumental extension and sublimation of a musical idiom that, in its melodic, if not its rhythmic, characteristics, is fundamentally vocal. . . . Louis Armstrong is often said to sing the way he plays, but it would be more accurate, I think, to say that he plays the way he sings. . . . It is evidence of the jazz musician's instinctive feeling for his music as a sublimation of song that Lester Young, one of the most eloquent of saxophonists, could say that before improvising on any song, he first memorized the words.[46]

Mention Lester Young, of course, and the name Billie Holiday comes to mind. Find us a Holiday, the neoclassicists might say, and we'll gladly accompany her. The finest singers belong to the older generation: Tony Bennett, Carmen McCrae, Peggy Lee, Mel Tormé, Joe Williams. Even if the neoclassicists wanted to accompany younger singers capable of pleasing both the jazz and the popular audience, where would they look?

Not in contemporary R&B, where most gifted singers, such as Luther Vandross, end up pampered—and smothered—by all the twinkling glitz in the high-tech boutique. But not in the 1950s candy store, either. Despite the singular triumph of *Unforgettable*, Natalie Cole's tribute to her famous father, which combines top-notch singing with unsyrupy arrangements, the current revival of 1950s pop is not the answer. One need only heed the efforts of Linda Ronstadt, Barry Manilow, Carly Simon, Harry Connick, Jr., and (no kidding) Sinead O'Connor to recall the hard-won lesson of the 1950s: that lush orchestrated settings do not bring out the best in American popular singers. Certainly they do not develop vocal talent the way performing with jazz instrumentalists does.

Hence my focus on the new wave survivors, folkies, country outlaws, and root doctors discussed herein. As vocalists, none of these people possesses the bebop facility of a Carter, Fitzgerald, or Vaughan. But neither did the majority of singers who made their names with the big bands and small combos of the 1940s and 1950s. The finest performers discussed in this chapter possess the two qualities most essential to the Afro-American idiom: individuality of style, and depth of emotional expression. And they acquired those qualities the old-fashioned way: through years of performing for the same casual but discriminating audience that made jazz great in the first place. That is why they just might have something to teach the neoclassicists.

It is outlandish, I admit, to talk about narrowing the gap between today's revitalized jazz and the best popular music to have survived the rock era. But really, I'm seeking nothing more outlandish than John Hammond asking Tony Bennett to record a song by Hank Williams, Sr.; Dave Bartholomew adapting big band arrangements for Fats Domino; Horace Silver borrowing Cape Verdean rhythms for "Song for My Father"; or Sonny Rollins delivering a stunning rendition of "Tennessee Waltz." The most timely ideas are routinely resisted by the commercial powers that be, with their tidy categories and rigid marketing systems. But if commerce is the logjam, it is also the river. Break things up, I say, and let the fresh current flow.

Chapter 21

Coda: Escape from Postmodernism

he term *postmodernism* is superfluous, I have argued, because the tendencies it describes have been present since the dawn of modernism. Specifically, the postmodernist injunctions to break with the past, to attack aesthetic standards, to shock the audience, and to erase the line between art and life, are the essence of perverse modernism. We latch onto *postmodernism* because it seems to encompass an aspect of our situation that the older term *modernism* does not: the existence of a powerful and invasive popular culture, seemingly bent on undermining whatever artistic, social, and moral virtues we have left.

Yet here, too, postmodernism is simply updating what perverse modernism has been doing all along: commandeering the popular media in the hope of reaching the public with messages of radical transformation. Originally commandeered were the newspapers, the theater, the circus, and the cabaret; seized later were film, radio, advertising, and popular music. There is, of course, a difference between Marinetti placing his futurist manifesto on the front page of *Le Figaro* and MTV beaming Ice-T's latest "revenge fantasy" to millions of American teenagers. But there's also a connection, which the term *postmodernism* does nothing to illuminate.

The enemies of postmodernism see this commandeering as the crux of the matter. Indeed, they agree with the champions of postmodernism that, in essence, the term means the triumph of popular culture over high. Yet this notion makes sense only if we take "high" and "popular" to be opposites. The situation looks quite different if we make a logical distinction between popularity (as measured by commercial success) and artistic merit (as measured by critical and audience acclaim). Surely it is no longer possible to deny that certain works of popular culture, such as classic Hollywood films or jazz performances, excel by both measures. Yet our critical discourse continues to be ruled by two categories, the bad/popular and the good/unpopular. We know that two others exist: the bad/unpopular and the good/popular. But we don't readily admit them, because of our inherited conviction that commerce and the electronic media automatically debase art. In Martin Williams's memorable phrase, we cannot see what is "hidden in plain view."[1]

Recall that our antimedia bias arose in the visual arts, where the possibility of mass reproduction has long bred concern about the value and uniqueness of the original art object. The question is, How relevant is this concern outside the visual arts? In what other field is the original object so sacred? Not in literature, where, however precious and irreplaceable an author's manuscript, it is not wholly identified with the work. As long as a legible copy exists, the loss of a manuscript is not considered the loss of a work. The reasons for literature's decline are many and complex, and they include competition from movies and television. But reproducibility is not the issue, because since the 1830s, books have been just as reproducible as their electronic rivals.[2]

As for music, its reproducibility is more recent, developing in the 1920s with photography and film. Yet music has survived the transition most handily. Does anyone still take seriously Adorno's insistence on the degraded quality of recorded and broadcast music? His ignorance of the Afro-American idiom led him to explain its distinctive characteristics as a function of capitalism and the electronic media—a contrived argument that deserves no further attention. Still, Adorno was right about one thing: the fate of Afro-American music has been intertwined with that of commercialized recording and broadcasting. Indeed, like film, it came to artistic maturity within that environment.

And to be sure, it was also corrupted there. Commerce and the electronic media did not create perverse modernism and neoprimitivism, but they have certainly magnified, amplified, and popularized them. What remains to be seen is whether this is good news or bad news.

Some people derive comfort from the marginality of the worst offenders. Ice-T's loyal fans, for example, number in the hundreds of thousands, not millions. Were it not for his headline-grabbing antics, his obnoxiousness would remain a specialized taste. But the headline grabbing is exactly the point. Performers such as Ice-T and Madonna are not working in the medium of music, hoping to attract a critical mass of listeners who like what they're doing. They're working in the medium of publicity, testing the resistance of a public that generally dislikes what they're doing, but that can be forced to pay attention through the skillful application of sexual, sometimes violent, obscenity. I need not reiterate that being shocked by these applications does not make the average person either a prude or a philistine. Indeed, these performers are the true puritans, incapable of depicting sex as anything other than a soulless or sadistic transaction between strangers. And they're also philistines, flaunting their simpleminded notion of art as superior to all that has gone before.

Thus, the cult of obscenity and brutality described in this book *is* a mass phenomenon, whether or not Ice-T's records happen to go platinum. Yet, if Dr. Johnson was right in saying that art is best judged by the test of time—that is, by popularity gradually achieved over time—then perhaps there is a silver lining to this ominous cloud. Consider the following scenario: As obscenity and brutality cease to be the preoccupation of an elite, and become the steady diet of the public at large, they will be judged by a broader, more traditional standard. By entering the mainstream of American popular culture, this kind of art will face something it has never had to face before: a plebiscite, conducted over time, through the mechanism of the market. Naturally, one hesitates to place too much faith in the aesthetic judgment of the ordinary people who will cast the deciding votes. But better they than the elite, breathing nothing but the rarified ozone of Art. At least the public is apt to weigh the claims of art against those of civility, decency, and morality—exactly what the elite strives not to do.

But such judgments will founder in philistine censoriousness if they are not guided by a better understanding of what art can and cannot do. And such an understanding will not come about until we re-examine certain decrepit ideas bequeathed to us from modernism. It is ironic that, in this age of multiculturalism, so many people seem intent upon ignoring the fact that the West is the only civilization to have created a form of art whose sole purpose is to attack morality. Now, by "morality" I do not mean either sexual probity or the fancy dilemmas cooked up by teachers of "values clarification." I mean simply the difference between good and evil as understood by most human beings. As the philosopher Isaiah Berlin writes:

> The laws and principles to which we appeal, when we make moral and political decisions of a fundamental kind, have, unlike legal enactments, been accepted by the majority of men, during, at any rate, most of recorded history; we regard them as being incapable of being abrogated; we know of no court, no authority, which could, by means of some recognised process, allow men to bear false witness, or torture freely, or slaughter fellow men for pleasure; we cannot conceive of getting these universal principles or rules repealed or altered; in other words, we treat them not as something that we, or our forefathers, freely chose to adopt, but rather as presuppositions of being human at all, of living in a common world with others.[3]

Too often artistic modernism has sought just such a repeal of morality—in the name of the radical freedom needed to create a radical new culture (in both senses) without any of the old culture's imperfections. Here, too, the West is unique, because no other culture asks human beings to live without cultural continuity. Art is timeless when it touches aspects of human life that do not change. But modernism has dreamed of the most disruptive possible change, the greatest discontinuity between past, present, and future. It is no accident that this dream was conceived in the *fin-de-siècle* atmosphere of the late nineteenth century, and delivered, under the banner of "futurism," into the dawn of the twentieth. As we approach the end, not just of our century but of an entire millennium, it is bound to undergo a resurgence.

Yet here, too, there is a ray of hope. These are the 1990s, not the 1890s, and only a fool would stake the world's future on sudden, drastic social change. Only a fool would ignore the message coming from the survivors of the collapsing revolutionary regimes of the twentieth century, articulated here by Berlin:

> The search for perfection does seem to me a recipe for bloodshed, no better even if it is demanded by the sincerest of idealists, the purest of heart. No more rigorous moralist than Immanuel Kant ever lived, but even he said, in a moment of illumination, 'Out of the crooked timber of humanity no straight thing was ever made.'[4]

It is mostly in the arts that the dream of radical change still perpetuates its cruel hoax. To see through that hoax, we must reassess the position of art in our scale of values.

In a nutshell that position is both too high and too low. Art has been raised too high by the introverted-modernist tendency to put it on a quasi-religious pedestal, where its purely formal properties are credited with being able to enlighten and transform society. False gods invite blasphemy, and pomposity attracts ridicule—which is why art has also been brought too low, through the perverse-modernist tendency to knock down the pedestal, to erase the line between art and life, to reduce inspiration and creativity to spontaneous self-expression, and to sever the bonds of talent, craft and virtue that have always connected art with the rest of human life.

Those bonds are in bad shape partly because we think it is somehow philistine to connect the aesthetic and the moral. The legacy of Plato is to conflate the two, which has led historically to severe restrictions on art in the name of virtue: philosophical virtue, religious virtue, and more recently, politico-ideological virtue. Hence the late-romantic tendency to insist on a total separation between the aesthetic and the moral; and finally the modernist tendency to grant art the ultimate legitimacy and authority that were previously reserved for morality. This is the legacy of Nietzsche: art as radically autonomous, able to generate its own values and truths in total freedom.

Of course, Nietzsche distinguished between the genius, who created new truths out of a profound connection with nature, and the merely immoral type who used the concept of genius as a cloak for his lack of self-control—a distinction that, needless to say, has been forgotten. The result has been a gross oversimplification of discourse about art that again admits only two categories where four are possible. The two admitted are: the morally good/aesthetically bad, and the morally bad/aesthetically good. Obviously, the terms can be recombined two other ways: the morally bad/aesthetically bad, and the morally good/aesthetically good. But these we fail to admit, so persuaded are we that indifference or hostility to morality is both a necessary and a sufficient condition of the highest artistic merit.

The logic of the problem is really not all that complicated: We can admire the moral intention of a work that is aesthetically formulaic or bad, just as we can admire the skill and power of a work that is morally reprehensible. Ultimately, aesthetic judgments are blended from different ingredients, only one of which is moral. Yet, as I say, respect for morality is a necessary, if not sufficient, condition of the *highest* artistic achievement.

From the history of totalitarianism's attacks on modernism, cultural intellectuals derive their gut-level assumption that simple, vulgar, or formulaic works cannot possibly be morally virtuous; and that complex, refined, or original works cannot possibly foster evil. Intellectuals also associate public outrage at immoral content in art with philistinism. Yet the public is not always wrong, and when the work in question is neither complex, refined, nor original—merely morally offensive—the charge of philistinism is irrelevant. If this were clearer to our elites, then they would not so easily be persuaded that, just because a record by 2 Live Crew succeeds in shocking a philistine like Reverend Donald Wildmon, that doesn't automatically make it art.

The philosophical legacy we need to remember is that of Aristotle, who made more room for art than Plato, giving it freedom to make its own rules and even, at times, mock goodness and sympathize with evil. Yet, ultimately, Aristotle saw art's relation to good and evil as the same as that of all other human endeavors; he certainly did not give it the exclusive power to redefine, or re-create, good and evil. Plato's view has repeatedly asserted itself, but during the greatest periods of Western culture, Aristotle's has prevailed.

I am convinced that one of the attractions of multiculturalism, both for people whose backgrounds are not Western and for those whose are, is simply that most non-Western cultures do not conceive of art as above morality. Instead of lumping multiculturalism together with perverse modernism in all its arrogance and folly, we would do well to note that at least some multiculturalism contains a profoundly conservative element—a groping, however misguided, toward an older, and wiser, conception of art.

I say "misguided" because what multiculturalism tends to overlook is that our contemporary civilization has more to offer than a fruitless battle between too-high introverted modernism and too-low perverse modernism. It also has extroverted modernism, in which the elevation of good over evil is seen as a necessary, but not a sufficient, condition of greatness. It is precisely such a human aesthetic that informs the Afro-American idiom, with its peculiar history of having matured and blossomed in the modern world without being stricken by the perverse-modernist blight. It is stricken now, of course, and many people declare its time to be past. This declaration would be more convincing if there were something genuinely new on the horizon. But all I see is a repertory of postures and gestures that are more than a century old, and much the worse for the wear.

The music, by contrast, is a perennial. Its roots run deep and its bloom stays pungent, because it does not ignore, insult, or abuse its audience. It does not distrust its own vitality. It does not strive to purge itself of those musical elements that give pleasure to the untutored ear. It does not regard its own tradition as exhausted. It does not pursue the goal of innovation to enervating, self-destructive, or nihilistic extremes. It does not place the value of art above all other human values, only to tear it down again in a fit of "negative transcendence." Above all, it does not forget that its original purpose was to affirm the humanity of a people whose humanity was being denied.

Notes

Chapter 1. Introduction

1. Tipper Gore, *Raising PG Kids in an X-Rated Society* (Nashville, Tenn.: Abingdon Press, 1987), pp. 26–29.
2. Allan Bloom, *The Closing of the American Mind* (New York: Simon & Schuster, 1987), pp. 74–76.
3. See W. Jackson Bate, *Samuel Johnson* (New York: Harcourt Brace Jovanovich, 1977), p. 210.
4. Neil Postman, *Technopoly: The Surrender of Culture to Technology* (New York: Alfred A. Knopf, 1992).
5. Michele Wallace, "Invisibility Blues," in *Multi-Cultural Literacy*, Rick Simonson and Scott Walker, eds. (Saint Paul, Minn.: Graywolf Press, 1988), p. 170.
6. T. S. Eliot, "Notes Toward a Definition of Culture," in *Christianity and Culture* (New York: Harcourt Brace Jovanovich, 1968), p. 94.
7. Robert Warshow, *The Immediate Experience: Movies, Comics, Theatre, and Other Aspects of Popular Culture* (New York: Doubleday, 1962), p. 28.
8. Ibid., p. 29.
9. Henry Pleasants, *Serious Music—and All That Jazz!* (New York: Simon & Schuster, 1969), p. 25.
10. Bloom, *The Closing of the American Mind*, p. 73.
11. Quoted in Penelope Spheeris, director, *The Decline of Western Civilization, Part 2: The Metal Years* (documentary film), 1988.
12. Jacques Barzun, *The Use and Abuse of Art* (Princeton: Princeton University Press, 1974), p. 148.

Chapter 2. Why Music Is The Wild Card

1. Quoted in Christopher Headington, *History of Western Music* (New York: Schirmer, 1974), p. 311.
2. Henry Pleasants, *Serious Music—and All That Jazz!* (New York: Simon & Schuster, 1969), p. 43.
3. Ibid., p. 25.

4. Ibid., p. 43.
5. André Hodeir, *Jazz: Its Evolution and Essence* (New York: Grove Press, 1956; revised reprint, New York: Grove Press, 1980), p. 139.
6. Ibid., pp. 141, 142.
7. Pleasants, *Serious Music*, p. 45.
8. See Martin Williams, *The Jazz Tradition* (New York: Oxford University Press, 1987), p. 58.
9. See Henry Pleasants, *The Great American Popular Singers* (New York: Simon & Schuster, 1974), p. 29.
10. Headington, *History of Western Music*, p. 97.
11. Pleasants, *Serious Music*, p. 65.
12. Spoken by Groucho's character, Dr. Quackenbush, in Sam Wood, director, *A Day at the Races* (feature film), 1937.
13. Quoted in Neil Leonard, *Jazz: Myth and Religion* (New York: Oxford University Press, 1987), p. 179.
14. Williams, *The Jazz Tradition*, p. 7.
15. Gunther Schuller, *Early Jazz: Its Roots and Musical Development* (New York: Oxford University Press, 1968), p. 11.
16. Ibid., p. 8.
17. A. M. Jones, "African Music," quoted in Leonard B. Meyer, *Emotion and Meaning in Music* (Chicago: University of Chicago Press, 1990), p. 242.
18. Hodeir, *Jazz*, p. 197.
19. Schuller, *Early Jazz*, p. 8.
20. Eileen Southern, *The Music of Black Americans: A History* (New York: Norton, 1971), p. 51.
21. Albert Murray, *Stomping the Blues* (New York: McGraw-Hill, 1976), pp. 114–18.
22. Schuller, *Early Jazz*, pp. 56–57.
23. Quoted in Robert Jacobson, *Reverberations: Interviews with the World's Leading Musicians* (New York: William Morrow, 1974), p. 239.
24. Pleasants, *Serious Music*, p. 86.
25. Charles Keil, *Urban Blues* (Chicago: University of Chicago Press, 1966), p. 44.
26. See Albert Murray, *The Omni-Americans* (New York: Vintage, 1970).
27. Samuel Charters, *The Roots of the Blues* (New York: Perigee, 1981).
28. Ibid., p. 125.
29. John Collins, *Music Makers of West Africa* (Washington, D.C.: Three Continents, 1985), p. 1.
30. Keil, *Urban Blues*, p. 33.
31. Ralph Ellison, *Shadow and Act* (New York: Signet, 1966), p. 248.
32. Ibid., p. 246.
33. See Lawrence W. Levine, *Highbrow, Lowbrow: The Emergence of Cultural Hierarchy in America* (Cambridge: Harvard University Press, 1988).
34. LeRoi Jones, *Blues People* (New York: William Morrow, 1963), p. 84.
35. Southern, *The Music of Black Americans*, p. 104.
36. Ibid., p. 169.
37. Ibid., p. 170.

38. Robert Palmer, *Deep Blues* (New York: Penguin, 1981), p. 225.

39. Quoted in Lawrence W. Levine, *Black Culture and Black Consciousness* (New York: Oxford University Press, 1978), p. 194.

40. Southern, *The Music of Black Americans*, p. 269.

41. Ibid., p. 266.

42. Ibid., pp. 311ff.

43. Ibid., pp. 262, 341; chap. 12.

44. Ibid., p. 365.

45. Ibid., p. 357.

46. See James Lincoln Collier, *Louis Armstrong: A Biography* (London: Pan Books, 1985), p. 55.

47. Ibid., p. 100.

48. Thomas Mann, *Death in Venice and Seven Other Stories*, translated by M. T. Lowe-Porter (New York: Alfred A. Knopf, 1939; reprint, New York: Vintage, 1957), p. 201.

Chapter 3. The Three Strains of Modernism

1. Thomas Mann, *Death in Venice and Seven Other Stories*, translated by M. T. Lowe-Porter (New York: Alfred A. Knopf, 1939; reprint, New York: Vintage, 1957), pp. 207–208.

2. Ibid., pp. 209, 201.

3. Ibid., p. 208.

4. See Gerald Graff, *Literature Against Itself: Literary Ideas in a Modern Society* (Chicago: University of Chicago Press, 1979), chap. 2.

5. See W. Jackson Bate, *Samuel Johnson* (New York: Harcourt Brace Jovanovich, 1977).

6. M. H. Abrams, *The Mirror and the Lamp: Romantic Theory and Critical Tradition* (New York: Oxford University Press, 1971), p. 299.

7. Ibid., pp. 326–7.

8. Ibid., pp. 335, 327.

9. Edmund Wilson, *Axel's Castle: A Study In The Imaginative Literature of 1870–1930* (New York: Charles Scribner's Sons, 1969), p. 25.

10. Jacques Barzun, *The Use and Abuse of Art* (Princeton: Princeton University Press, 1975), p. 58.

11. Oscar Wilde, "The Critic as Artist, Part II," in Oscar Wilde, *Intentions* (London: The Unicorn Press, 1974), p. 131.

12. Barzun, *The Use and Abuse of Art*, pp. 138–9, 149.

13. Jacques Barzun, *Classic, Romantic, and Modern* (Chicago: University of Chicago Press, 1961), pp. 151–2.

14. See William Barrett, *Time of Need: Forms of Imagination in the Twentieth Century* (New York: Harper Torchbooks, 1973).

15. John Rewald, *Paul Cézanne: A Biography* (New York: Schocken Books, 1968), p. 200.

16. See Arnold Hauser, *The Social History of Art*, translated in collaboration with the author by Stanley Goodman (New York: Vintage, 1951), vol. 4.

17. Renato Poggioli, *The Theory of the Avant-Garde*, translated by Gerald Fitzgerald (Cambridge: Harvard University Press, 1982).
18. Quoted in Jane Kallir, catalog for Arnold Schoenberg's Vienna, Galerie St. Étienne, New York, November 13, 1984–January 5, 1985, p. 80.
19. Quoted in Joan Peyser, *The New Music: The Sense Behind the Sound* (New York: Delta Books, 1971), p. 67.
20. Wassily Kandinsky, "Reminiscences," in Robert L. Herbert, ed., *Modern Artists on Art*, (Englewood Cliffs, N.J.: Prentice-Hall, 1964), pp. 40–41.
21. Ibid., pp. 20–44.
22. Kasimir Malevich, "Suprematism," in Herbert, *Modern Artists*, p. 97.
23. Quoted in William Gaunt, *The Observer's Book of Modern Art* (London: Frederick Warne, 1968), pp. 55–56.
24. Arthur Schopenhauer, *The World as Will and Idea*, translated by R. B. Haldane and J. Kemp (London: Kegan Paul, Trench, Trübner & Co., 1896; reprint, New York: AMS Press, 1977), p. 232.
25. Paul Hindemith, *A Composer's World*, quoted in Christopher Headington, *History of Western Music* (New York: Schirmer Books, 1974), p. 315.
26. For a cogent discussion of this question, see Anthony Storr, *Music and the Mind* (New York: Free Press, 1992), chap. 3.
27. Quoted in Dona Mack, "Schoenberg and the Battles of Modern Music," *The New Criterion* 6:6 (February 1988), p. 19.
28. See Mack, "Schoenberg," p. 18.
29. Barbara Rose, *American Art Since 1900* (New York: Praeger, 1967), p. 235.
30. Kandinsky, "Reminiscences," p. 35.
31. Erwin Stein, quoted in Peyser, *The New Music*, p. 69.
32. Hilton Kramer, *The Revenge of the Philistines* (New York: Free Press, 1985), p. 150.
33. Samuel Lipman, "Redefining Culture and Democracy," *The New Criterion* 8:4 (December 1989), p. 17.
34. Henry Pleasants, *Serious Music—and All That Jazz* (New York: Simon and Schuster, 1969), p. 234.
35. Wilson, *Axel's Castle*, p. 275.
36. Ibid., p. 279; and Arthur Rimbaud, *A Season in Hell and the Drunken Boat*, translated by Louise Varèse (New York: New Directions, 1961), pp. xv–xx.
37. Arthur Rimbaud, quoted in Wilson, *Axel's Castle*, p. 280.
38. Filippo Tommaso Marinetti, "The Founding and Manifesto of Futurism," quoted in Caroline Tisdall and Angelo Bozzola, *Futurism* (New York: Oxford University Press, 1977), p. 9.
39. Barzun, *Classic, Romantic and Modern*, p. 154; and Poggioli, *Theory of the Avant-Garde*, pp. 61ff.
40. Luigi Russolo, "The Art of Noises," quoted in Tisdall and Bozzola, *Futurism*, p. 114.
41. Tisdall and Bozzola, *Futurism*, p. 115.
42. Ibid., p. 8.
43. Rimbaud, *A Season in Hell*, p. 49.
44. Tisdall and Bozzola, *Futurism*, pp. 91, 101–2.
45. See RoseLee Goldberg, *Performance Art: From Futurism to the Present* (New York: Harry N. Abrams, 1988), p. 38.

46. Ibid., p. 50.
47. Tisdall and Bozzola, *Futurism*, p. 115.
48. Lionel Trilling, quoted in Mark Krupnick, *Lionel Trilling and the Fate of Cultural Criticism* (Evanston, Ill.: Northwestern University Press, 1986), p. 110.
49. Kevin Mulcahy, "The Public Interest in Public Culture," *Journal of Arts Management, Law, and Society* 21:1 (Spring 1991), p. 21.
50. Martha Wilson, "What Shall We Do? Here's One Suggestion," *Wall Street Journal*, letter to the editor, Apr. 20, 1992.
51. *Miller v. California*, quoted in Donald Alexander Downs, *The New Politics of Pornography* (Chicago: University of Chicago Press, 1989), p. 17.
52. See Harry M. Clor, *Obscenity and Public Morality: Censorship in a Liberal Society* (Chicago: University of Chicago Press, 1985), pp. 212–14.
53. Ibid., pp. 231–32.
54. Ibid., p. 225.
55. Rimbaud, *A Season in Hell*, pp. 37–43.
56. Barzun, *The Use and Abuse of Art*, p. 57.
57. Quoted in Goldberg, *Performance Art*, pp. 50–52.
58. Carl E. Schorske, *Fin-de-Siècle Vienna: Politics and Culture* (New York: Vintage Books, 1981), p. 334.
59. Robert W. Corrigan, ed., *Masterpieces of the Modern German Theatre* (New York: Collier Books, 1967), p. 222.
60. Martin Green, *The Von Richthofen Sisters: The Triumphant and Tragic Modes of Love* (Albuquerque, N. Mex.: University of New Mexico Press, 1974), p. 54.
61. See Paul Delany, *The Neo-Pagans: Rupert Brooke and the Ordeal of Youth* (New York: Free Press, 1987), p. 114.
62. Green, *The Von Richthofen Sisters*, p. 47.
63. D. H. Lawrence, *Sex, Literature and Censorship*, edited by B. Harry T. Moore (New York: The Viking Press, Compass Books Edition, 1959), p. 69.
64. Stephen Spender, *The Struggle of the Modern* (Berkeley: University of California Press, 1965), pp. 50–51.
65. Georges Bataille, *Death and Sensuality* (New York: Ballantine Books, 1969), p. 12.
66. Ibid., p. 263.
67. Abrams, *The Mirror*, p. 327.
68. Spender, *The Struggle of the Modern*, pp. 79–80.
69. See Kramer, *The Revenge of the Philistines*, pp. 70–75.
70. Peyser, *The New Music*, pp. 86–90.
71. T. S. Eliot, "Tradition and the Individual Talent," in T. S. Eliot, *The Sacred Wood* (New York: University Paperbacks, 1966), p. 49.
72. Kramer, *The Revenge of the Philistines*, p. 81.
73. Quoted in Abrams, *The Mirror*, p. 328.
74. Kramer, *The Revenge of the Philistines*.
75. See Hauser, *The Social History of Art*, p. 176.
76. See Barzun, *Classic, Romantic, and Modern*, p. 117.
77. Christopher Green, *Cubism and Its Enemies* (New Haven: Yale University Press, 1988), p. 231.

78. Quoted in Hilton Kramer, "Modernism and Its Enemies," *The New Criterion* 4:7 (March 1986), p. 2.

79. S. Frederick Starr, *Red and Hot: The Fate of Jazz in the Soviet Union* (New York: Limelight, 1985), p. 31.

80. André Hodeir, *Jazz: Its Evolution and Essence* (New York: Grove Press, 1956; revised reprint, New York: Grove Press, 1980), pp. 261–2.

81. Quoted in Ibid., p. 249.

82. Hodeir, *Jazz*, p. 249.

83. Samuel Lipman, *Music After Modernism* (New York: Basic Books, 1979), p. 67.

84. Quoted in Headington, *History of Western Music*, p. 356.

85. Hodeir, *Jazz*, p. 263.

Chapter 4. The Obstacle of Race

1. Christopher Headington, *History of Western Music* (New York: Schirmer Books, 1974), p. 16.

2. Ibid., p. 20.

3. See Allan Bloom, "Interpretive Essay," in Plato, *The Republic of Plato*, translated by Allan Bloom (New York: Basic Books, 1968), p. xiii.

4. Headington, *History of Western Music*, p. 25.

5. Julius Portnoy, *The Philosopher and Music* (New York: Humanities Press, 1954), pp. 86–87, 107, 143–45.

6. Johann Wolfgang von Goethe, *The Sorrows of Young Werther*, translated by Victor Lange (1774; reprint, New York: Holt, Rinehart and Winston, 1968), p. 43.

7. Quoted in Headington, *History of Western Music*, p. 236.

8. Allan Bloom, *The Closing of the American Mind* (New York: Simon & Schuster, 1987), p. 73.

9. Ibid., p. 71.

10. See Edith Hamilton, *Mythology* (Boston: Little, Brown, 1940; reprint, New York: Mentor Books, 1962), pp. 57ff.

11. Carl E. Schorske, *Fin-de-Siècle Vienna: Politics and Culture* (New York: Vintage Books, 1981), p. 354.

12. Neil Leonard, *Jazz: Myth and Religion* (New York: Oxford University Press, 1987), p. 11.

13. Headington, *History of Western Music*, p. 356.

14. Eduard Hanslick, quoted in Norman Lebrecht, *Discord* (London: André Deutsch, 1982), p. 40.

15. Aaron Copland, *What to Listen for in Music* (New York: McGraw-Hill, 1957), pp. 247–48.

16. See Jane Addams Allen, "Post-Modernism and the Romantic Temper," *The World & I* (December 1988), p. 199.

17. See Anthony Storr, *Music and the Mind* (New York: Free Press, 1992), chaps. 2, 3.

18. Ezra Pound, *ABC of Reading* (1934; reprint, New York: New Directions Paperback, 1960), p. 61; and Arnold Schoenberg, quoted in Igor Stravinsky and Robert Craft, *Dialogues and A Diary* (Garden City, New York: Doubleday, 1963), p. 56.

19. For a notable exception, see Leonard Bernstein, *The Infinite Variety of Music* (New York: Simon & Schuster, 1966), pp. 49–64.

20. Leonard, *Jazz*, p. 11.
21. Quoted in Leonard, *Jazz*, p. 12.
22. Hermann Hesse, *Steppenwolf* (New York: Henry Holt, 1929; reprint, New York: Bantam Books, 1969), pp. 43, 141–42, 66.
23. André Hodeir, *Jazz: Its Evolution and Essence* (New York: Grove Press, 1956; revised reprint, New York: Grove Press, 1980), p. 31.
24. Quoted in Josef Skvorecky, *The Bass Saxophone* (New York: Alfred A. Knopf, 1979), p. 5.
25. Skvorecky, *The Bass Saxophone*, pp. 8–9.
26. Maxim Gorky, "On the Music of the Gross," quoted in S. Frederick Starr, *Red and Hot: The Fate of Jazz in the Soviet Union* (New York: Limelight, 1985), pp. 90–91.
27. *The Rite of Spring*, performed by the Joffrey Ballet on PBS, *Great Performances* Jan. 12, 1990.
28. Eugene D. Genovese, *Roll, Jordan, Roll: The World the Slaves Made* (New York: Pantheon Books, 1974), p. 458.
29. Arthur Rimbaud, *A Season in Hell and the Drunken Boat*, translated by Louise Varèse (New York: New Directions, 1961) p. 19.
30. Caroline Tisdall and Angelo Bozzola, *Futurism* (New York: Oxford University Press, 1977), pp. 11, 14.
31. Phyllis Rose, *Jazz Cleopatra: Josephine Baker in Her Time* (New York: Doubleday, 1989), p. 41.
32. Paul Wingert, *Primitive Art: Its Traditions and Styles* (New York: Meridian Books, 1965), pp. 371–72.
33. Ibid., p. 370.
34. Rose, *Jazz Cleopatra*, pp. 46–47.
35. Christopher Ralling, director, *Chasing a Rainbow: The Josephine Baker Story* (documentary film), 1986.
36. Rose, *Jazz Cleopatra*, p. 6.
37. Ibid., p. 31.
38. Nathan Huggins, *Harlem Renaissance* (New York: Oxford University Press, 1971), quoted in Jim Haskins, *The Cotton Club* (New York: New American Library, 1977), p. 39.
39. Lewis A. Erenberg, *Steppin' Out: New York Nightlife and the Transformation of American Culture, 1890–1930* (Westport, Conn.: Greenwood Press, 1981), p. 254.
40. Haskins, *The Cotton Club*.
41. Genovese, *Roll, Jordan, Roll*, pp. 428–29.
42. Albert J. Raboteau, *Slave Religion: The "Invisible Institution" in the Antebellum South* (New York: Oxford University Press, 1978), p. 66.
43. Benezeri Kisembo, Laurenti Magesa, and Aylward Shorter, *African Christian Marriage* (London: Geoffrey Chapman, 1977), p. 115.
44. Genovese, *Roll, Jordan, Roll*, p. 459.
45. Mary B. Chesnut, *Diary from Dixie*, quoted in ibid., p. 467.
46. Genovese, *Roll, Jordan, Roll*, pp. 423, 466.
47. Ibid., p. 462.
48. Calvin C. Hernton, *Sex and Racism in America* (New York: Grove Press, 1966).
49. Ibid., p. 113.

50. Toni Morrison, *The Bluest Eye* (New York: Holt, Rinehart and Winston, 1970; reprint, New York: Pocket Books, 1976), p. 117.
51. James Lincoln Collier, *Louis Armstrong: A Biography* (London: Pan Books, 1985), pp. 87–88.

Chapter 5. The Taint of Commerce

1. Jacques Barzun, *The Use and Abuse of Art* (Princeton: Princeton University Press, 1975), p. 63.
2. Ivan Narodny, "The Birth Processes of Ragtime," quoted in S. Frederick Starr, *Red and Hot: The Fate of Jazz in the Soviet Union* (New York: Limelight, 1985), pp. 34–35.
3. Starr, *Red and Hot*, p. 102.
4. Ibid., pp. 102–3.
5. Ibid., p. 97.
6. Ibid., p. 181.
7. Quoted in ibid., pp. 92–93, 99.
8. Samuel Lipman, address delivered at "Philanthropy and the Arts After Mapplethorpe: What Standards For Private Funders?", conference of the Philanthropic Roundtable, November 14, 1989, Washington, D.C.
9. Paul Connerton, "Introduction," in Paul Connerton, ed., *Critical Sociology* (New York: Penguin Books, 1976), pp. 24–25.
10. Martin Jay, *The Dialectical Imagination* (Boston: Little, Brown, 1973), p. 185.
11. Ibid., chap. 6.
12. Theodor Adorno, "On the Fetish Character in Music and the Regression of Listening," in Andrew Arato and Eike Gebhardt, eds., *The Essential Frankfurt School Reader* (New York: Continuum, 1990), p. 296.
13. Adorno, quoted in Jay, *The Dialectical Imagination*, p. 185.
14. Adorno, "On the Fetish Character," p. 292.
15. Clement Greenberg, "Avant-Garde and Kitsch," in *Art and Culture: Critical Essays* (Boston: Beacon Press, 1965), pp. 9, 11, 10.
16. Ibid., p. 15.
17. Ibid., p. 11.
18. Carl Dalhaus, *Between Romanticism and Modernism*, translated by Mary Whittall (Berkeley: University of California Press, 1989), p. 12.
19. See Hilton Kramer, "Clement Greenberg in the Forties," *The New Criterion* 5:5 (January 1987), pp. 1–6.
20. Dwight MacDonald, "Masscult & Midcult," in Dwight MacDonald, *Against the American Grain: Essays on the Effects of Mass Culture* (New York: Da Capo, 1983), p. 37.
21. For a vivid account of those criticisms, see Andrew Ross, *No Respect: Intellectuals and Popular Culture* (New York: Routledge, 1989), p. 48.
22. MacDonald, "Masscult & Midcult," passim.
23. Ibid., p. 7.
24. Ibid., pp. 19, 20, 28, 50.
25. Ibid., p. 73.
26. Ibid., p. 8.

27. David Riesman, Nathan Glazer, and Reuel Denney, *The Lonely Crowd* (New Haven: Yale University Press, 1966), p. 297ff.
28. Ibid., pp. 298–99.
29. MacDonald, "Masscult & Midcult," p. 54.
30. Ibid., pp. 29, 14.

Chapter 6. Cubists and Squares: Jazz as Modernism

1. Nat Hentoff, *Jazz Is* (New York: Limelight, 1984), p. 68.
2. Gary Giddins, *Satchmo* (New York: Doubleday, 1988), p. 2.
3. Ibid., p. 34.
4. Quoted in ibid., p. 32.
5. Quoted in Hentoff, *Jazz Is*, p. 68.
6. Quoted in Giddins, *Satchmo*, p. 33.
7. Quoted in Derek Jewell, *Duke* (London: Elm Tree Books, 1977), p. 140.
8. Gunther Schuller, *Early Jazz: Its Roots and Musical Development* (New York: Oxford University Press, 1986), pp. 55, 89, 103.
9. Ibid., p. 125.
10. Quoted in John A. Kouwenhoven, *The Arts in Modern American Civilization* (New York: Norton, 1967), p. 222.
11. Quoted in Hilton Kramer, "Stuart Davis at the Met," *The New Criterion*, 10:5 (January 1992), pp. 4–5.
12. Kramer, "Stuart Davis at the Met," pp. 5–7.
13. Quoted in ibid., p. 7.
14. Barbara Rose, *American Art Since 1900* (New York: Praeger, 1967), p. 141.
15. Ibid., p. 141.
16. Ralph Ellison, *Going to the Territory* (New York: Random House, 1986), pp. 219, 225.
17. Jacques Barzun, *Classic, Romantic, and Modern* (Chicago: University of Chicago Press, 1961), p. 152.
18. Philip Larkin, *All What Jazz: A Record Diary 1961–1971* (New York: Farrar, Straus & Giroux, 1985), pp. 62, 27.
19. Walter Benjamin, "The Work of Art in the Age of Mechanical Reproduction," in John Hanhardt, ed., *Video Culture: A Critical Investigation* (New York: Visual Studies Workshop Press, 1986), pp. 33, 43.
20. See Gerald Mast, *A Short History of the Movies* (Indianapolis: Pegasus, 1971), p. 189.
21. Benjamin, "The Work of Art," p. 39.
22. Theodor Adorno, "On the Fetish Character in Music and the Regression of Listening," in Andrew Arato and Eike Gebhardt, eds., The Essential Frankfurt School Reader (New York: Continuum, 1990), passim.
23. See interview with Milt Gabler in Ted Fox, *In the Groove* (New York: St. Martin's Press, 1986), p. 92.
24. Henry Pleasants, *The Great American Popular Singers* (New York: Simon & Schuster, 1974), p. 39.
25. Ibid., p. 26.
26. Albert Murray, *Stomping the Blues* (New York: McGraw-Hill, 1976), p. 131.

27. Billie Holiday and William Dufty, *Lady Sings the Blues* (New York: Penguin, 1984), pp. 10–11.
28. Ibid., p. 176.
29. Murray, *Stomping the Blues*, p. 126.
30. Quoted in James Lincoln Collier, *Louis Armstrong: A Biography* (London: Pan Books, 1985), p. 96.
31. See "Eighteenth-Century Newspapers: Slave Advertisements," in Eileen Southern, ed., *Readings in Black American Music* (New York: Norton, 1983), pp. 31–35.
32. See Louis Hartz, *The Founding of New Societies* (New York: Harcourt Brace & World, 1964).
33. Jacques Barzun, *The Use and Abuse of Art* (Princeton: Princeton University Press, 1975), p. 63.
34. Giddins, *Satchmo*, front matter.
35. See Ben Sidran, *Black Talk* (New York: Da Capo, 1986), chap. 4.
36. Gary Giddins, *Celebrating Bird: The Triumph of Charlie Parker* (New York: Beech Tree Books, 1987), p. 60.
37. Ibid., p. 66.
38. Robert George Reisner, *Bird: The Legend of Charlie Parker* (New York: Da Capo, 1987), p. 25.
39. Ted Joans, "I Love a Big Big Bird," quoted in ibid., p. 118.
40. Norman Mailer, *The White Negro* (San Francisco: City Lights Books, 1970), p. 4.
41. See Giddins, *Celebrating Bird*, passim.
42. Ralph Ellison, *Shadow and Act* (New York: Signet Books, 1966), p. 223.
43. Ibid., p. 220.
44. James Weldon Johnson, "The Dilemma of the Negro Author," *The American Mercury* XV:60 (December 1928), p. 477.
45. For a description of popular black attitudes toward bebop, see LeRoi Jones, *Blue People* (New York: William Morrow, 1963), p. 199.
46. Gary Giddins, *Rhythm-a-ning: Jazz Tradition and Innovation in the 80's* (New York: Oxford University Press, 1986), p. xii.
47. Henry Pleasants, *Serious Music—and All That Jazz!* (New York: Simon & Schuster, 1969), p. 52.
48. Neil Leonard, *Jazz: Myth and Religion* (New York: Oxford University Press, 1987), pp. 99–100.
49. Quoted in ibid., p. 100.
50. Ibid., pp. 96–97.
51. Martin Williams, *The Jazz Tradition* (New York: Oxford University Press, 1983), p. 253.
52. Sydney Smith, letter to the Countess of Carlisle, in Nowell C. Smith, ed., *The Letters of Sydney Smith*, vol ii (London: Oxford University Press, 1953), p. 847.

Chapter 7. The Strange Career of 1950s Rock 'n' Roll

1. Herbert London, *Closing the Circle: A Cultural History of the Rock Revolution* (Chicago: Nelson Hall, 1984), pp. 32–33.

2. Robert Palmer, "The 50's," *Rolling Stone*, 576 (April 19, 1990), p. 48.
3. See Charlie Gillett, *The Sound of the City: The Rise of Rock 'n' Roll* (New York: Pantheon, 1983), pp. 7–8.
4. Quoted in Donald Clarke, ed., *The Penguin Encyclopedia of Popular Music* (New York: Viking, 1989), p. 288.
5. See Nelson George, *The Death of Rhythm & Blues* (New York: Pantheon, 1988), p. 17.
6. Quoted in Ted Fox, *In the Groove* (New York: St. Martin's Press, 1986), pp. 39–40.
7. See interview with Jerry Wexler in ibid., p. 126.
8. Gillett, *The Sound of the City*; and (passim) Charles Keil, *Urban Blues* (Chicago: University of Chicago Press, 1975).
9. George, *The Death of Rhythm & Blues*, pp. 11–12.
10. Albert Goldman, *Elvis* (New York: McGraw-Hill, 1981), p. 104.
11. Ibid., p. 102.
12. See George T. Nierenberg, director, *That Rhythm, Those Blues* (documentary film), 1987.
13. Peter Guralnick, *Sweet Soul Music: Rhythm & Blues and the Southern Dream of Freedom* (New York: Harper & Row, 1986).
14. Gillett, *The Sound of the City*, p. 13.
15. Ibid., pp. 39–40.
16. Quoted in Arnold Passman, *The DeeJays* (New York: Macmillan, 1971), p. 203.
17. Carl Belz, *The Story of Rock* (New York: Harper Colophon Books, 1973), pp. 34–36.
18. Quoted in Gillett, *The Sound of the City*, p. 19.
19. Ed Ward, Geoffrey Stokes, and Ken Tucker, *Rock of Ages: The Rolling Stone History of Rock & Roll* (New York: Rolling Stone/Summit Books, 1986), p. 89.
20. Gary Giddins, *Riding on a Blue Note: Jazz and American Pop* (New York: Oxford University Press, 1982), p. 27.
21. See James Gilbert, *A Cycle of Outrage: America's Reaction to the Juvenile Delinquent in the 1950's* (New York: Oxford University Press, 1986), p. 185.
22. Ward, Stokes, and Tucker, *Rock of Ages*, pp. 106–7.
23. Mark Thomas McGee and R. J. Robertson, *The JD Films: Juvenile Delinquency in the Movies* (Jefferson, N.C.: McFarland, 1982), p. 25.
24. Bosley Crowther, review of *The Blackboard Jungle*, *Film Daily* (Mar. 4, 1955).
25. David Meeker, *Jazz in the Movies* (New York: Da Capo, 1981), entry W-3638.
26. McGee and Robertson, *The JD Films*, p. 32.
27. Gilbert, *A Cycle of Outrage*, 64.
28. Ibid., chap. 2, pp. 26–29.
29. Quoted in ibid., p. 40.
30. Gilbert, *A Cycle of Outrage*, pp. 114, 234.
31. See ibid.; and Robert Warshow, *The Immediate Experience: Movies, Comics, Theatre, and Other Aspects of Popular Culture* (New York: Doubleday, 1962).
32. Quoted in Henry Pleasants, *The Great American Popular Singers* (New York: Simon & Schuster, 1974), p. 273.
33. Goldman, *Elvis*, pp. 81, 129, chap. 5.
34. Ibid., p. 205.

35. Gilbert, *A Cycle of Outrage*, pp. 136–42.
36. See William L. O'Neill, *American High: The Years of Confidence* (New York: Free Press, 1986).
37. Quoted in Peter Guralnick, *Lost Highway: Journeys and Arrivals of American Musicians* (New York: Vintage, 1982), p. 332.
38. Quoted in Goldman, *Elvis*, pp. 219–20.
39. Quoted in Peter Guralnick, liner notes to Elvis Presley, *Elvis Presley: The Sun Sessions CD* (BMG/RCA 6414-2-R, 1987).
40. Guralnick, liner notes to *Elvis Presley: The Sun Sessions*.
41. Pleasants, *The Great American Popular Singers*, p. 276.
42. Jimmy Snow, quoted in Goldman, *Elvis*, p. 155.
43. Quoted in Pleasants, *The Great American Popular Singers*, p. 271.

Chapter 8. Rock 'n' Rollers or Holy Rollers?

1. Charles White, *The Life and Times of Little Richard* (New York: Harmony Books, 1984), p. 16.
2. See Acts 2, 4.31, 10.44–48, 11.15–17, 19.1–7; 1 Cor. 12–14; and Sydney E. Ahlstrom, *A Religious History of the American People* (New York: Image Books, 1975), vol. 2, p. 291.
3. See Ahlstrom, *A Religious History*, vol. 1, pp. 353–54, 50.
4. Quoted in Eileen Southern, *The Music of Black Americans: A History* (Chicago: University of Chicago Press, 1970), p. 99.
5. Southern, *The Music of Black Americans*, p. 99.
6. Quoted in ibid.
7. Ahlstrom, *A Religious History*, vol. 2, p. 294.
8. Ibid., p. 294.
9. Ibid., p. 167.
10. See Anthony Heilbut, *The Gospel Sound* (New York: Limelight, 1985), pp. 21–36.
11. See Nick Tosches, *Hellfire: The Jerry Lee Lewis Story* (New York: Dell, 1985), pp. 36–37; and Myra Lewis and Murray Silver, *Great Balls of Fire* (London: Virgin, 1982), p. 14.
12. Quoted in Tosches, *Hellfire*, p. 74.
13. Lewis and Silver, *Great Balls of Fire*, p. 32.
14. W. J. Cash, *The Mind of the South* (New York: Vintage Books, 1969), p. 56.
15. Quoted in Tosches, *Hellfire*, pp. 130–32.
16. Tosches, *Hellfire*, p. 141; and Lewis and Silver, *Great Balls of Fire*, p. 34.
17. Quoted in White, *Little Richard*, pp. 68–69.
18. White, *Little Richard*, pp. 80–11.
19. Quoted in ibid., p. 197.
20. See Parke Puterbaugh, interview with Little Richard in *Rolling Stone* 576 (Apr. 19, 1990); and Robert Gordon, "Little Richard Comes Home," *Musician* 146 (Dec. 1990), p. 126.
21. Quoted in White, *Little Richard*, p. 104.
22. See Larry Geller, Joel Spector, and Patricia Romenowski, *If I Can Dream: Elvis's Own Story* (New York: Avon, 1990), pp. 339–42.
23. See mocking tone in Goldman, *Elvis*, p. 369.

24. Geller, Spector, and Romenowski, *If I Can Dream*, p. 44.

25. Greil Marcus, *Mystery Train: Images of America in Rock 'n' Roll* (New York: E. P. Dutton, 1982), pp. 165–66, 15, 11–40.

26. Ibid., pp. 164, 155, 207, 179.

27. Ibid., p. 167.

28. Ibid., pp. 154, 285, 157–60.

29. Quoted in ibid., p. 287.

30. Marcus, *Mystery Train*, p. 288.

31. Jacques Barzun, *Classic, Romantic, and Modern* (Chicago: University of Chicago Press, 1961), p. 127.

32. William O'Neill, *American High: The Years of Confidence* (New York: Free Press, 1986), p. 46.

33. Marcus, *Mystery Train*, p. 18.

34. Cash, *Mind of the South*, p. 56.

35. See Michael Mason, ed., *The Country Music Book* (New York: Charles Scribner's Sons, 1985), pp. 23, 60; and Henry Pleasants, *The Great American Popular Singers* (New York: Simon & Schuster, 1974), pp. 238–39.

36. Calvin C. Hernton, *Sex and Racism in America* (New York: Grove Press, 1966), pp. 102–4.

37. Ibid., p. 103.

Chapter 9. Reaction and Revitalization

1. Quoted in Paul Montgomery, producer, *Rock 'n' Roll: The Early Days* (documentary film), PBS air date December 8, 1986.

2. See Ed Ward, Geoffrey Stokes, and Ken Tucker, *Rock of Ages: The Rolling Stone History of Rock & Roll* ((New York: Rolling Stone/Summit, 1986), p. 176.

3. Quoted in ibid., p. 105.

4. Quoted in Mike Jahn, *The Story of Rock from Elvis Presley to the Rolling Stones* (New York: Quadrangle, 1975), pp. 40–41.

5. Dwight MacDonald, "A Caste, a Culture, a Market," *The New Yorker* (Nov. 22, 1958).

6. Carl Belz, *The Story of Rock* (New York: Harper Colophon Books, 1973), pp. 112–14.

7. Donald Clarke, ed., *The Penguin Encyclopedia of Popular Music* (New York: Viking, 1989), p. 242.

8. Robert Palmer, "The Fifties," *Rolling Stone* 576 (Apr. 19, 1990), p. 48.

9. Jahn, *Rock from Elvis*, p. 82.

10. Herbert London, *Closing the Circle* (New York: Harper Colophon, 1973), p. 59.

11. Jahn, *Rock from Elvis*, p. 11.

12. See Ward, Stokes, and Tucker, *Rock of Ages*, pp. 209, 210.

13. Quoted in Chuck Berry, *Chuck Berry: The Autobiography* (New York: Harmony Books, 1987).

14. Charlie Gillett, *The Sound of the City: The Rise of Rock 'n' Roll* (New York: Pantheon, 1983), p. 80.

15. Quoted in Taylor Hackford, director, *Hail, Hail, Rock 'n' Roll* (documentary film), 1987.

16. Quoted in Peter Guralnick, *Feel Like Going Home: Portraits in Blues and Rock 'n' Roll* (New York: Perennial Library, 1989), p. 235.
17. Berry, *Chuck Berry*, p. 90.
18. Ibid., p. 89.
19. Quoted in *Hail, Hail, Rock 'n' Roll*.
20. Quoted in Richard Harrington, "Chuck Berry's Rock of Ages," *Washington Post*, Oct. 9, 1987, p. B9.
21. See Paul McCartney, producer, *Real Story of Buddy Holly* (documentary film), 1987.
22. Belz, *The Story of Rock*, p. 65; and Jahn, *Rock from Elvis Presley*, p. 33.
23. For an example of the latter, see the scorekeeping in Bill Wyman, *Stone Alone* (New York: New American Library, 1991).
24. Quoted in *Hail, Hail, Rock 'n' Roll*.
25. London, *Closing the Circle*, pp. 41, 45.
26. Berry, *Chuck Berry*, chap. 12.
27. Quoted in *Hail, Hail, Rock 'n' Roll*.
28. See Bill Flanagan, *Written in My Soul: Conversations with Rock's Great Songwriters* (Chicago: Contemporary, 1987), p. 78.
29. See Peter Herbst, *The Rolling Stone Interviews 1967–1980: The Classic Oral History of Rock and Roll* (New York: St. Martin's/Rolling Stone Press, 1981), p. 228.
30. Quoted in Clarke, *The Penguin Encyclopedia of Popular Music*, p. 258.
31. Quoted in *Hail, Hail, Rock 'n' Roll*. Actually, Berry is mistaken: Christian played with Goodman's band, not Dorsey's.
32. Charles Keil, *Urban Blues*, (Chicago: University of Chicago Press, 1970), p. 43.
33. See Nelson George, *Where Did Our Love Go?: The Rise and Fall of Motown* (New York: St. Martin's Press, 1985), chap. 1.
34. Ibid., p. 29.
35. Ibid., p. 59.
36. Quoted in ibid., pp. 87–91.
37. Andy Mackay, *Electronic Music: The Instruments, the Music, the Musicians* (Minneapolis: Control Data Publishing, 1981), p. 90.
38. George, *Where Did Our Love Go?*, p. 114.
39. Quoted in David Ritz, *Divided Soul: The Life of Marvin Gaye* (New York: Paper Jacks, 1986), p. 100.
40. Jahn, *Rock from Elvis*, p. 11.
41. George, *Where Did Our Love Go?*, p. 38.
42. Nelson George, *The Death of Rhythm & Blues* (New York: Pantheon, 1988), p. 70.
43. See Paul Oliver, "Gospel," in Paul Oliver, Max Harrison, and William Bolcom, *The New Grove Gospel, Blues and Jazz* (New York: Norton, 1986), pp. 204ff.
44. See Peter Guralnick, *Sweet Soul Music: Rhythm & Blues and the Southern Dream of Freedom* (New York: Harper and Row, 1986), p. 417.
45. See Anthony Heilbut, *The Gospel Sound* (New York: Limelight, 1985), pp. 48, 116, 206.
46. Henry Pleasants, *The Great American Popular Singers*, (New York: Simon & Schuster, 1974), p. 253.
47. Iain Chambers, *Urban Rhythms: Pop Music and Popular Culture* (New York: St. Martin's Press, 1985), p. 143.

48. Quoted in Herbst, *The Rolling Stone Interviews*, p. 262.
49. Quoted in ibid., p. 263.
50. For a trenchant discussion of this mystique as the product of both European and African influences, see Kwame Anthony Appiah, *In My Father's House: Africa in the Philosophy of Culture* (New York: Oxford University Press, 1992).
51. See Michael J. Budds, *Jazz in the Sixties: The Expansion of Musical Resources and Techniques* (Iowa City: University of Iowa Press, 1990), p. 10.
52. See Gillett, *The Sound of the City*, p. 202.
53. Quoted in Guralnick, *Sweet Soul Music*, p. 99.
54. See King Curtis, "Memphis Soul Stew," *Atlantic Rhythm & Blues 1947–1974*, vol. 6 (Atlantic 7 81298-1-F, 1985).
55. Gillett, *The Sound of the City*, p. 232.
56. Guralnick, *Sweet Soul Music*, p. 57.

Chapter 10. Another Country Heard From

1. See Ed Ward, Geoffrey Stokes, and Ken Tucker, *Rock of Ages: The Rolling Stone History of Rock & Roll* (New York: Rolling Stone/Summit, 1986), p. 272.
2. Ibid., p. 272; and Charlie Gillett, *The Sound of the City: The Rise of Rock 'n' Roll* (New York: Pantheon, 1983), pp. 283–84.
3. Gillett, *The Sound of the City*, p. 257.
4. Iain Chambers, *Urban Rhythms: Pop Music and Popular Culture* (New York: St. Martin's Press, 1985), pp. 47–48.
5. See Donald Clarke, ed., *The Penguin Encyclopedia of Popular Music* (New York: Viking, 1989), p. 1233.
6. Paul Oliver, *Blues Fell This Morning: Meaning in the Blues* (New York: Cambridge University Press, 1990), p. 3.
7. Robert Palmer, *Deep Blues* (New York: Penguin, 1981), p. 256.
8. Charles Keil, *Urban Blues* (Chicago: University of Chicago Press, 1966), p. 37.
9. Quoted in ibid., p. 37.
10. Palmer, *Deep Blues*, p. 257.
11. Quoted in ibid., p. 258.
12. Gillett, *The Sound of the City*, pp. 250–51.
13. Quoted in Clarke, *The Penguin Encyclopedia of Popular Music*, p. 840.
14. Gillett, *The Sound of the City*, pp. 251–53; see also Ithiel de Sola Pool, *Technologies of Freedom* (Cambridge: Belknap/Harvard University Press, 1983), pp. 109–12.
15. Gillett, *The Sound of the City*, p. 254.
16. Ibid., p. 255.
17. Simon Frith and Howard Horne, *Art into Pop* (New York: Methuen, 1987), p. 33.
18. Carol Anne Mahsun, *Pop Art and the Critics* (Ann Arbor, Mich.: U.M.I. Research Press, p. 1987), p. 5.
19. Frith and Horne, *Art into Pop*, pp. 71–73.
20. Quoted in Theodore Forstmann, "American Document: The Indispensable Entrepreneur," *American Spectator* 24:2 (February 1991), pp. 26–27.
21. See Irwin Stambler, *The Encyclopedia of Pop, Rock and Soul* (New York: St. Martin's Press, 1974), p. 474.

22. Chambers, *Urban Rhythms*, pp. 45–46.
23. See John Lennon and Jann Wenner, *Lennon Remembers: The Rolling Stone Interviews* (New York: Popular Books, 1971), p. 184; and Ed Ward, Geoffrey Stokes, and Ken Tucker, *Rock of Ages: The Rolling Stone History of Rock & Roll* (New York: Rolling Stone/Summit, 1986), p. 263.
24. Quoted in Stambler, *Pop, Rock and Soul*, 1974 ed., p. 211.
25. Gillett, *The Sound of the City*, p. 265.
26. Quoted in Clarke, *The Penguin Encyclopedia of Popular Music*, p. 85.
27. Clarke, *The Penguin Encyclopedia of Popular Music*, p. 840.
28. Mike Jahn, *The Story of Rock From Elvis Presley to the Rolling Stones* (New York: Quadrangle, 1975), p. 141.
29. Ward, Stokes, and Tucker, *Rock of Ages*, p. 263.
30. Frith and Horne, *Art into Pop*, pp. 80–81.
31. See Chambers, *Urban Rhythms*, p. 65; and Anthony Heilbut, *The Gospel Sound* (New York: Limelight, 1985), pp. 146, 155.
32. Gillett, *The Sound of the City*, p. 263.
33. Lennon and Wenner, *Lennon Remembers*, p. 72.
34. Jahn, *Rock from Elvis*, p. 140.
35. Quoted in ibid., p. 40.
36. See Lennon and Wenner, *Lennon Remembers*, p. 184.
37. Quoted in Nelson George, *Where Did Our Love Go?: The Rise and Fall of Motown* (New York: St. Martin's, 1985), pp. 121, 123.
38. Hilton Kramer. *The Revenge of the Philistines* (New York: Free Press, 1985), pp. 5–11.
39. Ibid., p. 6.
40. Lennon and Wenner, *Lennon Remembers*, p. 12.
41. Quoted in Jahn, *Rock from Elvis*, pp. 135, 141.
42. Chuck Berry, *Chuck Berry: The Autobiography* (New York: Harmony Books, 1987), p. 150.
43. Richard Poirier, "Learning from the Beatles," *Partisan Review* 34:4 (1967).
44. See Paul Gambaccini, interview with Paul McCartney in Peter Herbst, ed., *The Rolling Stone Interviews 1967–1980: The Classic Oral History of Rock and Roll* (New York: St. Martin's/Rolling Stone, 1981), p. 306.
45. Gillett, *The Sound of the City*, p. 266.
46. Ibid., p. 266.
47. Quoted in Bill Flanagan, *Written in My Soul: Conversations with Rock's Great Songwriters* (Chicago: Contemporary, 1987), p. 19.

Chapter 11. Blues, Blacks, and Brits

1. Quoted in Gerri Hirshey, *Nowhere to Run: The Story of Soul Music* (New York: Penguin Books, 1985), p. 52.
2. Charlie Gillett, *The Sound of the City: The Rise of Rock 'n' Roll* (New York: Pantheon, 1983), p. 233.
3. Quoted in Charles Shaar Murray, *Crosstown Traffic: Jimi Hendrix and the Rock 'n' Roll Revolution* (New York: St. Martin's Press, 1989), p. 164.

4. Gillett, *The Sound of the City*, p. 237.

5. Quoted in Peter Guralnick, *Sweet Soul Music: Rhythm & Blues and the Southern Dream of Freedom* (New York: Harper and Row, 1986), p. 332.

6. Quoted in Ted Fox, *In the Groove* (New York: St. Martin's, 1986), p. 14.

7. Quoted in Guralnick, *Sweet Soul Music*, p. 340.

8. Quoted in Hirshey, *Nowhere to Run*, pp. 243–44.

9. Fox, *In the Groove*, p. 140.

10. Henry Pleasants, *The Great American Popular Singers* (New York: Simon & Schuster, 1974), pp. 328–32.

11. Ibid., pp. 328–32.

12. Ibid., p. 328.

13. Ray Charles and David Ritz, *Brother Ray: Ray Charles' Own Story* (New York: Dial, 1978), p. 239.

14. Ibid., p. 242.

15. Hirshey, *Nowhere to Run*, p. 312.

16. Philip Norman, *Symphony for the Devil: The Rolling Stones Story* (New York: Linden Press/Simon & Schuster, 1984), p. 77.

17. Simon Frith and Howard Horne, *Art into Pop* (New York: Methuen, 1987), p. 80.

18. Ibid., p. 81.

19. Norman, *Symphony for the Devil*, p. 90.

20. Ibid., p. 96.

21. Quoted in Ed Ward, Geoffrey Stokes, and Ken Tucker, *Rock of Ages: The Rolling Stone History of Rock & Roll* (New York: Rolling Stone/Summit, 1986), p. 283.

22. Quoted in Donald Clarke, ed., *The Penguin Encyclopedia of Popular Music* (New York: Viking, 1989), p. 1217.

23. Quoted in Ward, Stokes, and Tucker, *Rock of Ages*, p. 283.

24. See Paul Oliver, "Blues," in Paul Oliver, Max Harrison, and William Bolcom, *The New Grove Gospel, Blues and Jazz* (New York: Morrow, 1989), p. 43.

25. See, for example, Tony Scherman, "The Hellhound's Trail: Following Robert Johnson," *Musician* 147 (January 1991).

26. Johnny Shines, quoted in Peter Guralnick, *Searching for Robert Johnson* (New York: Dutton, 1992), p. 22.

27. Robert Palmer, *Deep Blues* (New York: Penguin, 1981), p. 177.

28. Quoted in Lawrence W. Levine, *Black Culture and Black Consciousness* (New York: Oxford University Press, 1978), p. 26.

29. Quoted in Pleasants, *Great American Popular Singers*, p. 199.

30. Paul Oliver, *Blues Fell This Morning: Meaning in the Blues* (New York: Cambridge University Press, 1990), p. 255.

31. Albert Murray, *Stomping the Blues* (New York: McGraw-Hill, 1976), pp. 38–42.

32. Robert Johnson, "Me and the Devil Blues," copyright King of Spades Music, 1990. Used by permission.

33. Ibid., "Last Fair Deal Gone Down." Used by permission.

34. Oliver, *Blues Fell This Morning*, passim.

35. Charles Keil, *Urban Blues* (Chicago: University of Chicago Press, 1966), p. 70.

36. Oliver, *Blues Fell This Morning*, p. 98.

37. Johnson, "Traveling Riverside Blues." Used by permission.

38. See Gillett, *The Sound of the City*, p. 172.

39. See Peter Guralnick, *Feel Like Going Home: Portraits in Blues and Rock 'n' Roll* (New York: Perennial Library, 1989), p. 85.

40. Charles S. Murray, *Crosstown Traffic*, p. 136.

41. Norman, *Symphony for the Devil*, p. 99.

42. Charles S. Murray, *Crosstown Traffic*, p. 136.

43. Quoted in Stanley Booth, *The True Adventures of the Rolling Stones* (New York: Vintage, 1985), p. 146.

44. Quoted in Guralnick, *Feel Like Going Home*, p. 85.

45. I am indebted to Al Basile for the comparison with Covay.

46. Charles S. Murray, *Crosstown Traffic*, 144.

47. Quoted in Palmer, *Deep Blues*, p. 260.

48. Norman, *Symphony for the Devil*, p. 113.

49. Iain Chambers, *Urban Rhythms: Pop Music and Popular Culture* (New York: St. Martin's, 1985), p. 56.

50. Chuck Berry, *Chuck Berry: The Autobiography* (New York: Harmony, 1987), pp. 97–98.

51. The Rolling Stones, *Our Own Story*, quoted in Frith and Horne, *Art into Pop*, p. 88.

52. Chambers, *Urban Rhythms*, p. 67.

53. Quoted in Norman, *Symphony for the Devil*, p. 59.

54. Norman, *Symphony for the Devil*, p. 93.

55. Quoted in ibid., p. 88.

56. Norman, *Symphony for the Devil*, pp. 120–21.

57. Ibid., p. 351.

58. Quoted in ibid., p. 91.

59. Mike Jahn, *The Story of Rock From Elvis Presley to the Rolling Stones* (New York: Quadrangle, 1975), p. 146.

60. James Brown and Bruce Tucker, *James Brown: The Godfather of Soul* (New York: Macmillan, 1986), p. 166.

61. Quoted in Booth, *Rolling Stones*, p. 192.

62. Booth, *Rolling Stone*, p. 11.

63. Ibid., pp. 176–179.

64. Norman, *Symphony for the Devil*, p. 317.

65. See Tina Turner and Kurt Loder, *I, Tina: My Life Story* (New York: Avon, 1986), chs. 4, 9.

66. Ibid., p. 49.

67. Quoted in Peter Herbst, ed., *The Rolling Stone Interviews 1967–1980: The Classic Oral History of Rock and Roll* (New York: St. Martin's/Rolling Stone, 1981), p. 28.

68. Norman, *Symphony for the Devil*, p. 351.

Chapter 12. Words and Music: The Rise of the Counterculture

1. See Nathan Glazer, *Remembering the Answers: Essays on the American Student Revolt* (New York: Basic Books, 1970), pp. 195–96.

2. Paul Goodman, *Growing Up Absurd* (New York: Vintage, 1960).

3. Morris Dickstein, *Gates of Eden: American Culture in the Sixties* (New York: Basic Books/Harper Colophon, 1977), pp. 78.

4. Ibid., p. 81.
5. Ibid., pp. 70–71.
6. Norman Podhoretz, *Breaking Ranks: A Political Memoir* (New York: Harper and Row, 1979), p. 45.
7. Dickstein, *Gates of Eden*, p. 70.
8. Allan Bloom, *The Closing of the American Mind* (New York: Simon & Schuster, 1987), p. 223.
9. Ibid., p. 149.
10. Walter Kaufmann, *Nietzsche: Philosopher, Psychologist, Antichrist*, 4th ed. (Princeton: Princeton University Press, 1974).
11. Quoted in Mark Krupnick, *Lionel Trilling and the Fate of Cultural Criticism* (Evanston, Ill: Northwestern University Press, 1986), pp. 144–45.
12. Lionel Trilling, "On the Teaching of Modern Literature," in *Beyond Culture* (New York: Harcourt Brace Jovanovich, 1978), p. 23.
13. Ibid., pp. 26–27.
14. Quoted in Krupnick, *Lionel Trilling*, p. 145.
15. Ibid., p. 145.
16. Dickstein, *Gates of Eden*, pp. 254–55.
17. Arthur M. Schlesinger, Jr., *The Crisis of Confidence* (New York: Bantam Books, 1969), pp. 167, 153, 173, 178.
18. The authors mentioned are those on Trilling's syllabus. See Trilling, "Modern Literature," pp. 13–23.
19. Schlesinger, *Crisis of Confidence*, p. 178.
20. Dickstein, *Gates of Eden*, pp. 189–90.
21. Quoted in Podhoretz, *Breaking Ranks*, p. 276.
22. See Ibid., pp. 276–82, 295–304.
23. Krupnick, *Lionel Trilling*, pp. 187–88.
24. Donald Clarke, ed., *The Penguin Encyclopedia of Popular Music* (New York: Viking, 1989), p. 497.
25. Quoted in ibid., p. 1047.
26. Clarke, *Encyclopedia of Popular Music*, p. 659.
27. Ibid., p. 909; and Mike Jahn, *The Story of Rock from Elvis Presley to the Rolling Stones* (New York: Quadrangle, 1975), pp. 93–96.
28. Jahn, *Rock from Elvis*, p. 96.
29. Ibid., pp. 106–7.
30. Quoted in ibid., pp. 107, 106.
31. Quoted in Ted Fox, *In the Groove* (New York: St. Martin's, 1986), p. 15.
32. Charlie Gillett, *The Sound of the City: The Rise of Rock 'n' Roll* (New York: Pantheon, 1983), p. 301.
33. Ibid., p. 338.
34. Clarke, *Encyclopedia of Popular Music*, p. 1048; and Jahn, *Rock from Elvis*, p. 161.
35. Clarke, *Encyclopedia of Popular Music*, p. 1048.
36. Quote in Bill Flanagan, *Written in My Soul: Conversations with Rock's Great Songwriters* (Chicago: Contemporary, 1987), p. 89.
37. Dickstein, *Gates of Eden*, p. 194.
38. Ed Ward, Geoffrey Stokes, and Ken Tucker, *Rock of Ages: The Rolling Stone History of Rock & Roll* (New York: Rolling Stone/Summit, 1986), p. 306.

39. Gillett, *The Sound of the City*, p. 301.
40. John Clellan Holmes, quoted in Jahn, *Rock from Elvis*, p. 194.
41. Dickstein, *Gates of Eden*, p. 196.
42. Quoted in Peter Herbst, ed., *The Rolling Stone Interviews 1967–1980: The Classic Oral History of Rock and Roll* (New York: St. Martin's/Rolling Stone, 1981), p. 84.
43. Quoted in Nat Hentoff, liner notes to Bob Dylan, *The Freewheelin' Bob Dylan* (Columbia CS 8786, CL 1986, 1963).

Chapter 13. Art and Religion, 1960s Style

1. See Andy Mackay, *Electronic Music: The Instruments, the Music, the Musicians* (Minneapolis: Central Data Publishing, 1981), p. 32.
2. Ibid., p. 32.
3. Philip Norman, *Symphony for the Devil: The Rolling Stones Story* (New York: Linden Press/Simon & Schuster, 1984), p. 248.
4. See Charles Shaar Murray, *Crosstown Traffic: Jimi Hendrix and the Rock 'n' Roll Revolution* (New York: St. Martin's, 1989), p. 209.
5. Quoted in Jon Wiener, *Come Together: John Lennon in His Time* (New York: Random House, 1984), p. 38.
6. Bob Merlis, interview Aug. 2, 1987.
7. See Ed Ward, Geoffrey Stokes, and Ken Tucker, *Rock of Ages: The Rolling Stone History of Rock & Roll* (New York: Rolling Stone/Summit, 1986), pp. 404, 480; and Charlie Gillett, *The Sound of the City: The Rise of Rock 'n' Roll* (New York: Pantheon, 1983), p. 397.
8. Gillett, *The Sound of the City*, p. 397.
9. See Ward, Stokes, and Tucker, *Rock of Ages*, p. 482; and Donald Clarke, ed., *The Penguin Encyclopedia of Popular Music* (New York: Viking, 1989), passim.
10. John Rockwell, *All American Music: Composition in the Late 20th Century* (New York: Alfred A. Knopf, 1983), p. 234.
11. Murray, *Crosstown Traffic*, p. 183.
12. Mackay, *Electronic Music*, p. 58.
13. Quoted in Irwin Stambler, *The Encyclopedia of Pop, Rock and Soul*, 1977 ed., (New York: St. Martin's), p. 400.
14. Stambler, *Pop, Rock, and Soul*, p. 519.
15. Quoted in ibid., p. 519; see also Edwin Wilson, "The Who's *Tommy*," *Wall Street Journal*, Apr. 27, 1993. Wilson was one of the few reviewers to note that the 1993 Broadway revival of *Tommy* was less a musical improvement than an MTV-style visual orgy.
16. See Gillett, *The Sound of the City*, pp. 277–78.
17. See Paul Goodman, *The New Reformation* (New York: Random House, 1970).
18. Morris Dickstein, *Gates of Eden: American Culture in the Sixties* (New York: Basic Books/Harper Colophon, 1977), p. 19.
19. Arthur M. Schlesinger, Jr., *The Crisis of Confidence* (New York: Bantam Books, 1969), p. 174.
20. See Michael J. Budds, *Jazz in the Sixties: The Expansion of Musical Resources and Techniques* (Iowa City: University of Iowa Press, 1990), p. 52.
21. See Rockwell, *All American Music*, p. 111.

22. Quoted in Clarke, *The Penguin Encyclopedia of Popular Music*, p. 467.
23. See Mackay, *Electronic Music*, p. 107.
24. Quoted in ibid., p. 107.
25. See Rockwell, *All American Music*, p. 110.
26. Clarke, *The Penguin Encyclopedia of Popular Music*, p. 1055.
27. See Ward, Stokes, and Tucker, *Rock of Ages*, p. 332.
28. See Clarke, *The Penguin Encyclopedia of Popular Music*, p. 487; and Fred Good-man, "The Grateful Dead," *Rolling Stone* 585 (Aug. 23, 1990), pp. 21ff.
29. See Stambler, *Pop, Rock and Soul*, 1977 ed., p. 270.
30. Gillett, *The Sound of the City*, p. 357.
31. See Ward, Stokes, and Tucker, *Rock of Ages*, p. 330.
32. Anthony Heilbut, *The Gospel Sound* (New York: Limelight, 1985), pp. 297–98.
33. Quoted in Peter Guralnick, *Sweet Soul Music: Rhythm & Blues and the Southern Dream of Freedom* (New York: Harper and Row, 1986), p. 46.
34. Gillett, *The Sound of the City*, p. 221.
35. Charles S. Murray, *Crosstown Traffic*, pp. 174–75.
36. See Sly and the Family Stone, *Stand!* (Epic 26346, 1969).
37. See Gillett, *The Sound of the City*, pp. 358–59.
38. See The Temptations, *The Temptations Anthology* (Motown M782A3, 1973). The attitude that good lyrics cannot sell is summed up by folkies Peter, Paul & Mary in their parody song, "I Dig Rock 'n' Roll Music," *Album 1700* (Warner Brothers 1700, 1967).
39. David Ritz, *Divided Soul: The Life of Marvin Gaye* (New York: Paper Jacks, 1986), pp. 152–53.
40. Ibid., p. 157.
41. See Nelson George, *Where Did Our Love Go?: The Rise and Fall of Motown* (New York: St. Martin's, 1985), p. 177.
42. Ibid, p. 178.
43. See Budds, *Jazz in the Sixties*, pp. 135–36.
44. Nat Hentoff, *Jazz Is* (New York: Limelight, 1984), p. 206.
45. Heilbut, *Gospel Sound*, pp. xiv–xv.
46. Greil Marcus, *Mystery Train: Images of America in Rock 'n' Roll* (New York: Dutton, 1982), p. 83.
47. Ritz, *Divided Soul*, p. 348.
48. Quoted in David Henderson, *'Scuse Me While I Kiss the Sky: The Life of Jimi Hendrix* (Toronto: Bantam Books, 1983), p. 277.
49. See Schlesinger, *Crisis in Confidence*, pp. 174–77.
50. See Steven M. Tipton, *Getting Saved from the Sixties* (Berkeley: University of California Press, 1982).
51. See Edward Shils, "Totalitarians and Antinomians," in John H. Bunzel, ed., *Political Passages: Journeys of Change Through Two Decades, 1968–1988* (New York: Free Press, 1988), pp. 1–31.
52. Quoted in Henderson, *'Scuse Me*, p. 44, 242.
53. Charles S. Murray, *Crosstown Traffic*, pp. 40–42, 43.
54. See Henderson, *'Scuse Me*, p. 91; and Gary Carey, *Lenny, Janis and Jimi* (New York: Pocket Books, 1975), p. 240.

55. Quoted in Henderson, *'Scuse Me*, p. 246.
56. Quoted in Carey, *Lenny, Janis and Jimi*, pp. 245–47.
57. Mackay, *Electronic Music*, p. 56.
58. Quoted in Henderson, *'Scuse Me*, pp. 190–91.
59. Charles S. Murray, *Crosstown Traffic*, p. 195.
60. Quoted in Joan Peyser, *The New Music: The Sense Behind the Sound* (New York: Delta, 1971), p. xi.
61. Charles S. Murray, *Crosstown Traffic*, p. 151.
62. See Henderson, *'Scuse Me*, p. 76.
63. Quoted in Carey, *Lenny, Janis and Jimi*, p. 288.
64. Henderson, *'Scuse Me*, p. 268.
65. Charles S. Murray, *Crosstown Traffic*, pp. 199–201.
66. Henderson, *'Scuse Me*, p. 370.
67. Quoted in Charles S. Murray, *Crosstown Traffic*, p. 161.
68. Carey, *Lenny, Janis and Jimi*, p. 295, 297–98.
69. See Jerry Hopkins and Danny Sugarman, *No One Gets Out of Here Alive* (New York: Warner Books, 1980), p. 188.
70. Jac Holzman, "Memories of Morrison," *Spin* 7:1 (April 1991), p. 72.
71. See Carey, *Lenny, Janis and Jimi*, pp. 118–19.
72. Hopkins and Sugarman, *No One*, pp. 321–23.
73. Ibid., chap. 1.
74. Ibid., p. 18.
75. See Pat H. Broeske, "A Rebel's Verse," *Los Angeles Times*, Mar. 10, 1991, pp. E1, E11; and Tom Baker, "Morrison," *Spin* 6:5 (Aug. 1990), p. 30.
76. Friedrich Nietzsche, *The Gay Science*, quoted in Walter Kaufmann, *Nietzsche: Philosopher, Psychologist, Antichrist*, 4th ed. (Princeton: Princeton University Press, 1974), pp. 420–21.
77. See Hopkins and Sugarman, *No One*, p. 96.
78. I am indebted to Michael S. Joyce for this point.
79. Ralph Ellison, *Shadow and Act* (New York: Signet, 1966), p. 223.
80. Quoted in Henderson, *'Scuse Me*, p. 373.
81. Lester Bangs, *Psychotic Reactions and Carburetor Dung*, Greil Marcus, ed. (New York: Alfred A. Knopf, 1987), p. 172.

Chapter 14. Hard Rock Becomes a Hard Place

1. Gary Carey, *Lenny, Janis and Jimi* (New York: Pocket Books, 1975), cover copy.
2. Quoted in Irwin Stambler, *The Encylopedia of Pop, Rock and Soul*, 1977 ed. (New York: St. Martin's), p. 279.
3. Carey, *Lenny, Janis and Jimi*, p. 144.
4. See Chris Albertson, *Bessie* (New York: Stein and Day, 1985), pp. 234–35.
5. See Henry Pleasants, *The Great American Popular Singers* (New York: Simon & Schuster, 1974), pp. 74–75.
6. I am indebted to Ruth Pillsbury for suggesting the comparison with Smith.
7. Pleasants, *The Great American Popular Singers*, p. 308.
8. See Charles Shaar Murray, *Crosstown Traffic: Jimi Hendrix and the Rock 'n' Roll Revolution* (New York: St. Martin's, 1989), p. 90.

9. David Dalton, *Piece of My Heart: The Life, Times, and Legend of Janis Joplin* (New York: St. Martin's, 1985), pp. 35, 38.

10. Quoted in Ortiz M. Walton, *Music: Black, White, and Blue* (New York: Morrow, 1972), p. 122.

11. David Henderson, *'Scuse Me While I Kiss the Sky: The Life of Jimi Hendrix* (Toronto: Bantam, 1983), p. 133.

12. Ed Ward, Geoffrey Stokes, and Ken Tucker, *Rock of Ages: The Rolling Stone History of Rock & Roll* (New York: Rolling Stone/Summit, 1986), p. 396.

13. Donald Clarke, ed., *The Penguin Encyclopedia of Popular Music* (New York: Viking, 1989), p. 297.

14. Ward, Stokes, and Tucker, *Rock of Ages*, p. 397.

15. Clarke, *The Penguin Encyclopedia of Popular Music*, p. 997.

16. Jon Pareles, "Heavy Metal, Weighty Words," *New York Times Magazine*, July 10, 1988, p. 26.

17. Quoted in Penelope Spheeris, director, *The Decline of Western Civilization, Part 2: The Metal Years* (film documentary), 1988.

18. Charlie Gillett, *The Sound of the City: The Rise of Rock 'n' Roll* (New York: Pantheon, 1983), pp. 396–97.

19. George Trow, quoted in Peter Guralnick, *Sweet Soul Music: Rhythm & Blues and the Southern Dream of Freedom* (New York: Harper and Row, 1986), p. 71.

20. Pareles, "Heavy Metal, Weighty Words," p. 47.

21. Stephen Davis, *Hammer of the Gods: The Led Zeppelin Saga* (New York: Ballantine, 1985), p. 116.

22. Tipper Gore, *Raising PG Kids in an X-Rated Society* (Nashville: Abingdon Press, 1987), pp. 50–51.

23. Quoted in Henderson, *'Scuse Me*, p. 373.

24. Quoted in Peter Herbst, ed., *The Rolling Stone Interviews 1967–1980: The Classic Oral History of Rock and Roll* (New York: St. Martin's/Rolling Stone, 1981), p. 35.

25. Quoted in Carey, *Lenny, Janis and Jimi*, p. 250.

26. See Michael Shore, *The Rolling Stone Book of Rock Video* (New York: Quill/Rolling Stone, 1984), pp. 29–33.

27. See Bowie's early performance style in D. A. Pennebaker, director, *Ziggy Stardust and the Spiders From Mars* (film documentary), 1982.

28. Quoted in Stambler, *Pop, Rock, and Soul*, 1977 ed., p. 57.

29. Clarke, *The Penguin Encyclopedia of Popular Music*, p. 112.

30. Sol Stern, quoted in Philip Norman, *Symphony for the Devil: The Rolling Stones Story* (New York: Linden/Simon & Schuster, 1984), p. 328.

31. See Norman, *Symphony for the Devil*, pp. 325–39; and Stanley Booth, *The True Adventures of the Rolling Stones* (New York: Vintage, 1985), pp. 488–525.

32. Norman, *Symphony for the Devil*, p. 326.

33. Ibid., pp. 268–69.

34. See Davis, *Hammer of the Gods*, pp. 106–7, 154.

35. Ibid., pp. 119–22, 120.

36. Quoted in Booth, *The Rolling Stones*, p. 525.

37. Georgia (Jo) Bergman, interview, Jan. 13, 1993.

38. G. G. Coulton, *The Medieval Panorama*, quoted in Eugene Genovese, *Roll, Jor-*

dan, Roll: The World the Slaves Made (New York: Pantheon, 1974), p. 721.

39. See Genovese, *Roll, Jordan, Roll*, pp. 209–32.

40. Paul Oliver, *Blues Fell This Morning: Meaning in the Blues* (New York: Cambridge University Press, 1990), p. 123.

41. See Lawrence W. Levine, *Black Culture and Black Consciousness* (New York: Oxford University Press, 1978), p. 57; and Genovese, *Roll, Jordan, Roll*, pp. 218–19.

42. Levine, *Black Culture and Black Consciousness*, p. 40, 403.

43. Quoted in Billy Dwight, *Monsters of Metal: Mötley Crüe* (New York: Ballantine Books, 1986), p. 35.

44. Charles S. Murray, *Crosstown Traffic*, p. 60.

45. See Gore, *Raising PG Kids*, pp. 451–52, 94.

46. See ibid., p. 94; and David Mandelman, "The Devil and Sam Kineson," *Rolling Stone* 543 (Feb. 23, 1989), pp. 24ff.

47. Quoted in Toby Goldstein, *Monsters of Metal: Twisted Sister* (New York: Ballantine, 1986), p. 122.

48. Davis, *Hammer of the Gods*, p. 63.

49. See Mikal Gilmore, "Heavy Metal Thunder," *Rolling Stone* 608–609 (July 11 and 25, 1991), pp. 52–53.

50. Charles S. Murray, *Crosstown Traffic*, pp. 59–60.

51. Bergman interview.

52. Iain Chambers, *Urban Rhythms: Pop Music and Popular Culture* (New York: St. Martin's, 1985), pp. 113–14.

53. Roy Hollingsworth, quoted in Davis, *Hammer of the Gods*, p. 175.

54. Goldstein, *Twisted Sister*, p. 42.

55. Quoted in Dennis Hunt, "Three New Heroes in the Hard Rock Parade," *Los Angeles Times*, Nov. 12, 1989, pp. 65–66.

56. See Davis, *Hammer of the Gods*, pp. 302–3.

57. Clarke, *The Penguin Encyclopedia of Popular Music*, p. 831.

58. Robert Hilburn, "Rockers on an Anti-Drug 'Stairway,'" *Los Angeles Times*, Dec. 23, 1989, pp. F1–F2.

59. Quoted in Richard Harrington, "W.A.S.P. Lewd and Clear," *Washington Post*, Feb. 8, 1987, pp. F1–F3.

60. Quoted in Robert Hilburn, "A New Just Say No Mötley Crüe," *Los Angeles Times*, Feb. 13, 1990, pp. F1–F2.

61. Quoted in Harrington, "Lewd and Clear"; see also Gore, *Raising PG Kids*, p. 52.

62. See Edward Donnerstein, Daniel Linz, and Steven Penrod, *The Question of Pornography: Research Findings and Policy Implications* (New York: Free Press, 1987).

63. For reservations expressed by social scientists themselves, see Donnerstein, *The Question of Pornography*, chap. 1; Donald Alexander Downs, *The New Politics of Pornography* (Chicago: University of Chicago Press, 1989), pp. 23–24, 169–75; and James Q. Wilson, "Violence, Pornography, and Social Science," *Public Interest* 22 (Winter 1971), pp. 45–61.

64. Danny Goldberg, interview, September 1987.

65. Quoted in Matt Neufeld, "Outrageous? Just '3 Dimensional,'" *Washington*

Times, June 25, 1991, Life section.

66. Quoted in Joan Peyser, *The New Music: The Sense Behind the Sound* (New York: Delta, 1971), p. 104.

67. Lionel Trilling, "From the Notebooks of Lionel Trilling," selected by Christopher Zinn, *Partisan Review* 54:1 (January 1987), p. 17.

68. Quoted in Dennis Hunt, "Hot Heavy Metal Dad," *Los Angeles Times*, Dec. 20, 1987, p. 74.

69. Quoted in Christopher Phillips, "To Be Whole Again," *Parade Magazine*, Aug. 11, 1991, pp. 11–12.

70. Gilmore, "Heavy Metal Thunder," p. 52.

71. Pareles, "Heavy Metal, Weighty Words," p. 47.

72. See Spheeris, *Decline of Western Civilization, Part 2*; Janet Maslin, "The Personal Side of Heavy Metal," *New York Times*, June 17, 1988; and David Wharton, "Heavy Going," *Los Angeles Times*, Aug. 9, 1987, pp. 1, 4.

Chapter 15. Soul Loses Its Soul

1. See Iain Chambers, *Urban Rhythms: Pop Music and Popular Culture* (New York: St. Martin's, 1985), pp. 144–50.

2. See Donald Clarke, ed., *The Penguin Encyclopedia of Popular Music* (New York: Viking, 1989), p. 1098; and Peter Guralnick, *Sweet Soul Music: Rhythm & Blues and the Southern Dream of Freedom* (New York: Harper and Row, 1986), p. 355.

3. Guralnick, *Sweet Soul Music*, pp. 357–59.

4. Quoted in Frederic Dannen, *Hit Men: Power Brokers and Fast Money Inside the Music Business* (New York: Vintage Books, 1991), p. 65.

5. See Nelson George, *The Death of Rhythm & Blues* (New York: Pantheon, 1988), pp. 135–38.

6. Dannen, *Hit Men*, pp. 87–88.

7. Both quoted in Guralnick, *Sweet Soul Music*, p. 355.

8. George, *Death of Rhythm & Blues*, pp. 111–14.

9. Guralnick, *Sweet Soul Music*, p. 383.

10. Quoted in ibid., p. 384.

11. George, *Death of Rhythm & Blues*, p. 115.

12. See Nelson George, *Where Did Our Love Go?: The Rise and Fall of Motown* (New York: St. Martin's, 1985); and George, *Death of Rhythm & Blues*, pp. 142–46.

13. George, *Death of Rhythm & Blues*, p. 200.

14. Quoted in Guralnick, *Sweet Soul Music*, p. 245.

15. George, *Death of Rhythm & Blues*, pp. 115, 114.

16. Dannen, *Hit Men*, pp. 87–88, 105–6.

17. George, *Death of Rhythm & Blues*, p. 140.

18. Quoted in Guralnick, *Sweet Soul Music*, p. 369.

19. Quoted in Gerri Hirshey, *Nowhere to Run: The Story of Soul Music* (New York: Penguin, 1985), p. 355.

20. See David Ritz, *Divided Soul: The Life of Marvin Gaye* (New York: Paper Jacks, 1986), p. 151.

21. Lester Bangs, *Psychotic Reactions and Carburetor Dung*, Greil Marcus, ed. (New York: Alfred A. Knopf, 1987), p. 153.

22. Ritz, *Divided Soul*, p. 80.
23. Marvin Gaye, liner notes to Marvin Gaye, *Let's Get It On* (Motown 5192, 1973).
24. Ritz, *Divided Soul*, pp. 226–27.
25. Ibid., p. 258.
26. Quoted in Robert Mugge, director, *The Gospel According to Al Green* (film documentary), 1988.
27. Quoted in Kristie McKenna, "Al Green: The Prince of Love," *Los Angeles Times*, July 30, 1989, pp. 61, 66.
28. See James Brown and Bruce Tucker, *James Brown: The Godfather of Soul* (New York: Macmillan, 1986), pp. 196, 278, and chap. 34.
29. Ibid., p. 202.
30. David Levering Lewis, quoted in Guralnick, *Sweet Soul Music*, p. 240.
31. LeRoi Jones, "The Changing Same (R&B and New Black Music)," in *The Black Aesthetic*, Addison Gayle, Jr., ed. (New York: Anchor Books, 1972), p. 118.
32. Guralnick, *Sweet Soul Music*, p. 240.
33. Brown and Tucker, *James Brown*, p. 267.
34. See Clarke, *The Penguin Encyclopedia of Popular Music*, p. 444.
35. Brown and Tucker, *James Brown*, p. 158.
36. Quoted in George, *Where Did Our Love Go?*, p. 177.
37. Guralnick, *Sweet Soul Music*, pp. 232–233.
38. Quoted in Ed Ward, Geoffrey Stokes, and Ken Tucker, *Rock of Ages: The Rolling Stone History of Rock & Roll* (New York: Rolling Stone/Summit, 1986), p. 533.
39. Ibid., p. 534.
40. Brown and Tucker, *James Brown*, p. 252.
41. Quoted in Jim Greer, "Free at Last," *Spin* 7:3 (June 1991), p. 52.
42. See Charles Shaar Murray, *Crosstown Traffic: Jimi Hendrix and the Rock'n'Roll Revolution* (New York: St. Martin's, 1989), p. 180.
43. See Radcliffe A. Joe, *The Business of Disco* (New York: Billboard Books, 1980), pp. 12–15.
44. Ibid., pp. 20–21, 30–31.
45. Brown and Tucker, *James Brown*, pp. 242–43.
46. Ward, Stokes, and Tucker, *Rock of Ages*, p. 530.
47. Bernard Holland, "What is Truth? Ask a Recording Crew," *New York Times*, Nov. 27, 1988, p. 29.
48. Quoted in Ted Fox, *In the Groove* (New York: St. Martin's 1986), p. 334.
49. Ibid.
50. George, *Death of Rhythm & Blues*, p. 154.
51. See Stambler, *The Encyclopedia of Pop, Rock and Soul*, 1989 ed., p. 387.
52. David Toop, *Rap Attack: African Jive to New York Hip Hop* (Boston: South End Press, 1984), p. 130.
53. See Dannen, *Hit Men*, chap. 9.
54. See Steve Perry, "Ain't No Mountain High Enough: The Politics of Crossover," in Simon Frith, ed., *Facing the Music: A Pantheon Guide to Popular Culture* (New York: Pantheon, 1988), p. 53.
55. For reservations about this life-style even before AIDS, see Stanley Crouch, "Gay Pride, Gay Prejudice," in *Notes of a Hanging Judge: Essays and Reviews 1979–1989* (New York: Oxford University Press, 1990), pp. 113–28.

56. Joe, *Business of Disco*, p. 77.

57. See Ward, Stokes, and Tucker, *Rock of Ages*, p. 532.

58. Joe, *Business of Disco*, pp. 185, 161.

59. Peter Watrous, "Look Out New Jack, The Love Man's Back," *New York Times*, May 5, 1991, Arts & Leisure section; see also Geoffrey Himes, "Vandross: Romancing the Soul," *Washington Post*, Sept. 28, 1988, p. C7.

60. André Hodeir, *Jazz: Its Evolution and Essence*, Rev. ed. (New York: Grove, 1980), p. 197.

61. Harold Childs, interview, August 1987.

Chapter 16. *Their Art Belongs to Dada*

1. RoseLee Goldberg, *Performance Art: From Futurism to the Present* (New York: Harry N. Abrams, 1988), p. 144.

2. See ibid., p. 149. For a contemporary version of the same stunt, see "Rear-Action Avant-Garde," *Harper's* 286:1716 (May 1993), pp. 23–24.

3. Susan Sontag, "Happenings: An Art of Radical Juxtaposition," in Susan Sontag, *Against Interpretation* (New York: Dell, 1969), p. 274.

4. Goldberg, *Performance Art*, pp. 129–38.

5. See Caroline Tisdall and Angelo Bozzola, *Futurism* (New York: Oxford University Press, 1977), p. 11.

6. See Alan W. Watts, *The Way of Zen* (New York: Vintage Giant, 1957), passim.

7. Filippo Tomasso Marinetti, quoted in Tisdall and Bozzola, *Futurism*, p. 89.

8. Sontag, "Happenings," pp. 275–76.

9. Goldberg, *Performance Art*, pp. 133–34.

10. Sontag, "Happenings," pp. 267–68.

11. See Charlie Gillett, *The Sound of the City: The Rise of Rock'n'Roll* (New York: Pantheon, 1983), pp. 306–9.

12. Irwin Stambler, *The Encyclopedia of Pop, Rock and Soul*, 1989 ed. (New York: St. Martin's), p. 716.

13. Quoted in Lester Bangs, *Psychotic Reactions and Carburetor Dung*, Greil Marcus, ed. (New York: Alfred A. Knopf, 1987), p. 159.

14. See John Rockwell, *All American Music: Composition in the Late 20th Century* (New York: Alfred A. Knopf, 1983), p. 235.

15. Gillett, *The Sound of the City*, p. 309.

16. Karen Schoemer, "The Legacy of the Velvets: Rock'n'Roll as Pop Art," *New York Times*, Dec. 3, 1989, Arts & Leisure section.

17. See Jack Anderson, "Baker Zaps Rocker Critical of His Wife," *Washington Post*, Feb. 6, 1992, p. B11.

18. "The New Rock," quoted in Stambler, *Pop, Rock and Soul*, 1989 ed., p. 763.

19. Quoted in Donald Clarke, ed., *The Penguin Encyclopedia of Popular Music* (New York: Viking, 1989), p. 1277.

20. Iain Chambers, *Urban Rhythms: Pop Music and Popular Culture* (New York: St. Martin's, 1985), p. 95.

21. Frank Zappa, *Hot Rats* (Capitol D4-74211, 1969).

22. See Zappa, "Tengo Na Minchia Tanta," *Uncle Meat* (1969, Rykodisc 10064.65 reissue, 1987).

23. Jon Wiener, *Come Together: John Lennon and His Time* (New York: Random House, 1984), p. 165.

24. Quoted in Tipper Gore, *Raising PG Kids in an X-Rated Society* (Nashville: Abingdon Press, 1987), p. 25.

25. Dave Marsh, *The Heart of Rock and Soul: The 1001 Greatest Singles Ever Made* (New York: New American Library, 1989), p. 588.

26. Anderson, "Baker Zaps Rocker."

27. Quoted in Matt Resnicoff, "Poetic Justice: Frank Zappa Puts Us in Our Place," *Musician* 157 (Nov. 1991), p. 70.

28. Goldberg, *Performance Art*, p. 145.

29. Wiener, *Come Together*, pp. 30–31.

30. Quoted in ibid., p. 129.

31. Wiener, *Come Together*, pp. 84–85, 105.

32. Quoted in ibid., p. 105.

33. See this performance in D. A. Pennebaker, director, *Sweet Toronto* (film documentary), 1971.

34. Quoted in Peter Herbst, ed., *The Rolling Stone Interviews 1967–1980: The Classic Oral History of Rock and Roll* (New York: St. Martin's/Rolling Stone, 1981), p. 133.

35. Bangs, *Psychotic Reactions*, p. 303.

36. Quoted in Stambler, *Pop, Rock and Soul*, 1989 ed., p. 145.

37. See Marsh, *The Heart of Rock and Soul*, pp. 157–58.

38. Ed Ward, Geoffrey Stokes, and Ken Tucker, *Rock of Ages: The Rolling Stone History of Rock & Roll* (New York: Rolling Stone/Summit, 1986), p. 550.

39. Quoted in Stambler, *Pop, Rock and Soul*, 1989 ed., pp. 532–33.

40. Mike Jahn, *The Story of Rock from Elvis Presley to the Rolling Stones* (New York: Quadrangle, 1975), pp. 274–75.

41. Jim Sullivan, "An Intense Iggy, Madcap Mondays Rock Through the Night," *Boston Globe*, Apr. 18, 1991, Arts section.

42. Goldberg, *Performance Art*, p. 164.

43. Ibid., pp. 164–65.

44. Bangs, *Psychotic Reactions*, p. 38.

45. Marsh, *The Heart of Rock and Soul*, p. 593.

46. Bangs, *Psychotic Reactions*, p. 195.

47. I am indebted to Isaac Green for this observation.

48. Quoted in Bangs, *Psychotic Reactions*, p. 191.

49. Roman Kozak, *This Ain't No Disco: The Story of CBGB* (Boston: Faber & Faber, 1988), chap. 1.

50. Quoted in Stambler, *Pop, Rock and Soul*, 1989 ed., p. 719.

51. Quoted in ibid., p. 288.

52. On Smith's hard rock phase, see Rockwell, *All American Music*, p. 236.

53. Robert Hilburn, "Patti Smith is Back—With New Priorities," *Los Angeles Times*, July 24, 1988, p. 60.

54. See Tom Carson, "Patti Smith Dream On," *Village Voice*, Aug. 9, 1988, pp. 67, 70.

55. See Kozak, *This Ain't No Disco*, p. 65.

56. Bangs, *Psychotic Reactions*, pp. 277–78.

57. Quoted in ibid., p. 279.

58. Bangs, *Psychotic Reactions*, p. 278.
59. Quoted in Stambler, *Pop, Rock and Soul*, 1989 ed., p. 551.
60. Ibid.
61. Ward, Stokes, and Tucker, *Rock of Ages*, p. 554.
62. For an example of this approach, see Penelope Spheeris, director, *The Decline of Western Civilization* (film documentary), 1981.
63. Theodor W. Adorno, "On the Fetish Character in Music and the Regression of Listening," in Andrew Arato and Eike Gebhardt, eds., *The Essential Frankfurt School Reader* (New York: Continuum, 1990), p. 292.
64. For an example of such undeserved praise, see Simon Frith and Howard Horne, *Art into Pop* (New York: Methuen, 1987), p. 124.
65. Quoted in Kozak, *This Ain't No Disco*, p. 15.

Chapter 17. Punk: The Great Avant-Garde Swindle

1. See "Impresario: Malcolm McLaren and the British New Wave," 1988, Paul Taylor (guest curator), New Museum of Contemporary Art, New York, Sept. 16, Nov. 20, pp. 72–73.
2. Quoted in ibid., p. 12.
3. "Impresario," pp. 18, 20.
4. See Greil Marcus, *Lipstick Traces: A Secret History of the 20th Century* (Cambridge: Harvard University Press, 1989); and Jon Savage, *England's Dreaming: Anarchy, Sex Pistols, Punk Rock, and Beyond* (New York: St. Martin's, 1991), p. 473.
5. See Bob Geldof, *Is That It?: The Autobiography* (New York: Ballantine, 1986), p. 143.
6. For Savage's concession on this point, see *England's Dreaming*, p. 196.
7. Quoted in "Impresario," p. 37.
8. Savage, *England's Dreaming*, pp. 210, 64.
9. Susan ("Siouxsie") Jane Dallon, quoted in ibid., p. 241.
10. Savage, *England's Dreaming*, pp. 86–88.
11. Quoted in ibid., p. 92.
12. Savage, *England's Dreaming*, p. 71.
13. Ibid., p. 62.
14. Ibid., pp. 98, 120–21.
15. Simon Frith and Howard Horne, *Art into Pop* (New York: Methuen, 1987), p. 127.
16. Savage, *England's Dreaming*, pp. 240, 347.
17. Frith and Horne, *Art into Pop*, p. 124.
18. Savage, *England's Dreaming*, p. 100.
19. Ibid., pp. 102, 158.
20. Quoted in "Impresario," p. 37.
21. See Savage, *England's Dreaming*, pp. 101, 189, and (quote from Jane ["Suck"] Jackman) 331.
22. Ibid., pp. 47–48.
23. Ibid., p. 167.
24. John Ingham, quoted in ibid., p. 167.
25. Savage, *England's Dreaming*, p. 168.

26. Jane Withers, in "Impresario," pp. 39–40.

27. Geldof, *Is That It?*, p. 145.

28. Savage, *England's Dreaming*, p. 194.

29. Geldof, *Is That It?*, pp. 140–41.

30. Ibid.

31. Quoted in Savage, *England's Dreaming*, p. 513.

32. Jello Biafra, quoted in Peter Belsito, ed., *Notes From the Pop Underground* (Berkeley, Calif.: Last Gasp, 1985), p. 117.

33. See Savage, *England's Dreaming*, pp. 473–89. By the early 1990s, this distinction had evolved into "punk" (meaning protest oriented) vs. "hard-core" (meaning nihilistic). I am indebted to Isaac Green for this observation.

34. See Jon Pareles, "Heavy Metal, Weighty Words," *New York Times Magazine*, July 10, 1988.

35. Robert Palmer, "Dark Metal: Not Just Smash and Thrash," *New York Times*, Nov. 4, 1990, Arts & Leisure section, p. 31.

36. See Morris Dickstein, *Gates of Eden: American Culture in the Sixties* (New York: Basic Books/Harper Colophon, 1977), pp. 23–24.

37. William S. Burroughs, "Rock Magic," quoted in Stephen Davis, *Hammer of the Gods: The Led Zeppelin Saga* (New York: Ballantine, 1985), pp. 267–68.

38. Quoted in Mikal Gilmore, "Heavy Metal Thunder," *Rolling Stone* 608–609 (July 11 and 25, 1991), p. 124.

39. Quoted in Gilmore, "Heavy Metal Thunder," p. 124.

40. Steven Blush, "Grindcore," *Spin* 7:3 (June 1991).

41. Justin Broadrick, quoted in ibid., p. 36.

42. Quoted in Jon Pareles, "Nirvana, the Band That Hates to Be Loved," *New York Times*, Nov. 14, 1993, p. 32.

43. Eric Bentley, *In Search of Theater* (New York: Vintage Books, 1954), pp. 62–63.

44. Eamon Dunfy, *Unforgettable Fire: Past, Present, and Future—The Definitive Biography of U2* (New York: Warner, 1987), pp. 276, 277–78.

45. Ibid., p. 244.

46. See Thomas Day, *Why Catholics Can't Sing: The Culture of Catholicism and the Triumph of Bad Taste* (New York: Crossroads, 1990). Passim.

47. Quoted in Bill Flanagan, *Written in My Soul: Conversations with Rock's Greatest Songwriters* (Chicago: Contemporary, 1987), p. 448.

48. Quoted in Robert Hilburn, "From Rage to Reason," *Los Angeles Times*, May 13, 1990, Calendar section.

49. Quoted in Flanagan, *Written in My Soul*, p. 450.

50. Jon Pareles, "When Self-Importance Interferes with the Music," *New York Times*, Oct. 16, 1988, Arts & Leisure section.

Chapter 18. High on High Tech

1. Quoted in Jon Savage, *England's Dreaming: Anarchy, Sex Pistols, Punk Rock, and Beyond* (New York: St. Martin's, 1991), p. 425.

2. See Frith and Howard Horne, *Art into Pop* (New York: Methuen, 1987), pp. 115–18.

3. Quoted in Ted Fox, *In the Groove* (New York: St. Martin's, 1986), p. 311.

4. Dave Marsh, *The Heart of Rock and Soul: The 1001 Greatest Singles Ever Made* (New York: New American Library, 1989), p. 339.

5. Ibid., p. 339.

6. Ibid., p. 123.

7. Allan Bloom, *The Closing of the American Mind* (New York: Simon and Schuster, 1987), p. 74.

8. Georgia Bergman, interview, May 22, 1991.

9. See Michael Shore, *The Rolling Stone Book of Rock Video* (New York: Quill/Rolling Stone, 1984), pp. 89–90.

10. See Gerald Mast, *A Short History of the Movies* (New York: Pegasus, 1971), p. 228.

11. Aaron Copland, "Second Thoughts on Hollywood," *Modern Music* 17:3 (March-Apr. 1940), p. 141.

12. Shore, *Rock Video*, p. 110.

13. Brigid Brophy, "A Literary Person's Guide to Opera," *Opera* 16:5 (May 1965), p. 321.

14. Shore, *Rock Video*, p. 22.

15. Quoted in ibid., p. 235.

16. Midge Ure, quoted in Shore *Rock Video*, p. 240.

17. See Shore, *Rock Video*, p. 88–89.

18. Quoted in Pat Aufderheide, "The Look of the Sound," in Todd Gitlin, ed., *Watching Television: A Pantheon Guide to Popular Culture*, (New York: Pantheon, 1086), p. 124.

19. Aufderheide, "The Look of the Sound," p. 125.

20. Quoted in Shore, *Rock Video*, p. 165.

21. Shore, *Rock Video*, p. 266.

22. Quoted in ibid., p. 190.

23. J. Randy Taraborrelli, *Michael Jackson: The Magic and the Madness* (New York: Birch Lane Press, 1991), p. 322.

24. Ibid., pp. 294-295.

25. Greil Marcus, *Mystery Train: Images of America in Rock'n'Roll* (New York: Dutton, 1982), p. 110.

26. Both comments appear in "TRB From Washington: The Prisoner of Commerce," *New Republic*, Apr. 16, 1984, p. 4.

27. See, for example, Taraborrelli, *Michael Jackson*, p. 422; and Stanley Crouch, "Man in the Mirror," in Stanley Crouch, *Notes of a Hanging Judge: Essays and Reviews 1979-1989* (New York: Oxford University Press, 1990), pp. 209–12.

28. Jon Pareles, "They Sing, They Dance, They're Utterly Different," *New York Times*, Oct. 11, 1988, Arts & Leisure section.

29. Quoted in Taraborrelli, *Michael Jackson*, p. 428.

30. Tipper Gore, *Raising PG Kids in an X-Rated Society* (Nashville: Abingdon Press, 1987, p. 17.

31. Quoted in Irwin Stambler, *The Encyclopedia of Pop, Rock and Soul*, 1989 ed. (New York: St. Martin's), p. 538.

32. Chris Moon, quoted in Steve Perry, "Prince and the Purple Decade," *Musician* 121 (Nov. 1988), p. 90.

33. Quoted in Taraborrelli, *Michael Jackson*, p. 453.
34. Taraborrelli, *Michael Jackson*, pp. 489–90.
35. See Marsh, *The Heart of Rock and Soul*, p. 501.
36. Quoted in Alek Keshishian, director, *Truth or Dare* (film documentary), 1991.
37. See Roman Kozak, *This Ain't No Disco: The Story of CBGB* (Boston: Faber & Faber, 1988), p. xiv.
38. See Savage, *England's Dreaming*, p. 250.
39. Quoted in Savage, p. 423.
40. Donald Clarke, ed., *The Penguin Encyclopedia of Popular Music* (New York: Viking, 1989), p. 189.
41. Karen Woods, "Industrial Index," *Spin* 7:12 (Mar. 1992), p. 43.
42. See Robert Tomsho, "As Sampling Revolutionizes Recording, Debate Grows Over Aesthetics, Copyrights," *Wall Street Journal*, Nov. 15, 1990, pp. B1–B3.
43. Emile Subirana, quoted in ibid., p. B3.
44. Tomsho, "As Sampling Revolutionizes Recording," p. B3.
45. See Jon Pareles, "Mix-and-Match Music For a Zap! Age," *New York Times*, Apr. 21, 1991, Arts & Leisure, pp. 1, 28.
46. Robert Schumann, *On Music and Musicians*, translated by Paul Rosenfild (1854; reprint, New York: Pantheon, 1946), p. 51.

Chapter 19. Rap: Trying to Make It Real (Compared to What?)

1. David Toop, *Rap Attack: African Jive to New York Hip Hop* (Boston: South End Press, 1984), pp. 60–61.
2. Quoted in ibid., pp. 63–65.
3. Ibid., p. 73.
4. See Donald Clarke, ed., *The Penguin Encyclopedia of Popular Music* (New York: Viking, 1989), p. 195.
5. For a cogent discussion of these differing perceptions, see Nathan Glazer, "On Subway Grafitti in New York," *Public Interest* 54 (Winter 1979), pp. 3–11.
6. Toop, *Rap Attack*, p. 90.
7. Quoted in Jim Greer, "Free at Last," *Spin* 7:3 (June 1991), p. 50.
8. See Alan di Perna, "Locking in Loops," *Musician* 160 (Feb. 1992), pp. 43, 45.
9. See Jonathan Gold, "Why Rap Doesn't Cut It Live," *Los Angeles Times*, June 3, 1990, Calendar section.
10. See Gerald David Jaynes and Robin M. Williams, Jr., ed., *A Common Destiny: Blacks and American Society*, Report of the Committee on the Status of Black Americans, Commission on Behavioral and Social Sciences and Education, National Research Council (Washington, D.C., National Academy Press, 1989).
11. See Andrew Hacker, *Two Nations: Black and White, Hostile and Unequal* (New York: Ballantine, 1992).
12. See William Julius Wilson, *The Declining Significance of Race: Blacks and Changing American Institutions* (Chicago: University of Chicago Press, 1980).
13. See Elijah Anderson, *Street Wise: Race, Class, and Change in an Urban Community* (Chicago: University of Chicago Press, 1990); and Nicholas Lehman, *Promised Land: The Great Black Migration ans How It Changed America* (New York: Alfred A. Knopf, 1991).

14. Anderson, *Street Wise*, pp. 69, 73.
15. Ibid., pp. 103–5.
16. Ibid., pp. 243, 115, 175.
17. See Alex Kotlowitz, *There Are No Children Here: The Story of Two Boys Growing Up in the Other America* (New York: Doubleday, 1991), p. 151.
18. Toop, *Rap Attack*, p. 137.
19. See Michael Shore, *The Rolling Stone Book of Rock Video* (New York: Quill/Rolling Stone, 1984), p. 106.
20. Toop, *Rap Attack*, pp. 40–41.
21. Kathleen M. Sullivan, "2 Live Crew and the Cultural Contradictions of Obscenity Law," *Reconstruction* 1:2 (1990), p. 20.
22. See Harry M. Clor, *Obscenity and Public Morality: Censorship in a Liberal Society* (Chicago: University of Chicago Press, 1985), chaps. 3 and 5.
23. Chuck D, quoted in Ice Cube, "Black Culture Still Getting a Bum Rap," *Los Angeles Times*, June 25, 1990, p. F3.
24. See Clor, *Obscenity and Public Morality*, chap. 4.
25. See Russell Simmons, interviewed in Robert Hilburn, "Rap—The Power and the Controversy," *Los Angeles Times*, Feb. 4, 1990, Calendar section, p. 78.
26. Orlando Patterson (responding to Rhonda Datcher), "The Ongoing Struggle over Clarence Thomas: An Exchange of Correspondence," *Reconstruction* 1:4 (1992), p. 76.
27. See Henry Louis Gates, Jr., "2 Live Crew, Decoded," *New York Times*, June 19, 1990, op-ed page.
28. Lee May, "2 Live Crew's Teen Club Crew Does the Nasty Singing in Georgia," *Los Angeles Times*, June 16, 1990, pp. F1, F9.
29. James Brown and Bruce Tucker, *James Brown: The Godfather of Soul* (New York: Macmillan, 1986), p. 227.
30. David Ritz, *Divided Soul: The Life of Marvin Gaye* (New York: Paper Jacks, 1986), p. 267.
31. Quoted in David Mills, "Lusting for Laughs," *Washington Post* June 22, 1992, p. B8.
32. Quoted in Mills, "Lusting for Laughs," p. B8.
33. Toop, *Rap Attack*, p. 29.
34. Quoted in Mills, "Lusting for Laughs," p. B8.
35. Daniel Goleman, "Hope Seen for Curbing Youth Violence," *New York Times*, Aug. 11, 1993, p. A10.
36. Mark Naison, "Outlaw Culture and Black Neighborhoods," *Reconstruction* 1:4 (1992), p. 130.
37. Greg Tate, "Posses in Effect," *Village Voice*, Jan. 10, 1989, p. 67.
38. Eazy-E, quoted in Dennis Hunt, "The Rap Reality: Truth and Money," *Los Angeles Times*, Apr. 2, 1989, Calendar section, p. 80.
39. Lawrence W. Levine, *Black Culture and Black Consciousness* (New York: Oxford University Press, 1978), pp. 417–18.
40. Ibid., p. 420.
41. Ibid., p. 426–27.
42. Ibid., p. 438.
43. David Mills, "Rappers' Violent Reality," *Washington Post*, July 31, 1991, Style section.

44. Quoted in Patrick Goldstein, "Geto Boys' Raunchy Rap Gets the Green Light," *Los Angeles Times*, Sept. 16, 1990, Calendar section, p. 70.

45. See David Samuels, "The Rap on Rap," *New Republic*, Nov. 11, 1991, pp. 24–29.

46. Hans Dodson ("Prime, the Hip Hop Advisor"), interview, June 22, 1992.

47. Quoted in David Mills, "Rap's Hostile Fringe," *Washington Post*, Sept. 2, 1990, p. G2.

48. Jonathan Gold, "The Day of Dre," *Rolling Stone* 666 (September 30, 1993), p. 38.

49. Quoted in Goldstein, "Geto Boys' Raunchy Rap," p. 70.

50. Bushwick Bill, quoted in Jon Pareles, "Distributor Withdraws Rap Album Over Lyrics," *New York Times* Aug. 28, 1990, p. C18.

51. Gerald Early, "'And I Will Sing of Joy and Pain for You': Louis Armstrong and the Great Jazz Traditions," in Gerald Early, *Tuxedo Junction: Essays on American Culture* (New York: Ecco Press, 1989), p. 296.

52. See Jon Savage, *England's Dreaming: Anarchy, Sex Pistols, Punk Rock, and Beyond* (New York: St. Martin's, 1992), chap. 32.

53. Steve Hochman, "Rappers Go to the Source for Anti-Gang Video," *Los Angeles Times*, Apr. 19, 1990, pp. F1, F4.

54. Tone Loc, quoted in Hochman, "Rappers Go to the Source," p. F4.

55. Stanley Crouch, "The Failure of Black Power," in Crouch, *Notes of a Hanging Judge: Essays and Reviews, 1979–1989* (New York: Oxford University Press, 1990), p. 105.

56. Samuels, "The Rap on Rap," p. 26.

57. Quoted in Hilburn, "Rap—The Power," p. 79.

58. Hilburn, "Rap—The Power," p. 79.

59. Quoted in Richard Harrington, "The End of Public Enemy?," *Washington Post*, June 28, 1989, p. C7.

60. See Jon Pareles, "Public Enemy Rap Group Reorganizes After Anti-Semitic Comments," *New York Times*, Aug. 11, 1989, Arts section.

61. See Public Enemy, *Fight the Power: Live* (film documentary), 1989.

62. Eldridge Cleaver, *Soul On Ice* (New York: McGraw-Hill, 1968), p. 55.

63. Wilbert Nelson, quoted in Richard Harrington, "Public Enemy's Twisted Tribute," *Washington Post*, Jan. 19, 1992, p. G5.

64. Quoted in Harrington, "Twisted Tribute," p. G5.

65. Zak Kondo, quoted in Harrington, "Twisted Tribute," p. G5.

66. "Chuck D—The Interview," with Robert Hilburn, *Los Angeles Times*, Feb. 4, 1990, Calendar section, p. 65.

67. Ibid., p. 66.

68. Quoted in David Mills, "Sister Souljah's Call to Arms," *Washington Post*, May 13, 1992, p. B1.

69. Stanley D. Henderson, *Washington Post*, May 23, 1992, op-ed letter, p. A29.

Chapter 20. You Don't Miss Your Water (Till Your Well Runs Dry)

1. Dominic Milano, quoted in Robert Tomsho, "As Sampling Revolutionizes Recording, Debate Grows Over Aesthetics, Copyrights," *Wall Street Journal*, Nov. 5, 1990, p. B1.

2. Henry Pleasants, *Serious Music—and All That Jazz!* (New York: Simon & Schuster, 1969), pp. 233–234.

3. See Stanley Crouch, "Play The Right Thing," *New Republic* (February 12, 1990) pp. 30–37; and "Miles Davis: A Life in Four Scores," interviews by Cheryl McCall, Tom Moon, Mark Rowland, and Peter Watrous, *Musician* 158 (Dec. 1991), pp. 52–63.

4. See Michael J. Budds, *Jazz in the Sixties: The Expansion of Musical Resources and Techniques* (Iowa City, IA: University of Iowa Press, 1990), pp. 39, 93.

5. Crouch, "Play The Right Thing."

6. Charles Shaar Murray, *Crosstown Traffic: Jimi Hendrix and the Rock'n'Roll Revolution* (New York: St. Martin's, 1989), p. 203.

7. Quoted in Ted Fox, *In the Groove* (New York: St. Martin's, 1986), p. 118.

8. I am indebted to Isaac Green for this observation.

9. See Gary Giddins, "Bensonality," in Gary Giddins, *Riding on a Blue Note: Jazz and American Pop* (New York: Oxford University Press, 1982), p. 272.

10. Quoted in *Parade Magazine*, Nov. 18, 1990, p. 26.

11. See Gary Giddins, "Stan Getz's Transfusion," in Gary Giddins, *Rhythm-A-Ning: Jazz Tradition and Innovation in the 80's* (New York: Oxford University Press, 1986), p. 128.

12. Quoted in Nat Hentoff, "A Magical Night With Duke," *Wall Street Journal*, Sept. 11, 1991, Leisure & Arts page.

13. Ken Barnes, "Top 40 Radio: A Fragment of the Imagination," in Simon Frith, ed., *Facing the Music: A Pantheon Guide to Popular Culture* (New York: Pantheon, 1988), p. 45; and Ken Barnes, interview, June 1991.

14. Donald Clarke, ed., *The Penguin Encyclopedia of Popular Music* (New York: Viking, 1989), p. 1277.

15. Ibid., p. 972.

16. Quoted in Irwin Stambler, *The Encyclopedia of Pop, Rock, and Soul*, 1989 ed. (New York: St. Martin's), p. 173.

17. Bill Flanagan, "The Age of Excess," *Musician* 133 (Nov. 1989), p. 32.

18. Bob Geldof, *Is That It?: The Autobiography* (New York: Ballantine, 1986), p. 132.

19. Quoted in Bill Flanagan, *Written in My Soul: Conversations With Rock's Greatest Songwriters* (Chicago: Contemporary, 1987), p. 231.

20. See Byrne and the Talking Heads at their best in Jonathan Demme, director, *Stop Making Sense* (film documentary), 1984.

21. See Timothy White, *Catch a Fire: The Life of Bob Marley* (New York: Henry Holt, 1983), p. 294.

22. Dave Marsh, *The Heart of Rock and Soul: The 1001 Greatest Singles Ever Made* (New York: New American Library), p. 78.

23. Quoted in Stambler, *Pop, Rock, and Soul*, 1989 ed., p. 653.

24. Dave Marsh, *Glory Days: Bruce Springsteen in the 80's* (New York: Pantheon, 1987) p. 233.

25. Ibid., p. 347.

26. Jon Pareles, "World Beat Music Struggles with Identity Crisis," *New York Times*, July 2, 1989, Arts & Leisure section.

27. John Collins, *Music Makers of West Africa* (Washington: Three Continents Press, 1985), passim.

28. Charlie Gillett, *The Sound of the City: The Rise of Rock'n'Roll* (New York: Pantheon, 1983), pp. 302–03.

29. See Jim Fusilli, "Paul Simon Hits Troubled Water Over Apartheid," *Wall Street Journal*, Jan. 30, 1987, Leisure & Arts page; and Janet McBride, "Paul Simon Under Fire at Howard," *Washington Post*, Jan. 9, 1987, pp. B1–B2.

30. See Fernando Gonzalez, "Paul Simon's World Beat," *Boston Globe*, Oct. 14, 1990, pp. B1, B28.

31. Quoted in Gonzalez, "Paul Simon's World Beat," p. B28.

32. I am indebted to John McDonough for this recollection.

33. Quoted in Ben Fong-Torres, *Hickory Wind: The Life and Times of Gram Parsons* (New York: Pocket Books, 1991), p. 60.

34. Robert K. Oermann, "Listening to Country Music," in ed., Michael Mason, *The Country Music Book* (New York: Charles Scribner, 1985), p. 105.

35. Ibid., p. 84.

36. Ibid., p. 88.

37. Peter Guralnick, *Lost Highway: Journeys and Arrivals of American Musicians* (New York: Vintage, 1982), p. 210.

38. See Bill C. Malone, *Country Music U.S.A.* (Austin TX: University of Texas Press, 1968).

39. Quoted in Iain Chambers, *Urban Rhythms: Pop Music and Popular Culture* (New York: St. Martin's, 1985), p. 243.

40. See James Ring Adams, "Country Music Foundation: Mecca with a Mission," *Wall Street Journal*, Sept. 1, 1988, Leisure & Arts page.

41. See, for example, the June 1992 opinion survey of 750 black Americans, conducted by Omnifacts, Inc., and cosponsored by Home Box Office and the Joint Center for Political and Economic Studies, Washington, DC.

42. Quoted in Peter Guralnick, *Sweet Soul Music: Rhythm & Blues and the Southern Dream of Freedom* (New York: Harper and Row, 1986), p. 405.

43. For an account of Parker's liking for country music, see Nat Hentoff, *Jazz Is* (New York: Limelight, 1976), pp. 192–93.

44. Quoted in Richard Harrington, "Cleve Francis: Country Doctor," *Washington Post*, Mar. 15, 1992, p. G5.

45. See Henry Pleasants, *The Great American Popular Singers* (New York: Simon & Schuster, 1974), p. 177; and Quincy Jones commenting on Jimmy Scott, quoted in Ishmael Reed, "A Voice That Tweaks Souls," *New York Times*, June 13, 1993, p. 28.

46. Pleasants, *Serious Music*, pp. 167–68.

Chapter 21. Coda: Escape from Postmodernism

1. See Martin Williams, *Hidden in Plain View* (New York: Oxford University Press, 1992).

2. See W. Russell Neuman, *The Future of the Mass Audience* (New York: Cambridge University Press, 1992), p. 7.

3. Isaiah Berlin, *The Crooked Timber of Humanity: Chapters in the History of Ideas* (New York: Vintage Books, 1992), p. 204; see also James Q. Wilson, *The Moral Sense* (New York: The Free Press, 1993).

4. Berlin, *The Crooked Timber of Humanity*, pp. 18–19.

Index